Meyer

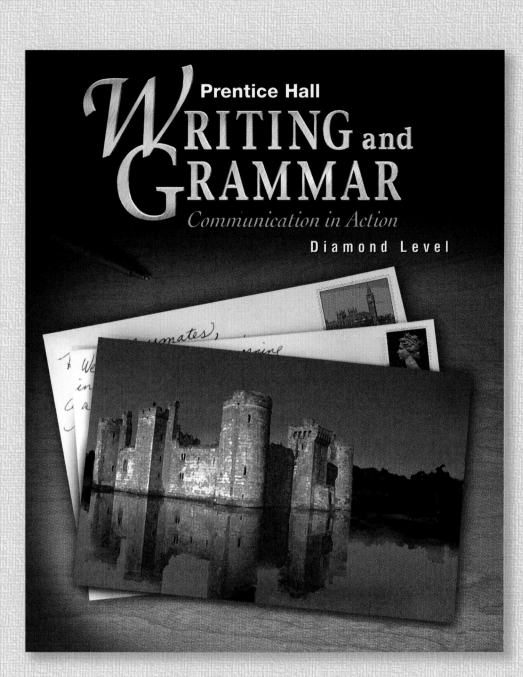

Prentice Hall

WRITING and GRAMMAR

Communication in Action

Diamond Level

Diamond Level

Prentice
Hall

Upper Saddle River, New Jersey
Needham, Massachusetts
Glenview, Illinois

ISBN 0-13-436971-8

3 4 5 6 7 8 9 10   04 03 02 01 00

WRITING and GRAMMAR
Communication in Action

Copper
Bronze
Silver
Gold
Platinum
Ruby
Diamond

Program Authors

The program authors guided the direction and philosophy of *Prentice Hall Writing and Grammar: Communication in Action*. Working with the development team, they contributed to the pedagogical integrity of the program and to its relevance to today's teachers and students.

Joyce Armstrong Carroll

In her forty-year career, Joyce Armstrong Carroll, Ed.D., has taught on every grade level from primary to graduate school. In the past twenty years, she has trained teachers in the teaching of writing. A nationally known consultant, she has served as president of TCTE and on NCTE's Commission on Composition. More than fifty of her articles have appeared in journals such as *Curriculum Review, English Journal, Media & Methods, Southwest Philosophical Studies, Ohio English Journal, English in Texas,* and the *Florida English Journal.* With Edward E. Wilson, Dr. Carroll co-authored *Acts of Teaching: How to Teach Writing* and co-edited *Poetry After Lunch: Poems to Read Aloud.* Beyond her direct involvement with the writing pedagogy presented in this series, Dr. Carroll guided the development of the Hands-on Grammar feature. She co-directs the New Jersey Writing Project in Texas.

Edward E. Wilson

A former editor of *English in Texas*, Edward E. Wilson has served as a high-school English teacher and a writing consultant in school districts nationwide. Wilson has served on the Texas Teacher Professional Practices Commission and on NCTE's Commission on Composition. With Dr. Carroll, he co-wrote *Acts of Teaching: How to Teach Writing* and co-edited the award-winning *Poetry After Lunch: Poems to Read Aloud.* In addition to his direct involvement with the writing pedagogy presented in this series, Wilson provided inspiration for the Spotlight on Humanities feature. Wilson's poetry appears in Paul Janeczko's anthology *The Music of What Happens.* Wilson co-directs the New Jersey Writing Project in Texas.

Gary Forlini

Gary Forlini, a nationally known education consultant, developed the grammar, usage, and mechanics instruction and exercises in this series. After teaching in the Pelham, New York, schools for many years, he established Research in Media, an educational research agency that provides information for product developers, school staff developers, media companies, and arts organizations, as well as private-sector corporations and foundations. Mr. Forlini was co-author of the *S.A.T. Home Study* program and has written numerous industry reports on elementary, secondary, and post-secondary education markets.

National Advisory Panel

The teachers and administrators serving on the National Advisory Panel provided ongoing input into the development of *Prentice Hall Writing and Grammar: Communication in Action.* Their valuable insights ensure that the perspectives of teachers and students throughout the country are represented within the instruction in this series.

Dr. Pauline Bigby-Jenkins
Coordinator for Secondary English
  Language Arts
Ann Arbor Public Schools
Ann Arbor, Michigan

Lee Bromberger
English Department Chairperson
Mukwonago High School
Mukwonago, Wisconsin

Mary Chapman
Teacher of English
Free State High School
Lawrence, Kansas

Jim Deatheridge
Language Arts Department
  Chairperson
Richland High School
Richland, Washington

Luis Dovalina
Teacher of English
La Joya High School
La Joya, Texas

JoAnn Giardino
Teacher of English
Centennial High School
Columbus, Ohio

Susan Goldberg
Teacher of English
Westlake Middle School
Thornwood, New York

Jean Hicks
Director, Louisville Writing Project
University of Louisville
Louisville, Kentucky

Karen Hurley
Teacher of Language Arts
Terry Meridian Middle School
Indianapolis, Indiana

Karen Lopez
Teacher of English
Hart High School
Newhall, California

Marianne Minshall
Teacher of Reading and Language Arts
Westmore Middle School
Columbus, Ohio

Nancy Monroe
English Department Chairperson
Bolton High School
Alexandria, Louisiana

Ken Spurlock
Assistant Principal
Boone County High School
Florence, Kentucky

Dr. Debi Sulzer
Senior Administrator for Instruction
Orange City Public Schools
Orlando, Florida

Cynthia Katz Tyroff
Staff Development Specialist
  and Teacher of English
Northside Independent School District
San Antonio, Texas

Holly Ward
Teacher of Language Arts
Campbell Middle School
Daytona Beach, Florida

Grammar Review Team

The following teachers reviewed the grammar instruction in this series to ensure accuracy, clarity, and pedagogy.

Kathy Hamilton
Paul Hertzog
Daren Hoisington
Beverly Ladd

Karen Lopez
Dianna Louise Lund
Sean O'Brien

CONTENTS IN BRIEF

CONTENTS
PART 1: WRITING

Chapter 5 — Narration

Short Story 74

Student Work IN PROGRESS

Featured Work:
"Butterbee the Wise"
by Cormac Levenson
Palmetto Senior High School
Pinecrest, Florida

Creating a Character
"History" 81
Using SEE to Provide
Elaboration 83
Building Audience Interest
Through Foreshadowing . . 84
Final Draft. 90

INTEGRATED SKILLS

▶ **Grammar in Your Writing**
Using Phrases to Create
Sentence Variety 86
Punctuating Direct
Quotations and Dialogue . . 88
▶ **Spotlight on the Humanities**
Making Connections in the Arts
Focus on Theater:
Sir Noel Coward 94
▶ **Media and Technology Skills**
Video Adaptation of a Short
Story
Activity: Create
a Short Film 95
▶ **Standardized Test
Preparation Workshop**
Responding to Questions
About Short Stories 96

Persuasion
Persuasive Speech. 122

Student Work
IN PROGRESS

Featured Work:

"Four-Day School Week"
by Marvin Astorga
Bel Air High School
El Paso, Texas

INTEGRATED SKILLS

Student Work
IN PROGRESS

Featured Work:
"Are Local Music Stores Obsolete?"
by Catherine Bailey
and Zach Bucek
L. C. Anderson High School
Austin, Texas

INTEGRATED SKILLS

Chapter 10 Exposition

Cause-and-Effect Essay 194

INTEGRATED SKILLS

Chapter 13

Research

Research Paper 274

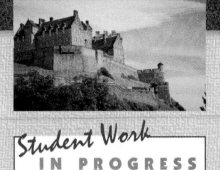

Student Work
IN PROGRESS

Featured Work:
　"Seamus Heaney: A Literary
　　Biography"
　by Ian Pritchard
　Buena High School
　Ventura, California

INTEGRATED SKILLS

Chapter 14 Response to Literature 306

Student Work IN PROGRESS

Featured Work:
"'Kubla Khan': A Response"
by Emily Elstad
Tupelo High School
Tupelo, Mississippi

INTEGRATED SKILLS

Chapter 15 Writing for Assessment 330

Student Work
IN PROGRESS

Featured Work:
   "Dream and Dreamer"
   by Scott Sang-Hyun Lee
   Duncanville High School
   Duncanville, Texas

INTEGRATED SKILLS

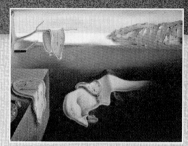

PART 2: GRAMMAR, USAGE, AND MECHANICS

Writing

Josephine and Mercie, Edmund Tarbell, The Corcoran Museum of Art, Washington, DC

The Writer in You

▲ **Critical Viewing**
What type of writing do you imagine that this student is doing? Why? **[Speculate]**

Writing is an activity like any other. You improve through practice and reflection. Just as you can't run a marathon if you haven't been training, your writing won't be effective if you haven't devoted time and energy to honing your writing skills. As Samuel Johnson said, "What is written without effort is in general read without pleasure."

Writing in Everyday Life

Writing is probably already an integral part of your daily routine. Consider everything you might write in one day: messages or reminders at home, e-mail at the computer, notes in school, and ideas in a journal. Your school life also includes many different forms of writing—from creative short stories and poems to well-researched reports and presentations. Short-answer quizzes and essay tests are also a familiar challenge.

Why Write?

There is nothing you will ever learn in school that is more important than learning to be a good writer. That is because you will be called on to use your writing skills throughout your life—both in work situations and in your life outside of work. In addition to helping you achieve success in your life, writing can also enable you to express your feelings and observations to others. As you go through life, you'll discover that the opportunities that writing can provide for you are almost limitless.

What Are the Qualities of Good Writing?

Ideas Think about the most captivating pieces of writing you've read. Most interesting writing begins with a good idea—an unusual perspective or viewpoint. The first step toward making your own writing captivating is coming up with interesting ideas to write about. Think about the topics that fascinate you most and that you think would be of interest to others. Then, decide how you can present topics in unique ways.

Organization Once you have some interesting ideas to present in your writing, it is essential to present them in a logical, organized way. Think about your topic and the type of writing that you are doing, and choose the organization that makes the most sense to you. For example, if you are comparing and contrasting two items, you may want to present all of the similarities first and then present all of the differences.

Voice Voice refers to all of the qualities that set your writing apart from the work of others. The qualities include the words you use, the way you put your words together, the topics you explore, and more. Focus on developing your voice to give your writing a personal touch.

Word Choice Words are the most essential components of writing. Choosing the right word can make a difference in whether a reader understands what you are trying to convey or is willing to accept your viewpoint. Take care in choosing your words so that they convey the exact meaning you intend and stir up the types of emotions you desire from your audience.

Sentence Fluency Use transitions and a variety of sentence lengths and structures to produce a rhythm in your writing and to ensure that one sentence flows smoothly into the next.

Conventions Make sure that all of your writing follows the conventions of English grammar, usage, mechanics, and spelling.

Writers in
ACTION

For many writers, the process of creation is a journey of discovery. Through writing, you can explore new ideas and new approaches. Poet Derek Walcott says that writing is "a process not of knowing, but of unknowing, of learning again. The next word or phrase that's written has to feel as if it's being written for the first time, that you are discovering the meaning of the word as you put it down."

Developing Your Writing Life

You will communicate with writing throughout your life. Long after you finish your last school essay, you will be applying the writing skills you are developing now. You will write in your future career to prepare clear reports, notes, and correspondence. Writing will help you organize your personal life, too.

Keep Track of Your Ideas

A writer cannot write without ideas any more than a mason can build a brick wall without bricks. You need to collect, select, and develop ideas throughout any writing project. Here are some methods you can use to keep track of your inspirations:

Writer's Notebook You need to be ready for inspiration when it strikes. Carry a small notebook to record writing ideas or thoughts wherever you go. You might use it to record thoughts that pique your interest, subjects for further research, or snippets of overheard conversation. You can include quotations from the media or the Internet. Some writers prefer to carry a small audio recorder to dictate their thoughts. When you transcribe them into writing, new connections and relationships may jump out at you.

Clipping File You can store a wide variety of materials in a clipping file. Include anything from a newspaper article to a printout from a Web page. Look in unusual sources like daily calendars, "junk" mail, and travel brochures, too.

Personal Journal Write regularly in a personal journal. You can write about anything you observe or feel or anything that captures your interest. The act of writing regularly will help you improve as a writer.

Style Journal Keep a Style Journal in which you experiment with different writing forms and ways of writing. For example, you might try writing the opening sentence for three different kinds of novels. You might take an idea and write it in three or four different poetic forms, as in the sample to the right.

▲ **Critical Viewing**
What activity do you think this student is performing? Why? **[Analyze]**

Inspiration:
I saw a gnat get out of a spider's web and fly away.

Blank Verse:
A gnat was caught inside a spider's web.
But struggled free and flew into the clouds.
No trap is sure. No fight is without hope.

Free Verse:
My eye falls on the swift small pulse
Of a tiny bug struggling to be free.
It pulls against the silken cord
And suddenly flies.
No web catches everything.

Haiku:
Struggling in the web.
Fighting all restraints and bonds.
Suddenly, aloft.

Sharing Your Work

Work With Others

Working with others can help you come up with ideas, discover ways of improving your work that you have missed, and find new strategies for approaching your work.

Group Brainstorming A group brainstorming session is a free-flowing discussion on a broad topic. Encourage participants to share any ideas that come to mind. Don't critically evaluate the ideas that are expressed. Instead, let the discussion flow. Let one idea lead to the next. Take notes as the discussion progresses. Use your notes as a source of writing topics.

Collaborative Writing In collaborative writing, a group works together to complete a writing project. Every team develops its own dynamics. Some teams divide the work into tasks, such as researching, drafting, and revising. Others divide a large topic into subtopics, with each member responsible for writing about one subtopic.

Peer Reviewers Even if you are writing independently, you might decide to ask a partner to read a draft to help you catch mistakes and identify ideas that need further elaboration. Listen carefully to your reviewer's advice. Discuss comments you don't agree with, and then make your own final decisions.

Writing doesn't begin with a pen—it begins with a mental spark. Poet W. H. Auden said that the first act of writing is "noticing." Novelist John Irving agrees that inspiration comes from a "vision—not so much what we make up but what we witness."

▼ **Critical Viewing**
Does this look like an effective peer-review session? Why or why not? **[Analyze]**

Publishing

For sheer satisfaction, few experiences can match reaching an audience with your writing. Seeing your work in print can boost your self-confidence as a writer and inspire you to set and achieve even more challenging writing goals. Look for opportunities to publish your writing, whether through a student Web site or by submission to a magazine contest. Here are a few places that publish student work:

Periodicals

- *Merlyn's Pen: The National Magazine of Student Writing,* P. O. Box 910, East Greenwich, RI 02818

- *Writing!,* 3001 Cindel Drive, P.O. Box 8012, Delran, NJ 08075-9819

On-line Publications

- MidLink Magazine: **http:www.cs.ucf.edu/~Midlink/**

Contests

- National Written & Illustrated By . . . Awards Contest for Students: Landmark Editions, Inc., P.O. Box 270169, Kansas City, MO 64127

- *Seventeen* Magazine Fiction Contest, *Seventeen* Magazine, 850 Third Avenue, New York, NY 10022

- The Young Playwrights Festival National Playwriting Competition, Young Playwrights Inc., 321 West 44th Street, Suite 906, New York, NY 10036

Reflecting on Your Writing

You can foster your own growth as a writer by asking yourself questions about your writing successes and obstacles. Here are some questions to begin your reflection:

- Which of your writing projects makes you feel most proud? Why did you connect so well with this project?

- What specific challenges have you faced when writing? What strategies might you try in order to overcome these challenges?

- What writers do you admire? How does reading their work suggest ideas you can apply to your own writing?

- What advice would you give to a beginning writer?

- What was the most valuable writing "mistake" you ever made?

Share your responses with a partner, and then note your ideas in your writer's journal.

Writers in Action

Careers in Writing, Writing in Careers

Professional writers—such as screenwriters, journalists, novelists, and copywriters—earn their living through words. Many other occupations also require workers to use their writing skills every day. A politician may write a powerfully persuasive speech. A businessperson may write a résumé that catches the eye of a potential employer. An artist may create a Web site advertising a new graphics service. The ability to write effectively will serve you well in just about any occupation you choose.

Meet the Professionals

The chapters that follow include insights from a variety of professional writers, including the following:

Guy Garcia, travel writer
In his travel writing, Garcia provides vivid descriptions to convey the experience of his journeys to his readers.

James Berry, fiction writer and poet
Berry's life experiences provide rich inspirations for the colorful settings, interesting characters, and compelling plots of his narratives.

Anne Billson, film critic
Billson uses writing to help moviegoers decide which films to see and which to avoid.

Cary Bricker, defense lawyer
Bricker relies on persuasive writing and speaking to convince juries and judges of his clients' innocence.

Peter Ginsburg, sportswriter
As a researcher and sportswriter for a television network, Ginsburg uses both primary and secondary research to gather accurate and current information about sporting events and athletes.

Derek Walcott, poet and playwright
Nobel Prize-winning writer Derek Walcott draws on both his imagination and his impressions of his Caribbean homeland, St. Lucia, for inspiration in creating poems and plays.

Eavan Boland, critic and poet
In both her writing and teaching, Boland incorporates her belief that the response to literature can be as important as the literature itself.

Jeff Christian, personal trainer
Christian uses technical writing to record fitness procedures and to communicate with other trainers at his health club.

Seeing how these professionals use writing may help you imagine the role that writing will play in your professional life.

Writers at Work Videotape

You can view these Writers at Work demonstrating their writing process in the Writers at Work videos.

Derek Walcott

James Berry

Eavan Boland

Spotlight on the Humanities

Analyzing How Meaning Is Communicated Through the Arts
Introducing Spotlight on the Humanities

Whether woven in the moving notes of a great composer, in the storyline of a classic drama, or in the brilliant colors of a painted masterpiece, self-expression can be exhibited through several different media. As artists experiment and challenge boundaries, definitions of various art forms grow and change. However, to give you a framework for a study of the humanities, consider these broad categories:

- **Fine Art** fashions meaning through color, line, texture, and subject. It includes paintings, sketches, sculpture, and collage.

- **Photography** captures still images of people, places, and events. Photographers can express ideas through their choice of subjects and their use of composition and lighting.

- **Theater** is designed to be performed by actors on a stage. Using props, scenery, sound effects and lighting, drama brings a story to life.

- **Film** records sound and motion. Like dramatic theater, most films tell a story and use setting and characterization to develop it. A filmmaker can also portray a unique point of view using camera angles and lighting and sound techniques.

- **Music** creates meaning through pitch and rhythm. Whether presented as an oboe solo, an operatic aria, or a symphony, music can create moods or present variations on a theme.

- **Dance** generates meaning through organized movement. It can be performed by a single person, a pair, or larger groups.

Writing Activity

Think about a classic work of art that you like from any of the categories in the above list. Write an explanation of why you believe this work of art has stood the test of time and still inspires audiences today.

Media and Technology Skills

Making Technology Work for You
Activity: Experiment With a Variety of Tools

Writers use tools that range from a simple pencil to a complex computer network. Experimenting with a wide variety of technologies will help you develop many useful writing strategies. Spend some time learning how these tools work.

Word-Processing Software Many writers prefer to draft and revise their work using a word processor because this software includes many powerful writing functions. For example, using cut-and-paste tools, a writer can easily try different arrangements of sentences or paragraphs.

Desktop-Publishing Software Use desktop-publishing software to produce newsletters, brochures, or other forms that incorporate text and art. You might add art using graphics software or digital photos. Interesting and bold fonts can also heighten the appeal of your final document. This software allows you to easily plan and change the layout of a document.

The Internet Writers need access to information. The Internet provides millions of ideas, facts, data, images, and sounds. When you sign on, you connect your computer to this network and can collect information stored throughout the world.

E-mail Sending electronic mail, called e-mail, from your computer to another computer, is a great way to swap ideas with friends or students in other areas. You can also share early or final drafts of your current writing projects.

Tracking Your Use of Technology Over the course of the year, keep a log of the different types of technology that you use in writing, and note whether they are effective and why.

Standardized Test Preparation Workshop

Responding to Writing Prompts

As you must have already discovered in your experience as a student, writing plays a critical role in assessment. For example, writing is often a major component of both national and local standardized tests.

When you are asked to write on standardized tests, you will most often have to work within a limited amount of time. As a result, it is important to budget your time among gathering ideas, drafting your essay, and revising it.

To do well on standardized test essays, it is essential to do the following:

- Respond directly to the prompt.

- Make your writing thoughtful and interesting.

- Make sure your essay has a clear main idea that is supported by facts, examples, and other types of details.

- Make sure that your essay has a clear, logical, and consistent organization.

- Include only ideas or materials that relate directly to the prompt.

- Take care to avoid errors in grammar, usage, mechanics, spelling, and sentence structure.

Following is an example of one type of writing prompt that you might find on a standardized test. Use the suggestions on the following page to help you respond. The clocks next to each stage show a suggested plan for organizing your time.

Sample Writing Situation

Certain books can have a major influence on our lives. Some books are so important that they may even change the way we think. Write an essay about a book you've read that made you change the way you thought about something. Explain your viewpoint on the issue before you read the book. Then, tell how your point of view changed and why it changed.

Prewriting

Allow about one quarter of your time for prewriting.

Choose Your Topic Begin by searching your memory for books you have read that had a major influence on you. Choose one of these books. Then, jot down some notes about how the book affected you and why it affected you.

Gather Specific Details The success of your essay will depend on how well you explain how the book brought about the changes in your thinking. To make your explanation effective, you need to provide as much detail as possible. Jot down details from the book that support your points about the book's impact. Then, arrange the details in an order that makes sense.

Drafting

Allow almost half of your time for drafting.

Write Your Introduction Begin with an introductory paragraph in which you state your main point about how the book affected you. If possible, begin your introduction with a question or a quotation that will grab your reader's interest.

Use a Personal Tone Since you are writing about your own experiences, it is appropriate to use a personal, somewhat conversational, tone in your writing.

Provide Examples to Support Your Points Back up your points with details from the book. Describe characters, settings, and events that affected you, and tell why they affected you. Be as specific as possible.

Revising, Editing, and Proofreading

Allow the remainder of your time for this part of the process.

Make Sure Your Point Comes Across Check carefully to see that you have presented your main points clearly and directly and that you have thoroughly backed them up with details from the book.

Proofread Your Work Errors in grammar, usage, mechanics, and spelling can detract from the impact of your essay and hurt your score. Allow time to proofread your work carefully. Place a line through text that you want to delete. Add words or phrases neatly in the space above the text, using a caret [^] to indicate the exact placement.

A Walk Through the Writing Process

From prewriting through publishing and presenting, knowing and using the stages of the writing process will help you produce better writing.

▲ **Critical Viewing**
What is your favorite part of writing—the planning shown here, the drafting, or the polishing? Explain. **[Connect]**

Types of Writing

Writing can be categorized by **mode**—the form or shape that it takes. Each type has characteristics that are unique and qualities it shares with other types. For example, narration tells a story, but it may also incorporate elements of description. This chart shows several common modes you'll encounter in this book.

As you work on any piece of writing, you should consider its audience and purpose as well as its form. **Reflexive writing** is from yourself and for yourself. When you write reflexively, you choose what to write, what format to use, and whether to share your writing with others. Because it is for yourself, this type of writing can be tentative and exploratory.

In contrast to reflexive writing, the ideas of **extensive writing** are generated by others and intended for others. With extensive writing, you purposely write something for someone else to read. Therefore, you pay closer attention to conventions, and your writing is less exploratory and more definitive.

Modes of Writing
Narration
Description
Persuasion
Exposition
Research
Response to Literature
Poems and Plays
Writing for Assessment
Workplace Writing

The Process of Writing

These are the stages of the writing process:

• **Prewriting** Freely exploring topics, choosing your topic, and beginning to gather and organize details before you write

• **Drafting** Getting your ideas down on paper in roughly the format you intend

• **Revising** Correcting any major errors and improving the writing's form and content

• **Editing and Proofreading** Polishing the writing; fixing errors in grammar, spelling, and mechanics

• **Publishing and Presenting** Sharing your writing

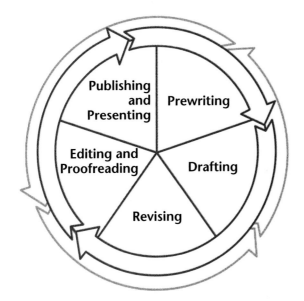

While these steps may seem sequential, writers may jump back to earlier stages as they work. For example, as you draft, you may realize you want to learn more about your topic. Similarly, during revision, you may need to conduct additional prewriting to refine or elaborate upon an idea. You may even leave a piece of writing in the prewriting stage, save it in your portfolio, and come back to it several weeks later.

A Guided Tour

This chapter introduces you to skills and strategies that you may find useful at each stage of the writing process. As you complete the guided tour the chapter offers, consider the ways each step and each suggested technique could enhance your writing process, and ultimately, your writing.

What Is Prewriting?

Just as competitive swimmers need to warm up by stretching before a major race, writers prepare for writing with their own techniques. Before you dive into a first draft, take the time to test the waters by considering the topic you'll address, gathering the details you'll include, and identifying the main idea you'll convey. In this book, each writing chapter will offer several strategies for getting started.

Choosing Your Topic

Before you can write the great American novel, argue persuasively, or respond to a work of literature, you need a topic. Each chapter begins with strategies to help you choose a topic that interests you. Try the sample strategies here to explore the process of choosing your topic.

SAMPLE STRATEGY

Brainstorming Whenever you answer the question, "What should we do today?" you are using the technique of brainstorming. Using a formalized version of this strategy can help you find a writing topic. Make a list of potential ideas that a category suggests, allowing each idea to prompt another. By freeing your mind to make quick connections between ideas for several minutes, you generate a wide list of topics from which to choose. In this sample, a group brainstormed for ideas related to the word *history,* and then, chose to pursue "Winston Churchill" as a writing topic.

BRAINSTORMING TOPICS ABOUT HISTORY		
elections	fortresses	yesterday
wars	Tower of London	historians
castles	stories	-textbooks
ancient:	leaders:	-questions
-Egypt	-Churchill	-interpretations
-Rome	-FDR	-argument
-pyramid	-Lincoln	
technology	followers	
	law	

Learn More

For additional prewriting strategies suited to specific writing tasks, see Chapters 4–16.

Challenge

When you brainstorm with classmates, you get the benefit of their ideas and the connections they see among responses. This is why brainstorming is most effective in a group.

Narrowing Your Topic

The scope of your topic will dictate the amount of detail and explanation you'll need to provide. For example, if your topic is food, you could write a 300-page book comparing the cuisines of the world, a 10-page paper on the unique features of French cuisine, or a 3-page essay explaining the process of making crepes. To identify the topic you'll want to develop, narrow your general topic to one you can address adequately in the time and space you anticipate. You will find a topic-narrowing activity in each lesson.

SAMPLE STRATEGY

Using a Pentad To examine your topic as if it were a drama, use the pentad. This strategy lets you analyze your subject by identifying these five key elements:

- **Actors:** *Who* did the action?
- **Acts:** *What* was done?
- **Scenes:** *When* or *where* was it done?
- **Agencies:** *How* was it done?
- **Purposes:** *Why* was it done?

In the model pentad below, the writer analyzed a summer job as a tour guide to narrow the focus of an autobiographical essay.

PENTAD

Broad Topic: My job as a tour guide

Actors: Me, the tour guides, the tourists

Purpose: To share knowledge with others

Action: Overcoming stage fright to describe tall ships

Agency: My enthusiasm

Scene: At the seaport historic district

Narrow Topic: How my job helped me overcome stage fright and gain self-confidence

Considering Your Audience and Purpose

To make your writing more effective, take time to consider your audience or the people you intend to address. Then, focus on a purpose, or your specific reason for writing.

Analyzing Your Audience The knowledge level, background, and interest your audience has will affect their ability to understand and respond to the points you make. For example, if you are writing to show young children how to train a pet, you would choose a specific level of vocabulary and detail. In contrast, if you are addressing the same topic for an audience of adults, your word choice and sophistication would be different. Whenever you write, take a moment to answer questions like the ones presented below. Then, use your responses to target your specific audience.

- What does my audience already know about my topic?
- What background or context do they need to understand my main ideas?
- What details will interest or influence my audience?

Refining Your Purpose The reason you are writing will influence the kinds of information you include about your subject. For example, you may want to entertain, persuade, inform, or reflect on an experience. Look at this example.

Writing Lab CD-ROM

To analyze your audience for a specific writing project, use the Audience Profile activity. You can find it in the Toolkit.

REFINING YOUR PURPOSE

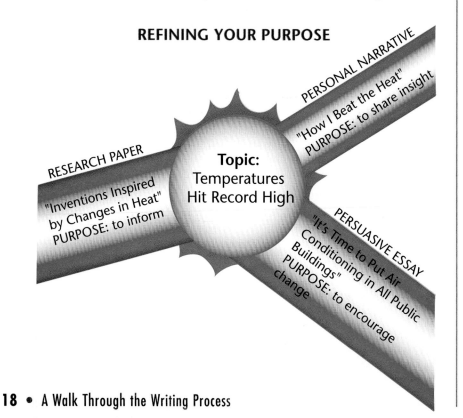

PERSONAL NARRATIVE
"How I Beat the Heat"
PURPOSE: to share insight

RESEARCH PAPER
"Inventions Inspired by Changes in Heat"
PURPOSE: to inform

Topic: Temperatures Hit Record High

PERSUASIVE ESSAY
"It's Time to Put Air Conditioning in All Public Buildings"
PURPOSE: to encourage change

Gathering Details

If you collect the information you need before you begin to write, you'll make the writing task easier. Gather facts, details, examples, or any other information that will help you prove the point you want to make in your draft. Each writing chapter offers a strategy for gathering details for the specific mode of writing.

SAMPLE STRATEGY

Using Hexagonal Writing When writing about literature, use hexagonal writing to gather the details you'll need in order to address your subject in a thoughtful, thorough analysis. The instructions in the illustration at right show you how to complete a hexagonal diagram.

As you complete your hexagonal diagram, use your responses as a springboard for collecting more of the information you'll need to support your ideas.

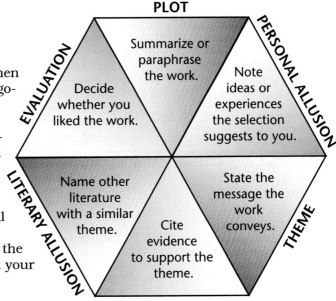

PLOT — Summarize or paraphrase the work.

PERSONAL ALLUSION — Note ideas or experiences the selection suggests to you.

THEME — State the message the work conveys.

ANALYSIS — Cite evidence to support the theme.

LITERARY ALLUSION — Name other literature with a similar theme.

EVALUATION — Decide whether you liked the work.

SAMPLE STRATEGY

Analyzing by Cubing Use cubing to study your subject from many angles. The experience of looking closely at your subject will improve the depth of your writing. Follow these steps to analyze your subject by cubing:

- **Describe it:** Explain the physical attributes of your subject.
- **Associate it:** List ideas or objects your subject suggests.
- **Apply it:** Tell how your topic can be used or what it does.
- **Analyze it:** Break your subject into smaller components.
- **Compare and contrast it:** Explain how other ideas or objects are similar to and different from yours.
- **Argue for or against it:** Promote or reject the idea.

While you may not use all the ideas you generate through cubing, the act of careful consideration may reveal connections you hadn't imagined previously.

SAMPLE STRATEGY

Making a Timeline When you are planning a narrative, use a timeline to help you gather, outline, and organize details about the events you'll describe. In the timeline below, the writer identifies information to plan how the story will unfold:

USING A TIMELINE TO GATHER DETAILS

Conflict: A hiking trip is ruined by bad weather.

Lightning strikes.	Heavy rains fall for hours.

| Hikers start five-mile hike. | | | | | Hikers return home, glad to be safe and warm. |

| Weather seems threatening; hikers continue. | Hikers find a cave to wait out the storm. | Hikers emerge, exhausted and cold. |

▶ **APPLYING THE PREWRITING STRATEGIES**

1. Using the word *movies* as a prompt, get together with a group of classmates to brainstorm for as many ideas as you can. Then, review your list to identify a writing topic you might choose to develop into an essay.
2. Complete a pentad to narrow a broad topic like "the current or recent election" or "my favorite sport." When you complete the pentad, identify a focused idea you could develop in a paper.
3. Develop two different audience profiles for an essay on courage. Complete one audience profile for a national newsmagazine audience. Make a second profile for a group of sixth-grade students.
4. For each type of writing in the following list, identify a specific purpose you could apply to a paper on school spelling bees: (a) narration, (b) persuasion, (c) research.
5. Complete a hexagonal for a short story or novel you have recently read.
6. Prepare a timeline for an autobiographical narrative about a challenge you recently faced.

2.2 *What Is Drafting?*

Shaping Your Writing

Focusing on the Form Each type of writing follows a set of expectations and conventions. For example, persuasion provides details meant to convince, exposition provides elaboration in order to explain, and narration tells a story. Whatever your final product, identify the expectations of the form you've chosen, and keep this focus in mind as you draft.

Grabbing Readers' Interest With a Powerful Lead
The opening sentences of your writing present you with an opportunity to grab your readers' attention and invite them to keep reading. Consider a quotation, a compelling fact, or an intriguing description, and then link the lead to your topic. Look at these examples from literature:

 **Learn More**

Each writing chapter presents and elaborates the conventions for a specific mode of writing. For more information, see Chapters 4–16.

WRITING MODELS

Man will never conquer space. Such a statement may sound ludicrous, now that our rockets are already 100 million miles beyond the moon and the first human travelers are preparing to leave the atmosphere. Yet it expresses a truth. . . .

—Arthur C. Clarke, "We'll Never Conquer Space"

> Arthur C. Clarke presents a contrast in his opening paragraph, following a stark declarative statement with the evidence that might disprove it.

In Moulmein, in lower Burma, I was hated by large numbers of people—the only time in my life that I have been important enough for this to happen to me.

—George Orwell, "Shooting an Elephant"

> George Orwell leads off with an intriguing statement that makes the reader curious about the events that caused it to be true.

It was the best of times, it was the worst of times, it was the age of wisdom, it was the age of foolishness, it was the epoch of belief, it was the epoch of incredulity, it was the season of Light, it was the season of darkness, it was the spring of hope, it was the winter of despair, we had everything before us, we had nothing before us . . .

—Charles Dickens, *A Tale of Two Cities*

> In one of the most famous leads in British fiction, Charles Dickens uses contrasts to establish the setting of *A Tale of Two Cities*.

Providing Elaboration

Whether you want to convince an audience of your position on a controversial topic or show readers all the atmosphere of a festive holiday evening, elaboration of your ideas will help your writing succeed. The SEE method can help you add details, facts, and examples to any writing you do. You will find an elaboration strategy in each of the writing chapters in this book.

SAMPLE STRATEGY

Using the SEE Method The SEE method of Statement, Extension, and Elaboration can strengthen your writing by encouraging you to provide a greater depth of information. Begin with a statement that conveys a main idea. Write an extension by restating or explaining the first sentence. Elaborate further by providing even more details about the main idea. When you have completed these three steps, you will have shed more light on your subject.

STATEMENT: We decorated the room for a surprise party.

EXTENSION: The balloons and streamers we draped across the room transformed it.

ELABORATION: As soon as Belinda walked in, we tossed confetti into the air, showering her with sparkles and paper that completed the effect.

Statement   Extension   Elaboration

▶ APPLYING THE DRAFTING STRATEGIES

1. Write an interest-grabbing lead for an essay developing one of the following topics: (a) the importance of a varied diet; (b) a valuable lesson you've learned; (c) your response to a favorite piece of literature; (d) a description of a beach.
2. Complete each of the sentences below. Then, using the SEE method, elaborate on each one.
   a. Every student should know how to __?__.
   b. __?__ is my favorite television show.

2.3 *What Is Revising?*

Color-Coding Clues to Revision

To give your writing the best chance to succeed, devote attention to the revision stage of the writing process. **Ratiocination** (rash′ ē äs ə nā′shen) is a word that means "to think logically." Apply this approach to your writing by marking your draft with color-coded clues that will help you focus on one element of your writing at a time. When segments are highlighted, bracketed, or circled for your review, you can evaluate your draft and make informed revisions. As you work through the revision sections of the writing chapters, you will find ratiocination strategies to help you revise structure, paragraphs, sentences, and word choice.

Writers in ACTION

"Writing is hard work. A clear sentence is no accident. Very few sentences come out right the first time, or the third. Keep thinking and rewriting until you say what you want to say."

—*William Zinsser*

Revising Your Overall Structure

Whether you are revising a business letter, a research paper, or a short story, a logical first step of the revision process is to look at the overall structure of your draft. Before you begin analyzing word choice and polishing punctuation, make sure that the structure of your writing is sound.

SAMPLE STRATEGY

▶ **REVISION STRATEGY**
Color-Coding to Compare the Draft to Purpose

To be sure your draft achieves the effects you planned, return to your prewriting work. Write your purpose on a self-sticking note, and attach it to your draft for easy reference. Then, review your draft to highlight sentences, words, or phrases that address your purpose. If you can't identify at least one sentence in each paragraph, consider adding or revising a sentence to clarify how the paragraph supports your purposes. In this example, the writer added more details to make the writing achieve its intended purpose.

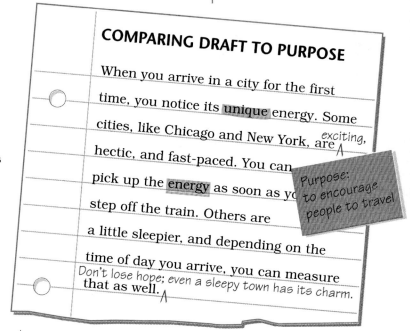

COMPARING DRAFT TO PURPOSE

When you arrive in a city for the first time, you notice its unique energy. Some cities, like Chicago and New York, are *exciting,* hectic, and fast-paced. You can pick up the energy as soon as you step off the train. Others are a little sleepier, and depending on the time of day you arrive, you can measure that as well. *Don't lose hope; even a sleepy town has its charm.*

Purpose: to encourage people to travel

Revising Your Paragraphs

To begin another layer of revision, look at each paragraph in your draft. Topical paragraphs that develop an idea should present information without introducing contradictions or distractions. To ensure unity, eliminate this type of information.

▶ REVISION STRATEGY
Circling Contradictory Information

For each topical paragraph in a draft, identify the main idea the paragraph develops. Read the paragraph, confirming that each sentence supports that idea. If you notice words, sentences, or phrases that distract from your main idea, circle these elements. When you have reviewed each paragraph, evaluate the circled information. Consider these revision options:

- If the circled items are important to your essay, write a new paragraph to address the information, revise the topic sentence, or introduce transitions to make the information fit.

- Eliminate items you cannot link to your essay's main idea.

Revising Your Sentences

Generate energy in your writing by analyzing and revising your sentence beginnings.

SAMPLE STRATEGY

▶ REVISION STRATEGY
Identifying Sentence Beginnings

To evaluate the variety of your sentence beginnings, list the first word of each sentence in your draft. Review your list to identify any pattern your draft includes. For example, you may have begun many sentences with the word *I* or *The.* To improve your draft, insert phrases or clauses that break the pattern. Look at this example:

LISTING SENTENCE BEGINNINGS

My
He
~~He~~ Even
He
~~He~~ Sam
It

My baby brother has an adorable habit of saying "yesh" to almost anything we ask him. He says "yesh" when we ask if he wants to go to bed. *Even if he was up all night,* He says "yesh" if we ask him if he slept well. He says "yesh" if we ask him if he signed the Declaration of Independence. *Sam* He doesn't understand the content of the questions, but he knows he is being asked. It keeps the family laughing.

Revising Your Word Choice

As you revise your writing, check to see whether each word is the best one for your purpose. In the writing chapters, you will learn about refining your word choice.

SAMPLE STRATEGY

▶ **REVISION STRATEGY**
Generating a Synonym Bank

When you write about a specific topic, you may find that you use the same words to name it each time. For example, if you write an editorial to state your position about school taxes, you may use the words *student* or *funding* frequently.

Identify the key words in your writing, and circle examples of them in your draft. Using a thesaurus, generate a synonym bank, and revise your draft as appropriate. Look at the examples shown on the cards at right.

> **students**
> young people
> adolescents
> teenagers

> **funding**
> financing
> subsidizing
> stocking

> **voters**
> citizens
> taxpayers
> community members

Peer Review

You may be your best editor; however, tapping the reactions of your peers can give you useful suggestions. Peer reviewers can help you see things from a distance, noticing strengths or weaknesses that you may not have seen. Each writing chapter offers specific suggestions for inviting a peer review.

Ask for Specific Feedback Instead of asking whether your paper was effective, focus your questions to get more specific feedback. This chart offers some suggestions:

Focusing Peer Review	
Purpose	**Ask**
Evaluate characterization	What kind of person was the main character?
Test your argument	Which reason was most convincing?
	Which point was least compelling?

▶ **APPLYING THE REVISION STRATEGIES**

Choose an early draft of an essay you have recently written. Experiment with each of the revision strategies presented in this chapter. Discuss your experiences with a partner.

What Are Editing and Proofreading?

Once you have revised your draft for content, edit and proof-read it to correct any errors. Each writing chapter offers a proofreading focus and a brief lesson on a related grammar, usage, or mechanics topic to help you hone your proofreading skills.

Focusing on Proofreading

Whether you work in an office and develop professional publications or you share your writing with others using a less formal technique, the care you take to identify and correct errors will show the pride you take in your work.

To help you develop strong editing and proofreading skills, each writing chapter offers a specific focus. Look at your draft with this specific element in mind. However, always review your work to correct any errors you see. These are the categories you should address as you revise your work:

Scrutinize Spelling Take a look at every word in your draft, consulting a dictionary to check words that raise doubt. Confirm the spelling of any proper nouns, such as the names of people and places.

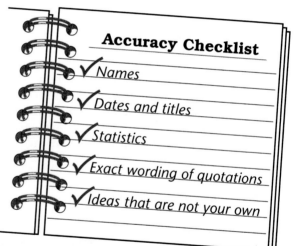

Accuracy Checklist
- ✓ Names
- ✓ Dates and titles
- ✓ Statistics
- ✓ Exact wording of quotations
- ✓ Ideas that are not your own

Follow Grammar, Usage, and Mechanics Rules Apply the conventions of grammar, usage, and mechanics to everything you write. For example, analyze your writing for its use of complete sentences, subject-verb agreement, and correct punctuation.

Fact Check When you include information from outside sources, confirm the accuracy of your work. Consult your research notes or double-check by using encyclopedias, the Internet, or other sources.

▶ **APPLYING THE EDITING AND PROOFREADING STRATEGIES**

Take a moment to consider the types of grammar, usage, and mechanics errors you frequently make. Add this list to your portfolio, revise it as you improve as a writer, and refer to it as you review the writing assignments you complete this year.

2.5 *What Are Publishing and Presenting?*

Moving Forward

This guided tour of the writing process has presented you with an overview of strategies and techniques that can enhance your writing. Each of the writing chapters in this section will extend your choices, introducing new strategies for each of the stages of the writing process. Here are the features you'll find in the Publishing and Presenting sections of each chapter:

PORTFOLIO

Building Your Portfolio A writing portfolio captures the successes and experiences of your life as a writer. Keep your finished writing products in a folder, box, or other organized container. Use it to record your progress and growth as a writer. In addition to providing a showcase of your finished work, your portfolio can also serve as a place for works in progress, records of peer conferences, documentation of presentations, and inspirations for future writing.

Reflecting on Your Writing Beyond learning about the varied topics you'll address through the writing chapters, strive to learn something about your own writing process with each assignment you complete. A Reflecting on Your Writing feature in each writing chapter will direct your thinking.

Assessing Your Writing While all writing should meet certain criteria for clarity, each type of writing must also meet requirements unique to its form. For example, a test response must answer a given question, but persuasive writing must present a fair and logical argument to convince readers. Use the Rubric for Self-Assessment in each writing chapter to be sure you are addressing the key features of each type of writing.

▶ ## APPLYING THE PUBLISHING AND PRESENTING STRATEGIES

1. Review the prewriting activities you used in this introductory walk-through. Choose one to put in your portfolio as an inspiration for a later piece of writing. Talk with a partner about the activity you selected.
2. To begin reflecting on your writing process, jot down a response to one of these questions. Save your writing in your portfolio:
   - What is your greatest strength as a writer?
   - Which writing experience in your life have you enjoyed most? Why?

Spotlight on the Humanities

Evaluating Photographic Techniques

Focus on Photography: Southworth and Hawes

Every step—from choosing and researching your topic to revising and editing—is crucial to a finished writing product. Similarly in photography, the developing process is critical to the quality of the final image. Two American photographers who pioneered in their field during the nineteenth century were pharmacist Albert Sands Southworth (1811–1894) and painter Josiah Johnson Hawes (1808–1901). Through their partnership, they refined an already existing process for creating daguerreotypes, early photographs in which images were captured on plates covered with silver iodide. In addition to their scientific advances with developing techniques, Southworth and Hawes also created exceptional portraits.

▲ **Critical Viewing**
How do the quality and texture of this daguerreotype influence your response to the picture of Henry Wadsworth Longfellow?
[Respond]

Art Connection Albert Sands Southworth learned about daguerrotypes through an agent of Louis Daguerre (1789–1851), the man whose name inspired the word. Daguerre was a French painter who invented the photographic technique of the daguerreotype. Working first as a painter of scenery for the opera, he later painted expansive panoramas that inspired the diorama form, a technique for three-dimensional scenes with figures.

Literature Connection One of the eminent individuals that Southworth and Hawes photographed was American author and poet Henry Wadsworth Longfellow (1807–1882). Longfellow brought poetry back to popularity with his clear, simple language and technically proficient style of writing. Among his most famous works are *The Song of Hiawatha* (1855), *Evangeline* (1847), and "Paul Revere's Ride" (1863).

Writing Process Activity: Using Photographs to Choose a Topic

Review photographs you have taken or flip through magazines to find images that inspire you. For each photograph you select, brainstorm to list several writing topic ideas. Keep this list in your portfolio for later development.

Media and Technology Skills

Using Technology for All Aspects of the Writing Process

Activity: Building an Electronic Portfolio

If you have ever saved a file on a computer and then were unable to find it again, you know how frustrating a disorganized computer drive can be. Setting up and maintaining an effective portfolio structure can help you access files more easily.

Think About It The structure you choose for your portfolio will depend on the types of writing you plan to do. Think about the classes for which you will complete writing assignments and the writing projects you will complete on your own.

Structure It Computer platforms differ, but your portfolio will be best organized using folders and files. You can nest subfolders within folders to create narrower topic groups. In the sample below, a folder for each work in progress and folders for finished projects and a writing journal makes the organization orderly.

- Works in Progress: College Essay
  - Prewriting
  - Drafting
  - Revising
  - Final Draft
- Works in Progress: Research Report
- Works in Progress: Letter to the Editor
- Finished Reports
- Writing Journal

> ### Computer Tips
> - If you store your portfolio on a hard drive, regularly back it up on a floppy disk.
> - Create two backup disks. Store one in a safe place at home in case you lose the first copy or it becomes damaged.
> - Print a hard copy of particularly important documents.
> - Consider "locking" a final draft to prevent others from making changes. You can always unlock it to add new revisions.
> - Use your computer system's Search or Find tool to locate a file that isn't where you thought it was.

Use It When creating a document, make sure to place it in the correct folder. To keep a trail of your revision work, consider renaming files as you revise them. You might use a point system to show the progress of one essay. For example, you could name the first draft "camp.1" and subsequent revisions "camp.2" and "camp.3."

Maintain It Your electronic portfolio is a flexible project. Take time at least once a month to evaluate and amend the structure. This can help you see your progress and preferences as a writer. After you've used the electronic portfolio long enough to become comfortable with it, decide what works for you and what does not.

Standardized Test Preparation Workshop

Using the Writing Process to Respond to Prompts

Using the writing process helps writers create well-organized, interesting, and coherent works. When responding to a test prompt for a standardized test, you can use the steps of the writing process to construct an effective response. Your response will be evaluated on your ability to do the following:

- Choose a logical, consistent organization.

- Elaborate with the appropriate amount of detail for your specific audience and purpose.

- Use appropriate transitions to show the connections among ideas.

- Use complete sentences and follow the rules of grammar.

- Use correct spelling and punctuation.

The process of writing for a test, or any kind of writing, can be divided into stages. As you write an essay for a standardized test, plan to spend a specific amount of time prewriting, drafting, revising, and proofreading.

Following is an example of a writing prompt that you might find on a standardized test. Use the suggestions on the following page to help you respond. The clocks next to each stage show a suggested plan for organizing your time.

> ## Test Tip
>
> When you want to be persuasive, create the proper *tone* for your argument by expressing your attitude toward your subject. For example, your tone may be humorous, angry, or sympathetic. Use a tone you think is best suited to your topic.

Sample Writing Situation

> The Internet was originally used as a research tool for the U.S. Department of Defense and educational institutions. Now anybody with a home computer and a modem can access the Internet. Regardless of age, background, or experience, anyone can have access to virtually any type of information easily. Should the Internet be monitored, or policed? If so, by whom—the FCC, parents, or Internet users themselves? Choose a position, and prepare a newspaper editorial presenting your point of view.

Prewriting

Allow one quarter of your time for prewriting.

Consider Both Sides Brainstorm to jot down facts or opinions that will help you clarify where you stand on the issue, Note any ideas that come to mind, both pro and con. Then, review your list, and decide which points reflect your position. Circle these ideas for full development. Then, identify one or two points that support the opposing argument. You may address and refute these in your writing, too.

Gather Examples Prepare to support your ideas by citing specific examples from your own personal experience or knowledge.

Drafting

Allow almost half of your time for drafting.

Remember Your Readers Since you are writing an editorial to be read by a wide audience, keep your ideas simple and concise. Explain the subject without assuming your readers even know what the Internet is, and be sure to provide information about the controversy.

Introduce Your Topic Start your editorial with a strong introduction. Make sure your opinion is included in the first paragraph. Then, summarize the points you'll cover in the editorial.

Use Evidence for Support In the following paragraphs, use the best examples you have collected in prewriting to support your position. Show how these examples back up your ideas.

Conclude Write a conclusion that effectively summarizes the points you have made and leaves your readers with something to consider long after they have finished reading.

Revising, Editing, and Proofreading

Allow about one quarter of your time for revising, editing, and proofreading your work.

Review the Clarity of Your Writing Read your draft to evaluate your ability to convey ideas clearly. Add transitional phrases and more persuasive language to communicate your ideas to readers.

Check for Errors Review your editorial for any mistakes you may have made in spelling, punctuation, and sentence structure. Finally, make sure your writing is neat and readable. Make deletions with a single line, and add corrected words or phrases neatly in the space above the text. Use a caret [^] to indicate the exact placement of inserts.

Paragraphs and Compositions
Structure and Style

▲ **Critical Viewing**
Explain how painting a picture is like producing an effective paragraph or composition.
[Connect]

What Are Paragraphs and Compositions?

A **paragraph** is one of the building blocks of writing. It presents a single main idea. Paragraphs may be as short as one sentence or contain several dozen sentences. Paragraphs are either indented or set off by extra space above and below.

When you put together a series of related paragraphs, you are constructing a **composition.** Like a good paragraph, an effective composition should focus on a single main idea. All of the sentences within a composition work together to introduce, develop, and support that main idea.

3.1 *Writing Effective Paragraphs*

Main Idea and Topic Sentence

Many paragraphs are built around a **topic sentence**, a single sentence that directly states the paragraph's main idea. The other sentences support, explain, or illustrate the topic sentence. Some paragraphs, however, have an **implied main idea**. This means that the paragraph's main idea is not directly stated. Instead, the sentences work together to suggest a main idea, and it is left up to the reader to piece together the sentences to draw a conclusion about the main idea.

WRITING MODELS

from **We'll Never Conquer Space**
Arthur C. Clarke

To our ancestors, the vastness of the earth was a dominant fact controlling their thoughts and lives. In all earlier ages than ours, the world was wide indeed, and no man could ever see more than a tiny fraction of its immensity. A few hundred miles—a thousand, at the most—was infinity. Only a lifetime ago, parents waved farewell to their emigrating children in the virtual certainty that they would never meet again.

> This paragraph contains a topic sentence, which appears in blue. Notice that all of the other sentences support and develop the topic sentence.

from **Shooting an Elephant**
George Orwell

I had halted on the road. As soon as I saw the elephant I knew with perfect certainty that I ought not to shoot him. It is a serious matter to shoot a working elephant—it is comparable to destroying a huge and costly piece of machinery—and obviously one ought not to do it if it can possibly be avoided. And at that distance, peacefully eating, the elephant looked no more dangerous than a cow. I thought then and I think now that his attack of "must" was already passing off; in which case he would merely wander harmlessly about until the mahout came back and caught him. Moreover, I did not in the least want to shoot him. I decided that I would watch him for a little while to make sure he did not turn savage again, and then go home.

> This paragraph does not contain a topic sentence. Instead, Orwell presents an implied main idea: that the elephant did not appear to pose a threat and that it should be left alone.

Writing a Topic Sentence

A good **topic sentence** conveys the subject of the paragraph and the point the writer wants to make about the subject. It should accurately capture the paragraph's range of ideas. If a topic sentence is too broad, it will lead readers to expect that the paragraph will cover more than it actually does. If, on the other hand, a topic sentence is too narrow, it will fail to express the entire range of ideas in the paragraph.

To write an effective topic sentence, analyze the group of details and ideas that you plan to include in a paragraph, and come up with a statement that sums up the common features of the details and ideas. For example, if you were writing a paragraph about the number of careers involved with working on the Internet, you might write the topic sentence below.

SAMPLE TOPIC SENTENCE: There are a wide range of possible careers related to the Internet.

> **Exercise 1** **Identifying a Topic Sentence** Identify the stated topic sentence of the following paragraph:

Each friend contributed a special dish to our International Feast. There was a gargantuan bowl of the garlicky Middle Eastern chickpea dip called *hummus,* accompanied by wedges of toasted pita bread for dipping. There was a luscious tray of the Greek dish *spanakopita,* thin tiers of spinach and feta cheese nestled between layers of crisp, buttery phyllo pastry. Best of all, there was the Spanish caramel custard, flan—and enough for second helpings.

> **Exercise 2** **Identifying an Implied Main Idea** Identify the implied main idea of the following paragraph:

The lake sparkles, bright as a newly minted quarter tossed among gently sloping hills. At the shallow water's edge, small children frolic; while out in deeper waters, smiling people drift by peacefully in weathered canoes. A gentle breeze rustles the leaves of majestic trees whose branches reach like graceful arms across the lake. The laughter of children mingles with birdcalls to create a joyful summer song.

> **Exercise 3** **Writing Topic Sentences** Write a topic sentence for a paragraph on each of the following subjects:
> 1. An older friend or relative you admire
> 2. A place you love
> 3. The importance of recycling
> 4. A memorable meal
> 5. The funniest movie you have ever seen

Writing Supporting Sentences

Your topic sentence contains the paragraph's main idea and guides the rest of that paragraph. The remaining sentences in the paragraph should develop, explain, or illustrate the topic sentence. These are called supporting sentences. You can use one or more of the following strategies to support and develop your topic sentence:

Use Facts Facts are statements that can be proved. They support your main idea by offering backup or proof.

TOPIC SENTENCE:	This movie is likely to do very well at the Academy Awards ceremony.
SUPPORTING FACT:	It received positive reviews from virtually every prominent film critic.

▲ Critical Viewing
What type of movie would you expect these teenagers to go to see? Why?
[Analyze]

Use Statistics A statistic is a fact stated using numbers.

TOPIC SENTENCE:	This movie is likely to do very well at the Academy Awards ceremony.
SUPPORTING STATISTIC:	It has already won twelve other major awards.

Use Examples, Illustrations, or Instances An example, illustration, or instance is a specific person, thing, or event that demonstrates a point.

TOPIC SENTENCE:	This movie is likely to do very well at the Academy Awards ceremony.
ILLUSTRATION:	Jane, who is very critical when it comes to films, even raved about it.

Use Details Details are the specifics—the parts of the whole. They make your main idea or key point clear by showing how all the pieces fit together.

TOPIC SENTENCE:	This movie is likely to do very well at the Academy Awards ceremony.
DETAIL:	So far, it has been nominated in almost every category, including Best Screenplay, Best Director, Best Actor, and Best Supporting Actress.

▶ **Exercise 4** **Writing Topic Sentences** Write two supporting sentences for each topic sentence in Exercise 3.

Placing Your Topic Sentence

Topic sentences conveying your main idea usually appear at the beginning of a paragraph. A topic sentence placed at the beginning of a paragraph focuses the reader's attention before the supporting details are presented. Sometimes, however, you will want to place your topic sentence in the middle or at the end of a paragraph. By placing a topic sentence in the middle of a paragraph, you can lead into it with some introductory statements. Placed at the end, the topic sentence summarizes the paragraph's details or draws a conclusion.

Paragraph Patterns The placement of your topic sentence will determine the pattern your paragraph follows. One possible pattern is the TRI pattern (Topic, Restatement, Illustration). You can construct a paragraph with the following elements:

TOPIC SENTENCE: State your key idea.

RESTATEMENT: Restate your key idea in other words.

ILLUSTRATION: Support your key idea with illustrations and examples.

> **T**   Physical activity is not only good for you; it is absolutely essential if you are to remain healthy. **Studies have shown**
>
> **R**   **that people who regularly engaged in activities such as walking, climbing stairs, or dancing have lived longer.** Since they were physically active, they significantly reduced
>
> **I**   their risk of coronary heart disease, certain types of cancer, and various chronic diseases.

By placing your topic sentence in different locations, you can form other paragraph patterns, such as TIR, TII, or ITR. Experiment with paragraph patterns to use different effects in your writing.

Exercise 5 **Placing a Topic Sentence** Arrange the following sentences in a paragraph. First, choose your topic sentence to express the main idea. Then, rearrange the sentences, using the TRI pattern or a variation.

Others park in garages because they can't find parking spaces elsewhere or because they're in a hurry and don't want to look. Parking your car in a congested city can present a challenge. It's often difficult to find a parking spot on the street. Some people park their cars in expensive parking garages because they don't want to leave their cars on the streets.

Grammar and Style Tip

Varying the placement of your topic sentences will make your writing flow more smoothly and will help sustain your readers' interest.

3.2 *Paragraphs in Essays and Other Compositions*

Unity and Coherence
Maintain Unity

A paragraph has unity, or singleness of effect, when all of its sentences relate to the main idea. All of the sentences should either support, explain, or develop the topic sentence. When you revise, strengthen a paragraph's unity by deleting those details or sentences that do not support, develop, or explain the main idea. Look at this example.

EXAMPLE: If we were to choose a single symbol to evoke the image of the modern American city, it would be the skyscraper. From San Francisco's Transamerica Pyramid to Chicago's Sears Tower to the twin towers of New York's World Trade Center, "skyscraper" means "city." ~~Other symbols for American cities include Gateway Arch in St. Louis and the Astrodome in Houston.~~ If we accept the idea that "skyscraper" means "city," then we can be very precise about the place and time that the modern city was born, because the first skyscraper was built in Chicago in 1885.

For a composition to have unity, all of the paragraphs should develop the thesis statement. The **thesis statement** of a composition is a sentence or two that sums up the main idea you are trying to express.

▶ **Exercise 6** **Revising for Unity** On a separate sheet of paper, copy the following paragraph. Mark for deletion any sentences that detract from the unity of the paragraph.

In the United States, cities have grown dramatically since the late nineteenth century. Over the same period, the general population has increased, making the population growth in the cities even more dramatic. The percentage of the population living in urban areas has continually increased, while the percentage of people living in rural areas has declined. A person's choice to live in an urban or a rural area may be voluntary or it may depend on employment opportunities or other controlling factors. In 1890, about 35 percent of the population lived in cities; but by 1990, more than 75 percent of the population was urban. The population figures for Chicago illustrate how dramatic the growth of cities has been: Chicago's population, increased through annexation, surpassed 1 million for the first time in 1890; by 1990, it had surpassed 2.7 million. Urban life may offer cultural advantages that rural life does not, while rural life may proceed at a more relaxed pace.

▼ **Critical Viewing**
Come up with a topic for a paragraph based on this photograph.
[Connect]

Organize for Coherence

In a paragraph or a composition that has **coherence**, the supporting ideas are logically connected and the reader is able to see how one idea is related to another. Order the sentences in a paragraph so that one leads logically to the next, and organize the paragraphs in a composition in a logical order. Following are some methods for organizing your ideas:

- **Chronological Order** Details are arranged in time order.
- **Spatial Order** Details are presented according to their physical relationship to one another.
- **Order of Importance** Details are arranged from least to most important or vice versa.
- **Comparison and Contrast** Details are grouped according to corresponding points of comparison.

Use transitional words and phrases appropriate to your organization to help readers follow the flow of information.

🕔 Learn More

In the chapters that follow, you will learn more about each of these types of organizations, along with other possible organizations.

COMMON TRANSITIONS

Comparison and Contrast	Chronological Order	Spatial Order	Logical Relationships	Order of Importance
along with	first	alongside	whether or not	first of all
also	second	above	unless	most of all
as well as	third	beneath	in fact	more
similarly	next	in front of	in essence	importantly
although	then	behind	therefore	less
in spite of	finally	on the right	to conclude	significantly
yet	before	on the left	as proof	primarily
nevertheless	afterward	in the northeast	for example	secondarily
unless	simultaneously	in the west	as you can see	best of all
on the other	soon	on top of		worst of all
hand	later	inside		the main reason
in contrast	recently	outside		more
except for				outstanding
				the most vital

▶ **Exercise 7** Revising for Coherence Revise this paragraph to make it more coherent.

Practice your scales and chord changes every day so you'll develop the necessary technical skills. If you keep practicing, you'll find that persistence pays off. Take lessons with an experienced guitar player so that you can avoid a lot of the mistakes beginners tend to make. Remember, Rome wasn't built in a day, and you won't become a good musician overnight. If you start practicing the guitar now and keep working at it for the next ten years, someday you'll become an accomplished musician.

The Parts of a Composition

A composition is a series of related paragraphs that focus on a single topic and develop a single **thesis**, or main idea. Compositions can assume a wide variety of different forms and can have a range of purposes. However, most compositions have the following common features.

Introduction

The **introduction** usually consists of a single paragraph, although a long composition may have two or more. The introduction presents opening remarks on the topic, establishes the writer's attitude toward the topic, presents the thesis statement, and previews the subtopics to be covered in the paragraphs that follow. The **thesis statement** is the most important sentence in the introduction because it presents the controlling idea or main point of the composition.

Body

The **body** consists of a series of paragraphs that support, explain, and elaborate on the thesis. The number of body paragraphs in a composition depends on the complexity of the thesis statement, the number of subtopics into which the writer divides the main topic, and the quantity of available supporting information.

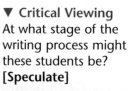

▼ Critical Viewing
At what stage of the writing process might these students be? [Speculate]

Conclusion

The **conclusion** wraps up the composition with a reminder of the main point and closing remarks. It leaves the reader satisfied that the topic has been fully covered.

▶ **Exercise 8** Planning a Composition Outline the parts of a composition on a topic related to something you are studying in one of your other classes.

Types of Paragraphs

There are a number of different types of paragraphs you can use in your compositions and creative writing:

Topical Paragraphs

A topical paragraph consists of a group of sentences containing one main idea and several sentences that support or illustrate that main idea.

Functional Paragraphs

Functional paragraphs serve a specific purpose within a piece of writing. Though they may not contain a topic sentence, they have unity and coherence because the sentences are clearly connected and logically ordered. Functional paragraphs can be used for the following purposes:

To arouse or sustain interest A few vivid sentences can work together to capture the reader's attention.

To create emphasis A short paragraph of one or two sentences can be an effective way of restating or reinforcing one of your key points.

To make a transition A short paragraph can help readers move between the main ideas in two topical paragraphs.

To indicate dialogue In written dialogue, a new paragraph begins each time the speaker changes.

WRITING MODEL

from **The Rocking-Horse Winner**
D. H. Lawrence

"But what are you going to do with your money?" asked the uncle.

"Of course," said the boy, "I started it for mother. She said she had no luck, because father is unlucky, so I thought if *I* was lucky, it might stop whispering."

"What might stop whispering?"

"Our house! I *hate* our house for whispering."

"What does it whisper?"

"Why—why"—the boy fidgeted—"why, I don't know! But it's always short of money, you know, uncle."

"I know it, son, I know it."

In this excerpt, a young boy explains to his uncle why he has wanted to make money. Each time the speaker changes, a new paragraph begins.

Paragraph Blocks

Sometimes, you have more information about a single idea than you can include in one manageable paragraph. When this occurs, you may develop that idea over several paragraphs. These "blocks" of paragraphs all support the same main idea or topic sentence. By separating the contributing ideas into blocks, you make your ideas clearer and more accessible.

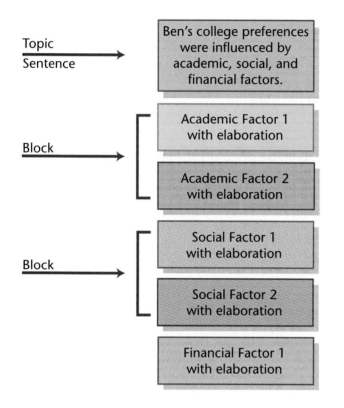

Exercise 9 **Identifying Functional Paragraphs** Skim a short story, persuasive essay, or review. Find one example of a functional paragraph that sustains interest or creates emphasis and one example of a functional paragraph that either indicates dialogue or makes a transition. Explain how these paragraphs work in the context of the complete piece of writing.

Exercise 10 **Creating Paragraph Blocks** Write a "block" of three to five paragraphs in which you explain one of your favorite hobbies.

Writing Style

Just as no two people are exactly alike, no two writers are exactly alike. Every writer has his or her unique style. **Style** refers to the way a writer puts his or her ideas into writing. It includes everything about the writing, except for the ideas on which the writing focuses. It includes such features as the way the writer uses sentences, the types of words that a writer uses, and the attitude that a writer conveys toward his or her subject and audience.

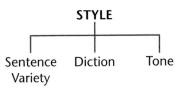

STYLE

Sentence Variety   Diction   Tone

Sentence Variety One of the key elements of your style is the types of sentences you use. When you want your writing to come across as scholarly or sophisticated, you might rely mainly on longer, more complex sentences. When you want your writing to be simple and easy to follow, focus on using shorter sentences. Most often, however, you will want to use a blend of long and short sentences; also, try to vary the sentence structures you use.

Diction Diction, which refers to a writer's choice of words, is one of the most immediately noticeable aspects of a writer's style. Choose language that you find appealing and that conveys the exact meaning you intend. Also, be aware of the connotations, or associations, that your words bring to mind. Some words, for example, might convey a positive impression of a topic, while others convey a negative impression.

Tone Your attitude toward your subject is conveyed in the tone of your writing. You may approach your subject in many ways: with delight, reverence, or understatement. A note to a friend or relative will probably have a casual and lighthearted tone, while a warning about the need to drive safely will be stern and cautionary.

> **Exercise 11** Read the two Writing Models on page 33. Study the sentence lengths and structures, the word choice, and the tone of each. Discuss with a partner how the styles of the two paragraphs are similar and different. Then, write a paragraph of your own, modeled on the style of one of them. See if your partner can tell which style you used as a model.

 **Learn More**

For more on sentence variety, see Chapter 20, "Effective Sentences."

Formal and Informal English

Standard English may be either formal or informal. Formal English is appropriate for serious and academic purposes. Informal English is appropriate for casual writing or when you want your writing to resemble conversation.

Use the Conventions of Formal English

You will use formal English for business communications, college-application essays, newspaper editorials, and most school assignments. When writing in formal English, you should observe these conventions:

- Avoid contractions.
- Do not use slang.
- Use standard English and grammar.

Use Informal English

Informal English is the language of everyday speech. You can use informal English in friendly letters, in journal entries, and—to create realistic dialogue—in personal narratives. In informal English, you can:

- Use contractions.
- Use slang and popular expressions, especially to capture the natural sounds of speech.

FORMAL ENGLISH:	Key West, Florida, boasts beautiful beaches, exciting water sports, and international shopping with a local flair. Tourists can stroll the grounds at Ernest Hemingway's house or visit a monument marking the southernmost tip of the continental United States. Visitors and natives alike gather to watch Key West's famous sunsets.
INFORMAL ENGLISH:	I had a super weekend in Key West, Florida. We spent a lot of time on the beach, soaking up the amazing rays. While I was chilling-out on the sand, I saw lots of brave souls parasailing! No way would you ever get me to try that! I did other cool stuff, too. We bought these tacky souvenirs, ate conch fritters, and checked out the sunset.

▲ **Critical Viewing**
Write two descriptions of this photograph: one in formal English and one in informal English. **[Connect]**

▶ **Exercise 12** **Using Formal and Informal English** Find a paragraph written in formal English and rewrite it in informal English. Then, find a paragraph written in informal English and rewrite it in formal English.

Spotlight on the Humanities

Exploring Cultural History Through the Arts

Focus on Theater: Greek Drama

If you were to write a brief overview of Greek drama, your overview would contain at least one paragraph on tragedies and at least one paragraph on comedies. A Greek tragedy involved an individual who was above average, like a king or a god. Comedy centered on average or below-average individuals. In tragedy, language was elevated; and in comedy, the language was like that spoken in everyday life. A central part of all Greek drama was the chorus who, under a leader, sang to the audience and imparted important facts about the plot and action of the play.

Literature Connection In 1872, the German author and philosopher Friedrich Nietzsche (1844–1900) had his first book published, entitled *The Birth of Tragedy*. His study of the components of Greek tragedy led him to assert that two types of cultures existed: the Apollonian and the Dionysian. He believed that true creativity grew from Dionysian cultures, which emphasized emotion and instinct, rather than Apollonian cultures, which accentuated reason and logical thought.

Theater Connection The Greek chorus evolved into the singers and dancers in American musical theater who comprise the chorus behind the lead performers. An examination of the musical chorus appeared in the 1976 Pulitzer Prize-winning musical *A Chorus Line*. For many years, *A Chorus Line* was the longest-running show on Broadway, playing to audiences for fifteen years.

Writing Activity: Acceptance Speech

Imagine that you are a dramatic actor who has just won an award. Write an acceptance speech for the award to read to the audience. Break down your speech into several paragraphs, first discussing your part and your inspiration, next discussing the significance of the award, and finally thanking all of the people who helped strengthen your performance.

▲ **Critical Viewing** How does the production of this Greek drama look different from what you know about performances in today's American theater? [Compare]

Media and Technology Skills

Recognizing the Varieties of Media Sources of Information

Activity: Conduct a Media Survey

Everyone uses technology differently. Some people rely heavily on traditional sources of information, such as books, newspapers, and magazines. Others depend mostly on newer technologies, such as the Internet, e-mail, and CD-ROMs. Conducting a media survey will help you evaluate your classmates' research patterns.

Think About It You will survey your class or school to identify how your peers use different media sources of information. Devise an action plan for your survey, including these features:

- **Sample group:** Decide whether you will survey all students or a representative sample.

- **Survey scope:** Choose a specific focus for your survey, such as what source students use when researching history or science topics.

- **Question format:** The results of your survey need to be tabulated and analyzed. Choose a format that produces measurable data, such as multiple-choice questions, a ratings scale, or a checklist.

Design It Write enough survey questions to get a significant amount of information, but don't make your survey too long. Participants may lose interest and rush through a long survey, giving careless or inaccurate responses.

Collect Data and Analyze It Collect data from your chosen survey sample. Make sure you give respondents enough time to answer each question on your survey. Then, tabulate and analyze the results. Look for trends, and make generalizations based on your findings.

Report It Write a short paragraph summarizing your survey results. Include a graph showing the most significant or interesting data you collected. Publish your report in a classroom, school, or community bulletin.

Types of Media

Print
- Books
- Magazines
- Newspapers
- Photography

Broadcast
- Film
- Radio
- Television
- Internet Broadcasts

Which of the following sources provided you with information

yesterday?

___ book
___ catalog
___ CD-ROM
___ e-mail
___ Internet
___ magazine
✓ newspaper
___ radio
___ telephone call
___ television

within the last week?

___ book
___ catalog
___ CD-ROM
✓ e-mail
___ Internet
___ magazine
___ newspaper
___ radio
___ telephone call
___ television

Standardized Test Preparation Workshop

Analyzing Strategy, Organization, and Style

Questions on standardized tests frequently measure your knowledge of writing skills. In these tests, items may include a passage in which part of a sentence is marked for your analysis. You will be asked to analyze strategy, organization, sequence of sentences, and style within a passage. The following are three types of questions you may encounter:

- **Strategy questions** ask whether a given revision is appropriate in the context of the passage.

- **Organization questions** ask you to choose the most logical sequence of ideas or to decide whether a sentence should be added, deleted, or moved.

- **Style questions** focus on your ability to identify the writer's point of view or evaluate the use of language for an intended audience.

The sample test item that follows will give you practice in answering these types of questions.

Test Tips

- Read the passage through at least once, and then go back and mark places where you think a transitional phrase or sentence is needed.
- If you become confused as you read a passage, think about rearranging sentences to make it more logical.

Sample Test Item

Directions: Read the passage, and then answer the question that follows.

[1]Relieved and surprised, Andrea found that the noise was actually her two cats chasing each other around the couch. [2]After leaving her room, she decided to grab the phone in case she needed to call for help. [3]Frightened by a noise in her living room, Andrea tiptoed out of her bedroom.

1 Choose the sequence that will make the passage the most logical.

    A 1, 2, 3

    B 2, 3, 1

    C 3, 2, 1

    D 2, 1, 3

Answer and Explanation

The correct answer is **C**. This sequence begins with Andrea being frightened by a noise and ends with her discovering the source of the noise.

▶ **Practice 1** **Directions:** Read the passage, and then answer the questions that follow. Choose the letter of the best answer.

¹Born in Ireland in 1900, my grandmother boarded a ship to the United States when she was just twenty-three years old. ²Her family in Ireland needed financial help, and since she was the oldest child, she felt that it was her responsibility to help her family.

³After a short time in New York, she found work as a nanny and cook for a family in Manhattan. ⁴In return, she received room and board and a small paycheck. ⁵Each month, she mailed a majority of her pay back to her family.

⁶Born and raised on a farm, my grandmother endured some culture shock while living in a big city. ⁷The crowded streets, the apartment buildings, and the noise were overwhelming at times. ⁸In addition to the cultural changes, she felt homesick. ⁹Ireland was very far away, and the only communication she had with her family was through letters. ¹⁰She looked forward to the day she could return to Ireland.

¹¹After seven years in New York, she packed up her bags for her return to Ireland. ¹²It was a rainy and windy day. ¹³She had worked hard and supported her family well, but by then, her younger siblings were older and more capable of supporting her family. ¹⁴In 1930, she returned to her homeland as an even stronger, more independent woman, with a much wider knowledge of the world.

1 Which of the following would be the best order of the paragraphs?

A 1, 3, 2, 4

B 2, 3, 1, 4

C 1, 2, 3, 4

D 4, 3, 2, 1

2 Which would be the best sentence to add at the beginning of the third paragraph to show a transition from the previous paragraph?

A Although she knew that she needed to be in New York to support her family, it was a difficult time for many reasons.

B She became great friends with the family she worked for in New York.

C She wrote letters to her family twice a week.

D My grandmother was a courageous woman.

3 If the author wanted to include more information about the culture shock experienced by the grandmother, which of the following would be an appropriate addition?

A The variety of food available in New York was very surprising to my grandmother, who had never even heard of a pizza pie.

B The journey by ship to the United States was fun but also filled with anxiety.

C The family was kind to my grandmother and treated her like part of the family.

D She kept a journal every day because she knew that one day she would want to share her experiences with her children.

4 Which best identifies the author's purpose?

A To evaluate

B To entertain

C To inform

D To persuade

5 Which of the following draws attention away from the main focus?

A Part 3

B Part 8

C Part 10

D Part 12

Narration
Autobiographical Writing

In Front of the Mirror, K. N. Istomin

Autobiographical Writing in Everyday Life

"What did you do on your vacation?" "What happened in school today?" "How was work?" Whether you realize it or not, everyday questions like these are an invitation to tell an **autobiographical narrative**—a true story from your life. In response to these questions, you would explain what you did or experienced and tell the story from your own point of view, using *I* and *my*. The unique experiences and perspectives of a person's own life form the essence of autobiography.

Autobiographical writing comes in many forms, ranging in formality and length. For example, you might write a humorous letter to a friend, telling about your experiences on your vacation; or you might describe your past job experiences in a cover letter to an employer; or you could relate an incident from your past in a college-application essay.

▲ Critical Viewing
If the character in this painting were to write an autobiographical narrative, how might she describe herself? **[Analyze]**

What Is Autobiographical Writing?

The telling of stories—whether real or imagined—is called **narration. Autobiographical stories** are stories we tell about ourselves or our experiences. In most autobiographical writing, you'll find

- characters, including the writer as a character.

- settings, drawn from real life.

- a series of events that form a plot.

- conflict or tension between characters or between a character and another force.

- insights that the writer gained from the experience.

To preview the criteria on which your autobiographical writing may be evaluated, see the Rubric for Self-Assessment on page 65.

Writers in ACTION

It is the rare writer who does not draw from his or her life in some form. Acclaimed writer Isaac Bashevis Singer often drew upon his own life as inspiration for his stories. He believed that one's life experience would find its way into one's writing:

"Writers always go back to their young days, to their young lives. If a writer writes about his life, and he is serious, he will go back there. . . ."

Types of Autobiographical Writing

You may be familiar with full-length autobiographies that are often featured in bookstore windows. Following are other types of autobiographical writing:

- **Personal narratives** tell a true story about an important experience, relationship, or period in the writer's life.

- **Autobiographical incidents** capture and explore in detail a short episode or moment in time from the writer's life.

- **Memoirs** are written records of people and events as experienced and remembered by the writer.

- **Anecdotes** are episodes in the writer's life that usually are amusing and end with a punch line or general insight.

PREVIEW Student Work IN PROGRESS

In this chapter, you'll read the autobiographical writing of Melissa Sanborn, a student at Seneca High School in Louisville, Kentucky. You'll see how Melissa used prewriting, drafting, and revising techniques to shape her memoir "Where Are You When the Dandelions Bloom?"

Model From Literature

Pulitzer Prize-winning author Annie Dillard often draws upon her own life in her writing. In the following memoir, Dillard describes a turning point in her life during which she came to realize her full potential.

◄ Reading Writing Connection ►

Reading Strategy: Use Context Clues The personal narrative that follows is full of scientific terminology. When you come across unfamiliar terms, look for **context clues**—definitions, restatements, or descriptions in the surrounding text—to help you figure out their meanings.

▲ Critical Viewing
In what way do microscopes, such as the one pictured, help us understand our world? **[Apply]**

from

An American Childhood

Annie Dillard

After I read *The Field Book of Ponds and Streams* several times, I longed for a microscope. Everybody needed a microscope. Detectives used microscopes, both for the FBI and at Scotland Yard. Although usually I had to save my tiny allowance for things I wanted, that year for Christmas my parents gave me a microscope kit.

In a dark basement corner, on a white enamel table, I set up the microscope kit. I supplied a chair, a lamp, a batch of jars, a candle, and a pile of library books. The microscope kit supplied a blunt black three-speed microscope, a booklet, a scalpel, a dropper, an ingenious device for cutting thin segments of fragile tissue, a pile of clean slides and cover slips, and a dandy array of corked test tubes.

One of the test tubes contained "hay infusion." Hay infusion was a wee brown chip of grass blade. You added water to it, and after a week it became a jungle in a drop, full of one-celled

Because this is a piece of autobiographical writing, the writer uses the first-person "I" to tell the story.

animals. This did not work for me. All I saw in the microscope after a week was a wet chip of dried grass, much enlarged.

Another test tube contained "diatomaceous earth." This was, I believed, an actual pinch of the white cliffs of Dover. On my palm it was an airy, friable chalk. The booklet said it was composed of the silicaceous bodies of diatoms—one-celled creatures that lived in, as it were, small glass jewelry boxes with fitted lids. Diatoms, I read, come in a variety of transparent geometrical shapes. Broken and dead and dug out of geological deposits, they made chalk, and a fine abrasive used in silver polish and toothpaste. What I saw in the microscope must have been the fine abrasive—grit enlarged. It was years before I saw a recognizable, whole diatom. The kit's diatomaceous earth was a bust.

All that winter I played with the microscope. I prepared slides from things at hand, as the books suggested. I looked at the transparent membrane inside an onion's skin and saw the cells. I looked at a section of cork and saw the cells, and at scrapings from the inside of my cheek, ditto. . . .

All this was very well, but I wanted to see the wildlife I had read about. I wanted especially to see the famous amoeba, who had eluded me. He was supposed to live in the hay infusion, but I hadn't found him there. He lived outside in warm ponds and streams, too, but I lived in Pittsburgh, and it had been a cold winter.

Finally late that spring I saw an amoeba. The week before, I had gathered puddle water from Frick Park; it had been festering in a jar in the basement. This June night after dinner I figured I had waited long enough. In the basement at my microscope table I spread a scummy drop of Frick Park puddle water on a slide, peeked in, and lo, there was the famous amoeba. He was as blobby and grainy as his picture; I would have known him anywhere.

Before I had watched him at all, I ran upstairs. My parents were still at table, drinking coffee. They, too, could see the famous amoeba. I told them, bursting, that he was all set up, that they should hurry before his water dried. It was the chance of a lifetime.

▲ **Critical Viewing**
Judging from this photograph, why might some people find amoebas interesting to study?
[Connect]

Dillard uses vivid details to bring to life both the setting and the event she is describing.

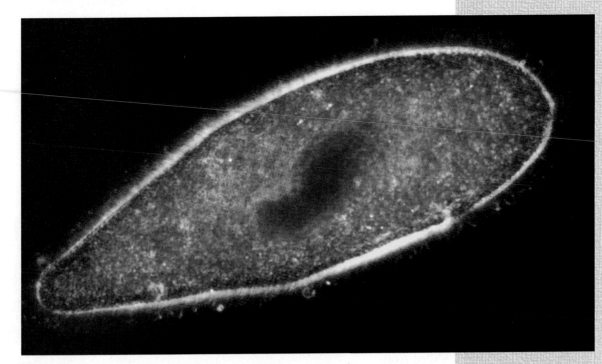

▲ **Critical Viewing** How would you describe a paramecium to someone who had never seen one before? **[Analyze]**

Father had stretched out his long legs and was tilting back in his chair. Mother sat with her knees crossed, in blue slacks. . . . The dessert dishes were still on the table. My sisters were nowhere in evidence. It was a warm evening; the big dining-room windows gave onto blooming rhododendrons.

Mother regarded me warmly. She gave me to understand that she was glad I had found what I had been looking for, but that she and Father were happy to sit with their coffee, and would not be coming down.

She did not say, but I understood at once, that they had their pursuits (coffee?) and I had mine. She did not say, but I began to understand then, that you do what you do out of your private passion for the thing itself.

I had essentially been handed my own life. In subsequent years my parents would praise my drawings and poems, and supply me with books, art supplies, and sports equipment, and listen to my troubles and enthusiasms, and supervise my hours, and discuss and inform, but they would not get involved with my detective work, nor hear about my reading, nor inquire about my homework or term papers or exams, nor visit the salamanders I caught, nor listen to me play the piano, nor attend my field

This is the climax, or high point of interest, in the story.

hockey games, nor fuss over my insect collection with me, or my poetry collection or stamp collection or rock collection. My days and nights were my own to plan and fill.

When I left the dining room that evening and started down the dark basement stairs, I had a life. I sat next to my wonderful amoeba, and there he was, rolling his grains more slowly now, extending an arc of his edge for a foot and drawing himself along by that foot, and absorbing it again and rolling on. I gave him some more pond water.

I had hit pay dirt. For all I knew, there were paramecia, too, in that pond water, or daphniae, or stentors, or any of the many other creatures I had read about and never seen: volvox, the spherical algal colony; euglena with its one red eye; the elusive, glassy diatom; hydra, rotifers, water bears, worms. Anything was possible. The sky was the limit.

This is the insight offered in the memoir: Annie Dillard's young world had opened up.

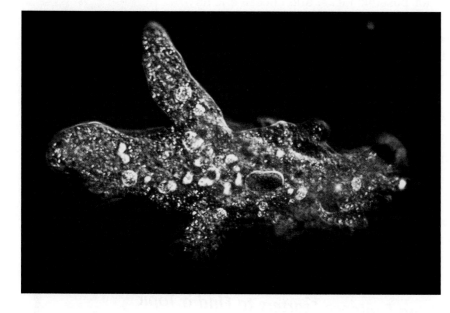

◀ **Critical Viewing** Why are one-celled animals so fascinating to many students? **[Relate]**

Reading Writing Connection

Writing Application: Give Context Clues If you were writing an autobiographical narrative about a special interest of yours, what terms might you use that readers would need to have defined in context?

To read another autobiographical account, read George Orwell's "Shooting an Elephant" in *Prentice Hall Literature: Timeless Voices, Timeless Themes,* The British Tradition.

4.2 Prewriting

Choosing Your Topic

Sift through your memories to come up with a topic for your autobiographical narrative, or try one of these strategies for choosing a topic:

Strategies for Generating Topics

1. **Blueprint** Draw a diagram of your home or school. Label each room. Then, jot down memories or associations that come to mind when you recall each place. Choose one of these ideas as the basis for an autobiographical narrative.

2. **Timeline of Your Life** Beginning with your earliest memory, write important events and dates in chronological order on a timeline. Include significant people and places. Review the timeline for possible ideas, and choose one as your topic.

3. **Sentence Starters** Finishing an unfinished sentence helps generate writing ideas. Complete these sentence starters. Then, choose one as the starting point for your narrative.

The funniest thing happened when ___?___ .

My favorite holiday was ___?___ .

The strongest memory from childhood ___?___ .

Writing Lab CD-ROM

For more help finding a topic, explore the activities and topic suggestions in the Choosing a Topic section of the Narration lesson.

IN PROGRESS

Name: Melissa Sanborn
Seneca High School
Louisville, KY

Using Sentence Starters to Find a Topic

Melissa Sanborn used sentence starters to generate a topic for her memoir. She reviewed her responses and decided to write about her grandfather.

The funniest thing happened when <u>I fell off the stage during a ballet recital.</u>

My favorite holiday is <u>Independence Day.</u>

The strongest memory from childhood involves <u>my grandfather.</u>

TOPIC BANK

For more specific topic ideas, consider the following suggestions:

1. **Narrative About a Discovery** Think about a time in your life when you discovered something wonderful in nature. For example, maybe you discovered a family of chipmunks in your yard or spotted a hawk roosting on top of your apartment building. In your narrative, tell of the events leading up to and following your discovery.

2. **Memoir of a Person or an Event** Write a memoir that captures a special time or person in your life. Include details about why that time or person was so memorable.

Responding to Fine Art

3. What reaction does *Highway Patrol* by James Doolin evoke in you? Write a narrative about an exciting car trip or getting your driver's license. Bring your experience to life through description and dialogue.

Responding to Literature

4. Read "Follower" by Seamus Heaney, in which the poet describes following the plow as his father tilled the fields. Then, write a memoir describing someone you, as a young child, followed around and wanted to be like. You can find "Follower" in *Prentice Hall Literature: Timeless Voices, Timeless Themes*, The British Tradition.

✍ Cooperative Writing Opportunity

5. **Collected Memoirs** With a group of classmates, draw up a list of experiences that everyone in the group has shared. The list might include a teacher, class, extracurricular activity, or a school or townwide event. Choose a topic from the list. Each group member should write a memoir of that event or person. Then, assemble the completed memoirs into a collection.

Highway Patrol, James Doolin, Courtesy of Koplin Gallery, Los Angeles, CA

▲ **Critical Viewing**
What words would you use to bring to life the color and movement depicted in this image? **[Analyze]**

Narrowing Your Topic
Describe Your Focus

If the topic you have chosen is very specific—for example, the time a cake you baked exploded in the oven—you may not need to narrow it further. On the other hand, if your topic is fairly general—such as your first year in high school—you'll need to narrow it down. You can do this by writing a sentence in which you describe the highlight or main focus you want your narrative to reveal. Refer to this focus as you gather details for and revise your writing.

Considering Your Audience and Purpose

Decide who your audience is and how you want them to respond to your writing. For example, if you plan to share your autobiographical writing with your family, you may want to include lots of "inside information" that they will understand and appreciate. If, on the other hand, you plan to share your narrative with a general audience, you may have to more fully explain the characters and situations you describe.

Choose Details to Suit Your Purpose

In real life, you automatically adjust your word choice depending on your purpose. If, for example, you were telling someone about getting a terrible case of the flu and wanted to get sympathy from that person, you'd choose dramatic words and emphasize details about your illness; if, however, you wanted to reassure your audience, you'd choose more neutral language and de-emphasize details about your illness.

Following is a chart that shows how your purpose affects the types of details you'll gather for your writing.

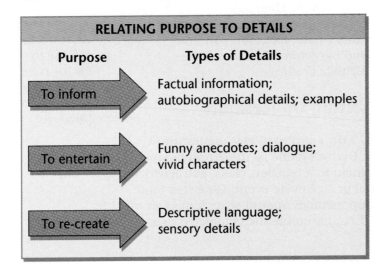

RELATING PURPOSE TO DETAILS	
Purpose	**Types of Details**
To inform	Factual information; autobiographical details; examples
To entertain	Funny anecdotes; dialogue; vivid characters
To re-create	Descriptive language; sensory details

Gathering Details

As the writer of an autobiographical narrative, you have an advantage: an intimate knowledge of your subject. This can help you create a compelling story, but only if your writing is vivid and detailed. Consider the following strategy for gathering specific details that will bring your writing to life.

Interview Yourself

On talk shows, guests often relate stories from their lives. If you were being interviewed about the topic of your narrative, what would you have to say about it? Make a list of interview questions, and answer them in writing in as much detail as you can recall. Below is an example of a self-interview you could use to generate details for your narrative:

**Writing Lab
CD-ROM**

For more help gathering details about characters, use the Character Traits Word Bin in the Developing Narrative Elements section of the Narration lesson.

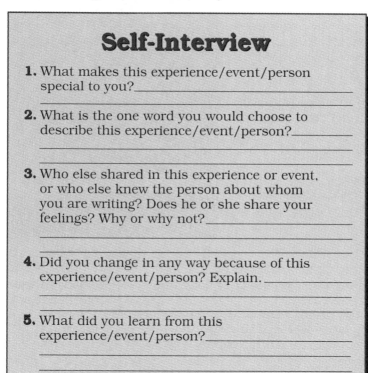

Self-Interview

1. What makes this experience/event/person special to you?_____

2. What is the one word you would choose to describe this experience/event/person?_____

3. Who else shared in this experience or event, or who else knew the person about whom you are writing? Does he or she share your feelings? Why or why not?_____

4. Did you change in any way because of this experience/event/person? Explain. _____

5. What did you learn from this experience/event/person?_____

Review Your Responses

Read through your responses to the Self-Interview. Note where there are gaps of information. Fill those gaps by using the following strategies:

• Look through photo albums and memorabilia that relate to your pick. Jot down details that relate to your topic.

• Interview someone who was also present during the time and place of your autobiographical narrative. If you like, base your questions on the Self-Interview form.

4.3 Drafting

Shaping Your Writing

Using the notes and ideas you have gathered, begin drafting your narrative. Consider the following approaches to help you identify the starting point for your story.

Find a Starting Point

Because your narrative is autobiographical, its organization can be at least partially determined by the order of actual events. The starting point, however, is up to you. Here are some ideas for beginning your narrative:

• **Start With a Character** If your personal narrative centers around a relationship, begin with a vivid description or revealing anecdote about the dominant character.

EXAMPLE: My Aunt Estelle wrapped her arms around my life, sheltering me from a world she believed was too harsh for her beloved niece.

• **Start With Dialogue** Opening with dialogue immediately captures your readers' interest while, at the same time, provides insight into a key character or situation.

EXAMPLE: "Hold on to the reins, honey!" shouted my father as he angled to get a snapshot of me and my sister on our first pony ride.

• **Start With the Setting** If the setting—the time and place in which your narrative takes place—is a critical element of your personal narrative, begin with a colorful description that evokes the time and place.

EXAMPLE: Sunlight blistered the walls of the shed in back of our little cottage by the seashore.

• **Start With Your Theme** Beginning your narrative with a statement of your theme—the story's main message—can focus your readers' attention as well as whet their curiosity about what's to come.

EXAMPLE: Don't count your chickens until they've hatched. On the morning of my tenth birthday, I woke to the sound of party preparations. . . .

▲ **Critical Viewing** Why might photographs such as this one inspire autobiographical writing? **[Analyze]**

Providing Elaboration

As you write your draft, flesh out your narrative by incorporating the details you gathered earlier as well as new details that come to mind as you write. Another way to give your narrative depth is to include dialogue through "thought shots."

Add Dialogue With "Thought Shots"

A "thought shot" is a passage that reveals the inner workings of a character's mind. One of the most effective ways to bring forth a character's thoughts is through dialogue. Dialogue enables you as the writer to show, not tell about, interesting aspects of characters.

To create a thought shot, write lines of dialogue that reveal a character's inner thoughts, motivations for his or her actions, or personal reactions to what is happening in the narrative. If you finish a paragraph and then decide to add a thought shot, write the dialogue on a self-sticking tag and place it according to where it will go.

⚙ Grammar and Style Tip

When writing dialogue, keep in mind that people often speak in incomplete sentences and use contractions and slang.

Student Work IN PROGRESS

Name: Melissa Sanborn
Seneca High School
Louisville, KY

Adding Dialogue With Thought Shots

As she drafted, Melissa provided insight into her grandfather's character with a thought shot. She then added another one to further show his personality.

By that time we were hungry and went out to eat. After we stuffed our bellies completely full, we would return to the camper and, once again, admire our site. "Best site in the park, huh, Squirt?" he would comment proudly. I always agreed, because it was, and because it was the only one that was ours. . . . After rest time, Poppop would watch me swim for a couple of hours.

This line of dialogue provides insight into Poppop's personality through a "thought shot."

"Leave some water in the pool for everyone else," he'd say with a slight grin and a chuckle.

Revising

Revising Your Overall Structure

Review your narrative to be sure that it has a definite beginning, middle, and end. Its beginning should capture the readers' interest, its middle should develop the story, and its end should leave the readers satisfied with the story's conclusion.

▶ **REVISION STRATEGY**
Strengthening Your Narrative's Ending

Does your narrative end on a strong note or does it trail off? Give your narrative an effective and memorable ending. Below are some ideas for ending your narrative:

- **Write an Epilogue** Tell what ended up happening to you or another character since the events of the story took place. This can be a satisfying conclusion to an autobiographical narrative.

- **Sum Up** Another way to end a personal narrative is to sum up your feelings or insights about your experience or state what you learned from your experience.

- **Pose a Question** It is sometimes effective to leave the readers with a question, especially when your narrative explores the conflict in a situation or relationship.

Revising Your Paragraphs
Create Functional Paragraphs

In contrast to topical paragraphs that develop the point of a topic sentence, functional paragraphs serve another purpose. They may arouse or sustain interest; present a special effect; emphasize a point; indicate dialogue; or make a transition.

▶ **REVISION STRATEGY**
Analyzing Paragraphs

As you revise, analyze your paragraph structure. Look for places where material from a longer paragraph may be more effective as a functional paragraph. Restructure your paragraphs accordingly.

Evaluate	Revise
"This storm is especially fierce, Brian," Stacey said in a wavery voice. That's when the lights went out.	"This storm is especially fierce, Brian," Stacey said in a wavery voice. That's when the lights went out.

 **Learn More**

To learn more about writing effective paragraphs, see Chapter 3.

Revising Your Sentences

Review the sentences in your draft to be sure you have no unintentional fragments or run-on sentences. Add transitions where necessary to connect the ideas in your narrative, and check to be sure that you've chosen correct verb tenses.

▶ **REVISION STRATEGY**
Using Color-Coding Clues to Check Verb Tenses

Writing about your past can be tricky, especially if your narrative moves back and forth in time. Use different color highlighters to call out verb tenses in your draft. For example, use pink for present tense, yellow for past tense, and green for future tense. Then, review your draft to be sure that if you've switched tenses, you've done so intentionally. Avoid switching verb tenses in mid-sentence unless you mean to show that the events in the sentence did not occur at the same time.

Language Lab CD-ROM

To learn more about using verb tenses, see the section on Verb Tenses.

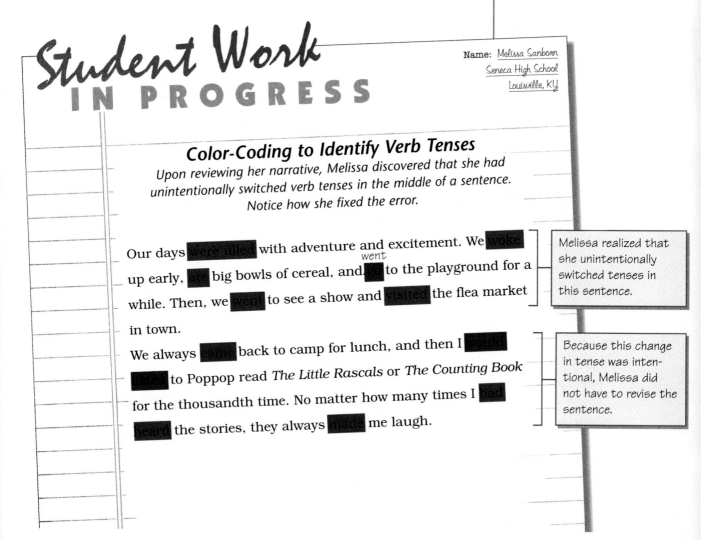

Student Work
IN PROGRESS

Name: *Melissa Sanborn*
Seneca High School
Louisville, KY

Color-Coding to Identify Verb Tenses
Upon reviewing her narrative, Melissa discovered that she had unintentionally switched verb tenses in the middle of a sentence. Notice how she fixed the error.

Our days ⬛were filled⬛ with adventure and excitement. We ⬛woke⬛
up early, ⬛ate⬛ big bowls of cereal, and ⬛*went*⬛ to the playground for a
while. Then, we ⬛went⬛ to see a show and ⬛visited⬛ the flea market
in town.
We always ⬛came⬛ back to camp for lunch, and then I ⬛would⬛
⬛listen⬛ to Poppop read *The Little Rascals* or *The Counting Book*
for the thousandth time. No matter how many times I ⬛had⬛
⬛heard⬛ the stories, they always ⬛made⬛ me laugh.

> Melissa realized that she unintentionally switched tenses in this sentence.

> Because this change in tense was intentional, Melissa did not have to revise the sentence.

Revising • 61

Grammar in Your Writing
Verb Tenses

As the narrator of an autobiographical story, you need to be able to move between the past and present with clarity. Proper use of verb tenses will enable you to do this. The **tenses** of verbs are the forms that show time. There are six main tenses:

THE BASIC FORMS OF THE SIX TENSES		
Tense	**Explanation**	**Example**
Present	This tense tells of an action or a condition that exists at the present time.	I *am looking* for the old camper.
Past	This tense tells of an action or a condition that began and ended at a given time in the past.	I *looked* for the old camper yesterday.
Future	This tense tells of an action or a condition that has not yet occurred.	I *will look* for the old camper tomorrow.
Present Perfect	This tense tells of an action or a condition that occurred at an indefinite time in the past or that began in the past and has continued into the present.	I *have looked* for the old camper wherever I go.
Past Perfect	This tense tells of a past action or condition that ended before another past action began.	I *had looked* for the old camper before leaving.
Future Perfect	This tense tells of a future action or condition that will have ended before another begins.	By nightfall I *will have looked* for the old camper.

Find It in Your Reading Review the excerpt from Annie Dillard's *An American Childhood* on pages 50–53. Identify five different examples of verb tenses. Describe when the action or condition in each example took place.

Find It in Your Writing Review the verb tenses in your writing. If you find that you've relied too much on a particular tense, add depth and sophistication to your story by using another tense to show time relationships between events.

To learn more about verb tenses, see Chapter 21.

Revising Your Word Choice

▶ **REVISION STRATEGY**
Circling the *I*'s

Go through your draft, and circle every use of the pronoun *I*. As a general rule, avoid beginning more than two sentences in a row with *I*. Use the same strategy to evaluate your use of *we* and *my*.

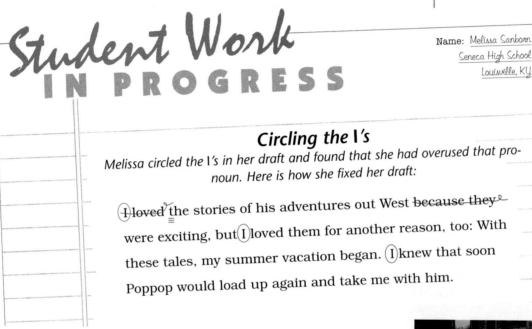

Student Work
IN PROGRESS

Name: Melissa Sanborn
Seneca High School
Louisville, KY

Circling the I's

Melissa circled the I's in her draft and found that she had overused that pronoun. Here is how she fixed her draft:

~~I loved~~ the stories of his adventures out West ~~because they~~ were exciting, but (I) loved them for another reason, too: With these tales, my summer vacation began. (I) knew that soon Poppop would load up again and take me with him.

Peer Review

Work with a group of peer reviewers to get different perspectives on your writing. Peer reviewers may spot weaknesses or confusing jumps in your narrative that you missed. Use the following idea to get feedback from your peers:

Analytical Talk

In a group, read your narrative twice, pausing between readings. Direct the other members of the group to simply listen the first time. The second time, tell them to listen and jot down words, phrases, images—whatever catches their interest. Then, ask your group to respond to the following questions:

1. Which parts of the narrative do you find most interesting?
2. Which parts of the narrative, if any, need improvement?

Editing and Proofreading

You want your readers to become completely absorbed in your narrative. Don't let them become distracted by a glaring error in spelling, mechanics, grammar, or usage. Check for errors before you create your final draft.

Focusing on Correct Spelling

Proofread your narrative carefully to locate mistakes in spelling. Because this narrative is autobiographical, be especially careful to spell the names of people and places correctly.

💡 Spelling Tip

Keep in mind that the spell-check feature on a word-processing program is a great tool, but it is not a substitute for careful proofreading.

Grammar in Your Writing
Spelling Homophones

Homophones are words that sound alike but have different spellings and meanings. They are a common source of spelling errors and need careful proofreading. While you are probably aware of the differences in spelling and meaning among most homophones, it is easy to make a mistake when you are writing quickly. The following homophones are frequently misspelled:

COMMONLY USED HOMOPHONES

there	to	its	accept	affect
their	too	it's	except	effect
they're	two			

Find It in Your Reading Look through the excerpt from *An American Childhood* to find the sentences containing the homophones *weak* and *here*. Think about how the meaning of those sentences would change if Dillard had chosen the wrong homophone.

Find It in Your Writing As you proofread your autobiographical narrative, double-check the spelling of homophones. If you are unsure whether you have spelled a homophone correctly, look it up in a dictionary.

To learn more about homophones, see Chapter 29.

4.6 Publishing and Presenting

The story of your life is unique. Share it with others. Consider these possibilities for publishing or presenting your work:

Building Your Portfolio

1. **Share With People Who Were There** Send your personal narrative to people who played a part in the story you told. Possible recipients might include family members, relatives, old friends, teachers, or employers.

2. **Send to a Student Publication** Submit your work to a student magazine for publication. This might be a school publication or a literary magazine for young people.

Reflecting on Your Writing

Take a moment to reflect on the experience of writing your autobiographical narrative. Then, answer the following questions. Save your answers in your portfolio.

- How did writing the narrative affect your attitude toward the topic you chose?

- Which part of the writing process—prewriting, drafting, revising, or editing—did you find most challenging? Why?

🖥 Internet Tip

To review essays scored with this rubric, visit **www.phschool.com**

Rubric for Self-Assessment

Use these criteria to evaluate your autobiographical narrative.

	Score 4	Score 3	Score 2	Score 1
Audience and Purpose	Contains details that engage the audience	Contains details appropriate for an audience	Contains few details that appeal to an audience	Is not written for a specific audience
Organization	Presents events that create an interesting narrative; told from a consistent point of view	Presents sequence of events; told from a specific point of view	Presents a confusing sequence of events; contains a point of view that is inconsistent	Presents no logical order; is told from no consistent point of view
Elaboration	Contains details that create vivid characters; contains dialogue that develops characters and plot	Contains details that develop character and describe setting; contains dialogue	Contains characters and setting; contains some dialogue	Contains few or no details to develop characters or setting; no dialogue provided
Use of Language	Uses language to create a tone; contains no errors in grammar, punctuation, or spelling	Uses vivid words; contains few errors in grammar, punctuation, and spelling	Uses clichés and trite expressions; contains some errors in grammar, punctuation, and spelling	Uses uninspired words; has many errors in grammar, punctuation, and spelling

FINAL DRAFT

Where Are You When the Dandelions Bloom?

Melissa Sanborn
Seneca High School
Louisville, Kentucky

"I'll be home when the dandelions bloom." Those were my grandfather's words as he loaded up the camper to head out on his annual trip. Sure enough, every spring, as soon as I caught sight of the first dandelion, I'd see the trusty old camper pushing down the lane. My "Poppop" was home, and right on time.

We sat and talked for hours about the exciting places he had traveled, tracing his journey on the brightly colored map tacked to the inside of the camper door. "See, Squirt, it's right here. . . . This is Kentucky—where we are—the green state. I went over this way, across the blue, that's Illinois, to the red, Iowa, then through

▲ **Critical Viewing**
Why might Melissa have chosen to mention dandelions in the title of her autobiographical narrative? **[Connect]**

This opening line of dialogue makes an interesting beginning to Melissa's narrative.

Melissa is the writer as well as the main character in her narrative.

the purple, South Dakota, and over to the big yellow state, Montana. Follow it with your finger."

The stories of his adventures out West were exciting, but I loved them for another reason, too: With these tales, my summer vacation began. I knew that soon Poppop would load up again and take me with him. Every vacation I can remember was spent with Poppop in the blue-and-beige camper. Whether we were headed up north, down south, or to the Horse Park down the street, I was thrilled to spend time with my grandfather.

Making our way into a campground on the first day, my heartbeat seemed to race. Poppop was anxious to find our site.

"Let's see, I know that number twenty-two is a good one. It's real close to the store, so it will be easy for us to go get ice cream sandwiches after dinner. . . . Oh, it's taken. What else is there? Ohhh, I forgot about number twenty-seven. It's right across from the swimmin' pool and game rooms. There it is, and there's even a big shade tree for the really hot days."

It was perfect, as were all the sites he picked out. Poppop always knew the best lots in the park.

He backed the camper slowly into the space, making sure we were far enough from the tree to set up the awning. He got out to make sure the trailer was straight and to chock the tires. Then, we set up. Out came the brightly striped blue awning. We pulled the picnic table over into the shade and strung the old lantern lights—green, red, and yellow—along the edge of the awning. The finishing touch was the old blue duck, wooden with propellers for wings, which spun around when the wind blew. It had our last name on it. We always marked our spot this way.

By that time, we were hungry and went out to eat. After we had stuffed our bellies completely full, we returned to the camper and, once again, admired our site.

Long passages of dialogue give the reader a sense of Poppop's personality.

Vivid description helps the reader visualize the campsite setting.

◀ **Critical Viewing** Why does camping appeal to many vacationers? Use details from the photograph to support your response. **[Analyze]**

"Best site in the park, huh, Squirt?" he would comment proudly. I always agreed, because it was, and because it was the only one that was ours.

Our days were filled with adventure and excitement. We woke up early, ate big bowls of cereal, and went to the playground for a while. Then, we went to see a show and visited the flea market in town.

We always came back to camp for lunch, and then I would listen to Poppop read *The Little Rascals* or *The Counting Book* for the thousandth time. No matter how many times I had heard the stories, they always made me laugh.

After rest time, Poppop would watch me swim for a couple of hours. "Leave some water in the pool for everyone else," he'd say with a slight grin and a chuckle.

By the time we got back to the motor home, it was dinner time. We had the best dinners, too: pot roast, corn on the cob, green beans, mashed potatoes, and spaghetti (my favorite). After dinner, we'd stay up late, laughing and playing Yahtzee or Dominoes.

This was our routine, every day for the rest of the summer. Then, September came, and it was time for me to go back home. That was the worst part, but I always knew we would do it again the next year.

Every spring, as the dandelions begin to bloom, I still look for Poppop's old camper coming down the lane, but it never comes. Our adventures and summers together have gone, but the memories remain. The summertime camping trips with Poppop were the highlight of my childhood. They brought me sunshine, fun times, and a whole bunch of laughs.

▲ **Critical Viewing**
If you were to use a dandelion as a symbol, what would it symbolize? Explain. **[Apply]**

This detail vividly captures the personality of Poppop.

Melissa concludes her narrative by sharing this insight with readers.

Connected Assignment *Firsthand Biography*

Chances are, you often tell stories from your life. In school, you've been taught how to use research to tell the life stories of notable people. There is, however, another kind of storytelling, in which you combine your own firsthand knowledge with research. This is called a **firsthand biography.** In this type of writing, you blend firsthand observations and experiences with researched information to recount the life of someone you know well. For example, subjects for a firsthand biography may include your neighbor or a coach at your school.

Write your own short firsthand biography with the writing process steps suggested below:

Prewriting Because a firsthand biography depends on first-hand observations, it's important to choose a person you know well. Consider writing about a close friend, a person with whom you have worked, or a member of your family.

Once you choose your subject, create a K-W-L chart like the one below. This will help you identify what you already know about your subject as well as things you will need to research to find out.

What I Know	What I Want to Know	What I've Learned
Grandma's birthday	Where she was born	Grandma was born in Poland during WWII

Drafting Use the first-person point of view to include yourself in the story. Start with your first experience or memory of your subject. Refer to your prewriting notes to organize additional events in chronological sequence and to check facts.

Revising and Editing Have a classmate read your firsthand biography. Discuss passages of the paper in which the subject's actions or words seem unrealistic or don't make sense. Insert transitions or modifiers to clear up these confusing passages. Also, check to be sure that you have consistently used the first-person point of view.

Publishing and Presenting Make a cover for your firsthand biography and give it as a gift to the person about whom you wrote.

Spotlight on the Humanities

Examining Media Portrayals of a Character
Focus on Film: *Throne of Blood*

The life stories of historical figures, whether autobiographical or told by others, are often fascinating. In 1957, Akira Kurosawa directed his classic film *Throne of Blood*, an adaptation of Shakespeare's historical play *Macbeth*. This powerful film moves the story of Macbeth to medieval Japan. After a great military victory, lords Washizu and Miki are lost in the dense Cobweb Forest, where they meet a mysterious old woman who predicts great things for Washizu and even greater things for Miki's descendants. Once out of the forest, Washizu and Miki are immediately promoted by the emperor. Washizu, encouraged by his ambitious wife, plots to make even more of the prophecy come true, even if it means killing the emperor.

Art Connection Considered one of the precursors of Symbolism and Surrealism in painting, Swiss artist Henry Fuseli often used Shakespearean subjects in his work. His 1784 painting of Lady Macbeth is one example. The work now hangs in the Louvre in Paris, France.

Music Connection In 1847, Italian composer Giuseppe Verdi wrote his famous opera *Macbeth* based upon the Shakespearean play. The musical work premiered in Florence, Italy, and is known for its complex orchestral themes that challenge its principal performers.

Narrative Writing Activity: Autobiography of a Famous Villain Choose a film that you've watched recently or a book you have read that had a memorable villain. Imagine that you are that person. Based on what you saw or read, write an autobiography in his or her voice. In your autobiography, be sure to explain your motivation for your actions, as well as your inner feelings about your actions. Share your autobiography with your classmates.

▲ Critical Viewing Study these photographs of two portrayals of Lady Macbeth. In what ways do the actresses' costumes help to convey Lady Macbeth's personality? **[Distinguish]**

Media and Technology Skills

Conveying Messages Using Visuals

Activity: Create a Video Scrapbook

Scrapbooks, which may contain photographs, report cards, play-bills, or awards, are a popular way to capture and revisit your special memories and experiences. Technology tools may help you effectively capture your memories and, if you choose, share them with others. Choose a memorable event, and create a video scrapbook or capture a current experience in your scrapbook.

Think About It Choose a focused topic for your video. Rather than try to capture your whole summer vacation, for example, capture the side trip you took to a folk festival.

Gather It Gather artifacts, mementos, and photographs related to your topic. These items will be used in filming your video scrapbook. Also, choose shooting locations and obtain permission to film there. Once you have gathered items and located filming sites, create a storyboard or chart that shows the order in which you will videotape the items. Also on your storyboard, jot down ideas for the way you will use the camera. You might, for example, use a soft focus for some scenes or a kaleidoscope special effect for another.

> ### What You'll Need
> - Video recorder
> - Single-deck or double-deck videocassette recorder
> - CD or audiocassette player
>
> ### Special Techniques
> **Use special lighting:**
> - Use a desklamp as a spotlight.
>
> **Use camera angles:**
> - Pan across a series of objects arranged on a piece of fabric.
> - Shoot a scene through a window.
>
> **Use camera effects:**
> - Fade in and out as you go through a series of snapshots.
> - Use special framing devices, as provided by your video recorder.

STORYBOARD

Series of pictures

Soft focus on postcard

Funny Music as I show swim gear photos

Shoot It Follow your storyboard plan, and shoot your film. Set up each shot individually. Film it until you are satisfied with the results. Then, refer to your storyboard and complete the next shot.

When you have completed filming, use a double-deck videocassette recorder, or hook up your video camera to a single-deck recorder and edit your video. To do this, record the scenes you like best in the order you like onto a fresh tape. Select appropriate music to help create a mood or atmosphere for your video.

Standardized Test Preparation Workshop

Responding to Narrative Writing Prompts

Test Tip

While describing your experiences, remain focused on your purpose. Eliminate details that do not directly relate to helping students prepare for high school.

Standardized tests often measure your ability to use the elements of narrative writing when responding to a prompt. The following are the criteria upon which your narrative writing will be evaluated:

- Words and constructed sentences that are appropriate for the purpose and audience named in the response
- Details of your narrative that are organized in a meaningful and coherent way
- Appropriate transitions that enable ideas to flow and that unify your narrative
- Elaboration that makes effective use of description, characterization, and other details
- Correct grammar, spelling, and punctuation

When writing for a timed test, devote a specified amount of time to prewriting, drafting, revising, and proofreading.

Following are examples of narrative writing prompts. Use the suggestions on the following page to help you respond. The clocks next to each stage show a suggested percentage of time to devote to each stage.

Sample Writing Situation

As a senior, you are eligible to take part in a mentor program for freshmen at your school. The program includes sharing your experiences: what you have learned from them about being a successful high-school student and how to prepare for the future. You may also offer advice based on your experiences on how to make the most of the high-school experience. Think about the ways you could positively influence these students and then respond to one of the following prompts.

Prepare an application essay to be submitted to your school principal. In the essay, outline your achievements, the lessons you have learned, and how your experiences could influence students in a positive way.

Write a speech that you would give to incoming high-school students, in which you describe what you have learned from your experiences in high school and offer advice to others that will help them meet the challenges of high school.

Prewriting

Allow close to one fourth of your allotted time for prewriting.

Focus Your Topic Don't try to cover four years of high school in your essay or speech. Narrow your topic by using a timeline to plot significant events. Then, choose to write about those events that taught you the most and would most likely have a positive impact on your audience.

Consider Your Audience As you gather details for your narrative, keep in mind the audience indicated in the prompt you have chosen. For example, if you were writing to the principal, you would use more formal language than if you were writing to incoming high-school students.

Identify Your Purpose Decide on your purpose for writing, and choose words and details that will help you to achieve that purpose. For example, if your purpose is to encourage, you might choose to write many imperative sentences that contain words with positive connotations.

For a sample purpose planner, see page 56.

Drafting

Allow almost half of your time for drafting.

Choose a Structure and Organization Write an introduction, body, and conclusion in which you state and develop your main idea. In this type of writing, you will most likely organize the body of your essay or speech chronologically, listing events in time order.

Elaborate To convey the significance of your experience, give examples, comparing your experience to another, providing a telling quotation, or describing your sensory experience.

Put It on Paper Neatly write your response on your test paper. Begin with a statement of your opinion. Pause occasionally to review your outline or list, and make sure you continue to follow the logical sequence you have chosen.

Revising, Editing, and Proofreading

Allow almost one fourth of your time to revise and edit. Use the last few minutes to proofread your work.

Add Transitions As you review your work, mark places where the connections between ideas is not obvious. Then, use appropriate transitions to make ideas flow.

Make Corrections Review your response for errors. Change language that is inappropriate for your audience, and correct errors in spelling, grammar, and punctuation.

5 Narration
Short Story

▲ Critical Viewing
What sort of story
might this photo-
graph inspire?
Explain. **[Analyze]**

Storytelling in Everyday Life

What would your world be like without stories? Think for a moment about the stories you hear and tell each day. For example, did you read an adventure story before going to sleep last night? On your way to school, did your friend tell you about his exciting weekend?

Stories can thrill, teach, and inspire their readers. Some stories are true, some are based on truth, and some are completely fictional. Some contain a single character, and some contain casts of hundreds. Some stories revolve around a single plot, whereas others contain intricately intertwined plots and subplots.

Despite the wide variety of stories around us, however, they often teach us something about ourselves and our world.

What Is a Short Story?

A **short story** is a short piece of fiction that has a simple plot and few settings. Short stories often revolve around a key incident that reveals insights about its main character. Short stories frequently contain

- a narrator—either a character or an impersonal voice—who tells the story from a particular point of view.
- characters—fictional people who participate in the events—whose personalities may be revealed through dialogue.
- plot—a sequence of events that creates tension or suspense and that usually centers on one particular struggle or conflict.
- setting—the time and place in which the plot unfolds.

To preview the criteria on which your short story may be evaluated, see the Self-Assessment Rubric on page 89.

Types of Short Stories

Short stories can take many forms, from realistic tales to fantastic ones. Following are descriptions of types of short stories you may encounter:

- **Adventure stories** tell about a character who faces a huge challenge—either from nature or from other people.
- **Fantasies** are set in a time and place that is invented by the writer.
- **Science-fiction stories** often take place in the future, in outer space, or in some other environment that helps us see how science affects our lives.

Writers in
ACTION

Author James Berry bases the elements of his narratives on his life experiences. His Caribbean childhood and life in England provide rich inspirations for colorful settings, interesting characters, and compelling plots. To gather and develop his ideas, Berry jots down his thoughts in a notebook:

"I have over the years had dozens and dozens and dozens of notebooks. . . . When I read something, when I see something, [when] somebody has said something to me or I overhear a conversation, [or] I see something in the newspaper or on television—I want to write my own story about that particular thing."

PREVIEW
Student Work
IN PROGRESS

In this chapter, you'll follow the work of Cormac Levenson, a student at Palmetto Senior High School in Pinecrest, Florida. Cormac used prewriting, drafting, and revising techniques to develop his story "Butterbee the Wise," which appears in its entirety at the end of the chapter.

Model From Literature

Writer Italo Calvino was born in Cuba but moved with his parents to Italy when he was young. His works have been called "modern fables" because they use elements of the fable form to comment on modern life.

 **Reading Strategy: Identify With a Character** When you identify with a character from fiction, you use your own experiences to imagine how you would think, feel, or act in the character's situation. This strategy allows you to understand and participate more fully in the story. As you read this story, identify with its main character.

The Man Who Shouted Teresa

Italo Calvino

I stepped off the pavement, walked backwards a few paces looking up, and, from the middle of the street, brought my hands to my mouth to make a megaphone and shouted towards the top stories of the block: "Teresa!"

My shadow took fright at the moon and huddled between my feet.

Someone walked by. Again I shouted: "Teresa!" The man came up to me and said: "If you don't shout louder she won't hear you. Let's both try. So: count to three, on three we shout together." And he said: "One, two, three." And we both yelled, "Tereeeesaaa!"

A small group of friends passing by on their way back from the theater or the cafe saw us calling out. They said: "Come on, we'll give you a shout too." And they joined us in the middle of the street and the first man said one two three and then everybody together shouted, "Te-reee-saaa!"

Somebody else came by and joined us; a quarter of an hour later there were a whole bunch of us, twenty almost. And every now and then somebody new came along.

Organizing ourselves to give a good shout, all at the same time,

The story's main character, who is unnamed, is also the narrator, the voice telling the story.

In the story's second paragraph, Calvino uses personification to help create a mood.

This story's plot is simple and has few events: The main character is joined by others as he calls out for Teresa.

▲ **Critical Viewing** What clues in the photograph above help reveal where it was taken? [Analyze]

wasn't easy. There was always someone who began before three or who went on too long, but in the end we were managing something fairly efficient. We agreed that the "Te" should be shouted low and long, the "re" high and long, the "sa" low and short. It sounded great. Just a squabble every now and then when someone was out.

We were beginning to get it right, when somebody, who, if his voice was anything to go by, must have had a very freckly face, asked: "But are you sure she's at home?"

"No," I said.

"That's bad," another said. "Forgotten your key, have you?"

"Actually," I said, "I have my key."

"So," they asked, "why don't you go on up?"

"Oh, but I don't live here," I answered. "I live on the other side of town."

"Well then, excuse my curiosity," the one with the freckly voice asked carefully, "but who does live here?"

"I really wouldn't know," I said.

People were a bit upset about this.

"So could you please explain," somebody with a very toothy voice asked, "why you are standing down here calling out Teresa?"

"As far as I'm concerned," I said, "we can call another name, or try somewhere else. It's no big deal."

The others were a bit annoyed.

"I hope you weren't playing a trick on us?" the freckly one asked suspiciously.

"What?" I said, resentfully, and I turned to the others for confirmation of my good faith. The others said nothing, indicating they hadn't picked up the insinuation.

There was a moment's embarrassment.

"Look," someone said good-naturedly, "why don't we call Teresa one last time, then we'll go home."

So we did it again. "One two three Teresa!" but it didn't come out very well. Then people headed off home, some one way, some the other.

I'd already turned into the square, when I thought I heard a voice still calling: "Tee-reee-sa!"

Someone must have stayed on to shout. Someone stubborn.

Writing Application: Give Readers Characters With Whom They Can Identify As you prepare to write your short story, think of ways in which the story's characters will be understood or appreciated by your readers.

LITERATURE

To read another short story that has an unusual twist, read "A Shocking Accident," by Graham Greene. You can find the story in *Prentice Hall Literature: Timeless Voices, Timeless Themes,* The British Tradition.

Through dialogue, Calvino "shows," rather than tells, about the characters.

Here, the conflict develops as the characters begin to suspect the motives of the main character.

Calvino uses a series of functional paragraphs to indicate speakers of dialogue and to make transitions.

The resolution, which begins here, provides a finish to the story.

Prewriting

Choosing Your Topic

Choose a topic for your short story. Select a topic that will reach your audience, making them laugh, think, feel, or see things in a new way.

Strategies for Generating Topics

1. **Choosing a Story Type** Select a type of story to tell. For example, you may want to write a mystery, a western, or a fable or folk tale. Then, write a sentence or two telling about the story: where it takes place, who is involved, what the conflict is, and what happens at the story's end. Use these ideas as the basis for your short story.

2. **Naming Characters** Jot down the names of characters that you might like to write about. These might be ordinary names or fantastic names, such as Winky McPluto and Parsep IV. Then, write a few phrases about each character you've named. Choose the character that most interests you as the central character of your short story.

3. **Drawing a Setting** Interesting settings can sometimes trigger story ideas. Start by sketching a setting. It can be an actual setting, like a schoolroom; a historical setting, like a mining camp in the Old West; or a fantasy setting, like an undiscovered planet. Then, look at your drawing, and think of a conflict that may occur in the scene and the characters who might be in the conflict. Use these ideas to build your short story.

4. **Using Real Life** Some short stories are loosely based on real life. Think of a real-life incident that had an impact on you, and adapt it into a short story. Make a chart like the one below to help you adapt elements from real life into fiction.

**Writing Lab
CD-ROM**

For more help finding a topic, explore the activities and topic suggestions in the Choosing a Topic section of the Narration lesson.

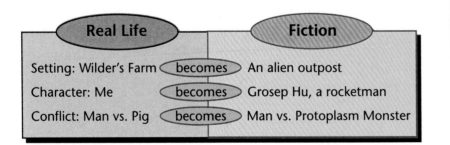

Real Life		Fiction
Setting: Wilder's Farm	becomes	An alien outpost
Character: Me	becomes	Grosep Hu, a rocketman
Conflict: Man vs. Pig	becomes	Man vs. Protoplasm Monster

TOPIC BANK

For help coming up with a topic for your story, consider these ideas:

1. **Story Set in the Past** Choose a past time period and place that interests you, and write a short story that takes place then and there. Develop a main character with a problem to solve, and tell how he or she solves it.

2. **Continuation of a Story or Movie** Think of an interesting story, movie, TV show, or play that you've read or seen. Then, in a short story, tell what happened *after* the ending.

Responding to Fine Art

3. Use the image in *Informal Evening* by Milton Avery to spark a short-story idea. Who are these people? What has just happened? Focus your storytelling by identifying a conflict among the characters in which one person wants something that the other two oppose, and let your imagination run free as you imagine what happens next.

Informal Evening, Milton Avery, D C Moore Gallery

Responding to Literature

4. Read "Araby," by James Joyce. Then, write your own version of the story, using the events that Joyce describes but setting your story in the present day, in settings with which you're familiar. You can read "Araby" in *Prentice Hall Literature: Timeless Voices, Timeless Themes,* The British Tradition.

Cooperative Writing Opportunity

5. **Stories With a Common Theme** In a group, decide on a single theme to explore. For example, you may select as a theme loyalty, sacrifice, or ambition. Once you agree on a theme, have each group member write a short story in which that theme is central. When the stories are completed, select images or pictures to enhance them. Then, bind the stories together, and share the anthology with your classmates.

Narrowing Your Topic

Once you've chosen a topic, focus your story. Use the technique known as CASPAR to help you identify important elements you'll need for your story.

Character	Who is your main character? What does he or she want?
Adjectives to describe character	What type of person is your main character?
Setting	When and where does your story take place?
Problem (conflict)	What does your character want? What is preventing him or her from getting it?
Actions (plot)	What does your character do to get what he or she wants? What happens as a result?
Resolution	How do things finally turn out?

Considering Your Audience and Purpose

How do you want your short story to affect your audience? For example, do you want them to laugh, cry, or learn something important? First, identify your purpose, and then choose details that will help you to accomplish it.

Identify Your Purpose and Create a Plan

To help you craft an effective story, identify your purpose for writing and create a plan to achieve that purpose. The chart below shows different plans to help you fulfill your purpose:

If You Want Your Audience to . . .	Then You Might . . .
. . . laugh	. . . have your characters say witty things . . . put your characters into absurd situations . . . give the narrator a dry, humorous tone
. . . cry	. . . show your characters' pain so that the audience can feel it, too . . . make your characters likeable and understandable
. . . see things in a new way	. . . create a character who learns an important lesson . . . set up events so that your audience expects one thing, and then show why something quite different must happen

Gathering Details

Choose details to make your short story come alive. Vivid, specific details help make plot events more believable and characters more interesting.

Capture Details About Characters and Setting

The more thought you put into your characters and settings, the better you'll be able to capture them on paper when it comes time to draft your short story. Following are some strategies for gathering details about character and setting:

- **Tape-Record Your Ideas** Talk about the story's characters and its settings. You could base your ideas on reality or let your imagination run free. Just talking aloud about your story will help you identify important details.

- **Sketch Your Characters and Settings** Sometimes, you can crystallize your ideas about characters and settings by sketching them. As you work, let one idea lead to another, until you have a completed vision to draw from as you draft.

- **Fill in a Character "History"** Create a history for your main character(s). Start by giving details about his or her family and background. Then, get more creative, and jot down your character's likes, dislikes, habits, and eccentricities. Refer to this "history" as you draft your short story.

Research Tip

If you've set your story in an unfamiliar time or place, do some research so that you can provide authentic details within the story.

Student Work
IN PROGRESS

Name: Cormac Levenson
Palmetto Senior High School
Pinecrest, FL

Creating a Character "History"

Cormac created a character history to help make the character Butterbee come alive for his readers.

Character name: George Butterbee

Age: Young man through 70's

Family: Only child of Doris and Alvin Butterbee of
  Breekenwood, Massachusetts

Background: Public-school education; Rossiter College,
  B.A. degree

Likes: Pistachio ice cream, rugby, and science fiction . . .

Drafting

Shaping Your Writing

Stories can take various shapes—they sometimes begin in the middle of the action, they sometimes contain stories within stories, and they sometimes contain flashbacks that interrupt the narrative to tell of events that happened earlier in time. Most stories, however, conform to a traditional plot structure, which never grows stale and enables the writer to fulfill and satisfy the expectations of the reader. Following is an example of how to use a plot diagram to shape your narrative:

Make a Plot Diagram

Making a plot diagram can help you shape your plot. A plot diagram contains the following elements: an **exposition,** which introduces the characters and setting; **rising action,** which introduces the conflict and builds gradually in intensity; and the **climax,** during which the **conflict** reaches its peak. The **falling action** refers to the events that immediately follow the climax and lead to the **resolution,** in which any unfinished issues within the story are resolved.

▲ **Critical Viewing**
If this dog were a character in a short story, what would you name him, and why? **[Analyze]**

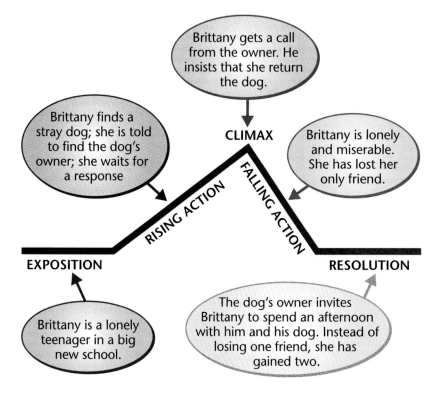

Brittany gets a call from the owner. He insists that she return the dog.

Brittany finds a stray dog; she is told to find the dog's owner; she waits for a response

CLIMAX

Brittany is lonely and miserable. She has lost her only friend.

RISING ACTION

FALLING ACTION

EXPOSITION

RESOLUTION

Brittany is a lonely teenager in a big new school.

The dog's owner invites Brittany to spend an afternoon with him and his dog. Instead of losing one friend, she has gained two.

Writing Lab CD-ROM

For more help laying out story events, fill in a Story Line Diagram in the Developing Narrative Elements section of the Narration lesson.

Providing Elaboration

As you draft, use the SEE structure to help you develop incidents in your plot or to flesh out descriptions of characters, events, and settings.

Use SEE: Statement, Extension, Elaboration

This technique, also known as "layering," can help you add depth to your writing. Each layer should help you understand more about the subject of your original statement.

S: Write a **statement** that conveys a basic idea.

E: Next, write an **extension** of that statement. An extension should take the basic thought and "go a little further" toward explaining it or defining it.

E: Finally, **elaborate** on your original statement by giving more information about it.

IN PROGRESS

Name: _Cormac Levenson_
Palmetto Senior High School
Pinecrest, FL

Using SEE to Provide Elaboration

By extending and elaborating his initial statement, Cormac helps us better understand the character of Phyllis McKinney, a waitress in a diner.

Old Phyllis had a mouth on her. When she was a ⎤ Statement

waitress at the diner, people would go there not so ⎤ Extension

much to eat as to hear Phyllis tell stories. Her

stories were about good things that happened to

people in town. (I still hear the story about the ⎤ Elaboration

time Tommy Dillers was chosen for the state

all-star baseball team and hit a home run

against Florida.)

 Revising

Once you have drafted your short story, revise it to make it more effective. Start by looking at its overall structure. Then, make sure that each paragraph and every sentence works the way you want it to. Finally, reread your story carefully to see whether your word choices support your purpose.

Revising Your Overall Structure
Build Suspense

Consider altering the structure of your short story to build suspense. For example, if your story has a very long exposition in which the setting and characters are introduced, you could eliminate some descriptive detail to more fully develop the story's conflict. Following is another strategy for making your short story interesting and suspenseful:

▶ **REVISION STRATEGY**
Adding Details to Create Foreshadowing

One way to create reader interest is to add details to create **foreshadowing,** a writer's use of clues to hint at story events that might happen next. These clues cause readers to think about what might happen next and keep them involved and interested in the story.

Student Work
IN PROGRESS

Name: _Cormac Levenson_
Palmetto Senior High School
Pinecrest, FL

Building Audience Interest Through Foreshadowing
Cormac decided to increase tension in his story by adding foreshadowing. The use of foreshadowing helps build the readers' interest in upcoming plot events.

Eventually, it was my turn to go see Butterbee, but I
What if he gave me advice that I didn't want to take—advice that ruined my
didn't really want to go.ᴧI was supposed to see   *whole life?*
                                                            What if he
George Butterbee the same day as a Greg Brown   *turned out to*

concert that I had eagerly anticipated for almost a   *be a phony?*

year. My mother didn't care; she felt you weren't

really an adult until you went to see what Mr.

Butterbee had to teach.

Revising Your Paragraphs

Create Functional Paragraphs

Functional paragraphs are short paragraphs written for effect. They can arouse or sustain interest, emphasize a point, indicate dialogue, and make transitions.

▶ **REVISION STRATEGY**
Creating Functional Paragraphs to Set Off Dialogue

Review your draft, and begin a new paragraph each time a new character begins speaking. You could give just the words of the dialogue or add a description about how the character felt, behaved, or spoke.

"Well, I guess you'll be taking your dog home now," Brittany said.

> This functional paragraph reveals a character's words.

"Sure. I guess I will."

> When the speaker changes, start a new paragraph.

"Goodbye, Goldie." Brittany's voice was very small. "Be good."

> The paragraph does not break after the description of Brittany's voice because she continues speaking.

"Actually, his name is Max."

Revising Your Sentences

Work with the sentences in your story to be sure they flow together and convey your intended meaning.

▶ **REVISION STRATEGY**
Varying Sentences

If many sentences in your story begin the same way and are of the same approximate length, vary them to liven up your story. To do this, you might throw in a long question or a short exclamation. Start a few sentences with an introductory word or phrase, or add emphasis by inverting the word order.

REPETITIVE SENTENCES: Tryson walked into the room. He looked around. He saw his long-lost baseball glove. It was on the shelf, next to the trophy.

VARIED SENTENCES: As soon as Tryson walked into the room, he looked around for his long-lost baseball glove. Would it be there? Yes! There it was, on the shelf, next to the trophy.

Technology Tip

Select the Show Invisibles option in your word-processing program to allow you to readily see paragraph breaks within your story.

Writing Lab CD-ROM

For more help, use the Revision Checker for Sentence Length in the Narration lesson.

Grammar in Your Writing
Using Phrases to Create Sentence Variety

When sentences fall into a pattern, such as subject-verb-object, it can have a dulling effect on writing. One way to inject variety into your writing is to use a variety of sentence patterns. Following are ways to begin sentences with phrases, rather than with subjects:

Prepositional Phrases: When you begin a sentence with a prepositional phrase, it stirs interest in what follows. Adjective phrases modify nouns or pronouns. Adverb phrases modify a verb, an adjective, or another adverb by pointing out *where, when, in what way,* or *to what extent.*

Adjective Phrase: With her head held high, Lana glowed as she was presented to the audience.

Adverb Phrase: Before the end of school, several students were already headed for the soccer field.

Gerund Phrases: A gerund is a form of a verb that acts as a noun. For example, in the sentence "Running is my favorite sport," *running* is a gerund. A gerund with modifiers or a complement is called a gerund phrase. Gerund phrases may contain a variety of modifiers and complements.

Gerund Phrase With Adjective: Loud hammering broke the quiet of the dawn.

Gerund Phrase With Direct Object: Delivering mail has its rewards.

Infinitive Phrases: An infinitive is a form of a verb that generally appears with the word *to* and acts as a noun, an adjective, or an adverb. An infinitive phrase is an infinitive with modifiers, a complement, or a subject, all acting together as a single part of speech.

Infinitive Phrase With an Adverb: To succeed quickly, Ned had to drop his initial plans.

Infinitive Phrase With Indirect and Direct Objects: To warn others of the danger, the group posted fliers.

Find It in Your Reading Choose a long paragraph from Italo Calvino's "The Man Who Shouted Teresa," on pages 76–77. Write out the paragraph on a sheet of paper, and identify its sentence patterns. Then, analyze the variety of sentences. Are they varied or similar in length and pattern? Why might Calvino have made the choices he made?

Find It in Your Writing Review your draft to find at least three different sentence patterns. If you can't find three different patterns, challenge yourself to add at least two more sentence patterns to your writing. You might like your story better once you've added a bit more variety!

For more on phrases, see Chapter 19.

Revising Your Word Choice
Revising Words to Suit the Characters

Not everyone speaks the same way. As you revise your characters' dialogue, make sure they use the words that fit their age, background, and personality, as well as the time and place in which they live and their relationships with the other characters. Below are three basic types of speech, which might help you identify your characters' distinct voices:

> **Formal:** People who are in business situations, unfamiliar situations, or simply proper in their manner tend to use formal speech. Their word choice is precise and carefully considered.
>> "The short story you wrote is superb, Ms. Lopez."

> **Informal:** Many people use informal speech when they speak with acquaintances or peers.
>> "Your short story is pretty amazing, Marisol."

> **Casual:** People may use nicknames and slang when they speak with family members and close friends.
>> "Mari! That was a great story!"

REVISION STRATEGY
Adding Partial Sentences, Contractions, and Slang

Most people—no matter their age, educational background, and circumstances—use some degree of informality when they speak. Review the passages of dialogue in your short story. Then, consider adding the following elements to any passages that seem stilted or overly formal.

- **Partial Sentences:** "Sure, enough . . ."
- **Contractions:** "I can't find the clicker."
- **Slang:** "You're kidding me, right?"

Peer Review
Read Aloud

Another way to evaluate the dialogue in your story is to hear it read aloud. Ask a small group of peers to read your story aloud, assigning each character to a different reader. Listen closely as your characters speak, to make sure they're using the words that suit their personalities. Ask your readers for feedback, too. When you've finished working with your peers, revise your dialogue based on their responses.

Editing
and Proofreading

Errors in your short story can distract your audience and reduce the impact of your story. To make your writing error-free, fix all errors in spelling, punctuation, and grammar.

Focusing on Punctuation

Carefully review the punctuation in your story. Be especially sure you have punctuated your dialogue correctly. Review the rules for punctuating direct quotations, paying particular attention to which punctuation marks go inside quotation marks and which appear outside them.

Grammar in Your Writing
Punctuating Direct Quotations and Dialogue

Use the following guidelines to help you punctuate your dialogue correctly:

1. Only direct quotations are enclosed in quotation marks.

   Direct Quotation: "Please help me clean up," said Brian.

   Indirect Quotation: Brian said that he wanted his friend to help him clean up.

2. Enclose the actual words spoken by a character in quotation marks. Note, however, that only the beginning of each sentence is capitalized, not the beginning of every quotation.
   "Give me the keys," said Stella, "and I'll lock up."

3. Use a comma or colon after an introductory expression.
   The boy said slowly, "I hate to see you so upset."

4. Use a comma, question mark, or exclamation point after a quotation followed by a concluding expression.
   "I'll never be happy again!" shouted Brittany.
   "That's too bad," said her mother. "What if we got you another dog?"

Find It in Your Reading Find an instance of a direct quotation and an indirect quotation within Italo Calvino's "The Man Who Shouted Teresa" on pages 76–77. Explain the difference between them.

Find It in Your Writing As you proofread your short story, double-check your punctuation of dialogue.

For more on punctuating dialogue, see Chapter 27.

5.6

Publishing and Presenting

Part of the fun of writing a short story is sharing it with others. Consider these ideas for publishing and presenting:

Building Your Portfolio

1. **Record Your Story** Alone or with a group of classmates, read your story aloud, speaking the dialogue as your characters might speak it. Tape-record your reading, and make the recording available for others to borrow.

2. **Enter a Literary Contest** Many magazines for young people or adults sponsor short-story contests. Find out the rules, submit your work, and see what happens!

Reflecting on Your Writing

Think about your experience writing a story. Then answer these questions and record your responses in your portfolio.

- As you created your story, what did you learn about yourself?

- If a friend were writing a story and wanted your advice, what would you suggest?

 **Internet Tip**

To see other stories scored with this rubric, go to **www.phschool.com**

Rubric for Self-Assessment

Use the following criteria to evaluate your short story.

	Score 4	Score 3	Score 2	Score 1
Audience and Purpose	Contains details that create a tone to engage the audience	Contains details and language that appeal to an audience	Contains few details that contribute to its purpose or appeal to an audience	Contains no purpose; is not written for a specific audience
Organization	Presents events that create an interesting, clear narrative; told from a consistent point of view	Presents sequence of events; told from a specific point of view	Presents a confusing sequence of events; contains inconsistent points of view	Presents no logical order; is told from no consistent point of view
Elaboration	Contains details that provide insight into character; contains dialogue that reveals characters and furthers the plot	Contains details and dialogue that develop character	Contains characters and setting; contains some dialogue	Contains few or no details to develop characters or setting; no dialogue provided
Use of Language	Uses word choice and tone to reveal story's theme; contains no errors in grammar, punctuation, or spelling	Uses interesting and fresh word choices; contains few errors in grammar, punctuation, and spelling	Uses clichés and trite expressions; contains some errors in grammar, punctuation, and spelling	Uses uninspired word choices; has many errors in grammar, punctuation, and spelling

Student Work
IN PROGRESS

FINAL DRAFT

Butterbee the Wise

**Cormac Levenson
Palmetto Senior High School
Pinecrest, Florida**

◀ **Critical Viewing**
Does the man in the photograph look like a "Butterbee"? Explain why or why not. **[Make a Judgment]**

I live in the small town of Breckenwood, Massachusetts, population 248. Anyway, in the town we have a legend, the legend of George Butterbee.

As the story goes, at the age of twenty-five, George Butterbee simply decided to stop talking. No one knows why, but he just stopped. At first, everyone thought he was crazy. He even tried to keep his job as a teacher. Some people think that he was so smart that they should have let him stay on anyway. But everyone at the diner was always talking about how much of a loon he was.

Luckily for all of us, old Phyllis McKinney had a crush on him, and old Phyllis had a mouth on her. When she was a waitress at the diner, people would go there not so much to eat as to hear Phyllis tell stories. Her stories were about good things that happened to people in town. (I still hear the story about the time Tommy Dillers was chosen for the state all-star baseball team and hit a home run against Florida.) Anyway, old Phyllis didn't like people talking badly about her George, so she would always stick into any conversation, whenever she could, stories about all of the smart things Butterbee had done.

Finally, after two years of telling everyone how great George was, Phyllis finally persuaded her mother's best friend, Mary Lou, to send her Mikey to get a little bit of wisdom from Butterbee. No one knew what Mr. Butterbee did, but Mikey insisted that it was the most enlightening experience he ever had. It wasn't long before everyone called him Butterbee the Wise, and all the

Because the story's narrator is a character in the story, the story is told from the first-person point of view.

Cormac uses elaboration to provide an in-depth look at Phyllis, one of the story's characters.

parents began waiting impatiently for their children to come of age so they, too, could go learn from Butterbee the Wise.

Eventually, it was my turn to go see Butterbee, but I didn't really want to go. What if he gave me some advice that I really didn't want to take—advice that I followed and that then ruined my whole life? What if I believed everything he said and he turned out to be a big phony?

I was supposed to see George Butterbee the same day as a Greg Brown concert that I had eagerly anticipated for almost a year. My mother didn't care; she felt you weren't really an adult until you went to see what Mr. Butterbee had to teach.

My mother eventually did make me go and see him. He was exactly what I expected, all long gray hair and sunken eyes, with leathery skin folding over itself. He smelled horrible. He waved me in hastily, making me feel very unwanted. He took me into the bathroom, grabbing four paper cups, a notepad, and a pen on the way. He turned the nozzle on his bathtub and on his bathroom sink. Then, he simply put a cup under both of them and ushered me into the kitchen.

I was confused: I had noticed there wasn't any water coming out of either tap. In the kitchen, he put a third cup under the faucet and turned the nozzle. The water came out with such force that both of us and everything else in the kitchen became very, very wet. He wrote on his notepad, "This is not what I want." Then, he took a pitcher and poured water from it slowly into the fourth cup.

He was trying to teach me about moderation. I was very disappointed, more so than I thought I would be. He wrote on his pad, "This is what I want."

I frowned deeply and said, "I already know about that."

He smiled deeply and took me into the bathroom, where it seemed the bathroom sink was working, just barely, so that the cup was only half full of water. The bathtub wasn't working at all, and its cup was, of course, empty. Butterbee took a long, satisfied sip of the half-full cup and wrote, "It's better than nothing."

I left, very disappointed. But with every day and every drop, I became less and less disappointed with his teachings. That was, of course, until I found out the truth about them. Two years later, Butterbee the Wise became very sick. Finally, when rumor was that he had only a day or two left, a large group of friends and I went to see him. He died looking into my eyes, asking me a question that left me forever disenchanted with his teachings. I often think back to those words and smile a sad smile. He had simply asked, "Why didn't you fix my plumbing?"

Here, Cormac uses fore-shadowing, dropping hints about the story's ending, to build suspense.

At this point, the plot takes an important turn: The main character is to visit Butterbee.

▲ **Critical Viewing**
If you were to capture the essence of water in a photograph, would your photo resemble this one? Explain. **[Compare and Contrast]**

This functional paragraph contains dialogue.

The story's final sentence serves two purposes: It provides a humorous surprise ending as well as reveals the story's theme.

Connected Assignment
Drama

When you tell a story through dialogue for a live audience, you are performing **drama.** Stories and dramas have a lot in common. What distinguishes the two is that drama is written to be performed, whereas stories are meant to be read. Actors in a drama get directions from a script, which tells them what to say—their dialogue. Stage directions tell actors how and where to move and what the setting looks like.

Below is an excerpt from a drama. Notice how the dialogue and stage directions are formatted.

Bring a story to life by writing a dramatic scene. Use the strategies on the following page to guide you as you write.

▲ Critical Viewing
This still photo is of the character Juliet from the movie *Romeo and Juliet.* What lines of dialogue do most people associate with this character? [Interpret]

MODEL

Pygmalion
George Bernard Shaw

ACT I

London at 11:15 P.M. Torrents of heavy summer rain. Cab whistles blowing frantically in all directions. Pedestrians running for shelter into the portico of St. Paul's Church (not Wren's cathedral but Inigo Jones's church in Covent Garden vegetable market), among them a lady and her daughter in evening dress. All are peering out gloomily at the rain, except one man with his back turned to the rest, wholly preoccupied with a notebook in which he is writing. The church clock strikes the first quarter.

The Daughter (*in the space between the central pillars, close to the one on her left*) I'm getting chilled to the bone. What can Freddy be doing all this time? He's been gone twenty minutes.

The Mother (*on her daughter's right*) Not so long. But he ought to have got us a cab by this time.

A Bystander (*on the lady's right*) He won't get no cab, not until half-past eleven, missus, when they come back after dropping their theater fares.

Prewriting

Find an Idea You may start with a setting, character, or plot idea. If you like, you can base your drama on another work and adapt it to suit the needs of the stage.

Plan a Plot Decide on the conflict your main character will face and how it will be resolved. Then, organize plot events in chronological order, and think about how you will tie up loose ends.

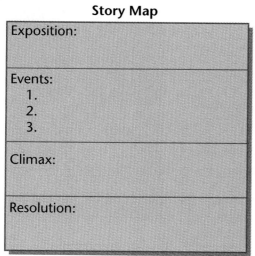

Story Map

Exposition:

Events:
  1.
  2.
  3.

Climax:
Resolution:

Develop Characters Consider physical appearance, personality traits, likely skills, and speech style as you jot down ideas about each character. Before you begin writing, pause to listen in your head to the characters' dialogue. Try to hear the way each character speaks.

Drafting Look at the excerpt from *Pygmalion* on page 92 for clues to script formatting. Craft your story as much as possible through the actors' words and actions. To do this, experiment with dialects, slang, and informal speech. Say each line of dialogue aloud, and then transcribe it exactly as you spoke it. Once you establish a speech style for a character, keep it consistent throughout the drama, unless you have a particular reason for showing how a character has grown or changed over time.

Revising and Editing Reread your script, focusing first on what happens to whom. Make sure the plot events make sense, that they forward the action of the play, and that they are interesting. Then, revise dialogue to make it realistic and to help develop characters' personalities and reveal their motivations. Also, add or revise stage directions as necessary to provide actors and directors with information about sets, movements, lighting, sound effects, and so on.

Publishing and Presenting Make a clean copy of your script and photocopy it. Distribute copies to peers and hold a script reading for your class.

Spotlight on the Humanities

Making Connections in the Arts

Focus on Theater: Sir Noel Coward

Short stories can be read in books, shared in the oral tradition, told through song, or acted out in plays and films. Sir Noel Coward was a master storyteller who wrote in several different media. Not only was Britain's Coward (1899–1973) a playwright, producer, composer, and singer, but he was also an actor. He starred in many of his own plays, which were known for their wit, sophistication, and charm. His first play was produced in 1917, when he was eighteen, and he published his first song at age twenty. Coward's most famous plays include *Private Lives*, *Blithe Spirit*, *Present Laughter*, and *Design for Living*.

▲ **Critical Viewing**
Re-create this scene by writing a description of its characters and their costumes. **[Apply]**

Music Connection Noel Coward wrote more than three hundred songs in his career. Known for their ingenious story lines and plays upon words, Coward's songs were inspired by the work of Gilbert and Sullivan. William Gilbert (1836–1911) and Arthur Sullivan (1842–1900) wrote a series of comic operas called the Savoy Operas, which were originally produced at the Savoy Theatre in London during the late nineteenth century. Among their best-known operas are *H.M.S. Pinafore* (1878), *The Pirates of Penzance* 1879), and *The Mikado* (1885).

Film Connection Written by Noel Coward, the film *Brief Encounter* (1945) has become a cinematic classic. Starring Trevor Howard and Dame Celia Johnson, *Brief Encounter* was directed by the legendary David Lean. Dame Celia Johnson was awarded the Best Actress Oscar for her performance in the film as well as the New York Film Critics Circle Award for Best Actress. An accomplished actress on the British stage, Dame Johnson went on to become one of the most famous British actresses of the 1940's based upon her role in this popular, timeless film.

Narrative Writing Activity: Short Story Inspired by a Song

Noel Coward often said that the music of Gilbert and Sullivan inspired many of his songs and story lines. Choose a song that you find particularly inspirational, and write a short story based on it. When finished, read your short story aloud for your classmates.

Media and Technology Skills

Video Adaptation of a Short Story
Activity: Create a Short Film

Many film professionals agree that short stories are ideal source material for effective films. They often contain a clearly focused structure that can be enhanced and illuminated by a transfer to film. The writer, director, designers, and actors work together to bring words on the page to life on a screen.

Think About It Choose a short story of your own or by another writer. Beginning filmmakers should look for stories that are direct and uncomplicated. Even the simplest story will take on layers of complexity when adapted for video. Brainstorm for a list of possibilities. Narrow the list to three strong choices. Have each member of your production team read the stories, and then select one to adapt.

Script It Use these two techniques to build a script for your video adaptation:

- **Storyboard the Action** A storyboard is an illustrated sequence of sketches that shows each scene in your film. Directors use storyboards to plan a film's flow of scenes.

- **Improvise Dialogue** After you decide the flow of scenes, improvise the dialogue by acting out the events in the scene. Transcribe the best lines for use in your script. Improvise an important scene several times with different actors to generate a wealth of possible lines.

What You'll Need
- video camera
- single-deck or double-deck videocassette recorder

Styles of Editing
- **In-Camera Editing** Film the scenes in the order of your storyboard. Use fade in/fade out features to form transitions.
- **Post-Shooting Editing** Shoot several versions of each scene. Then, use your recorder's editing features to copy the best takes onto a new tape.

"B. Wordsworth" by V. S. Naipaul: Storyboard

Boy plays alone in his yard   B. Wordsworth appears   Boy hears noise

Shoot It Follow your storyboard as you shoot your film. Make sure that you film each scene in your storyboard, but allow time and tape for unexpected "happy accidents." For example, if you are filming at sunset, think about how this atmospheric setting can enhance your film.

Standardized Test Preparation Workshop

Responding to Questions About Short Stories

Understanding the basic elements of a short story helps you write about them. Some standardized tests will present you with questions evaluating your interpretation of and response to what you have read. Your answers may be in the form of a brief response or a longer essay.

To respond effectively, you should become familiar with the components of a short story. These include its plot—the story's sequence of events; characters—people, animals, or other beings performing the action in the story; setting—the time and place in which the story occurs; and theme—the subject or reoccurring message of the story. Your response will be measured by the following criteria:

- a clearly stated main idea that answers the response

- writing that is focused

- proper language and use of details that skillfully elaborate upon your focus

- correct spelling, grammar, punctuation, and sentence structure

Choose one of the prompts in the following sample writing situation for the short story "The Man Who Shouted Teresa," and write a brief response.

Test Tips

- If you are responding in a timed test, allow yourself enough time to prewrite, revise, and proofread your draft.
- Keep your focus while writing your response. Make sure that you specifically answer the question being asked.

Sample Writing Situations

Italo Calvino's short stories are famous, in part, for their quirky humor and unique messages about life. "The Man Who Shouted Teresa" fits that mold: It conveys a message about life in a strangely humorous way.

Explain the ways in which Italo Calvino uses humor to get across the message of "The Man Who Shouted Teresa."

Would the impact of "The Man Who Shouted Teresa" be different if it were told from the third-person point of view? Why or why not?

Prewriting

Allow about one quarter of your time for prewriting.

Gather Details Writing down details you know about the story will help you give shape to and support your response. The details can consist of character traits, personal observations on theme or setting, or any specific feature you notice in the story (style of writing, overlapping themes, and so on). Taking note of these details will help give shape to your response.

Organize Details Organize your details according to the kind of response you are writing. For example, if you are writing about plot events, you will want to organize details chronologically; if you are comparing and contrasting, you will want to use point-by-point or subject-by-subject organization. If you are making an evaluation, you may want to list your details in order of importance so that your argument builds in intensity.

Drafting

Allow approximately half of your time for drafting.

Use the Story as Support Use details you have from the story to support your opinions. If your topic is about the relationship between the central characters, your details may include examples of dialogue between them, other story characters' observations about the couple, and passages from the story that help indicate their relationship.

Conclude Effectively Write a concluding paragraph that summarizes your main idea. To make your conclusion memorable, you may want to end with a tantalizing question, an astute observation, or an appropriate quotation.

Revising, Editing, and Proofreading

Allow about one quarter of your time for the revising and editing of your paper.

Check Language and Details Carefully review the language in your response to be sure your usage is academic and precise. Keep only those details that are essential to your response; eliminate any unnecessary details you find.

Make Corrections Above all, be sure that your response precisely answers the prompted question. If it does not, fix your response as best you can by crossing out irrelevant details and adding details that answer the question. Then, edit your writing for errors. After fixing errors in grammar, critique the content and style of your response.

Description

▲ Critical Viewing
What descriptive
words would you
choose to describe
this landscape?
[Interpret]

Description in Everyday Life

Words can bring worlds to life. All around you, in day-to-day life, you use words to describe what you see, hear, smell, taste, touch, imagine, and remember. Through the power of description, you can amaze, horrify, or gladden your listeners. You may also use description as a tool, guiding others step by step through a process or in giving directions.

Descriptive writing is part of many other types of writing: You might use description to report on a scientific experiment; explain a historic event; or discuss a painting, story, or movie. Later in life, you might have to describe yourself in a college essay or job application; tell about a product you're trying to sell; write a progress report; or provide a job description.

What Is Description?

Description is writing that appeals to one or more of the five senses—sight, sound, smell, taste, and touch. It can make you smell the smoke from a dying campfire, hear the crickets sing, or see the face of the author's friend. Description can stand on its own or breathe life into other types of writing, such as poems or stories.

Many descriptions contain

- sensory language, appealing to the five senses, which helps create a dominant impression.
- figurative language, such as simile, metaphor, hyperbole, and personification.
- vivid verbs and precise nouns.
- a logical organization.

To preview the criteria on which your description may be evaluated, see the Rubric for Self-Assessment on page 114.

Types of Description

Following are some specific types of description:

- **Functional descriptions** include precise details that objectively describe basic physical characteristics of people, places, and things.
- **Character profiles** describe actual people—their appearance, thoughts, history, accomplishments, and goals.
- **Character sketches** are detailed descriptions of fictional characters. The writer reveals a character's personality and history through description and dialogue.
- **Observations** are firsthand, factual accounts of an event or experience the writer has personally witnessed.

Writers in ACTION

Almost all writers use the power of description in their writing. Travel writer Guy Garcia, for example, uses description to enable readers to envision the places, people, and sights he has encountered on his travels throughout the world:

"What I'm trying to convey is the actual experience of being in a new place, ... of looking at what's around you with a very open appreciation for the sounds, the sights, the emotions that are being triggered by your environment. ... And if I'm doing that with honesty and clarity, the reader will be drawn along on the journey that I experienced."

PREVIEW *Student Work* **IN PROGRESS**

In this chapter, you'll follow the work of Laura Emily Goldblatt of Princeton High School, in Princeton, New Jersey. Laura's descriptive piece, "Final Night," uses sensory details to convey what a summer at camp meant to her.

Argentinian Jorge Luis Borges's writings, both fiction and nonfiction, are renowned throughout the world. The following excerpt is from an autobiographical essay entitled "Blindness."

Reading Strategy: Form Mental Images
When you read descriptions, pause occasionally to form a mental image of what the author is describing. By doing so, you will be able to more fully understand and appreciate what the author is conveying.

from *Blindness*

Jorge Luis Borges

In the course of the many lectures—too many lectures—I have given, I've observed that people tend to prefer the personal to the general, the concrete to the abstract. I will begin, then, by referring to my own modest blindness. Modest, because it is total blindness in one eye, but only partial in the other. I can still make out certain colors; I can still see blue and green. And yellow, in particular, has remained faithful to me. I remember when I was young I used to linger in front of certain cages in the Palermo zoo: the cages of the tigers and leopards. I lingered before the tigers' gold and black. Yellow is still with me, even now. I have written a poem entitled "The Gold of the Tigers," in which I refer to this friendship.

People generally imagine the blind as enclosed in a black world.

In his opening paragraph, Borges tells readers what his descriptive essay will be about. The remaining paragraphs clearly describe what it is like to "see" through Borges's eyes.

There is, for example, Shakespeare's line: "Looking on darkness which the blind do see." If we understand *darkness* as *blackness,* then Shakespeare is wrong.

One of the colors that the blind—or at least this blind man—do *not* see is black; another is red. *Le rouge et le noir* are the colors denied us. I, who was accustomed to sleeping in total darkness, was bothered for a long time at having to sleep in this world of mist, in the greenish or bluish mist, vaguely luminous, which is the world of the blind. I wanted to lie down in darkness. The world of the blind is not the night that people imagine. (I should say that I am speaking for myself, and for my father and my grand-mother, who both died blind—blind, laughing, and brave, as I also hope to die. They inherited many things—blindness, for example—but one does not inherit courage. I know that they were brave.)

The blind live in a world that is inconvenient, an undefined world from which certain colors emerge: for me, yellow, blue (except that the blue may be green), and green (except that the green may be blue). White has disappeared, or is confused with gray. As for red, it has vanished completely. But I hope some day—I am following a treatment—to improve and to be able to see that great color, that color which shines in poetry, and which has so many beautiful names in many languages. Think of *scharlach* in German, *scarlet* in English, *escarlata* in Spanish, *écarlate* in French. Words that are worthy of that great color.

Vivid words like "bluish mist" and "luminous" help Borges create a mental image for readers.

The use of repetition, such as the word "blind," throughout the essay creates a memorable, domi-nant impression.

LITERATURE

For another nonfic-tion work containing vivid description, read Mary Wollstonecraft Shelley's introduction to *Frankenstein*. The introduction to *Frankenstein* appears in *Prentice Hall Literature: Timeless Voices, Timeless Themes,* The British Tradition.

Writing Application: Create Mental Images
Before you begin to write your description, think about the words you'll choose to help your readers create mental images.

6.2 Prewriting

Choosing Your Topic

The best topics for description are those that are especially vivid or those with which you have a personal connection. Use the following strategies to help you choose a topic:

Strategies for Generating Topics

1. **Choose an Unusual Point of View** Sometimes, it's fun to describe something from a new perspective. What would the ocean look like to a high-flying gull or to a crab burrowing in the sand? Make a list of familiar people, places, and experiences—and then, imagine two or three new perspectives from which you might view each one. Choose the most interesting one as the topic for your description.

2. **Blueprint** Memories associated with places can be especially strong and vivid. Sketch a building or place that holds a special meaning for you. Label each area, and then jot down ideas that spring to mind when you remember that place. Choose your topic from among your notes.

3. **Freewrite** A great way to find out what you want to write about is to just start writing. Write nonstop for five minutes. Then, review your writing, and look for repeated ideas or for interesting ideas. Choose one to use as the topic for your description.

Writing Lab CD-ROM

For more help finding a topic, explore the activities and topic suggestions in the Choosing a Topic section of the Description lesson.

Name: Laura Emily Goldblatt
Princeton High School
Princeton, NJ

Freewriting to Generate a Topic
Laura Emily Goldblatt used the freewriting strategy to help her come up with a descriptive writing topic.

What what what what to write about? I'm not sure nothing interesting ever happens around here. School bus, school fuss. I wish I was back at camp. Crickets, trees, clouds, campfire. Making new friends. Sharing, sharing, sharing. The way we all sat together, what it felt like to be part of a teem. I mean a team. The Red Team. My Team.

TOPIC BANK

If no topic for your description comes to mind, consider these topic suggestions:

1. **Description of an Exam Room** Think of a place where you recently took a test. What did you see, hear, and smell? Use specific sensory details in a description that helps your readers join you in that room.

2. **Character Profile of a Friend** Decide on a special friend to portray. Include descriptive details that bring your friend's personality to life. You also may want to include quotations from your friend to illustrate his or her personality and views on life.

Responding to Fine Art

3. Study *Boats on the Beach* by Vincent van Gogh. Using descriptive details, first describe the painting itself and then describe its mood.

Responding to Literature

4. Samuel Pepys's *Diary* describes the Great Fire of London. Read the diary entry dated September 2, 1666, noting the ways in which Pepys brought that historic event to life. Then, think about an important or exciting event you've witnessed, and write a descriptive account of it. You can find Pepys's *Diary* in *Prentice Hall Literature: Timeless Voices, Timeless Themes*, The British Tradition.

Fishing Boats on the Beach at Saintes-Maries, Vincent van Gogh, Amsterdam, Van Gogh Museum

☑ Cooperative Writing Opportunity

5. **Travel Brochure** Create a travel brochure describing local sites of interest in your area. Each group member should pick a site and write an article describing it. Then, collect the group's finished articles, and combine them into a brochure.

Narrowing Your Topic

Once you know the general topic you want to describe, take time to narrow your description. You might choose to describe just one moment of an event or experience, just one part of a place, or just one aspect of a person.

Drawing can also help you narrow your topic.

Draw to Narrow a Topic

Make a sketch of the person, place, or event you're describing to help you bring details into focus. Don't worry about how well you draw—you never have to show your sketch to anyone else. Just think about the details that you'd like to include when you paint a picture in words.

Refer to your completed drawing as you gather details, draft, and revise your description.

Considering Your Audience and Purpose

Think about who will read your description and your purpose for writing it. What do you want your audience to feel, think, or understand when they have finished reading your description? Choose words and details that will appeal to your audience and help you to achieve your purpose for writing.

In the examples below, notice how different word choices help to achieve different purposes.

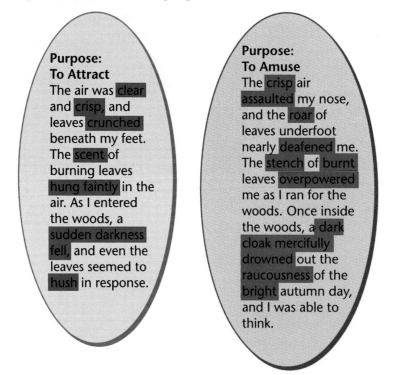

Purpose:
To Attract
The air was clear and crisp, and leaves crunched beneath my feet. The scent of burning leaves hung faintly in the air. As I entered the woods, a sudden darkness fell, and even the leaves seemed to hush in response.

Purpose:
To Amuse
The crisp air assaulted my nose, and the roar of leaves underfoot nearly deafened me. The stench of burnt leaves overpowered me as I ran for the woods. Once inside the woods, a dark cloak mercifully drowned out the raucousness of the bright autumn day, and I was able to think.

Gathering Details

Details bring a description to life. Sensory details can help your readers see, hear, smell, taste, and touch—right along with you. Use the following strategy to generate sensory details:

Use All Five Senses

Sometimes, we rely so much on our eyes that we forget about our other senses. Think of what you're describing. Then, shut your eyes. What do you hear, smell, taste, and feel? Sit inside the experience for a few minutes. Next, list the other four senses, and jot down at least two details relating to each.

Writers in **ACTION**

Famed writer Joseph Conrad says this about the power of description:

"My task ... is, by the power of the written word, to make you hear, to make you feel—it is, before all, to make you see."

Student Work **IN PROGRESS**

Name: *Laura Emily Goldblatt*
Princeton High School
Princeton, NJ

Using All Five Senses

Laura listed each of the five senses and challenged herself to come up with at least two details relating to each. Although Laura didn't use all of these images in her final draft, she liked having them there to choose from.

SIGHT	HEARING	SMELL	TASTE	TOUCH
clouds hang suspended like marionettes	crickets singing a duet with the wind	tang of smoke in the air	taste of smoke in your mouth as you smell it	crushed leaves between our fingers
red and white uniforms side by side	crackle of the campfire	the smell of rich earth	the clean, fresh air	cold autumn air
glancing across the schism to see a friend's face	wind whistling	burnt wood	mountain water	hard earth

6.3 Drafting

Shaping Your Writing
Choose a Point of View

Choose a point of view from which to write your description. Different points of view will give you access to different kinds of details and create different emotional effects. Choosing to write in the first person, using the pronoun *I,* may bring your readers closer to your experience. The third-person limited point of view gives your writing less of a personal feel. The third-person omniscient point of view allows you to show the same event or person from many different angles.

If you're describing a person—for example, your best friend—you might write from the *first-person point of view:*

> I was glad to be able to attend the concert, which was sure to be a record-breaking event. As I watched, thousands upon thousands of people streamed into the park, lugging hampers. . . .

If you were to write the same passage from the *third-person limited point of view,* you would adhere to a single point of view, but avoid the use of the pronoun *I.*

> The concert at the park was a record-breaking event. Thousands upon thousands of concert-goers streamed into the park at six o'clock, lugging hampers and chairs. . . .

Yet another choice is the *third-person omniscient point of view,* with a narrator who sees and knows everything. This point of view is usually used in fiction.

> The concert at the park was a record-breaking event. Stephanie Othaller and her children felt very lucky to have tickets. Her neighbor, however, was extremely envious, although she tried to hide her feelings from Stephanie.

▲ **Critical Viewing**
From what point of view would you choose to write a description of the scene in this photograph? Why? **[Analyze]**

Providing Elaboration

As you draft your description, help your readers feel that they know, have seen, or have experienced your topic for themselves. One way to provide such depth in your writing is to use a technique known as "depth charging."

Use Depth Charging

When you use depth charging, you provide explanations and examples that develop or support your observations or ideas. This strategy also helps ensure that your writing will be unified—that the details given all flow together in a logical way.

To use the depth charging strategy:
- Write a sentence about your topic.

- Identify a word or idea within that sentence to further develop, and write a sentence that does so.

- Identify a word or idea within the second sentence that you would like to further develop, and write a sentence that does so.

- Repeat the process until the paragraph is complete.

Student Work
IN PROGRESS

Name: *Laura Emily Goldblatt*
Princeton High School
Princeton, NJ

Using Depth Charging to Elaborate

Laura used depth charging as she began drafting her description.

Our (friends) are the reason we come back year after year. They have (shared) our joys, defeats, sorrows, and triumphs. There are few people who will ever know us with the same (intensity) as the friends we've formed bonds with here. We all fear that they will slip through our fingers like crushed leaves when the solitude of autumn sets in.

When depth charging, Laura circled key words as she drafted, then wrote sentences that elaborated on those key ideas.

6.4

Revising

Read your draft critically, and revise it where necessary. Check to be sure that your description's overall structure, paragraphs, sentences, and words work together to create a unified whole.

Revising Your Overall Structure
Create a Dominant Impression

The details in your description should work together to shape a dominant impression—the main idea or overall impact you want to form in the minds of your readers.

▶**REVISION STRATEGY**
Circling Details to Identify the Function

Circle in red pencil the details in your draft that contribute to your description's dominant impression. Circle in blue pencil any details that do not directly convey that main impression. Consider replacing or deleting passages circled in blue to give your description a specific focus and to strengthen the dominant impression you'd like to make.

Student Work
IN PROGRESS

Name: *Laura Emily Goldblatt*
Princeton High School
Princeton, NJ

Circling Details to Identify Function
Laura used circling to identify details that did not help create a dominant impression. Notice how she revised her description accordingly.

The red team and white team sit ~~parallel to~~ (across from) each other, and yet there is such a sense of unity that is ~~stifling.~~ (a powerful sense of togetherness.) For ten weeks, we have been ~~a single unit~~ (as one). No longer are we only for ourselves, (but for everyone) and thus we ~~are forced to be~~ ('ve learned) unselfish~~ness~~. Leaders emerge and we accept their authority, (allowing) ourselves to follow their ~~command.~~ (lead) The emphasis is placed on (spirit and sportsmanship,) not just winning.

> Laura wanted to create a harmonious dominant impression. She rewrote passages that did not add to the piece's sense of harmony.

Revising Your Paragraphs
Revise for Impact and Unity

Read through your description, and locate topical paragraphs—paragraphs that are organized around a topic sentence. Check to be sure that your topic sentence is placed effectively within the paragraph. Also, check to be sure that each sentence in your paragraph supports its topic sentence.

A topic sentence may appear anywhere in the paragraph: at the beginning, in the middle, or at the end. The topic sentence may create different effects on the reader, depending on its position within the paragraph.

Topic sentence as opener: *The twentieth century will be known as the Information Age.* The advent of the radio, television, fax machine, business and personal computers, and the Internet all serve to share information and speed its transmission. Via television satellites, we watch wars unfold before our eyes, and vast stores of knowledge are a mouse click away on the Internet.

Topic sentence as closer: The advent of the radio, television, fax machine, business and personal computers, and the Internet all serve to share information and speed its transmission. Via television satellites, we watch wars unfold before our eyes, and vast stores of knowledge are a mouse click away on the Internet. *In fact, the twentieth century will be known as the Information Age.*

▶ **REVISION STRATEGY**
Color-Coding Topic Sentences and Support

Read through your draft, and use a highlighter to call out topic sentences. Then, examine the placement of the topic sentences to be sure they are in the most logical, effective positions. Then, in another color, highlight the details that support the topic sentence. Delete or move to another paragraph any details that do not support the topic sentence.

I like Dale a lot, because she's someone I can count on. Once I was home sick for three weeks with pneumonia. Dale came by my house every single day to make sure I was all right, even when she wasn't allowed to see me. ~~My mother is sometimes overprotective.~~ When I started getting better, she brought me comic books and videotapes to help me pass the time. She even brought me my homework assignments—though I wished she hadn't!

Technology Tip

In a word-processing program, highlight and drag topic sentences to various positions within a paragraph. Then, examine how each position affects the impact of the topic sentence on your writing.

Revising Your Sentences
Add Descriptive Details to Your Sentences

Read through the sentences in your description, and add descriptive details, where necessary, to further explain, identify, or describe your topic. Descriptive details may include vivid nouns and verbs, adjectives and adverbs, quotations, and figurative language. Use the following strategy to add a specific type of descriptive detail to your writing.

▶ **REVISION STRATEGY**
Adding Details With Appositives

Appositives—nouns or pronouns that identify or rename other nouns or pronouns—are a good way to offer more detail about the person, place, or object being described. Examine your draft, and add appositives where more detail is necessary.

Original Sentence:

Dale finally finished the climb.

Sentence With an Appositive Phrase:

Dale, *my best friend*, finally finished the climb.

Student Work
IN PROGRESS

Name: Laura Emily Goldblatt
Princeton High School
Princeton, NJ

Adding Details With Appositives

As she reread her work, Laura began to feel that she had not fully conveyed how deep the camp friendships ran or how profound her experience had been. She added some appositives to develop her ideas.

A phoenix rising from the ashes, we, *the Red Team,* emerge, reborn and fresh after each trial, prepared to face the world again with our friends beside us.

Grammar in Your Writing
Descriptive Phrases

There are many ways to add descriptive details to your writing. Adjective phrases are prepositional phrases that modify a noun or pronoun by telling *what kind* or *which one*. Appositives and appositive phrases rename, identify, or explain the nouns or pronouns they are near.

Below, you'll learn how to identify appositives and appositive phrases and use them in your writing.

Appositives The word *appositive* comes from a Latin verb that means "to put near or next to." An **appositive** is, literally, a noun or pronoun that is put next to another noun or pronoun in order to identify, rename, or explain it.

His best quality, honesty, had always served him well.

The writer Ursula LeGuin is known for her science fiction.

Appositive Phrases When an appositive is accompanied by its own modifiers, it forms an appositive phrase. An **appositive phrase** is a noun or pronoun with modifiers, placed next to another noun or pronoun, in order to add information and details. The modifiers can be adjectives, adjective phrases, or other groups of words that function as adjectives.

Wilma Rudolph, my favorite athlete, was a great runner.

Marc introduced us to The Half-Baked Band, a group of musicians who had just returned from their world tour.

Find It in Your Reading Like appositive phrases, which rename nouns and pronouns, adjective phrases also add descriptive details to writing. Read through the excerpt from "Blindness" by Jorge Luis Borges on pages 100–101, and locate two adjective phrases. Why might Borges have chosen to use adjective phrases rather than appositive phrases there? Explain.

Find It in Your Writing Review your draft to find at least two appositives. If you can't find two appositives, challenge yourself to add them. See whether adding appositives makes your description stronger.

For more on appositives and appositive phrases, see Chapter 19.

Revising Your Word Choice

Revise Word Choice to Create a Tone

Different words evoke different moods and emotions, allowing writers to create various tones, or attitudes, toward their writing subjects. You may have heard this word joke:

> I am *strong-minded.* (admiring tone)
>
> You are *stubborn.* (neutral tone)
>
> He is *pig-headed.* (critical tone)

Although "strong-minded," "stubborn," and "pig-headed" all mean more or less the same thing, each word conveys a different tone, or attitude, the writer has toward "I," "you," and "he." Use the following strategy to give your description a definite tone:

▶ REVISION STRATEGY
Circling and Replacing Words to Create a Tone

Read through your description, and circle words or passages that don't adequately convey your attitude. Use a dictionary, thesaurus, or your own memory to locate two or three synonyms or equivalent phrases. Then, make the choice that best projects the tone you intend.

Peer Review

Share Responses

Show your revised work to a group of peers, asking them to read your description carefully with an open mind. Then, ask them the following:

- Did I use enough sensory language and descriptive details to describe my subject fully? Explain.

- Was my point of view consistent and appropriate? Explain.

- What dominant impression did the description leave?

If your classmates understood your work differently from the way you intended, consider revising your draft to better achieve your original purpose.

▼ Critical Viewing
How does this peer conference compare to ones with which you've been involved? **[Compare and Contrast]**

6.5 **Editing and Proofreading**

Errors in your description might mean that your audience will pay more attention to your mistakes than to the topic about which you're writing. Fix errors in spelling, punctuation, and grammar before you create your final draft.

Focusing on Mechanics

As you proofread, check to be sure that you have used commas in sentences correctly. Pay particular attention to appositives and appositive phrases to be sure you've correctly punctuated them.

Grammar in Your Writing
Commas With Appositives

To punctuate appositives and appositive phrases correctly, refer to the following rules:

> 1. An **essential appositive** is one that is necessary to the meaning of the sentence. It does not need commas.
>
> **Example:** The movie star Cary Grant is one of my favorites.
>
> Since the sentence does not make sense without the words *Cary Grant,* you don't need commas around the appositive.

> 2. A **nonessential appositive** or **appositive phrase** is one that can be removed without changing the sentence's meaning. It must always be set off with commas.
>
> **Example:** The real name of Cary Grant, one of my favorite stars, was Archibald Leach.
>
> **Example:** After the movie, we ate at Mr. Louis's, the restaurant with the best fries in the city.

Find It in Your Writing As you proofread your short story, double-check your punctuation of appositives and appositive phrases.

For more on punctuating appositives, see Chapter 19.

Publishing and Presenting

Share your finished description with others. Following are some ideas for publishing and presenting your work:

Building Your Portfolio

1. **Illustration of Your Description** Illustrate your description with a drawing, sketch, photograph, or painting. Then, protect your work with a binder, and display it in the class library.

2. **Local Publication** Look through local publications to see whether your profile of a resident or your description of the county fair might find a home. Call or write to the editor for information on how to submit your work.

Reflecting on Your Writing

Reflect on your experience of writing a description by answering these questions. Save your responses in your portfolio.

- What strategies for finding and narrowing a topic seem most useful to you? Explain.

- What advice would you give to someone who was going to write a description?

 **Internet Tip**

To see a descriptive essay scored with this rubric, go to
www.phschool.com

Rubric for Self-Assessment

Use the following criteria to evaluate your description.

	Score 4	Score 3	Score 2	Score 1
Audience and Purpose	Contains details that work together to create a single, dominant impression of the topic	Creates through use of details a dominant impression of the topic	Contains extraneous details that detract from the main impression	Contains details that are unfocused and create no dominant impression
Organization	Is organized consistently, logically, and effectively	Is organized consistently	Is organized, but not consistently	Is disorganized and confusing
Elaboration	Contains creative use of descriptive details	Contains many descriptive details	Contains some descriptive details	Contains no descriptive details
Use of Language	Contains sensory language that appeals to the five senses; contains no errors in grammar, punctuation, or spelling	Contains some sensory language; contains few errors in grammar, punctuation, and spelling	Contains some sensory language, but it appeals to only one or two of the senses; contains some errors in grammar, punctuation, and spelling	Contains no sensory language; contains many errors in grammar, punctuation, and spelling

6.7 Student Work IN PROGRESS

FINAL DRAFT

Final Night

**Laura Emily Goldblatt
Princeton High School
Princeton, New Jersey**

▲ Critical Viewing
Why might an event
like the one in the
photograph provide
lasting memories?
[Connect]

Summer's end 1999

I look around the campfire at the friends I've made this summer, and I wonder how I'll ever be able to say goodbye to these people, this place. There is so much here that I love. At night you can hear the crickets singing a duet with the wind as it swirls past the trees, while the clouds hang suspended like marionettes. In fact, if you hold still a moment, you can smell the rich earth on which you sit.

Sensory details such as "crickets singing a duet with the wind," "clouds hang suspended like marionettes," and "smell the rich earth on which you sit" help to create a dominant impression.

This past week, the red team and white team were challenged to the utmost, vying for "The Golden Branch," the camp's highest honor. Now, in the glow of firelight, the red team and white team sit opposite each other, yet there is a powerful sense of togetherness.

For ten weeks, the teams have shared triumph and failure. We no longer look out only for ourselves; we've learned unselfishness. Leaders emerge and we accept their authority, allowing ourselves to follow their lead. Emphasis is placed upon spirit and sportsmanship, not just upon winning. We take our losses with smiles and cheer for the winning team. Our pride expands infinitely until everything seems possible.

This camp is no ordinary place. The fields are alive; they move with us in silent cycles that only those of us willing to watch patiently can see. Each of us has had a moment that we felt the earth around us, closed our eyes, and thought, "This is perfection."

Unlike other competing groups, we are small, closely united.

Everyone knows everyone, if not by name, by sight. Even now, divided as we are, people sneak glances at one another across the schism. Camp, this camp, teaches us more about who we are, where we're going, and who we're taking with us than an entire lifetime can. Soon, a single glance reveals exactly what a person is feeling. Words become unnecessary as we sit knowing that no matter how far we fall, there will always be someone there to catch us. Like a phoenix, we, the red and white teams, rise from the ashes, reborn and refreshed after each trial, prepared to face the world again with our friends beside us.

Our friends are the reason that we come back year after year. They have shared in our joys, defeats, sorrows, and triumphs. There are few people who will ever know us with the same intensity as the friends we've formed bonds with here. We all fear that they will slip through our fingers like crushed leaves when the solitude of autumn sets in. But even if not a word is exchanged between us after that final good-bye, the emotions we have shared will last a lifetime. And so, at night, as we lie alone in our rooms, barren without the presence of our friends, our memories will creep up from under our eyelids, fly to the heavens, kiss the distances between us away, and we will once again be here together at camp.

Laura has logically organized her description, presenting one main idea with its accompanying details in each paragraph.

This instance of personification—"the fields are alive"—creates a vivid image in readers' minds.

A vivid verb and a precise noun are provided in the phrase "sneak glances."

This simile, in which campers are compared to a phoenix, helps readers understand how this experience transformed the people who shared it.

The final sentence of Laura's description is powerful and memorable.

Connected Assignment *Poem*

Successful descriptive writing makes readers feel as if they are seeing, hearing, feeling, smelling, or tasting just what the writing describes. Poems can achieve a similar effect, with words carefully chosen to create a picture for readers. Poets, too, focus particularly on the form and sound of words, and because poetry is generally brief, each word really counts.

Let the writing process skills described below guide you in writing your own poem.

Prewriting Read over journal entries to recall experiences that generated strong emotions, or talk with a friend about what makes you especially optimistic or somber. Choose one of those ideas to be the subject of your poem.

Then, brainstorm for sensory images that will help you bring the subject of your poem to life. Push yourself to go beyond visual images by completing a sensory language chart like the one shown here.

▲ **Critical Viewing**
Why might this picture inspire a poem?
[Connect]

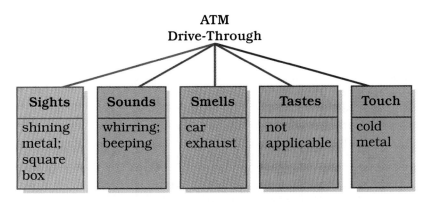

ATM
Drive-Through

Sights	Sounds	Smells	Tastes	Touch
shining metal; square box	whirring; beeping	car exhaust	not applicable	cold metal

Drafting As you draft, string words together, listening to how the combinations sound. Experiment with various rhythms and sound combinations. Focus on expressing a specific mood, and choose descriptive modifiers, verbs, and nouns that support the mood.

Revising and Editing Test your poem by reading it to some peers and asking for feedback. Take notes as they give advice. If necessary, use a thesaurus to find words to replace weak or inappropriate words. A rhyming dictionary can help you to find alternative rhymes.

Publishing and Presenting With a few peers, hold a poetry reading for a group of friends or family. Ask for feedback, and answer questions when the reading is over.

Spotlight on the Humanities

Appreciating Art
Focus on Art: Art Deco

The style of Art Deco—with its emphasis on geometric shapes and sleek, slender lines—revealed itself in jewelry, furniture, and interior design in the 1920's and 1930's. The name *Art Deco* came from the title of a Paris design show in 1925: *Exposition Internationale des Arts Decoratifs et Industriels Modernes.* One of the early artists who created in the Art Deco style was glassmaker René Lalique. The style quickly became popular in the United States, and its characteristics were soon to be found not only in interior design but in roadside diners, skyscrapers, trains, and jukeboxes.

Connection to Dance An important influence on the development of Art Deco was the ballet company Ballets Russes, founded by Russian director and art critic Sergei Diaghilev (1872–1929) in 1909. Centered in Paris, the Ballets Russes was noted for the magnificent Oriental designs in its stage decor as well as for its use of exotic colors in the production designs. Diaghilev experimented with music, costume design, and painting, as well as dance, and his work inspired such artists as Pablo Picasso, Henri Matisse, Anna Pavlova, and Vaslav Nijinsky to contribute to the company.

Connection to Architecture One of the great examples of the Art Deco style is Radio City Music Hall in New York City, pictured above. Opening its doors in 1932, Radio City Music Hall was known as "The Showplace of the Nation" with its lavish musical productions. A console organ sits on each side of the largest proscenium stage in the world. Each console weighs 2.5 tons and requires eleven rooms to house its pipes. The stage consists of four elevators that can be lowered twenty-seven feet into the basement. The hydraulic system that runs the elevators was considered so inventive that the U.S. Navy came to Radio City during World War II to study it for use on U.S. aircraft carriers.

Descriptive Writing Activity: Criticize a Design
Study the photograph above, which shows the interior of Radio City Music Hall in New York City. Then, write a review of the new theater, describing what it felt like to sit in such a massive Art Deco hall.

Media and Technology Skills

Evaluating Images

Activity: Analyzing Propaganda Images

Images in print and broadcast media are often used as propaganda to support or renounce a specific cause, institution, or person. Some propaganda is strictly political, such as the campaign advertisements in a presidential race. Other propaganda, such as public-service announcements, support a specific cause, such as smoking prevention or home safety.

Whether or not you agree with a piece of propaganda, you should always take time to evaluate the images being used. Because these issues are often highly emotional, the images used in propaganda are often loaded with positive or negative associations.

Think About It Choose a poster, magazine advertisement, or television commercial that you suspect contains propaganda. Select a piece that uses strong images to capture your attention. Your analysis will help you understand how these images work.

Describe It Begin by making a list of words that you associate with the images in the work. Your list can take the form of the list that follows, which was created in response to a political advertisement featuring workers on a construction site. Use the words in your list to create an overall description of the images used in the propaganda.

Image Shown	Inner Meaning
construction site	building and growth
	progress
	productivity
sunny day	prosperity
	comfort and warmth
	happiness

Analyze It After describing the images, analyze them to determine how effectively and fairly they persuade an audience. Consider whether or not some images are overly "weighted," or loaded with emotional appeals. Highly sentimental or sensational images can provoke a strong reaction, but one that might not be solidly supported by facts. Write a brief but complete assessment of the propaganda you have investigated.

Symbols and Propaganda

Symbols are potent images because viewers associate a wide range of meanings with common symbols. Think about what the following symbols might mean in various forms of propaganda:

- American flag
- rainbow
- babies or children
- Uncle Sam
- elephant
- donkey
- eagle
- Statue of Liberty
- dollar bill
- skull
- heart

Standardized Test Preparation Workshop

Strategy, Organization, and Style

Writing segments on standardized tests often measure your knowledge by asking you to evaluate a piece of writing. You may be asked to assess the writer's organizational strategy, the complexity of the language used, and the overall style of the passage. You will typically be given a descriptive passage to read in which each sentence is numbered. Following the passage will be several specific questions based on the reading.

Some of the types of questions you should expect follow:

- Style questions focus on the use of appropriate and effective language for the intended audience.

- Organization questions ask you to look at the order of sentences and paragraphs in the context of the overall organizational strategy of the passage.

- Strategy questions offer several options for revising words and phrases and ask you to select the best option within the context of the essay.

The sample test items that follow will give you practice answering questions on writing strategy, organization, and style.

Test Tip

If you are unsure of an answer, try eliminating one or more obviously incorrect answers and then choose between those remaining.

Sample Test Items

Directions: Read the passage, and then answer the questions that follow.

(1) It is a clear lake, devoid of the dangerous crocodiles and parasites found in many African lakes. (2) Lake Kivu, located on the border between Rwanda and the Democratic Republic of Congo in central Africa, is unique among African lakes. (3) Kivu is set among towering volcanoes. (4) It is a tragedy that political upheaval has led to widespread violence in Rwanda.

1. Which part does not support the main idea of the passage?
   A. part 1
   B. part 2
   C. part 3
   D. part 4

2. What revision would **best** improve the passage?

A. Add a transition at the beginning of part 2.

B. Change the present tense to the past tense.

C. Delete part 4.

D. Correct as is

Answers and Explanations

The correct answer for item 1 is *D*. It does not help describe Lake Kivu.

The correct answer for item 2 is *C* because part 4 does not support the topic sentence.

Practice 1 **Directions:** Carefully read the passage below. Select the letter that best answers each of the questions following the passage.

(1) Vehicles with advanced technologies are being designed now and will be available in the near future. (2) Several automobile manufacturers are already able to make <u>very advanced cars</u>. (3) Cars of all colors with on-board navigation, personal computers, infrared night-vision displays, and lane-sensing video cameras are the automotive wave of the future. (4) Some automobile makers are even researching collision-avoiding vehicles in which an on-board computer will be able to sense danger and automatically steer the car to safety.

(5) <u>The technological advances of the late twentieth century</u> surpass all of those in previous centuries combined. (6) The next ten years will make the accomplishments of the 1900's seem like child's play. (7) Researchers formerly dedicated only to military and space technologies are using their discoveries to enhance and even create new consumer products. (8) Advances in all areas, especially vehicle technology, will be exciting to watch and to use.

(9) Scientists and engineers are spending much of their time making the machines around us faster, safer, and easier to use. (10) Technology will guarantee an exciting twenty-first century. (11) More sophisticated automotive technology will mean decreased drive times and increased <u>performance</u> on the road.

1. Choose the **most logical** paragraph order.
   A. 1, 3, 2
   B. 3, 2, 1
   C. 2, 1, 3
   D. Correct as is

2. In which part should the underlined phrase be replaced by more precise language?
   A. part 2
   B. part 5
   C. part 11
   D. Correct as is

3. In part 3, which of the following should be deleted to eliminate irrelevant information?
   A. of all colors
   B. and lane-sensing video cameras
   C. automotive wave of the future
   D. personal computers

4. If the author wanted to rewrite part 4 for an audience of college engineering students, which of the following would be the **best** revision?
   A. A sophisticated on-board computer will be able to sense danger and automatically steer the car to safety.
   B. A computer will be able to sense danger. It will then automatically steer the car to safety.
   C. Collision-avoidance radar will improve safety statistics by sensing and correcting the vehicle's position relative to lane markings and other vehicles.
   D. Correct as is.

Persuasion
Persuasive Speech

Persuasion in Everyday Life

Persuasive communication is a powerful tool that is useful throughout life, in all types of situations. At home, for example, you might persuade your family to work together on a community project. At school, you might persuade classmates to vote for a student politician. Later, in the working world, you might convince an employer that you are the right person for a job. Once you have that job, you may need persuasion to convince buyers of the value of a product or to gain a raise or promotion.

▲ **Critical Viewing**
Presenting a persuasive speech successfully involves effective writing as well as presenting skills. What presenting skills does the woman pictured seem to be employing? **[Analyze]**

What Is a Persuasive Speech?

A **persuasive speech** is a spoken statement that presents a position and tries to convince an audience to accept that position or to take action. An effective persuasive speech

- addresses an issue of concern or importance to the speaker.
- clearly states the speaker's position and goal.
- supports the position with clearly organized facts, examples, and statistics.
- addresses the knowledge level, experiences, needs, and concerns of the intended audience.
- uses rhetorical, or speaking, devices to grab and hold the audience's attention.

To preview the criteria on which your persuasive speech may be evaluated, see the Rubric for Self-Assessment on page 139.

Writers in **ACTION**

Many professionals, such as politicians and ad writers, use persuasion in work situations. Public defender Cary Bricker relies on persuasion to get the best possible results for her clients:

"To be persuasive in writing, I have to focus on word usage. I focus on issues. I have to be very clear in my writing. I have to tailor my writing toward the issues that I'm taking on. . . . The idea is to persuade, through my writing, through every step of the case."

Types of Persuasive Speeches

There are many types of persuasive speeches. Following are some examples:

- **Campaign speeches** attempt to persuade voters in local, state, or national elections.
- **Public-service announcements** use advertising techniques to focus on important public issues such as wearing seat belts or getting an education.
- **Inspirational speeches** seek to persuade an audience to strive to reach specific goals.

PREVIEW *Student Work* **IN PROGRESS**

In this chapter, you'll follow the work of Marvin Astorga, a student at Bel Air High School in El Paso, Texas. Concerned about a proposal to adopt a four-day school week, Marvin prepared a speech to present at a school board meeting. A completed version of Marvin's speech appears at the end of the chapter.

In 1873, Susan B. Anthony was tried for breaking the law that forbade women to vote. Before her trial, she went on a speaking tour during which she delivered the following powerful persuasive speech.

Reading → **Writing**
Connection

Reading Strategy: Evaluate an Argument *When you read a piece of persuasion, evaluate the writer or speaker's argument by weighing the evidence that is presented and deciding whether you find the argument convincing.*

Woman's Right to Suffrage

Susan B. Anthony

Friends and Fellow-citizens: I stand before you to-night, under indictment for the alleged crime of having voted at the last Presidential election, without having a lawful right to vote. It shall be my work this evening to prove to you that in thus voting, I not only committed no crime, but, instead, simply exercised my citizen's right, guaranteed to me and all United States citizens by the national Constitution, beyond the power of any state to deny.

Our democratic-republican government is based on the idea of the natural right of every individual member thereof to a voice and a vote in making and executing the laws. We assert the province of government to be to secure the people in the enjoyment of their unalienable rights. We throw to the winds the old dogma that governments can give rights. Before governments were organized, no one denies that each individual possessed the right to protect his own life, liberty, and property. And when 100 or 1,000,000 people enter into a free government, they do not barter away their natural rights; they simply pledge themselves to protect each other in the enjoyment of them, through prescribed judicial and legislative tribunals. They agree to abandon the methods of brute force in the adjustment of their differences, and adopt those of civilization.

* * *

▲ **Critical Viewing**
What can you learn about the time in which Anthony lived by looking at this photograph? **[Analyze]**

Anthony clearly states her purpose in her opening paragraph.

L̲ITERATURE

For another example of a persuasive speech, see Winston Churchill's stirring "Wartime Speech" in *Prentice Hall Literature: Timeless Voices, Timeless Themes*, The British Tradition.

"All men are created equal, and endowed by their Creator with certain unalienable rights. Among these are life, liberty, and the pursuit of happiness. That to secure these, governments are instituted among men, deriving their just powers from the consent of the governed."

Here is no shadow of government authority over rights, nor exclusion of any from their full and equal enjoyment. Here is pronounced the right of all men, and "consequently," as the Quaker preacher said, "of all women," to a voice in the government. And here, in this very first paragraph of the declaration, is the assertion of the natural right of all to the ballot; for, how can "the consent of the governed" be given, if the right to vote be denied?

* * *

The preamble of the federal constitution says:

"We, the people of the United States, in order to form a more perfect union, establish justice, insure domestic tranquillity, provide for the common defense, promote the general welfare and secure the blessings of liberty to ourselves and our posterity, do ordain and establish this constitution for the United States of America."

It was we, the people, not we, the white male citizens, nor yet we, the male citizens; but we, the whole people, who formed this Union. And we formed it, not to give the blessings of liberty, but to secure them; not to the half of ourselves and the half of our posterity, but to the whole people—women as well as men. And it is downright mockery to talk to women of their enjoyment of the blessings of liberty while they are denied the use of the only means of securing them provided by this democratic-republican government—the ballot.

* * *

For any State to make sex a qualification that must ever result in the disenfranchisement of one entire half of the people is to pass a bill of attainder, or an *ex post facto* law, and is therefore a violation of the supreme law of the land. By it, the blessings of liberty are forever withheld from women and their female posterity. To them, this government has no just powers derived from the consent of the governed. To them, this government is not a democracy. It is not a republic. It is an odious aristocracy; a hateful oligarchy of sex; the most hateful aristocracy ever established on the face of the globe.

Citing a familiar passage from the Declaration of Independence helps Anthony connect her ideas to the audience's background knowledge and experiences.

Repetition of the word we creates a stirring rhythm that supports Anthony's analysis of the Constitution.

Anthony ends this portion of her speech with a stirring restatement of her position.

Reading Writing Connection

Writing Application: Building an Argument
Build a strong argument in your speech by providing thorough supporting evidence.

Choosing Your Topic

To write an effective persuasive speech, it helps to believe in the argument that you are making. Start with a topic that truly interests or concerns you, and develop it into a persuasive speech. Use the following strategies to find a topic that you can develop with honest commitment:

Strategies for Generating Topics

1. **Find a "Hot Topic"** When controversy flares up in the news, the debate usually centers on important political or social issues. Scan newspaper headlines, and listen to newscasts for controversial topics that evoke strong reactions in you. In a chart like the one below, note the specific conflict, the underlying issues, and your opinion about the topic. Review your chart to find a topic for your speech.

Topic	Underlying Issues	My Opinion
A student who missed four rehearsals is allowed to play in the winter concert.	◆ student responsibility ◆ appropriate punishments	It's not fair to let one student get away with breaking a rule, even if it seems minor.

2. **Hold a Discussion Group** Tap into school or community issues by holding a discussion with students, neighbors, or other local residents. Find out what key issues and concerns really get people talking. Note topics that generate the most controversy or disagreement. You may find that one topic is particularly interesting. If so, choose that as the topic for your persuasive speech.

3. **List and Respond** Make a list of the speeches you hear in one day or one week. You can include everything from advertisements and public-service announcements to campaign and pep-rally speeches. Briefly describe each speech, and note your response. Then, review your list of descriptions and responses, and choose the topic about which you have the strongest feelings.

Writing Lab CD-ROM

For more help finding a topic, explore the activities and topic suggestions in the Choosing a Topic section of the Persuasion lesson.

TOPIC BANK

If you have trouble coming up with a topic on your own, try one of these:

1. **Address About Violence in Video Games** Plan a speech in which you present your opinions about the amount of violence in today's most popular video games. Choose a specific goal for your speech, such as regulating the games, instituting a stronger rating service, or eliminating current restrictions.

2. **Speech Concerning the Portrayal of Women on Television** When television became popular in the 1950's, women's roles were mostly restricted to housewives and entertainers. Give a speech in which you analyze how television portrays women today. In it, convince your audience that your analysis is accurate, and encourage them to take a specific action, such as writing letters or boycotting a network.

Responding to Fine Art

Grand Voyages (Part Four, Plate VIII), DeBry, Courtesy of the John Carter Brown Library at Brown University

3. This painting of Christopher Columbus departing from Spain in 1492 suggests the artist's opinion of the explorer's achievements. Do you agree with the artist? Write a speech in which you argue for or against celebrating Columbus and his accomplishments with a national holiday.

Responding to Literature

4. Read "Defending Nonviolent Resistance" by Mohandas K. Gandhi. Write a persuasive speech in which you respond to Gandhi's ideas, arguing for or against his philosophy. You can find this piece in *Prentice Hall Literature: Timeless Voices, Timeless Themes*, The British Tradition.

Cooperative Writing Opportunity

5. **Driving-Age Debate** Form two teams to debate this resolution: In the interest of public safety, the driving age should be raised to nineteen. Members of each team should work together to plan their debate strategy, with each student assigned to speak on a specific aspect of the topic. Stage the debate, and have classmates act as judges.

Narrowing Your Topic

After selecting a broad topic, focus on a specific element or aspect of it that you can fully and completely support. If, for example, you choose a topic such as "Health Care," you would need many hours to identify every important issue. A narrower related topic, such as "The Importance of Preventive Care," would be a more suitable topic for a short persuasive speech. Use the following strategy to help you narrow your topic.

Create an Outline

You may be familiar with outlining a topic as a way of organizing an essay, but you can also use this strategy to narrow your topic. Creating an outline helps to divide your topic into smaller parts. Begin by writing your broad topic as the main level of an outline. Divide the topic into lettered heads (A, B, C, and so on). Then, divide those headings into numbered subheads (1, 2, 3, and so on.) Review your outline, and choose a single subheading to be the narrowed topic for your persuasive speech.

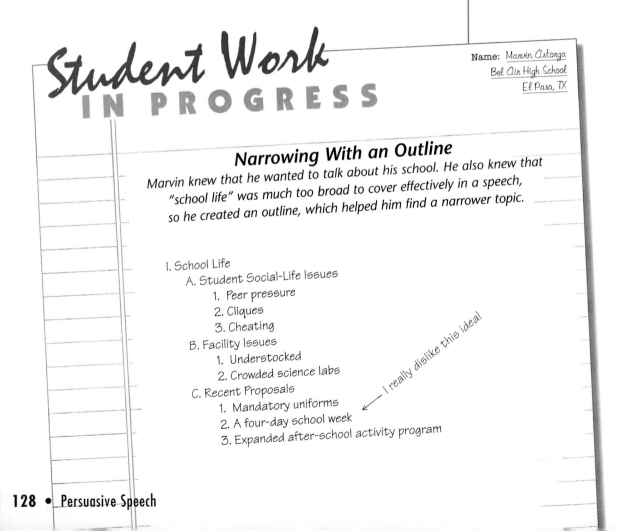

Student Work
IN PROGRESS

Name: Marvin Astorga
Bel Air High School
El Paso, TX

Narrowing With an Outline

Marvin knew that he wanted to talk about his school. He also knew that "school life" was much too broad to cover effectively in a speech, so he created an outline, which helped him find a narrower topic.

I. School Life
    A. Student Social-Life Issues
        1. Peer pressure
        2. Cliques
        3. Cheating
    B. Facility Issues
        1. Understocked
        2. Crowded science labs
    C. Recent Proposals
        1. Mandatory uniforms
        2. A four-day school week   ← I really dislike this idea!
        3. Expanded after-school activity program

Considering Your Audience and Purpose

As you plan your speech, it is important that you consider both your audience and your purpose. Your audience might be one person, such as a friend, parent, or boss, or a large crowd, such as a school assembly or the readers of a newspaper. Your basic purpose is to persuade your audience, but you need to set a more specific goal to be able to assess the success of your speech.

Suit Your Audience's Needs

Putting yourself in your audience is a good way to make sure that you have gathered enough information about a topic. Imagine that you are an audience member, and make a list of the things you would like to find out when listening to a speech on your topic. As you gather ideas, use your list to help you make sure that you are tailoring your speech to your audience's specific concerns and expectations.

Identify a Specific Purpose

It's not enough to say that your purpose is to persuade. You need to state a specific purpose for your speech and then gather details that will help you to achieve that purpose. For example, do you want your listeners to sign a petition? To volunteer at a local recycling plant? Use a chart like the one below to state a general purpose, and then refine it into a definite action that you would like your audience to take.

General Purpose	Specific Purpose
Persuade people to support the school theater department.	Persuade parents to attend the opening-night benefit performance of the play.
Inspire students to achieve success at school.	Inspire every student in your class to set five specific school goals that they can achieve by the end of the month.
Convince people that animals have rights.	Convince students to support animal rights by writing letters to businesses discouraging testing on animals.

Writing Lab CD-ROM

To see audio-annotated models written for different purposes, see the Considering Audience and Purpose section of the Persuasion lesson.

Gathering Evidence

The strength of your persuasive speech will depend on the quality of your analysis and evidence. You won't persuade anyone unless you have facts, details, anecdotes, and personal experiences to support your statements. Use the following strategies to collect information you will use to support your claims.

Conduct Research

Unless you're already an expert on your topic, explore reliable sources to collect facts, statistics, and examples you can use to support your argument. The following are suggestions to guide your research:

- Consult books by experts, respected magazines, and influential periodicals.
- Visit Internet sites that are sponsored by well-known organizations or prominent individuals.
- Set specific goals and stay on track so your research time will be most effective.
- Scan indexes, tables of contents, and summaries for the information you need.
- Don't ignore facts that contradict your position. Keep track of them, and hunt down additional information that answers each assertion. You can use a T-chart to collect and categorize the details you uncover.

Complete a T-Chart

Use a two-sided T-chart to organize information for and against your position. This is particularly effective when you plan to talk about a controversial subject. It is important to collect information on both sides of an issue so that you can weigh the relative strengths of each position.

List your position in one column and the opposing position next to it. If you have more evidence against your position than for it, reconsider your position or find more evidence that supports your opinion.

Reasons to Vote for the Library Tax Levy	Reasons to Vote Against the Library Tax Levy
Library is understocked and overcrowded	Expensive
Reference sources are outdated	The library is used by only 43% of the town
The expansion will create a new multimedia center	

Research Tip

Make a research plan before you begin gathering evidence. Doing so will help you to stay focused on your topic. It will also help ensure that you gather evidence from a variety of sources.

Conduct Interviews and Surveys

In addition to conducting research, you may want to conduct live interviews—if appropriate for your topic. If you decide to conduct an interview, keep these tips in mind:

- Prepare a list of questions that will help you focus the interview.

- Always speak politely, and allow the subject enough time to respond.

- Use a tape recorder, if possible, or take accurate notes.

⚙ Grammar and Style Tip

Create survey questions that are unbiased. For example, instead of asking "Will you vote against the tax levy?" ask "How will you vote on the tax levy: for or against?"

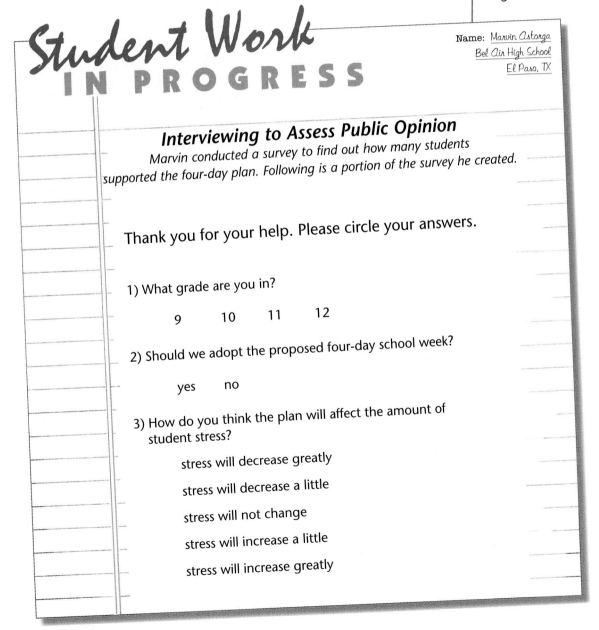

Student Work
IN PROGRESS

Name: Marvin Astorga
Bel Air High School
El Paso, TX

Interviewing to Assess Public Opinion

Marvin conducted a survey to find out how many students supported the four-day plan. Following is a portion of the survey he created.

Thank you for your help. Please circle your answers.

1) What grade are you in?

   9   10   11   12

2) Should we adopt the proposed four-day school week?

   yes   no

3) How do you think the plan will affect the amount of student stress?

   stress will decrease greatly

   stress will decrease a little

   stress will not change

   stress will increase a little

   stress will increase greatly

Drafting

Shaping Your Writing

Once you've finished gathering evidence to include in your speech, write out a first draft. In preparing your draft, keep in mind that your argument will be presented orally. Pay attention to the sound of the language, as well as to its meaning.

Focus on Your Appeal

An effective persuasive speech presents a clear and specific appeal. Remember that your audience is listening to your ideas, not reading them. Begin with a precise and emphatic statement of your position.

SAMPLE APPEALS:	I adamantly oppose the four-day school week proposal.
	I urge you to vote for Vincent Hernandez, clearly the strongest candidate for Senior Class President.

After stating your appeal, present the facts and ideas that support your position. Finally, conclude your speech with a restatement of your original appeal. Because the final words of your speech will have a particularly strong effect on your audience, use this opportunity to present your most direct and attractive appeal.

▲ **Critical Viewing**
What sorts of appeals have you seen on flyers like the one the student above is distributing? **[Relate]**

Providing Elaboration

Use "Layering"

A unified paragraph, in which the ideas flow logically, is much easier for an audience to understand than a paragraph of disjointed ideas. As you draft, use layering to help you create unified, effective paragraphs.

The acronym SEE can help you remember the three parts of a successfully layered paragraph.

- **S** stands for **Statement.** Begin by stating the topic of the paragraph.

- **E** stands for **Extension.** Extend the topic by connecting it to the original statement.

- **E** stands for **Elaboration.** Provide the facts, statistics, and other elements that support your topic statement.

7.4 Revising

Once you've finished your first draft, revise it by focusing on its overall structure, paragraphs, sentences, and words.

Revising Your Overall Structure
Check for Unity

Your speech should leave listeners with a strong, lasting impression. To achieve this goal, you need to present a unified argument—one that focuses on a single important or main idea. Each paragraph in your speech should contribute to its main idea. Likewise, each sentence within each paragraph should support the main idea of the paragraph.

▶ **REVISION STRATEGY**
Outlining and Reflecting

Just as you can use outlining to narrow a topic, you can also use it to evaluate the structure of a first draft. First, summarize the main point of each paragraph. In the margin of your paper, write a heading that describes it. Then, organize the headings into an outline, and use this to review the unity of your overall structure. Eliminate paragraphs that are not directly related to your topic. Also, consider reordering your points to strengthen the flow of your ideas.

Name: Marvin Astorga
Bel Air High School
El Paso, TX

Outlining to Check Unity

After writing his first draft, Marvin created an outline and adjusted the order in which he presented his arguments.

I. Why I Am Against the Four-Day School Week Proposal
 A. Parents' schedules
 B. Hard for students to adjust
 C. Student fatigue
II. Survey Results

Revising Your Paragraphs

▶ **REVISION STRATEGY**
Revising to Create Parallelism

Speakers use a variety of techniques to help them communicate effectively. One common strategy is to use parallelism, the repetition of words, phrases, or grammatical structures. Like repetition, parallelism helps speakers establish ear-catching rhythms that help listeners stay focused and attentive.

One of the most trusted strategies for effective speaking is the "rule of three." Look in your draft to find sets of three facts or elements. Then, place them in parallel structures.

Paragraph Without Parallelism

The new library will help our community in many ways. The media center will be a vital place to study and learn. Emphasizing the connection between reading and technology sends an important message to children growing up in our area. The improved library will help us all gain the skills we need every day.

Paragraph With Parallelism

The new library will help our community in many ways. The media center will be a vital place to study, to learn, and to explore. By emphasizing the connections among reading, research, and technology, we send an important message to children growing up in our area. The improved library will help us all gain the skills we need in our daily lives, at school, and in an increasingly competitive marketplace.

Student Work IN PROGRESS

Name: Marvin Astorga
Bel Air High School
El Paso, TX

Revising to Create Parallelism

Marvin revised the final sentence of his opening paragraph to include a set of parallel ideas that establish an effective flow of ideas.

I adamantly oppose the new proposal because it will increase student fatigue, ~~create potentially dangerous disorientation, and interfere with parents' schedules.~~ The plan will also be disorienting, which could be dangerous. Parents' schedules will be disturbed, too.

Revising Your Sentences

▶ **REVISION STRATEGY**
Eliminating Errors in Logic

Look for the following errors in logic as you review your draft. Correct any and all instances you find.

- **Circular reasoning** is an attempt to prove a statement by restating it in a new way. Example: *This recommendation is illegal because it is against the law.*

- An **either/or argument** allows for only two possibilities, when, in fact, there are many others. Example: *If we advertise on television, people will buy our magazine.*

- A **questionable cause-and-effect** statement gives a cause that did not necessarily result in the stated effect. Example: *Most offices today use computers instead of typewriters because typewriters are so noisy.*

- An **overgeneralization** is a broad statement that is all-inclusive but cannot be true. Example: *Everyone believes that this soup will cure the common cold.*

Grammar in Your Writing
Parallelism

Whenever you present a comparison or a series of ideas that are equal in importance, express them in parallel grammatical structures.

Parallel Words: The board reviewed three aspects of the plan: economic, social, and educational.

Parallel Phrases: Surveys were available at the library, in the cafeteria, and on the Internet.

Parallel Clauses: We learned who approved of the plan, who disapproved, and who had no opinion.

Avoid faulty parallelism, which results when ideas of equal importance are not expressed in equal grammatical structures. To correct faulty parallelism, make sure that each idea is expressed with the same grammatical structure.

Find It in Your Reading Review "Woman's Right to Suffrage" on pages 124–125. Identify three sentences that contain parallel words, phrases, or clauses.

Find It in Your Writing Review your draft, correcting faulty parallelism. Then, add parallel structure to emphasize key points.

For more on parallelism, see Chapter 20.

Revising Your Word Choice

Trim Unnecessary Words and Phrases

Few things are as tiring as listening to someone go on and on about a topic. Avoid boring your audience—trim unnecessary words and phrases from your persuasive speech. Doing so will ensure that your audience hears only the strong, important points in your speech.

▶ **REVISION STRATEGY**
Deleting Empty Phrases and Hedging Words

Empty phrases say nothing. Hedging words and phrases lessen the impact of what you say. Read through your draft, and, whenever you come across an empty or hedging word or phrase, delete it. Then, reread the surrounding text to be sure that it still makes sense.

Following are some examples of empty phrases and hedging words:

Empty Phrases: as I said before, needless to say, in my opinion, it is a fact that, it is also true that, there are, the reason was that, the thing is, what I mean is, given the fact that

Hedging Words and Phrases: almost, it seems, kind of, quite, rather, somewhat, sort of, tends, probably, fairly

Student Work
IN PROGRESS

Name: Marvin Astorga
Bel Air High School
El Paso, TX

Deleting Unnecessary Words
*Marvin revised these sentences to delete unnecessary qualifiers
and to revise an overgeneralization.*

Finally, ~~probably~~ one of the most important reasons for rejecting this

proposal is that parents' schedules will be ~~fairly~~ drastically affected.

Working parents will have ⟨difficulty accommodating the new school hours.⟩ ~~no way of picking up their kids from~~ school.

Consider Connotations

A word's dictionary definition is called its **denotation.** The feelings or associations the word suggests are its **connotations.** As you review your word choices, consider the positive or negative associations of each word.

Negative	Neutral	Positive
nosy	inquisitive	curious
relentless	unyielding	determined
trendy	in style	fashionable
bossy	firm	assertive

 REVISION STRATEGY
Annotating Word Choices

Use + or – signs to mark the positive or negative connotations of important words in your speech. You might use ++ or – – to indicate words with particularly strong connotations. After marking each important word, look at the overall pattern. If you have too many + or – symbols, consider changing some words to create a less emotional appeal.

Peer Review

Replay

Practicing your speech for a partner is one of the most valuable strategies you can use to review a persuasive speech. After practicing your speech, assess its impact by asking questions such as the following:

- What was your main impression of the speech?
- What do you think my goal was? Did I achieve it?
- Which connections confused or misled you?
- What arguments did I leave out?

You may want to make revisions in your speech based on your partner's suggestions. Then, practice delivering your speech once more before you make your formal presentation.

Writers in
ACTION

When it comes to persuading an audience, the words you choose are just as important as your argument or position. Joseph Conrad is acknowledged as a writer who used words brilliantly. Conrad emphasized the impact of words over meaning when he wrote,

"He who wants to persuade should put his trust not in the right argument, but in the right word."

Editing and Proofreading

Before you present your speech aloud, check your grammar, usage, and spelling carefully.

Focusing on Proofreading

As you proofread your draft, look for words that are commonly mistaken for one another. Check for words that have similar sounds, such as *adapt* and *adopt*. Then, consult a dictionary to make sure you are using the correct word.

Grammar in Your Writing
Commonly Mistaken Words

The following words are commonly confused because of similar sounds, spellings, or meanings. When you use these words, make sure that you have chosen the correct one.

accept, except

Accept is a verb meaning "to receive." *Except* is a preposition meaning "other than" or "leaving out."

affect, effect

Affect is almost always a verb and means "to influence."
Effect may be used as a noun meaning "result."

than, then

Use *than* in comparisons. *Then,* an adverb, usually refers to time.

Find It in Your Reading Find three words in the "Woman's Right to Suffrage" on pages 124–125 that might be confused with other terms. Explain why each chosen word is correct.

Find It in Your Writing As you proofread, check that you have used each of these words correctly: *accept, except, affect, effect, than, then.*

For more on choosing the correct words, see Chapter 29.

7.6 Publishing and Presenting

Building Your Portfolio

1. **Speech** Deliver your speech to your classmates or to another audience. While making your presentation, make frequent eye contact with your audience and use hand gestures to emphasize your key points. Speak slowly and clearly, and vary the tone and volume of your voice to match the content of your speech. If possible, record your delivery so that you can evaluate your own presentation.

2. **School Paper** Reformat your speech into a persuasive essay. Send it to your school newspaper to be published as an article.

Reflecting on Your Writing

After you have completed your persuasive speech, take some time to think about the experiences you had while writing and presenting it. Use these questions to direct your reflection, and record your responses in your portfolio:

- What aspects of the topic did you discover while collecting evidence for your speech?

- What specific techniques did you learn for persuading an audience?

Internet Tip

To see model essays scored with this rubric, go to **www.phschool.com**

Rubric for Self-Assessment

Use the following criteria to evaluate your persuasive speech:

	Score 4	Score 3	Score 2	Score 1
Audience and Purpose	Chooses highly effective words; clearly focuses on persuasive task	Chooses effective words; focuses on persuasive task	Occasionally uses effective words; is minimally focused on persuasive task	Poor word choice shows lack of attention to persuasive task
Organization	Uses clear, consistent organizational strategy	Uses clear organizational strategy with occasional inconsistencies	Uses inconsistent organizational strategy and illogical presentation	Lacks organizational strategy; gives confusing presentation
Elaboration	Contains specific, well-elaborated reasons that provide convincing support for the writer's position	Contains two or more moderately elaborated reasons in support of the writer's position	Contains several reasons, but few are elaborated	Contains no specific reasons
Use of Language	Contains no empty or hedging words; makes no errors in grammar, spelling, and punctuation	Contains few empty or hedging words; makes few errors in grammar, spelling, and punctuation	Contains some empty and hedging words; makes errors in grammar, spelling, and punctuation	Contains many empty or hedging words; makes many errors in grammar, spelling, and punctuation

FINAL DRAFT

◀ **Critical Viewing**
How would you describe the emotional state of the student pictured? What clues helped you decide? **[Interpret]**

Four-Day School Week

Marvin Astorga
Bel Air High School
El Paso, Texas

Before I begin, I would like to compliment you and the entire school board on the wonderful job you are doing. I am a sophomore at Bel-Air High School, and it has recently come to my attention that the school board is considering a plan that would have students attend a four-day school week instead of the current five-day schedule. Each school day would be lengthened so that students would spend the same total amount of time in school each week. This may seem like a good idea at first, but a little reflection will reveal serious drawbacks. I adamantly oppose the new proposal because it will increase student fatigue, create potentially dangerous disorientation, and interfere with parents' schedules.

In the opening paragraph, Marvin respectfully and clearly states his opposition to the proposal.

Although it sounds like less time in school, this plan will actually exhaust even the best of students. The new plan calls for approximately two more hours per school day, which will leave students less time at home for homework and rest. If students are not given time to meet these needs, they will come to school tired and without their homework. The current five-day week is already as crammed with work as a stray dog is with fleas. Why burden kids with a heavier load to carry? In fact, a recent survey in the September 27, 1997, issue of *Newsweek* sternly states that 78 percent of students with two or more hours of homework a night fail not one, not two, but all of their core classes, which includes math, English, social studies, and science. Add a sleepy disposition to this calculation and students are even more likely to fail. Subtracting a day from the work week and adding the time to the other days is an aberration that will have students working toward failure. I doubt that even the mighty Hercules could handle this four-day proposition.

Marvin gains the audience's attention by using a light-hearted and humorous analogy when he compares the five-day week to a dog with fleas.

Another reason for not adopting this plan is that adjusting to the new schedule will be disorienting and possibly dangerous. Students will be confused by the new hours, as well as distracted by plans they will be making for their newly acquired free day. Disrupting the sequence of a person's biological clock can be harmful, especially to young people like ourselves; such disruption can be the catalyst for a breakdown. Dr. Robert Heely of the National Institute for Physiological Observation illustrates my point. In the April 1997 issue of *Parenting Magazine*, he writes, "When there is an abrupt change in a child's biological clock, it can often lead to migraine headaches, stomachaches, weakness, irregular eating habits and sleep patterns." Why create a situation that can contribute to such a wide range of potential health problems?

Marvin uses statistics to support the main idea of this paragraph.

Finally, one of the most important reasons for rejecting this proposal is that parents' schedules will be drastically affected. Working parents will have difficulty accommodating the new school hours. Since their schedules revolve around their kids, a new schedule will disorient them as much as it will us. Confusion leads to frustration, and frustration to anger. I am sure that the school board does not want to create a band of angry parents.

At the end of his speech, Marvin widens the perspective from his own opinion to the collective opinion of his school.

For these reasons, I am totally against accepting the four-day plan. My research also indicates that I am not alone. I surveyed 80 of my fellow students and found that 79 percent were against the plan. An even greater percentage thought the plan would increase student stress. I urge you to consider their responses and reject this proposal. I know the school board is very busy, and I thank you for your time.

Marvin concludes with a strong restatement of his position and a polite ending sentence.

Connected Assignment
Editorial

Like persuasive speeches, editorials seek to influence readers or listeners about a particular issue. They appear in newspapers or magazines and on television or radio. Editorials may present the opinions of the media's management or those of guest writers or speakers. Writers construct a persuasive argument and then support it with facts, details, and examples.

An effective editorial contains

- a clearly stated position on a subject.

- details such as facts, statistics, and other examples to help support the opinion.

- a respectful yet persuasive tone.

- a clear and effective method of organization.

Write an editorial presenting your views on an issue. Use the writing process skills to guide your work.

▲ **Critical Viewing** Besides editorials, what types of persuasive writing might you find in a newspaper? **[Generalize]**

Prewriting

Choosing Your Topic Because effective persuasion stems from conviction, choose an issue that is important to you. Then, chat with a group of friends about controversies in your school or community and in the nation as a whole. Note any issues that spark your interest, and choose one as your topic.

Narrowing Your Topic Narrow your topic to a manageable size to increase the persuasive impact. You cannot address everything about global pollution, for example, in an editorial, but you can respond to a specific law about pollution. Choose an aspect of your topic that you can adequately discuss in a brief paper. Keep narrowing your topic until you can hit all your main points quickly.

Gathering Your Details

Before you begin drafting your editorial, take time to gather details that will support your argument and help you achieve your purpose. Gather details from a variety of sources. The details themselves should also vary.

Types of details may include:

- factual details or ststistical details

- quotations

- personal opinions

Drafting

Choosing an Organizational Strategy Present your ideas effectively and logically. When writing persuasively, you may find order-of-importance organization particularly effective. Following is a sample outline that shows how to build an argument or build to a point using order-of-importance organization.

I. Introductory paragraph

II. Least important point

III. Points that build in importance

IV. Most important point

V. Concluding paragraph

Creating a Tone Use engaging and enthusiastic language to convey your idea's appeal. While it is appropriate to argue against specific aspects of the opposing viewpoint, keep a respectful tone and avoid name-calling. To do this, choose your words carefully, and address the opposition's views with respect.

Revising and Editing

Carefully check your editorial to be sure that it is free of faulty logic. Look for examples of overgeneralization, bandwagon appeals, begging the question, and circular reasoning within your editorial, and rewrite or delete them.

Then, reread your editorial, and evaluate its language. Make sure that you've chosen words that your audience will understand—especially if your topic is technical or is unfamiliar to the audience.

Confirm that you've provided sufficient supporting detail. Add details where lacking, and delete details that are unnecessary. Also, check to be sure that the details you've chosen help to create a tone.

Proofread your editorial carefully to be sure that it is free of errors in grammar, spelling, and punctuation.

Publishing and Presenting

Neatly print out a copy of your editorial and sign it. Then, mail it to your school paper or to a local newspaper. If you like, you can post a copy of your editorial on a bulletin board if you obtain permission to do so.

🖊 Spelling Tip

Use a spell-check feature if you are working in a word-processing program. Then, reread the printout to be sure that you haven't left out any words and to catch errors that the spell check does not find, such as incorrect word usage.

Spotlight on the Humanities

Appreciating the Arts

Focus on Art: Patron of the Arts, Isabella Gardner

Persuasion—getting others to agree with your opinion—is an essential skill for those who believe that the preservation of art and artifacts is important to history and culture. One of the nineteenth and twentieth centuries' most influential patrons of the arts was Bostonian Isabella Stewart Gardner (1840–1924). Born in New York City, Mrs. Gardner collected art from abroad, filling the Venetian palace that she built in Boston's Fenway Court with these great works. The museum still exists and is filled with Renaissance furniture, art, and tapestries. Raphael, Rembrandt, Botticelli, and Monet are just a few of the great painters whose works hang on the walls of Fenway Court.

Literature Connection American author Henry James (1843–1916) was a friend of Isabella Stewart Gardner in the late nineteenth century. James perfected the use of the sentence in literature, molding a single sentence into a work of art. His emphasis on moral themes and the difference between innocence and experience can be identified in all his novels and short stories. *The American, Daisy Miller, The Bostonians,* and the novelette *The Turn of the Screw* are among his best-known works.

Isabella Stewart Gardner (1840–1924), 1888, Isabella Stewart Gardner Museum, Boston, MA, USA

▲ Critical Viewing
What do clues in the portrait reveal about Isabella Stewart Gardner, the portrait's subject? [Interpret]

Art Connection A friend of Henry James and Isabella Stewart Gardner, the American painter John Singer Sargent (1856–1925) was known for elegant, distinctive portraiture. Born in Florence, Italy, Sargent spent his early years in the major European capitals. In the 1880's, Venice, Italy, was a favorite spot for him, and he painted the city's extraordinary architecture and daily life. Experimenting with the depiction of light, Sargent painted with individual strokes of pure color that made the canvas seem to flicker. His portrait of Isabella Stewart Gardner was done in 1888.

Persuasive Writing Activity: Essay on the Importance of Museums

Write a persuasive essay supporting state and public funding for additional museums in the cities or suburbs in your area. Cite reasons why you think the preservation of art and artifacts is so important. Present your persuasive essay to your class.

Media and Technology Skills

Recognizing Persuasion in Media

Activity: Evaluating Internet Advertising

If you have spent much time surfing the Internet, you know that almost every Web site you visit is dotted with eye-catching, sometimes distracting advertisements. However, you might not realize just how many ads you see. Researchers estimate that you will see 360 ads during one hour of using the Internet.

Learn About It Advertisements on Web pages are called banners. Each banner is linked to an advertisement called a "target ad." A target ad can be one Web page or a complete site. For example, a banner ad might take you to an on-line clothing store.

Collect It Conduct an Internet survey to classify the Internet advertising you encounter in a fifteen- or thirty-minute Web session. Complete a chart to describe each advertisement.

Banner Ad	Images	Text	What It Is Advertising

Analyze It After describing each, see how the elements work together to persuade an audience. Look for these examples of persuasive strategies as you analyze the ads you've collected:

- **Animation and Imagery** Many banners use animation and vivid imagery to draw your attention and make you curious about what will happen when you click on the ad.

- **Deceptive or Misleading Layout** Some banner ads try to blend in with the Web page. You may not even be aware that an image is an advertisement until you have already clicked on it.

- **Product Positioning** Even if you never click a banner ad, you can still be affected by Internet advertising. Some Internet advertising is designed to build a product's image or reputation. If you see a name at the top of every Web page in a search engine, you might think that the product being advertised is well known or highly respected.

- **Site Registration** Some Web sites require you to register. The site owners might use your demographic information to target you with specific advertisements.

Watch Where You're Going

Many Internet surfers have experienced this surprise: You click on links without thinking and, before you know it, you're in a Web site that you don't want to be in.

To avoid the problem:
- Pay attention to your cursor, and read before you click.
- Beware of radio buttons that are preset to take you to a site when you hit Back.

To fix the problem:
- Hit GO on the Task Bar, and select from the list of sites already visited the point to which you want to return.

Standardized Test Preparation Workshop

Responding to Persuasive Writing Prompts

On some standardized tests, you will be evaluated according to your ability to write persuasively. Following are the criteria upon which your persuasive response will be assessed:

- a clearly stated position that directly responds to the essay prompt
- language that appropriately addresses the audience you are targeting
- details that help you achieve your purpose for writing
- a logical and effective organization of ideas
- correct use of grammar, spelling, and punctuation

As you generate standardized test responses, rely on the basic writing process stages—prewriting, drafting, revising, editing, and proofreading—to lead you through the task. Keep an eye on time, however, as you work through each stage.

Below is an example of a standardized test persuasive writing prompt. Before developing your response, read the tips on the next page. Consider them as you write, also noting the time-planning suggestions on the clocks next to each stage.

Sample Writing Situation

Your school grounds are next to a wooded area inhabited by various forms of wildlife. Recently, the school board decided to expand the school's parking lot into this area in order to solve the congested parking situation. This would have some consequences on the wildlife. What is your position on the situation? Compose a letter to your school newspaper stating your opinion and defending it with compelling reasons.

Prewriting

Allow about one quarter of your time for shaping your argument and providing supporting details.

Look at Both Sides To provide you with a fully rounded picture of the topic you are addressing, enter your ideas onto a Pro-and-Con chart. To make a Pro-and-Con chart, write details that support your position in the left column and details that support the opposition's opinion in the right column. Take the opposition's points into account, and address them in your argument, pointing out why your position makes more sense.

Drafting

Allow about half of your time for drafting. Remember to leave space for text you may want to add when revising.

Elaborate State your position clearly at the beginning of the essay, and present your supporting reasons in order of importance. Also, cite specific examples from your personal experience that will help readers visualize the situation as you see it.

Create a Tone The tone of your argument should be persuasive. It should not simply attack any opposing viewpoints. Support your argument with convincing reasons, and present your case in as positive a light as possible. For example, if you are opposed to the expansion of the parking lot onto wildlife-inhabited areas, explain the ways in which the construction would injure the presence of the animals.

Revising

Allow almost one quarter of your time for revising.

Review the Tone Read over your work, and listen to its tone. Replace words with negative, overly critical connotations, which may alienate undecided readers. If possible, recopy your work. Otherwise, insert changes neatly.

Editing and Proofreading

Allow about five minutes to review your work for spelling, punctuation, and grammar errors.

Take Time Work steadily and carefully to review your essay for spelling or punctuation errors. Sometimes reading backward makes these errors easier to spot. Make all changes with proofreader's marks and neatly drawn deletion lines.

Greetings from Route 66, Beth Nobles, Courtesy of the artist

Advertisements in Everyday Life

Take a moment to think about how many advertisements you see or hear every day. What was your guess? Nine? Ninety? Every time you open a newspaper, turn on the television, flip through a magazine, log on the Internet, listen to the radio, check your mail, walk into a store, or drive past a billboard, you are exposed to advertising.

Advertisements (or *ads,* for short) are a form of **persuasion**—writing or speaking that attempts to convince others to accept a position or to take an action. Ads, it seems, are everywhere today.

▲ **Critical Viewing**
In what way does this artwork make Route 66 seem appealing? Explain. **[Interpret]**

What Is an Advertisement?

An **advertisement** tries to persuade an audience to buy a product or service, accept an idea, or support a cause or candidate. Most advertisements have

- an attention-getting opener, such as a startling headline, catchy slogan, or surprising statistic.
- a memorable ending or tag line.
- persuasive and/or informative text.
- striking visual or aural images.

To preview the criteria on which your advertisement may be evaluated, see the Rubric for Self-Assessment on page 160.

Types of Advertisements

Advertisements range from those that sell consumer products to those that educate the public. Whatever the focus, most advertising takes one of the following forms:

- **Print ads** are written advertisements that appear in newspapers and magazines.
- **Posters, flyers, and mailers** are printed on sheets of paper and are either posted or delivered.
- **Television and radio commercials** convey their persuasive messages through dialogue and visual or aural images.
- **On-line ads** contain persuasive messages, some of which employ animation, video, and sound effects.
- **Product packaging,** besides listing a product's contents, may also contain promotional messages and attractively designed labels to entice consumers.

Writers in
ACTION

English actor John Cleese is also an expert comedian who was part of the renowned Monty Python troupe. Cleese believes that humor can play an important role in the art of persuasion:

"If I can get you to laugh with me, you like me better, which makes you more open to my ideas. And if I can persuade you to laugh at the particular point I make, by laughing at it you acknowledge its truth."

PREVIEW

Student Work
IN PROGRESS

Matt Bezerman, a student at General Douglas MacArthur High School in Seaford, New York, created an advertisement for a yard sale in his neighborhood. Follow his progress as he gathers details, drafts, and revises his advertisement. Matt's finished advertisement appears at the end of the chapter.

The following advertisement was placed by a university. The ad promotes the university's Semester at Sea program.

The advertisement features the catchy title of the university's program. The title helps capture readers' interest.

Photographs such as these help convince the audience that the program is interesting and worthwhile.

Words like "voyage" and "discovery" conjure up exciting associations in readers.

Boldfaced text makes exotic country names stand out.

Reading Writing Connection

Evaluate Visuals When you look at an advertisement, identify the message that is being conveyed by visual elements such as photographs and art. Then, decide whether or not that message is realistic and truthful.

8.2 Prewriting

Choosing Your Topic

Before you can create an advertisement, you need to have a product, a service, or an idea to sell. Use the following strategies to generate a topic:

Strategies for Generating a Topic

1. **Blueprint** Sketch rooms in your home. Then, list the products that you use daily in the various rooms. For example, you might list dish soap and sponges when you consider the kitchen. Then, write an advertisement for the product you like the most.

2. **Listing** Write the heading "Things I Can Do," and list as many items in this category as you can. For example, you might list *play the piano, walk the dog, cook,* and *baby-sit,* among other things. Then, choose an item from the list, and write an advertisement for that service.

Writing Lab CD-ROM

For more help finding a topic, explore the activities and topic suggestions in the Choosing a Topic section in the Persuasion lesson.

TOPIC BANK

Following are more topic ideas for advertisements:

1. **Favorite Restaurant** When you get to choose where to eat out, where do you go? Choose to advertise your favorite restaurant.

Responding to Literature

2. Samuel Taylor Coleridge's "Kubla Khan" contains descriptive details that make Xanadu seem magical. Create your own "Xanadu," using your imagination. Then, write an advertisement to encourage tourism to that place. "Kubla Khan" appears in *Prentice Hall Literature: Timeless Voices, Timeless Themes,* The British Tradition.

☑ Cooperative Writing Opportunity

3. **Public-Service Announcement** Public-service announcements (PSAs) are a type of advertisement that educates the public about health risks and other concerns. With a group, choose an issue (for example, the environment or voter registration) and create a PSA. Then, work together to complete and present the ad.

Narrowing Your Topic

Narrow and Focus Your Topic

If you have chosen a particular product or service to advertise, you will not need to narrow your topic further. If your topic is general, however, such as chocolate chip cookies, narrow it by choosing to advertise a specific brand.

It is also helpful to focus your topic. To do this, analyze the product, service, or idea to get a clear sense of what it is you're selling, who might buy it, and why someone might buy it. Keep the answers to those questions in mind as you begin to gather details for your advertisement.

Considering Your Audience and Purpose

Identify Your Audience

Before you begin to gather details to sell your idea, service, or product, think about your audience—the people you are trying to convince. The details you choose to emphasize and the word choices you make will have a great impact on how well your audience responds to your ad.

Fill out an audience profile like the one below to pinpoint the details that will appeal to your audience. Take their responses into consideration as you gather details.

Research Tip

Before you write your advertisement, look at ads for products or services similar to the one you plan to advertise. Then, make your advertisement different, so that it stands out from the rest.

Audience Profile

What age group are you trying to convince to buy your product, service, or idea?

| 3–7 | 8–12 | 13–18 | 19–25 | 26–30 | 30 or over |

Are potential buyers at all familiar with the product, service, or idea you're selling?

| Not at all familiar | Somewhat familiar | Very familiar |

Do you think potential buyers will be resistant or receptive to the product, service, or idea you're selling?

| Resistant | Neutral | Receptive |

What in life do you think is most important to potential buyers?

| Making or saving money | Comfort |
| Fun and excitement | Success |

Consider Your Audience's Taste

Once you have identified your audience, think about what type of word choice or language style will most appeal to the audience you've identified. Then, plan your ad carefully, choosing details, words, and phrases that will help you achieve your purpose: to sell your product, idea, or service.

This chart gives examples of how your language might vary in an advertisement for a restaurant depending on your audience.

	Families With Children	Older, Upscale Crowd	Young Singles
Food	hearty plentiful kids' menus all-you-can-eat salad bar	traditional cuisine	innovative sensational updated nouvelle
Service	fast friendly	attentive discreet experienced	relaxed knowledge-able
Atmosphere	family fun relaxed	quiet elegant classical luxury reservations required	lively hip new young

Identify Your Audience's Questions

Think about the questions your audience—potential buyers—might have about the product, service, or candidate that you are advertising. Make a list of those questions, and be sure to answer them as you draft and develop your advertisement. Questions that your audience might have may include the following:

- How can I be sure the product, service, or person is reliable?

- Is this product, service, or person recommended by others?

- What do I have to do to learn more about this product, service, or person?

Gathering Details

To sell a product or idea successfully, you need to learn everything you can about it and about the people you hope will buy it. Use the following strategy to help you gather detailed information:

Create and Distribute a Questionnaire

One way to find out how people view a product is to create a questionnaire. Distribute the questionnaire to people you think make up the potential market for your product. Use the questionnaire results to help you determine the approach you will take in your ad.

Below, you can see how Matt grouped the responses he received to his questionnaire.

Name: Matt Bezerman
General Douglas MacArthur High School
Seaford, NY

Creating and Distributing a Questionnaire

Matt Bezerman had been to yard sales before, but he was interested in other people's experiences. He distributed a short questionnaire to several friends and relatives. The results gave him a direction for his advertisement.

6 out of 13 had attended a yard sale in the last two months.

> Matt realized he needed to target the people who don't go to yard sales.

Of those 6:
2 had bought something at the sale they attended.
3 said: "there was nothing good for sale."
1 said: "didn't have any money."

> Matt decided to target this market to those who might not attend based on past experience.

Of the 7 who had not attended a yard sale in the last two months:
5 said: "there's never anything worth buying."
2 said: "too busy."

> This told Matt that he needed to convince the doubters that this was not a typical yard sale. This one would have high-quality merchandise.

8.3 *Drafting*

Shaping Your Writing

Because advertisements usually have little time or space to make an impression, create a structure that will allow you to capture the audience's attention right away and to underscore your message at the close.

Develop a Main Idea

To shape a written advertisement, develop a main idea to feature. One way to do this is to create a slogan. A good slogan sums up a product or an idea in a few words and is easily recognizable and catchy. Not every product has one, but a good one may make your advertisement more effective. Here are some ways to make a slogan memorable:

- **Word Play** Rhyme, pun, repetition, or other forms of word play can make a slogan memorable. For example, a company that makes baby-food products may use: "Give a Cookie to Your Cookie."

- **Alliteration** Using the same sound for most of the words in a phrase or sentence will grab your readers' attention. For example, "The Cocoa Cookies That Crunch" contains alliteration.

- **Pithiness** *Pith* means "essence" or "gist"; a pithy slogan is one that is short but full of meaning. For example, "Your Favorite Cookie" contains one essential idea about the product.

▲ **Critical Viewing** What main idea might you convey in a slogan for an ad about this cookie? **[Analyze]**

Providing Elaboration

As your advertisement takes shape, add details to support the claims you make about your product.

Cite Statistics and Experts

Collect and include in your advertisement data about your topic—the percentage of people who use it, the number of doctors who recommend it, awards given to it, and so on. Following is an example:

In a recent poll conducted by Pollard University, 87% of cardiologists recommend swimming to improve health. It strengthens the muscles, especially the back muscles, and it is less damaging than aerobics or jogging.

> This is a statistic.

> Cardiologists are doctors who are experts in the field of heart and health.

Now that you've given your advertisement its rough form, find ways to improve it. Look at it critically, as if you were the audience seeing or hearing the advertisement for the first time.

Revising

Revising Your Overall Structure

Your advertisement will not be very persuasive if your main point is hidden where the audience can't find it. Check that your advertisement is structured—both textually and visually—so that the key ideas stand out.

▶ REVISION STRATEGY
Highlighting Key Ideas

Using a highlighter, identify the key ideas in your advertisement. Make sure these key points are the most prominent ideas in your advertisement. If they are not, restructure the advertisement to feature your most important points.

Revising Your Paragraphs

Although it is common to see advertisements that are almost completely visual, with just a line or two of text, many advertisers, particularly on the radio, use words skillfully. If your advertisement depends heavily on words, make sure that its message is clear and to the point.

▶ REVISION STRATEGY
Cutting Extraneous Information

Read your advertisement, and evaluate each sentence or paragraph carefully. Ask yourself: What is the single most important idea in this paragraph? If it is not obvious, take out unnecessary words and phrases. Cut and rewrite until just the most important ideas are left.

The following paragraph from a radio advertisement contained extraneous information, which was cut to make it more focused and concise.

Galliard High School Marching Band has held an award-winning reputation since it was formed. Over the years, it has won several awards, including ~~Second Prize in the Festival of colors and~~ last year's First Prize at the Boone County Competition of the Bands. Support this band, which has enhanced our local reputation. ~~The students work really hard and deserve the community's support.~~

▲ **Critical Viewing**
If you were to write an ad for a marching band like the one shown, what key idea would you choose to feature? Why? **[Connect]**

Revising Your Sentences
Correcting Run-on Sentences

In your advertisement, you may find that you have run two or more main clauses together into a run-on sentence. Run-on sentences are confusing and will detract from the impression you want to make. You can correct this problem by breaking the sentence into two sentences or by revising the sentence so that it becomes a complex or a compound sentence.

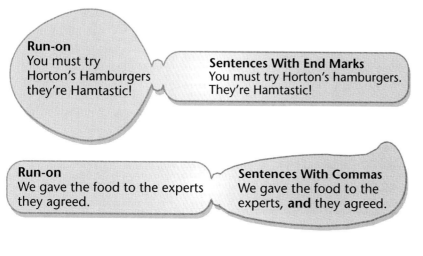

Run-on
You must try Horton's Hamburgers they're Hamtastic!

Sentences With End Marks
You must try Horton's hamburgers. They're Hamtastic!

Run-on
We gave the food to the experts they agreed.

Sentences With Commas
We gave the food to the experts, **and** they agreed.

▶ **REVISION STRATEGY**
Circling Sentence Subjects

A run-on sentence is two or more complete sentences that are punctuated as if they were one. One way to spot a run-on sentence is to circle all the sentence subjects you come across in your draft. Then, examine each sentence that contains two or more subjects to be sure that it is not a run-on.

Student Work
I N   P R O G R E S S

Name: *Matt Bezerman*
General Douglas MacArthur High School
Seaford, NY

Circling to Identify Run-on Sentences
Matt discovered this run-on sentence in the opening of his draft. To fix the problem, he decided to break the run-on sentence into two distinct sentences:

(Everybody) knows yard sales can be a waste of time, however all your preconceived (notions) about yard sales are about to change.

Matt fixed this run-on by making it two sentences.

Revising Your Word Choice

Choose Words to Achieve Your Purpose

Check the words in your advertisement. Do they achieve the purpose you have set? If not, experiment with other word choices until you are satisfied that you have found just the right ones.

▶ **REVISION STRATEGY**
Revising Weak Words

Your advertisement will have more impact if you avoid using weak or vague adjectives to describe the product or service you are selling.

Peer Review

The goal of advertising is to persuade others to do what you want them to do—whether it is to make a purchase, attend an event, or donate money to a cause. Therefore, the best way to find out whether your advertisement works is to show it to a potential audience. Here's a strategy for getting constructive feedback:

Distribute a Survey and Discuss It

Share your advertisement with a peer group, and distribute a short survey about the effectiveness of the advertisement. Your survey questions might resemble the following:

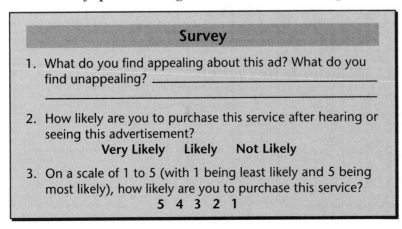

Survey

1. What do you find appealing about this ad? What do you find unappealing? _____

2. How likely are you to purchase this service after hearing or seeing this advertisement?
   Very Likely   Likely   Not Likely

3. On a scale of 1 to 5 (with 1 being least likely and 5 being most likely), how likely are you to purchase this service?
   5 4 3 2 1

8.5 Editing and Proofreading

Advertisements are meant to positively impress others. Carefully check spelling, grammar, usage, and mechanics to ensure that your advertisement is error-free.

Focusing on Dates and Times

You do not want to persuade people to attend an event only to have them come on the wrong day! Proofread your advertisement carefully to make sure dates and times are correct.

Grammar in Your Writing
Abbreviating Dates and Ordinals

To save space in your advertisement, abbreviate *dates* and *ordinals* (numbers that rank items in a series, like third and thirtieth). Following is a chart showing correct abbreviations for months and days.

DAYS	Sun.	Mon.	Tues.	Wed.	Thurs.	Fri.	Sat.

MONTHS	Jan.	Feb.	Mar.	Apr.	May	June
	July	Aug.	Sept.	Oct.	Nov.	Dec.

ORDINALS		
Add *-st* after 1	*1st* Annual Roadrace
Add *-nd* after 2	*2nd* Prize
Add *-rd* after 3	*3rd* Day of the Month
Add *-th* after all other numbers	*16th* Squadron

Find It in Your Reading Read the advertisement on page 150 to locate an abbreviation of a country name.

Find It in Your Writing As you proofread your advertisement, check to see that all of the dates and ordinals are correctly abbreviated.

For more on abbreviations, see the Abbreviation Guide.

8.6 Publishing and Presenting

Now that your advertisement is finished, share it with the public. Here are some ideas for presenting your ad:

Building Your Portfolio

1. **Post It** If you've created a print advertisement for an actual product or service of your own, get permission to post it in your classroom, school, and around town. You'll soon find out if your ad is effective by the response you get.

2. **Ad Book** Gather together ads your classmates have completed, and bind them together into an ad book. Leave a copy in the classroom for everyone to flip through.

Reflecting on Your Writing

When you've finished your advertisement, think about what it was like to create it. Answer the following questions, and save your responses in your portfolio.

• How did creating your own ad change your view of the advertising you see around you?

• With which aspect of creating an advertisement did you feel more comfortable, the verbal or the visual?

 **Internet Tip**

To see an advertisement scored with this rubric, go to **www.phschool.com**

Rubric for Self-Assessment

Use the following criteria to evaluate your persuasive writing.

	Score 4	Score 3	Score 2	Score 1
Audience and Purpose	Presents effective slogan; clearly addresses persuasive task	Presents good slogan; addresses persuasive task	Presents slogan; minimally addresses persuasive task	Does not present slogan; shows lack of attention to persuasive task
Organization	Uses clear, consistent organizational strategy; clearly presents key ideas	Uses clear organizational strategy with few inconsistencies	Uses inconsistent organizational strategy; creates illogical presentation	Demonstrates lack of organizational strategy; creates confusing presentation
Elaboration	Successfully combines words and images to provide convincing, unified support for a position	Combines words and images to provide unified support for a position	Includes some words or images that detract from a position	Uses words and images that do not support a position
Use of Language	Successfully communicates an idea through clever use of language; includes very few mechanical errors	Conveys an idea through adequate use of language; includes few mechanical errors	Misuses language and lessens impact of ideas; includes many mechanical errors	Demonstrates poor use of language and confuses meaning; includes many mechanical errors

8.7 Student Work IN PROGRESS

FINAL DRAFT

Not Your Everyday Yard Sale

Matt Bezerman
General Douglas MacArthur High School
Seaford, New York

NOT YOUR EVERYDAY YARD SALE

Everybody knows yard sales can be a
waste of time.
However, all your preconceived notions
about yard sales are about to change.

THIS WILL BE THE. . .

BIGGEST Four households' worth of goods!

BEST Like-new appliances, never-worn clothes,
antiques, collectibles!!!

CHEAPEST Low prices are flexible; make us an offer!

YARD SALE YOU HAVE EVER SEEN!

Saturday, July 20th
10:00 A.M.–5:00 P.M.
Johnson Avenue, Seaford

YOU CAN'T AFFORD TO MISS IT!

The opening line of Matt's ad helps and arouses readers' curiosity.

Matt used an unusual visual element— the yard sign—to make his ad interesting to look at.

These details are persuasive and are centrally placed to catch the readers' eyes.

The ad's ending line is memorable. It also is a pun—the word "afford" makes a connection with the yard sale.

Connected Assignment
Ad Campaign

Ad campaigns, like other ads, seek to sell you something. Ad campaigns, however, seek to reach potential buyers through various places and forms; for example, through print ads, radio and television ads, T-shirts, bumper stickers, and so on. Usually, an ad campaign focuses on a central idea, slogan, issue, or position, creating a key idea that carries through all the ads.

Create an ad campaign for a real or imaginary product, idea, service, or candidate. Use the writing process tips to guide you as you create your ad campaign.

▲ **Critical Viewing**
What aspect of an ad campaign do these students seem to be working on? **[Connect]**

Ad Campaign for FIZZ COLA

Slogan: Put Some Fizz In Your
(Life, Work, Step, and so on)!

Radio ad:
[Sound of Fizz cola being opened followed by the sound of someone drinking and saying "Ah." Lively music in background.]

WOMAN'S VOICE: Put some Fizz in your life. Nothing else can compare.

Billboard:
Picture of a giant bottle of Fizz Cola on a desk. Enthusiastic, determined group—professionally dressed —gathered around in intense discussion. Underneath photo is the slogan: "Put Some Fizz In Your Work."

T-shirt giveaway:
Photo of Fizz Cola bottle centered on the front of the shirt. On the back will read: "Put Some Fizz In Your Step."

Prewriting To choose a topic, decide on a product, a service, an idea, or a candidate on which to build your ad campaign. To come up with topic ideas, think about the products or services you use often or the people in politics or those who seek public office.

Examples of Products: soap, car, alarm clock, food, towel

Examples of Services: public transportation, gas stations, hair salons

Examples of People: city mayor, school principal, union leader

Focusing Your Ad Campaign Choose an aspect of your product, service, or candidate to build your campaign around. Then, focus on getting that message out. Jot down every advertising outlet you can list in which to sell your product or candidate. Group them into categories, and note the type of details (visual, text, music, sound effect, and so on) that will best work within that medium.

Television	Radio	Magazines	T-shirts
visual aural	aural sound effects	visual text	visual some text

Drafting Experiment with jingles or rhymes to make your slogan memorable. Then, create three ads that are built around this slogan. Use positive and persuasive language to highlight what it is you're selling. Include visuals, if appropriate. Finally, develop and complete a presentation chart to show how the overall campaign will work.

Revising and Editing Post your presentation chart and sample ads on a bulletin board and review them. Enlarge the text for readability, and position the main idea of each ad prominently. Read any text aloud to gauge its aural impact, and punch up language to achieve a friendly but direct tone. Ask a friend or family member to scan your presentation for errors or areas of confusion.

Publishing and Presenting Place your presentation chart and the sample ads in a portfolio. If you have created radio or television ads, consider taping or filming them with the help of your peers. Then, "broadcast" the ads for your class.

Technology Tip

To make your sample advertisement look professional, work in a page-layout program. Scan in photographs or other visual aids. Then, use interesting fonts and type treatments—such as boldface, italics, and drop shadows—to make your ad's main idea stand out.

Spotlight on the Humanities

Identifying Themes in Media
Focus on Film: *Camille*

Today, film producers release aggressive ad campaigns on television, radio, and in newspapers, touting their films as "must sees" and persuading audiences to flock to see them. This was true even in 1936, when *Camille* was released. Starring legendary actress Greta Garbo, it is one of the great romance classics of the twentieth century. Originally a novel written in 1848 by the French novelist Alexandre Dumas, *Camille* is the story of a woman with a questionable past who falls in love with a gentleman, played by Robert Taylor. The heroine, Marguerite (or Camille, as she is known to American audiences) ultimately sacrifices her happiness for his good. George Cukor directed the film, and the New York Film Critics gave Garbo the award for best actress.

Music Connection Italian composer Giuseppe Verdi (1813–1901) immortalized the story of Camille (whom he renamed Violetta) in his opera *La Traviata*. Written in 1853, *La Traviata* is one of Verdi's most popular works and brought him fame on an international scale. Verdi was one of the first operatic composers to combine drama and music into one unified composition.

Theater Connection The actress who made the lead role of Dumas's play famous on the stage was France's Sarah Bernhardt (1844–1923). Educated in a convent and at the Paris Conservatoire, Bernhardt made her acting debut at the Comedie Française. Her first noticeable success came in 1869, in François Coppée's *Le Passant*. Bernhardt went on to become one of the most famous stage actresses of her time. In 1914, she was given membership in the Legion of Honor and continued to act until her death.

Persuasive Writing Activity: Poster for a Film
Create a poster advertising your favorite film. Decide what details from the film to highlight on the advertisement. For example, you may include lines of dialogue, a still photograph from the movie, or feature the names of the starring actors. Also, be sure to include information about where and when the film is playing.

▲ **Critical Viewing** Judging from this photograph, what makes the character of Camille so interesting? **[Connect]**

Media and Technology Skills

Using Technology to Extend Meaning

Activity: Enhance a Video

Even beginning filmmakers can learn to create sophisticated and effective videos. Most video cameras have many built-in special effects; you can create others using sounds, lights, and a little imagination. For your next video project, challenge yourself to use several new techniques that will enhance the overall effect.

Think About It Choose a basic project for a short video. For example, you might create an advertisement for a school event or produce a brief "welcome" video for new students. You might also decide to reshoot a video you previously produced. You can apply several new strategies to create a more effective video.

Plan It Begin by planning the new techniques you will try. Read your camera's manual to find out what effects are built into it. Consider trying the following strategies and tools.

> **Framing Devices:** Your camera might allow you to fade in and out of scenes, as well as to decide on the shape of a frame, such as circular or oval.
>
> **Color Effects:** Shoot a scene in black and white, or choose a sepia tint for an old-fashioned look.
>
> **Titles:** Create titles using an in-camera function, or film hand-drawn or computer-printed titles of your own.
>
> **Lighting Effects:** Use natural lighting effects, such as a sunrise or sunset, to create an intense atmosphere. Artificial lighting, such as a single bare bulb or a desk lamp shining up from the floor, can create unusual or other-worldly effects.

Choose an Unusual Point of View

Filming a scene from an unusual point of view can make the difference between a drab video and an exciting one. Suppose you are filming two friends talking in your school parking lot. Any of these angles might make the scene stand out:

- Film from inside a parked car, framing the action with the car window.
- Place the camera on the ground, making the actors loom.
- Use a ladder to view the scene from above.
- Have different students walk past the scene, holding the camera in their hands to create a hand-held, documentary quality.

Film It After choosing your techniques, begin filming. Be ready to take advantage of "happy accidents." A sudden storm might produce an effective mood, as might a gust of wind.

Edit It You can create some special effects, like quick cutting between shots, while editing your video. During editing, you can also select the best of several takes, or filmed versions.

Standardized Test Preparation Workshop

Reading Critically

Standardized test questions often measure your ability to evaluate an advertisement objectively. All advertisements have the same goal—to get you to believe or do something. As an educated reader, you must discern what information is valid by seeing past the attempts to persuade you. The following strategies will help you evaluate an advertisement:

Test Tip

Consider what the writer does not say. Omitting details can slant information in a particular direction.

- See if the argument or claim is supported with facts.
- Check for missing information, vague statements, or partial truths.
- Recognize faulty logic, such as overgeneralizations, circular reasoning, questionable cause-and-effect statements, either/or arguments, or bandwagon appeals.

The following sample test item will give you practice with these types of questions.

Sample Test Item	Answer and Explanation
Directions: Read the passage, and then choose the letter of the best answer. Buy Brighter toothpaste for a brighter, whiter smile! Three out of five dentists recommend that you use it every day for a healthier, whiter smile.	
1 What important information has been left out of this advertisement? A the name of the toothpaste B the total number of dentists surveyed C how often it should be used D the results of using the toothpaste	The correct answer is *B*. While the advertisement implies that many dentists were asked, it does not tell you how many dentists were asked overall. An advertiser could make this claim even if only five dentists were asked.

Practice 1 **Directions:** Read the passage, and then choose the letter of the best answer to each question.

How are your tax dollars best used? Are they best used to paint police cars a new color? Are they best used to replace the functional trash cans on main streets with prettier ones? Either the money goes to these projects or to the schools. Our town's priority should be caring for its children. Town officials have allocated our tax dollars for frivolous expenditures. All of the taxpayers in this town have been given the opportunity to attend school without being deprived of teachers, textbooks, and supplies, yet we would deprive our children of the same. If we don't support education, the children won't have a chance at being successful. Everyone who cares about children will be voting YES for next year's school budget. Vote YES for next year's school budget and give today's children a fair chance at tomorrow.

1 The statement "Either the money goes to these projects or to the schools" is an example of—

A a bandwagon appeal

B circular reasoning

C questionable cause and effect

D either/or argument

2 Which of the following is an example of an overgeneralization—a statement too broad to be backed up by evidence?

F "Vote YES for next year's school budget and give today's children a fair chance at tomorrow."

G "Town officials have allocated our tax dollars for frivolous expenditures."

H Our town's priority should be caring for its children.

J None of the above

3 You can tell from this political advertisement that the writer intends to—

A vote against the school budget

B vote for the school budget

C encourage people to make private donations

D find ways to allocate money to town projects as well as education

4 Which of the following appeals to the emotions and not to logic?

F "All of the taxpayers in this town have been given the opportunity to attend school without being deprived of teachers, textbooks, and supplies, yet we would deprive our children of the same."

G "Either the money goes to these projects or to the schools."

H "Everyone who cares about children will be voting YES . . ."

J None of the above

5 The author implies but does not provide proof that—

A an inadequate amount of money is allocated to education

B the community plans on painting police cars

C the school budget is supported by most town members

D none of the above

6 Which of the following is an example of a bandwagon appeal?

F "Either the money goes to these projects or to the schools."

G "Town officials have allocated our tax dollars for frivolous expenditures."

H "Our town's priority should be caring for its children."

J "Everyone who cares about children will be voting YES for next year's school budget."

Exposition
Comparison-and-Contrast Essay

Comparisons and Contrasts in Everyday Life

Many psychologists say that you can learn about dogs by studying cats. Comparing and contrasting the two animals, rather than studying one in isolation, will give a richer under-standing of both animals.

Besides enriching your knowledge, skills in comparing and contrasting also help you make decisions in daily life. You could, for example, compare and contrast sports equipment in order to select the brand that's best for you, or you could choose a college or university to attend by comparing and contrasting several possibilities.

▲ **Critical Viewing**
What physical simi-larities do this dog and cat share? What differences do you see? **[Compare and Contrast]**

What Is a Comparison-and-Contrast Essay?

A **comparison-and-contrast essay** is an expository nonfiction essay that explains how two or more subjects are similar and different. An effective comparison-and-contrast essay

- explores two or more topics that are similar enough to make an effective comparison.

- clearly shows through details and examples how two or more subjects are similar and different.

- is logically and effectively organized.

- clearly indicates the connections among ideas.

- closes with a summary of main points or an evaluation of the subject's overall points of similarity and difference.

To preview the criteria on which your comparison-and-contrast essay may be evaluated, see the Rubric for Self-Assessment on page 186.

Types of Comparison-and-Contrast Essays

Comparison-and-contrast essays exist in a number of specialized forms, including the following:

- **Comparisons of literary works** examine similarities and differences between literary elements, such as characters, setting, or theme, in different works.

- **Consumer reports** may compare and contrast two or more products or services from different companies to evaluate the positive and negative qualities of each.

- **Comparative reviews** evaluate or compare two or more related books, movies, albums, or television programs.

An effective comparison-and-contrast essay addresses both similarities and differences. Poet Percy Bysshe Shelley emphasized the importance of addressing both aspects when he said: "Reason respects the differences, and imagination the similitudes of things."

Catherine Bailey and Zach Bucek, students at L. C. Anderson High School in Austin, Texas, used various writing strategies to write a comparison-and-contrast article about shopping for music on-line versus shopping for music in a store. A completed draft appears at the end of this chapter.

◀ **Critical Viewing**
If you were to compare and contrast this computer with another, what features might you use as points of comparison? **[Connect]**

The following article by James Gorman originally appeared in The New Yorker *magazine.*

Reading **Writing**
Connection

Reading Strategy: Identify Author's Tone
Recognizing an author's tone—his or her attitude toward a subject—can help you better understand and appreciate what you read. As you read the following article, look for clues that reveal Gorman's attitude toward the topic of his comparison-and-contrast essay. Clues may include word choice, formality of language, and types of examples given.

Man, Bytes, Dog

James Gorman

Many people have asked me about the Cairn Terrier. How about memory, they want to know. Is it IBM compatible? Why didn't I get the IBM itself, or a Kaypro, Compaq, or Macintosh? I think the best way to answer these questions is to look at the personal computer and the Cairn head on. I almost did buy the personal

Gorman introduces the subjects of his comparison-and-contrast essay: a personal computer and a dog. This essay is humorous because the two subjects are not often thought of as similar enough to compare.

computer. It has terrific graphics, good word-processing capabilities, and the mouse. But in the end I decided on the Cairn, and I think I made the right decision.

Let's start out with the basics:

Personal Computer	Cairn Terrier
Weight (without printer): 20 lbs.	Weight (without printer): 14 lbs.
Memory (RAM): 128 K	Memory (RAM): Some
Price (with printer): $3,090	Price (without printer): $250

Charts such as this one allow readers to see supporting details at a glance.

Just on the basis of price and weight, the choice is obvious. Another plus is that the Cairn Terrier comes in one unit. No printer is necessary, or useful. And—this was a big attraction to me—there is no user's manual.

Here are some of the other qualities I found put the Cairn out ahead of the personal computer.

Portability: To give you a better idea of size, Toto in *The Wizard of Oz* was a Cairn Terrier. So you can see that if the young Judy Garland was able to carry Toto around in that little picnic basket, you will have no trouble at all moving your Cairn from place to place. For short trips it will move under its own power. The personal computer will not. . . .

Compatibility: Cairn Terriers get along with everyone. And for communications with any other dog, of any breed, within a radius of three miles, no additional hardware is necessary. All dogs share a common operating system.

Software: The Cairn will run three standard programs, SIT, COME, and NO, and whatever else you create. It is true that, being microcanine, the Cairn is limited here, but it does load the programs instantaneously. No disk drives. No tapes.

Admittedly, these are peripheral advantages. The real comparison has to be on the basis of capabilities. What can the personal computer and the Cairn do? Let's start on the personal computer's turf—income-tax preparation, recipe storage, graphics, and astrophysics problems:

Gorman chose point-by-point organization for his comparison-and-contrast essay.

LITERATURE

To read another comparison-and-contrast essay, see "Birds on the Western Front," in which Saki compares and contrasts the reactions of various birds to wartime conditions. The essay appears in *Prentice Hall Literature: Timeless Voices, Timeless Themes,* The British Tradition.

◀ Critical Viewing How does this dog compare and contrast with a dog you know? [Compare and Contrast]

	Taxes	Recipes	Graphics	Astrophysics
Personal Computer	yes	yes	yes	yes
Cairn	no	no	no	no

At first glance it looks bad for the Cairn. But it's important to look beneath the surface with this kind of chart. If you yourself are leaning toward the personal computer, ask yourself these questions: Do you want to do your own income taxes? Do you want to type all your recipes into a computer? In your graph, what would you put on the x-axis? The y-axis? Do you have any astrophysics problems you want solved?

Then consider the Cairn's specialties: playing fetch and tug-of-war, licking your face, and chasing foxes out of rock cairns (eponymously). Note that no software is necessary. All these functions are part of the operating system:

	Fetch	Tug-of-war	Face	Foxes
Cairn	yes	yes	yes	yes
Personal Computer	no	no	no	no

Another point to keep in mind is that computers, even the personal computer, only do what you tell them to do. Cairns perform their functions all on their own. Here are some of the additional capabilities that I discovered once I got the Cairn home and housebroken:

Word Processing: Remarkably, the Cairn seems to understand every word I say. He has a nice way of pricking up his ears at words like "out" or "ball." He also has highly tuned voice recognition.

Education: The Cairn provides children with hands-on experience at an early age, contributing to social interaction, crawling ability, and language skills. At age one, my daughter could say "Sit," "Come," and "No."

Cleaning: This function was a pleasant surprise. But of course cleaning up around the cave is one of the reasons dogs were developed in the first place. Users with young (below age two) children will still find this function useful. The Cairn Terrier cleans the floor, spoons, bib, and baby, and has an unerring ability to distinguish strained peas from ears, nose, and fingers.

Heads like the ones that appear in front of these paragraphs help clarify the point being compared and contrasted.

Psychotherapy: Here the Cairn really shines. And remember, therapy is something that computers have tried.

There is a program that makes the computer ask you questions when you tell it your problems. You say, "I'm afraid of foxes." The computer says, "You're afraid of foxes?"

The Cairn won't give you that kind of echo. Like Freudian analysts, Cairns are mercifully silent; unlike Freudians, they are infinitely sympathetic. I've found that the Cairn will share, in a nonjudgmental fashion, disappointments, joys, and frustrations. And you don't have to know BASIC.

This last capability is related to the Cairn's strongest point, which was the final deciding factor in my decision against the personal computer—user-friendliness. On this criterion, there is simply no comparison. The Cairn Terrier is the essence of user friendliness. It has fur, it doesn't flicker when you look at it, and it wags its tail.

Transitions such as "like" and "unlike" allow readers to clearly connect what's being compared and contrasted.

Reading Writing Connection

Writing Application: Identify Author's Tone
Before you begin writing your comparison-and-contrast essay, think for a moment about what subject you might write about and how you would reveal your attitude toward that subject. What words and phrases might you choose to create a tone revealing your attitude?

 **Prewriting**

Choosing Your Topic

You need to find two or more related things or ideas to form the topic of your comparison-and-contrast essay. Use these strategies to select a topic you would like to develop:

Strategies for Generating Topics

1. **Word Association** Work with a partner to create a list of pairs. Your pairs might be opposites or closely related subjects. Take turns suggesting a person, character, subject, idea, or product, and allow your partner to respond with the first related idea that comes to mind. After listing ideas and responses, choose as a topic a pair that you could understand better through comparing and contrasting.

Idea	Response
high school	college
Keats	Shelley
Frankenstein	Dracula
sonnet	soliloquy
e-mail	World Wide Web
satire	parody

2. **Writing Marathon** If you have a single subject that interests you but do not know to what you could compare it, perform a "writing marathon." To do this, freewrite about your topic for at least ten minutes. Jot down everything that comes to mind about the subject. When you're finished writing, read what you have written to see if you have generated any possible topics for a comparison. If so, focus your comparison-and-contrast essay on that topic.

3. **Mental Shopping** Imagine yourself shopping in a store. What products might you compare before making a buying decision? You can concentrate on a large purchase, such as a bicycle or jacket, or a small purchase that affects your daily life, such as toothpaste or shampoo. As you visualize the store, jot down notes or sketches to help you focus on two or more products. Choose as a topic the products you find most interesting.

Writing Lab CD-ROM

For help finding a topic, explore the activities and topic suggestions in the Choosing a Topic section of the Exposition lesson.

TOPIC BANK

Use one of these topics if you are having trouble coming up with your own:

1. **Comparison of Political Leaders** Choose two political leaders who held the same position, and compare their governing style and overall effectiveness. For example, you might choose two U.S. presidents from the same era, such as Abraham Lincoln and Ulysses S. Grant. As an alternative, choose two world leaders who ruled at the same time, such as King George III and George Washington.

2. **Consumer Report** Write a consumer report for a student newspaper. Choose as a topic a specific type of product that many students are interested in buying, such as in-line skates or jeans. Then, compare and contrast two or more brands of that product.

Responding to Fine Art

3. Closely examine *Song of Many Colors* by Michael Woodbury. Then, write a comparison-and-contrast essay in which you discuss the ways in which the artist uses color, shapes, and texture to depict various aspects of nature.

Song of Many Colors, Michael Woodbury, Courtesy of the artist

Responding to Literature

4. Read William Shakespeare's Sonnets 116 and 130. Compare the views of love presented in each sonnet. You can find these sonnets in *Prentice Hall Literature: Timeless Voices, Timeless Themes*, The British Tradition.

☑ Cooperative Writing Opportunity

5. **Consumer Magazine** Work with a team to create a consumer magazine. Each team member should be responsible for choosing two or more types of a particular product or service and writing a brief comparison-and-contrast article about them. When the articles are finished, assign one team member to illustrate them, another to bind them together into a single volume, and another to create a table of contents. Share the completed magazine with your classmates.

Evaluating Your Topic

Choose subjects to compare that share enough similarities and have enough differences to make the comparison useful.

Evaluate Similarities and Differences

To evaluate your subjects, use a chart to note similarities and differences. Review your chart to make sure your subjects share enough qualities to make an effective topic for comparison.

Ineffective Comparison
Romeo and Juliet
and
Guys and Dolls

Similarities	Differences
both have been made into movies	one is a tragedy; one is a comedy
both include love stories	written in different eras
	characters have little in common
	plots are different
	themes are different

Effective Comparison
Romeo and Juliet
and
West Side Story

Similarities	Differences
both tell the same story	settings are different
both are plays that have been filmed	time periods are different
	one is a drama; one is a musical
related characters	
both explore the theme of love overcoming differences	backgrounds of characters are different

Considering Your Audience and Purpose

Select details and choose a style of language that will appeal to your audience and help you achieve your purpose.

Consider Your Purpose

When writing exposition, your general purpose is to inform. However, you must have a more specific purpose to guide your choices as you collect ideas, draft, and revise.

For example, if you are writing a consumer report and your purpose is to educate readers, use words and details that are formal, precise, and factual. If your purpose is to warn readers, include details and language that have strong connotations and a serious impact.

Gathering Details

To create a balanced comparison, make sure you collect details in similar categories about each of your subjects. Remember that your essay will investigate both similarities and differences.

List Your Questions

Write a list of questions to help guide your prewriting investigation. Your questions should focus on specific categories or aspects of your subjects. To achieve a balanced essay, be sure you answer each question relating to both subjects.

For example, suppose you are writing an essay comparing and contrasting two different colleges. You might use some of the following questions to help you gather details:

- Where is each college located?

- How many students attend each school?

- What subject areas are particular strengths for each college?

- How does each school determine financial aid?

- What is the estimated cost of attending each school?

Write each question on note cards or paper, and record answers for each subject. Keep your research plan flexible, because your answers may lead you to additional questions.

Technology Tip

Use the "table" feature in your word-processing program to create a chart in which you list similarities and differences between your subjects.

Student Work IN PROGRESS

Name: Catherine Bailey
and Zach Bucek
L. C. Anderson High School
Austin, TX

Listing Questions to Gather Details

Catherine and Zach wrote a list of questions before they began researching their article about on-line and traditional music stores

1. What is the procedure for buying CDs?

2. How much does a CD cost?

3. How do you search for a CD?

4. What are the benefits?

Drafting

9.3

Shaping Your Writing
Choose an Effective Organization

During prewriting, you uncovered various details about the subjects you are comparing and contrasting. Now, decide on a clear organizational strategy to keep those details from becoming jumbled and confusing.

Two common approaches are used to write a comparison-and-contrast essay:

- **Point-by-Point Comparison:** Discuss one feature or aspect of both subjects, and then move on to another feature. Continue until you have covered all of your points.

- **Subject-by-Subject Comparison:** Discuss one subject fully, and then move on to the next subject. Make sure that the sequence of details in the second discussion mirrors that of the first.

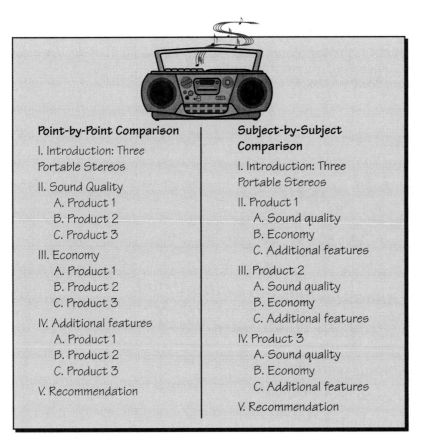

Point-by-Point Comparison

I. Introduction: Three Portable Stereos

II. Sound Quality
    A. Product 1
    B. Product 2
    C. Product 3

III. Economy
    A. Product 1
    B. Product 2
    C. Product 3

IV. Additional features
    A. Product 1
    B. Product 2
    C. Product 3

V. Recommendation

Subject-by-Subject Comparison

I. Introduction: Three Portable Stereos

II. Product 1
    A. Sound quality
    B. Economy
    C. Additional features

III. Product 2
    A. Sound quality
    B. Economy
    C. Additional features

IV. Product 3
    A. Sound quality
    B. Economy
    C. Additional features

V. Recommendation

Providing Elaboration

As you draft, create a complete picture of each subject you are comparing and contrasting. Use specific details to show the extent to which or the ways in which your subjects are similar and different.

Support Your Statements

Provide details that emphasize how your subjects are similar and different, and then prove or illustrate those points of similarity or difference. Following are examples of details you could use:

- **Example:** Hugger Jeans faded after just ten washings.
- **Statistic:** Nine out of ten mechanics recommend Ignite Spark Plugs.
- **Quotation:** Skating commentator Dirk Leeland stated, "Romanov is exquisite, but Lewis is perfection."

Student Work
IN PROGRESS

Name: *Catherine Bailey
and Zach Bucek*
*L. C. Anderson High School
Austin, TX*

Providing Support

Catherine and Zach drafted a paragraph about the kinds of information available at on-line stores. They used elaboration to provide support for their topic statement.

On-line stores also offer a substantial amount of information that is not available at a local store. For example, many sites link to professional reviews that provide up-to-date commentary on the recording artists, the record labels, and other professionals involved in creating the CD. Many on-line buyers have told me that these professional reviews are very helpful in making purchasing decisions and that "they are more knowledgeable than your average store clerk."

> This detail is an example.

> Quotations, like this one, are another type of detail.

Revising

Improve your first draft by reviewing it from a variety of perspectives. Start by evaluating the big picture, making sure that the overall structure is complete and effective. Once you are sure that the basic structure is solid, evaluate your paragraphs, sentences, and word choices.

Revising Your Overall Structure

Strengthen Unity

A comparison-and-contrast essay needs a strong sense of unity, or singleness of effect, to keep it from seeming like two separate essays. Your overall structure should help make clear how your subjects are related.

▶ **REVISION STRATEGY**
Circling Topic Sentences

With a colored pencil, circle the topic sentence of each paragraph of your essay. Then, review each topic sentence to make sure it directly supports or connects to your essay's topic. If you find a topic sentence that does not belong, delete the sentence and the paragraph in which it appears.

Student Work
IN PROGRESS

Name: *Catherine Bailey and Zach Bucek*
L. C. Anderson High School
Austin, TX

Circling Topic Sentences to Strengthen Unity
Catherine and Zach noticed a break in the unity of their first draft.

Another advantage of on-line record stores is their extensive collection of albums. Web sites sell hundreds of thousands of titles. Although it may take some rare selections a few weeks to ship, at least on-line stores can get them for you. No local store can stock such a vast inventory, and many are reluctant to try to locate rare selections for their customers.

MP3s have also contributed to the on-line music boom. MP3 is a format that allows users to download music directly to their hard drives. Songs in MP3 format are available on many Web sites. Because of this innovation, downloading music has become more convenient.

The topic of MP3s is not directly related to the comparison of on-line record stores and retail stores. Catherine and Zach cut the paragraph to create unity.

Revising Your Paragraphs

To make your comparison-and-contrast essay effective, make sure you have effectively grouped your thoughts, details, and support into paragraphs.

Identify and Revise Paragraphs

Paragraphs present a unit of thought. Some units are expressed in a single sentence; some are expressed through several. Following are explanations of several types of paragraphs you may use in your comparison-and-contrast essay.

Topical Paragraphs: A topical paragraph revolves around a main idea that is expressed in its topic sentence. All other sentences within this type of paragraph should support or relate to the paragraph's topic sentence.

Functional Paragraphs: A functional paragraph serves a specific purpose. For example, it may emphasize a single point, create a special effect, show a shift from one speaker to another, or provide a transition.

Paragraph Blocks: A paragraph block refers to a topic sentence that is supported by several paragraphs in sequence. Paragraphs blocks are useful when presenting characteristics of a subject, citing causes, distinguishing features, or enumerating components of something.

 **Learn More**

To learn more about effective paragraphs, see Chapter 3.

▶**REVISION STRATEGY**
Underlining Main Ideas and Checking Paragraphs

Read through your draft, and underline each main idea.

- If you have more than one main idea within a paragraph, break that paragraph into two paragraphs.

- If a paragraph has no main idea, read it carefully. If it contains support for a main idea presented in another paragraph, combine the two paragraphs. If the paragraph serves a specific function, leave it as is. If the paragraph is part of a paragraph block, leave it as is.

On our road test, we found that <u>the Greystone Lynx X321 is a pleasure to drive</u>. The cab is quiet, even when the engine is pushed to perform. It accelerates swiftly and smoothly and handles curves like a dream. On wet roads, on bumpy roads, on curved roads and straight ones, the Lynx out drives all others in its category.

> This paragraph is topical. Its sentences support the main idea expressed in its topic sentence.

Now, let's look at the price factors—what you'll get for your money.

> This is a functional paragraph. It makes a transition from the previous paragraph to the next.

Revising Your Sentences

Vary Your Sentences

During revision, identify sentence patterns that you rely on too heavily and make adjustments. An effective essay uses sentences of various lengths as well as types to create interest and flow.

▶ **REVISION STRATEGY**
Coding to Identify Sentence Type

Read your essay, and bracket each simple sentence you have used. Put a box around compound sentences. Underline the compound-complex sentences. Then, review your draft. If you have relied too heavily on one type of sentence, add complexity to your sentences or simplify them.

To add complexity:
- Combine sentences.
- Add transitions to link ideas.
- Insert clauses into simple sentences.
- Use a question to create variety.

To simplify:
- Separate one sentence into two or more sentences.
- Add a short, emphatic statement between long sentences.
- Delete unnecessary phrases.

Writing Lab CD-ROM

To analyze the lengths of sentences in your draft, use the Revision Checker for Sentence Length in the Toolkit.

Student Work
IN PROGRESS

Name: *Catherine Bailey and Zach Bucek*
L. C. Anderson High School
Austin, TX

Coding to Improve Sentence Variety

Catherine and Zach noticed that every sentence in this paragraph was a simple sentence. They decided to combine some sentences to improve sentence variety and the overall flow of the paragraph.

Although
∧[On-line record stores have created a ∧convenient more
experience.][However, the atmosphere and feel of ∧tangible record an ordinary
store is absent.][For many people, a local record store is like a
favorite coffee shop or bookstore.][Clerks ∧ are familiar with the who
stock.][They can offer personal recommendations.]

Grammar in Your Writing
Compound and Complex Sentences

Creating sentence variety means using different sentence types. Become familiar with various sentence types so that you know your options as you revise.

A **simple sentence** consists of a single independent clause:

Last night, we watched a movie.

The critic enjoyed the film and recommended it.

Laughing all the way to the bank, the director parodies modern society.

A **compound sentence** consists of two or more independent clauses joined by a comma and a coordinating conjunction or by a semicolon.

Hamlet becomes a tragic hero, but Macbeth becomes a villain.

The two calculators are nearly identical; therefore, I purchased the cheaper model.

A **complex sentence** consists of one independent clause and one or more subordinate clauses.

Independent Clause	Subordinate Clause

She created the Web site that was profiled in *The New York Times*.

Independent Clause

Lady Macbeth encourages her husband to criminal actions, but

Subordinate Clause	Independent Clause

after he kills his enemies, she loses her sanity.

Find It in Your Reading Read through "Man, Bytes, Dog" on pages 170–173 of this chapter. Identify two simple, two compound, and two complex sentences within it. Then, explain how the author's use of sentence variety makes his writing lively.

Find It in Your Writing Classify each sentence in two or three paragraphs of your essay according to its type. If you find too many examples of one type, combine or split several sentences to create greater variety.

For more on sentence variety, see Chapter 20.

Revising Your Word Choice

Strengthen Connections

It's especially important in a comparison-and-contrast essay to make connections between the similarities and differences you are discussing. Review your draft critically, and strengthen connections between your ideas.

▶ **REVISION STRATEGY**
Adding Transitions

Transitions make the relationships among your ideas clearer to readers. They are words, phrases, and even sentences that help explain the similarities and differences between your subjects or emphasize the relative importance of the details you present. As you review your choice of words, consider adding transitional words, phrases, and sentences to strengthen the connections you are describing.

Transitional Word: The Traveler brand backpack held up under tough conditions, *although* it did get extremely dirty.

Transitional Phrase: The Take-It brand backpack, *on the other hand,* fell apart after getting soaked by rain.

Peer Review

Make a Summary Report

Ask a partner to read your draft and summarize the essay aloud. Listen to your partner's summary to help you evaluate the overall effectiveness of your writing, as well as the points that stand out the most.

After discussing the summary, have your partner respond to specific questions about your essay, like the ones that follow. Then, consider his or her responses as you prepare your final draft.

- Is my topic clear and well supported? Explain.

- Are there enough points of comparison and contrast? If not, explain.

- Which, if any, sections of the essay confused you?

- Was my writing exciting or predictable? Explain.

- If you could make one change to this essay, what would it be?

▼ **Critical Viewing** Who is the peer reviewer in this photograph? How can you tell? **[Analyze]**

9.5 Editing and Proofreading

Read your draft carefullly. Make your essay error-free by fixing errors in spelling, punctuation, and grammar.

Focusing on Punctuation

Read your draft carefully, and fix any errors you find in punctuation. Check especially to make sure you have correctly used commas in sentences in which ideas have been combined.

Grammar in Your Writing
Using Commas in Compound and Complex Sentences

A **comma** tells a reader to take a short pause before continuing the sentence. Here are some of the rules you can follow when using commas in compound and complex sentences:

Use a comma before the conjunction that separates two independent clauses in a compound sentence:

I enjoyed the film, but the ending was unbelievable.

Use commas to separate three or more words, phrases, or clauses:

The report stated that security was lax, that lighting was inadequate, and that exits were not clearly marked.

Use commas to set off an introductory adverb clause:

When the bus stopped, the passengers got off.

Do not use a comma to set off adverb clauses in other positions:

The passengers got off when the bus stopped.

Find It in Your Reading Find one example of each of the above usages of the comma in "Man, Bytes, Dog" on pages 170–173. Label each example, and explain why it is punctuated as it is.

Find It in Your Writing Review your draft to find two compound sentences and two complex sentences. Decide whether or not the sentences require commas.

To learn more about using commas, see Chapter 27.

Publishing and Presenting

No matter how you share your comparison-and-contrast essay, you will learn a lot from the reaction of your audience. Use the following ideas for publishing and presenting your essay:

Building Your Portfolio

1. **School Bulletin** Publish your consumer review in a school bulletin to share your findings with an audience. Talk with readers to see whether or not they agree with your conclusions.

2. **Class Essay Contest** Hold a class contest with a panel of student judges to determine the most effective comparison-and-contrast essays. Winning essays can be read aloud, posted, or printed in a pamphlet. Talk as a class about the qualities shared by each of the best entries.

Reflecting on Your Writing

Think about the strategies you used to complete your essay. Then, respond to the following questions, and save your responses in your portfolio.

- What did you learn about your topic as you gathered details?
- What advice would you give to a student who is about to begin a comparison-and-contrast essay?

 **Internet Tip**

To see essays scored with this rubric, go to www.phschool.com

Rubric for Self-Assessment

Use the following criteria to evaluate your comparison-and-contrast essay.

	Score 4	Score 3	Score 2	Score 1
Audience and Purpose	Clearly provides a reason for a comparison-contrast analysis	Adequately provides a reason for a comparison-contrast analysis	Provides a reason for a comparison-contrast analysis	Does not provide a reason for a comparison-contrast analysis
Organization	Clearly presents information in a consistent organization best suited to the topic	Presents information using an organization suited to the topic	Chooses an organization not suited to comparison and contrast	Shows a lack of organizational strategy
Elaboration	Elaborates several ideas with facts, details, or examples; links all information to comparison and contrast	Elaborates most ideas with facts, details, or examples; links most information to comparison and contrast	Does not elaborate all ideas; does not link some details to comparison and contrast	Does not provide facts or examples to support a comparison and contrast
Use of Language	Demonstrates excellent sentence and vocabulary variety; includes very few mechanical errors	Demonstrates adequate sentence and vocabulary variety; includes few mechanical errors	Demonstrates repetitive use of sentence structure and vocabulary; includes many mechanical errors	Demonstrates poor use of language; generates confusion; includes many mechanical errors

9.7 Student Work IN PROGRESS

FINAL DRAFT

Are Local Music Stores Obsolete?

**Catherine Bailey and Zach Bucek
L. C. Anderson High School
Austin, Texas**

▲ Critical Viewing
What might you find to compare and contrast within a music store, such as this one? **[Connect]**

The opening paragraph clearly states what Catherine and Zach will compare and contrast: on-line music stores and local music stores.

In recent years, the fusion of the Internet and the music industry has revolutionized the way many people buy music. Today, Web sites that sell music compete directly with local music stores. But what are the advantages and disadvantages of each shopping experience?

On-line shopping offers unprecedented convenience. Customers can search for and purchase music without leaving their homes. Travel time to these on-line stores is based not on speed limits, location, or traffic, but on the agility of your fingers and the speed of your computer connection. You don't have to check the store hours, either. Web sites operate twenty-four hours a day.

The sentences of various lengths in the second paragraph help make it lively and interesting.

Another advantage of on-line record stores is their extensive collection of albums. Web sites sell hundreds of thousands of titles. Although it may take a few weeks to ship some rare selections, at least on-line stores can get them for you. No local store can stock such a vast inventory, and many are reluctant to try to locate rare selections for their customers.

On-line stores also offer a substantial amount of information that is not available at a local store. For example, many sites link to professional reviews that provide up-to-date commentary on the recording artists, the record labels, and other professionals involved in creating the CD. Many on-line buyers have told me that these professional reviews are very helpful in making purchasing decisions and that "they are more knowledgeable than your average store clerk." There is a lot of information stored in on-line search engines, too. For example, you can search for a specific song title and find out what album it is on. Of course,

The essay uses point-by-point organization. Each paragraph discusses one feature or point and how it relates to the two subjects being compared and contrasted.

many record stores have computers that work in the same way, but you might have to wait in line to use it.

Although on-line record stores have created a more convenient experience, the atmosphere and feel of an ordinary record store is absent. For many people, a local record store is like a favorite coffee shop or bookstore. Clerks, who are familiar with the stock, can offer personal recommendations.

Prices are often, but not always, cheaper at on-line stores. You usually have to pay a shipping cost, which decreases the more items you buy. Depending on where the CDs are shipped from, you may not have to pay a sales tax. In our survey, the total cost of a CD was about one dollar less at on-line sites. That's not a huge difference, but it can add up if you are a music collector.

Don't think, however, that on-line stores are impersonal. They, too, can offer personalized services, based on your purchases or album ratings. To shop at most on-line stores, you create an account by giving them information about yourself. You might also provide some album ratings so the database can determine your musical preferences. Once your account is established, the site will keep records of what you buy and provide you with customized recommendations and special offers.

Some on-line stores provide a personalized experience that local stores cannot match: They let you buy single songs to create your own CD. Do you want a CD with your favorite dance music or maybe one with your list of the ten best jazz songs? Some sites allow you to assemble your own CD by choosing songs and selecting the order. Your finished CD will cost much less than it would cost to buy all of the albums that include those songs.

Of course, if you want a CD right away, you'll still have to drive, cycle, or walk to your nearest music store. "People love impulse buying," Bill Jeffrey, the buyer at Waterloo Records, said. "We often hear complaints from our customers concerning the time it takes to receive the product [when ordering on-line]. We have considered starting a Web site because of the competition, but I don't think these on-line music sites are any threat to us or other record stores in general."

For now, however, on-line stores offer an attractive and economical alternative, not a replacement. Even with the convenience and personalization offered by on-line sites, we don't think physical stores are going to disappear any time soon. For many shoppers, the experience of flipping through albums with their glossy packaging is just as vital as convenience.

Results of a statistical survey create support for the main point of this paragraph.

Transitions such as "too," "also," and "once" clarify the connections among ideas.

Catherine and Zach support this topic sentence with a lengthy quotation from a professional in the music industry.

The conclusion presents a recommendation based on Catherine and Zach's findings.

Connected Assignment

Consumer Report

Being an informed consumer helps you maximize your spending dollars and avoid costly mistakes. One way to become informed is to read consumer reviews. These articles compare and contrast features of a product or service, drawing on factual information such as testing, experts' opinions, or user surveys. Report writers then reach a conclusion or make a recommendation to readers.

Write your own consumer report, following the writing process steps below to guide you.

Questionnaire

1. Which service do you find more useful?

2. What kind of savings do you get by using that service?

3. How long have you used the service?

Prewriting Make a questionnaire like the one at right, and poll friends or family about their favorite or least favorite services in your community. Ask at local stores about the products people are buying most frequently. Then, choose a product or service to analyze in a consumer report.

Devise a note-taking system, such as index cards or a chart, building your system around such criteria as durability, appearance, and cost. Then, visit stores, conduct surveys, or talk with an expert to gather information about the product or service about which you are reporting.

Drafting In your report's introduction, identify what you are evaluating and introduce the criteria on which it will be judged. Use transitions such as *more, less, equally, identically,* or *differently* to indicate relationships. Also, be sure to include supporting information from your prewriting fact-gathering.

Revising and Editing As you revise, change any language that is unsuitable for your audience, and check to ensure that you've explained technical terms clearly. Delete any details that are unnecessary or misleading, and double-check survey or test results, quotations, and other supporting information.

Publishing and Presenting Share your report with interested friends or peers. To share your report with a wider audience, send it to your school newspaper and ask its editorial board to publish it.

Spotlight on the Humanities

Connecting Themes in the Arts
Focus on Theater: *Pygmalion*

Pygmalion Makeovers are great examples of visual comparison and contrast. British playwright George Bernard Shaw (1856–1950) explored such a comparison and contrast in *Pygmalion*, one of his most famous plays. In the play, Shaw tells the story of Professor Henry Higgins and his student, Eliza Doolittle. In the play, Professor Higgins, who teaches phonetics, transforms Eliza from a flower girl with a Cockney accent into a well-spoken, elegant woman.

Literature Connection The myth of Pygmalion and Galatea appears in Ovid's (43 B.C.?–A.D. 17) *Metamorphoses*. Pygmalion was a sculptor who adored his statue of Aphrodite. He appealed to the goddess Venus to give life to the statue— which she did. In 1871, W. S. Gilbert wrote a comedy, *Pygmalion and Galatea*, based upon the myth.

Film Connection In 1964, George Cukor directed a film adaptation of *My Fair Lady*, a Broadway musical that was based on Shaw's *Pygmalion*. Composer Frederick Loewe created the music, and Alan Jay Lerner wrote the book and lyrics. Cukor's film, starring Audrey Hepburn and Rex Harrison, won eight Academy Awards.

Comparison-and-Contrast Writing Application: Before-and-After Chart or Pictorial

Choose as a topic something that has changed over time. For example, has a playground in your town been refurbished? Perhaps Main Street has undergone a renewal, or a remake of a classic film has just been released. Once you find a topic, visually represent the before-and-after relationship with a chart, illustrations, or photographs. Then, write captions that point out the features that changed for the better or worse over time. When your chart or pictorial is finished, share it with your class.

▲ **Critical Viewing** Based on clues in this photograph, in what time period do you think this photo of George Bernard Shaw was taken? Explain how you arrived at your answer. **[Analyze]**

Media and Technology Skills

Analyzing Relationships Between Media

Activity: Compare Newspapers' Editorial Positions

The people who edit and produce newspapers have opinions that become clear when you read many issues. A newspaper's editorial position might be conservative or liberal, Democratic or Republican, mainstream or progressive. Examining a newspaper's editorial position can help you interpret the articles you read.

Think About It Choose two newspapers to analyze. Then, read several issues of each paper to evaluate each paper's editorial position. Before you begin, write down your first impression of each paper. When you have finished your research, you will be able to decide whether your first impressions were justified.

Bowen Wins in a Landslide

Dvafj vasflm hxncadm xxjdfs vvstk bsc nvd ndk jn pchevxa ndc ycvnmk vasflm hxncadm xxj dfs vvstk bsc nvd ndk jn

Yvafj vasflm hxncadm xxjdfs vvstk bsc nvd ndk jn pchevxa ndc ycvnmk vasflm hxncadm xxjdfs vvst

Four More Years for Bowen

Wvafj vasflm hxnca xxjdfs vvstk bsc nvd jn pchevxa ndc ycvnn vasflm hxncadm xxjd vvstk bsc nvd ndk jn

> ### Statistical Analysis
>
> Numerical data can help you draw conclusions about a newspaper's editorial preferences. Here are a few examples of statistical data you might collect to help you compare two newspapers:
>
> • During a political race, count the number of times each candidate is mentioned in the headlines. Is the paper's preferred candidate mentioned more often?
>
> • Determine what percentage of the paper's political endorsements support each major party.

Plan It Use several strategies to compare the two newspapers you have selected. Consider these action plans:

• Read issues from the same date. Evaluate the stories that are covered in each paper.

• Keep a list of editorials presented by each paper for one week.

• Research the paper's history of political endorsements.

• Compare published photographs of prominent politicians. Evaluate each photograph to determine whether it presents a positive or negative view of the subject.

Evaluate It After collecting information from several issues of each newspaper, analyze your findings to draw a conclusion about each source's editorial position. For example, a paper might be conservative on financial issues but progressive on conservation.

Create a chart or paragraph to compare your evaluation of the two newspapers. Share your work by displaying the finished project or by holding a presentation for the class.

Standardized Test Preparation Workshop

Responding to Comparison-and-Contrast Prompts

Standardized writing tests measure your ability to compare-and-contrast two or more subjects. The types of samples you will be prompted to compare and contrast might include two models of literature, two views on a controversial issue, or two reviews of a work of art. Whatever prompt you are offered, your goal is to illuminate both the similarities and differences of the subjects given. You may also be asked to state a position on which of the two you prefer. Within your comparison-and-contrast writing, make sure to address the following:

- similarities and differences among the two or more subjects

- a neat and logical organization of the points of comparison and contrast

- details that successfully support and elaborate upon your comparisons and contrasts

- proper use of spelling and grammar

Use the writing process stages—prewriting, drafting, revising, editing, and proofreading—as you draft your response. Assign a rough amount of time to perform each stage of the writing process.

Following is an example of a comparison-and-contrast writing prompt you may encounter. Use the writing process steps on the next page to guide you as you respond to the prompt. The clocks next to each stage recommend the amount of time you should spend on each suggestion.

Test Tips

- Create an introduction, body, and conclusion. Introduce your thesis or main point in the introduction, develop your main idea in the body paragraphs, and restate your thesis or main idea in the conclusion.
- When drafting, allow extra space between lines so you will be able to insert corrections neatly during revision.

Sample Writing Situation

Read the following prompt, and provide an answer in essay form.

In an essay, compare and contrast two or more economic philosophies, ranging from *laissez faire* to total government regulation. Also, point out in your essay which economists supported which philosophies.

Prewriting

 Allow about one quarter of your time for developing your position and identifying comparison-and-contrast details.

Identify Details Select two or three criteria against which to evaluate the two opposing views. List details that show the ways in which the subjects are similar and different.

Organize Details Create a two-column chart to help organize the details you have collected in a comparison-and-contrast format. Make sure that you have a balanced number of details that show similarities and differences.

Drafting

 Allow about half of your time for drafting. Write neatly, and leave space for any text you may want to insert when revising.

Write an Introduction, Body, and Conclusion As you draft, introduce your thesis, or main idea, and grab the interest of your audience. Also, provide a transition into the first body paragraph of your essay. In the body of your essay, develop your main idea and provide support in the form of details. Conclude memorably by restating your main idea and then posing an interesting question or providing a thought-provoking quotation or observation.

Elaborate As you draft, support your statements by giving specific examples. You should present a variety of support, such as details that show personal observations, statistical data, quotations, and historical facts.

Revising, Editing, and Proofreading

 Allow almost one quarter of your time for revising.

Close the Gaps Solidify your argument by adding important details you omitted. Review your prewriting notes to make sure that you have included the details you had planned to include.

Stengthen Unity Read your essay carefully to be sure that each detail relates to your topic. If you find a detail that is beside the point, delete it or add a clarifying sentence to show its connection to your topic.

Clarify Relationships Smooth connections and clarify relationships between your subjects by inserting transitions such as *in addition, as well,* and *unlike.*

Fix Errors Take time to proofread carefully. Look first to catch errors that you make frequently. Then, proofread and correct all errors you find in spelling, punctuation, and grammar.

Exposition
Cause-and-Effect Essay

Cause-and-Effect Relationships in Everyday Life

Have you ever tried to explain to a friend how a series of mishaps caused you to be late? Perhaps you have recounted for your family the game events that led to a basketball victory. In these situations, you explained the cause-and-effect relationships among events. Understanding such relationships helps you to learn about past events as well as to predict future ones.

Cause-and-effect relationships are often explored in various types of writing. For example, a self-help book may explain how certain attitudes produce poor outcomes in life and then tell you why new attitudes might lead to better results. A biography of a rock star might explain what caused each of the ups and downs in her career or tell you what caused her to leave one record label for another.

▲ **Critical Viewing**
Judging from clues in this photograph, what might cause a phenomenon like the Northern Lights? **[Analyze Causes and Effects]**

What Is a Cause-and-Effect Essay?

Writing that explains or informs is called **expository writing.** One type of expository writing is the **cause-and-effect essay,** which explains the relationship between events or situations that took place in the past and the events or situations that occurred as a result. Sometimes, these essays may look forward, cautioning readers about the likely results of certain current events or situations.

Effective cause-and-effect essays usually contain

- an explanation of how particular causes produced or might produce particular effects.

- examples and other details that support the essay's main ideas.

- transitions that show how various causes and effects are linked.

- a logical organizational strategy.

To preview the criteria on which your cause-and-effect essay may be evaluated, see the Self-Assessment Rubric on page 209.

The Greek philosopher Aristotle was renowned for his wisdom. An astute observer of human nature, Aristotle noted the following: "Every action must be due to one or other of seven causes: chance, nature, compulsion, habit, reasoning, anger, or appetite."

Types of Cause-and-Effect Essays

Cause-and-effect essays may take the following forms:

- **Historical cause-and-effect essays** may explain causes and effects of major events such as war, drought, and elections.

- **Scientific cause-and-effect essays** often explore the causes of natural phenomena such as hurricanes and volcanoes.

- **General interest cause-and-effect essays** center around the cause-and-effect relationships in the everyday world, such as exercise and fitness or education and success.

Follow along as student Carl Byers of Muncie Central High School in Muncie, Indiana, writes an article for his school paper explaining why swing music has risen in popularity. A final draft of Carl's article appears at the end of this chapter.

Mario Salvadori is the author of *Why Buildings Stand Up,* as well as *Why Buildings Fall Down,* from which this selection was taken. Matthys Levy, a master of structural design, collaborated with Salvadori on this book.

Reading Strategy: Look for Authors' Main Points As you read, look for the main points the authors are making to help you more thoroughly understand and evaluate their ideas.

from *"Miracle on 34th Street"*

Matthys Levy and Mario Salvadori

On July 28, 1945, nearly three months after the defeat of the Nazi government and the end of the war in Europe, on the very day the U.S. Senate ratified the United Nations Charter, Lieutenant Colonel W. F. Smith, Jr., took off at 8:55 A.M. from Bedford, Massachusetts, in a B-25 bomber for a flight to Newark, New Jersey. With two other occupants, the plane flew on the gray morning at an estimated 250 mph, arriving in the New York area less than an hour later. Lieutenant Colonel Smith was advised by the control tower at La Guardia Airport that the ceiling, the distance from the ground to the clouds, was less than 1,000 feet. This implied that clouds and fog would have obscured the tops of New York's skyscrapers, especially the then tallest, the Empire State Building.

The pilot, flying under visual rules, was required to maintain 3 miles forward visibility. If unable to do so between La Guardia and Newark airports, he was required to land at La Guardia. Smith ignored that requirement. Continuing toward Newark, he was seen heading in a southwesterly direction, weaving through the maze of skyscrapers over Manhattan and crossing low-hanging clouds. Heading toward Forty-second Street, the plane

▲ Critical Viewing Is the damage visible in the photograph more extensive or less extensive than you would have imagined following a plane crash? Explain. **[Analyze]**

Here, the first cause-and-effect relation-ship is revealed: Because of the war, bomber planes were in use by the air force.

Among the details that explain the various causes are those describing the weather conditions.

flew down out of a cloud at no more than 400 feet above the ground, at which point it started climbing in a right turn. In an effort to slow the plane, the wheels were lowered moments before the plane struck the Empire State Building on the north face of the seventy-ninth floor, 913 feet above the ground, ripping a hole 18 feet wide and 20 feet high in the outer wall of the building. The force of the impact sheared off the wings of the plane and propelled one of the two motors across the width of the building, through the opposite wall, and down through the twelfth-story roof of a building across Thirty-third Street, starting a destructive fire. Two women in an elevator fell seventy-five stories when the cable holding their cab snapped, cut by flying shrapnel. Miraculously they escaped with their lives, although they were seriously injured, when automatic devices sufficiently slowed the free fall of the cab. Flames from the burning gasoline killed most of the thirteen victims, including the crew of the plane.

"I couldn't believe my own eyes," said a witness, looking out from the 103rd-story observatory, "when I saw the plane come out of the overcast. Then it struck the building with a force that sent a tremor through the whole structure." The crash spilled gasoline from the ruptured tanks, which immediately ignited, illuminating the tower of the building for a brief instant before it disappeared again in the mist and the smoke from the burning plane. As the spilled gasoline burned, flaming debris rained down the face of the building. The ebullient mayor of the city, Fiorello La Guardia, arriving, as usual right behind his firefighters, on the scene of the inferno at the seventy-ninth floor, was seen shaking his fist and muttering: "I told them not to fly over the city."

The center of impact aligned almost exactly with a column on the face of the tower. The right motor passed on one side of the column and the left motor on the opposite side. The column itself was barely damaged, although a steel beam supporting the masonry wall struck by the right motor was torn out, and a second beam supporting the floor slab was bent back 18 inches. The plane apparently struck the seventy-ninth floor dead-on, which explains the lack of damage to the column. Had the plane been just a bit higher or lower, it might have struck and bent the column, and then . . .

Supporting details are arranged in chronological order, making it easy to follow the cause-and-effect relationships.

LITERATURE

"We'll Never Conquer Space," an essay by Arthur C. Clarke, examines cause-and-effect relationships as he predicts space travel possibilities. "We'll Never Conquer Space" appears in *Prentice Hall Literature: Timeless Voices, Timeless Themes,* The British Tradition.

Elaboration in the form of quotations by eyewitnesses helps bring the event to life for readers.

These details, which help explain the effects of the crash, are factual and statistical.

The final sentence poses an intriguing cause-and-effect "what if" question.

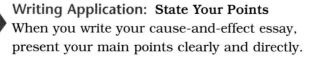

Writing Application: State Your Points
When you write your cause-and-effect essay, present your main points clearly and directly.

Choosing Your Topic

Choose a topic for your cause-and-effect essay by selecting a subject or recent event that can be broken down into specific causes and effects.

Following are some strategies that can help you find a topic for a cause-and-effect essay:

Strategies for Generating a Topic

1. **Scan a Newspaper or Magazine** Read quickly through a favorite newspaper or magazine. When you find an interesting topic, ask yourself "What caused this situation?" and "What effects will it have?" Jot down a few notes in answer to those questions. Then, if you find the topic has possibilities, use it for your cause-and-effect essay.

2. **Freewrite** Sometimes, the best way to come up with a topic is to just start writing. Find a quiet place to work, glance at your watch or set a timer, and write without stopping for five minutes. When the time is up, read over what you have written. Choose the idea that interests you most as a topic for your cause-and-effect essay.

Writing Lab CD-ROM

For more help choosing a topic, explore the activities and topic suggestions in the Choosing a Topic section of the Exposition lesson.

Name: Carl Byers
Muncie Central High School
Muncie, IN

Freewriting to Find a Topic

Carl Byers used the freewriting strategy to help him find a topic for his cause-and-effect essay. After he wrote for five minutes, he read though his writing and found a suitable topic. (Because he was freewriting, he jotted down words and phrases. When he drafts, he will use complete sentences.)

Rock music—how it came into being. Elvis Presley, blues bands, Carl Perkins, Cab Calloway, Glenn Miller, and swing music. Jitterbugging, Lindy Hop. Big bands—Harry Connick, Jr. New swing bands. Why swing is popular again today.

TOPIC BANK

If you are having difficulty coming up with a topic on your own, consider one of the following:

1. **Analysis of a War** Write about the causes that led to a particular war or about the effects that the war had. For example, if you were writing about the Civil War, you might explain how disagreements over slavery, arguments over states' rights, and economic competition all helped cause the war.

2. **Prediction** Advances in technology—television, microwave ovens, the Internet—have had a huge impact on our lives. Think of an invention yet to be created, and explain the effects it will have on the way people live.

Responding to Fine Art

3. *Breakers on the Promontory at Granville* is an artist's depiction of ocean waves. Write an essay explaining the causes and effects of the ocean's tides or the effects that storm tides have on shorelines.

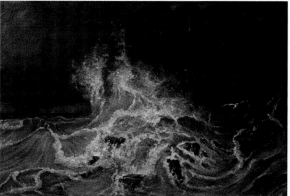

Breakers on the Promontory at Granville,
Paul Huet, Musée du Louvre, Paris

Responding to Literature

4. In Samuel Pepys's *Diary,* he gives an eye-witness account of the Great Fire of London. In a cause-and-effect essay, examine the causes and effects of a notable fire like the one Pepys describes or the ones that devastated Chicago and San Francisco. You can read Pepys's *Diary* in *Prentice Hall Literature: Timeless Voices, Timeless Themes,* The British Tradition.

☑ Cooperative Writing Opportunity

5. **Cause-and-Effect Presentation** With a group, choose an important event or a scientific phenomenon to explore. Then, brainstorm to create two lists: factors that caused the event or phenomenon and effects resulting from it. Then, have each group member choose one cause or effect to learn more about. As a group, compile your information and create visual aids that clearly show the cause-and-effect relationships. Present your findings to the class.

Narrowing Your Topic

Once you have a general topic, decide how much of that topic can be covered effectively in a short paper. If you are analyzing a war, for example, you probably can't describe all of its causes fully in a single essay. You could give a general overview of the most important causes, or you could focus on one type of cause, such as economic conditions.

Create a Web to Narrow Your Topic

Make a web to help you consider ways of narrowing your focus. Start by listing your topic in the center. Surround it by connected subtopics. Then, list details connected to each subtopic. Review your web to see whether any of the subtopics would make a suitable topic for your paper.

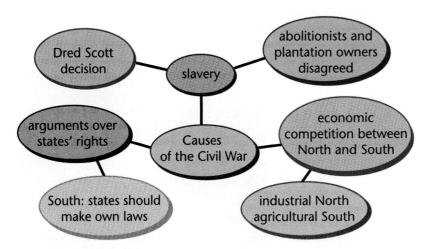

Considering Your Audience and Purpose

Your audience is the people who will read your essay; your purpose is the way you want your writing to affect your audience. As you write, choose details and language that will engage and interest your audience and help you accomplish your purpose.

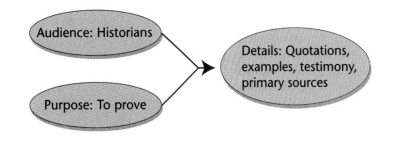

Gathering Details

Your general purpose in a cause-and-effect essay is to show how one action or situation led to another. Include concrete, specific details so your readers can see exactly how this process happened.

Research to Gather Details

Of course, you might not know all the details you need in order to write an effective essay. You might need to do research—reading books, magazines, or newspapers; interviewing experts in the field; or looking up a topic on the Internet.

One way to direct your research is to begin with an effect. List all the causes of that effect that you know. Then, use printed materials, interviews, and the Internet to verify those causes and to discover more.

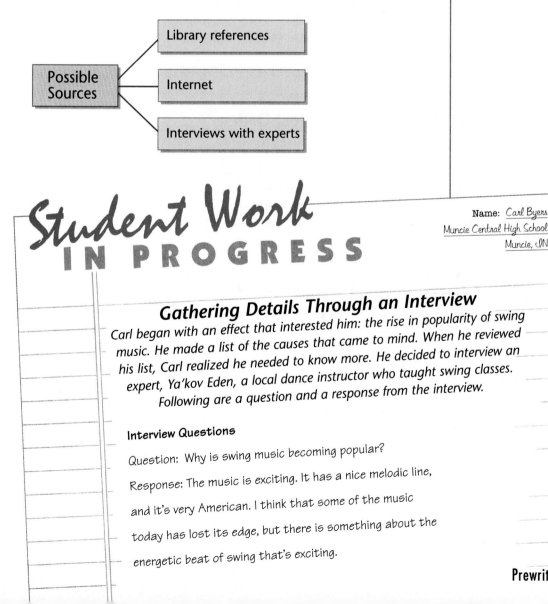

Library references

Possible Sources

Internet

Interviews with experts

Student Work
IN PROGRESS

Name: Carl Byers
Muncie Central High School
Muncie, IN

Gathering Details Through an Interview

Carl began with an effect that interested him: the rise in popularity of swing music. He made a list of the causes that came to mind. When he reviewed his list, Carl realized he needed to know more. He decided to interview an expert, Ya'kov Eden, a local dance instructor who taught swing classes. Following are a question and a response from the interview.

Interview Questions

Question: Why is swing music becoming popular?

Response: The music is exciting. It has a nice melodic line, and it's very American. I think that some of the music today has lost its edge, but there is something about the energetic beat of swing that's exciting.

Drafting

Shaping Your Writing

Before you begin writing, decide how you want to organize your details. Consider which of the following organizational strategies will be most effective in enabling readers to follow causes and effects.

Organize Details in Order of Importance

One effective way to organize details is to begin with the least important cause and move up to the most important one. Readers' interest builds as they feel that they are getting closer and closer to the heart of the matter.

If you were writing about the causes of a baseball team winning the World Series, for example, you might choose the following order, from least to most important:

1. Good outfield
2. Outstanding pitcher
3. New coach, who reorganized the team and totally improved morale

Organize Details in Chronological Order

Another logical organization is to give causes or effects in the order in which they occurred. This is especially useful when one cause or effect leads to another. If you were writing about the causes of a rock band's rise to fame, for example, you might want to begin at the beginning of their formation, listing each important milestone to their destination—the top of the charts.

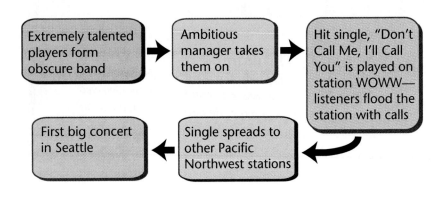

Providing Elaboration

As your cause-and-effect essay takes shape, use elaboration—the addition of details—to help your readers understand more clearly the nature of each cause or effect and how they relate to each other.

Provide Data

Specific statistics, dates, names, or places can help your readers fully understand what you are describing. The use of data also adds authority to your writing.

Give Examples

Examples help readers connect information you have given with their own experiences. For example, if you were describing the horrors of a battle, you might compare the battle to one your audience may have seen in a film.

Share Insights

Your own insights and predictions will give your writing a personal touch and help you to convey a tone, or your attitude toward your subject.

Student Work
IN PROGRESS

Name: *Carl Byers*
Muncie Central High School
Muncie, IN

Elaborating by Adding Insights

Carl included hard data on the causes for swing's popularity, but he decided that giving his own insights would help get his main idea across.

                            type of
"The Swing" is not only a dance step. It's also an attitude,
a way of dressing—and a type of very appealing music.

Some of the reasons have to do with the dance itself.

"The Swing" is based on the smooth movement of the

ballroom step the foxtrot.

10.4 Revising

Revising Your Overall Structure

Review Your Essay's Organization

Review the method of organization you chose to be sure it works effectively and that you've used it consistently throughout the essay.

▶ **REVISION STRATEGY**
Making a New Outline

Make a new outline of your work to see whether all the information you have included is in the right place. At the top of the page, write the form of organization you have chosen. Then, make a numbered list, one number for each paragraph in your work. Beside each number, write a few words or a sentence summarizing what's in the paragraph.

Now, look at the list to be sure the ideas are presented in an effective or logical order. If necessary, rearrange paragraphs or sentences within paragraphs.

Revising Your Paragraphs

Improve Paragraph Flow

A coherent essay contains paragraphs that flow together. Review your paragraphs, and revise them so that they work together to develop your main idea.

▶ **REVISION STRATEGY**
Circling the First and Last Sentences

Read through your cause-and-effect essay, using a colored pen to circle the first and last sentences in each paragraph. Then, look at your work, focusing on paragraph flow. Ask yourself whether each sentence that begins a paragraph flows naturally out of the sentence that came before it. If necessary, rewrite one or both sentences in order to show the connection.

Writers in
ACTION

Samuel Johnson was known for his brilliant prose style and his keen wit. His famous quotation on the revising process works particularly well for cause-and-effect essays, in which every sentence should contribute to the reader's understanding and nothing should be included simply because it "sounds good":

"Read over your compositions and, when you meet a passage which you think is particularly fine, strike it out."

Order of Importance
1. Poverty
2. Restrictive Laws
3. Revolution in France

Revising Your Sentences

Fix Faulty Coordination

Clauses can be connected in various ways. When a writer fails to show the relationship between two clauses in a sentence, it is known as faulty coordination. Changing the connecting words can help make the relationship more clear.

▶**REVISION STRATEGY**
Changing or Adding a Conjunction

To fix faulty coordination, change an inappropriate conjunction or add a conjunction to better show relationships.

Coordinating conjunctions connect similar kinds of words or groups of words that are grammatically alike. Examples include: *and, but, for, nor or, so,* and *yet.*

Correlative conjunctions are similar to coordinating conjunctions except that they are always used in pairs. Examples include: *but . . . and; either . . . or; neither . . . nor; not only . . . but also.*

Subordinating conjunctions connect two complete ideas by making one of the ideas subordinate to, or less important than, the other. Examples include: *consequently, furthermore, however, indeed, otherwise, therefore, fortunately,* and *moreover.*

Student Work
IN PROGRESS

Name: *Carl Byers*
Muncie Central High School
Muncie, IN

Improving Sentence Coordination
As he reread his work, Carl corrected instances of faulty coordination he found in his writing.

"The Swing" is based on the smooth movement of the ballroom step the foxtrot. ~~And,~~ "the Swing" ,however, is not only a type of dance ~~step~~. It's also an attitude, a way of dressing—and a a type of very appealing music.

> By deleting And and adding however, Carl highlights the fact that "The Swing" is more than a dance step.

Grammar in Your Writing
Independent and Subordinate Clauses

A **clause** is a group of words with its own subject and verb. An **independent clause** can stand by itself as a complete sentence. An independent clause can be used in several ways:

By Itself

That cat has a striped tail.

With Another Independent Clause

I hope it's true that cats have nine lives; my cat has used up eight.

With a Subordinate Clause

My cat yowled to be helped from the tree because it was scared.

A **subordinate clause,** although it has a complete subject and verb, cannot stand by itself as a complete sentence; it can only be part of a sentence. Subordinate clauses show relationships of time, result, comparison, contrast, or condition; or they simply add information. They begin with conjunctions, such as *while, because, as if,* and *which.*

Relationship of Time

While they were in the store shopping, we were becoming bored.

Relationship of Result

We became bored *because* they spent so much time shopping.

Relationship of Comparison

They shopped *as if* the world were coming to an end tomorrow.

Relationship of Condition

Shopping, *which* is my family's favorite pastime, is not one of my favorite things to do.

Find It in Your Reading Read through "Miracle on 34th Street" on pages 196–197, and locate three sentences containing subordinate clauses. Identify the conjunctions that help indicate the relationship of the subordinate clause to the main clause of the sentence.

Find It in Your Writing Review your draft to find at least two independent and two subordinate clauses. If you can't find them, challenge yourself to add them. Then, make sure that you have used the correct connecting words to show the relationship between clauses.

To learn more about clauses, see Chapter 19.

Revising Your Word Choice
Eliminate Qualifying Words and Phrases

Unnecessary words clutter up writing, making the main points less clear to readers. Qualifying words and phrases are almost always unnecessary. Read your draft, and eliminate all qualifying words and phrases that are not essential to the point you are trying to convey.

> **UNNECESSARY QUALIFIERS**
>
> almost; it seems; kind of; quite;
>
> rather; somewhat; sort of; tends

▶**REVISION STRATEGY**
Underlining Unnecessary Qualifiers

Read through your cause-and-effect essay, looking for the qualifiers listed in the chart above. Underline with red ink those you find. Then, think about whether you simply want to cut them or whether the sentence needs to be rewritten.

Original sentence: The group's rise was somewhat fast, but so was its fall.

Revised sentence: The group's rise was fast, but so was its fall.

Rewritten sentence: The group's rise was fast by today's standards, but so was its fall.

Peer Review
Ask Peers to Summarize

Share your revised work with a group of peers. Once they've read through your essay, ask them to summarize for you the major causes and effects that they understood from reading your work.

If your classmates have not understood the main cause-and-effect relationships, revise your writing to make it more clear.

🖥 Technology Tip

Use the Find option in your word-processing program to locate qualifiers. Then, edit on the spot and search for more.

Editing and Proofreading

Edit your work carefully, correcting errors in spelling, punctuation, and grammar before you write your final draft.

Focusing on *Which* and *That*

Which and *that* are frequently misused, even by experienced writers. *That* offers essential information, and *which* indicates nonessential information. As you proofread your work, check your usage to be sure that it is correct.

Grammar in Your Writing
Commas in Essential and Nonessential Expressions

An **essential expression** is a word, phrase, or clause that provides information that cannot be removed without changing the meaning of the sentence. **Nonessential expressions** provide additional, but not essential, information.

1. Essential information does not need to be enclosed in commas. Since the following sentence does not make much sense without the essential expression *Brain*, you don't need commas.

The rock band Brain is one of my favorites.

2. Nonessential information must be set off with commas. The following sentence makes sense without the italicized phrase. Therefore, that nonessential expression is set off by commas.

Brain, one of my favorite bands, now rarely plays in concert.

Find It in Your Reading Look for one example each of essential and nonessential expressions in "Miracle on 34th Street" on pages 196–197. Then, explain why each expression is punctuated as it is.

Find It in Your Writing As you proofread your cause-and-effect essay, double-check to be sure your punctuation of essential and nonessential information is correct.

For more on punctuating essential and nonessential information, see Chapter 27.

10.6 Publishing and Presenting

Building Your Portfolio

Following are some ideas for publishing and presenting your cause-and-effect essay:

1. **Discussion Group** Share your essay with interested peers. Then, lead a discussion about your work. Note which strategies you'll repeat and which you'll change the next time you write a cause-and-effect essay.

2. **Community Publication** If you've written about an event or a situation that affects your community, a community publication might be interested in publishing your work. Find out the guidelines for submitting your writing and prepare your manuscript accordingly.

Reflecting on Your Writing

Think back on your writing experience. Then, respond to the following questions, and save your responses in your portfolio.

- What new information about your topic did you learn as you gathered details for your essay?

- If a friend were writing a cause-and-effect essay, what three pieces of advice would you give to him or her?

Internet Tip

To see model essays scored with this rubric, go to **www. phschool.com**

Rubric for Self-Assessment

Use the following criteria to evaluate your cause-and-effect essay.

	Score 4	Score 3	Score 2	Score 1
Audience and Purpose	Consistently targets an audience; clearly identifies purpose in thesis statement	Targets an audience; identifies purpose in thesis statement	Misses a target audience by including a wide range of word choice and details; presents no clear purpose	Addresses no specific audience or purpose
Organization	Presents a clear, consistent organizational strategy to show cause and effect	Presents a clear organizational strategy with occasional inconsistencies; shows cause and effect	Presents an inconsistent organizational strategy; creates illogical presentation of causes and effects	Demonstrates a lack of organizational strategy; creates a confusing presentation
Elaboration	Successfully links causes with effects; fully elaborates connections among ideas	Links causes with effects; elaborates connections among most ideas	Links some causes with some effects; elaborates connections among some ideas	Develops and elaborates no links between causes and effects
Use of Language	Uses words precisely; presents very few mechanical errors	Uses words precisely; presents few mechanical errors	Contains some imprecise words; presents many mechanical errors	Demonstrates poor use of words; presents many mechanical errors

Student Work
IN PROGRESS

FINAL DRAFT

▶ **Critical Viewing** If you were describing this dance move to someone, what phrases would you use? **[Interpret]**

Why Swing Is Here to Stay

**Carl Byers
Muncie Central High
School
Muncie, Indiana**

We live in an age in which music is bought and sold by major labels and marketed to the public until nothing is left, after which the majors move on to the next trend and repeat the process. Well, it looks as if the public has done the picking this time. Swing music and its dances have had a renewed interest—and with almost no help from the major labels. I mean, who hasn't heard the latest covers of swing classics by modern rock bands?

You don't see tons of swing bands turning up on the covers of popular music magazines or on music television. Yet swing is everywhere: on TV commercials, in fashion, and in movies. Popular culture is full of swing nowadays.

How did this happen? It was a combination, really: Certain people were in the right place at the right time.

Some of the reasons have to do with the dance itself. "The Swing" is based on the smooth movement of the ballroom step the foxtrot. "The Swing," however, is not only a dance step. It's also

In his introduction, Carl reveals his topic: the causes behind the rise in popularity of swing music.

Carl's essay is organized consistently and logically: He discusses each causative factor, one at a time.

an attitude, a way of dressing—and a type of very appealing music.

"I think that, when you listen to the music, it's exciting. It has a nice melodic line, and it's very American," said swing instructor Ya'kov Eden. "I think that some of the music today has kind of lost its edge, but there is something about the rock-and-roll beat of swing that's exciting. The nineties swing bands are so exciting in their instrumentation that when you hear them, you can't sit still."

Another factor in the rise of swing was the "Khakis Swing" commercial produced by a popular clothing chain. The popular ad featured "Jump, Jive and Wail," leading to a radio renaissance of singles from various rock bands.

An interest in swing has filtered down to our very own school. Eden offers swing classes to the public at his studio on Monday and Thursday nights, and several Central students have attended.

By mentioning that Central High School students are studying swing, Carl shows his audience—readers of the school newspaper—how they, too, are affected by the rise in swing's popularity.

"I took the class because it sounded like fun," said senior Monica Young.

By offering a fresh, new alternative to the dead-end trends of popular music, swing music is guaranteed to leave a lasting impression.

This conclusion predicts an effect swing music will have in the future.

▼ **Critical Viewing** Why might the dance depicted in the photograph be so popular among young and old? **[Analyze]**

Connected Assignment
Documentary

Documentaries are films that examine people's lives, historical events, and scientific phenomena. Today's television schedules are filled with documentaries on every topic from sports to politics to celebrity lifestyles. Many focus on cause-and-effect relationships, such as those that influence a person's career path or lead a country into war.

The writers of documentaries create scripts that help filmmakers shape and mold visual and textual information into the finished film you view. Documentaries can include interviews, historical and current film clips, sound bites and audio excerpts, information footage explained by narration, or primary source documents, such as legal court papers. Stage directions outline the organization of these different elements, while narration is indicated as dialogue.

Imagine that you're a scriptwriter for a popular television newsmagazine. Develop a documentary script using these suggested writing process steps.

▲ **Critical Viewing**
What sort of documentary might the people pictured be working on? How can you tell? **[Connect]**

MODEL

Scene 1
Interior. Fade in.

Close-up of female hand writing a letter with a quill pen. A voice-over (Jane Austen character) reads as letter is written:

Dearest Fanny,

I feel quite as doubtful as you could be my dearest Fanny as to *when* my Letter may be finished, for I can command very little quiet time at present, but yet I must begin, for I know you will be glad to hear as soon as possible . . .

Fade out.

NARRATOR: Jane Austen was born in Steventon, Hampshire. Her father was a clergyman . . .

Choosing a Topic Brainstorm for possible documentary topics by scanning the newspaper or talking with neighbors about issues of interest. You might also choose to center your documentary around a person or place within your own community.

Creating a Plan Decide on a plan for your documentary. Make a chart like the one that follows, and show how various elements from your plan will work together as you develop your documentary.

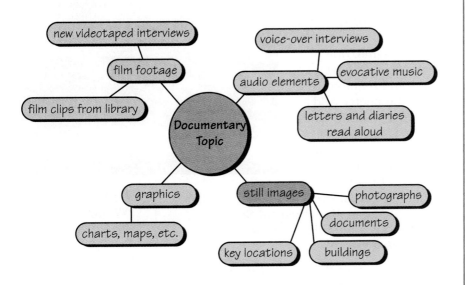

Drafting Follow your plan as you draft, visualizing the images viewers will see as you describe them in words on your script. Orient the filmmaker (and other script readers) to the events by clearly indicating what images are shown when. Add voice-overs to bind the elements into a smooth narrative that emphasizes a cause-and-effect relationship. Keep the narration neutral in tone, even when explaining disturbing or surprising events.

Revising and Editing Have a peer read your script and comment on its coherence and visual impact. Add transitional narration to smoothly move from element to element. Check to be sure that people and places are well explained and that your language suits the audience's knowledge level. Avoid overly emotional appeals; trust viewers to reach reasonable conclusions when presented with compelling evidence.

Publishing and Presenting Film your documentary or a portion of it, and hold a screening for your family and friends.

Appreciating Music

Focus on Music: Ralph Vaughan Williams

In a cause-and-effect essay, you consider the reasons something did happen or might happen. According to Ralph Vaughan Williams, one of the reasons he became a composer was that he was profoundly influenced and inspired by English folk songs, as well as the poetry and music of the seventeenth century. British composer Ralph Vaughan Williams (1872–1958) was one of the most important composers of the twentieth century. With a voice all his own and inspired by poetry in much of his work, Vaughan Williams wrote music of almost every type. Some of his major works include *Serenade to Music*, *Five Mystical Songs*, and *10 Blake Songs*. His nine symphonies include the *London Symphony* and the *Pastoral Symphony*.

▲ **Critical Viewing** What type of music might you expect these musicians to play? Why? **[Infer]**

Theater Connection Ralph Vaughan Williams's *Serenade to Music*, written in 1938, is based upon a passage in William Shakespeare's *The Merchant of Venice*. Written in 1596–1597, *The Merchant of Venice* is the story of the Venetian merchant Antonio; Portia, a wealthy single woman; and Shylock, the man who has loaned Antonio money. In the drama, the money must be repaid in three months or Shylock may take a pound of flesh from Antonio. However, it is a disguised Portia who brings the plot to an unexpected end.

Literature Connection In 1920, Ralph Vaughan Williams revised a musical piece entitled *The Lark Ascending*, which was based upon the poem of the same name by British author and critic George Meredith (1828–1909). Meredith was a prolific writer who believed that comedy and laughter kept in check the excesses of sentimentality and egotism. Meredith, who began as a newspaper writer and reader for a publisher, became the author of novels and poetry. He was awarded the Order of Merit in 1905.

Cause-and-Effect Writing Activity: Musical Analysis

Listen to a symphony or other work by Ralph Vaughan Williams. Then, describe the effect the music had on you, and analyze how various musical elements—tempo, instruments, volume, or intensity, for example—contributed to that effect.

Media and Technology Skills

Examining the Effect of Media on Perceptions of Reality

Activity: Create a Musical Tour of Current Styles

Popular music is a primary component of our culture. When a song becomes a hit, its musicians become cultural trendsetters through their appearances in videos, television, and magazines. Identify trendsetters of the moment by creating an audio tour of currently popular, "cutting edge" music.

Learn About It Begin by researching which songs are most popular at this time. If you want to analyze how your school's students are affected by their favorite music, conduct a survey to identify the most popular current songs or artists.

Record and Reflect on It Record and listen to three or four popular songs. Use a chart to describe each song. Then, use sources such as television interviews, music and entertainment magazines, and Internet sites to collect information about the performers.

Song Title	Style of Song	Summary of Lyrics	Performers	Performers' Styles (clothing, speech, hair, etc.)

Select and Annotate It Create an anthology tape of influential music to share with classmates. Also, include an annotated track list that contains the information that you gathered in the chart above.

Present It Share your audio tour in a presentation. To create a visual impact, use an overhead projector to show photographs from magazines or other sources. In your presentation, emphasize how the music you are playing has affected current styles and trends.

Standardized Test Preparation Workshop

Responding to Cause-and-Effect Writing Prompts

Writing prompts on standardized tests measure your ability to identify and analyze cause-and-effect relationships. For example, you may be asked to analyze the causes of the Great Depression or explain the phenomena that causes a tornado. Your writing will likely be evaluated on the following criteria:

- a clearly stated thesis that answers the prompt

- details that support your thesis

- a logical and effective organizational strategy

- language that is appropriate for your audience and that helps you to achieve your purpose

- appropriate transitions that clearly indicate connections between ideas

- correct grammar, spelling, and punctuation

When writing for a timed test, plan to devote a specified amount of time for prewriting, drafting, revising and proofreading.

Following is an example of a writing prompt that probes your understanding of cause-and-effect relationships. Respond to the prompt, using the writing process steps on the following page as a guide. The clocks next to each stage give a suggestion for how much time you should devote to each step.

Test Tips

- Organize your thoughts before you begin writing your response.
- Just before you begin drafting, reread the question to be sure that you answer it in your response.

Sample Writing Situation

Read the excerpt from "Miracle on 34th Street" on pages 196–197. Then respond to the following prompt in the form of an essay.

In "Miracle on 34th Street," Levy and Salvadori analyze the causes leading up to and the effects following a plane crash. Read the essay, and then comment upon the thoroughness and effectiveness of the authors' work. Use details from the essay to support your evaluation.

Prewriting

Allow about one quarter of your time for prewriting.

Write a Thesis Statement Read the prompt and come up with a thesis statement in response. For example, you might think that the cause-and-effect relationships within "Miracle on 34th Street" could be more clear. If so, your thesis statement might read, "Although Levy and Salvadori provide ample details showing cause and effects, they fail to clearly show the relationships among them." Once you develop your thesis statement, gather details to support it.

Outline Details Take a few moments to outline the details you plan to use in your essay. Rough out the order in which you plan to present your ideas. For example, you may prefer to lead off with your second-most important point, followed by points in descending order of importance, and end with your most important point.

Drafting

Allow about one-half hour to draft your essay.

Create an Introduction, Body, and Conclusion Use a classic essay structure as you draft your response. In your introduction, state your thesis and lead into the body of the essay. In the body of your essay, develop and support your thesis. Then, in the essay's conclusion, restate your main points and conclude with a memorable or intriguing closing statement.

Elaborate As you draft the body of your essay, elaborate on your ideas by providing examples from the text as well as personal observations and examples from real life.

Revising, Editing, and Proofreading

Allow almost one fourth of your time to revise and edit. Use the last few minutes to proofread your work.

Delete Unnecessary Details Read through your draft and delete details that do not support your thesis or that detract from your purpose.

Revise Your Introduction and Conclusion Make sure that your introduction and conclusion match and that they work together to create a unified essay. Be sure that in your introduction that you state your thesis and that in your conclusion you reinforce that statement.

Fix Errors Read carefully through your essay and fix all errors in grammar, spelling, and punctuation that you find. Neatly cross out passages containing errors and write corrections above or in the margins.

Exposition
Problem-and-Solution Essay

His Grandmother's Quilt, 1998, Phoebe Beasley, Courtesy of the artist

Problems and Solutions in Everyday Life

Like most people, you probably face major and minor problems every day. You may, for instance, have limited time and too many obligations, or maybe your two closest friends are having a dispute. No matter what the problem is, it won't go away if you ignore it. As commentator Alan Saporta said, "The best way to escape a problem is to solve it."

Writing about problems can help you face difficult challenges and turn them into opportunities. In this chapter, you will learn how to analyze and discuss problem-and-solution topics.

▲ **Critical Viewing** Quilting is a craft that involves skill as well as creativity. What sort of problems might you encounter while quilting? **[Analyze]**

What Is a Problem-and-Solution Essay?

Exposition is writing that explains or informs. A **problem-and-solution essay** is a piece of exposition that describes a problem and one or more likely solutions. An effective problem-and-solution essay

- clearly states a specific problem.
- identifies the most important aspects of the problem.
- presents one or more possible solutions.
- supports each solution with specific details and logical reasons.
- is logically and effectively organized.

To preview the criteria on which your problem-and-solution essay may be evaluated, see the Rubric for Self-Assessment on page 236.

Writers in **ACTION**

Inventor R. Buckminster Fuller once said: "When I'm working on a problem, I never think about beauty. I think only how to solve the problem. But when I have finished, if the solution is not beautiful, I know it is wrong."

Types of Problem-and-Solution Essays

Problem-and-solution essays may address a variety of issues, including the following:

- **Business issues**, which include problems facing a business, such as inventory control and increased competition.
- **Community issues,** which revolve around problems that directly affect the residents of and visitors to your community.
- **Consumer issues,** which address problems related to the operation of products or the quality of services rendered.

PREVIEW
Student Work
IN PROGRESS

Follow along as Gabrielle Frame, a student at Northeast High School in Omaha, Nebraska, writes a problem-and-solution essay about the fear that many students feel when faced with speaking in public. A final draft of her essay appears at the end of this chapter.

"Warding Off Wildlife" appears in The Practical Gardener *by Roger B. Swain. Swain is the science editor of* Horticulture *magazine, as well as the host of* The Victory Garden, *a popular gardening show on PBS.*

Reading Strategy: Evaluate the Writer's Statements Don't accept as fact everything a writer offers. As you read the following essay, evaluate the details and statements that are given as evidence. Then, decide whether each detail or statement has merit.

▲ Critical Viewing
What sort of wildlife might the fence shown in this photograph ward off? **[Draw Conclusions]**

Warding Off Wildlife

Roger B. Swain

I am no hunter. It doesn't really matter how many legs are involved—two, four, six, eight. I don't even like to kill slugs, and they have no legs at all. . . . Not that I am unbloodied. I have done my share of squashing, drowning, poisoning, clubbing, and shooting. It was all, however, in self-defense. My garden was being attacked. Even pacifist vegetarians will reach for a rock when their own beans are at stake.

Because I don't have the temperament of a hunter, and because even if I did I doubt whether I could kill all the animals that have a taste for my fruits and vegetables, I put my effort into excluding the larger animals rather than exterminating them. This means finding ways to keep animals at a safe distance from my young lettuce and ripening grapes.

Woodchucks, rabbits, raccoons, porcupines, and assorted birds have all troubled my gardens at one time or another. These can all do a devastating amount of damage in a short time. For completeness I ought to add deer, but, though deer wreak havoc in some people's gardens, so far they haven't in any of mine.

The introduction reveals Swain's problem. Swain uses humor to capture the interest of his audience.

Here, Swain explains a problem—large animals invade his garden.

I have learned as have generations of gardeners before me, that as long as I am actually working in the garden, animals stay away. But if I am gone even a few minutes, let alone a whole night, they move in to feed. Stand-ins for myself, old-fashioned straw men, are notoriously ineffective. Scarcely better are the more modern scarecrows, those vinyl snakes or inflatable owls. All too quickly the enemy becomes habituated to their presence and recognizes these dummies for what they are.

The only practical way to ward off wildlife, I am now convinced, is to erect barriers: fences against the ones that walk, nets against those that fly. These barriers are put up each year before the animals begin to feed in the garden. A naïve woodchuck will be turned back by a wire fence; not so one that has tasted peas.

Over the years I have used different materials for fencing my main vegetable garden, but the one that I have settled on is 48-inch–high chicken wire with a 1-inch mesh. Historically, chicken wire was indestructible stuff. I have been trying to tear up some that has been outdoors for at least half a century, and it is hardly tarnished. But the current lot lasts scarcely five years before it disintegrates into rusty fragments. The falling quality has not, however, prevented a rise in price. Chicken wire now sells for roughly $25 per 50-foot length, or 50¢ a foot. My vegetables are valuable, but my garden is not Fort Knox. To keep the costs of fencing within bounds, I now dismantle the fence every fall, rolling the wire up and storing it under cover until spring. I am hoping that by exposing the wire to weather for only six months of every year it will last at least twice as long.

For fence posts I use 6-foot wooden stakes that are no thicker than a bean pole. Indeed, some of them are ex–bean poles that rotted off at ground level. Instead of trying to drive these slender posts into the ground with a mallet, I ram them into conical holes made by jamming a crowbar 18 inches into the soil and rotating it. I space these posts 8 feet apart, a generous distance that

LITERATURE

For a variation of a problem-and-solution essay, see Winston Churchill's "Wartime Speech," in which he addresses the monumental problem of war in Europe. The speech is included in *Prentice Hall Literature: Timeless Voices, Timeless Themes,* The British Tradition.

These details clearly explain how to make a barrier fence to solve the problem of invading wildlife.

Within this paragraph is another problem-and-solution relationship: Because the posts were so slender, the author found an alternate method of putting them into the ground.

◄ **Critical Viewing** What sorts of problems might a raccoon like the one pictured cause in a garden? **[Speculate]**

saves on the number of posts needed and guarantees a floppy fence. Animals, I have found, are more reluctant to climb a floppy fence than a taut one.

Once the posts are in, I unroll the fence, leaning it up against the posts. Originally I then bent the bottom foot of the wire at a 90-degree angle because this made a barrier much more difficult for animals to burrow under (because when they began tunneling at the edge of the fence they were stymied by the wire beneath them). This left me with a three-foot-high fence that required no gate, since it was low enough to step over. . . .

My fence does a good job of keeping woodchucks and rabbits and porcupines at bay. It does not, however, keep out raccoons. Raccoons are ordinarily not a problem in the vegetable garden— unless you are growing corn, whereupon they are guaranteed to show up the first night the corn is ripe and begin breaking down even the most robust stalks in pursuit of the sweet kernels.

Innumerable ploys for keeping raccoons away from corn have been tried. The only one that has worked for me is an electric fence, which I use in conjunction with the chicken wire. It need not be up until the corn is nearing maturity, but installing it earlier helps keep out other animals. I purchased a standard electric fence charger intended for livestock, one that runs off a house current, though battery-powered models exist. I then made a large number of 16-inch–long stakes, each topped with a porcelain or plastic insulator. These I drive in a row around the garden about a foot outside the chicken-wire fence. Their height and distance from one another are such that when I string electric-fence wire from insulator to insulator it is always 6 to 8 inches above the ground. The only difficulty with a wire this low is that the grass and weeds grow up and short-circuit the fence. But by using a string trimmer I keep the vegetation down with only a few minutes of attention a week.

The shock that the animal, or for that matter human, gets from an electric fence of this sort is painful but not dangerous. I find it works better to leave mine on all the time, and risk an occasional zap, than to turn it off when I am working in the garden and risk forgetting to turn it on. . . .

My two-ply fence—one woven, the other electrified— stops only those animals that walk. For those that fly, I turn to netting. My introduction to the virtues of netting came when in desperation I covered a bed of strawberries

At this point, the organization of the essay becomes clear: The author is introducing one related problem at a time and then discussing in detail its solution.

▼ **Critical Viewing** Judging from this photograph, would you expect wood-chucks to be garden pests? Why or why not? [**Draw Conclusions**]

◀ **Critical Viewing**
What sort of barrier might be effective in keeping crows out of gardens? Explain.
[Speculate]

with some salvaged fish netting picked up at a nearby seaport. Draped across the bed on low-lying poles, it cut my avian losses enormously. Since then I have purchased netting intended for the purpose, some of which is made of black polypropylene, some from white nylon. I now consider it indispensable in assuring a harvest of grapes, cherries, or blueberries.

Again, netting should be installed before the crop is ripe and birds have acquired a taste for the fruits. And there must be no gaps through which birds can pass. The larger the piece of netting, the less splicing and tying will be needed. Netting that is 14 feet wide is sufficient to drape over a 6-foot-high grape trellis. A medium-size cherry tree can use a piece that is 20 feet or more square. I've found that a long pole with a forked tip serves best to put such a big piece on and take it off a tree.

Netting is even more susceptible to the elements than chicken wire. Plastic, especially polypropylene, breaks down eventually from exposure to sunlight. So I am careful to roll up and store the netting indoors as soon as the crop of fruit has been picked.

All this may sound like a huge endeavor. In season my garden—the fruit trees wrapped in netting, the vegetables encircled by chicken wire and an electric fence—is reminiscent of a Christo project. But now that I know what I am doing the fences and nets go up and down in only a few hours. And the beauty of it is knowing that I am going to be the one who gets to enjoy what I am growing. Some days I can even relax enough to admire a woodchuck eating clover outside the fence.

Swain gives specific details that explain how to install netting, which helps solve the problem of birds invading the garden.

This paragraph introduces another related problem.

The concluding paragraph emphasizes the easiness and successfulness of the solutions.

Writing Application: Prepare Your Work for Evaluation As you prepare to write your problem-and-solution essay, remember to support your statements, so that your readers will give them a positive evaluation.

Choosing Your Topic

Your essay should address an important problem. Challenge yourself to select a topic that has a complex solution. Use the following strategies for help finding a topic:

Strategies for Generating Topics

1. **Scan a Newspaper** Newspapers can provide you with countless examples of issues and problems. For example, you might read about a conflict between a mayor and the school board. After investigating the situation, you might propose a fair compromise. Use a highlighter or self-sticking notes to mark possible articles as you flip through the newspaper. Then, choose the topic you like best for your essay.

2. **Work With a Peer** Work with a partner to find a topic for your problem-and-solution essay. Each of you should create a list of problems. Then, take turns reading each item on your list aloud to your partner. After each item is read, allow time for your partner to write down one or two possible solutions to each problem. Review your responses to find a topic.

3. **Make a List** Make a list to help you find and evaluate a wide variety of possible topics. Once your list is finished, choose the entry you find most promising as the topic for your problem-and-solution essay. Following is an example:

Writing Lab CD-ROM

For more help choosing a topic, explore the activities and topic suggestions in the Choosing a Topic section of the Exposition lesson.

Individual	School	Country	World
• Not enough time to exercise • Too much information about colleges • High levels of stress reduce productivity	• Two student groups want to use the auditorium on the same day • Overenrollment in many school activities	• Crime • Political apathy • Crumbling infrastructure	• Endangered animals • Pollution • Ozone depletion • Oil spills • Unequal distribution of wealth

TOPIC BANK

If you are having difficulty finding a topic, choose one of the topics below:

1. **Essay About Overcoming an Obstacle** Many people face obstacles that restrict and complicate their lives. For example, a person may not have a car, yet need to drive to hold a job. Choose such a situation, and solve it in a problem-and-solution essay.

2. **Letter Resolving a Dispute** Identify a conflict that has occurred within your school or community. Analyze the situation, and determine the best solution to the dispute. Write a letter to both sides explaining why you think your solution is both fair and practical.

Responding to Fine Art

3. Consider how the workers in *Tunnel Workers* by William Low solve problems every day on the job. Write an essay in which you evaluate one problem that workers might face on the job: anything from a dangerous work environment to an unreasonable supervisor.

Tunnel Workers, William Low, Courtesy of the artist

Responding to Literature

4. Read "The Train from Rhodesia" by Nadine Gordimer, and use it as a springboard to consider the problem of conflict between different cultures. Write a problem-and-solution essay based on your reflections. You can find Gordimer's story in *Prentice Hall Literature: Timeless Voices, Timeless Themes*, The British Tradition.

☑ Cooperative Writing Opportunity

5. **Freshman Handbook** Work with a group to list the problems that a high-school freshman faces. Write a handbook that provides practical advice about how to handle each problematic situation. Each writer on your team should address a different problem. Ask permission to leave a copy of the handbook in your school's library.

Narrowing Your Topic

Many problems are too complex to be described and solved effectively in a single problem-and-solution essay. You may need to narrow your topic to focus on one aspect.

Create a Web

Make a web to help you narrow a topic. Write your broad topic in the center and specific topics in circles branching off from the center. Then, review the specific topics, and choose one as your narrowed topic.

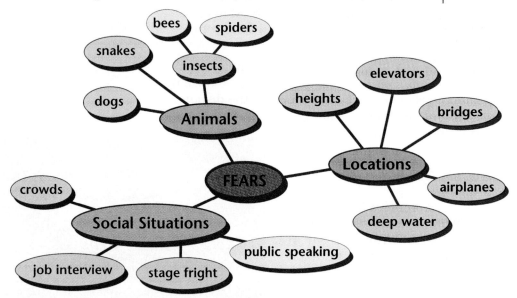

Considering Your Audience and Purpose

Your general purpose for writing a problem-and-solution essay is to share your ideas about how to solve a problem. The way that you share your ideas depends on your specific purpose and on the audience you are addressing.

Suit Details to Your Audience

Always consider your audience's level of familiarity with your topic, and choose details that are appropriate for that audience. For example, if you were writing for an audience of computer experts, you would not need to define computer terminology; but if you were writing for beginning computer students, you would have to explain computer terms in detail.

Gathering Evidence

Once you have narrowed your topic, gather details about both the problem and the solution. The deeper you explore your problem, the more likely you are to come up with truly successful solutions. Begin your research and preparation by getting to know each important aspect of your problem.

Complete a T-Chart

Complete a T-chart to collect ideas for your essay. In the left column of the chart, list the problem or problems you will address in your essay. In the right column, list your solution or solutions. Refer to the details that you gather as you draft your problem-and-solution essay.

Writers in

ACTION

Edwin Bliss is the author of self-help books. He has the following advice to give when dealing with problems and solutions:

"The precise statement of any problem is the most important step in its solution."

Student Work
IN PROGRESS

Name: *Gabrielle Frame*
Northeast High School
Omaha, NE

Using a T-Chart to Gather Evidence
Gabrielle used a T-chart to gather ideas for her essay on overcoming a fear of public speaking.

Problem	Solution
Fear of public speaking is one of the most common fears	Use note cards (if they're allowed)
Nerves	Practice a lot
Fear of forgetting what you are going to say	Memorize the beginning and end
Classmates become very critical, even if they are your friends	Change your attitude

Shaping Your Writing

The most common organization for a problem-and-solution essay is suggested by the name itself. Most writers begin by describing the problem and then present one or more solutions. Begin your draft with a clear statement of the problem. Depending on your audience, you might decide to include background information or explanations about how the problem developed, as well as specific descriptions of each important aspect of the problem.

Choose an Appropriate Organization

When describing the solution, choose an organization that will most effectively present to readers the details you have gathered.

- If your solution has several steps, use **chronological order.** Describe all steps completely, in the logical order that they will be carried out, so that your audience will be able to follow your step-by-step description.

- If you are presenting more than one solution, place them in **order of importance.** Begin with the least effective solution, and build to the solution that you believe is most effective. This organization is particularly useful when you are trying to persuade readers that your solution is the best option.

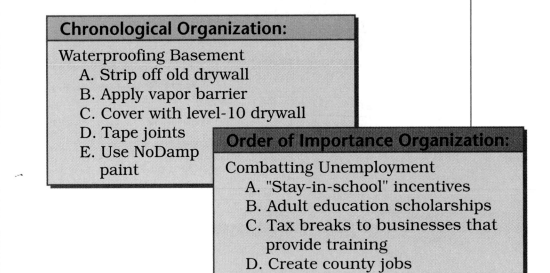

Chronological Organization:

Waterproofing Basement
   A. Strip off old drywall
   B. Apply vapor barrier
   C. Cover with level-10 drywall
   D. Tape joints
   E. Use NoDamp paint

Order of Importance Organization:

Combatting Unemployment
   A. "Stay-in-school" incentives
   B. Adult education scholarships
   C. Tax breaks to businesses that provide training
   D. Create county jobs

Providing Elaboration

Use Points to Illuminate

As you write your first draft, elaborate on your major points by providing a variety of supporting details. One way to ensure that you use various types of elaboration is to use the Five Points of Illumination strategy as you draft.

Five Points of Illumination When you illuminate something, you reveal its features or qualities. Do the same as you draft your essay. To do so, create the following graphic, and keep it nearby as you draft your essay. As you write each paragraph, try to incorporate at least two different types of details.

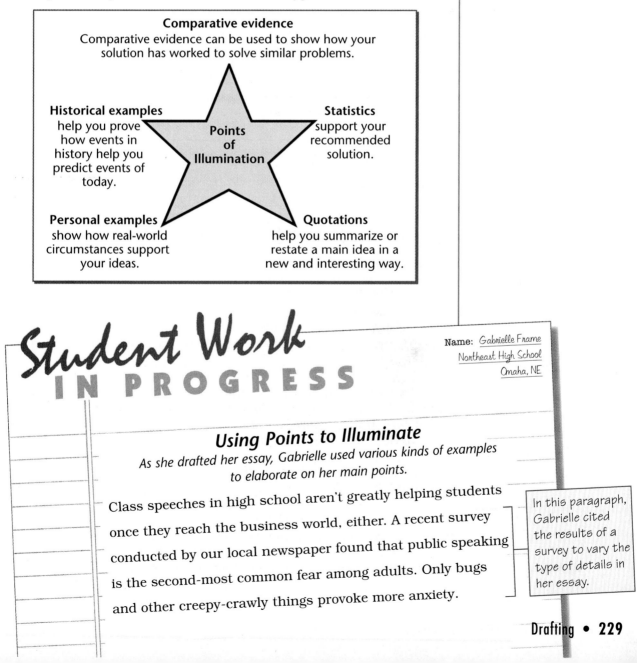

Comparative evidence
Comparative evidence can be used to show how your solution has worked to solve similar problems.

Historical examples
help you prove how events in history help you predict events of today.

Points of Illumination

Statistics
support your recommended solution.

Personal examples
show how real-world circumstances support your ideas.

Quotations
help you summarize or restate a main idea in a new and interesting way.

Student Work
IN PROGRESS

Name: *Gabrielle Frame*
Northeast High School
Omaha, NE

Using Points to Illuminate

As she drafted her essay, Gabrielle used various kinds of examples to elaborate on her main points.

Class speeches in high school aren't greatly helping students once they reach the business world, either. A recent survey conducted by our local newspaper found that public speaking is the second-most common fear among adults. Only bugs and other creepy-crawly things provoke more anxiety.

In this paragraph, Gabrielle cited the results of a survey to vary the type of details in her essay.

Revising Your Overall Structure

Analyze the Balance of Information

Your essay should present details that explain a problem, as well as details that describe one or more solutions to that problem. If your essay contains lots of details describing a problem and fewer details proposing a solution, fix the balance of details.

▶ **REVISION STRATEGY**
Color-Coding Details to Analyze Balance

Use a highlighter or colored pencil to call out details that relate to the problem you are addressing. If you are discussing more than one problem, use a highlighter or pencil of a different color for each. Use a highlighter or pencil of a different color to call out details that describe your solution or solutions. Then, review your draft. Add details where necessary to improve the balance of information you provide.

Fixing an Unbalanced Essay

The biggest problem related to air travel is getting to the plane. Airport access highways are always crowded, and it's virtually impossible to park in long-term parking, let alone in short-term parking. Once in the terminal, long lines at the baggage check-in torture passengers, as do long lines at the boarding gate.

When rows are called for boarding, everyone rushes to the gate, heedless of whether or not their row has been called. And carry-on bins are always filled with the excess baggage of thoughtless fellow travelers.

How do we solve this problem? Make available public transportation to the airport, make curbside check-in mandatory, and enforce one-per-customer limit on carry-on bags.

Make available better public transportation to the airport. Designate area hotels as bus stops, allowing travelers to take public transportation rather than driving rental cars to the airport. Give residents a book of coupons, encouraging them to ride the bus rather than driving to area airports. Make curbside check-in mandatory. When airline tickets are sent to customers, also send along a book of forms for baggage check-in for filling out. That way there will be no delays at curbside. Once at the gate, flight attendants should be made to enforce the one-bag-per-customer limit on carry-on bags. If necessary, security can be increased to deal with belligerent customers. However, once an airline commits to enforcing the rules, fewer and fewer customers will expect the rules to be broken in their favor.

Revising Your Paragraphs

Each topical paragraph in your essay should focus on a single main idea. Functional paragraphs should perform a specific function, such as making a transition or emphasizing a point. In your problem-and-solution essay, many of your paragraphs will be topical. Consider the following strategies as you revise your topical paragraphs:

▶ **REVISION STRATEGY**

Adding, Strengthening, or Moving Topic Sentences

- **Add a topic sentence.** If you find a topical paragraph without a topic sentence, read it carefully. If the point of the paragraph is vague, add a topic sentence to make its meaning clear.

- **Use a subject complement in your topic sentence.** Use a short defining statement as a topic sentence. The following statements, each containing a subject complement, make a strong, clear point: *Teamwork is essential. The only viable solution is recycling.*

- **Change the positions of some topic sentences.** For variety and impact, change the positions of some topic sentences. Although many paragraphs begin with topic sentences, others build to a powerful close by saving the topic sentence for the last statement.

Student Work

IN PROGRESS

Name: *Gabrielle Frame*
Northeast High School
Omaha, NE

Adding a Topic Sentence

Gabrielle added a short, emphatic topic sentence to strengthen this paragraph. She also deleted a sentence that was not related to the paragraph's main idea.

Anyone who has ever stood in front of a class and felt numb or panicky has probably had the same thought: "Why didn't I practice more?" The more familiar you are with your material, the more comfortable you'll be when the dreaded hour strikes. ~~Remember to wear something comfortable.~~ Practice in the morning before you go to school. Practice on the bus. Practice in front of the mirror before you go to bed. Keep at it until you feel as if you are speaking in your sleep. ∧ *Practice is the most effective fear-buster.*

Grammar in Your Writing
Subject Complements

A **subject complement** is a noun, pronoun, or adjective that appears with a linking verb and tells something about the subject of the sentence. A **linking verb** is a verb that connects a word at or near the beginning of a sentence with a word at or near the end. Common linking verbs are *be, appear, seem, sound, feel, grow,* and *look.*

There are two kinds of subject complements: predicate nominatives and predicate adjectives. A **predicate nominative** is a noun or pronoun that appears with a linking verb and renames, identifies, or explains the subject of the sentence.

The essay in the morning newspaper is an *editorial.*

The best person for the job is *you.*

A **predicate adjective** is an adjective that appears with a linking verb and describes the subject of the sentence.

The problem is *complex.*

The solution to our predicament seems *obvious* to me.

Find It in Your Reading "Warding Off Wildlife" by Roger B. Swain appears on pages 220–223. Read through the essay, and find three predicate nominatives and three predicate adjectives. Explain how they help Swain communicate with the reader.

Find It in Your Writing Look for linking verbs in your draft, and identify whether they connect subjects to predicate nominatives or to predicate adjectives. If your essay is lacking in predicate nouns or predicate adjectives, consider rewriting some sentences to include linking verbs and subject complements.

To learn more about subject complements, see Chapter 18.

Revising Your Sentences

Sentences are an important part of an essay. Review each sentence in your draft to be sure that it contains a subject and verb. If a sentence lacks either a subject or verb, it is a fragment and should be rewritten.

Vary Sentence Lengths

Edit your draft to include sentences of various lengths. A series of short sentences can sound choppy and un-connected. A series of long sentences can be tiring to read. Use the following strategy to help you analyze sentence lengths within your draft.

▶ **REVISION STRATEGY**
Underlining to Code Sentence Length

Read through your draft, and underline in one color sen-tences containing fewer than six words. Underline in another color sentences that contain six or more words. Then, review the markings in your draft. If most of your sentences are underlined in the same color, rewrite some of them to add variety to your essay.

For example, to add sophistication, combine some short sentences into longer, complex ones; to add clarity, break some long sentences into shorter, simpler sentences.

Student Work
IN PROGRESS

Name: *Gabrielle Frame*
Northeast High School
Omaha, NE

Underlining to Code Sentence Length

When she used the underlining strategy, Gabrielle discovered that she almost always wrote long sentences. She edited her draft to include a greater variety of sentence lengths.

Of course, once you stand in front of the class, all your preparation can fly right out the window. Utter terror can leave even the best prepared student with a blank mind, a dry mouth, and a roomful of staring eyes. The only way to combat this is to stay calm. ~~and~~ concentrate on your breathing. ~~A brain with oxygen is a happy brain, so use~~ can calm breathing ~~to~~ make remembering easier and ~~to~~ keep you from passing out, which is not a good thing.

Revising Your Word Choice

Read your draft, and examine your choice of words. Replace imprecise words with more precise ones, and double-check to be sure you've used unfamiliar words correctly. Be on the lookout for redundancies, and delete them when they occur.

▶ **REVISION STRATEGY**
Eliminating Redundancies

Redundancy is the unnecessary repetition of an idea. To identify a redundancy, look for a passage in your essay that seems wordy or weak. Within that passage, look for repeated words that take away from the impact or meaning of your statement. Eliminate the redundant words and phrases.

Example	Revised Sentence
You can solve the problem *alone by yourself*.	You can solve the problem by yourself.
The flag is a brilliant *red in color*.	The flag is a brilliant red.

Some Common Redundancies

free gift; past history; completely finished; surrounded on all sides; various different; usual custom; first begins; referred back; reflected back; repeated again; advanced forward; speak out loud; unknown stranger

Peer Review
Use "Double Vision"

Ask two partners to read and review your problem-and-solution essay. Give each partner a specific focus. You might try one of these divisions of responsibility:

- **Problem and Solution** One partner evaluates your description of the problem; the other evaluates your presentation of the solution.

- **Clarity and Style** One partner assesses the clarity of what you say; the other considers the effectiveness of the way you say it.

- **Overview and Details** One partner looks at your overall structure; the other inspects the details you present.

11.5 Editing and Proofreading

Carefully read your essay to make sure it is free from errors in grammar, spelling, and punctuation.

Focusing on Punctuation

Proofreading is an important part of the writing process. When you proofread your problem-and-solution essay, check especially to see whether you have used punctuation marks correctly. If you have used hyphens and dashes, check the rules for usage to make sure that you have used them correctly.

Grammar in Your Writing
Using Hyphens and Dashes

Although they look similar, **hyphens** and **dashes** are used for different purposes. Below are some of the most common uses for these punctuation marks:

Use a **dash** to indicate an abrupt change of thought, a dramatic interrupting idea, or a summary statement.

> Examples: The problem is challenging—no, it's impossible!
> The mayor's speech—did you hear it?—was impressive.

Use a **hyphen** to connect a compound modifier that comes before a noun.

> Examples: well-prepared student
> grayish-blue sky
> all-night diner

Use a **hyphen** in words with the prefixes *all-*, *ex-*, and *self-*.

> Examples: all-powerful
> ex-mayor
> self-addressed

Find It in Your Reading Find two dashes and two hyphens in "Warding Off Wildlife" on pages 220–223. Explain why each punctuation mark is used.

Find It in Your Writing As you proofread, check your usage of dashes and hyphens, and correct any errors.

To learn more about dashes and hyphens, see Chapter 27.

Publishing and Presenting

Share your problem-and-solution essay with an audience to provide a meaningful conclusion to your writing process.

Building Your Portfolio

1. **Local Publication** If your essay addresses a vital contemporary problem, submit it to a local newspaper or student magazine. In your cover letter, you might suggest that the publication could use the essay on an editorial page.

2. **Discussion** Read your essay to students, teachers, and community members who are concerned about your topic. Your essay can be the launching point for an in-depth discussion about the problem and potential solutions.

Reflecting on Your Writing

Pause to reflect on your writing experience. Then, answer the following questions, recording your responses in your portfolio:

• Which strategy did you try for the first time, and how successful was it?

• What discoveries did you make during the revision process that strengthened your writing?

 **Internet Tip**

To see essays scored with this rubric, go to **www.phschool.com**

Rubric for Self-Assessment

Use the following criteria to evaluate your problem-and-solution essay:

	Score 4	Score 3	Score 2	Score 1
Audience and Purpose	Contains language and details to engage audience and accomplish purpose	Contains language and details appropriate for audience and that help contribute to overall effect	Contains some language and details not suited for audience; contains some details that detract from purpose	Contains language and details that are not geared for a particular audience; has an unclear purpose
Organization	Is organized consistently, logically, and effectively	Has consistent organization	Has inconsistent organization	Is disorganized and confusing
Elaboration	Has a solution that is clearly laid out, along with details that support or explain it	Has a solution that is supported with details	Has a stated solution, but it contains few details to support it	Has unclear solution, and no details are given to support it
Use of Language	Contains precise words and no redundancies; contains no errors in grammar, punctuation, or spelling	Contains effective words and few redundancies; contains few errors in grammar, punctuation, and spelling	Contains few precise words and some redundancies; contains some errors in grammar, punctuation, and spelling	Contains imprecise words and many redundancies; contains many errors in grammar, punctuation, and spelling

11.7 Student Work IN PROGRESS

FINAL DRAFT

◀ **Critical Viewing**
How well does the student pictured seem to be handling the pressure of public speaking? Explain. **[Analyze]**

Fear of the Speech

Gabrielle Frame
Northeast High School
Omaha, Nebraska

High school can be a scary place. Deadlines loom like stone sentinels in the future. Previous grades and papers haunt the past. Besides academic anxieties, social scares also abound. Above all of these, there is one event that can strike terror into even the most confident student's heart; something that can make the prom queen's knees shake and the valedictorian's hair stand on end. This dreaded occurrence is, yes, a speech in English class.

In theory, classes in public speaking provide an excellent opportunity to become accustomed to speaking in front of people before having to conduct presentations in the business world. After all, one gets to speak in a familiar classroom environment in

Gabrielle's introduction humorously reveals the topic of her problem-and-solution essay.

front of friends, right? Wrong. First of all, sitting at a desk is completely different from standing in front of the room looking at everyone with everyone looking back. Second, those sweet best friends, no matter how close they are, will enjoy teasing and heckling a poor stuttering classmate all too much. It's all in good fun, but the teasee often doesn't realize the teaser is teasing until his or her feelings are already hurt.

Gabrielle provides a description of the various aspects of the problem.

Class speeches in high school aren't greatly helping students once they reach the business world, either. A recent survey conducted by our local newspaper found that public speaking is the second-most common fear among adults. Only bugs and other creepy-crawly things provoke more anxiety.

So, what can be done? Is there anything that can keep a normal, talkative student from becoming absolutely speechless once she steps up to the lectern? You may not be able to completely overcome your fear, but preparation, a strong will, and some relaxed breathing can help you keep your fear from getting the best of you.

The organization of the essay becomes clear at this point. The essay first discussed aspects of the problem; from this point on, it will address solutions to the problem.

Fear of forgetting is a major cause of anxiety for almost all speakers. There are a few things you can do beforehand to make remembering the speech easier. If note cards are allowed, write down key points and statistics, and keep it short. Too much detailed information on the note cards will just get in the way when you are delivering your speech. If the speech must be completely memorized, your best bet is to memorize the opening and closing statements and have a good idea of what you need to say in between. It is almost impossible to try to memorize a speech word for word, and it is better to have a solid, logical outline that can easily be modified on the spot.

Each aspect of the solution is described in a separate paragraph.

Anyone who has ever stood in front of a class and felt numb or panicky has probably had the same thought: "Why didn't I practice more?" The more familiar you are with your material, the more comfortable you'll be when the dreaded hour strikes. Practice in the morning before you go to school. Practice on the bus. Practice in front of the mirror before you go to bed. Keep at it until you feel as if you are speaking in your sleep. Practice is the most effective fear-buster.

Of course, once you stand in front of the class, all your preparation can fly right out the window. Utter terror can leave even the best-prepared student with a blank mind, a dry mouth, and a roomful of staring eyes. The only way to combat this is to stay calm. Concentrate on your breathing. Calm breathing can make remembering easier and keep you from passing out, which is not a good thing. However, don't overdo it—hyperventilating won't help. Take a few deep breaths before starting the speech, and try to concentrate on speaking slowly and clearly. Do not drink massive doses of soda beforehand. Not only will this energy overload make you nervous and excitable, but the sugar can coat the back of your throat and vocal cords, making it difficult to speak clearly.

Sometimes, a simple psychological placebo can make the difference between a stuttering utterance and a stunning speech. Wearing a "lucky" shirt or necklace or performing a prespeech mental ritual can soothe your nerves. If props or visual aids are allowed, by all means use them. Props give your hands something to do and help shift the audience's gaze away from your face.

There are a few gifted people who have no problems getting up in front of crowds and talking until the cows come home. For the rest of us, learning to speak comfortably in class is an inevitable challenge that we have to face and conquer. Like parachuting out of an airplane, you may not feel truly relieved until it's over, but after one or two jumps, you might even begin to enjoy the journey.

Humor adds to the friendly and supportive tone of the essay.

A brief conclusion summarizes the essay's overall message.

◄ **Critical Viewing** If you were to speak in front of this audience, how might you react? Explain. **[Relate]**

Connected Assignment
Proposal

Suppose that you want to suggest some ways to solve a problem shared by yourself and others in a group. A **proposal**—which presents a plan of action for acceptance— is the writing tool you need. In a proposal, you explain the plan in detail and provide specifics on how the plan will solve the problem or meet the identified need. You should also discuss requirements such as human effort, financial contributions, or supplies you'll need to put the plan into action. Proposals sometimes take the form of business letters, memos, or even letters to the editor.

An effective proposal

- clearly defines the problem and the solution or solutions to rectify the problem.

- contains details that appeal to the writer's audience and help achieve a specific purpose.

- provides details that support and explain the writer's main idea.

- is clearly and effectively organized.

- is free from mistakes in grammar, spelling, and punctuation.

Develop a proposal to solve a problem you've identified. Write it in a format that fits your audience. As you prepare your proposal, use the writing process stages to guide you.

▲ Critical Viewing
Do you think this group is likely to accept the speaker's proposal? Why do you think as you do? **[Relate]**

Prewriting

Choosing Your Topic To come up with a topic for a proposal, jot down ideas you have about improving your school, neighborhood, or town. Review what you have written, and choose as a topic the idea that interests you most.

Considering Your Audience and Purpose Defining your audience is critical when writing a proposal. Choose a business-letter format if you are writing to a local business or organization with whom you have had no previous experience. Write a memo to your employer, school, or neighborhood. Then, decide on the details you must emphasize to gain the audience's interest and support.

Gathering Details Once you have a topic for your proposal, gather details that show why your ideas are good ones. For example, gather statistics that prove that there is a problem that needs solving. Then outline, step by step, your proposed solution to the problem—your proposal. You may want to use index cards like the one at right on which to gather and organize details.

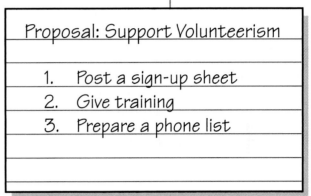

Proposal: Support Volunteerism

1. Post a sign-up sheet
2. Give training
3. Prepare a phone list

Drafting As you draft, outline the steps of your proposal in a logical and effective way. For example, if your proposal consists of three stages, present them in the order in which they must occur. Also, make connections as you draft to ensure that your audience will be able to follow your ideas and understand what you are proposing.

Revising and Editing Review your proposal carefully to be sure that it makes sense. Add details where your argument seems thin, and remove details if they are unnecessary. Next, examine your proposal's overall organization. Move chunks of text and details, where necessary, to create a consistent structure. Finally, add transitions to link your ideas and to help the flow of your sentences.

Publishing and Presenting Proofread your proposal carefully, and correct all errors in grammar, spelling, and punctuation. Also, check to be sure that you have consistently and correctly formatted your proposal. Share your completed proposal with interested peers and family members.

Spotlight on the Humanities

Recognizing Inspirations for Art
Focus on Film: *A Room With a View*

Just as a problem-and-solution essay focuses on solving a problem, many films are based on a characters' problems and conflicts that require resolution. Released in 1986 and a winner of three Academy Awards, the Merchant-Ivory film *A Room With a View* is a beautifully photographed story of a Victorian girl, Lucy Honeychurch, who must decide whether to follow through with her marriage to her stoic fiancé or follow her heart and her growing attraction to a young man she met on a trip to Florence, Italy. Filmed in England and Florence, the period film is based upon the 1908 novel by British author E. M. Forster (1879–1970).

Literature Connection E. M. Forster's *A Room With a View* was inspired by Forster's first trip to Italy, during the winter of 1901–1902. Over the course of the trip, Forster sketched out ideas for the novel. The novel, however, took several years to finish, and it was finally published in 1908. Although Forster was not entirely satisfied with *A Room With a View,* most critics of the time responded positively to the story.

Art Connection In E. M. Forster's *A Room With a View,* the main character, Lucy Honeychurch, falls under the spell of Florence, Italy, an ancient and beautiful city in Tuscany. One of the main attractions of Florence is the Uffizi, which houses one of the world's largest and most impressive art collections. Masterpieces by Raphael, Botticelli, Caravaggio, and Titian belong to its collection.

Problem-and-Solution Writing Activity: Advice Column

Lucy Honeychurch, the main character in *A Room With a View,* travels with an older companion who does not hesitate to dispense advice. Imagine that you are an advice columnist for your high-school newspaper, and write questions that you have received from students who need advice. Then, provide answers or solutions to them in your column. Share your advice column with your classmates.

▲ Critical Viewing
What do the details in this photograph reveal about this character and her circumstances? **[Infer]**

Media and Technology Skills

Using Technology to Find Answers
Activity: Rate Help Resources

Getting help when you need it is often a matter of knowing where to look. Consulting the wrong source can be a waste of time. Familiarize yourself with the many help resources available. Then, share your knowledge and opinions of those resources in a ratings guide. Make your guide available in your school computer center to help other students get the help they need.

Think About It Choose a common situation in which you might need informational help. Consider these circumstances, or select one that you have experienced:

- A software program is not compatible with your computer.

- You are trying to locate a friend or relative with whom you have lost touch.

- You would like information about how to plan a camping trip.

Research It Consult a variety of sources to get the help you need. You might use any of the following resources:

On-line support: Many companies offer on-line support to their customers. Look for Internet addresses in manuals or advertisements.

Manuals: Many products—from computer hardware and software to audio equipment—come with manuals that provide essential information and list other help resources.

Search engines: These Internet sites can help you locate specific information. Enter a key word or words to search for your topic.

E-mail: Write to a company or expert listed in a manual or on an Internet site. Using a courteous tone, explain your problem completely in your e-mail note.

Telephone hotlines: Many hotlines provide useful information about handling health, safety, or other problems.

Evaluate It After consulting each help source, provide a rating that assesses its ease of use and efficiency. When you have finished researching, write a comparative review that describes your findings. Post your completed ratings guide in your classroom or in your school's computer center.

FAQs
Many Web sites use the abbreviation *FAQ* to stand for Frequently Asked Questions. Take the time to read these entries before you ask a question. You may find the answer is already posted in the FAQs.

Software Help
Remember that most software programs have built-in Help functions that can answer many common questions. Select Help from the software's menu to access this feature.

Standardized Test Preparation Workshop

Responding to Expository Writing Prompts

Standardized test prompts often measure your ability to clearly state a problem and offer several solutions. Your response will be evaluated on the following criteria:

- a clearly stated problem, with appropriate language that suits the purpose and audience identified in the response

- a method of organization that allows you to organize your solution in a meaningful and coherent sequence, such as order-of-importance, chronological order, or pro-and-con organization

- appropriate transitions that contribute to your essay's unity and coherence

- clear descriptions, facts, and other details that support your main points

- correct grammar, spelling, and punctuation

When writing for a timed test, plan to devote a specific amount of time to prewriting, drafting, revising, and proofreading.

Following is an example of an expository writing prompt. Use the strategies following to help you respond. The clocks next to each stage show a suggested amount of time to devote to each stage.

Test Tip

When writing a problem-and-solution response, first identify your personal intention. Are you trying to present an impartial or a persuasive solution? Once you know your purpose, your essay will be easier to complete.

Sample Writing Situation

Directions: Read the following prompt, and write an essay in response. Use details to support your response.

Different people have different tastes. This can present a real problem, particularly when it is your job to satisfy many people at once. You are on the organizing committee for a school dance. It is your decision to choose what form the music will take. Write an open essay to the student body, to be published in the school newspaper, in which you clearly state the problem you are facing and possible solutions for selecting the right type of musical format for the dance.

Prewriting

Allow close to one quarter of your time for prewriting.

Choose a Topic Sentence Because you are writing an essay for a wide audience, it is important to clearly identify the issue so that everyone who reads it understands it. A topic sentence explains what your essay is about. This is your opportunity to summarize the problem and provide yourself with a foundation for the essay.

Brainstorm There is usually more than one solution to any given problem. Write down every solution you can think of that would solve your problem. Then, decide which solution or solutions are the most practical and why.

Prepare an Outline Once you have arrived at your solution, outline your thought process and how you came to this particular solution. Not only will an outline help you organize your ideas, but it may also serve as a rough sketch for your first draft.

Drafting

Allow half of your time for drafting.

Start Creatively Begin your essay in a creative way. For example, if you begin your essay with a thought-provoking question, you have an immediate attention-grabber.

Present Solutions Let your audience know that you have thought the problem through. Choose several of your choices from your prewriting, and explain each thoroughly. Use examples, details, and anecdotal evidence to support your concern.

Link Your Ideas Coherence makes your essay easier for readers to understand. You can achieve this by using clear transitions between paragraphs. Transitions are words that will help you link ideas from one paragraph or sentence to the next.

Revising, Editing, and Proofreading

Allow almost one quarter of your time to revise and edit.

Revise Where Necessary Delete repetitive or nonvital information. Be honest with yourself about what does and does not belong in your essay. A point may be well written, but it may also be nonessential.

Proofread Your Essay Use the last few minutes to check your writing for errors in spelling, grammar, and punctuation. Add words or phrases neatly in the space above the text, using a caret [^] to indicate the exact placement.

12 Research
Documented Essay

Documentation in Everyday Life

"Where did you hear that?" "What makes you so sure?" You probably encounter questions like these from time to time in everyday life. In response, you may furnish a name, book, or news article to reveal your source of information.

The same holds true in journalism. When you switch on the radio and hear a news report, chances are you don't question its truthfulness. Perhaps that's because most reporters and journalists, as part of their job, provide documentation to help ensure that what you hear and read in newspapers, news programs, magazines, and journals is accurate.

▲ **Critical Viewing**
Scientists like those pictured often write reports on their findings. What sort of documentation might they provide in their reports? **[Hypothesize]**

What Is a Documented Essay?

A **documented essay** is writing, based on research, about a particular subject. Though it may make use of personal observations and illustrations, the documented essay is a form of research writing and is therefore more formal and authoritative than a personal essay. Most documented essays

- provide detailed information about a specific topic, usually one of current interest.

- are based on research that can be documented, or proved, to be accurate by means of supporting references.

- contain references to source material within the text of the essay.

- have fewer than four sources of information.

- are clearly and effectively organized.

To preview the criteria on which your documented essay may be evaluated, see the Rubric for Self-Assessment on page 266.

Writers in **ACTION**

Many writers perform research when preparing their manuscripts. Zora Neale Hurston, author and story-teller, showed her understanding of the usefulness of research skills when she said: "Research is formalized curiosity. It is poking and prying with a purpose."

Types of Documented Essays

Documented essays may be about a variety of subjects:

- **Biographical profiles** give information about the life, experiences, and career of a notable person.

- **Science articles** explore a wide range of subjects—from weather occurrences to discoveries in outer space to brain research.

- **General information articles** may provide up-to-the-minute information on current fads, fashions, or cultural events.

PREVIEW *Student Work* **IN PROGRESS**

Tameeka Mitchem, a student at the Satellite Academy in New York City, wrote a documented essay about volunteerism among teenagers. Her essay was published in a student newspaper called *Spectrum*. Tameeka's completed documented essay appears at the end of this chapter.

Bill Bryson is the author of several collections of essays, among them A Walk in the Woods and The Mother Tongue, *from which the following excerpt comes.*

Reading Strategy: Read Ahead or Back As you read the following essay, you may encounter unfamiliar words or references. To figure out their meaning, read ahead or read back to see whether clues within the text can help you figure out the meaning of troublesome words, phrases, and references.

from

The Mother Tongue

Bill Bryson

▲ Critical Viewing What language is printed on the sign in this photograph? How might you find out? **[Hypothesize]**

Bryson presents his thesis in the first sentence of his essay. It is an effective thesis because it is concise and clear.

All languages have the same purpose—to communicate thoughts—and yet they achieve this single aim in a multiplicity of ways. It appears there is no feature of grammar or syntax that is indispensable or universal. The ways of dealing with matters of number, tense, case, gender, and the like are wondrously various from one tongue to the next. Many languages manage without quite basic grammatical or lexical features, while others burden themselves with remarkable complexities. A Welsh speaker must choose between five ways of saying *than: na, n', nag, mwy,* or *yn fwy.* Finnish has fifteen case forms, so every noun varies depending on whether it is nominative, accusative, allative, inessive, comitative, or one of ten other grammatical conditions. Imagine learning fifteen ways of spelling *cat, dog, house,* and so on. English, by contrast, has abandoned case forms, except for possessives, where we generally add *'s,* and with personal pronouns which can vary by no more than three ways (e.g., *they, their, them*), but often by only two (*you, your*). Similarly, in English *ride* has just five forms (*ride, rides, rode, riding, ridden*); the same verb in German has sixteen. In Russian, nouns can have up to twelve inflections and adjectives as many as sixteen. In English adjectives have just one invariable form with but, I believe, one exception: *blond/blonde.*

Estimates of the number of languages in the world usually fix on a figure of about 2,700, though almost certainly no one has ever made a truly definitive count. In many countries, perhaps the majority, there are at least two native languages, and in some cases—as in Cameroon and Papua New Guinea—there are hundreds. India probably leads the world, with more than 1,600 languages and dialects (it isn't always possible to say which is which). The rarest language as of 1984 was Oubykh, a highly complex Caucasian language with eighty-two consonants but only three vowels, once spoken by 50,000 people in the Crimea. But as of July 1984 there was just one living speaker remaining and he was eighty-two years old.

The number of languages naturally changes as tribes die out or linguistic groups are absorbed. Although new languages, particularly creoles, are born from time to time, the trend is towards absorption and amalgamation. When Columbus arrived in the New World, there were an estimated 1,000 languages. Today there are about 600.

Almost all languages change. A rare exception is written Icelandic, which has changed so little that modern Icelanders can read sagas written a thousand years ago, and if Leif Ericson appeared on the streets of Reykjavik he could find his way around, allowing for certain difficulties over terms like *airport* and *quarter-pound cheeseburger*. In English, by contrast, the change has been much more dramatic. Almost any untrained person looking at a manuscript from the time of, say, the Venerable Bede would be hard pressed to identify it as being in English—and in a sense he or she would be right. Today we have not only a completely different vocabulary and system of spelling, but even a different structure.

Nor are languages any respecters of frontiers. If you drew a map of Europe based on languages it would bear scant resemblance to a conventional map. Switzerland would disappear, becoming part of the surrounding dominions of French, Italian, and German but for a few tiny pockets for Romansh (or Romantsch or Rhaeto-Romanic as it is variously called), which

Bryson's essay is well organized. Each paragraph is devoted to exploring and developing a single aspect of his thesis.

To make his essay interesting and slightly humorous, Bryson cites "rare exceptions"—that the words airport *and* cheeseburger *would be unfamiliar to Leif Erickson.*

The topic sentence of this paragraph is supported by several details.

is spoken as a native language by about half the people in the Graubünden district (or Grisons district—almost everything has two names in Switzerland) at the country's eastern edge. This steep and beautiful area, which takes in the ski resorts of St. Moritz, Davor, and Klosters, was once effectively isolated from the rest of the world by its harsh winters and forbidding geography. Indeed, the isolation was such that even people in neighboring valleys began to speak different versions of the language, so that Romansh is not so much one language as five fragmented and not always mutually intelligible dialects. A person from the valley around Sutselva will say, "Vagned nà qua" for "Come here," while in the next valley he will say, "Vegni neu cheu." [Cited in *The Economist,* February 27, 1988] In other places people will speak the language in the same way but spell it differently depending on whether they are Catholic or Protestant.

German would cover not only its traditional areas of Germany, Austria, and much of Switzerland, but would spill into Belgium, Czechoslovakia, Romania, Hungary, the Soviet Union, and Poland, and it could be further divided into high and low German, which have certain notable differences in terms of vocabulary and syntax. In Bavaria, for instance, *Samstag* is the name for Saturday, but in Berlin it is *Sonnabend*; a plumber in Bavaria is a *spengler*, but a *klempner* in Berlin.

Italy, too, would appear on the map not as one language entity but as a whole variety of broadly related but often mutually incomprehensible dialects. Italian, such as it is, is not a national language, but really only the dialect of Florence and Tuscany, which has slowly been gaining preeminence over other dialects. Not until 1979 did a poll show for the first time that Italian was the dialect spoken at home by more than 50 percent of Italians.

Much the same would be the position in the Soviet Union, which would dissolve into 149 separate languages. Almost half the people in the country speak some language other than Russian as a native tongue, and a full quarter of the people do not speak Russian at all.

Some languages are not so distinct as we are sometimes led to believe. Spanish and Portuguese are closely enough related that the two peoples can read each other's newspapers and books, though they have more difficulty understanding speech. Finns and Estonians can freely understand each other. Danes, Swedes, and Norwegians often insist that their languages are quite distinct and yet, as Mario Pei puts it, there are greater differences between Italian dialects such as Sicilian and Piedmontese than

Since Bryson is a language expert, he needed to cite only two sources in this essay. This internal citation reveals the source of Bryson's information.

The supporting details in this paragraph are statistical and easily proved.

there are between any of the three main Scandinavian languages. Romanian and Moldavian, spoken in the Soviet Union, are essentially the same language with different names. So are Serbian and Croatian, the only real difference being that Serbian uses the Cyrillic alphabet and Croatian uses Western characters.

In many countries people use one language for some activities and a second language for others. In Luxembourg, the inhabitants use French at school, German for reading newspapers, and Luxemburgish, a local Germanic dialect, at home. In Paraguay, people conduct business in Spanish, but tell their jokes in Guarani, the native Indian tongue. In Greece, for a long time children were schooled only in Katharevousa, a formal language so archaic that it was (and indeed still is) no longer spoken anywhere in the country. The language for common discourse was Dhimotiki, yet perversely this everyday language was long held in such low esteem that when the Old Testament was published in Dhimotiki for the first time in 1903, riots broke out all over the country. [Peter Trudgill, *Sociolinguistics*, page 115+] . . .

LITERATURE

To read an essay that contains research, see the excerpt from Bede's *A History of the English Church and People*, which appears in *Prentice Hall Literature: Timeless Voices, Timeless Themes*, The British Tradition.

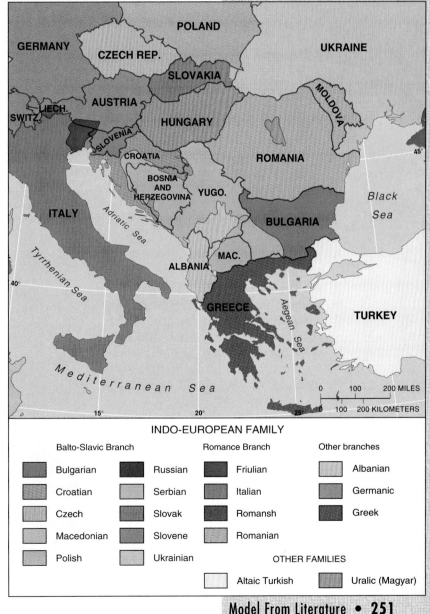

INDO-EUROPEAN FAMILY

Balto-Slavic Branch		Romance Branch		Other branches	
Bulgarian	Russian	Friulian		Albanian	
Croatian	Serbian	Italian		Germanic	
Czech	Slovak	Romansh		Greek	
Macedonian	Slovene	Romanian			
Polish	Ukrainian				

OTHER FAMILIES

Altaic Turkish   Uralic (Magyar)

Reading ▶ Writing ◀ Connection

Writing Application: Give Clues to Help Readers Understand As you draft your documented essay, include details about your topic to help readers understand it better.

▶ **Critical Viewing** Does any of the information shown on this map surprise you? Explain. **[Relate]**

Prewriting

Choosing Your Topic

To choose a topic for a documented essay, start with subjects that interest you and that you would like to research. Also, think about whether there are likely to be sources of information available about the particular topic you're considering. Use the following strategies for help in choosing a topic:

Strategies for Generating Topics

1. **Write "Invisibly"** When you use the Invisible Writing strategy, you brainstorm for ideas without editing or judging them as you write them down. To perform this activity, turn off your computer monitor or insert carbon paper between two sheets of writing paper and write with an empty pen. When you have finished writing, turn on the monitor or look at the sheet of paper under the carbon paper. Review what you have written, and choose an idea for your documented essay.

2. **Perform a Flip Test** Magazines can be a source of ideas for research. Choose one or more magazines that explore an area of interest to you, such as art or science. Flip through the magazines, and jot down topics that interest you. Consider whether or not you will be able to find information on these topics through library or other sources. Choose to develop the topic that both interests you and for which sources can be found.

3. **Imagine an Address Book** Mentally flip through a book containing the names and addresses of interesting people. Then, write down the names of those you would like to research. Review the list, and base your documented essay on the person about whom information is available or who would be available for an interview.

▶ **Critical Viewing** What strategy for choosing a topic might this student be using? **[Infer]**

TOPIC BANK

If you are having difficulty coming up with a topic, consider these ideas:

1. **Inspiration From an Inspirational Person** Is there someone you admire for his or her ability to inspire others? Do research, including a personal interview if possible, and write a documented essay about that person.

2. **Essay on a New Trend** Identify a trend that you would like to research. For example, is there a new sports craze, fitness routine, or development in fashion that is significant? Write a documented essay about it based on research and interviews.

Responding to Fine Art

3. The *Chrysler Building Composite at Dusk* depicts a world-famous skyscraper located in New York City. Think about a building you admire, and reveal what makes it special in a documented essay.

Responding to Literature

4. Read "The Chimney Sweeper" by William Blake. This poem deals with a serious problem of Blake's time—child labor. Write a documented essay that centers on one aspect of child labor. Blake's poem appears in *Prentice Hall Literature: Timeless Voices: Timeless Themes*, The British Tradition.

Chrysler Building Composite at Dusk, Yvonne Jacquette, DC Moore Gallery

☑ Cooperative Writing Opportunity

5. **Documented Essay About a Newsmaker** With a group, choose a newsmaker about whom to write. You might choose, for example, a sports star, a politician, or a local hero. Divide among group members the tasks of researching, interviewing, collecting photos or creating visuals, writing captions to photos or visuals, and writing up the notes. Submit the finished, documented essay to your school newspaper for publication.

Narrowing Your Topic

Think about your topic and whether it is narrow enough to fully develop in the confines of your planned essay. If your topic can be divided into significant subheads, each with its own focus, then it is probably too broad. One way to narrow your topic is by looping.

Narrow by Looping

First, write freely on your topic for two or three minutes, based on what you already know or have learned. Read what you have written, and circle the most important idea. Write for a few minutes on that idea. Again, read what you have written, and circle the most important idea. Continue this process until you arrive at a topic that is narrow enough for your essay.

Space shuttle missions are interesting. There are many shuttlecraft in the fleet. How dangerous are the missions? How have the shuttle's goals changed since *Challenger?* Who is likely to be the (visionary) behind missions of the twenty-first century?

Visionaries. Gene Roddenberry. John F. Kennedy. Bill Gates. (George Lucas.) Making special effects realistic. Matching sci-fi with possible reality.

▲ **Critical Viewing**
What topic for a documented essay does this photograph inspire? **[Assess]**

Considering Your Audience and Purpose

Before you begin to draft, identify your audience (who will read your essay) and your purpose (what effect you want your writing to have on your audience). Then, begin to gather details that are appropriate for your audience and that will help you to achieve your purpose.

	Family	Friends	Teacher
Audience ➡	Casual language	Slang	More formal language
	To amuse	**To warn**	**To educate**
Purpose ➡	lighthearted language funny comparisons	serious word choice; short, direct sentences	definitions; examples; illustrations

Gathering Details

Make a search plan to direct your search for information from a variety of sources. Use the following tips to help you:

Make a Research Plan

The best way to prepare for research is to list the information you want to find and where you hope to find it. Libraries contain information in both printed and electronic formats.

- To locate **nonfiction books,** use the library's card or computer catalog. In either catalog, you can search for books about your topic by author, title, or subject.

- To locate **current magazine articles,** use the *Readers' Guide to Periodical Literature.* Use a microfiche machine to read the appropriate articles.

- Libraries also have reference sections in which you will find a variety of useful sources, including **indexes, bibliographies, almanacs, atlases,** and **encyclopedias.**

- **CD-ROM encyclopedias** give multimedia presentations on a number of topics.

- The **World Wide Web** contains a wealth of Web pages that give information about a multitude of subjects.

Research Tip

If you're not sure where to look for what you need, ask a librarian. Librarians are trained to know various places in which to locate information.

Student Work IN PROGRESS

Name: Tameeka Mitchem
Satellite Academy
New York, NY

Creating a Research Plan

To direct her search for information, Tameeka first made a research plan.

Topic: Volunteerism

Question: How many students volunteer?

Plan: Readers' Guide: Search for "volunteering, volunteerism, volunteers, teen volunteering"

Question: What kind of volunteering experiences have local students had?

Plan: Interview two or three local teens who volunteer; contact volunteer groups to get names and numbers of possible interview subjects

Conduct Interviews

If your documented essay is about a person, interview him or her if you can. If the topic of your essay isn't a person, you still may benefit from interviewing experts, eyewitnesses, or others who have firsthand knowledge about your subject. Follow these tips for interviewing:

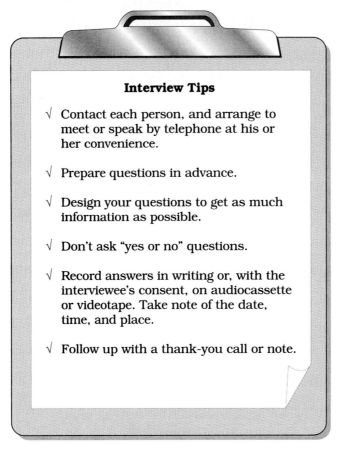

Interview Tips

√ Contact each person, and arrange to meet or speak by telephone at his or her convenience.

√ Prepare questions in advance.

√ Design your questions to get as much information as possible.

√ Don't ask "yes or no" questions.

√ Record answers in writing or, with the interviewee's consent, on audiocassette or videotape. Take note of the date, time, and place.

√ Follow up with a thank-you call or note.

◎ Technology Tip

If you plan to tape-record an interview, be sure that your tape recorder has fresh batteries. Also, check sound levels prior to the interview to ensure that both you and the interviewee can be clearly heard.

Conduct On-line Research

The World Wide Web contains a vast source of information, both reliable and unreliable. To conduct research on-line, keep the following tips in mind:

• Use a search engine to speed and focus your search.

• Always look for the originator of the Web site. Doing so will help you spot biased or one-sided coverage of issues.

• Web addresses with **.gov** are government sponsored; Web addresses with **.edu** stem from educational organizations. They are good places to find information.

• Download and print out pages you plan to use as source material. Double-check facts you plan to use to make sure they are accurate.

 12.3 Drafting

Shaping Your Writing
Write an Introduction, Body, and Conclusion

As you draft, give your writing shape by writing an introduction, a body, and a conclusion.

Introduction Starting to read an essay is like meeting a new
person: First impressions count, so plan your introduction
carefully. An effective introduction serves two key purposes:
It states the essay's main idea, letting readers know what you
are planning to discuss, and it captures readers' interest,
making them eager to keep reading.

Body The body of an essay is composed of paragraphs that
develop and support a main idea. Normally, each body paragraph presents a single main idea that is supported by details.
Some paragraphs, however, perform a specific function, such
as making a transition or emphasizing an important point.
Sometimes, too, when dealing with a long or complicated
issue, a single aspect of a topic may be explored over a number of paragraphs known as a paragraph block.

Conclusion Conclusions should leave a lasting, vivid impression on the reader. An effective conclusion sums up or
restates an essay's main idea and gives the reader something
to think about. Consider ending your essay by offering a recommendation, an intriguing question, or a personal insight.

Student Work IN PROGRESS

Name: Tameeka Mitchem
Satellite Academy
New York, NY

Writing an Introduction
*Tameeka's introduction was designed to capture her
audience's interest immediately.*

Each day after school, eighteen-year-old Courtney
Cauthett of Manhattan spends two hours counseling
and tutoring young children at a local community
center. Kajal Angras, eighteen, a senior at Curtis High
School in Staten Island, volunteers three hours a day,
two days a week at Project Hospitality, an organization
that helps needy mothers and their kids.

By giving two
examples of local
teens who currently
volunteer, Tameeka
draws the interest
of her audience,
New York-area
teenagers.

Providing Elaboration

As you draft, elaborate by defining, explaining, or illustrating the points you are making.

Provide Details and Elaborate

In your documented essay, cite facts and statistics and explain how they relate to your main idea. For example, suppose you are writing about the growing popularity of ferrets as house pets. Prove your point by citing a survey (Twenty-five percent of today's teens would like to own a ferret.) or a fact found in your research (Ferrets are banned as house pets in some states). Then, follow up by restating, explaining, defining, or illustrating the fact (Although ferrets can be house pets in one state, in another, they are considered to be wild animals.).

Whenever you cite a fact within your essay, be sure to document it. Immediately following details you got from a source, place in parentheses the title, author, and copyright information of the corresponding source material.

 **Learn More**

To learn how to format citations within text, see Citing Sources and Preparing Manuscript on pages 886–892.

Student Work
IN PROGRESS

Name: Tameeka Mitchem
Satellite Academy
New York, NY

Providing Details and Elaboration
As she drafted, Tameeka cited and elaborated on specific details she found while researching her topic.

Many teenagers devote their free hours to volunteering. Last year, for example, nearly 60% of the nation's teens volunteered 2.3 billion hours to a social or political cause. Of those hours, 1.8 billion were given to national organizations while the other 500 million were given to people in their communities. (Philanthropy Journal Online) These statistics are compelling evidence that teenagers care about others.

*Philanthropy Journal Online
nearly 60% of U.S. teens
volunteered 2.3 billion hours
to causes:
1.8 billion to national
organizations / 500 million to
communities*

12.4 *Revising*

Now that you have completed your first draft, look at it critically. Then, take steps to improve it.

Revising Your Overall Structure

Improve Unity and Coherence

Effective essays are unified—each paragraph relates to the essay's thesis or main point. Paragraphs should also be coherent—they should link together to build meaning. As you reread your draft, improve your essay's unity and coherence by using the following strategies:

▶ **REVISION STRATEGY**
Eliminating Unnecessary Details to Improve Unity

Read through your draft, and circle your thesis statement or main idea. Then, using another color, circle all details in your draft that support or relate to your main idea. When you are finished, review the details that have not been circled. Either rewrite them to connect with or support your main idea or eliminate those details altogether.

The historic district of Philadelphia has a lot to offer visitors and residents alike. Elfreth's Alley, off 2nd Street, is hailed as being the narrowest street in the United States. ~~Philadelphia is home to some great sports teams, too, like the Phillies and the Eagles.~~ The Liberty Bell can be viewed close up at Independence Park. At the end of the park is Independence Hall, where our nation's founders hammered out the details of the Declaration of Independence. To see some tall ships, stroll over to Penn's Landing, a waterfront park along the Delaware River. . . .

▶ **REVISION STRATEGY**
Linking Paragraphs to Improve External Coherence

External coherence refers to the connections that link paragraphs together. To make your paragraphs coherent:

- Repeat a word or thought from the previous paragraph to emphasize the connection between paragraphs.

- Add sentences or phrases that build bridges, making the connection between paragraphs more clear.

Writing Lab CD-ROM

If you are working electronically, consider using the Revision Checker for Unity and Coherence in the Reports lesson.

Revising Your Paragraphs

Place Topic Sentences Effectively

Topical paragraphs contain topic sentences. Functional paragraphs perform a specific function, such as making a transition or emphasizing a point. Each topical paragraph of your essay should contain a topic sentence and supporting details, but the placement of these elements is up to you. The topic sentence doesn't necessarily have to come first. You may express your main idea in the first sentence, the last sentence, or the body of the paragraph.

Learn More

To learn more about writing effective paragraphs, see Chapter 3.

▶**REVISION STRATEGY**
Bracketing Topic Sentences

Reread each paragraph of your essay carefully. If the paragraph is topical, place a bracket around its topic sentence. Then, review the placement of each topic sentence, considering whether it is positioned effectively. If a paragraph seems dull or unclear, or if a transition between paragraphs can't be made, your topic sentence may need to be moved.

EXAMPLE: Topic Sentence Begins Paragraph

[Prior to the construction of the Newmill Market, there had been several community protests aimed at halting the developer's project.] For example, residents were primarily concerned about increased traffic and the disappearance of wildlife. Built in 2000 on what had been a cow farm, the mall has since been hailed as an example of how the community and developers can work together to erect a well-planned shopping area.

EXAMPLE: Topic Sentence Within Paragraph

The Newmill Market was built in 2000 on the site of what had been a cow farm. [Prior to construction, there had been several community protests aimed at halting the developer's project.] For example, residents were primarily concerned about increased traffic and the disappearance of wildlife. Since its completion, however, the mall has been hailed as an example of how the community and developers can work together to erect a well-planned shopping area.

Revising Your Sentences

Improve Sentence Variety

One of the most common problems in writing sentences is the careless repetition of certain words. For example, if you were writing about the United States mail, you might repeat the word *letter* several times. In order to add variety to your sentences, replace some repeated words with synonyms or pronouns to enliven your writing.

DRAFT: The company president receives thousands of *letters* a day. Many *letters* are from companies and corporations, and many *letters* are from private individuals.

REVISION: The company president receives thousands of *letters* a day. Many *of them* are from companies and corporations, and many are from private individuals.

▶ **REVISION STRATEGY**
Color-Coding to Locate Repeated Words

Read through your draft, and highlight or circle all repeated words you find. Then, replace some of those words with synonyms (words with similar meanings) or with pronouns (words that stand for nouns). When you insert pronouns to take the place of nouns, be sure that you do not introduce errors in pronoun-antecedent agreement.

Student Work
IN PROGRESS

Name: Tameeka Mitchem
Satellite Academy
New York, NY

Color-Coding to Locate Repeated Words
In revising her draft, Tameeka replaced some repeated words with pronouns.

A survey conducted by The Gallup Organization in January said ~~teens~~ are four times more likely to volunteer when asked than when ^{they} ~~teens~~ are not asked. And, according to a recent on-line poll in *Youth Magazine*, 96 percent of ^{young people} ~~teens~~ feel that they can make a difference and change the world.

> Tameeka replaced the repeated word *teens* with a pronoun, *they*, and a synonym, *young people*, to add variety to her writing.

Grammar in Your Writing
Pronoun-Antecedent Agreement

Pronouns are an indispensable writing tool. Most pronouns replace words that have already been used and thus help avoid repetition. The word or group of words to which the pronoun refers is called the *antecedent*. **Pronouns and their antecedents must agree in number and gender.**

When the antecedent is an indefinite pronoun, it may be difficult to tell whether the pronoun and antecedent agree. **Indefinite pronouns** refer to nouns or pronouns that are not specifically named. They may be singular or plural or either.

NUMBER	INDEFINITE PRONOUN
Singular ⟶	another, anybody, anyone, anything, each, either, everybody, everyone, everything, much, neither, no one, nothing, one, other, somebody, someone, something
Plural ⟶	both, few, several, many, others
Singular or Plural ⟶	all, any, most, none, some

When an indefinite pronoun is used as an antecedent, make sure the pronoun that refers to it agrees with it in number and gender.

Examples:
Each of the students was given **his or her** own book.

One of the dogs had **its** bowl upside down.

Several guests asked that **their** rooms be changed.

Some of the initial confusion had **its** source in a computer malfunction.

Some decided not to register **their** complaints after all.

Find It in Your Reading Review the excerpt from "Mother Tongue" on pages 248–251. Then, identify two indefinite pronouns used as antecedents and the pronouns that refer to them. Label each *singular* or *plural*.

Find It in Your Writing Review your draft to identify any indefinite pronouns used as antecedents. Be sure that the pronouns that refer to them agree with them in number and gender. Make any necessary corrections.

To learn more about pronoun-antecedent agreement, see Chapter 23.

Revising Your Word Choice

Revise to Convey a Tone

Tone is the writer's attitude toward his or her subject. Although most research papers are academic and lack a personal tone, documented essays may be less formal and convey an attitude toward the subject. For example, a writer's tone may be satirical, humorous, or one of warning.

▶ **REVISION STRATEGY**
Color-Coding to Check Word Choice

A writer's tone is achieved through his or her word choice. Read through your draft, and circle in color the key words, such as verbs or adjectives and adverbs. Then, review your word choice. Ask yourself the following:

- Do the words work together to create a specific picture?

- Which words, if any, do not fit with the others?

- What other word choice might I make to better convey a single attitude?

Based on the answers to the questions above, revise your draft to create a single, specific tone.

Student Work
IN PROGRESS

Name: Tameeka Mitchem
Satellite Academy
New York, NY

Color-Coding to Identify Word Choice

Tameeka color-coded the words in her essay to get a better idea of her tone. She decided to change her choice of words to better achieve a single tone.

Courtney was told that in order to graduate, she had to do one

hundred hours of community service over the summer.

    was determined   showed up
Courtney ~~decided~~ to make the most of it. She ~~went~~ the first day

on time and nervous.

Check Connotation and Denotation

In research writing, accuracy is important. Therefore, you need to be very aware of both the denotation and connotation of the words you choose. A word's *denotation* is its explicit meaning or dictionary definition. A word's *connotation* is its underlying emotional association.

Following are the various denotations and connotations for three similar words:

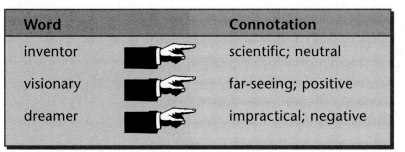

Word		Connotation
inventor		scientific; neutral
visionary		far-seeing; positive
dreamer		impractical; negative

▶ **REVISION STRATEGY**
Underlining Words and Using a Dictionary and a Thesaurus

Reread your draft, and underline words that have a denotation or connotation of which you are unsure. Then, use a dictionary to check the denotation and a thesaurus to look up alternate word choices and their connotations. Revise your word choices where necessary to make sure you are communicating exactly what you intend.

Peer Review

One of the best ways to find out whether your essay succeeds is to have peers read and respond to it. Your peers may give you a fresh perspective and point out ways to sharpen your ideas and express them more clearly.

Get Group Feedback

Distribute your documented essay to a few of your classmates in advance of meeting as a group. Ask them to read your essay and to jot down their comments about what they have read. Then, when you meet as a group, use these questions to generate discussion:

• How well was the essay's main idea supported?

• How could the essay be made more interesting to a reader?

After you've heard from your classmates, consider using their suggestions to improve your essay.

12.5 Editing and Proofreading

Before sharing your documented essay with others, proofread it carefully. Correct all errors you find in grammar, spelling, and punctuation.

Focusing on Quotation Marks

Cite sources for all information in your documented essay that does not come directly from you. To avoid plagiarism—using other people's words or ideas without crediting them—be sure you use quotation marks around words, phrases, and sentences that come directly from someone other than yourself. As you proofread, compare each quotation in your essay with the source to make sure that you have recorded exactly what your source said or wrote.

Technology Tip

Use the Find feature in your word-processing program to quickly locate quotation marks within your draft. Then, check each quoted passage against the original to be sure that you have accurately transcribed it.

Grammar in Your Writing
Direct and Indirect Quotations

A **direct quotation** is a word-for-word repetition of what someone said or wrote. Set off direct quotations in one of two ways:

• When a direct quotation is short, enclose it in quotation marks.

Example: Director L. C. Woodgrange remarked, "Shooting a film in an urban location is extremely complicated. That's why we built a set on a soundstage."

• When a direct quotation is four lines or more, precede the quotation with a colon, start the quotation on a new line, and write or type the quoted material to a narrower measure than that used in the rest of the report.

An **indirect quotation** is a restatement, or paraphrase, of someone else's words. It should not be put in quotation marks. However, the source of an indirect quotation must be acknowledged in your essay.

Example: According to director L. C. Woodgrange, he chose to build a set on a soundstage because urban film shoots are complicated.

Find It in Your Writing As you proofread your essay, check that you have set off and correctly punctuated all direct quotations. If you have no direct quotations in your essay, challenge yourself to add a few.

For more on punctuating direct quotations, see Chapter 27.

Publishing and Presenting

Building Your Portfolio

Consider these ideas for publishing and presenting your documented essay:

1. **Class Presentation** Contact a teacher who might be interested in having you present your essay to his or her class. Discuss the form of presentation—reading aloud or distributing copies—with the teacher.

2. **Library** If several of your classmates have written profiles of individuals, compile them into an anthology. Protect the essays by putting them in a plastic binder, and put the binder in an accessible place so others can borrow it.

Reflecting on Your Writing

Consider your experience writing a documented essay. Then, respond to the following questions. Record your responses in your portfolio.

- In the process of writing, what did you learn about the topic you chose?

- If you had to research and write a documented essay again, what would you do differently?

 **Internet Tip**

To see model essays scored with this rubric, go to **www.phschool.com**

Rubric for Self-Assessment

Use the following criteria to evaluate your documented essay:

	Score 4	Score 3	Score 2	Score 1
Audience and Purpose	Consistently targets a unique audience; clearly identifies purpose in thesis statement	Targets a specific audience; identifies purpose in thesis statement	Misses target audience by including too many details; presents no clear thesis	Addresses no specific audience or purpose
Organization	Presents a clear, consistent organizational strategy	Presents a clear organizational strategy with few inconsistencies	Presents an inconsistent organizational strategy; creates illogical presentation	Demonstrates a lack of organization; creates confusing presentation
Elaboration	Supports thesis statement with several documented sources; elaborates all main points	Supports thesis statement with some documented sources; elaborates most points	Supports the thesis statement with one documented source; elaborates some points	Provides no documented sources; does not provide thesis
Use of Language	Clearly integrates researched information into the writing; presents very few mechanical errors	Integrates most researched information into the writing; presents very few mechanical errors	Does not integrate researched information into the writing; presents many mechanical errors	Demonstrates poor use of language; presents many mechanical errors

12.7 Student Work
IN PROGRESS

FINAL DRAFT

▼ Critical Viewing
What benefits does reading to children provide for the children? For the volunteer? [Generalize]

Youths Offer a Helping Hand

**Tameeka Mitchem
Satellite Academy
New York, New York**

Each day after school, eighteen-year-old Courtney Cauthett of Manhattan spends two hours counseling and tutoring young children at a local community center. Kajal Angras, eighteen, a senior at Curtis High School on Staten Island, volunteers three hours a day, two days a week at Project Hospitality, an organization that helps needy mothers and their children.

Courtney and Kajal are among the growing number of teens across the country who are getting up, going out, and getting

Tameeka captures the interest of her audience by giving examples of teenagers who are actively participating in volunteering.

involved to help others. Last year, nearly 60 percent of the nation's teens volunteered 2.3 billion hours to a social or political cause. (*Philanthropy Journal Online.* Philanthropy News Network Online. 3 May 20_ **<http://www.pj.org**) Of those hours, 1.8 billion were given to national organizations, while the other 500 million were given to people in their communities. These statistics present compelling evidence that teenagers care about others.

"The kids make you feel needed," says Courtney McAllister, a senior at The Beacon School, referring to the children she works with in a Police Athletic League program in Harlem. "They really open your eyes to so many things. It feels good when you help them with their homework and they thank you. It is so rewarding." (McAllister, Courtney, Personal interview, 25 March 2000)

Courtney was told that in order to graduate, she had to do 100 hours of community service over the summer. Courtney was determined to make the most of it. She showed up the first day on time and nervous. "I didn't know what to expect from the kids," she says. But

after getting to know them, she became more relaxed and even stayed on after her 100 hours were up.

Kajal says she never expected to be a volunteer. She had been to Project Hospitality once, but only to interview someone for her school paper. After reading about the organization and seeing it in action, she became intrigued and decided to pitch in. Kajal has now been a counselor and tutor there for two years. "I love the kids," said Kajal. "They remind me to be humble and help me to realize what I take for granted."

A survey conducted by The Gallup Organization in January said teens are four times more likely to volunteer when asked than if they are not asked. And, according to a recent poll, 96 percent of teens feel that they can make a difference and change the world.

"Getting out there and helping to contribute something to this planet is what it's all about," says Courtney.

Tameeka follows with her main idea: The number of students volunteering in their communities is increasing.

Source information is provided within parentheses.

The body of Tameeka's essay is clearly organized. Here, she illustrates her thesis with anecdotes and quotations, identifying the source each time.

◄ **Critical Viewing** What sort of volunteer work is this student performing? How can you tell? **[Analyze]**

In conclusion, Tameeka reemphasizes her thesis by citing two surveys that support it.

Ending with this quotation leaves the reader with something to think about.

Connected Assignment *Statistical Report*

A **statistical report** relies on numerical evidence—often presented in tables, charts, or graphs—to make and support its main idea. Sometimes, the main idea may be presented last as a conclusion drawn from the statistical evidence. Other times, writers may state a thesis and use statistical evidence to support it.

Use the writing process skills outlined below to write your own statistical report.

Prewriting

Choosing Your Topic To find a topic for a statistical report, you can either start with the statistics or with a more general topic. To start with statistics, look at a newspaper's business report or flip through an almanac until some numbers catch your eye. To start with a more general topic, think of an event from history or a scientific breakthrough that interests you.

Narrowing Your Topic Once you've chosen a topic, narrow it by asking yourself what you want readers to learn about that topic. Then brainstorm for places to find statistical information. Try subject-linked reference sources, general and specific almanacs, specialty magazines, newspaper articles, and even expert interviews. Respond to the statistics by writing a thesis statement that is supported by the data you have found.

▲ **Critical Viewing** At which stage of the writing process is this student? What makes you think so? **[Speculate]**

Drafting State your topic and your main idea in the first paragraph. Then, develop your main idea in the body of the report. Support each paragraph's main idea with the evidence you have found. As you draft, connect your statistics to the ideas you've stated. Don't use statistics unless they directly relate to the point you are making.

Revising and Editing Reread your report. If it seems unconvincing, insert more statistical evidence from your sources or from the library if necessary. Replace argumentative language with objective statements that are supported by facts. Review your evidence for accuracy, and check to be sure that charts and graphs are legible and consistently labeled.

Publishing and Presenting Make a neat copy of your report and its accompanying charts, graphs, or other visual evidence. Present your report to a group of interested peers. Keep a copy of your finished report in your portfolio.

Spotlight on the Humanities

Examining Messages in Film

Focus on Film: *Grand Illusion*

Documentary essays tell about real-life people, things, and events. War is a real-life event that is often explored in films and documentaries. French director Jean Renoir (1894–1979), considered to be one of the great filmmakers of all time, directed the masterpiece *Grand Illusion* in 1937. This moving war film defies the characteristics of the genre of war films in that it does not contain a single combat scene. Rather, it focuses on the relations between human beings, both friend and foe. This focus conveys the message that war is an illusion. Renoir's meaningful use of the moving camera, his use of plain yet emphatic music, and his use of middle gray tones to convey meaning make *Grand Illusion* a masterwork in the world of cinema.

Art Connection Jean Renoir's father was French Impressionist painter Pierre-Auguste Renoir (1841–1919). Pierre-Auguste Renoir was famed for his use of brilliant color, his harmony of lines, and his wide range of subjects, to which he brought great intimacy. His early influences were the painters Claude Monet and Eugène Delacroix. Although he was crippled by arthritis for the last years of his life, Renoir continued to paint by strapping a brush to his arm.

Music Connection In 1939, Jean Renoir directed a film version of the classic Italian opera *Tosca* by Giacomo Puccini (1858–1924). *Tosca*, first performed in Rome in 1900, is the operatic tale of a woman whose beloved friend is killed by a heartless sheriff for hiding a fugitive. *Tosca* brought Puccini recognition as the successor to composer Giuseppe Verdi, one of the most important composers of the nineteenth century.

Research Writing Application: Documented Essay on the Renoirs

Imagine that you had been able to interact with and interview Pierre-Auguste and Jean Renoir (instead, you can pull your information from library research). Write a documented essay about their exciting, prolific lives, complete with personal anecdotes about both men.

▲ **Critical Viewing**
Where and when might this scene from *Grand Illusion* have taken place? Explain. **[Analyze]**

Media and Technology Skills

Using Media to Produce a Documentary

Activity: Film a Video Documentary

As you collect information for a documented essay, you may uncover fascinating facts, images, and ideas that are best shared in another medium. Video allows you to combine various types of details to bring a subject to life for your audience.

Think About It Film a 10- to 12-minute documentary based on research into a topic. Choose a topic that will translate well into film. Because interviews are a key element of many documentaries, consider topics for which you know experts to interview.

Research It Collect information about your topic from a number of sources. Take careful notes that identify photographs, artwork, songs, sounds, or other media resources that you intend to include in your documentary.

Storyboard It Make a storyboard like the one shown below to plan and balance the elements you will include in your video.

Introduction: Testing Food Purity

Narrated discussion in the school cafeteria

Interview with Dr. Alana Klein in her food-testing lab

Script It Write a script that includes narration, a list of settings, and the images you will include. Write narration that provides essential background information, introduces settings and people, and links scenes. Conduct your video interviews, and select the best sections before finalizing your filming script.

Produce It Shoot the remaining video elements of your documentary. Look for opportunities to incorporate action into your film. Consider conducting an interview while walking, or have the camera pan across a photograph or landscape. Assemble the documentary elements during editing, and script to match your actual footage.

Standardized Test Preparation Workshop

Responding to Document-Based Writing Prompts

Your ability to use evidence from an article to support a response to a writing prompt is often assessed on standardized tests. For example, this type of prompt may require you to analyze an issue, evaluate a writer's position, or draw conclusions. In some cases, you may be required to synthesize information from several documents that are provided. When writing a response, you will be evaluated on your ability to do the following:

- respond directly to the prompt
- show a clear understanding of the included text
- elaborate, using details from the article to support your response
- compare and contrast several documents, where applicable
- organize details logically and effectively
- use correct grammar, spelling, and punctuation

The process of writing for a test, as for any kind of writing, can be divided into stages. Plan to use a specific amount of time for prewriting, drafting, revising, and proofreading.

Following is an example of one type of writing prompt that you might find on a standardized test. Use the suggestions on the following page to help you respond. The clocks next to each stage show a suggested plan for organizing your time.

Reread the excerpt from "Mother Tongue," by Bill Bryson, on pages 248–251. Then, respond to the following test prompt.

> **Test Tip**
>
> When analyzing a document provided in a test, don't overuse direct quotations. The basis of the response should be your interpretation of the text.

Sample Writing Situation

> In "Mother Tongue," Bill Bryson discusses how the world would be different if geographic boundaries were based on the languages spoken in different areas. How does language create boundaries between groups of people in the same country? Use details and information from the article in your response.

Prewriting

Allow close to one quarter of your time for prewriting.

Use a T-Chart Before you write, use a T-chart to gather details for your response. On the left side of the chart, list reasons that languages might create boundaries between people. For each reason, list on the right side details from the article that support it.

Make an Outline Review the information on your T-chart, and think about how to best present it. Make an outline that shows the order in which you plan to discuss each detail. Refer to your completed outline as you draft your response.

Drafting

Allow almost half of your time for drafting.

Write a Strong Beginning Begin your response with an effective introduction that lets readers know what you plan to discuss. Include a thesis statement that introduces the main idea of your response. Also, write a sentence that acts as a transition into the body of the response.

Elaborate in the Body In the body of your response, develop and support your thesis statement. In each paragraph, use specific details from the article to support your thesis; then, add your insights to support, explain, or illustrate those details.

Conclude Effectively In your final paragraph, summarize the main points of your essay by restating the thesis. Also, leave a lasting impression on readers by including a recommendation, a provocative question, or a statement of personal insight.

Revising, Editing, and Proofreading

Allow almost one quarter of your time to revise and edit. Use the last few minutes to proofread your work.

Quote Accurately Make sure that all the quotations included in your response are correctly punctuated and enclosed in quotation marks. Also, check to be sure that you have copied each quotation word for word from the article. Finally, make sure that all quotations are incorporated smoothly into the text.

Make Corrections Review your response for errors. Neatly cross out any details that do not support your thesis. Correct all errors you have made in grammar, spelling, and punctuation. When making changes, place one line through text that you want eliminated, and use a caret [^] to indicate where you are adding words.

Research

Research Paper

Research in Everyday Life

As a high-school student, you might think it's obvious how research papers fit into your daily life: They are a requirement for many courses. You may even be working on one right now. However, **research writing**—writing based on information gathered from outside sources—also has an important role to play in the world at large. News reports, documentary films, historical fiction, and business reports are an example of the various everyday items that involve some degree of research.

Other activities that involve research are not written at all. For example, checking a map to locate a city, running a web search to learn about a scientific breakthrough, and questioning a grandparent about life in the "olden days" are all forms of research. In the following chapter, you will become more familiar with how to conduct research and write a research-based paper.

▲ Critical Viewing
Study this photograph of Edinburgh Castle. What three questions come to mind that you would like to research? **[Analyze]**

What Is a Research Paper?

A **research paper** is an in-depth, written examination of a topic in which the writer puts forth a thesis, or main point, and supports it with information drawn from several outside sources. A research paper

- brings together factual information from a variety of credible sources.
- develops a thesis, which presents one or more key points or arguments about the topic.
- has a consistent and effective organization.
- uses footnotes, endnotes, or parenthetical notes to credit sources.
- includes a bibliography or "works-cited" page.

To preview the criteria on which your research paper may be evaluated, see the Rubric for Self-Assessment on page 296.

Types of Research Papers

Writing involving research varies in length, formality, and audience and can take many forms:

- **I-Searches** are research papers about a topic of special interest to the writer. An I-Search tells the story of the writer's research path.
- **Academic reports** help educators gauge a student's ability to use research skills as a learning tool.
- **Biographical reports** contain information—such as interview material, quotations, and family history—about a person.
- **Multigenre reports** share insights gained through research. Rather than presenting findings in a traditional report, the writer shares findings through writing spanning several genres, such as poetry, short story, and drama.

Writers in ACTION

Sportswriter Peter Ginsburg uses research in his work. He offers the following observations about the types of research that he performs:

"There are a couple of different types of research that I do, and I guess you could call them primary and secondary. Primary research occurs when we talk to the person on whom we want to do the story. . . . The best type of research you can do is going right to the source. Other types of research I do I would consider secondary. It takes place through the newspaper, talking to the sports information director, and then just reading articles and reading books."

PREVIEW
Student Work
IN PROGRESS

Ian Pritchard, a student at Buena High School in Ventura, California, researched and wrote a biographical report on Seamus Heaney, a Pulitzer Prize-winning poet. His completed research paper appears at the end of the chapter.

The following research report was written by Matthew Kachur as he pursued his doctorate in American history. Kachur is a writer and editor who works in New York City.

Reading → **Writing** **Connection**

Reading Strategy: Identify Causes and Effects As you read this paper, deepen your understanding by looking for cause-and-effect relationships.

▲ **Critical Viewing** Examine this photograph taken in the 1890's. In what ways are football uniforms similar to and different from football uniforms today? **[Compare and Contrast]**

Football at the Turn of the Twentieth Century

Matthew Kachur

The indexers for *The New York Times* decided to make a change when compiling the information for the year 1903. Previously, the heading "Football" had been sufficient for coverage of the subject matter. But in 1903, the newspaper had printed a group of related stories with such frequency that the index editors saw the need for a new category under the main head: "Football, Fatal Accidents." Below this subhead runs a list of people who had died while playing football that year (*New York Times Index* 664).

This addition to the index indicates that, by the turn of the twentieth century, football had become a sport of almost unmatched brutality. Fatal injuries, of course, occur in sporting events today. It appears that we as a people are prepared to accept the occasional fatality on the football field or the death of a prizefighter in the ring as long as they are isolated instances. It is difficult to imagine the American public sanctioning a sport in which participants are regularly killed. This last point must be emphasized: In the brand of football played in the 1890's, players

Kachur's introduction grabs the interest of the audience and introduces his topic.

The thesis statement leads off the second paragraph.

regularly sustained fatal injuries. And yet it was a sport that was defended and endorsed by many Americans, some of whom were members of the medical community.

In 1894, an American journal published a French visitor's description of a football game he had witnessed. The account was marked by phrases such as "young bulldogs" and "the demon of conflict." One passage was particularly telling:

> "The brutality with which they seize the bearer of the ball is impossible to imagine without having witnessed it. He is seized by the middle of the body, by the head, by the legs, by the feet. He rolls over and his assailants with him, and as they fight for the ball and the two sides come to the rescue, it becomes a whole heap of twenty-two bodies tumbling on top of one another, like a . . . heap of serpents with human heads . . . (*Boston Medical and Surgical Journal* 570–571)

American football has its origins in the English games of soccer and rugby. Indeed, the first American match game would seem to a modern observer more like soccer than American football. This game, played in 1869, pitted Rutgers against the College of New Jersey, with 25 players on each side. The ball was moved by kicking or slapping with the hand or head, but could not be carried or passed. By the 1870's, a game more familiar to us had developed, with ball carrying replacing kicking. Still, the game was basically a defensive affair in which serious injuries were common.

In 1882, a reform was instituted that halted play after the ball carrier was knocked down. Before this rule change, his teammates would have dragged him along if he hit the turf.

By the 1890's, football had become well established in the United States, especially at the intercollegiate level. Sixty colleges were playing the game in 1888, a figure that doubled by 1890. Already such institutions as the big Thanksgiving Day game had been established. College alumni supported the teams of their alma maters with the same enthusiasm they do today, and there were widespread rumblings of professionalism in the ranks of college athletes. (Danzig; Weyland)

In [an] essay, titled "The American Boy," [vice-president Theodore] Roosevelt addressed the importance of competitive athletics:

> "Nowadays, whatever other faults the son of rich parents may tend to develop, he is at least forced . . . to bear himself well in many exercises and to develop his body—and therefore, to a certain extent, his character—in the rough sports which call for pluck, endurance, and physical address." (Roosevelt 104)

The [supporters] of the game of football seized on Roosevelt's words, using his rhetoric in their defenses of the sport. Dr. J. William White, writing in *The Outlook*, quoted some remarks Roosevelt made before an audience of Harvard alumni:

Quotation marks around phrases like "young bulldogs" indicate that the words are someone else's.

This quoted passage is correctly set as an excerpt. The internal citation that follows gives the title of the source material because there was no author listed, plus the pages on which the quotation appears.

Historical data such as this help develop Kachur's thesis: that football was a brutal game.

The body of Kachur's report is organized chronologically.

This summary is based on information found in the two works cited.

"I do not mind in the least that they are rough games, or that those who take part in them are occasionally injured. I have no sympathy whatever with the overwrought sentimentality which would keep a young man in cotton wool, and I have a hearty contempt for him if he counts a broken arm or collarbone as of serious consequence when balanced against the chance of showing that he possesses hardihood, physical address, and courage." (*The Outlook*)

One of the leading critics of football was E. L. Godkin, who as early as 1893 was (protesting) against the sport in the editorials of *The Nation*. Describing a game between Harvard and Yale, it was pointed out that seven out of the twenty-two starting players were injured, a higher casualty rate than at Cold Harbor, Waterloo, or Gravelotte. How, the magazine asked, could the colleges [authorize] a sport in which litters and surgeons were required at every contest? (*The Nation*)

The numerous defenses of football were consistent on a number of points. First, the brutality and violence of football was overstated by its detractors, as were the number of injuries: It just was not as bad as it was said to be. Second, football was good exercise and beneficial to health. But the importance of football to physical health paled in importance to the moral benefits of football. Football built character; it turned boys into men.

William Lee Howard gave a spirited defense of football in "Football and Moral Health," published in 1906. In the article, Howard urged that no barriers beyond the basic minimum necessary to organize the game be placed on football. Indeed, he refers to the many "miserable beings" he has come across in his practice who he feels should have been forced to play football in their younger days (*The Medical Record* 546–547).

There were those doctors who condemned football. Dr. Germain See stated simply in *The American Physical Education Review* that "Football is a dangerous exercise without value." It was as an institution, however, that the medical journals expressed dissatisfaction with the sport. *The Medical News*, entitling an 1884 editorial "The Football Disgrace," stated:

"Our postman has brought us from many correspondents and from all over the land an amazing mass of news of deaths, broken bones, wrenches, concussions, dislocations, [and] gambling . . . of the victorious; tears and bellowing of the vanquished; and sluggings, sluggings, sluggings—without end. . . . Let us hear no more of . . . revision and reform . . . there is but one change demanded: abolish them absolutely!" (615)
[A] game between Harvard and Yale prompted *The Boston Medical and Surgical Journal* to write.

When no page number exists in source material, provide the title of the source or author name within parentheses.

Keeping his audience in mind, Kachur gives information about the people who are quoted.

▼ **Critical Viewing**
What sort of protection does this uniform offer the football player? **[Analyze]**

That a player may with impunity jump on an antagonist [lying] on the ground with the ball, after the whistle has blown, and dislocate his victim's [collarbone], should be an impossibility," the editors wrote. They argued that promises of reform had not been kept and that football would no longer be tolerated if the players were allowed to behave like "brutes." (543)

Finally, *The Journal of the American Medical Association* wondered if football was worth the twelve deaths and over eighty serious injuries, including "torn ears" and "brain injuries resulting in insanity," that occurred in the 1902 season. "To be a cripple or a lunatic for life is paying high for athletic (competition)." (39)

It is interesting to note that some of the strongest defenses of football, such as that of William Lee Howard, occurred after those in control of the sport at the college level were forced to reform the game. According to one source, seven football players died in 1901, fifteen in 1902, fourteen in 1903, fourteen again in 1904, and twenty-four in 1905. Theodore Roosevelt, new President of the United States, was moved by the mounting death toll to pressure those in charge of college football to begin a process of reform. The result was the gradual elimination of football's most vicious characteristics. Although the sport did not change overnight, rule changes that encouraged the pass and discouraged mass play gradually changed the character of the game.

When the source information is mentioned within the text of your paper, provide page number(s) within parentheses.

▲ **Critical Viewing** Does the violence in this illustration seem excessive to you? Would you rule it legal or illegal in a football rule book? [**Make a Judgment**]

A works-cited listing gives more information about Kachur's source material.

Works Cited

The Boston Medical and Surgical Journal. 29 Nov. 1894: 543.
The Boston Medical and Surgical Journal. Vol. 131, 1894.
Danzig, Allison. *The History of American Football.* Englewood Cliffs, NJ: Prentice Hall, 1956.
The Journal of the American Medical Association. 6 Dec. 1902: 39.
The Medical News. 1 Dec. 1884: 615.
The Medical Record. (7 April 1906): 546–547.
The Nation. (29 Nov. 1894).
The New York Times Index for the Published News of 1899–June 1905. New York: (1969).
The Outlook. (18 Nov. 1905).
Roosevelt, Theodore. *The Strenuous Life: Essays and Addresses.* New York: The Century Co., 1900.
Weyand, Alexander. *The Saga of American Football.* New York: Macmillan, 1955.

Reading Writing Connection

Writing Application: Give Causes and Effects As you prepare to write your research paper, consider the cause-and-effect relationships you could explore concerning your topic.

Prewriting

Choosing Your Topic

Because doing research means immersing yourself in a topic, choose one in which you have a genuine interest. If you are having trouble finding a topic, try one of these strategies:

Strategies for Generating Topics

1. **Scan News Headlines** Sometimes reading about events in the news can trigger a desire to find more in-depth information. Scan news headlines of the previous few days. Read articles of interest, and jot down your questions. Then, choose one of those questions, and base your research around it.

2. **Use Looping** Write freely about a general topic of interest for five minutes. Read what you've written, and circle the most interesting idea. Write for five minutes on that idea. Again, read what you have written, and circle the most important idea. Choose one of the circled items to be the topic for your research paper.

Writing Lab CD-ROM

For more help choosing a topic, explore the activities and topic suggestions in the Choosing a Topic section of the Research Writing lesson.

Student Work
IN PROGRESS

Name: Ian Pritchard
Buena High School
Ventura, CA

Looping to Generate a Topic

By using the looping strategy, Ian was able to find a topic for his research report: a biographical report on poet Seamus Heaney.

I love Britain. Scotland, (Ireland,) Wales. The Tower, Elizabeth I, and the Armada. Guy Fawkes Day and the Houses of Parliament. Westminster Abbey and Poet's Corner. The Plague.

The Potato Famine. The Industrial Revolution. Poverty. Child Labor and Dickens. Marlowe and Jonson. (The Troubles.)

Belfast and Dublin. James Joyce. Eavan Boland. (Seamus Heaney.)

Bombings. U2.

TOPIC BANK

If you're having trouble coming up with a topic, consider these ideas:

1. **Research Paper on Raising the *Titanic*** Perhaps no disaster in the twentieth century has inspired more interest than the sinking of the *Titanic*. Newly developed technology has kept that interest alive. Develop a thesis, and write a research paper about the raising of the *Titanic*.

2. **Research Paper on Your Town's Origins** Whether you live in New York, Los Angeles, or Anytown, U.S.A., your town has a history. Research and write a paper about your town's beginnings.

Responding to Fine Art

3. Study the people and setting in *Benedict Arnold Escapes on a British Frigate* by Brent Silverman. Then, write a research paper inspired by what you see. For example, you might research the British navy of the 1800's, or you could write a biography of Lord Nelson, a famous British naval hero.

Benedict Arnold Escapes on a British Frigate, Brent Silverman, Courtesy of Silverman Studios, Inc.

Responding to Literature

4. Read "Defending Nonviolent Resistance" by Mohandas K. Gandhi. Then, write a research paper about the influence of Gandhi's nonviolent philosophy on Dr. Martin Luther King, Jr. "Defending Nonviolent Resistance" appears in *Prentice Hall Literature: Timeless Voices, Timeless Themes*, The British Tradition.

☑ Cooperative Writing Opportunity

5. **Informational Display** As a group, list several colleges and universities that you would like to learn more about. For example, you may research a college's history, location, academic requirements, and famous graduates. Then, assign one list item to each group member to research. When research is finished, work as a group to make a chart on which you publish your research findings.

Narrowing Your Topic

Now that you've chosen a topic, consider whether it needs to be narrowed. For example, suppose you have chosen World War I as your topic. A glance at a card or computer catalog on this subject will show you that the research on such a vast topic could take years; the writing could fill volumes. If your own topic can be broken down into several subtopics, each pointing in a different direction for research, then you should narrow it. One technique for narrowing a topic is webbing.

Webbing to Narrow a Topic

Design a web, and write your topic in the center. In the outer circles, write the key aspects of your topic. One of these aspects may become the topic for your paper, or you may need to narrow it further. If so, choose an outer circle topic, and put it in the center of a second web. Repeat the process until you have arrived at a manageable topic for your research paper.

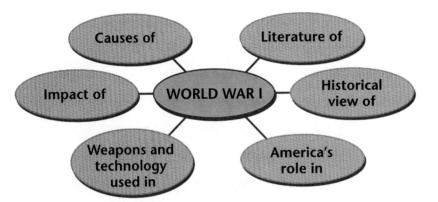

Research Tip

Do preliminary research to narrow a topic. Check card and computer catalogs, tables of contents of books, encyclopedia entries, and bibliographies to get a sense of the depth and breadth of a topic and its subtopics.

Considering Your Audience and Purpose

Consider your audience to identify the types of details and language they will understand and appreciate. Also, identify your purpose, so that you will be sure to choose details that will have a definite impact on your audience. Ask yourself:

- **For whom am I writing?** Consider the age, education level, and experience of your audience. For example, you would probably take one approach if your paper about pollution in a local lake is to be read by environmental scientists and a very different approach if it is to be read by high-school students.

- **Why am I writing?** Research papers are intended to inform or explain; but if your thesis is a controversial one, you may also have persuasion as a purpose.

Gathering Details

Before you start gathering details, make a research plan to guide you. A plan will help you to stay focused and use your time wisely as you make your way through the vast array of information sources available.

Develop a Research Plan

To develop a research plan, make a list of questions about your topic or areas of your topic you want to explore. Identify the types of sources that would be most useful, and find out where they are located. Plan to use a wide variety of sources, such as:

- Library sources
- Internet sites
- Media sources
- Interviews

One way to organize your research is to make a T-chart. Fold a piece of paper in half lengthwise to form two columns. In the left column, write down what you want to know. In the right column, write the possible sources for finding the information.

Student Work
IN PROGRESS

Name: *Ian Pritchard*
Buena High School
Ventura, CA

Planning Research With a T-Chart

Ian used a T-chart to help him plan and gather details for his research paper.

WHAT I WANT TO FIND OUT	POSSIBLE SOURCES
Where and when Heaney was born	Introduction to one of Heaney's books of poems
Political situations that existed	History books about Ireland; past issues of newspapers and journals
How other poets regard Heaney	Poets or poetry experts

Use Library Resources

The library contains extensive information in both print and electronic formats. Before you begin library research, use a T-chart to list the information or sources you want to find and use. Without such a list, you may waste valuable time browsing.

- **Nonfiction Books** Nonfiction books may provide broad overviews of topics, which can be useful when you are beginning your research, or they may explore specialized subjects. Use the library's card or computer catalog to locate nonfiction books. You can search for a topic by author, title, subject, or (in a computer catalog) key word.

- **Periodicals** To locate magazine articles, use the *Readers' Guide to Periodical Literature.*

- **Reference Books** The reference section of a library has a variety of sources that can provide interesting and current information on your topic. Types of reference works include bibliographies, almanacs, atlases, and encyclopedias.

Use Electronic Resources

Computers have become an indispensable research tool. There are two basic ways to use your computer for research:

- **On-line Research** The Internet, which you can access through an on-line service, offers a wealth of sources for information, including museums, news media, colleges and universities, special-interest groups, and government institutions. You can also find links to your topic by using a search engine.

- **CD-ROMs** Many information and reference sources are now available on CD-ROM. Check your library, bookstore, or electronics outlet to see what is available.

Conduct Investigative Research

Some research topics benefit from investigative research. If yours is one that does, consider these possibilities:

- **Interviews** Interview an expert in your topic. Prepare questions in advance, phrasing them to encourage the interviewee to answer at length. Conduct preliminary research if necessary. Follow up with a thank-you note or phone call.

- **Surveys** If the statistics you need are not available, conduct your own survey. Prepare questions in advance, framing questions as neutrally as possible to avoid biased results. Keep track of responses, and tabulate them carefully.

Writers in ACTION

The noted columnist for the New York Herald-Tribune *Franklin P. Adams* said the following about researching:

"I find that a great part of the information I have was acquired by looking up something and finding something else on the way."

Technology Tip

Many articles from past periodicals are stored on microfiche. The *Readers' Guide* will identify the file on which the article you want is located. Request the appropriate file from the librarian, and use a microfiche machine to locate and print out useful articles you find.

Take Notes

As you find information from sources, make note cards and source cards.

Source cards contain publication information of each source you consult in your research. This material will be used in your bibliography. Use one card for each source. Number each source card, and write that number on your note card.

Note cards contain details you might want to use in your report. To make organizing information easier, put only one piece of information on each card. Write the number of the source (written on the source card) on each note card.

Photocopy or Print Source Material

If resources are available, you may prefer to photocopy source material, including the book or journal's title page and copyright information. On the printout, highlight or circle the information you plan to use.

If you get your information from an on-line source or from a CD-ROM, print out the appropriate pages. Then, highlight or circle the information you plan to use.

Student Work
IN PROGRESS

Name: *Ian Pritchard*
Buena High School
Ventura, CA

Using Note Cards and Source Cards in Research

While researching Seamus Heaney, Ian created source cards and note cards.

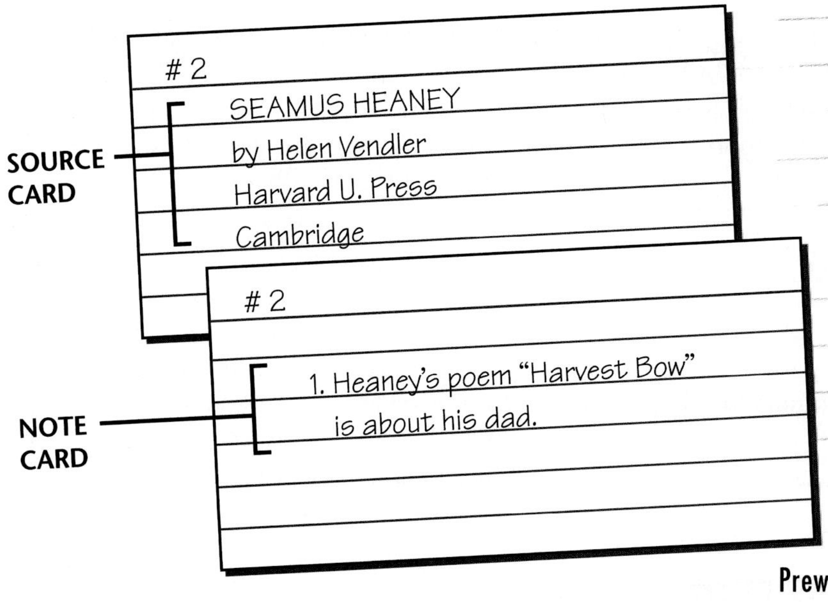

SOURCE CARD

2

SEAMUS HEANEY

by Helen Vendler

Harvard U. Press

Cambridge

NOTE CARD

2

1. Heaney's poem "Harvest Bow" is about his dad.

 **Drafting**

Shaping Your Writing

With your research finished, you may look at a stack of note cards or photocopied materials and wonder what to do with them. The task now is to organize your information. Start by sorting your notes into various groups. Label the groups, and write subheads, if necessary, beneath the general heads.

Develop a Thesis Statement

As you begin drafting, introduce your topic and state your thesis in the introduction. A *thesis* states the key point or argument you wish to make about your topic. Some writers have a thesis in mind before they even begin to research. Sometimes, the research will point a writer in a new direction.

To create a thesis statement, read your grouped notes carefully. Decide on the most important ideas you have gathered, and summarize them. After deleting unnecessary information, shape your summary into a single, clear statement.

Sample Thesis Statements
The space program of the 1960's helped to unite Americans. The childhood of Queen Elizabeth I of England had a great impact on decisions she made as a ruler.

Organize to Support Your Thesis

Having decided on a thesis, develop an organizational plan that will best support your thesis. There are several methods of organizing a paper, but the "right" plan for you is the one that best matches the content and purpose of your paper. Below are some suggestions for how to organize your research findings:

ORGANIZATIONAL IDEAS	
Use chronological organization if . . .	you are tracing the history of something; you are writing about someone's life.
Use cause-and-effect organization if . . .	you want to emphasize that certain events caused others to happen; you are making a prediction.
Use order-of-importance organization if . . .	you want to build an argument; there are various aspects to your topic.

Make an Outline

Once you've chosen an organizational approach, use an outline or graphic organizer to help you arrange the details to fit your organization. In an outline

- List each main point you will cover next to a Roman numeral.
- Under each main point, enter the topics you'll discuss next to capital letters.
- Under each topic, list details next to Arabic numerals.

Review your outline, and experiment with its organization until you are satisfied with it. Keep your completed outline handy, and refer to it as you draft and revise your research writing.

Writing Lab CD-ROM

You may want to use the Outliner tool in the Toolkit to help you prepare an outline for your research paper.

Student Work
IN PROGRESS

Name: *Ian Pritchard*
Buena High School
Ventura, CA

Organizing With an Outline
Here is the outline Ian created to support his thesis statement:
"The hard labor that he, his family, and other generations of Irish farmers endured in the cultivation and harvesting of potatoes has had a great influence on Heaney's poetry."

    I. Family Background
        A. Ireland
        B. "The Troubles"
        C. Relationship with parents

    II. Effect on Poetry
        A. Connection with homeland
        B. Allusion to parents
        C. Haunting imagery

Providing Elaboration

As you draft, follow your outline, making sure each body paragraph addresses an aspect of your thesis. Then, develop your ideas by providing supporting details. Insert citations as you draft, revealing the origin of source material.

Give Details and Cite Sources

Support your main points with various types of details:

Facts can be proved. General facts do not need to be cited.

Statistics give information about your topic. Cite the origin of your statistical information.

Examples include situations from life that illustrate the points you are making. Such examples do not need to be cited.

Quotations are word-for-word quotes from someone other than yourself. They must appear in quotation marks and be cited.

Paraphrased information is retelling in your own words information you learned while researching. If paraphrased information is not generally known, you must cite the source material.

Personal observations are your own ideas about what you have learned. Personal observations do not need to be cited.

Student Work
IN PROGRESS

Name: Ian Pritchard
Buena High School
Ventura, CA

Giving Details and Citing Sources

Ian incorporated the opinions of several authorities on the works of Heaney, using both direct and indirect quotations. In each case, he cited his sources.

He passed his days either at the local school in Anahorish or next to his father in the fields of Mossbawn, the family farm (Buttel 9). The hard labor that he, his family, and other generations of Irish farmers endured in the cultivation and harvesting of potatoes has had a great influence on Heaney's poetry. The land itself is mirrored in the strength of Heaney's words: As poet and editor Philip Fried has said, "He handles words as if they had the heft of potatoes." (Fried)

 13.4 *Revising*

Once you have completed your first draft, start looking for ways to improve it. Take a critical look at each level of writing, from the overall structure to individual word choices. Begin with the big picture.

Revising Your Overall Structure

Evaluate the Variety of Support

One of the hallmarks of an effective research paper is thoroughness. Review your paper to make sure you have completely explored your topic, using a variety of types of support.

▶ **REVISION STRATEGY**
Color-Coding to Identify Supporting Details

Using highlighters, identify the supporting facts and details in your paper. Use a different color of highlighter for each category of detail. Choose categories that suit your topic. You might choose to call out causes and effects in different colors, for example. Another system that works for many research papers is to make details that answer *Who? What? When? Where?* and *Why?* For example:

- *Whos,* or people, might be blue.
- *Whens*—dates, times, and periods in history—might be green.
- *Whats*—or events, developments, effects, things, and objects—might be yellow.
- *Wheres,* or places, might be red.
- *Whys*—or explanations, definitions, or causes—might be purple.

When you are finished, scan your paper. Is it a rainbow of color, or is it predominantly one color or two? If a category is underrepresented, consider why. It may be that your thesis requires you to focus on a particular type of data. On the other hand, it may mean that you've left something out. If that is the case, add details where they are lacking, to elaborate on your points.

▶ **Critical Viewing**
What are the benefits of revising on a computer? What are the benefits of revising in longhand? **[Generalize]**

Revising Your Paragraphs
Strengthen Your Paragraph Organization

When you are satisfied with the general structure of your paper, focus on individual paragraphs. In a research paper, body paragraphs are like building blocks: Arranged properly, they will provide solid support for your thesis. If the blocks aren't strong, your paper won't be either.

▶ **REVISION STRATEGY**
Identifying Paragraph Patterns: TRI/PS/QA

Identify the paragraph patterns you have used. Go through your draft, and jot down in the margin the organization pattern of each paragraph. If you cannot identify a specific pattern for a paragraph, reread it closely to make sure it makes sense. If not, revise it. You may want to use an organizational pattern like the ones that follow:

- **TRI: T**opic, **R**estatement, **I**llustration. In this pattern, the topic sentence comes first, followed by a restatement or extension of the main idea, followed by an illustration or an example. This pattern may be altered to TIR, TII, ITR, or TRIT.

- **PS: P**roblem/**S**olution. In this pattern, a problem is posed and one or several solutions follow.

- **QA: Q**uestion/**A**nswer. Paragraphs of this type generally start with a question that is then answered in subsequent sentences.

TRI

Rockefeller Center, an enormous complex of buildings located in midtown Manhattan, is named for its principal financial backers. These were John D. Rockefeller, Jr., and other members of that wealthy family. The Rockefeller family made most of its fortune in the oil industry. . . .

T
R
I

PS

Rockefeller Center is so big, it's hard to know where to begin to take a tour. If you begin, however, on Fifth Avenue between Forty-ninth and Fiftieth streets and follow this path, you will have an enjoyable tour of this fascinating piece of New York City. From Fiftieth Street and Fifth Avenue, walk down the flagstone path into the sunken plaza, which contains an ice rink and a statue of Prometheus.

P
S

QA

How did Rockefeller Center get its name? The building complex was named for its principal financial backers—John D. Rockefeller, Jr., and other members of that wealthy family.

Q
A

▲ **Critical Viewing**
Why do you think Rockefeller Center, pictured here, is such a popular destination for tourists? **[Infer]**

Revising Your Sentences
Create Sentence Variety

When too many sentences in a composition are of the same length, structure, and type, it has a numbing effect on its readers. Examine your draft closely, looking for patterns in your sentences. Provide variety where needed by interrupting patterns with sentences of different lengths or types.

▶ **REVISION STRATEGY**
Color-Coding to Identify Sentence Length

Read through your draft, using a highlighter of one color to mark sentences of fewer than twelve words. Use another highlighter color to mark sentences of twelve or more words.

Review your draft, and locate passages in which you have too many sentences of a particular length. Make those passages more interesting by rewriting or adding sentences to provide variety.

Student Work
IN PROGRESS

Name: *Ian Pritchard*
Buena High School
Ventura, CA

Color-Coding to Identify Sentence Length
Because the highlighting showed that all the sentences in this passage were long, Ian split some of them to add variety to his research paper.

The peat bogs that so fascinated Heaney as a child have come to be a consistent metaphor in his poetry; just as the bogs contain a catalog of objects buried for hundreds of years, Heaney's poems rely heavily on stories and people from the past, which give the reader a sense of modern-day Irish sentiment. These reflections on the past. Heaney writes about his country's and his countrymen's violated past in a voice that reflects upon the violence of the present. Persons, animals, and objects resurrected from the brown peat—indeed, the peat itself—have all become the source and subject of Heaney's writings (Tobin 91).

Grammar in Your Writing
Independent and Subordinate Clauses

When you combine sentences, you form a new sentence structure. The structure of a sentence is determined by the number and kind of clauses it contains. A **clause** is a group of words that contains a subject and a verb. There are two major types of clauses:

Independent Clause: An **independent clause** can stand alone as a sentence: Shakespeare's popularity has never waned.

Subordinate Clause: A **subordinate clause** cannot stand alone because it does not express a complete thought. It must be linked to a main clause: Because Shakespeare is so popular, his plays have been translated into dozens of languages.

Four sentence structures can be formed from these two types of clauses:

1. A **simple sentence** is a independent clause that stands alone:
      Sir Laurence Olivier was a great Shakespearean actor.

2. A **compound sentence** contains two or more independent clauses separated by a semicolon or linked by a comma and a coordinating conjunction such as *and, but, or, for, nor, so,* or *yet:*
      Olivier starred in many stage productions of Shakespeare plays, and he also starred in movies of these plays.

3. A **complex sentence** contains one independent clause and one or more subordinate clauses. The subordinate clauses in the following examples are underlined.
      Because he preferred the stage to film, Olivier made only a handful of films of Shakespeare's plays.

4. A **compound-complex sentence** contains at least one subordinate clause and at least two independent clauses:
      These films, though they were critically acclaimed, did not translate into box office success, so Olivier turned to more commercial films.

Find It in Your Reading Find one compound, one compound-complex, and two complex sentences in "Football at the Turn of the Twentieth Century" on pages 276–279. Identify the clauses in each example.

Find It in Your Writing Find two compound and two complex sentences in your research essay. Identify the clauses in each one. In the complex sentences, be sure the main idea of the sentence is contained in the main clause, not in the subordinate clause.

For more about independent and subordinate clauses, see Chapter 19.

Revising Your Word Choice

Review Your Use of *I* and *You*

Formal research papers are almost always written in the third person. Although the use of the first person is sometimes acceptable—in making a personal interpretation, for example—most times, the use of the third person is preferred. A common error, especially when writing about society and social issues, is to unintentionally lapse into the first or second person. For example:

FIRST PERSON: A 1989 study revealed that most of us vote for candidates of our own ethnic group.

THIRD PERSON: A 1989 study revealed that most people vote for candidates of their own ethnic group.

▶ **REVISION STRATEGY**
Circling Personal Pronouns

Carefully reread your paper. Identify and circle all first- or second-person pronouns: *I, my, we, us, our, you, your, yours.* If switches from third person to first person and second person are unintentional, revise them.

Peer Review

With the process of revision almost completed, step back to get a fresh perspective on your work. A good way to do this is to have a fellow student read your revised draft. At this stage, a peer can be more objective about your work than you can; he or she may help you see things you might have missed.

Work With a Partner

Pair up with another student, and exchange revised drafts. Take turns reviewing each other's work. Read through each other's drafts silently and then aloud before offering suggestions about content and style. You may want to prepare a list of questions such as the following to help your peer respond as he or she reads your report:

- What can make the introduction clearer and more interesting? What is my thesis statement?

- Which passages, if any, in the body could be better organized? Have I included enough facts and details to support the thesis?

- What revisions might make the conclusion stronger and more memorable?

- How can the writing be tightened or trimmed?

- What mistakes, if any, have I made in documenting resources?

▶ **Speaking and Listening Tip**

Slowly read your draft aloud to a partner while your partner jots down comments and suggestions for improvement.

Editing and Proofreading

Errors in spelling, punctuation, grammar, and usage indicate sloppiness and carelessness—qualities you do not want associated with your work. Before creating your final draft, proofread your essay to eliminate such errors.

Focusing on Quotations

Check each quoted line or passage in your research report to ensure that it is transcribed correctly and that it is enclosed in quotation marks or set as an excerpt. Also double-check the names, titles, and other reference information to be sure that each is accurate.

Focusing on Formatting

Research writing contains numerous citations. These may be in parenthetical form, in footnotes, or in endnotes. As you proofread, make sure you have formatted all citations correctly.

Formatting Excerpts Sometimes, the best way to incorporate another person's ideas into your research paper is to quote that person at length. Direct quotations of four lines or more are considered excerpts and must be formatted as such. Proofread your paper to make sure you have formatted excerpts correctly.

Formatting Citations When you credit your sources, it shows that your information is reliable. Use footnotes, endnotes, or parenthetical citations to document your sources whenever you directly or indirectly quote another person, present an idea that is not your own, or report a fact that is available only from one source. You should also prepare a works-cited page, which lists your sources alphabetically by author or, if a work has no credited author, by title.

Formatting a Works-Cited Listing Check your listing of works cited to be sure that it is complete and correctly formatted. Also, double-check the punctuation of entries to ensure that you've consistently and correctly punctuated each one. If in doubt, consult a manual or list of guidelines for preparing a works-cited list.

⊙ Technology Tip

Enter author names into the spell-check library of your software program. Then, run the spell-check feature to ensure that you have made no typographical errors in names.

Grammar in Your Writing
Formatting

Excerpts: When you have an excerpt of four lines or more, precede the excerpt with a colon; start the excerpt on a new line; write or type the excerpted material to a narrower measure than that used in the rest of the paper; and credit the source of the excerpt using a footnote, endnote, or parenthetical citation.

Parenthetical Citation: This appears in parentheses immediately after the relevant passage in the text of your paper. Include either the author's last name and page number (style of Modern Language Association, the MLA) or give the author's last name, date of publication, and page number (style of American Psychology Association, the APA).

MLA Style   (Coles 306)   **APA Style**   (Coles, 1990, p. 306)

Be sure to include a works-cited listing at the end of your paper.

Footnote: Place a raised number at the end of a cited passage. Place the same raised number at the bottom of the page; next to it, give details about the source of the information. Include the source documentation in full the first time you cite a source and a shortened version for every subsequent citation of that source.

Endnote: Place a raised number at the end of a cited passage. Instead of listing the source information next to a number at the bottom of the page, prepare a separate page for all endnotes.

Works-Cited Listing: This list comes at the end of your paper. It should contain an entry for each work cited in your text. Alphabetize entries by the authors' last names. If the author's name is unknown, alphabetize by the first word in the title of the work. Each entry has three parts: the author, the title, and the publication information. Each part is followed by a period and one space.

Ferrara, Jerry L. "Why Vultures Make Good Neighbors." *National Wildlife.* June–July, 1987: 16–20.

Gerrard, Tabitha. *A Guide to Eastern Seabirds.* Chicago: Agincourt Press, 1999.

Find It in Your Reading Find a passage and its accompanying citation in "Football at the Turn of the Twentieth Century" on pages 276–279. Identify the method of citation. Rewrite the citation using each of the two alternative methods shown above.

Find It in Your Writing Identify all the source citations in your paper. Double-check to make sure that you have included all the pertinent source information in the correct format.

For more about citing sources, see Citing Sources and Preparing Manuscript on pages 886–892.

Publishing and Presenting

Building Your Portfolio

Here are some suggestions for publishing and presenting your work:

1. **Internet** Millions of people around the world are connected electronically through the Internet; no doubt some of them will be interested in reading your paper. Try these ideas for using the Internet: e-mail your paper to a friend; publish it on an electronic bulletin board; submit it to a student publication.

2. **Oral Presentation** Present your research paper orally to your class or to another class that is studying a subject related to your topic. Instead of reading your paper word for word, speak from note cards with key ideas highlighted. Use visual aids to support your presentation.

Reflecting on Your Writing

After you've completed your research paper, spend a few minutes thinking about your writing experience. Then, answer the following questions, and record your answers in your portfolio.

- Did you learn anything about your topic that surprised you?
- If you had to do it over again, what would you do differently?

 **Internet Tip**

To see essays scored with this rubric, go to **www.phschool.com**

Rubric for Self-Assessment

Use the following criteria to evaluate your research paper.

	Score 4	Score 3	Score 2	Score 1
Audience and Purpose	Focuses on a clearly stated thesis, starting from a well-framed question; gives complete citations	Focuses on a clearly stated thesis; gives citations	Focuses mainly on the chosen topic; gives some citations	Presents information without a clear focus; few or no citations
Organization	Presents information in logical order, emphasizing details of central importance	Presents information in logical order	Presents information logically, but organization is poor in places	Presents information in a scattered, disorganized manner
Elaboration	Draws clear conclusions from information gathered from multiple sources	Draws conclusions from information gathered from multiple sources	Explains and interprets some information	Presents information with little or no interpretation or synthesis
Use of Language	Shows overall clarity and fluency; contains few mechanical errors	Shows good sentence variety; contains some errors in spelling, punctuation, or usage	Uses awkward or overly simple sentences; contains many mechanical errors	Contains incomplete thoughts and many mechanical errors

Student Work
IN PROGRESS

FINAL DRAFT

◀ **Critical Viewing**
Heaney is wearing the medal he received when he was awarded the Nobel Prize. How might you research the symbolism of the medal's design? **[Make a Plan]**

Seamus Heaney: A Literary Biography

Ian Pritchard
Buena High School
Ventura, California

The Irish poet Seamus Heaney spent his youth among fertile farmlands and peat bogs that make up the countryside of County Derry, a small farming community thirty miles northwest of Belfast. Born on April 13, 1939, to Margaret and Patrick Heaney, Seamus was the eldest of nine children. He passed his days either

In his report's intro-duction, Ian introduces the topic of his essay—Seamus Heaney—and his thesis—that Heaney's life has a direct influ-ence on his poetry.

at the local school in Anahorish or next to his father in the fields of Mossbawn, the family farm (Buttel 9). The hard labor that he, his family, and other generations of Irish farmers endured in the cultivation and harvesting of potatoes has had a great influence on Heaney's poetry. The land itself is mirrored in the strength of Heaney's words. Philip Fried, whose poetry collections include *Mutual Trespasses* and *Quantum Genesis,* has observed the earthiness of Heaney's poetry. In a recent interview, Fried said, "He handles words as if they had the heft of potatoes." (Fried) The tumultuous past and fervent present of Ireland's political situation have also lent substantially to Heaney's work.

The peat bogs that so fascinated Heaney as a child have come to be a consistent metaphor in his poetry: Just as the bogs contain a catalog of objects buried for hundreds of years, Heaney's poems rely heavily on stories and people from the past, which give readers a sense of modern-day Irish sentiment. Heaney writes about his country's and his countrymen's violated past in a voice that reflects upon the violence of the present. Persons, animals, and objects resurrected from the brown peat—indeed, the peat itself—have all become the source and subject of Heaney's writings (Tobin 91). Through his poems, Heaney's strong attachment to the soil is apparent; in "The Tollund Man," Heaney makes reference to the "Cauldron bog/Our holy ground," from which the well-preserved body of an old hunter was exhumed. The poet's captivation with things buried and times past parallels his search for answers to not only the Irish nature, but of the human condition as well (Vendler 42, 43). He compares the uncovering of layers upon layers of peat to his own pen "digging into the rich soil of his mind" (Interview 12/15/99), and discovers that the same holds true for both: "The wet centre is bottomless ("Bogland")."

A strong connection with his homeland and his family has given Heaney much material to write upon. His early life was filled with hardships, few of which did not leave an impression on his character, and, thus, on his work. Perhaps it was the joy he found in his life away from Mossbawn with Marie Devlin, whom he married in 1965, and their two children, Michael and Christopher, which made him realize that he had missed the fun of childhood.

Heaney, however, was grateful to his parents and actually in awe of them—his father, in particular. One of his best-known poems, "Harvest Bow," praises his father's creative impulse, glorifies the unspoken joy of shared experiences between father and son, and details the attachment Heaney felt toward his dad (Vendler 74). Among Heaney's more moving poems are those eight

Ian used various types of details to support his thesis. This paragraph contains information from a source, lines of poetry written by the subject, and personal observations.

Ian used MLA style documentation within his report.

Much of the body of Ian's report is organized chronologically, tracing the events of Heaney's life.

sonnets entitled *Clearances*, written shortly after his mother's death.

> When all the others were away at Mass
> I was all hers as we peeled potatoes.
> They broke the silence, let fall one by one
> Like solder weeping off the soldering iron:
> (from "In Memoriam M.K.H., 1911–1984")

After his parents' deaths, Heaney remarked that he felt, for a time, "as if the roof [had] blown off my life." Being thus released from both the weight and the shield of his parents was simultaneously freeing and frightening to Heaney. Heaney's latest volume of poetry, *Seeing Things* (1991), is largely a tribute to his father.

Ireland's turbulent past is also a common theme in Heaney's work, and he often returns to the peat bogs in his poetry to draw connections between himself and the past. Heaney relates the killings of those centuries-dead persons pulled from the peat to modern-day executions and martyrs, commenting that although the times have changed, very little in public action or sentiment has; the Irish are still as stubborn as they ever were, still as apt to "cast, I know,/The stones of silence."

Seamus Heaney, who, along with William Butler Yeats and Louis MacNeice, is considered among the best of all Irish poets, draws his vital and vivid images from the land he grew up in—Ireland's plagued past and its tormented present. Although Heaney has become successful and famous, it is nonetheless his past and the strong connection he feels with it that will be ever apparent in his poetry:

> Out here in Jutland
> In the old man-killing parishes
> I will feel lost,
> Unhappy and at home.

Because this quotation is four lines long, it is styled as an excerpt.

Ian chose to end his report with some lines of Heaney's poetry. These lines help prove Ian's thesis, and they create a memorable ending for the report.

Ian lists the source information for material that he cited in his report.

Works Cited

Buttel, Robert. *Seamus Heaney/Irish Writers Series.* Lewisburg: Bucknell University Press, 1975.

Fried, Philip. Personal Interview. 15 Dec. 2000.

Heaney, Seamus. *Opened Ground, Selected Poems,* 1966–1996. New York: Farrar, Straus, and Giroux, 1998.

Pellegrino, Joe. Web Page: Seamus Heaney. **http://metalab.unc.edu/ dykki/poetry/heaney/heaney.bio.html**

Tobin, Daniel. *Passage to the Center: Imagination and the Sacred in the Poetry of Seamus Heaney.* Lexington: University Press of Kentucky, 1999.

Vendler, Helen. *Seamus Heaney.* Cambridge: Harvard University Press, 1998.

Connected Assignment
Multimedia Report

A **multimedia report** is similar to a research paper in that it states a thesis that is supported with evidence. The difference is in the presentation—a multimedia report conveys its message through visual, auditory, and print media. The preparer of a multimedia report can therefore choose the most suitable medium for the presentation of research findings. For example, you could illustrate a painter's growth by showing slides of paintings completed at different points in the artist's career. If you wanted to make an observation about musical styles popular in the days of King Louis XIV, you could play a recording of such music for the class.

An effective multimedia presentation

- states, develops, and supports a thesis.
- contains a variety of supporting information.
- presents information through a variety of media.
- engages an audience and accomplishes a specific purpose.
- is error free.

Develop your own multimedia report by following the writing process suggestions explained below.

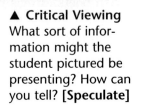

▲ Critical Viewing
What sort of information might the student pictured be presenting? How can you tell? **[Speculate]**

Prewriting

Choosing Your Topic Make a list of potential topics for your multimedia report. Then, choose two or three entries that interest you most. Copy those entries down on another list. For each, come up with ideas for how you would incorporate multimedia technology in its presentation. Finally, review your list and choose the topic most suited for a multimedia report.

Gathering Details Make a chart like the one on the following page to plan the types of media you will use in your presentation and the types of media you'll have to create and research. As you fill in the chart, strive to use a variety of types of media from a variety of sources.

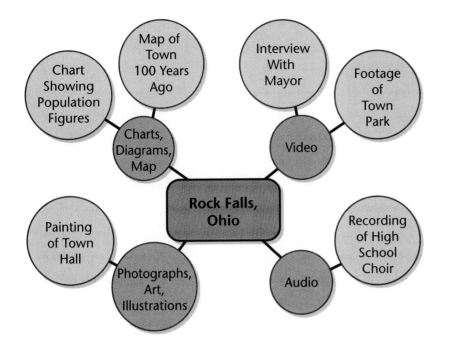

Drafting Because much of the information you find will be presented through visual or auditory media, shape your text in a script format, with your narration shown as dialogue. Within the script, explain the sequence and position of various media in stage direction format. Make sure to indicate what you or other helpers need to do to make alternative media accessible. For example, you may note in your report to point to specific elements or advance the slide projector.

Revising and Editing Critically examine the information you plan to present. Evaluate the information according to the following criteria: Make sure it is accurate; make sure it is interesting; and make sure it relates to your topic. Also, examine your word choice and choice of details to be sure that they are appropriate for your audience and help you to fulfill your purpose.

Publishing and Presenting Rehearse your multimedia presentation beforehand. Ask a family member or friend to watch your rehearsals. Practice using note cards and making eye contact with your audience. Also, make sure that you know how to operate all pieces of equipment you plan to use. Get feedback from your audience, and incorporate their suggestions wherever appropriate. Reduce or expand the time spent on each part of your presentation until it flows smoothly and retains audience interest.

Spotlight on the Humanities

Recognizing Art Forms

Focus on Dance: Agnes DeMille

If you were to do a research report on a famous family, the DeMille family would be an excellent choice. American choreographer and dancer Agnes DeMille (1905–1993) revolutionized the musical theater in 1943 with the Broadway show *Oklahoma!* by integrating choreography with plot. For the first time, dance numbers furthered the plot of a musical. In 1942, she created a major American ballet in *Rodeo,* which received twenty-two curtain calls at its premiere. The niece of Hollywood film producer Cecil B. DeMille, she danced and continued to tour with her dance company into the 1970's. In 1976, she received the Handel Medallion, which is New York's highest award for achievement in the arts.

Theater Connection Richard Rodgers (composer, 1902–1979) and Oscar Hammerstein (lyricist, 1895–1960) wrote eleven musicals in seventeen years, including the classic *Oklahoma!* with Agnes de Mille as choreographer. Beginning in 1943, Rodgers and Hammerstein created the musicals *Carousel, State Fair, South Pacific, The King and I,* and *Sound of Music.* In their lifetime, they garnered thirty-four Tony Awards, fifteen Academy Awards, two Pulitzer Prizes, and two Grammy Awards.

Film Connection Cecil B. DeMille (1881–1959), uncle of choreographer Agnes DeMille, is renowned for his monumental films, such as *Ten Commandments* (1923, 1956), *King of Kings* (1927), and *Greatest Show on Earth* (1952). Arriving in Hollywood in 1913 with Samuel Goldwyn and Jesse L. Lasky, he directed *The Squaw Man* that same year, which was one of the first full-length movies ever made.

Research Writing Application: Report on a Famous Family

Write a report on a famous family that you find interesting. You might choose to research a family active in politics, like the Roosevelts or the Kennedys, or you may choose to research a show-business family like the Bridgeses or the Baldwins.

▲ **Critical Viewing**
This photograph captures a moment from DeMille's Dream Ballet in *Oklahoma!* Does this scene seem realistic or dream-like to you? Explain. **[Criticize]**

Media and Technology Skills

Evaluating On-line Resources
Activity: Prepare an Annotated Web Index

Using the Internet successfully requires two complementary skills: finding the information you need and assessing the credibility of the information you locate. As you become an experienced Web surfer, you can share your evaluations of search engines and Web sites by building an annotated Web index to share with others.

Think About It Prepare a list of Web sites that you find particularly useful, misleading, poorly organized, or strongly biased. Identify your plan for your index before you sign on. For example, you might decide to review three search engines and six Web sites.

Locate It Search engines allow you to search the World Wide Web for specific information. The engine will search its database and present a list of every Web page that matches your search criteria. The number of matches, or hits, will vary because every engine uses a different search mechanism and has different Web sites in its database. Evaluate different search engines by trying the same search topic in three or four different search engines. Keep a chart like the one below to record the hits.

Search Engine	Search String	Number of Hits	Quality of Hits

Interpret It After evaluating search engines, analyze a set of related Web sites. For example, you might evaluate sites that relate to United States parks. When you enter a site for the first time, find out who has sponsored or produced the site. Evaluating authorship can help you uncover biases.

Many Web pages are written and published quickly. Do not assume that every fact on the Web has been verified. Always try to find at least one additional, reliable source for any fact or statistic you find.

Annotate It Finally, compile your annotated Web index. List the name and URL (address) of each site you visited. Describe the purpose of the content of the site, and explain any biases you uncovered. Finally, provide a rating to help your readers identify particularly helpful Web sites.

Varieties of Search Engines

Not every search engine on the Internet uses the same techniques. Notice the organization of your search results to evaluate a search engine and make use of its strengths.

- **Text searches:** Many search engines search through millions of Web pages to find the search string, or words, you entered. Sites using the string most frequently usually appear first on the list.
- **Category searches:** Some search engines group Web pages into related categories. Results are listed under topic classifications.
- **Group searches:** Some engines combine the results from several different search engines.

Standardized Test Preparation Workshop

Revising and Editing

One of the most important steps in writing a research paper is revising and editing. When taking a standardized test, you may be challenged by questions that test your ability to revise and edit a passage. Following are strategies that can help you address these types of questions:

- Critically evaluate a writer's word choice.
- Decide which information is irrelevant.
- When reading a passage, pay attention to how information could be clarified by adding more information.
- When reading a passage, note information that does not connect to the rest of the information being presented.
- Notice any commas that are placed incorrectly.
- Be sure that the proper tense is being used for verbs in the text.

The following sample test item will give you practice with questions on revising and editing.

Test Tip

Read the passage once and the questions that follow. Then, reread the passage before answering the questions. This will help you identify weaknesses and strengths in the paper.

Sample Test Item

Answer and Explanation

Sample Test Item	Answer and Explanation
Directions: Read the passage, and then answer the questions that follow. **1**Alexander Pope's mock-epic *The Rape of the Lock,* a tale about the theft of a lock of hair, are based on a real incident. **2**Two families, the Petres and the Fermors, became involved in a dispute when Robert Petre flirtatiously cut a lock of hair from the head of beautiful Arabella Fermor. **3**Pope wrote about this incident, in the hopes that a humorous poem would bring the families together.	

1. Which of the following changes is needed in the above passage?
 	
  A. Part 1: Change *are based* to *is based*.
 	
  B. Part 2: Change *became* to *becomes*.
 	
  C. Part 3: Change *wrote* to *written*.
 	
  D. Make no changes.
	The answer is *A*. Since the subject of the sentence *The Rape of the Lock* refers to a single poem, the verb must also be singular. Therefore, the singular verb phrase *is based* is correct.

Practice 1 **Directions:** Read the passage, and then answer the questions that follow. Choose the letter of the best answer.

1The obsession with fashion satirized by Alexander Pope in *The Rape of the Lock* was a genuine phenomenon of the upper classes in the 1700's. 2The world's first fashion magazine dates from 1785, and although it was French, fashion had become an international affair. 3Queen Marie Antoinette's hairdresser, Léonard, had stunned the world. 4He rolled her hair over pads of horse hair, then added accessories such as gauze and feathers to create elegant "hair statues" sometimes as high as four feet. 5His masterpiece, celebrating a French naval victory, transformed, waves of hair into a raging sea battering the sides of a French frigate in full sail. 6It was probably more difficult to do this with knotty hair. 7At war with France in fashion as well as on the battlefield, the English quickly responded to Léonard. 8English hairdressers decorated fashionable heads with horse-drawn carriages, zoos with miniature lions and tigers and, if accounts can be believed, a lit stove complete with pots and pans. 9For the most part, men of the period showed considerably less imagination when it came to hair. 10Among them are the Macaroni Club, a group of young men who wore bizarrely shaped wigs in order to annoy their conservative elders.

1. What is the best change, if any, to make in Part 1?
   A. Change *satirized* to *satirizes*.
   B. Change *lock* to *Lock*.
   C. Change *upper classes* to *upper class*.
   D. Make no change.

2. Which of the following changes, if any, is needed in the passage?
   A. Move Part 10 to the beginning of the passage.
   B. Delete Part 3.
   C. Delete Part 6.
   D. Make no change.

3. Which of the following should have a comma deleted?
   A. Part 2
   B. Part 10
   C. Part 5
   D. Part 8

4. Which of the following is the best way, if any, to combine the sentences in Part 3 and Part 4?
   A. Queen Marie Antoinette's hairdresser, Léonard, had stunned the world when he rolled her hair over pads of horse hair and added accessories such as gauze and feathers to create elegant "hair statues," some as high as four feet.
   B. Queen Marie Antoinette's hairdresser, Léonard, had stunned the world, and he rolled her hair over pads of horse hair, and then added accessories such as gauze and then he added feathers to create elegant "hair statues," sometimes as high as four feet.
   C. Queen Marie Antoinette's hairdresser, Léonard, had stunned the world; he rolled her hair over pads of horse hair and then added accessories such as gauze and feathers to create elegant "hair statues" sometimes as high as four feet.
   D. Make no change.

5. Which of these sentences would best fit after Part 9?
   A. Men weren't as interested in fashion.
   B. There were exceptions, however.
   C. They were very immature.
   D. A line from "Yankee Doodle" refers to these men.

Fond Memories, Michael Mortimer Robinson

Responding to Literature in Everyday Life

A talk-show host recommends a book she has been reading, and book sales skyrocket the next day. A rock band records a song based on an old Scottish folk tale. These responses to literature take place in everyday life. When you respond to literature, you might talk with friends about something you read, recommend it in an e-mail note, or write a letter to an author.

▲ Critical Viewing
Study the woman's expression in this painting. How would you describe her reaction to the book she's reading? **[Interpret]**

What Is a Response to Literature?

A **response to literature** is a nonfiction piece of writing that presents a reaction to or an analysis of one or more literary works. An effective response to literature usually

- identifies the work or works being discussed.

- supports the writer's interpretations with precise examples, citations, or quotations.

- is organized clearly and effectively.

- offers an opinion, a judgment, or an evaluation based on close scrutiny of specific elements.

To preview the criteria on which your response to literature may be evaluated, see the Self-Assessment Rubric on page 322.

Types of Responses to Literature

There are many different types of responses to literature. Your response might fall into one of these specific categories:

- **Reading journals** are notebooks in which to record your reactions and responses to works of literature.

- **Literary analyses** explain the literary elements that appear within a work, such as theme, character, plot, or meter.

- **Comparative analyses** compare two or more literary works, identifying relevant and instructive similarities and differences.

- **Critical reviews** identify a work's strengths and weaknesses and often present the reviewer's overall, supported evaluation.

Writers in ACTION

Poet and critic Eavan Boland emphasizes the strong mutual relationship between literature and readers that keeps texts fresh and vital:

"A poem or other work of literature is a little bit like a field that gets parched....The reader is like the rain, you see, so you want to keep bringing [literature] to the reader's attention and love and interest. This refreshes it. And every new generation brings a new view to it...."

PREVIEW Student Work IN PROGRESS

Samuel Taylor Coleridge's poem "Kubla Khan" has inspired a variety of responses in readers. In this chapter, you will see how Emily Elstad, a student at Tupelo High School in Tupelo, Mississippi, shaped her response to the poem into an effective essay. A completed draft of Emily's response can be found at the end of the chapter.

Eavan Boland's love of literature is reflected in her multifaceted writing, from poems to essays and criticism. This essay shares Boland's thoughts and feelings as she puzzled over a poem by Emily Dickinson.

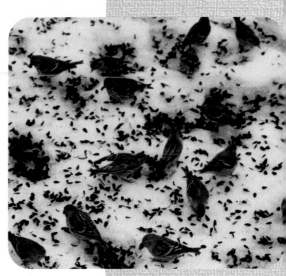

Reading Strategy: Draw Conclusions As you read, use clues within the text to draw conclusions about the author.

Reading Writing Connection

Meanings

Eavan Boland

 When I was seventeen my mother gave me a book of Emily Dickinson's poetry. We were standing in a room in a hotel when she handed it to me. It was summer. There was a gray, rainy light outside the window. She was returning to New York where she lived at that time with my father. I was staying in Dublin, getting ready to go back to boarding school for my last year.

She had a reason for giving it. I had gone to school for three years in New York, from age eleven to fourteen. I was beginning to forget the power and noise and drama of New York. I was beginning to forget the little of American poetry I had learned at school there. The whole experience of a different place was beginning to fade. And my mother wanted me to remember.

When she was gone and I was back in school I opened the book and began to read. Immediately I stumbled on one poem. It was so short it almost looked like a riddle:

> *Water is taught by thirst;*
> *Land, by the oceans passed;*
> *Transport by throe;*
> *Peace, by its battles told;*
> *Love by memorial mould;*
> *Birds by the snow.*

▲ **Critical Viewing** If you were to write a line of poetry inspired by this photograph, how would it go? **[Relate]**

Boland emphasizes the personal perspective of the essay by using the first-person point of view and opening with a description of how she first came to read Dickinson's poem.

Because this poem is short, Boland cites all of it. The citation allows readers to more fully understand Boland's response.

Now wait a moment, I said to myself—and, of course, by saying that I was already drawn into the poem. I can see perfectly well why you get to know something about water through being thirsty. I can see how you get to know about land by being on the sea. The little traveling I had done made me understand that you appreciated a car more when you had to walk. So that explained *Transport by throe.* And yes, peace became clearer in war. And love in memory. But what did the snow tell you about birds?

I couldn't forget the poem. Every time I opened the book it seemed to open at that page. I was so curious that I began to ask other people—friends, teachers—what they thought the line meant. No matter what they said, I was dissatisfied. I began to read about Emily Dickinson herself: that she lived in Amherst, Massachusetts, in the middle of the nineteenth century. That she was shy and solitary. That when she died her poems were found carefully sorted and tied by ribbon in what were called fascicles and looked like love letters. That out of the 1800 she kept, only ten were published in her lifetime. And that she said, in a letter describing herself, that her eyes were like "the sherry in the glass that the guest leaves."

Soon I knew the poem by heart and I was reading more. I loved the way her lines were short and out-of-breath and yet told so much, like someone who has run all the way to tell important news. And soon enough, the school term was ending. The autumn had become winter. I was excited because I was going back to New York for Christmas, for the first time since I had left. I packed my suitcase, stored her book away carefully.

Two days before I left, it began to snow. For a whole morning a crisp, light snow covered the grass and school buildings and obscured the blue of the Dublin hills. Snow was not an everyday part of an Irish winter. All morning, I kept looking out the window. And then I saw it: All at once I saw the line of poetry as if it had been written in the snow. There were birds outside on the grass. Blackbirds and thrushes, their wings tucked in, their beaks searching for food under the white crust. Suddenly I saw how they were made distinct—were *taught* just as the poem had said— in a way I had never seen before: Their wings. Their movements. Their dark heads. *Birds by the snow.* All at once the poem explained the world. And the world the poem.

Reading Writing Connection

Writing Application: As you prepare to write your response to literature, think about the conclusions you would like your readers to draw about you.

Boland presents a line-by-line analysis of the poem, explaining her interpretations.

This essay is organized chronologically, tracing Boland's efforts to assign meaning to the poem's final line.

Personal opinions, like this one, are one type of elaboration.

LITERATURE

"Outside History" is a poem by Eavan Boland. You'll find the poem in *Prentice Hall Literature: Timeless Voices, Timeless Themes,* The British Tradition.

Boland saves her final insight about the poem for the conclusion of her essay.

14.2 Prewriting

Choosing Your Topic

A response to literature begins with the literature itself. In some situations, the topic will be assigned. In others, you will choose the literature to which you will respond. Select works about which you feel strongly.

Strategies for Generating Topics

1. **Review Your Reader's Journal** Scan your reading journal to help you recall the works you have read and to revisit your initial reactions. As you browse through your notes, think about whether or not you still agree with everything you wrote. If you have changed your mind about a book or selection, you might write an essay to explain how your response has evolved over time. Choose to develop the topic about which you feel most strongly.

2. **Compile a List** Compile a list of possible works about which to write. When you make your list, add personal comments that record your instinctive reactions. For example, you might give your own ratings on a scale of one to five stars or assign three words that come to mind. When your list is complete, look for entries with high or low ratings or specific and intriguing words. Choose one such entry as a start for your response to literature.

Writing Lab CD-ROM

For more help finding a topic, explore the activities and topic suggestions in the Choosing a Topic section of the Response to Literature lesson.

Work	My Rating	Three Words
Frankenstein (Shelley)	★★★★★	fascinating, sad, mankind
The Tyger (Blake)	★★★	symbolic, illustrated, fearful
Infant Sorrow (Blake)	★	pessimistic, dark, depressing
The Rime of the Ancient Mariner (Coleridge)	★★★	rhythmic, long, guilt
Kubla Khan (Coleridge)	★★★★★	hypnotic, compelling, intense

3. **Flip Through a Source Book** You may have a literature anthology that contains works you have read and many that you would like to read. Read the introductory text to help you preview the literature, as well as the response questions to help you review selections you have already read. Use self-sticking notes to mark possible topics for your response. Then, review your notes, and select one topic to develop.

TOPIC BANK

For more specific topic suggestions, consider the ones below:

1. **Thematic Comparison** Choose two works that focus on a common theme. Then, describe similarities and differences in each presentation of the theme. You might, for example, consider comparing the theme of greed in Shakespeare's *Macbeth* and Milton's *Paradise Lost.*

2. **Literary Analysis of Character** Choose one literary character that had a strong impact on you, and describe that character's journey from the beginning to the end of the work. Explain how and why the character grew, identifying landmark events and realizations. You might consider title characters, such as Jane Eyre or Oliver Twist.

Responding to Fine Art

3. *Sean, Coco and Rumple,* by March Avery, depicts two interesting characters sharing a book. Study the painting, and then write a response that explores the growth of an interesting character.

Sean, Coco and Rumple, March Avery, Courtesy of the artist

Responding to Literature

4. Read "Sonnet 116," by William Shakespeare; "Love Among the Ruins," by Robert Browning; and "Sonnet 43," by Elizabeth Barrett Browning. Then, write a response in which you examine the speakers' ideas about love.

☑ Cooperative Writing Opportunity

5. **Readers' Guide** Work with a group to create a readers' guide to a number of selections in your literature anthology. Have each team member write a brief literary analysis of a different work. Then, collect and combine finished essays into a single volume. Share it with peers to give them an overview of a unit or chapter.

Narrowing Your Topic

Once you have chosen a work of literature to write about, focus your response. You might decide to concentrate on literary elements or on your personal reactions to the work. If you want to discuss literary elements, consider narrowing the scope of your response to a single important element, such as character, theme, setting, or tone. Use the strategy of looping to help you narrow your response to any work of literature.

Use Looping to Narrow a Topic

Looping is a brainstorming technique that helps you identify key ideas. Begin by writing freely on your response-to-literature topic for about five minutes. Read what you have written, and circle the most important or interesting idea. Then, write for five minutes on that idea. Continue this process until you discover a topic that is narrow enough to address fully and effectively in your essay.

Student Work
IN PROGRESS

Name: Emily Elstad
Tupelo High School
Tupelo, MS

Using Looping to Focus a Topic

Emily Elstad used looping to find a specific topic for her response to literature.

Broad topic: My response to "Kubla Khan"

Coleridge took medication before writing this poem. Then he fell asleep and when he woke up, wrote the poem. The landscape is very (dreamy.) Lots of detailed descriptions. Some references: Kubla Khan, Greek gods. When I read the poem I feel like I have entered his (dream.)

Dreams: How does Coleridge make me feel like I'm in his dream? He uses fragmented (images) that remind me of dreams. The (sounds) of the poem are hypnotic.

Narrowed topic: How Coleridge uses images and sounds to draw readers into a dream world.

Considering Your Audience and Purpose

Your general purpose in writing your response to literature is to share your reactions with an audience. Choose details and a writing style that will help you accomplish your purpose and appeal to your audience.

Satisfy Audience Expectations

Suppose that you talked about a piece of writing with a teacher, an author, and a friend. Consider how your conversation would change, depending on which person you were speaking to. You should be able to adjust your writing style to reach different audiences, too.

The following chart shows three specific audiences for whom you might write and provides strategies you can use to reach each audience.

Audience	Writing Examples	Audience Expectations	Strategies
Teacher	Class essays	A teacher is familiar with your previous work and will look for signs of growth and new accomplishments.	• Stretch yourself by choosing a more challenging topic. • If you are writing about a work discussed in class, relate additional insights.
Review Panel	Standardized tests College application essays	A review panel does not know your previous work. It is considering the quality of only one piece of your writing.	• Use formal language. • Exercise additional care when reviewing grammar and spelling.
Students	Book review for school newspaper	Students may or may not know you, but they expect that you will share your honest opinions.	• Use direct language that will appeal to student readers. • State your opinion clearly, and explain why you feel this way.

Gathering Details

Once you have decided on a narrow topic and considered your audience, gather details that will support your response.

Use the Hexagonal Writing Strategy

Use hexagonal writing to explore various aspects of your response to literature. Doing so will help you fully understand your response and will give maturity and depth to your writing. Following are the six levels of hexagonal writing:

Literal Level: Plot, Character, and Setting Give a concise retelling of plot events. Describe the characters and settings.

Personal Allusions Reveal the associations or memories this piece of literature brings to mind.

Themes Explore the theme or themes revealed in the literature.

Analysis of Literary Devices Explain the ways in which plot, setting, character, and theme work as separate elements, as well as how they work together.

Literary Allusions Describe other works that have similar elements or that come to mind when you read this work.

Evaluation Judge the work based on how well its literary elements combine to create an effective, fresh piece of literature.

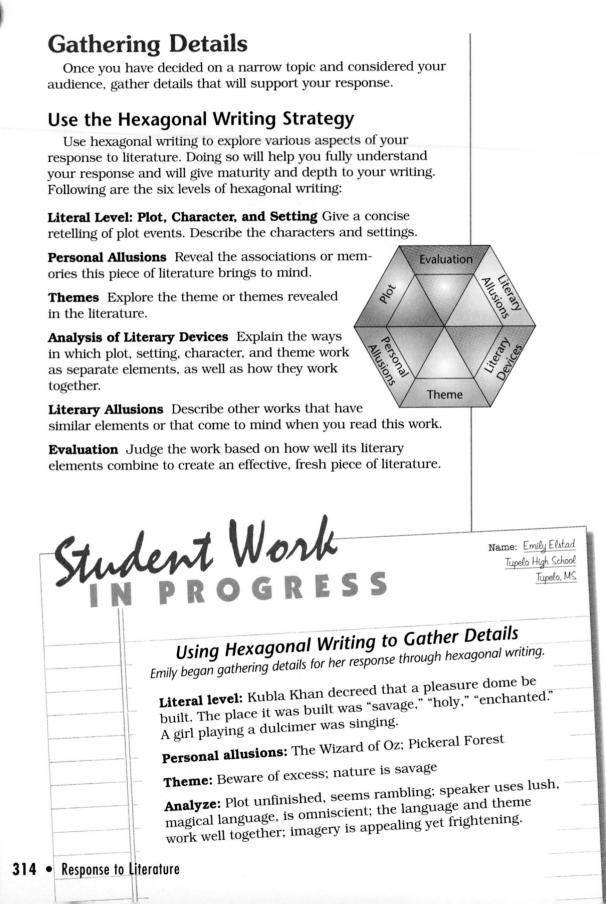

Student Work IN PROGRESS

Name: *Emily Elstad*
Tupelo High School
Tupelo, MS

Using Hexagonal Writing to Gather Details

Emily began gathering details for her response through hexagonal writing.

Literal level: Kubla Khan decreed that a pleasure dome be built. The place it was built was "savage," "holy," "enchanted." A girl playing a dulcimer was singing.

Personal allusions: The Wizard of Oz; Pickeral Forest

Theme: Beware of excess; nature is savage

Analyze: Plot unfinished, seems rambling; speaker uses lush, magical language, is omniscient; the language and theme work well together; imagery is appealing yet frightening.

14.3 Drafting

Shaping Your Writing
Use Nestorian Organization

"Saving the best for last" can be an effective organizational strategy for your response to literature. For example, in Nestorian organization, a proposition is presented in the introduction. Then, the second-best example or idea is developed, followed by reasons that decrease in impact or importance. The best example, the one that makes the strongest case, is saved for the conclusion.

SAMPLE OUTLINE SHOWING NESTORIAN ORGANIZATION

I. Introduction: Some readers believe that *Macbeth* shows the title character slowly losing his mind.

    A. "Some say he's mad," says one character.

    B. I disagree. I believe that Macbeth is weak, but not insane.   — Proposition

II. Lady Macbeth is mad.

    A. Lady Macbeth definitely goes mad, driven insane by her guilt.

    B. Shakespeare wants us to compare and contrast Macbeth and his wife. The contrast shows that Macbeth is not mad.   — 2nd most important point

III. Everything Macbeth does has a clear motivation.

    A. He kills the king to become king.

    B. He believes the witches because they tell him what he wants to hear.   — 3rd most important point

IV. Madness would weaken the point.

    A. The point of the play is that Macbeth was once noble, but is corrupted by ambition.

    B. That idea would be severely weakened if Macbeth is not accountable for his actions. Shakespeare clearly intends for us to hold Macbeth accountable.   — Most important point

Writing Lab CD-ROM

For help using various types of organizational strategies, use the interactive organizers in the Organizing Your Response section of the Response to Literature lesson.

Providing Elaboration

Elaborate on key ideas or statements by giving examples, referencing personal and literary allusions, and citing relevant passages from the text.

Cite Passages

You can use passages from the original text to provide an example of an author's style or tone, to highlight a specific literary device, or to support an interpretation. Consider these strategies when choosing passages to illustrate your ideas:

- Look for passages that are typical of the writer or work.
- Make sure the passages clearly show the characteristics you plan to discuss.
- Provide an introduction or context if your quotation needs it.
- Set off short passages with quotation marks. If you plan to use a quotation that is four lines or longer, set the passage off by using a narrower margin than you do for the rest of your response.

Student Work
IN PROGRESS

Name: Emily Elstad
Tupelo High School
Tupelo, MS

Citing Passages in a Draft

Emily incorporated lines from "Kubla Khan" as she drafted. She collected those lines earlier when she gathered details.

Coleridge uses alliteration to soothe the reader into a dreamy mood. Near the beginning of the poem, he describes the scene "Where Alph, the sacred river, ran/Through caverns measureless to man . . ." Coleridge conveys the never-ending flow of the river by the flow of words into one another. The repeated r sounds flow into the repeated m sounds, taking the reader to the dream world of Xanadu.

> These lines from the poem help Emily support the previous statement.

> Lines from the Poem
> "Where Alph, the sacred river, ran"
> "Through caverns measureless to man"
> Alliteration flows through these lines like the river flows.

 **Revising** (14.4)

During revision, find ways to strengthen your writing so that it communicates directly and effectively with your audience.

Revising Your Overall Structure

Consider Paragraph Order

As you review your draft, think about each paragraph as a unit, or chunk, of information. Ask yourself whether a different organization would strengthen the flow of ideas.

▶ **REVISION STRATEGY**
Rereading and Rearranging

If your response is organized in Nestorian order, evaluate the importance and effectiveness of each idea you present. You may find that what you thought would be your strongest argument or point is weaker than you had planned. If an earlier argument is more effective, move it to the end of the essay, to build to a powerful conclusion.

Revising Your Paragraphs

Eliminate Digressions

Each paragraph in your response should develop one central idea or perform a specific function, such as provide a transition. Identify the topic sentence or the function of each paragraph.

- If the paragraph has a topic sentence, make sure that all of the sentences and details relate directly to that topic. If not, eliminate or move unnecessary details.

- If the paragraph is functional, make sure that the details within it help it to perform that function. Eliminate any ideas that stray from the main purpose of the paragraph.

▶ **REVISION STRATEGY**
Coding Supporting Material in Topical Paragraphs

As you review topical paragraphs, use two different-colored pencils or use circling and underlining. Circle the topic sentence in each paragraph. Circle in another color or underline all the details within that paragraph that support the topic sentence.

When you have finished, examine your markings. Look closely at material that has not been circled or underlined. Consider eliminating that material, or revise it so that it has a purpose for being there.

 **Technology Tip**

If you are using a word processor, rearrange paragraphs using cut-and-paste tools. Try several different ways to present your paragraphs. Then, choose the organization you find most effective.

Revising Your Sentences
Clarify Your Comparisons

You will make many different kinds of comparisons when you write a response to literature. You might compare two works by the same author, two lines from the same poem, or two different techniques used in the same work. Regardless of what you are comparing, you need to make sure that your audience can easily understand your comparison.

▶ **REVISION STRATEGY**
Circling and Boxing Comparisons

Use this strategy to check that your comparisons are clear and logical:

1. Circle any comparisons you make in your draft. Look for adjectives or adverbs in the comparative or superlative (scan for *more, most, -er, -est,* and common irregulars).
2. When you find a comparison, draw a box around the names of the things being compared.
3. Make sure that if you have boxed two items, you use the comparative degree. If you have boxed three or more items, use the superlative degree.

Technology Tip

Use the Find feature in your word-processing program to locate words with *-er* and *-est* endings. Then, if the word found is a comparison, check to be sure you have used the correct comparative form.

Student Work
IN PROGRESS

Name: Emily Elstad
Tupelo High School
Tupelo, MS

Using Boxes to Check Comparisons

As she was revising her work, Emily strengthened two comparisons in order to make sure they were logical and clear.

Although the poem's images and characters are effective, Coleridge's use of sound effects is ~~more~~ the most effective as they create his dream world.

Grammar in Your Writing
Comparisons

You will use adjectives and adverbs to make **comparisons**. Most adjectives and adverbs have different forms to show degrees of comparison. The three degrees of comparison are the *positive*, the *comparative*, and the *superlative*.

	Positive	Comparative	Superlative
Regular			
Adjectives	fast	faster	fastest
	beautiful	more beautiful	most beautiful
Adverbs	quickly	more quickly	most quickly
Irregular			
Adjectives	bad	worse	worst
	good	better	best
Adverbs	much	more	most
	well	better	best

- Use the **comparative degree** to compare two people, places, or things:

  Lady Macbeth becomes corrupt **more** quickly than Macbeth.

- Use the **superlative degree** to compare three or more people, places, or things:

  Macbeth is the **most** fascinating character in the play. (The superlative degree is used to compare Macbeth with all the other characters in the play.)

- When comparing one of a group with the rest of the group, make sure that your sentence contains the word *other* or the word *else*. In the example below, you need to add the word *other* because the poem is one of the poems *she wrote:*

Illogical: The poem is **more** romantic than any poem she wrote.

Logical: The poem is **more** romantic than any **other** poem she wrote.

Find It in Your Reading Read through "Meanings" on pages 308–309 to find a comparison in the comparative degree. Explain why Boland chose the comparative rather than the superlative degree.

Find It in Your Writing Review your draft to identify any comparisons you make. Make sure that your comparisons are correct and logical.

For more on comparisons, see Chapter 24.

Revising Your Word Choice

Revise Words to Achieve Your Purpose

Review the word choices you have made in your response. Replace any words that are inaccurate, dull, or vague with better choices.

▶**REVISION STRATEGY**
Circling and Replacing Dull Words

Reread your draft, focusing on your choice of words. When you come to a word that seems dull, obvious, or predictable, circle it. When you have read through your entire draft, replace circled words with more effective alternatives. Be careful, however, not to select alternate words simply because they are interesting. Make sure that your vivid word choices really say what you mean to say.

Peer Review

A peer reviewer can make suggestions for improving your writing. Share your response to literature with a peer before you share it with the world.

Prepare a Response Sheet

Give a copy of your revised draft to a partner. When your partner has read your response, ask him or her to fill in a response sheet like the following to identify strong elements in your writing, as well as those that could use improvement.

> **Response Sheet**
>
> 1. What is the main idea of my essay?
>
> 2. Are any passages confusing? Explain.
>
> 3. Is my word choice interesting and appropriate? Explain.

14.5 Editing and Proofreading

Make sure that your writing is error-free by fixing errors in spelling, punctuation, and grammar.

Focusing on Proofreading

Double-check every text citation and quotation you have included. Make sure that you copied passages and quotations accurately from the original source. Also, check to be sure you have placed quotation marks around the author's exact words.

Grammar in Your Writing
Quotation Marks

Quotation marks are used frequently in responses to literature. Following are some guidelines for using quotation marks:

Titles of Short Works: Use quotation marks around the titles of short poems, stories, or essays.

> "Kubla Khan"   "The Rocking-Horse Winner"

Titles of Long Works—such as novels, plays, nonfiction books, or long poems. Underline or use italics to indicate these titles.

> Oliver Twist   Macbeth   Walden   Paradise Lost

Cited Passages: Use quotation marks around any words, lines, or passages you quote directly from another source.

> Coleridge refers to a "woman wailing."
>
> How did you feel when you first read "In Xanadu did Kubla Khan/A stately pleasure dome decree"?

Find It in Your Reading In "Meanings" by Eavan Boland, on pages 308–309, one passage is enclosed in quotation marks. Locate the passage, and explain why quotation marks are necessary.

Find It in Your Writing As you proofread your response to literature, review your usage of quotation marks to be sure they are correct.

To learn more about using quotation marks, see Chapter 27.

Publishing and Presenting

Consider these ideas for publishing and presenting your writing:

Building Your Portfolio

1. **Discussion Group** Share your responses with a group of readers. Allow all group members to read from their responses or to summarize their most important ideas. Then, take turns asking questions to compare and contrast opinions within the group.

2. **Critical Anthology** Compile responses in a classroom anthology. Decide on the order in which to present the responses, and compile a table of contents. Design a cover for the anthology, and put a copy in the school library.

Reflecting on Your Writing

Reflect on the experience of writing a response to literature. Use these questions to spark your reflection:

• How did your response to the work change or develop from the time you finished reading to the time you finished writing?

• What aspects of the work became clearer to you through writing about them?

 **Internet Tip**

To see model essays scored with this rubric, go to **www.phschool.com**

Rubric for Self-Assessment

Use the following criteria to evaluate your response to literature.

	Score 4	Score 3	Score 2	Score 1
Audience and Purpose	Presents sufficient background on the work(s); presents the writer's reactions forcefully	Presents background on the work(s); presents the writer's reactions clearly	Presents some background on the work(s); presents the writer's reactions at points	Presents little or no background on the work(s); presents few of the writer's reactions
Organization	Presents points in logical order, smoothly connecting them to the overall focus	Presents points in logical order and connects them to the overall focus	Organizes points poorly in places; connects some points to an overall focus	Presents information in a scattered, disorganized manner
Elaboration	Supports reactions and evaluations with elaborated reasons and well-chosen examples	Supports reactions and evaluations with specific reasons and examples	Supports some reactions and evaluations with reasons and examples	Offers little support for reactions and evaluations
Use of Language	Shows overall clarity and fluency; uses precise, evaluative words; makes few mechanical errors	Shows good sentence variety; uses some precise evaluative terms; makes some mechanical errors	Uses awkward or overly simple sentence structures and vague evaluative terms; makes many mechanical errors	Presents incomplete thoughts; makes mechanical errors that cause confusion

14.7 Student Work IN PROGRESS

FINAL DRAFT

Paisaje, (Cinco Pagodas), Alejandro Solar

"Kubla Khan": A Response

Emily Elstad
Tupelo High School
Tupelo, Mississippi

◄ **Critical Viewing**
What sort of poem
might this landscape
inspire? Explain.
[Analyze]

In his short but intense poem "Kubla Khan," Samuel Taylor
Coleridge envisions a dream world filled with exotic landscapes
and creatures. The cumulative effect of the poet's rich use of language and imagery is hypnotizing and nearly overwhelming. It
is a re-creation of a dark dream—a product of Coleridge's unique
imagination.

The origin of the poem explains the source of the dreamy
quality. Coleridge apparently wrote this poem while in a medicat-

*Emily identifies the
poem, author, and
her thesis in the
opening paragraph.*

ed daze. Falling asleep while reading about Kubla Khan, he awoke with his head filled with richly poetic lines. This background is sufficient explanation for the lack of narrative in the poem. The poet simply paints the picture of his dream.

These details came from researching the life of Coleridge.

The description of the landscape reminds me of the deep but fading details of a remembered dream. Coleridge describes a garden surrounded by a wall that encloses caves of ice. He envisions fountains, flowers, forests, and crevices. In addition to this lush and exotic scenery, Coleridge includes fragmented characters. He describes a "damsel with a dulcimer" playing "symphony and song." Coleridge (or the speaker) suggests that he could turn her song into the pleasure dome in the air. These odd and specific details contribute to the overall imagery of a dream.

In the final image, the dream turns into a nightmare. Coleridge gives a picture of Kubla Khan as a man with "flashing eyes" and "floating hair." He is diabolical; he has drunken the "milk of Paradise" and, one assumes, has gained some sort of magical or unworldly power—possibly immortality. He seems to have an inexorable power, one that casts a trance over the women in the poem.

Passages from the poem are cited to illustrate and support Emily's statements.

Although the poem's visuals are effective, Coleridge's use of sound effects is even more effective as they help create his dream world. The sounds and rhythms of the poem work together to hypnotize the reader. Repetition is one of the key devices Coleridge uses to create this effect. The phrase "the sacred river, ran through caverns measureless to man" is repeated twice, changed only slightly. This emphasizes the fact that the cavern, as well as the whole fantastical world, is incomprehensible to humans; it is a world for immortals only.

This paragraph opens with a statement of opinion, which Emily supports in the rest of the paragraph.

Alliteration, too, is a key device that transports the reader into Coleridge's dream world. Take, for example, the lines near the beginning of the poem, "Where Alph, the sacred river, ran/ Through caverns measureless to man . . ." The lines help convey the never-ending flow of the river because the words themselves flow into each other. The repeated r sounds flow into the repeated m sounds, lulling the reader into a dreamlike state. "Kubla Khan" contains many such examples of alliteration, such as "sunny spots," "woman wailing," and "meandering with a mazy motion."

Emily has chosen Nestorian organization for her response to literature. She began with her second-most important point, following with points in descending order of importance. She saved her strongest point for last.

Although "Kubla Khan" is said to have been written in one draft as a transcription of a dream of Coleridge, it is a short masterpiece, in which the poet's use of imagery and sound effects draws the reader into the realm of the fantastic. The kingdom of Xanadu is vivid and unforgettable—as, perhaps, was Coleridge's fateful dream.

Emily concludes with a restatement of her insights.

Connected Assignment *Music Review*

Before buying the latest CD by your favorite band, do you read the critic's reviews? Like other responses to literature, **music reviews** analyze the features of a work and put forth an opinion about that work. Rather than merely summarizing the work, music reviews analyze the music, the lyrics, the originality and effectiveness. Reviews also give credit to the album's key creative forces and recommend it (or not) to readers.

Write a music review about a song, concert, or CD you've heard. Use the writing process skills outlined below as a guide.

Prewriting Choose a song or CD about which to write a review. Then, begin gathering details about the work. As you gather details, organize them into "pro" and "con" categories, listing them, if you wish, on a two-column chart. For each entry, provide one or more specific details from the music that exemplify your reaction. Review your chart or list to decide whether it supports a positive or a negative recommendation to your readers.

▲ **Critical Viewing**
What unique aspects of this performance would you address in a music review? **[Analyze]**

Drafting Start by identifying the work's title and artist. Establish your opinion or recommendation to readers directly by stating it in the first paragraph. Then, describe the music, using descriptive nouns, verbs, and modifiers to help readers "hear" the music and understand its structure and message. Elaborate on your initially stated opinion by analyzing specific features such as lyrics, pacing, or arrangement.

Revising and Editing Ask a peer to read your review for clarity and impact. If necessary, reword your opinion statement, insert more precise evaluative modifiers, or add examples to support your views. Check your title punctuation, using quotation marks for specific song titles but underlining or italics for CD or album titles.

Publishing and Presenting Hold a music discussion group with classmates. Take turns playing selections of music that you are reviewing and reading your review aloud to peers. After each presentation, briefly discuss the opinions of group members.

Spotlight on the Humanities

Examining Various Media
Focus on Music: Tone Poems

Just as a good book or powerful painting may stir a response from the reader or viewer, artists often respond to other art forms by creating another work of art inspired by the original piece. Written from ideas that came from poems, paintings, dramas, natural landscapes, or sources other than music, the **tone poem** is a nineteenth- and twentieth-century musical phenomenon that consists of one movement, or section. Its early composers were the Hungarian piano virtuoso and composer Franz Liszt (1811–1886) and the French composer Hector Berlioz (1803–1869). Claude Debussy's tone poem *Prelude to the Afternoon of a Faun* (1894) was inspired by the French poet Stéphane Mallarmé.

Literature Connection French poet Stéphane Mallarmé (1842–1898) was a teacher most of his life who supplemented his income as a poet. His work explored the differences between an ideal world and the natural world. Rather than having a sunlit day in reality, Mallarmé believed that the poet could create the "notion" of a sunlit day. In 1876, he completed his dramatic poem "Afternoon of a Faun," which inspired Claude Debussy's tone poem years later.

Art Connection German painter and illustrator Wilhelm von Kaulbach (1805–1874) was a prolific artist who was part of the German Romantic movement in the nineteenth century. He illustrated the poetry of such great writers as William Shakespeare and Johann Goethe. On walls in Berlin and Munich, he created huge murals that resembled the work of the Renaissance artist Raphael. Composer Franz Liszt's tone poem *Hunnenschlacht* (1857) was inspired by Kaulbach's historical painting *The Battle of the Huns.*

Response Writing Activity: Response to a Tone Poem
Listen to one of the tone poems mentioned above or another tone poem that a music teacher recommends. Then, write a response to the piece. Discuss what you liked about it and how it differed from the music you usually listen to. Did the piece capture the feel of the art that influenced it? Why or why not?

Claude Debussy, Marcel Baschet

▲ **Critical Viewing**
What effect does this painting's colors have on its overall mood? Explain.
[**Examine Causes and Effects**]

Media and Technology Skills

Responding Using Technology

Activity: Video Adaptation of a Story

A memorable story, character, or theme can often be transplanted from a historical setting to a contemporary one in order to emphasize common threads between eras. Use your response to a short story or novel as a jumping off point to create a video adaptation set today.

Think About It Choose a work that you believe has a strong relevance for today's viewers, regardless of its original setting. Choose a short story or a section of a longer novel or play. For example, rather than update all of *Frankenstein*, you might produce an updated version of the scene in which the scientist confronts his creation.

Update It Begin by choosing an overall setting for your updated retelling. In addition to changing the setting, you might also alter the ages of the central characters to reflect your peer group. For example, you might update *The Tragedy of Macbeth* by writing a drama about the drastic steps a high-school student takes to achieve political power at school.

Next, brainstorm ideas for your modernization by listing the key elements of your source material. Think of how you can maintain the essential qualities of a character or background in your chosen environment.

Script It You might improvise with other students to help you write dialogue for your script. Use the original story as a launching point for key plot events, but try to generate dialogue that clearly reflects your new setting. Record your improvisations with audio- or video-cassettes, and then transcribe the best lines for use in your shooting script.

Film It Rehearse your script, and then film it in appropriate locations. Shoot several versions of each scene, selecting the best takes during editing. Share the finished film with an audience without identifying the original source. After the screening, discuss the project and see whether viewers recognized the inspiration for your film.

Materials
- video camera
- single-deck or double-deck video-cassette recorder
- audio recorder

Updating Tips
Try these strategies to remove any "old" feeling from the source you are modernizing.
- Use contemporary music in the soundtrack.
- Rename characters with historical or literary names. For example, you might change Hamlet to Henry or Hannah.
- Choose settings that feel modern, such as a computer lab, airport, or electronics store.

◀ **Critical Viewing** This still is from a film adaptation of Jane Austen's *Emma*. What details in this still reveal that it takes place in the past? **[Analyze]**

Standardized Test Preparation Workshop

Responding to Prompts About Literature

You will frequently be asked on standardized tests to write in response to a literary prompt—to comment on a provided piece of literature and support your analysis with examples. You will be evaluated on your ability to do the following:

- develop a clearly stated responsive position
- present effective supporting examples and details
- organize ideas in a logical manner
- apply proper grammar, usage, and mechanics

When you write for a test, use the same writing stages as you would for any writing assignment, but be aware of how much time you devote to each. Below is a poem followed by a standardized test writing prompt. Use the suggestions on the next page to help you formulate your response.

Test Tip

When writing a literary response for a test, place quotation marks around examples taken from the literary text.

Sample Writing Situation

> Read the following sonnet by William Shakespeare:
>
> #### Sonnet 130
>
> My mistress' eyes are nothing like the sun,
> Coral is far more red than her lips' red;
> If snow be white, why then her breasts are dun;
> If hairs be wires, black wires grow on her head.
> 5 I have seen roses damasked, red and white,
> But no such roses see I in her cheeks;
> And in some perfumes is there more delight
> Than in the breath that from my mistress reeks.
> I love to hear her speak. Yet well I know
> 10 That music hath a far more pleasing sound.
> I grant I never saw a goddess go;
> My mistress, when she walks, treads on the ground.
>   And yet, by heaven, I think my love as rare
>   As any she belied with false compare.
>
> Many traditional love sonnets place the object of their devotion upon a pedestal. "Sonnet 130" describes a different attitude toward love. Write a literary analysis of the poem in which you examine its structure, sentiment, and effectiveness. Use specific examples from the sonnet as support.

Prewriting

Allow about one quarter of your time for developing your response and identifying supporting details.

Write a Thesis Statement Your thesis statement lets your readers know the main idea of your response. Write a statement that clearly states your main idea about the sonnet.

List Details After writing your thesis statement, generate a list of details from the poem that directly support your main idea. Also, list your own opinions as well as personal and literary allusions and suitable examples and quotations.

Drafting

Allow about half of your time for drafting. Write neatly, and allow space for revision changes.

Organize Ideas Introduce your main idea or thesis statement in your introduction. Using the ideas in your list, organize them into groups. Discuss each of these groups in one of the body paragraphs. Finally, summarize your main points in your conclusion.

Elaborate As you draft, weave together details that reveal and support your ideas. Give examples, both from the sonnet as well as from your own experience and prior knowledge.

Revising

Allow about one quarter of your time for revising.

Check for Clarity As you review your work, make sure your references to the poem are clear. If a reference to the poem is not clearly explained, either omit it or neatly add necessary information.

Check Support Reread your response, and carefully discriminate between details that directly relate to the prompt and those that do not. Although some details may provide interesting insights, they may be distracting because they do not relate directly to the prompt. Eliminate these details by neatly drawing a line through them.

Editing and Proofreading

Allow about five minutes to review your essay for spelling, punctuation, and grammar errors.

Make Final Changes Read your response a final time, checking for errors in spelling or punctuation. Make changes by neatly placing a line through text to be omitted and using a caret [^] to show where new text should be inserted.

Writing for Assessment

Before the Nine O'Clock Bell, Jane Wooster Scott, Buckley School Collection

Assessment in School

How often have you heard or uttered these sentences: "Did you study for the science exam?" "Did you finish your history essay?" "I hope the test is multiple choice."

You have probably become used to being tested frequently. Tests may take many forms—from essays to short-answer quizzes to standardized timed tests. With some preparation and some basic test-taking skills, most students can perform well on tests—both timed and nontimed—enabling their teachers to evaluate accurately how much students have learned.

▲ **Critical Viewing**
Would you say this is a realistic portrayal of a classroom or an idealized one? Explain. **[Criticize]**

What Is Assessment?

An **assessment** is an evaluation. You might be assessed on the amount of information you have acquired, how well you can solve problems, or where you stand academically compared with other students in your class.

Most people who make assessments look for

- correct answers or responses that match the question asked.
- clearly stated main points that are supported with details.
- writing that is organized logically.
- correct grammar, spelling, and punctuation.

To preview the criteria on which your writing may be evaluated, see the Rubric for Self-Assessment on page 339.

No matter what type of writing you do, if it is read by someone, it will be assessed or evaluated. Writer Bill Wheeler has the following to say about what makes writing effective: "Good writing is clear thinking made visible."

Types of Assessment

Many types of tests and essays help educators assess your ability to write. Among the tests you may be asked to take are the following:

- **Timed tests** may take many forms. They access a student's familiarity with the tested topics.
- **Short-answer tests** require brief answers, ranging from a word or phrase to a few sentences for each question.
- **Analyses** are critical papers in which the structural components of a work are examined and evaluated or compared and contrasted.
- **Personal essays** reveal the unique experiences and insights of the writer.

Scott Sang-Hyun Lee, a student at Duncanville High School in Duncanville, Texas, wrote a personal essay for a college application. Follow along as he drafts and revises his essay. Scott's completed essay appears at the end of the chapter.

15.1 Prewriting

Choosing Your Topic

On some tests, you will be given one or more essay prompts to which you have to respond. In other instances, you will be given a choice of topics. Following are strategies to help you make this decision:

Strategies for Choosing an Essay Prompt

- **Read all of the prompts and then decide:** Don't simply read the first prompt and decide to answer it. Take the time to read all of the prompts. Then, choose to answer the prompt to which you can best respond.

- **Eliminate first:** Read the prompts and decide which questions baffle you or about which you're unsure, and avoid them.

- **Choose the question for which you have the most answers:** As you read the list of questions, rapidly think of evidence or details you could use to make your point. Choose to answer the question for which you have the most support.

- **Pay attention to what the question is asking:** If one question requires you to compare and contrast two or more topics and another asks you to trace the causes of an event, choose to answer the one you can organize more clearly in your mind.

TOPIC BANK

Following are some essay-test questions. If you plan to practice writing for assessment, choose one of these or ask your teacher to provide you with one.

1. In an essay, examine the impact that the Great Depression had on American politics in the decades that followed.
2. In a letter to the school board, argue for or against school newspapers being given absolute free speech, with no censorship from faculty advisors.
3. Explain "magical realism," and identify and examine a literary work that falls within that category.
4. Compare and contrast the literary contributions of the Romantic poets William Wordsworth and Samuel Taylor Coleridge.

Narrowing Your Response

Before you start writing your response, take a few moments to identify what the focus of your response will be.

Locate Key Words

Reread the question you're answering, and locate what you're being asked to do. For example, are you being asked to compare and contrast, analyze, reflect, trace the history of something, support an idea, or argue against an idea?

Form a Main Idea

Once you locate the key word, write down the main idea, or thesis, you will present in your response. Keep this idea in mind as you quickly gather details and plan an organization for your response.

Identify Your Audience and Purpose

Reread the prompt to see whether an audience or purpose has been specified. If so, keep them in mind as you gather details for your essay. If an audience and purpose have not been specified, identify them for yourself and gather details accordingly.

Student Work
IN PROGRESS

Name: *Scott Sang-Hyun Lee*
Duncanville High School
Duncanville, TX

Locating Key Words and Forming a Main Idea
Scott Sang-Hyun Lee wanted to make sure that he responded well to the question posed on the college application he was completing.

Scott jotted down key words in the essay question.

Personal Essay: Discuss a past experience that contributed in large part to who you are today.

Main Idea: My parents' struggle made me stronger.

This main idea will become the focus for Scott's essay.

Drafting

Shaping Your Writing

Plan a Structure

Before you draft, quickly sketch an organizational plan. You may want to make an outline or some other type of graphic organizer to be sure that your points are clearly and logically organized. Following are some organizations you might consider:

Comparison and Contrast Use this method of organization if you are asked to examine similarities and differences, choose one option from among several, compare an author's works, or argue for one thing over another.

Point by Point: Within each paragraph, examine one point of similarity or difference.

Subject by Subject: First examine all the features of one topic. Then, examine all the features of the second.

Chronological Organization This method of organization is effective when you're asked to trace causes and effects, examine the history of something, or tell a personal story.

Nestorian Organization When you are writing persuasively, this type of organization can be very effective.

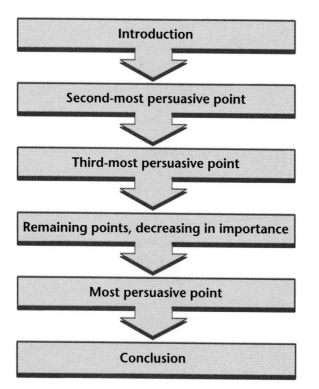

> ### 💿 Technology Tip
>
> If you are taking your test on-line, use the cut-and-paste feature to help you move around material to fit your organization.

Providing Elaboration

As you draft, make your writing convincing and give it depth by providing elaboration—details that define, explain, support, or illustrate your points.

Include Various Details

- **Details That Define** Be specific in your writing. Provide definitions to show that you fully understand the subject matter about which you're writing.

- **Details That Explain** Give reasons for your statements.

- **Details That Support** Cite statistics, expert testimony, and examples from life to make your arguments strong and convincing.

- **Details That Illustrate** Create graphs, sketches, or charts that present your points clearly and effectively.

Student Work
IN PROGRESS

Name: Scott Sang-Hyun Lee
Duncanville High School
Duncanville, TX

Providing Details

As he drafted his personal essay, Scott provided various types of elaboration.

This statement gives background information and explains why Scott's parents acted as they did.

My parents' mission was to sacrifice what would have been a comfortable life in their own country for a humble, and often humiliating, existence in a foreign world so that my brother and I could reap the benefits of their labor. Soon after arriving in the States, my father enrolled in graduate school, knowing so little English that entire lectures were blurry collages of unfamiliar sounds. Sometimes, I picture him—my father, my hero—feeling like a failure, disoriented by the swirl of foreign words. . . .

This sentence gives factual information about what happened next.

Here, Scott helps his readers identify with his father's experience.

 Revising

Revising Your Overall Structure

If you are writing under a time restriction, you may not be able to spend much time revising. Use your own knowledge of your writing habits to decide on the areas of your essay most likely to require revision.

▶ **REVISION STRATEGY**
Revisiting Your Introduction and Conclusion

Introductions and conclusions can have a great impact on how well your writing is judged. The following ideas can help you to strengthen your introduction and conclusion: (1) Add an interest-grabbing sentence to the introduction. (2) Write a transitional sentence to lead from the introduction to the body of your writing. (3) Reword the final sentence in the conclusion to give it more impact.

Revising Your Paragraphs

▶ **REVISION STRATEGY**
Deleting Unnecessary Details to Create Unity

Check to be sure that each paragraph helps develop or explain the main point of your essay. If not, delete or rewrite the paragraph. Then, read each paragraph carefully. If any sentences within the paragraph do not support the topic, move or delete them.

Student Work
IN PROGRESS

Name: Scott Sang-Hyun Lee
Duncanville High School
Duncanville, TX

Deleting Unnecessary Details to Create Unity
After reviewing his paragraphs, Scott made the following changes to create unity.

It is a challenge I accept because they first accepted it. ~~Their selfless love affects me in broader ways.~~ My fulfillment of their dream is not an idyllic state that I will reach only in adulthood; instead, it is something I achieve every day in who I am and what I do. ~~My happiness now comes in living humbly.~~

Revising Your Sentences

When writing quickly, it is easy to make mistakes. One common mistake is the unintentional switch of verb tenses. When you revise, be sure that you correct such mistakes.

▶**REVISION STRATEGY**
Scanning Verbs to Check for Unintentional Switches

One way to tell whether you've switched verb tenses is to scan your writing, looking for verbs. Identify the tense of each verb as you read. If, for instance, within one paragraph you find three past tense verbs and one present tense verb, you may have made an unintentional tense change.

EXAMPLE:

Participation in sports promotes teamwork, helps build leadership, and teaches players to strive for victory yet accept defeat gracefully. When you join a team, you learn life lessons. You ~~will have built~~ build self-confidence, too.

Revising Your Word Choice

Each word counts when you write for assessment. Critically examine the word choices you have made, and make sure that you have used transitions to connect your ideas.

▶**REVISION STRATEGY**
Adding Transitions to Make Connections Clear

Transitional words and phrases indicate relationships between ideas, enabling readers to follow your thoughts.

- If you have used comparison-and-contrast organization, you may want to add transitions such as *on the other hand, similarly, likewise,* or *contrary to.*

- If you have used chronological organization, you may want to add transitions such as *first, next, last, finally,* and *after that.*

- If you have used cause-and-effect organization, you may want to add transitions such as *consequently, because, after that,* and *due to.*

15.4 Editing and Proofreading

Focusing on Spelling

Misspellings and typographical errors convey to readers that your work is sloppy and carelessly written. Be sure to proofread carefully to catch such mistakes. Use the following strategies, depending on your assignment:

Open-Book and Nontimed Essays Use the spell-check tool if you are working electronically. Use a dictionary if you are writing in longhand.

Timed-Test Essays If you are aware of the mistakes you most often make in spelling, peruse your writing for such mistakes now. Otherwise, check for common errors, such as misspellings in "*i* before *e* words" and homophones.

Grammar in Your Writing
Homophones

Homophones are words that sound alike but have different spellings and meanings. When you write quickly, as in test-taking situations, you might mistakenly write the wrong homophone. Proofread your essay, and pay special attention to homophones such as *it's* and *its; there, their,* and *they're; to, too,* and *two;* and *your* and *you're.* Be sure that you've correctly spelled the homophone you intend.

its/it's	To give the organization **its** due, they employ many young students.
	It's a good idea to pack lightly.
your/you're	It is **your** responsibility.
	You're the only one who can make a difference.
hear/here	Can you **hear** the music?
	Put the empty boxes over **here.**
sight/cite	The tourist went to see the **sights.**
	Don't forget to **cite** your sources.

Find It in Your Writing As you proofread your essay, check that you have written all homophones correctly.

For more on spelling homophones, see Chapter 29.

15.5 Publishing and Presenting

Building Your Portfolio

1. **Portfolio** Save your completed essay in your portfolio. Attach a small note on which you describe when and where you took this test.

2. **Guidance Counselor** Give a copy of your writing to your guidance counselor for his or her review. Then, make an appointment with the counselor to discuss how best to take advantage of your writing skills.

Reflecting on Your Writing

Take a few moments to think about writing for assessment. Then, answer the following questions, and save your responses in your portfolio.

- Were you satisfied with the question you chose to answer? Why or why not?

- Which stage of the writing process did you find most useful as you wrote for assessment? Why?

💻 Internet Tip

To see essays scored with this rubric, go to
www.phschool.com

Rubric for Self-Assessment

Use the following criteria to evaluate your writing:

	Score 4	Score 3	Score 2	Score 1
Audience and Purpose	Uses appropriately formal diction; clearly addresses writing prompt	Uses mostly formal diction; adequately addresses writing prompt	Uses some informal diction; addresses writing prompt	Uses inappropriately informal diction; does not address writing prompt
Organization	Presents a clear, consistent organizational strategy	Presents a clear organizational strategy with few inconsistencies	Presents an inconsistent organizational strategy	Shows a lack of organizational strategy
Elaboration	Provides several ideas to support the thesis; elaborates each idea; links all information to thesis	Provides several ideas to support the thesis; elaborates most ideas with facts, details, or examples; links most information to thesis	Provides some ideas to support the thesis; does not elaborate some ideas; does not link some details to thesis	Provides no thesis; does not elaborate ideas
Use of Language	Uses excellent sentence and vocabulary variety; includes very few mechanical errors	Uses adequate sentence and vocabulary variety; includes few mechanical errors	Uses repetitive use of sentence structure and vocabulary; includes many mechanical errors	Demonstrates poor use of language; generates confusion; includes many mechanical errors

FINAL DRAFT

Dream and Dreamer

Scott Sang-Hyun Lee
Duncanville High School
Duncanville, Texas

◀ **Critical Viewing** What associations do the cap and diploma shown on this page call to mind? **[Relate]**

My parents, hoping to establish richer lives for my brother and me, moved the family to the United States when I was ten months old. We were the classic American immigrant family— poor and sustained only by the bread of hopes and dreams. My parents' mission was to sacrifice what would have been a comfortable life in their own country for a humble, and often humiliating, existence in a foreign world so that my brother and I could reap the benefits of their labor.

In the opening paragraph, Scott reveals the main point of his essay.

Soon after arriving in the United States, my father enrolled in graduate school, knowing so little English that entire lectures were blurry collages of unfamiliar sounds. Sometimes I picture him—my father, my hero—feeling like a failure, disoriented by the swirl of foreign words and unable to voice his confusion. My mother, needing to earn money as my father was studying, worked as a custodian at the local mall. Sometimes I picture her—my mother, my hero— cleaning up public restrooms. Thinking of her backbreaking task fills me with tears.

Scott's essay is logically and effectively organized. Each paragraph deals with a single main idea that he supports with examples and details.

My mother and father no longer have to work at jobs for which they are overqualified. Nevertheless, it is the memory of their past that pushes me forward. Every day, I strive to reward their sacrifice. Though it is not my only goal, nor my only motivation, I now consider it a duty to serve them as they have served me. I now willingly live with the weight of their dream upon my shoulders.

It is a challenge I accept because they first accepted it. My fulfillment of their dream is not an idyllic state that I will reach only in adulthood; instead, it is something I achieve every day in who I am and what I do. In one sense, I have already justified my parents' toils in committing myself to serving others. Yet commitment without deeds is meaningless; I still must equip myself in preparation for a life of service.

The memory of my past will serve as my vision for the future. I will always hold dearly my parents' dream and live to attain it— not only in submission to it, but also in ownership of it. The sacrifice of many years of their lives for my own is something I can never fully comprehend. However, I at least know that their lives have been planted in my heart, and that I have been entrusted as the deliverer of their defined hope. I am what they have sown, but I am also what I sow. I am both seed and reaper; I am both dream and dreamer.

Strong word choices, like "committing," "justified," and "serving" help Scott achieve his purpose.

The final sentences of Scott's conclusion are powerful and memorable.

▶ **Critical Viewing** How would you describe this student's mood upon graduation? Explain. **[Interpret]**

Connected Assignment
Open-Book Test

Do you feel anxious when taking a test? If you do, an open-book test may be a welcome change. In these tests, you're allowed to refer to specific materials such as textbooks and study notes. As a result, the process of developing supporting details rests more on scanning than on memory, but expectations for factual support may be higher. In most other ways, open-book tests require the same skills as traditional tests. You must plan your time, write efficiently, and express meaningful ideas and accurate information.

▲ **Critical Viewing** How does the chance to refer to textbooks change the way you approach an exam? Explain. **[Connect]**

Practice writing an essay for an open-book test by following the writing process steps identified below.

Prewriting

Gather Materials Before test time, verify the ground rules and then locate the books or materials that you are allowed to use during the test. If you know the test topics, think about these in advance and highlight relevant sections of your study materials. If topics are presented only at test time, choose to develop the topic about which you know the most.

Write Your Thesis Be sure that you write a thesis statement that matches the question being asked. Below is an example of an essay question for an open-book test followed by a thesis statement that addresses the question.

Sample Question: Was King Richard III of England indeed a murderous villain, as portrayed by Sir Thomas More and William Shakespeare, or was he falsely maligned, as many modern historians claim? Support your views using at least four reliable sources.

Sample Thesis: King Richard III of England was unfairly depicted as a murderer and villain. Indeed, he was a great counselor, battlefield commander, and trusted friend to many of his contemporaries.

Find Support Once you've written your thesis statement, make a plan for finding information that will support it. Use self-sticking tags to mark materials from books or in your notes that you plan to use in your essay.

Make an Outline Finally, prepare an outline to help you organize and present your ideas in an clear and effective way. When you are finished with your outline, use it as a guide as you gather supporting details.

SAMPLE OUTLINE

I. Introduction

    A. Quotation from Plato

    B. Thesis Statement: Jeremy Bentham's philosophies are ridiculed by Dickens in *Hard Times*

II. Utilitarianism

    A. Utilitarianism defined

    B. Utilitarianism—followers

III. Dickens

    A. Dickens's childhood

    B. Dickens's philosophies

Drafting Refer often to your outline and the earmarked reference materials as you draft. As with any essay, start by stating your thesis. Take full advantage of the open-book format to support your main idea with vivid, specific, and accurate details. If you cannot locate a particular fact or detail when you need it, leave yourself a reminder and continue drafting. As you write, look out for additional details or appropriate substitutes as you check notes and texts for information.

Revising and Editing Reread your essay, and adjust its organization, if necessary, to emphasize and develop your thesis. Use text resources to verify the accuracy of your supporting details. Add details where necessary to help support or explain your ideas. Delete details that stray from your purpose or the point you are making. Be sure to proofread your essay to locate and fix all errors you have made in grammar, spelling, and punctuation.

Publishing and Presenting Neatly write or print out a copy of your essay and hand it in when test time is over. To give your essay a professional look, enclose it in a folder or put a cover on it.

⚙ Grammar and Style Tip

Reread the test question and decide on an appropriate tone—a writer's attitude toward a topic—for your response. Then, choose words and phrases that will help create that tone.

Spotlight on the Humanities

Understanding History Through Media

Focus on Photography: Edward S. Curtis

While the history of Native Americans may form the subject for an essay-test question, artists, photographers, and playwrights have used our nation's history as a springboard for their creative work. American photographer Edward S. Curtis (1868–1952) took about 40,000 pictures of Native Americans over the span of thirty years. Theodore Roosevelt said that Curtis ". . . has been able to do what no other man has ever done; what, as far as we can see, no other man could do." Curtis spent more than thirty years in remote areas of the United States and Canada photographing Native Americans.

Film Connection In 1920, Edward S. Curtis moved to Los Angeles and assisted noted film director Cecil B. DeMille, whose first silent film in 1914 was called *The Squaw Man.* In 1976, film director Robert Altman brought Arthur Kopit's play *Indians* to the screen. The film, starring Paul Newman, was called *Buffalo Bill and the Indians.*

Literature Connection Author N. Scott Momaday has devoted himself to preserving Kiowa culture. Through essays, poetry, and retellings of Kiowa legends, Momaday provides his audience with a deeper understanding of Native American culture, both past and present.

Writing for Assessment Writing Activity: Essay on Native American History

Using several resources, research the history of a Native American group, perhaps one that originated in your home state. Then, write an essay—giving yourself a time limit as if you were being tested—discussing the history and tradition of the group.

▲ **Critical Viewing** What aspects of this photograph increase your understanding of Native American life? **[Distinguish]**

Media and Technology Skills

Taking Computerized Tests

Activity: Share Test-Taking Strategies

Many tests—from aptitude tests to driving exams—are computerized. Some test-taking skills can be easily applied to computerized situations, but some are specific to computerized testing. Talking about test-taking strategies can help you focus on the distinctions between computerized and traditional testing.

Think About It Review your own experiences with computerized tests. Think about what features helped ensure your success. List three points you would like to share during a team discussion.

Discuss It Share your ideas about computerized tests. In addition to talking about your team's ideas, discuss these strategies:

- **Read instructions:** Take time to read the test rules carefully. For example, find out what happens if you skip a question. How can you change an answer?

- **Read automatic feedback:** Some tests provide feedback while the test is in progress. Be sure to read feedback carefully, and apply any hints or suggestions provided.

- **Print out results:** After taking a test, print out the results. You might use the results to help you prepare for a final.

List It Compile a list of test-taking strategies. Use a chart like this one to organize strategies according to the type of test.

Computerized Tests Only	All Tests	Print Tests Only
• Print out your results to review later.	• Preview the test before you start answering. • Reserve some time to review your test.	• Underline key words in multiple-choice questions.

Share It Prepare a short presentation in which to share your test-taking strategies with your class. Identify the similarities and differences between forms of tests, and provide a list of the strategies you believe are most effective.

> **Your Computer Quotient**
> Many students who believe that they perform poorly on computerized tests are surprised by the results of comparative testing. If possible, keep track of your test scores on paper and on computer. For many students, the results indicate that their test results have little to do with the form of the test.

Standardized Test Preparation Workshop

Responding to Writing Prompts for Assessment

The writing prompts on standardized tests often measure your ability to write effectively. Some tests measure your ability to respond to literature; some measure your ability to write persuasively. The following are the criteria upon which your writing will be evaluated:

- varied word and sentence choice for the purpose and audience named in the response
- a method of organization that allows you to organize details in a meaningful and coherent sequence, such as pro-and-con organization or cause-and-effect organization
- appropriate transitions so ideas will flow and your persuasive writing will be unified and coherent
- elaboration through effective use of description, facts, and other details
- correct grammar, spelling, and punctuation

When writing for a timed test, plan to devote a specified amount of time to prewriting, drafting, revising, and proofreading.

Following is an example of a persuasive writing prompt. Use the suggestions on the following page to help you respond. The clocks next to each stage show a suggested percentage of time to devote to each stage.

Test Tip

Before you begin to write, reread the prompt to ensure that you answer it fully.

Sample Writing Situation

Space exploration has always been a hot topic for debate. Some people believe that government funding for space missions is a waste of money because there are so many domestic issues that need to be addressed. Yet some of our most innovative technology and advanced scientific understanding have evolved from the exploration of space.

Write a detailed letter to your state senator presenting your side of the argument for or against the federal funding of space exploration. Be sure to clearly state your position and to support it with reasons and facts.

Prewriting

Allow close to one quarter of your time for prewriting.

Identify Your Thesis A thesis reveals your main idea about the topic. Your thesis will help you summarize the issue and provide you with a foundation for the letter.

Gather Details Debatable statements are not factual statements but statements of opinion. When you are writing a persuasive letter, it is your job to convince your reader to agree with your thesis. You can do this by gathering details that support your position.

Drafting

Allow almost half of your time for drafting.

Write for Your Reader Since you are writing a letter to a senator, keep your language formal and your ideas concise. The choice and presentation of your words are important.

Introduce Your Topic Start your letter with a strong introduction. Although your premise does not have to be the first sentence, make sure it is included in the first paragraph. Then, give a brief description of the points you intend to make in the following paragraphs.

Present Your Argument In the letter's body paragraphs, present supporting arguments for your main premise. You may also address opposing arguments and illustrate why your argument is better. In your concluding paragraph, restate your topic sentence in a different way. Then, briefly summarize each of the points you've made, making sure that your last sentence will grab the reader's attention.

Revising, Editing, and Proofreading

Allow almost one quarter of your time to revise and edit. Use the last few minutes to check your work.

Review Your Writing Does what you've written make sense? If not, how can you reword it to sound more convincing? Delete any extra words, ideas, or sentences that repeat points already made or that don't belong.

Do a Final Check Use the last few minutes to check your letter for errors in spelling, grammar, and punctuation. Draw a line through the text you want to delete, and add the new choices neatly in the space above the text, using a caret [^] to indicate the exact placement.

Workplace Writing in Everyday Life

When you send a letter to the editor of the local newspaper or complete an application for financial aid for a summer-school program, you are using workplace writing skills. Workplace writing links the exits and entrances on today's information highway, and it keeps the lines of communication open between co-workers, classmates, businesses, and even governments. Effective workplace writing can lead to job advancement, ensure accurate and speedy financial trans-actions, persuade potential customers of a product's merit, or warn readers about an urgent problem.

In this chapter, you will examine various types of workplace writing and learn about the features that help make each successful.

▲ **Critical Viewing**
What sort of work-place skills do the people working in this office demon-strate? **[Analyze]**

What Is Workplace Writing?

The term **workplace writing** refers to fact-based written products that communicate specific information in a structured format. Effective workplace writing

- presents a core message and anticipates the readers' questions.
- communicates essential details in a concise way.
- is neatly and effectively organized.
- is free from errors in grammar, spelling, and punctuation.

Types of Workplace Writing

From the accident report a police officer generates at the scene of an accident to the memo a teacher submits requesting science lab supplies, workplace writing is an important part of life. Several types of workplace writing are listed below. Each reflects its own particular audience and purpose:

- **Business letters** introduce documents, communicate specific information, or discuss particular issues of concern to the writer.
- **Memorandums (memos)** are used to circulate information within a business.
- **Résumés** list a job applicant's skills, qualifications, and educational background.
- **Forms and applications** provide specific factual information requested by the issuing company or employer.

Writers in
ACTION

In 1978, writer Isaac Bashevis Singer was awarded the Nobel Prize for Literature. He had the following advice for aspiring writers:

"The wastebasket is a writer's best friend."

This may be especially true in workplace writing, where mistakes can cost more than merely injured pride. Revising and editing, and even starting over, are well worth the time they take.

PREVIEW

Chapter Contents

In this chapter, you will review and analyze several examples of workplace writing. These examples include real-life situations, such as a letter of recommendation for a school program, an office memo about appropriate dress, the résumé of a college student seeking employment after graduation, an application for college admission, and the forms typically used to accompany facsimiles (faxes) and record phone messages.

Business Letter

What Is a Business Letter?

Business letters are formally written letters in which the content is other than personal. Business letters can address any topic, in any industry, in any language. An effective business letter

- has six parts: the heading, the inside address, the salutation, the body, the closing, and the signature.

- follows one of several acceptable formats. In block format, each section of the letter begins at the left margin. In modified block format, the heading, the closing, and the signature are indented to the center of the page.

- contains formal and courteous language.

> The header should include the recipient's company name and address as well as the date.

Model Business Letter

This letter was written from one librarian to another, recommending a job applicant for a position.

Covington Consolidated Libraries
900 Baker Street
Covington, KY 41010

July 31, 20_ _

> A colon follows the name of the recipient. Address the recipients by title, if known.

Derek Henderson
Crowell Public Library
1400 Locke Lane
Charleston, SC 29407

Dear Mr. Henderson:

I would like to recommend Ericka Alonso for a position at your library. I am the children's librarian for the several branches of the Covington Library System. As the supervisor of her work in our libraries, I have seen Ericka's sense of responsibility, initiative, and humor in action.

> In the body, briefly communicate your purpose for writing as well as other important details.

Ericka began as an assistant in the story-hour program, helping children with projects. She quickly captivated her audiences with creative ideas and contagious enthusiasm. In addition, Ericka has mastered the complicated workings of our interlibrary loan, computer cataloging, and shelving systems and has acquired transferable skills in the process.

> Formal language is appropriate for business communications.

The independence Ericka has shown, paired with her strong intellectual curiosity, should serve her well in her library career. I am pleased to recommend Ericka to you, and I look forward to hearing about her successes.

> A polite closing should be followed by a signature as well as your typed name and title, if applicable.

Sincerely,

Kim Adams

Kim Adams
Head Children's Librarian

TOPIC BANK

To write a business letter that accomplishes your goals, choose a manageable and appropriate issue. If you're having trouble deciding on your own topic, consider these possibilities:

1. **Letter to an Author** Write a letter to an author in response to something he or she has written. In the letter, you may comment on the quality of the author's writing or the development of the book's main character or the work's theme.

2. **Community Service Letter** Many young people today have become involved in improving their communities and solving local problems. Think of a way you could help in your community. Then, write a business letter to residents or community officials introducing your idea and inviting their support.

Prewriting Jot down notes about your purpose for writing—what you want to accomplish. Then, gather the facts or statistics to ensure that your audience has the necessary information to respond to your letter. Also, take note of the recipient's name, title, and business address.

Drafting Decide on a format—block or modified block—and begin drafting. Refer to your prewriting notes to be sure you include necessary information.

Revising Review your letter critically. Be sure that you have clearly and briefly introduced yourself and stated your purpose for writing. Also, confirm that the details you've included support your main point and purpose. If not, delete them. Check your use of language, and change any words or phrases that are too informal.

Editing and Proofreading Use the model on the opposite page to check your letter's format. Verify the accuracy and correct spelling of names and addresses. Proofread to correct errors in spelling, grammar, and punctuation.

Publishing If you wrote your letter by hand, type or word-process it before mailing. Use 8 1/2 x 11 inch paper in a neutral color. Make sure to sign your finished letter. Then, fold it neatly and enclose it in an envelope that matches the paper. Apply correct postage, and mail it.

What Is a Memorandum?

Accurate communication of information among team members or co-workers is necessary for the successful completion of a task or a project. Memos (memorandums) are one tool colleagues can use to achieve that communication. Memorandums are usually brief letters or messages that offer information or communicate company policy. An effective memo

- communicates pertinent information.
- follows standard memo format to clearly present the topic and date along with names of sender(s) and addressee(s).
- quickly elaborates on the topic line and specifically directs any requested responses.

Angela uses the company letterhead for a professional appearance and to command respect.

Model Memo

Angela Schwers heads the Human Resources department for a large bank. In this memo, she clarifies the company's dress code.

Most memos follow this format: To, From, Date, and Re (Regarding). The memo's topic appears in the "Re:" line.

Memo

Global Bank

TO: Global Bank Employees
FROM: Angela Schwers
Vice President/Director
DATE: April 28, 1999
RE: Casual Business Dress

It has been several years now since we introduced the policy of "casual business attire" on Fridays. Most employees are pleased with this policy, and similar practices appear to be growing within our industry.

The objective of casual dress days is to be comfortable, while still maintaining a professional business environment. Casual businesswear encompasses many looks, but it really means casual clothing that is appropriate for an office environment. It is clothing that allows you to feel comfortable at work, yet always looks neat and professional. Clothing such as casual slacks, polo shirts, sweaters, and casual shoes would be appropriate. To maintain our professional image, we ask that you use discretion when determining what to wear. If you are expected to interact with customers, vendors, authors, or other business guests, you should dress in a manner that is professional and appropriate.

Please use good, professional judgment in selecting your casual business attire. Casual business dress is not an exemption from the Company's neat and appropriate standards of dress. If you have any questions regarding appropriate business attire, please direct them to your manager or your Human Resources representative.

Angela Schwers

The body of a memo should be brief and informative.

Most memos are signed to indicate that the contents have been approved by the sender.

TOPIC BANK

Choose a topic about which to write a memo. If you're having trouble finding a topic, consider these possibilities:

1. **Memo to Sports Director** In many communities, high-school students play important staff roles in intramural sports programs for children. As a staffer in such a program, write a memo to the regional sports director asking for clarification of program rules.

2. **Memo to Events Committee** Community organizations frequently raise funds through events such as auctions, fairs, and sponsored sporting events. Choose an organization or issue that interests you, and write a memo concerning plans for an upcoming fund-raiser.

Prewriting What would the title line for your memo's topic be? If you cannot easily summarize the topic this way, it's probably too broad for a memo. Think also about your audience's interest and knowledge level. How much do they know? How much do they need to know? Use questions such as *Who? What? When? Where?* and *Why?* to gather necessary details.

Drafting Present your main point as concisely and clearly as possible. Depending on the kind of information you need to communicate, charts or bulleted lists can convey a lot of information in a highly accessible format.

Revising Look to be sure that you have filled in the *TO:*, *FROM:*, *DATE:*, and *RE:* lines completely and accurately. Then, review the body of your memo to be sure that you have stated your main idea briefly and clearly. If your memo is long, delete unnecessary information. You might also reformat the information in a numbered or bulleted list for clarity.

Editing and Proofreading Revise inconsistent or confusing formatting. Also, proofread to correct errors in spelling, grammar, and punctuation.

Publishing Memos are useless unless they are shared with others. Print out and distribute your memo to interested peers. As an alternative, publish your memo via e-mail.

What Is a Résumé?

If you haven't compiled a résumé yet, you will probably need to do so soon. A *résumé* summarizes your educational background, work experiences, pertinent skills, and other employment qualifications. It also tells potential employers how to contact you. An effective résumé

- presents the applicant's name, address, and phone number.
- follows an accepted résumé organization, using labels and headings to guide readers.
- outlines the applicant's educational background, life experiences, and related qualifications using precise and active language.

> Put contact information such as name, address, telephone number, and e-mail address at the top of the résumé.

Model Résumé

With this résumé, college student Jon-Paul hoped to find a full-time job.

> Jon-Paul used heads with capital letters to identify each section of his résumé.

> Entries on a résumé should be brief and to the point, like those on Jon-Paul's.

JON-PAUL CIAMBRA
1234 Greene Street, Apt #3
Columbia, SC 29201

EDUCATION
University of South Carolina, Columbia, SC
Bachelor of Science in Administrative Information Management
Expected: December, 20_ _

SKILLS
Computer Languages: Cobol, HTML
Internet: Dial-Up Networking and most e-mail or WWWeb applications

WORK EXPERIENCE
Fall 1997 — Computer Services Department
University of South Carolina, Columbia, SC
<u>Computer Lab Technician</u>: Assisted students in the use of software and hardware; responded to user questions and problems

1995 – 1998 (summers and breaks) — **Gen X Wireless Services**
Paramus, NJ
<u>Receivables Management Representative</u>: Handled incoming accounts-receivable calls for cellular phone accounts in the New York, New Jersey, and Connecticut markets; trained and facilitated other representatives

Summer 1999 — P.E.S. Engineering
Charleston, SC
<u>Intern</u>: Designed a customized record management system for the engineers; trained in the data entry department

REFERENCES
Furnished on request

TOPIC BANK

Create a résumé that emphasizes the ways in which you are unique and special. If you're not sure how to write a résumé, practice with the following assignments:

1. **Résumé for a Job** Is there a job that needs to be done in your family, school, community, or part-time workplace? Define that job, and then write a résumé for the ideal candidate.

2. **Résumé for a Fictional or Historical Job** Find a job from your reading or from historical research that you would like to have. Write your own résumé for that job, using real and imaginary qualifications.

Prewriting Gather information with self-questioning. What skills do I have? Where and when did I use them? You might talk with a family member or friend to jog your memory about informal job experiences, such as tutoring a younger sibling with homework or driving in a carpool.

Drafting Experiment with the organization and design, but once you choose a format, stick with it consistently. Consider opening each job description with a vivid, active verb that describes your efforts. Consult a thesaurus to add variety and precision to these verbs.

Revising Review your organizing priorities, and make sure that your design supports your goals. For example, make sure that your most significant achievements are readily visible. Then, review the information you've provided. Cut out extraneous wording and add important details, if they're lacking.

Editing and Proofreading Verify names and addresses of former employers or educational institutions. If you are working on a computer, print out a copy of your résumé to check for centering, line spacing, and general readability.

Publishing Find out to whom the résumé should be sent. Print out a clean copy on good quality paper. Then, create a cover letter (see the Business Letter on page 350). Use a paper clip to attach the cover letter to your résumé. Mail both in a properly addressed and stamped matching business envelope.

16.4 Forms and Applications

What Are Business Forms?

Forms are preprinted documents that contain spaces in which the user enters specific information. Sometimes, forms contain directions or explanations to help users respond accurately. Two common forms in the workplace are **fax cover sheets** and **applications**. An effectively completed form

- is legible and neat so that reviewers can easily read information.
- responds specifically to the information requested by each instruction or heading.
- provides only the requested information.

Model Fax Cover Sheet

A fax (short for facsimile) is an electronically transmitted document. Most faxes are two part: They contain a cover sheet and an accompanying document. Below is an example of a fax cover sheet:

Fill in fax cover sheets completely, neatly, and accurately. This will ensure that the addressee actually receives the fax transmission.

PITTSBURGH SASH & DOOR
2 Kate Street • Pittsburgh, PA 15235
phone 151.773.8600 • fax 151.773.2104
e-mail: PSD@panct.com
PS&D

Fax

FACSIMILE COVER SHEET

DATE: 4/5/20--

TO: Marshall Burnett, Clinton Glass

FAX NUMBER: 860-669-1230

FAX SOURCE TRANSMISSION NUMBER: 151-773-2104

FROM: Rhonda Henebry

TOTAL NUMBER OF PAGES (including this cover sheet): 3

REMARKS:

A brief message tells the recipient what the fax is about and gives other important information.

Marshall-We need prices for the window glass in order to submit an important fee proposal. I've attached all the info and specifications you need. Can you get prices to me later today? Please call with questions. Thanks! Rhonda

Model Application

In recent years, colleges and universities around the country have accepted the Common Application. This straightforward form allows high-school students to complete one basic college application form and use it for several institutions. Below is an example:

1999-2000 Common Application

Application for Undergraduate Admission

Member colleges and universities encourage the use of this application. No distinction will be made between it and the college's own form. The accompanying instructions tell you how to complete, copy, and file your application with any one or several of the colleges.

Personal Data
Legal Name: _____Stelk_____ _____Samuel_____ _____Jacob_____ _____ ☐
             Last/Family   First   Middle (complete)   Jr, etc.

Prefer to be called: _____Sam_____ (nickname) Former Last name(s) if any: _____N/A_____
                             For the term beginning: _____

Applying as a ☒ Freshman ☐ Transfer

Permanent home address: _____45 Vincent Street_____

_____Eugene_____ _____OR_____ _____USA_____ _____97401_____
  City or Town   State   Country   Zip Code + 4 or Postal Code

E-mail address: _____SamJS@gene.com_____

Birth date (mm/dd/yy): _____1/25/83_____ ☒ Citizenship: U.S./dual U.S. citizen
                            If dual, specify other citizenship:_____

☐ U.S. Permanent resident visa. Citizen of: _____ ☐ Other citizenship.

Please specify country: _____

If you are not a U.S. citizen and live in the United States, how long have you been in the country?_____ Visa Type: _____

Possible area(s)of academic concentration/major: _____physics_____ ☐ Or undecided

Special college or division if applicable: _____

Possible career or professional plans: _____teaching_____ ☐ Or undecided

Will you be a candidate for financial aid? ☒ Yes ☐ No If yes, the appropriate form(s) was/will be filed on (mm/dd/yy): _____10/15/20--_____

> Because space is limited, print clearly and neatly in small letters,

> If any items do not pertain to your situation, write N/A for "not applicable" in the space provided.

> Use a check mark or an X to signal a choice.

> To avoid errors, double-check labels before filling in spaces.

Connected Assignment
E-mail

The pace of communication in today's workplace has gotten faster and faster due to technological innovations. E-mail, short for electronic mail, is an extremely effective workplace writing tool that enables messages and documents to be sent around the world to multiple recipients simultaneously and almost instantaneously. E-mail is composed in a software program and transmitted through a modem over the Internet.

Effective e-mails

- are brief and to the point.
- are simply formatted.
- contain a description of the contents in the Subject line.

Practice composing and sending effective e-mail messages with the help of the suggestions below.

▲ **Critical Viewing**
In what ways have computers changed people's lifestyles? **[Generalize]**

MODEL

From: Leland, Rebecca
Sent: Friday, March 11, 20_ _
To: Gandry, Evan; Jackson, Nicola; Parker, Theresa
Subject: Tuesday's Fund-raiser

Hello!

Only four days left until the "big night," so I'm checking with you to make sure that the arrangements are proceeding according to schedule. In particular, I want to confirm the following:

- Flowers have been ordered.
- The podium and microphone have been requisitioned from facilities.
- Programs have been printed and delivered.

Let me know immediately if you foresee any difficulties ahead.

Thanks.

Rebecca

Prewriting Identify a topic or main message you want to convey in your e-mail. Possible topics include conveying interest in a summer job or asking a research librarian for guidance. Then, think carefully about your audience before writing. How well do you know the recipient? What supporting information, such as your order number, might he or she need in order to respond effectively? Finally, review your e-mail program's format, consulting electronic or printed directions if necessary. Gather necessary information such as e-mail addresses to complete the memo-style address section.

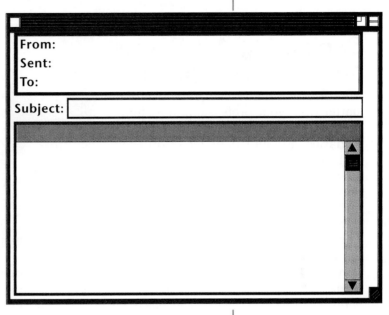

Drafting Although you'll need to be on-line to send your e-mail, consider drafting off-line to free up your phone line and limit on-line time. After completing the address section, open your letter much as you would a memo or personal note. For example, while you should address business recipients by their full name, you need not insert street addresses. Set a formality level appropriate to the recipient as you develop the letter's message. Keep the formatting simple to avoid translation problems at the receiving computer.

Revising and Editing Reread your letter carefully to be sure that its message is clearly stated. Change inappropriate language to better suit its recipients. Add details where it is lacking, and delete unnecessary information.

Also, check your e-mail for spelling and typographical errors. Use a pencil or your finger on the screen to verify e-mail addresses character by character. One mistake and your communication may come back undelivered.

Publishing and Presenting When you're satisfied with your e-mail message, find and attach any necessary documents. For important correspondence, print out or copy your letter into a desktop folder before sending it. To ensure that your e-mail gets delivered, you may want to click the optional Get Receipt feature from the software program you are using.

Grammar and Style Tip

When reading text on screen, shorter and simpler is better. Review the length and complexity of your sentences, and consider shortening and simplifying them to ensure that your message gets across to your readers.

Spotlight on the Humanities

Comparing Art Forms
Focus on Film: Luis Buñuel

Workplace writing skills can be useful no matter what your profession. Most film directors, for example, write memos, scenarios, and directions for setup shots in the course of producing a film. One of the greatest filmmakers of the twentieth century, Spanish film director Luis Buñuel (1900–1983), produced films with a simple narrative behind which he placed powerful on-screen imagery. In the 1960's and 1970's, Buñuel created some of his finest work, including *The Exterminating Angel* (1962), *The Discreet Charm of the Bourgeoisie* (1972), and *The Phantom of Liberty* (1974). *The Discreet Charm of the Bourgeoisie* won the Academy Award for Best Foreign Language Film of 1972.

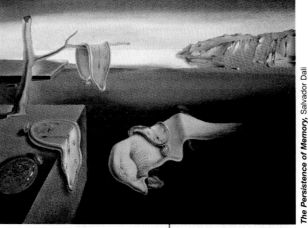

The Persistence of Memory, Salvador Dali

▲ **Critical Viewing**
What sort of film might this painting inspire? Why? **[Analyze]**

Art Connection Luis Buñuel collaborated with the Spanish artist Salvador Dali (1904–1989) on the 1928 film *Un Chien Andalou.* Dali's paintings are known for their strong depiction of dream imagery in which daily objects appear in unexpected forms. One of his most famous paintings, *The Persistence of Memory* (1931), shows limp, melting watches falling across the canvas. His later paintings reflect a more classical style. Using bright colors covered with transparent glazes, he is remembered as a master of the Surrealist art movement.

Literature Connection While at the University of Madrid, Luis Buñuel met the most popular poet of the Spanish-speaking world, Federico García Lorca (1898–1936). Lorca lived in Madrid from 1919 to 1934, where he often gave readings of his poems. In 1922, he organized the festival of the "deep song," or *cante jondo,* which was based upon an ancient Gypsy song, and this form heavily influenced his own poetry. Like Buñuel, Lorca's work is filled with startling images.

Workplace Writing Activity: E-mail That "Pitches" a Film

Even artists like filmmakers find workplace writing skills useful as they plan and produce their films. Think of an interesting idea you would like to make into a movie. Then, in an e-mail to a film production company, write a description of the movie, explaining why it would be a success and requesting financial backing.

Media and Technology Skills

Utilizing Business Technology
Activity: Compile a Technology Glossary

Understanding terminology is crucial when using technology. Whether you are learning to log onto a new computer system, operate a word processor, or search the Internet, you need to be familiar with specialized vocabulary. Creating a technology glossary can help you remember new words and phrases and share your knowledge with others.

Think About It Brainstorm for a list of technology terms. Include both terms you understand and those that confuse you. Keep in mind that your glossary may be used by people with little or no technology experience.

Expand It The best way to expand your list of terms is to work with several different technologies. As you work, add unfamiliar or specialized terms to your list. Find words from at least three of the following technologies:

- **Server:** If your school has access to a server, use this system to store material you have written.
- **Database:** Find information in a database, or prepare a database using your own information.
- **Page Layout Software:** Use the program to design a simple poster, greeting card, or flyer.
- **Graphics Software:** Create an original digital artwork or modify a scanned photograph.

Define It After exploring several technologies, review your list of terms. Write definitions for those you already understand. Use reference sources—such as instruction manuals, books, and the Internet—to find definitions for the other terms. Make sure that your definitions will be understood by someone who has not used the technology.

Organize It Finally, organize your glossary so that it will be easy to use. You might choose alphabetical order or a modified organization in which terms are grouped by category, such as the Internet or graphics, and then alphabetized. Make your final version available to students in your school's computer center.

Some Terms to Consider

Consider adding these terms to your technology glossary:

- bitmap
- cache
- central processing unit (CPU)
- daemon
- desktop
- domain
- e-mail attachment
- firewall
- footer
- footprint
- hardware
- header
- host
- HTML
- hypertext
- ISP
- memory
- menu
- MIME
- monitor
- network
- operating system
- peripheral
- RAM
- shareware
- software
- URL
- utility
- wallpaper

Standardized Test Preparation Workshop

Applying Usage Rules to Writing

Writing in the workplace should be error-free and follow the rules of grammar, usage, and mechanics. Standardized tests often measure your ability to recognize errors in grammar, spelling, or punctuation. The following strategies will help you address commonly tested usage problems:

- Check verbs to make sure they agree with their subjects.

- Make sure that verb tense is consistent.

- Look for homophones.

- Check pronoun-antecedent agreement.

Use the following sample test items to practice identifying usage problems.

Test Tip

Read each sentence to yourself several times. Each time, substitute one of the answer choices for the blank. Then, choose the word or group of words that best completes the sentence.

Sample Test Items

Directions: Read the passage, and choose the word or words that belong in each space. Choose the appropriate letter for your answer.

On Friday, Haley and I ___(1)___ to the meeting for the senior banquet.

1 **A** is going

    B were going

    C was going

    D are going

Directions: Read each passage, and decide which type of error, if any, appears in each underlined section. Choose the letter for your answer.

Both Haley and Caroline will <u>lead the Work</u>
(1)
<u>Group for the banquet.</u>

1 **A** Spelling error

    B Capitalization error

    C Punctuation error

    D No error

Answers and Explanations

The correct answer is *D, are going.* This verb phrase is correct in both tense—present progressive—and number—plural.

The correct answer is *B.* The words *work group* are not proper nouns and should not be capitalized.

> **Practice 1** **Directions:** Read the passage, and choose the word or group of words that belongs in each space. Choose the appropriate letter for your answer.

My first college interview ____(1)____ place last Friday afternoon at Grove University. I ____(2)____ nervous, but my mood ____(3)____ as soon as I entered the room. When I saw the posters for the school hockey team, I ____(4)____ I was in the right place. I then told the interviewer that I loved hockey and ____(5)____ out for the team if accepted to the school.

1 A take
  B have taken
  C took
  D will take

2 F were
  G is
  H was
  J are

3 A change
  B changes
  C changed
  D will change

4 F knew
  G know
  H will know
  J knowing

5 A tried
  B have been trying
  C would be trying
  D try

> **Practice 2** **Directions:** Read each passage, and decide which type of error, if any, appears in each underlined section. Choose the letter for your answer.

Our committee must <u>create a Proposal for</u>
                                (1)
<u>the March dance</u>. The first section will

describe the theme <u>of the dance and Marys</u>
                                              (2)
<u>plan for decorations</u>. Next, each member

should <u>write a description of his or her role</u>
                          (3)
<u>on the comittee</u>. Finally, let's include a
(4)
description <u>of our overall plan for the</u>
                          (5)
<u>evening</u>.

1 A Spelling error
  B Capitalization error
  C Punctuation error
  D No error

2 F Spelling error
  G Capitalization error
  H Punctuation error
  J No error

3 A Spelling error
  B Capitalization error
  C Punctuation error
  D No error

4 F Spelling error
  G Capitalization error
  H Punctuation error
  J No error

5 A Spelling error
  B Capitalization error
  C Punctuation error
  D No error

Grammar, Usage, and Mechanics

Waterfront Landscape, 1936, Stuart Davis, National Museum of American Art, Washington, D.C.

The Parts of Speech

There are thousands of words in the English language. Different combinations of these words in sentences can produce almost as many different meanings as there are stars in the sky.

On the other hand, every word in the English language can be assigned to at least one of only eight categories called the *parts of speech*, which are shown in the following chart.

THE EIGHT PARTS OF SPEECH		
nouns	adjectives	prepositions
pronouns	adverbs	conjunctions
verbs		interjections

The meaning of a word and the way it is used in a sentence determines its part of speech. This chapter discusses each of the eight parts of speech.

▲ **Critical Viewing** The Andromeda Galaxy contains as many as 200 billion stars. How many words do you think there are in the English language? Do you think the number is increasing or decreasing? Why? **[Deduce]**

Diagnostic Test

Directions: Write all answers on a separate sheet of paper.

Skill Check A. Write the pronouns and their antecedents (if any). Then, identify each pronoun as *personal, reflexive, intensive, demonstrative, relative, interrogative,* or *indefinite.*

(1) Which civilizations made the first discoveries about the stars? (2) It is the ancient Egyptians, Babylonians, and Greeks who made contributions to our knowledge of the stars. (3) The Greek astronomer Aristarchus of Samos found himself alone in the belief that the planets revolved around the sun. (4) According to Copernicus, the Earth revolved around the sun and the sun itself was the center of the universe. (5) However, in the eighteenth and nineteenth centuries, others would discover thousands of galaxies beyond this.

Skill Check B. Write the complete verb or verb phrase. Then, write *AV* or *LV* to indicate whether the word is an *action verb* or *linking verb* and *T* or *I* to indicate whether it is *transitive* or *intransitive.*

(6) Scientists classify galaxies by appearance. (7) Elliptical galaxies appear globular and have a bright center. (8) Spiral galaxies look flat. (9) Gravitational pull affects the appearance of irregular galaxies. (10) Large amounts of gas and dust exist in an irregular galaxy, but there are no spiral forms.

Skill Check C. Write the adjectives and adverbs in the following sentences. Beside each, write the word or words it modifies.

(11) Improved telescopes have greatly increased our knowledge. (12) In the 1960's, two British astronomers discovered pulsars. (13) Pulsars are widely believed to be the last stage in a star's life before eventual extinction as a black hole. (14) The Hubble Space Telescope provided very convincing evidence of a black hole's existence. (15) This Earth-orbiting telescope can peer through the deep recesses of space.

Skill Check D. Identify the conjunctions, prepositions, and interjections in the following sentences. Write whether the conjunctions are *coordinating, correlative,* or *subordinating.*

(16) The first images transmitted from the X-ray telescopes of the Chandra X-ray Observatory were of an exploding star. (17) Say, did you know that this star, Cassiopeia A, actually exploded around 300 years ago, but its light is only now reaching the Earth? (18) Not only did they capture a clear, detailed image of a supernova, they also found strong evidence of a black hole near its center. (19) In addition to this, a second image shows a long stream of X-rays jetting from a quasar about 6 billion light-years from Earth. (20) Wow! After I saw those pictures, I certainly felt small and insignificant in regard to my place in the universe.

Nouns and Pronouns

Nouns

Nouns constitute the largest category of the parts of speech.

> **KEY CONCEPT** A **noun** is the name of a person, place, or thing. ∎

The classification of things encompasses visible things, ideas, actions, conditions, and qualities.

VISIBLE THINGS: crater, rocket, camera
IDEAS: scholasticism, militarism, evolution
ACTIONS: exploration, research, ignition
CONDITIONS: excitement, command, anticipation
QUALITIES: courage, integrity, ability

Knowing the endings often attached to nouns can help you identify them. Some of the most common noun suffixes are *-dom, -ics, -ion, -ism, -ment, -ness,* and *-ship.*

EXAMPLES:
aeronau*tics*   free*dom*
cynic*ism*   fu*sion*
fit*ness*   commit*ment*
fellow*ship*

GRAMMAR IN LITERATURE

from **Outside History**
Eavan Boland

Read the following lines from Eavan Boland's poem. She uses concrete nouns such as light, stars, *and* inklings. *These things can be perceived with the sense of sight. She also uses an abstract noun,* history.

There are outsiders, always. These stars—
these iron inklings of an Irish January,
whose light happened

thousands of years before
our pain did: they are, they have always been
outside history.

▼ **Critical Viewing** The Lagoon Nebula is an interstellar cloud in the region of the constellation Sagittarius. What kind of a noun is *nebula?* Think of an adjective that is related. **[Classify]**

Concrete and Abstract Nouns

Nouns are sometimes grouped according to the characteristics of the things they name. A *concrete* noun names something that you can physically see, touch, taste, hear, or smell. An *abstract* noun names something that is nonphysical, or that you cannot readily perceive through any of your five senses.

Concrete Nouns	Abstract Nouns
nebula	distance
gas	light-year
scientist	discovery
telescope	infinity

Singular and Plural Nouns

Nouns can indicate number. *Singular* nouns name one person, place, or thing. *Plural* nouns name more than one. Most plural nouns are formed by the addition of -s or -es to the singular form. Some plural nouns, however, are formed irregularly and must be memorized.

SINGULAR: valley, sky, mouse
PLURAL: valleys, skies, mice

SINGULAR NOUNS	
Regular	**Irregular**
valley	mouse
lash	ox
sky	nucleus
PLURAL NOUNS	
valleys	mice
lashes	oxen
skies	nuclei

Collective Nouns

Nouns that name *groups* of people or things are called *collective nouns*. Although a collective noun looks singular, its meaning may be either singular or plural depending on how it is used in a sentence.

COLLECTIVE NOUNS	
council	orchestra
delegation	team
entourage	troop

Compound Nouns

A noun that is composed of two or more words acting as a single unit is called a *compound noun*. For example, the noun *space* and the noun *ship* can act together to name a particular object—a *spaceship*.

Compound nouns are usually entered in dictionaries because they name something other than what the individual words suggest. An expression such as *space movie*, on the other hand, is not generally considered a compound noun because it means nothing more than what the two words suggest: "a movie about space."

Compound nouns may appear in three forms: as separate words, as hyphenated words, or as combined words.

Grammar and Style Tip

Specific dates (*e.g.,* 1994) are also considered nouns.

COMPOUND NOUNS	
Separated	crab grass, player piano, space shuttle
Hyphenated	jack-in-the-box, light-year, sister-in-law
Combined	dragonfly, eardrum, earthquake

If you are in doubt about the spelling of a compound noun, check a dictionary.

Common and Proper Nouns

All nouns can be categorized as either common or proper. A *common noun* names any one of a class of people, places, or things. A *proper noun* names a specific person, place, or thing.

Common Nouns	Proper Nouns
astronomer	William Herschel, Charles Messier
nation	India, France
building	National Observatory, Taj Mahal

As you can see from these examples, proper nouns are always capitalized, whereas common nouns are not. (See Chapter 26 for rules on capitalization.)

A noun of direct address—the name of a person to whom you are directly speaking—is always a proper noun, as is a family title before a name.

COMMON NOUN: My aunt is a pilot.

DIRECT ADDRESS: Please, Dad, tell us about your spacewalk.

FAMILY TITLE: For years, Aunt Sarah has worked for NASA.

Exercise 1 Identifying the Types of Nouns Copy the following list of nouns. Then, identify each according to whether it (1) names a person, place, or thing, (2) is concrete or abstract, (3) is singular or plural, (4) is collective, (5) is compound, and (6) is common or proper.

EXAMPLE: light

ANSWER: (1) thing, (2) concrete, (3) singular, (4) not
             collective, (5) not compound, (6) common

▼ **Critical Viewing**
The Hubble Space Telescope is seen suspended in space above Earth. What nouns name images the telescope might transmit? **[Speculate]**

1. spacesuit
2. star
3. telescope
4. Alpha Centauri
5. astronomer
6. theory
7. light-year
8. Andromeda
9. universe
10. brown dwarf
11. cluster
12. Dr. Carl Sagan
13. cosmos
14. Milky Way
15. stargazer
16. astronomy
17. supernova
18. Pleiades
19. moonscape
20. system

Exercise 2 Recognizing Compound Nouns Look up the following expressions. If an expression is in your dictionary, write *compound* and give a brief definition. If an expression is not in your dictionary, simply define the expression from common knowledge.

EXAMPLE: word of honor   solemn promise
ANSWER: compound   oath

1. star tracker
2. star system
3. stellar voyage
4. stellar wind
5. white light
6. white dwarf
7. black light
8. black hole
9. cosmic dimensions
10. cosmic dust

▶ **More Practice**

Language Lab
CD-ROM
• Types of Nouns lesson
On-line
Exercise Bank
• Section 17.1
Grammar Exercise
Workbook
• pp. 1–2

Pronouns

Pronouns help people avoid awkward repetition of nouns.

> **KEY CONCEPT** **Pronouns** are words that stand for nouns or for words that take the place of nouns. ∎

In the examples below, the italicized words are pronouns. The arrows point to the words that the pronouns stand for.

EXAMPLES: Michelle and Ken went to the observatory. *They*

thought *it* was the clearest night so far this year.

The words that the arrows point to in the examples are called *antecedents*.

> **KEY CONCEPT** **Antecedents** are nouns (or words that take the place of nouns) for which pronouns stand. ∎

Although an antecedent usually precedes its pronoun, it can also follow the pronoun.

EXAMPLE: After their conference, the astronomers went to a party.

There are several kinds of pronouns in English. Most have antecedents; a few do not.

Personal Pronouns

> **KEY CONCEPT** **Personal pronouns** are used to refer to (1) the person speaking, (2) the person spoken to, or (3) the person, place, or thing spoken about. ∎

All of the personal pronouns are listed in the chart on the next page. *First-person pronouns* refer to the person speaking; *second-person pronouns* refer to the person spoken to; and *third-person pronouns* refer to the person, place, or thing spoken about. The personal pronouns in the chart that are italicized are sometimes called *possessive pronouns*.

PERSONAL PRONOUNS		
	Singular	**Plural**
First Person	I, me *my, mine*	we, us *our, ours*
Second Person	you *your, yours*	you *your, yours*
Third Person	he, she, it him, her *his, her, hers, its*	they, them *their, theirs*

The antecedent of a personal pronoun may or may not be directly stated. In the following examples, only the last one has a stated antecedent. In the first two, the antecedents are implied.

FIRST PERSON: *We* read about the origin of the universe.
SECOND PERSON: *You* must submit *your* paper soon.

THIRD PERSON: The technicians ate *their* lunch at noon.

Reflexive and Intensive Pronouns

▶ **KEY CONCEPTS** **Reflexive pronouns** are used to add information to a sentence by pointing back to a noun or pronoun near the beginning of the sentence. **Intensive pronouns** are used simply to add emphasis to a noun or pronoun. ■

REFLEXIVE: Cosmologists ready themselves for discovery.

INTENSIVE: You yourself agreed with the theory.

REFLEXIVE AND INTENSIVE PRONOUNS		
	Singular	**Plural**
First Person	myself	ourselves
Second Person	yourself	yourselves
Third Person	himself, herself, itself	themselves

Demonstrative Pronouns

▶ **KEY CONCEPT** A **demonstrative pronoun** is used to point out a specific person, place, or thing. ■

| DEMONSTRATIVE PRONOUNS ||
Singular	Plural
this, that	these, those

Demonstrative pronouns may be located before or after their antecedents.

BEFORE: *That* is a newly discovered galaxy.

AFTER: A star to steer by—*this* was all I had.

Relative Pronouns

▶ **KEY CONCEPT** A **relative pronoun** is used to begin a subordinate clause and relate it to another idea in the sentence. ■

RELATIVE PRONOUNS				
that	which	who	whom	whose

As the following sentences show, the antecedent for a relative pronoun is located in another clause of the sentence. Each relative pronoun links the information in a subordinate clause to a word in an independent clause.

Independent Clause	Subordinate Clause
We began reading *The Cyclops*,	*which* is a play by Euripides.
I wish to thank Sir John Herschel,	to *whom* we are grateful.
The show focused on scientists	*whose* discoveries changed our view of the universe.

Interrogative Pronouns

KEY CONCEPT An **interrogative pronoun** is used to begin a direct or indirect question. ■

The five interrogative pronouns are listed in the following chart.

INTERROGATIVE PRONOUNS
what   which   who   whom   whose

The antecedent for an interrogative pronoun may not always be known, as the first of the following examples illustrates.

DIRECT QUESTION: *What* fell from the sky?

INDIRECT QUESTION: He had two problems. I asked *which* needed to be solved first.

Indefinite Pronouns

KEY CONCEPT **Indefinite pronouns** are used to refer to persons, places, or things, often without specifying which ones. ■

NO SPECIFIC ANTECEDENT: *Nobody* was required to clean up, but *many* offered to assist.

SPECIFIC ANTECEDENT: I bought new book covers, but *none* was the right size.

The chart below lists the most commonly used indefinite pronouns.

INDEFINITE PRONOUNS				
Singular			**Plural**	**Singular or Plural**
another	everyone	nothing	both	all
anybody	everything	one	few	any
anyone	little	other	many	more
anything	much	somebody	others	most
each	neither	someone	several	none
either	nobody	something		some
everybody	no one			such

Grammar and Style Tip

For more on pronouns, see Chapter 22, "Pronoun Usage."

More Practice

Language Lab CD-ROM
• Pronouns and Antecedents lesson
On-line Exercise Bank
• Section 17.1
Grammar Exercise Workbook
• p. 3–4

Exercise 3 Identifying Antecedents of Pronouns Write each underlined pronoun and its antecedent. If a pronoun does not have an antecedent, write *none* after the pronoun. If the pronoun refers to the speaker, write *speaker*. Note that an antecedent may appear in a preceding sentence.

EXAMPLE: I know that a star gets hotter and denser near its core.

ANSWER: I (speaker)   its (star)

1. From the Earth, <u>one</u> can see about 3,000 stars without the assistance of a telescope.
2. However, there are actually hundreds of billions of <u>them</u> within the Milky Way alone.
3. The Milky Way <u>itself</u> is actually only one of hundreds of millions of galaxies in the universe.
4. A star is composed of extremely hot gases such as hydrogen and helium, <u>which</u> are held together by gravity.
5. Beneath <u>its</u> surface, nuclear reactions rumble, and <u>these</u> cause the gases to emit electromagnetic radiation, especially light.
6. Does <u>anybody</u> know <u>which</u> star is nearest?
7. <u>That</u> would be the sun, <u>which</u> is considered a typical star.
8. <u>Many</u> of the stars are actually multiple or binary systems.
9. A binary system comprises two stars <u>that</u> are in close proximity to <u>each other</u> and <u>that</u> orbit around <u>their</u> common center of mass.
10. These usually look like single stars when viewed from Earth, although <u>some</u> can be seen as doubles through a telescope.

Exercise 4 Supplying Pronouns Fill in each blank below with an appropriate pronoun.

1. __?__ of the stars have been in existence for millions—and, in some cases, billions—of years.
2. __?__ suspect that it is difficult for __?__ to imagine that new stars are still forming all across the galaxy.
3. An astronomer told __?__ that meteors, called "falling stars," are actually burning lumps of metal and rock.
4. __?__ should write an essay on the formation of meteors.
5. __?__ of __?__ stars can be called a supergiant?

> **Exercise 5** Identifying the Different Types of Pronouns
Identify each underlined pronoun as *personal, reflexive, intensive, demonstrative, relative, interrogative,* or *indefinite.*

EXAMPLE: We sat on the grass and gazed at the stars.

ANSWER: personal

When (1) you walk outside and look up at the stars, do you notice (2) that (3) their brightness often appears to fluctuate? Some of these variable stars change greatly, while (4) others vary only slightly. It can take hours, days, or even years for (5) them to return to their original brightness. All stars, even the sun (6) itself, are variable stars.

The nova, however, varies the most violently and fantastically of (7) all. (8) It may become thousands of times brighter than (9) our sun. The supernova, on the other hand, is an explosion (10) that, for all intents and purposes, marks the end of a star's life. (11) It may be billions of times brighter than the sun but burns out over time. In (12) its wake are left glowing gaseous clouds called nebulae or small stars known as pulsars.

A pulsar emits radio pulses that are so steady, (13) one could set a clock by them. Exactly (14) what are pulsars? Scientists think that (15) they are rotating neutron stars that are up to 10 miles in diameter. (16) This belies the fact, however, that they are among the densest objects known to (17) us.

A star's life generally ends when (18) nothing remains of it to produce energy. When all of their hydrogen is consumed, stars swell up to become red giants, but (19) those, too, do not last. As the high temperature causes fusion of its helium nucleus, a star contracts and becomes denser, and (20) many may ultimately become white dwarfs.

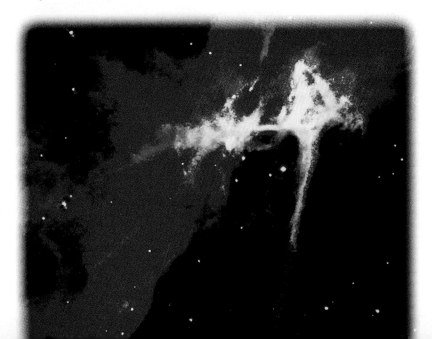

◀ **Critical Viewing**
This supernova, in a picture taken by the Hubble Space Telescope, is part of the Cygnus Loop. Ask three questions about the picture. Begin each question with an interrogative pronoun. **[Connect]**

Section Review

GRAMMAR EXERCISES 6–11

> **Exercise 6** **Identifying the Types of Nouns** Identify each noun according to whether it (1) is *concrete* or *abstract*, (2) is *singular* or *plural*, (3) is *collective*, (4) is *compound*, and (5) is *common* or *proper*.

1. magnitude
2. Stephen Hawking
3. cosmic ray
4. Proxima Centauri
5. neighbor
6. Barnard's Star
7. observatory
8. dog days
9. matter
10. sunspots

> **Exercise 7** **Recognizing Antecedents** Write each underlined pronoun and its antecedent. If a pronoun does not have an antecedent, write *none* after the pronoun.

1. <u>What</u> is the closest star to the Earth?
2. <u>That</u> is the sun, <u>which</u> helps sustain life on Earth.
3. <u>Its</u> nearest neighboring star system is the Alpha Centauri system.
4. <u>Many</u> say <u>it</u> looks like a single star when viewed with the unaided eye, but Alpha Centauri is really a triple star system.
5. <u>Which</u> of <u>these</u> is <u>our</u> sun's nearest neighbor?

> **Exercise 8** **Identifying Different Types of Pronouns** Identify each underlined pronoun in the paragraphs that follow as *personal*, *intensive*, *demonstrative*, *relative*, *interrogative*, or *indefinite*.

The sun is the star (1) <u>that</u> is at the center of (2) <u>our</u> solar system. Because (3) <u>it</u> is so near and is a typical star, (4) <u>many</u> consider it the greatest resource for cosmological study. Over the centuries, (5) <u>we</u> have studied and even worshiped the sun, but <u>it</u> is only relatively recently <u>that we</u> have gained in-depth knowledge about <u>it</u>.

(6) <u>Who</u> were the first people to gain quantitative knowledge about the sun? (7) <u>That</u> would have been Chinese astronomers more than 2,000 years ago. (8) <u>They</u> first reported the discovery of sunspots, (9) <u>which</u> are dark spots on the sun's surface. About 1,900 years later, German physicist Gustav Kirchhoff showed that the sun (10) <u>itself</u> was composed of ordinary matter by studying the light it emitted.

> **Exercise 9** **Find It in Your Reading** Reread the poem in the Grammar in Literature box on page 368. On your paper, write each pronoun and its antecedent. If a pronoun has no antecedent, write *none*.

> **Exercise 10** **Find It in Your Writing** Review a short story from your writing portfolio. Check to see that you have used pronouns correctly, and rewrite to clarify antecedents.

> **Exercise 11** **Writing Application** Write a description of a typical school week. Use pronouns to avoid repeating the same nouns over and over. Challenge yourself to use each category of pronouns discussed in this section.

Section 17.2 *Verbs*

Every complete sentence contains at least one verb, which may consist of as many as four words.

▶ **KEY CONCEPT** A **verb** is a word or group of words that expresses time while showing an action, a condition, or the fact that something exists. ■

Action Verbs and Linking Verbs

Action verbs, as their name suggests, express either physical or mental action—that is, what someone or something does, did, or will do. *Linking verbs* serve a more passive function, expressing a condition. Verbs used as linking verbs may also be used simply to show that something does exist.

▶ **KEY CONCEPT** An **action verb** tells what action someone or something is performing. ■

ACTION VERBS: The enemy *attacked.*
The soldiers *considered*
their position.

In the first example, the verb tells what the enemy did; in the second example, the verb describes a mental action of the soldiers. The person or thing that performs the action is called the *subject* of the verb. *Enemy* is the subject of *attacked. Soldiers* is the subject of *considered.*

▶ **KEY CONCEPT** A **linking verb** connects its subject with a word generally found near the end of the sentence and identifies, renames, or describes the subject. ■

LINKING VERBS: Augustus *was* emperor.

Augustus *was* powerful.

In the first example, *emperor* identifies or renames *Augustus.* In the second example, *powerful* describes *Augustus.*

The verb *be* is the most common linking verb. Study the many forms of this verb in the chart at the top of the next page.

▼ **Critical Viewing** Use linking verbs in sentences describing Caesar Augustus as rendered by the sculptor. **[Analyze]**

THE FORMS OF *BE*			
am	am being	can be	have been
are	are being	could be	has been
is	is being	may be	had been
was	was being	might be	could have been
were	were being	must be	may have been
		shall be	might have been
		should be	shall have been
		will be	should have been
		would be	will have been
			would have been

Research Tip

You can find lists of current and former world leaders in almanacs, which typically are published yearly.

When the forms of *be* act as linking verbs, they express the condition of the subject. Sometimes, however, they may merely express existence, usually by working with other words to show where the subject is located.

EXAMPLES: The queen *is* in the castle.
                  Alexander's armies *will be* here soon.

Other verbs can also function as linking verbs. The following list shows some of these verbs.

OTHER LINKING VERBS

appear	come	feel	grow	look	remain
seem	smell	sound	stay	taste	turn

EXAMPLES: Before the battle, the soldiers *grew* anxious.

                  The leader *looked* determined.

Most of these verbs can also serve as action verbs. To determine the function of such a verb, insert *am, are,* or *is* in its place. If the resulting sentence makes sense while linking two words, then the verb is serving as a linking verb.

LINKING VERB: Caesar *looks* busy. (Caesar *is* busy.)
ACTION VERB: The conspirators *looked* for an opportunity.

GRAMMAR IN LITERATURE

from **The Tragedy of Macbeth**
William Shakespeare

In the following passage from Macbeth, *the linking verbs are highlighted in blue.*

Good sir, why do you start, and *seem* to fear
Things that *do sound* so fair? I' th' name of truth,
Are you fantastical, or that indeed
Which outwardly ye show? My noble partner
You greet with present grace . . .

◀ **Critical Viewing**
Use three forms of *be* in three sentences about this statue of William Shakespeare. **[Compare]**

▶ **Exercise 12** **Identifying Action and Linking Verbs** Identify each underlined verb as an action verb or a linking verb.

EXAMPLE: Conspirators in the Roman senate <u>plotted</u> the assassination of Julius Caesar.

ANSWER: action verb

1. Born into a powerful family, Julius Caesar <u>seemed</u> destined for glory after an early career in public office.
2. His power <u>grew</u> when he formed an alliance with Pompey the Great and Marcus Licinius Crassus in 60 B.C.
3. After several successful foreign campaigns and the death of Crassus, Caesar and Pompey <u>turned</u> against each other in a quest for the ultimate power in Rome.
4. In 48 B.C., Caesar <u>crushed</u> Pompey's armies at Pharsalus, and Pompey himself was later assassinated.
5. It <u>appeared</u> that Caesar was set to assume power, but wary senators assassinated him on the Ides of March in 44 B.C.
6. Rome <u>was filled</u> with turmoil and unrest after his death.
7. The following year, Caesar's grandnephew Octavian, Mark Antony, and Marcus Aemilius Lepidus <u>banded</u> together to defeat the armies of the assassins.
8. Soon, however, Octavian <u>became</u> the first Roman emperor, after successively defeating Antony and then Lepidus.
9. Under Octavian, Rome <u>enjoyed</u> peace and prosperity.
10. Octavian <u>remained</u> emperor for the rest of his days, and in 27 B.C., the Roman senate gave him the name Augustus.

▶ **More Practice**

Language Lab CD-ROM
• Using Verbs lesson
On-line Exercise Bank
• Section 17.2
Grammar Exercise Workbook
• pp. 5–6

Transitive and Intransitive Verbs

All verbs can be described as either *transitive* or *intransitive*, depending on whether they transfer action to another word in a sentence.

> **KEY CONCEPTS** A verb is transitive if it directs action toward someone or something named in the same sentence. ■

A verb is intransitive if it does not direct action toward someone or something named in the same sentence. ■

The word toward which a transitive verb directs its action is called the *object* of the verb. Intransitive verbs never have objects. You can determine whether a verb has an object and is thus transitive by asking *Whom?* or *What?* after the verb. (See Section 18.3 for more about objects of verbs.)

TRANSITIVE:	He *wrote* a proclamation. OBJ Wrote *what? Answer:* proclamation
	The general *questioned* the soldier. OBJ Questioned *whom? Answer:* soldier
INTRANSITIVE:	The army marched south. Marched *what? Answer:* none
	He fights for his king. Fights *what? Answer:* none

Notice in the examples that the action of the transitive verbs is done *to* something. The writing is done to the proclamation; the questioning is done to the soldier. The action of the intransitive verbs, however, is just done. Nothing receives it.

Linking verbs, which do not express action, are always intransitive. Most action verbs, however, can be either transitive or intransitive, depending on their use in a sentence. Some are either always transitive or always intransitive.

TRANSITIVE OR INTRANSITIVE:	The commander *exercised* his authority. OBJ He *exercises* before battle.
ALWAYS TRANSITIVE:	A stone wall *encloses* the village. OBJ
ALWAYS INTRANSITIVE:	They *cringed* in fear.

⚙ Grammar and Style Tip

Remember: Verbs functioning as linking verbs are always intransitive.

▼ **Critical Viewing**
Alexander the Great possessed one of the greatest military minds. In this picture, he wears a crown of laurels. Explain why *wears* is a transitive verb in this sentence. **[Infer]**

Exercise 13 Identifying Transitive and Intransitive Verbs

Write the verb or verbs in the following sentences, and label each *transitive* or *intransitive*.

EXAMPLE: Alexander the Great conquered much of the Mediterranean world.

ANSWER: conquered (transitive)

1. Alexander the Great was the son of Philip II, king of Macedonia.
2. The great Greek philosopher Aristotle taught him rhetoric, literature, science, and philosophy.
3. Conspirators assassinated King Philip in 336 B.C.
4. At the young age of twenty, Alexander became the new king.
5. He quickly strengthened his position by quelling revolts at home and in Thessaly and Thebes.
6. His armies marched into Persia in 334 B.C. and defeated the main Persian army at Issus in northeastern Syria.
7. Alexander then traveled south, and by 332 B.C., he controlled much of the Middle East.
8. He next took Egypt and established the city of Alexandria at the mouth of the Nile River.
9. Alexandria quickly grew into the commercial and cultural center of the Greek world, and its culture and language spread throughout the lands.
10. After his armies waged war upon India, Alexander traveled to Babylon, where he contracted a fever and died.

Exercise 14 Using Verbs as Transitive or Intransitive

Write sentences using each of the following verbs. Use the verb as a transitive verb and as an intransitive verb. If the verb can be used only one way, identify that one way.

1. taste
2. fight
3. exist
4. leave
5. include
6. gather
7. encourage
8. march
9. pass
10. diminish
11. remember
12. travel
13. take
14. rise
15. name

More Practice

Language Lab CD-ROM
• Using Verbs lesson
On-line Exercise Bank
• Section 17.2
Grammar Exercise Workbook
• pp. 7–8

Verb Phrases

When a verb consists of more than one word, it is called a *verb phrase.*

> **KEY CONCEPT** A **verb phrase** is a verb with one, two, or three helping verbs before it. ■

Helping verbs, also known as *auxiliary verbs* or *auxiliaries*, add meaning to other verbs.

SINGLE VERB: The nation *instituted* a new law.
VERB PHRASES: The nation *will institute* a new law.
                 The nation *should have instituted* a new law.
                 A new law *might have been instituted* by the nation.

Any of the forms of the verb *be* that are listed on page 380 can be used as helping verbs, as can these words listed below.

HELPING VERBS OTHER THAN *BE*

do	have	shall	will	can	may
does	has	should	would	could	might
did	had				must

Verb phrases are often interrupted by other words. To find the complete verb in a sentence, locate the main verb first; then, check for helping verbs that may precede it.

INTERRUPTED
VERB PHRASES: They *will* probably not *institute* a new law.

> **Exercise 15** **Using Verb Phrases** Complete each of the following sentences with an appropriate verb phrase using a form of the verb in parentheses.

EXAMPLE: ___?___ you ___?___ the knight's tales? (hear)
ANSWER: Have you heard the knight's tales?

1. The son of a Frankish king, Charlemagne ___?___ probably ___?___ in Aachen about A.D. 742. (born)
2. King Charlemagne and his brother Carloman ___?___ ___?___ ___?___ power had not Carloman died in A.D. 771. (share)
3. ___?___ Charlemagne ___?___ without his brother? (rule)
4. Over the next 30 years, he ___?___ ___?___ most of Europe. (conquer)
5. His knights were extremely loyal and ___?___ ___?___ ___?___ anything for the glory of their king. (do)

Learn More

For more on verbs, see Chapter 21, "Verb Usage."

▶ **More Practice**

Language Lab CD-ROM
• Using Verbs lesson
On-line Exercise Bank
• Section 17.2
Grammar Exercise Workbook
• pp. 9–10

Section 17.2 Section Review

GRAMMAR EXERCISES 16–21

▶ **Exercise 16** **Identifying Action and Linking Verbs** Identify each of the underlined verbs or verb phrases in the following sentences as either an *action* or a *linking* verb.

1. Born in 1533, Elizabeth I <u>was</u> the daughter of King Henry VIII.
2. After Henry's death, her brother, Edward VI, <u>became</u> king.
3. Edward <u>ruled</u> briefly, and after his death, Mary I <u>ascended</u> to the throne.
4. Elizabeth <u>would have become</u> queen immediately, but Mary was older.
5. Queen Mary I <u>professed</u> Catholicism and had her Protestant sister jailed.

▶ **Exercise 17** **Identifying Transitive and Intransitive Verbs** Write the verbs or verb phrases in the following sentences, and label each *transitive* or *intransitive*.

1. During the French Revolution, Napoleon commanded the French forces.
2. A brilliant general, Napoleon defeated the Austrians in Italy.
3. He returned to France in 1798 and later led a successful coup d'état.
4. After years of successful warfare against the Austrians, peace was declared in 1801.
5. For two years, tranquillity reigned as Napoleon reorganized and simplified the government, courts, and schools.

▶ **Exercise 18** **Using Verbs in Sentences** Write sentences using the verb given as instructed in parentheses.

1. seem (linking verb phrase)
2. smell (action verb)
3. smell (linking verb phrase)
4. write (transitive verb)

5. write (intransitive verb phrase)
6. drive (intransitive verb)
7. drive (transitive verb phrase)
8. grow (linking and action verb phrases)
9. sound (intransitive, linking verb)
10. sound (action, transitive verb phrase)

▶ **Exercise 19** **Find It in Your Reading** Reread the excerpt from "Outside History" by Eavan Boland on page 368. Has Boland used transitive or intransitive verbs? Judging from this example, what differences might you expect to find between poetry that uses primarily transitive verbs and poetry that uses primarily intransitive verbs?

▶ **Exercise 20** **Find It in Your Writing** Review an autobiographical essay from your writing portfolio. In recounting events in your life, have you tended to use more action verbs or linking verbs? How do you think the verbs you use affect your reader? Consider revising your work to include more action verbs.

▶ **Exercise 21** **Writing Application** Draft a college application essay. As you write, monitor the balance of action and linking verbs and transitive and intransitive verbs. Why do you think successful applications tend to be those that make extensive use of action verbs and transitive verbs?

Adjectives and Adverbs

Adjectives and adverbs are the two parts of speech known as *modifiers*—that is, they slightly change the meaning of other words by adding description or by making them more precise.

Adjectives

An adjective qualifies the meaning of a noun or pronoun by providing information about its appearance, location, and so on.

▶ **KEY CONCEPT** An **adjective** is a word used to describe a noun or pronoun or to give it a more specific meaning. ■

An adjective answers one of four questions about a noun or pronoun: *What kind? Which one? How many?* and *How much?*

EXAMPLES: *green* fields (*What kind* of fields?)
             the *flower* garden (*Which* garden?)
             six roses (*How many* roses?)
             extensive rainfall (*How much* rainfall?)

When an adjective modifies a noun, it usually precedes the noun. Occasionally, though, the adjective may follow the noun.

EXAMPLES: The naturalist was *tactful* about my knowledge.

             I considered the naturalist *tactful*.

An adjective that modifies a pronoun usually follows it. Sometimes, however, the adjective may precede the pronoun.

AFTER: They were *brokenhearted* by the early frost.

BEFORE: *Brokenhearted* by the early frost, they left for Florida.

More than one adjective may modify a single noun or pronoun.

EXAMPLE: We hired a *competent, enthusiastic* gardener.

▲ **Critical Viewing**
List five adjectives you would use in a description of this picture. **[Describe]**

Theme: Gardens
In this section, you will learn about adjectives and adverbs. The examples and exercises in this section are about gardens.
Cross-Curricular Connection: Science

Articles

Three common *adjectives—a*, *an*, and *the*—are known as *articles*. *A* and *an* are called *indefinite articles* because they refer to any one of a class of nouns. *The* refers to a specific noun and, therefore, is called the *definite article*.

INDEFINITE:	*a* daisy
	an orchid
DEFINITE:	*the* stem

Nouns Used as Adjectives

Words that are usually nouns sometimes act as adjectives. In this case, the noun answers the questions *What kind?* or *Which one?* about another noun.

NOUNS USED AS ADJECTIVES	
flower	flower garden
lawn	lawn mower

Proper Adjectives

Adjectives can also be proper. Proper adjectives are proper nouns used as adjectives or adjectives formed from proper nouns. They usually begin with capital letters.

Proper Nouns	Proper Adjectives
Monday	Monday morning
San Francisco	San Francisco streets
Europe	European roses
Rome	Roman hyacinth

Compound Adjectives

Adjectives can be compound. Most are hyphenated; others are combined or are separate words.

HYPHENATED:	*rain-forest* plants; *water-soluble* pigments
COMBINED:	*airborne* pollen; *evergreen* shrubs
SEPARATED:	*North American* rhododendrons

Grammar and Style Tip

While some adjectives and nouns many seem interchangeable, that is not always the case. For example, *flower* can be both a noun and an adjective, but *flowery* is only an adjective.

Pronouns Used as Adjectives

Certain pronouns can also function as adjectives. The seven personal pronouns, known as either *possessive adjectives* or *possessive pronouns*, fill two capacities in a sentence. They act as pronouns because they have antecedents. They also act as adjectives because they modify nouns by answering *Which one?* The other pronouns become adjectives instead of pronouns when they stand before nouns and answer the question *Which one?*

> **KEY CONCEPT** A pronoun is used as an adjective if it modifies a noun.■

Possessive pronouns, demonstrative pronouns, interrogative pronouns, and indefinite pronouns can all function as adjectives when they modify nouns. The chart below shows examples of each type.

PRONOUNS USED AS ADJECTIVES

Possessive Pronouns or Adjectives	
my, your, his, her, its, our, their	The bride threw *her* bouquet.
Demonstrative Adjectives	
this, that, these, those	*This* lettuce and *these* dandelions are composite flowers.
Interrogative Adjectives	
which, what, whose	*Which* orchard do you own?
Indefinite Adjectives	
Used with singular nouns: another, each, either, little, much, neither, one	*Each* rose had thorns.
Used with plural nouns: both, few, many, several	*Several* plants bloomed this spring.
Used with singular or plural nouns: all, any, more, most, other, some	Buy *any* fertilizer that you want.
	We appreciate *any* donations.

> **More Practice**
>
> On-line
> Exercise Bank
> • Section 17.3
> Grammar Exercise
> Workbook
> • pp. 11–12

Verb Forms Used as Adjectives

Verb forms used as adjectives usually end in *-ing* or *-ed* and are called *participles*.

EXAMPLE: I pruned the *wilting* flowers.

Nouns, pronouns, and verb forms function as adjectives only when they modify other nouns or pronouns. The following examples show how their function in a sentence can shift.

	Regular Function	As an Adjective
Noun	The *deck* of the boat tilted.	I sat in the *deck* chair.
Pronoun	*This* was an idyllic life.	*This* life was idyllic.
Verb	I *arranged* the flowers.	The *arranged* flowers were admired.

Exercise 22 **Identifying Adjectives** Copy each underlined noun or pronoun in the following paragraph, and write all the adjectives, if any, that modify it. Write *none* if the noun or pronoun has no modifiers.

EXAMPLE: Collections of great art treasures have been preserved in many <u>places</u> around the world.

ANSWER: places (many)

(1) <u>Plants</u> are grown for scientific and educational (2) <u>purposes</u> in botanical (3) <u>gardens</u>. Living (4) <u>plants</u> are grown outdoors or in temperature-controlled (5) <u>greenhouses</u> and indoor (6) <u>conservatories</u>. The (7) <u>plants</u> are displayed in systematic, ecological, and geographic (8) <u>arrangements</u>. Rock, water, and wildflower (9) <u>gardens</u> are included at the larger botanical (10) <u>gardens</u>. In ancient (11) <u>Athens</u>, Aristotle founded one of the earliest botanical (12) <u>gardens</u>. Pisa, an Italian (13) <u>city</u>, houses the oldest public botanical (14) <u>gardens</u>. In the sixteenth and seventeenth (15) <u>centuries</u>, curious (16) <u>herbalists</u> cultivated medicinal (17) <u>herbs</u> in private (18) <u>gardens</u> for scientific (19) <u>research</u>. The (20) Chelsea Physic Garden provided research (21) <u>materials</u>. In the (22) <u>United States</u>, an American (23) <u>botanist</u> founded an experimental (24) <u>garden</u> near (25) <u>Philadelphia</u>.

Grammar and Style Tip

Numbers can also be used as adjectives. In formal writing, numbers are usually written out: *forty* acres or a *dozen* roses.

▼ **Critical Viewing** Compare this garden with the one pictured on page 386. Which adjectives could be used to describe both? Which adjectives would describe only one? **[Compare and Contrast]**

Adverbs

Adverbs, like adjectives, describe other words or make other words more specific.

> **KEY CONCEPT** An **adverb** is a word that modifies a verb, an adjective, or another adverb. ■

When an adverb modifies a verb, it will answer any one of the following questions: *Where? When? In what way?* or *To what extent?* An adverb answers only one question, however, when modifying an adjective or another adverb: *To what extent?* Because it specifies the degree or intensity of the modified adjective or adverb, such an adverb is often called an *intensifier*.

As the following charts show, the position of an adverb in relation to the word it modifies can vary in a sentence. If the adverb modifies a verb, it may precede or follow it or even interrupt a verb phrase. Normally, adverbs modifying adjectives and adverbs will immediately precede the words they modify.

Learn More

For more about correctly placing your modifiers within a sentence, see Chapter 24.

Adverbs Modifying Verbs	
Where?	**When?**
The plant grew *upward.*	She *never* raked the leaves.
The bushes were planted *there.*	*Later,* we toured the greenhouses.
In what way?	**To what extent?**
He *officially* announced it.	The bees were *still* buzzing.
She was *graciously* helping.	He *always* did it right.

Adverbs Modifying Adjectives	Adverbs Modifying Adverbs
To what extent?	**To what extent?**
The solution was *quite* logical.	He worked *very* competently.
It was an *extremely* overgrown garden.	I am *not* completely finished.

Adverbs as Parts of Verbs Some verbs require an adverb to complete their meaning. Adverbs used this way are considered part of the verb. An adverb functioning as part of a verb does not answer the usual questions for adverbs.

EXAMPLE: The tractor *backed up* alongside the field.

**Technology Tip**

To keep your writing fresh, use your word processor's thesaurus to find new and exciting modifiers.

Exercise 23 **Identifying Adverbs** Identify the adverb or adverbs in each sentence, and write whether each modifies a verb, another adverb, or an adjective, or whether it is itself part of a verb.

1. Japanese flower arranging is a very ancient art form.
2. Lately, westerners have taken up the practice.
3. It requires an exquisitely balanced sense of form.
4. When I tried it, I ran out of roses.
5. Nonetheless, I was so thrilled with the results.

More Practice

On-line
Exercise Bank
• Section 17.3
Grammar Exercise
Workbook
• pp. 13–14

Nouns Functioning as Adverbs

Several nouns can function as adverbs that answer the questions *Where?* or *When?* Some of these words are *home, yesterday, today, tomorrow, mornings, afternoons, evenings, nights, week, month,* and *year.*

NOUNS USED AS ADVERBS	
Nouns	**As Adverbs**
Evenings are restful times.	I work *evenings*.
My *home* is miles from here.	Let's head *home*.

Adverb or Adjective?

Adverbs usually have different forms from adjectives and thus are easily identified. Many adverbs are formed by the addition of *-ly* to an adjective.

ADJECTIVE: Our professor looked *pensive*.
ADVERB: The professor looked at her notes *pensively*.

Some adjectives, however, also end in *-ly*. Therefore, you cannot assume that every word ending in *-ly* is an adverb.

ADJECTIVES: an *ugly* scene
                      a *nightly* bloom

Some adjectives and adverbs share the same form. You can determine the part of speech of such words by checking their function in the sentence. An adverb will modify a verb, adjective, or adverb; an adjective will modify a noun or pronoun.

ADVERB: The concert ran late.

ADJECTIVE: We enjoyed the late dinners in Spain.

Adjectives and Adverbs • **391**

▶ **Exercise 24** Identifying Adverbs Each of the following sentences contains one or more adverbs. Write each adverb, and then write the word or words that it modifies.

EXAMPLE: We sailed the boat all afternoon.

ANSWER: all (afternoon)   afternoon (sailed)

1. Composite flowers are particularly well adapted to semi-arid regions.
2. Their name refers directly to the clusters of small flowers in their compact heads.
3. The flowers are always grouped into an "inflorescence," called the head, that resembles a single flower.
4. The numerous petals effectively make the flower more conspicuous to insects and other pollinators.
5. They are poorly represented in the tropical rain forests.
6. Also, composite flowers are not found on Antarctica, where only two species of grass grow.
7. The composite family contains nearly 10 percent of all flowering plants.
8. Economically, the importance of these plants is quite small.
9. Lettuce is certainly the most important crop, but the family also contains artichokes, endives, and tarragon.
10. Horticulturally important composite flowers include marigolds, daisies, dahlias, and zinnias.

▶ **Exercise 25** Revising Sentences by Adding Adverbs Add one adverb from the line below the example to each of the sentences below. Do not use an adverb more than once.

EXAMPLE: People visit botanical gardens.

ANSWER: People *often* visit botanical gardens.

then—later—also—actually—originally

(1) The Royal Botanical Gardens, known as Kew Gardens, is situated on the banks of the River Thames. (2) They consist of two estates, the Richmond Estate and Kew Estate. (3) Augusta, Dowager Princess of Wales, laid out a section of her estate as a botanical garden. (4) The architect Sir William Chambers designed several buildings for the gardens and grounds. (5) When King George III inherited the gardens, Sir Joseph Banks became the unofficial director.

More Practice

On-line
Exercise Bank
• Section 17.3
Grammar Exercise
Workbook
• pp. 13–14

▲ **Critical Viewing**
What adverb would you use to describe how this plant has been cared for? [Infer]

Section Review

GRAMMAR EXERCISES 26–31

▶ **Exercise 26** Identifying
Adjectives Write each noun, and list all
the adjectives, if any, that modify it. Write
none if the noun has no adjectives.

1. After visiting the Royal Botanical
   Gardens in London, a Columbia
   University botanist decided that New
   York should possess a similar garden.
2. A site was selected in the northern
   section of the Bronx.
3. The State Legislature set aside this
   land for the creation of "a public
   botanic garden of the highest class."
4. Many prominent civic leaders agreed
   to contribute funds.
5. At the New York Botanical Gardens,
   there are 250 acres of floral beauty
   and hands-on fun.

▶ **Exercise 27** Identifying Adverbs
Write each adverb, and then write the
word or words that it modifies.

1. The New York Botanical Garden has
   always had a commitment to public
   education.
2. Today, the garden effectively combines
   modern technology with traditional
   scientific research.
3. Its scientists travel extensively around
   the plant world.
4. They collect data to identify and save
   already endangered plant species.
5. Almost daily, schoolchildren visit and
   tour the garden.

▶ **Exercise 28** Identifying
Adjectives and Adverbs Write and label
each adjective (except articles) and adverbs
in the following paragraph. Then, write the
word each modifies.

(1) Gardens in medieval Europe were generally small and enclosed within fortified
walls. (2) Castles had a kitchen garden, a
private ornamental garden, and a large
grassy area for entertaining the entire
court. (3) Without the constant threat of
war and upheaval, gardens in Renaissance
Italy were extensively landscaped areas. (4)
The architect designed both the garden
and the house, for a harmonious relationship between the inside and outside.

▶ **Exercise 29** Find It in Your
Reading Reread the passage from
Macbeth in the Grammar in Literature on
page 381, and identify the adjectives and
adverbs in it. Tell which word is modified
by each adjective and adverb you find.

▶ **Exercise 30** Find It in Your
Writing Look through a personal-
response piece from your writing portfolio,
and find examples of adjective and adverb
usage. Challenge yourself to revise at least
two sentences to contain a verb form used
as an adjective and a noun that functions
as an adverb.

▶ **Exercise 31** Writing Application
Briefly describe a private or public garden in your community. Make sure your
descriptions contain examples of nouns,
pronouns, and verb forms as adjectives; of
nouns used as adverbs; and adverbs functioning as parts of verbs.

Prepositions, Conjunctions, and Interjections

Two of the final three parts of speech—prepositions and conjunctions—function in sentences as connectors. *Prepositions* express relationships between words or ideas, whereas *conjunctions* join words, groups of words, or even entire sentences. The last part of speech, *interjections*, functions by itself, independent of other words in a sentence.

Prepositions and Prepositional Phrases

Prepositions make it possible to show relationships between words. The relationships shown may involve, for example, location, direction, time, cause, or possession.

▶ **KEY CONCEPT** A **preposition** relates the noun or pronoun that appears with it to another word in the sentence. ■

See how the prepositions below relate to the italicized words.

	PREP
LOCATION:	Inventions *are made* around the *world*.
	PREP
DIRECTION:	Small discoveries *lead* toward new *inventions*.
	PREP
TIME:	Some inventions *last* for *centuries*.
	PREP
CAUSE:	People *invent* because of their *curiosity*.
	PREP
POSSESSION:	*Changes* from new *inventions* help many people.

▶ **KEY CONCEPT** A **prepositional phrase** is a group of words that includes a preposition and a noun or pronoun. ■

The noun or pronoun with a preposition is called the *object of the preposition*. Objects may have one or more modifiers. A prepositional phrase may also have more than one object.

EXAMPLES: Alexander Graham Bell and Elisha Gray applied
                              OBJ OF PREP   OBJ OF PREP
                for telephone patents *on* the same day.

                              OBJ OF PREP   OBJ OF PREP
                During his lifetime, Bell resided *in* Scotland and
                OBJ OF PREP
                Canada.

Theme: Inventions

In this section, you will learn about prepositions, conjunctions, and interjections. The examples and exercises in this section are about inventors and inventions.

Cross-Curricular Connection: Science

PREPOSITIONS

aboard	before	in front of	over
about	behind	in place of	owing to
above	below	in regard to	past
according to	beneath	inside	prior to
across from	beside	in spite of	regarding
across	besides	instead of	round
after	between	into	since
against	beyond	in view of	through
ahead of	but	like	throughout
along	by	near	till
alongside	by means of	nearby	to
along with	concerning	next to	together with
amid	considering	of	toward
among	despite	off	under
apart from	down	on	underneath
around	during	on account of	until
aside from	except	onto	unto
as of	for	on top of	up
at	from	opposite	upon
atop	in	out	with
barring	in addition to	out of	within
because of	in back of	outside	without

▶ **More Practice**

**On-line
Exercise Bank**
• Section 17.4
**Grammar Exercise
Workbook**
• pp. 15–16

▶ **Exercise 32** **Identifying Prepositional Phrases** Write the prepositional phrases in the following paragraph, and circle each preposition. If there are no prepositional phrases, write *none.*

EXAMPLE: The Machine Age began with the Industrial Revolution and continues to this day.

ANSWER: (with) the Industrial Revolution; (to) this day

(1) At the time, Thomas Edison was selling newspapers on the Grand Trunk Railway. (2) From a freight car, he started publishing a weekly newspaper called the *Grand Trunk Herald.* (3) After he saved the life of a child, Edison was taught telegraphy by the child's father. (4) Then, Edison made his first important invention, a telegraphic repeating instrument. (5) It could transmit messages over a second line without an operator.

▼ **Critical Viewing**
Describe the clutter in Thomas Edison's office. What prepositions would you use? [Analyze]

Preposition or Adverb?

Because prepositions and adverbs occasionally take the same form, they may be difficult to tell apart. Words that can function in either role include *around, before, behind, down, in, off, on, out, over,* and *up.* To determine the part of speech of these words, see whether an object accompanies the word. If so, the word is used as a preposition.

PREPOSITION: The Machine Age developed *around a*
                                                    OBJ
                group of inventions.

ADVERB: My thoughts went *around* and *around.*

Internet Tip

To find information about other inventions, use Internet search words like *inventions, patents,* and *Industrial Age.*

▶ **Exercise 33** **Distinguishing Between Prepositions and Adverbs** Identify the underlined word in each sentence as either a *preposition* or an *adverb.* If the word is a preposition, write its object on your paper as well.

EXAMPLE: They are waiting <u>near</u> the door.
ANSWER: preposition (door)

1. After Edison set up his own laboratory, his successful inventions took <u>off</u>.
2. In 1877, Edison announced <u>to</u> the public his invention of a phonograph.
3. Sound could be recorded <u>on</u> a tinfoil cylinder.
4. The incandescent electric light was ready <u>for</u> exhibition two years later.
5. <u>Before</u> its perfection, it required careful research and extensive experimentation.
6. He occupied himself <u>with</u> the improvement of the bulbs.
7. Edison <u>next</u> developed the first central electric-power station.
8. He experimented early with direct current, which was left <u>behind</u> when other inventors developed the alternating current system.
9. Later, he moved away <u>from</u> Menlo Park to West Orange, New Jersey.
10. In 1888, he invented the kinetoscope, which produced motion pictures <u>by</u> a succession of individual views.

▶ **More Practice**

On-line Exercise Bank
• Section 17.4
Grammar Exercise Workbook
• pp. 15–16

Conjunctions

There are three main kinds of conjunctions: *coordinating*, *correlative*, and *subordinating*. Sometimes a kind of adverb, the conjunctive adverb, is also considered a conjunction.

> **KEY CONCEPT** A **conjunction** is a word used to connect other words or groups of words. ■

Coordinating Conjunctions The seven coordinating conjunctions are used to connect similar parts of speech or groups of words of equal grammatical weight.

COORDINATING CONJUNCTIONS						
and	but	for	nor	or	so	yet

Correlative Conjunctions The five paired correlative conjunctions join elements of equal grammatical weight.

CORRELATIVE CONJUNCTIONS		
both . . . and	either . . . or	neither . . . nor
not only . . . but also	whether . . . or	

Subordinating Conjunctions Subordinating conjunctions join two complete ideas by making one of the ideas subordinate to or dependent upon the other.

SUBORDINATING CONJUNCTIONS			
after	because	lest	till
although	before	now that	unless
as	even if	provided	until
as if	even though	since	when
as long as	how	so that	whenever
as much as	if	than	where
as soon as	inasmuch as	that	wherever
as though	in order that	though	while

Spelling Tip

Be careful when writing some subordinating conjunctions. Words like *inasmuch* are written without spaces, but other words, like *as much as,* do have spaces.

The subordinate idea in a sentence always begins with a subordinating conjunction and makes up what is known as a subordinate clause. A subordinate clause may either follow or precede the main idea in a sentence.

Conjunctive Adverbs Conjunctive adverbs act as transitions between complete ideas by indicating comparisons, contrasts, results, and other relationships. The chart below lists the most common conjunctive adverbs.

CONJUNCTIVE ADVERBS		
accordingly	finally	nevertheless
again	furthermore	otherwise
also	however	then
besides	indeed	therefore
consequently	moreover	thus

As shown in the following examples, punctuation is usually required both before and after conjunctive adverbs.

EXAMPLES: The Marconi Wireless Telegraph Co., Inc., was very successful. *Nevertheless*, Marconi continued to pursue other inventions.

He also invented several types of aerials; *however*, he will be remembered for the wireless telegraph.

GRAMMAR IN
LITERATURE

from **Progress in Personal Comfort**
Sydney Smith

In the passage below, note how, by using coordinating conjunctions (highlighted in blue italics), the author presents a rapid series of images depicting a vanished way of life.

I can walk, by the assistance of the police, from one end of London to the other, without molestation; *or,* if tired, get into a cheap *and* active cab, instead of those cottages on wheels, which the hackney coaches were at the beginning of my life.

I had no umbrella! They were little used, *and* very dear. There were no waterproof hats, *and my* hat has often been reduced by rains into its primitive pulp.

Exercise 34 Identifying Conjunctions in Sentences Write the conjunctions in each sentence and label each *coordinating*, *correlative*, or *subordinating*.

EXAMPLE: They could not decide whether their films of everyday life would bore people or would interest people.

ANSWER: whether or (correlative)

1. Louis and Auguste Lumière contributed to the birth of film.
2. Their camera was a machine for both film projection and development.
3. Not only could the camera perform two tasks, but the box was much lighter than its rival, the Kinematoscope.
4. Because it was portable, the camera was suitable for outdoor use.
5. The camera was notable because it ran quietly and smoothly.

Exercise 35 Revising Sentences by Adding Conjunctive Adverbs Write the following pairs of sentences, adding appropriate conjunctive adverbs.

EXAMPLE: Many scholars believe that Homer wrote the *Iliad* and the *Odyssey*. Some scholars claim that he never existed.

ANSWER: Many scholars believe that Homer wrote the *Iliad* and the *Odyssey*. Some scholars, however, claim that he never existed.

1. A device called the Praxinoscope consisted of a revolving drum with mirrors at the center. When it revolved, the images appeared to be living.
2. People across Europe were working on similar theories at that time. In 1839, the photographic process was perfected.
3. Photographs replaced drawings in viewing machines. Coleman Sellers patented the Kinematoscope for this viewing.
4. The Kinematoscope made it possible to photograph movement instead of poses. In 1877, Eadweard Muybridge used multiple cameras to record the image of a running horse.
5. The chronophotographe moved a band of images past an opening at a steady speed. This invention was a major step toward the motion-picture camera.

More Practice

On-line
Exercise Bank
• Section 17.4
Grammar Exercise
Workbook
• pp. 17–18

▼ **Critical Viewing**
Use a conjunctive adverb in a sentence that contrasts the way this Kinematoscope technology would have been considered in the 1800's with the way we consider it today. [Contrast]

Interjections

Interjections express emotion. Unlike most words, they have no grammatical connection to other words in a sentence.

▶ **KEY CONCEPT** An **interjection** is a word that expresses feeling or emotion and functions independently of a sentence. ■

Interjections can express a variety of sentiments, such as happiness, fear, anger, pain, surprise, sorrow, exhaustion, or hesitation.

SOME COMMON INTERJECTIONS				
ah	dear	hey	ouch	well
aha	goodness	hurray	psst	whew
alas	gracious	oh	tsk	wow

Exclamation marks or commas usually set off an interjection from the rest of the sentence, as the following examples show.

EXAMPLES: *Ouch!* That machine is very hot.
Goodness, if you didn't see *The Great Train Robbery*, you haven't seen the first major American movie!

▶ **Exercise 36** **Using Interjections** Write five sentences containing interjections that express the following general emotions. Underline the interjections in your sentences.

EXAMPLE: surprise
ANSWER: <u>Oh</u>, was that by Edwin Porter?

1. indecision
2. sorrow
3. urgency
4. exhaustion
5. fear

▶ **Critical Viewing**
Thomas Edison inspects film as he sits next to an early projector. How do you think it would feel to discover that one of your inventions actually worked? What interjections might you use to express your feelings? **[Speculate]**

Grammar and Style Tip

When choosing the method of punctuating your interjections, be sure that your period, comma, question mark, or exclamation mark matches the content of your sentence.

▶ **More Practice**

On-line
Exercise Bank
• Section 17.4
Grammar Exercise Workbook
• pp. 19–20

Section 17.4 *Section Review*

GRAMMAR EXERCISES 37–42

Exercise 37 Identifying **Prepositional Phrases** Write the prepositional phrases from the following paragraph, and circle each preposition.

(1) A glider stays afloat by means of the aerodynamic forces acting upon it. (2) Glider wings, when compared to airplane wings, are longer and narrower. (3) Early experiments with gliders influenced the design of the first aircraft. (4) Starting in the 1870's, successful gliders provided information about wings and controls for flying. (5) Otto Lilienthal discovered the advantages of curved surfaces on wings.

Exercise 38 Distinguishing **Among Subordinating Conjunctions, Prepositions, and Adverbs** Identify each underlined word as a *subordinating conjunction*, *preposition*, *adverb*, or *conjunctive adverb*.

1. France and Germany focused <u>on</u> the internal-combustion engine.
2. Nikolaus Otto, who had already developed an efficient gas engine <u>before</u>, built a four-cycle engine in 1876.
3. <u>However</u>, it was Daimler's high-speed motor that aided development.
4. In 1891, Emile Levassor produced an automobile with parts arranged <u>in</u> the same order still used today.
5. Henry Ford brought <u>out</u> his first experimental car in 1896.

Exercise 39 Revising Sentences **by Adding Interjections** Insert an appropriate interjection into each sentence.

1. X-rays were discovered accidentally!
2. Wasn't Wilhelm Roentgen studying cathode rays?

3. The fluorescent light was quite a surprise!
4. He named the radiation "X ray" because it was so unknown.
5. I hope it didn't hurt him.

Exercise 40 Find It in Your **Reading** Identify the prepositions and conjunctions in the following excerpt from "Progress in Personal Comfort."

It is of some importance at what period a man is born. A young man, alive at this period, hardly knows to what improvements of human life he has been introduced; and I would bring before his notice the following eighteen changes which have taken place in England since I first began to breathe in it the breath of life—a period amounting now to nearly seventy-three years.

Exercise 41 Find It in Your **Writing** Review a comparison-and-contrast essay from your writing portfolio. How many correlative conjunctions did you use? Challenge yourself to revise at least five sentences to include correlative conjunctions.

Exercise 42 Writing Application Write a brief dialogue among three or more characters. Use at least three different interjections, four prepositions, and two conjunctions. Underline each of these words and identify the part of speech. For each conjunction, tell what kind it is.

Reviewing Parts of Speech

Words are flexible, often serving as one part of speech in one sentence and as another part of speech in another.

Words as Different Parts of Speech

A word's part of speech should be determined only by the way it is used in a sentence.

▶ **KEY CONCEPT** How a word is used in a sentence determines its part of speech. ■

Notice, for example, the many functions of the word *outside.*

AS A NOUN:	The *outside* of the house is brick.
AS AN ADJECTIVE:	It was an *outside* chance, but I took it.
AS AN ADVERB:	The children played *outside.*
AS A PREPOSITION:	We went sightseeing *outside* the city limits.

The following chart suggests questions to ask yourself when you are trying to identify a word's part of speech.

Parts of Speech	Questions to Ask Yourself
Noun	Does the word name a person, place, or thing?
Pronoun	Does the word stand for a noun?
Verb	Does the word tell what someone or something did? Does the word link one word with another word that identifies or describes it? Does the word merely show that something exists?
Adjective	Does the word tell *what kind, which one, how many,* or *how much?*
Adverb	Does the word tell *where, when, in what way,* or *to what extent?*
Preposition	Is the word part of a phrase that includes a noun or pronoun?
Conjunction	Does the word connect other words in the sentence?
Interjection	Does the word express emotion and function independently of the sentence?

Theme: Volcanoes
• •
In this section, you will practice using words as different parts of speech. The examples and exercises in this section are about volcanoes.
• •
Cross-Curricular Connection: Science

Grammar and Style Tip

In formal writing, try to vary your word choice rather than repeating the same words as different parts of speech.

Exercise 43 Identifying Parts of Speech Identify the part of speech of each underlined word.

EXAMPLE: Take <u>care</u> where you walk if you <u>care</u> about your safety

ANSWER: noun   verb

1. <u>Many</u> of us felt the <u>many</u> dangers brewing in the volcano.
2. <u>Well</u>, I think it would serve us <u>well</u> to evacuate.
3. If the Earth's <u>rock</u> layer is disrupted, the island <u>rocks</u>.
4. We tried to take everything <u>but</u> the furniture, <u>but</u> there was not enough time.
5. The volcano let out a mighty <u>groan</u> while the departing boat <u>groaned</u> under the weight of the fleeing residents.

Exercise 44 More Work With Parts of Speech Identify the part of speech of each underlined word.

EXAMPLE: In the distance, we saw the <u>smoking</u> volcano.
ANSWER: adjective

Volcanoes can erupt in (1) <u>different</u> ways at different times. (2) <u>Some</u> are more violent than (3) <u>others</u>. They blast ash, rock, and lava (4) <u>into</u> the atmosphere. Puffs of ash and gases (5) <u>are</u> released from the more gentle eruptions without causing much damage to the (6) <u>surrounding</u> landscape. The materials in the volcano's magma (7) <u>chamber</u> will determine the type of eruption. (8) <u>When</u> lava flows (9) <u>out of</u> a volcano, (10) <u>that</u> is called an effusive eruption. A (11) <u>steam</u> eruption, the more violent type, (12) <u>occurs</u> when water mixes with the molten rock. Some pieces of rock spin (13) <u>around</u> and (14) <u>become</u> more streamlined. These are called (15) <u>volcanic</u> bombs. Giant clouds of dust (16) <u>and</u> ash are produced in a (17) <u>Plinian</u> explosion. Pumice is a rock with holes (18) <u>where</u> there used to be gas bubbles. It is so (19) <u>light</u> that it can (20) <u>even</u> float on water.

More Practice
On-line
Exercise Bank
• Section 17.5
Grammar Exercise
Workbook
• pp. 21–22

◀ **Critical Viewing**
Compare this volcanic explosion with the explosion of the supernova on page 377. Which verbs apply to both events? [**Compare**]

Hands-on Grammar

Parts-of-Speech Points

Write each of the following words on an index card: *past, present, last, stop, opposite, after, dry, left, fast, beyond, outside, down, before, look, which.* Put the cards in a box, and shake them all around.

Divide your class into groups of three or four students so that there are an even number of groups. One group of students plays against another group. The object of the game is to use each word in as many ways as possible.

Noun:	They dug a deep well.
Adverb:	I did well on the test.
Interjection:	Well, what were you thinking?
Verb:	Emotion welled up inside her.

well

Pick a card. Set your timer for five minutes. See how many different ways the word can function. Students may brainstorm within their group for possible parts of speech the word may be used as. Each group is to write a sentence illustrating the use of the word as that part of speech.

The group that comes up with the most correct uses of the word within a sentence in five minutes gets a point. The team with the most points wins.

Find It in Your Writing Look through your portfolio to find examples of words used as more than one part of speech. Write the words on index cards, and add them to your collection for another round of the game.

Find It in Your Reading Record examples of words used as more than one part of speech as you discover them in your reading. Write them down, identify the parts of speech they are used as, and challenge yourself to think of other ways they could be used.

Section
17.5 *Section Review*

GRAMMAR EXERCISES 45–51

Exercise 45 **Identifying Parts of Speech** Identify the part of speech of each underlined word.

1. Volcanic explosions rock the area around <u>them</u>.
2. Lava <u>escapes</u> from cracks called fissures.
3. The lava floods <u>from</u> the fissures, which may be miles long.
4. It pours <u>down</u> the mountain.
5. As the lava continues to move <u>down</u>, it begins to cool.
6. <u>Cooling</u> lava cracks into columns with four, five, or six sides.
7. Basalt <u>is</u> a type of rock that forms when lava hardens.
8. <u>Flood</u> basalts may be hundreds of feet thick.
9. They will cover the <u>landscape</u>.
10. Much <u>basalt</u> cover was formed millions of years ago.

Exercise 46 **Supplying Parts of Speech** Supply the part of speech indicated in parentheses to complete each sentence.

1. Flowing (adv.), fluid lava races down a mountain at 660 feet per second.
2. Some lava resembles piles and coils (prep.) rope when it cools.
3. The speed of a lava flow (verb) upon its composition.
4. (Adj.) minerals and gases make up lava.
5. Silica, the most common mineral in the Earth's crust, is found more often in slowly flowing (noun).

Exercise 47 **Using Parts of Speech** Write sentences using each of the words that follow as the part of speech indicated.

1. like (verb)
2. like (preposition)
3. today (noun)
4. today (adverb)
5. after (preposition)
6. after (adverb)
7. train (verb)
8. train (noun)
9. early (adjective)
10. early (adverb)

Exercise 48 **Revising Sentences** Revise each sentence by adding adjectives, adverbs, and prepositional phrases.

1. The volcano exploded.
2. Lava is hot.
3. Lava is running.
4. The mountain is tall.
5. Eruptions are dangerous.

Exercise 49 **Find It in Your Reading** Identify the nouns, adjectives, adverbs, and prepositions in the excerpt from "Progress in Personal Comfort" on page 398.

Exercise 50 **Find It in Your Writing** Review a single paragraph from a finished piece of work in your writing portfolio. Determine the part of speech each word fills. Do you tend to use the same parts of speech over and over?

Exercise 51 **Writing Application** Revise the paragraph you reviewed for the preceding exercise to vary the parts of speech. Make a point of revising to include parts of speech that were missing or little used in the original.

Chapter Review

GRAMMAR EXERCISES 52–60

Exercise 52 Classifying Nouns

For each noun in the following list, identify it according to whether it (1) names a person, place, or thing; (2) is concrete or abstract; (3) is singular or plural; (4) is collective; (5) is compound; and (6) is common or proper.

1.	crater	6.	basalt
2.	Mount Vesuvius	7.	organization
3.	carbon monoxide	8.	gases
4.	volcano	9.	magma
5.	hot spots	10.	Mount Etna

Exercise 53 Identifying Pronouns and Their Antecedents Write each pronoun and identify it as *personal*, *reflexive*, *intensive*, *demonstrative*, *relative*, *interrogative*, or *indefinite*. Then, write its antecedent. If the pronoun does not have an antecedent, write *none*.

1. Volcanoes are not found everywhere. Their locations follow patterns.
2. Lines of volcanoes spread for miles. Sometimes, they are where a continent meets an ocean.
3. When a volcano is seen alone, it doesn't seem to belong to a chain.
4. Island arches are groups of volcanoes. Japan is one example of these.
5. There is a ridge in the middle of the Atlantic Ocean. That is where two of the Earth's plates meet.
6. As the plates move apart, they cause another line of volcanoes.
7. Their actions continue to move Europe and North American farther apart.
8. What produces the volcanic cones?
9. The magma cools into shapes that are called pillow lava.
10. Which volcanoes are still active?

Exercise 54 Identifying Verbs

Identify the verbs or verb phrases in the following sentences, and label them *action* or *linking*, *transitive* or *intransitive*.

1. Mount Pinatubo, a Philippine volcano, was not considered dangerous.
2. It had remained dormant for 600 years before it exploded in 1991.
3. The lava wrecked homes as it poured down the slopes.
4. The 30-mile-long stream forced 75,000 people to flee.
5. When a fissure opened on the side of the volcano, people in the 25-mile danger zone feared the worst.

Exercise 55 Identifying Adjectives and Adverbs Write each adverb and adjective, not including articles, in the following sentences. Write the word that each adverb or adjective modifies.

1. One giant eruption can completely change the shape of a volcano.
2. Mount St. Helens, before the 1980 eruption, was a perfect cone.
3. The violent eruption blew out one side.
4. The snowy mountain quickly lost 1,300 feet off the top.
5. The north side fell swiftly as an avalanche while ash clouds blasted out.
6. Mudflows and other debris filled in surrounding river valleys and lakes.
7. Entire forests of trees were blown flat.
8. Today, the shape continues to change.
9. Inside, there is now a new vent, and lava is building a new cone.
10. Rain and ice wear away the slopes to carve new valleys into the landscape.

> **Exercise 56** **Using Prepositions**
Complete each prepositional phrase with an appropriate preposition.

1. Earth is not the only planet __?__ volcanoes.
2. The highest and largest volcano, called Olympus Mons, is found __?__ Mars.
3. It is more than 16 miles high and 370 miles __?__ the base.
4. It may have been very active __?__ a very long period of time, longer than any volcanoes on Earth.
5. The entire area looks like it may have been formed __?__ lava flows.

> **Exercise 57** **Writing Sentences With Conjunctions** Write five sentences about volcanoes, earthquakes, or other natural phenomena, using at least eight of the conjunctions listed below. Make sure that each one functions correctly as a coordinating, correlative, or subordinating conjunction or as a conjunctive adverb.

and	but
or	yet
neither . . . nor	either . . . or
not only . . . but also	because
provided that	while
when	until
since	even though
therefore	consequently
moreover	finally
nevertheless	otherwise

> **Exercise 58** **Supplying All Parts of Speech** Fill in the blanks in the following paragraph with the appropriate parts of speech.

Flying into the __?__ of Managua, __?__ is the capital of Nicaragua, I __?__ see the volcanoes. There __?__ the middle of Lake Nicaragua was a volcano! Later, we __?__ a bus trip to the volcano. __?__ below, __?__ looked like a smoking cone. __?__ hiked to the top. Looking __?__ from the rim, __?__ view was obscured by the smoke. I just __?__ imagine living next to __?__ active volcano!

> **Exercise 59** **Recognizing All Parts of Speech** Identify the part of speech of the underlined word.

Pompeii, in ancient Italy, (1) <u>was located</u> a few miles south of Mount Vesuvius. Vesuvius is the only (2) <u>currently</u> active volcano on the (3) <u>European</u> mainland. Other (4) <u>nearby</u> cities included Herculaneum and Stabiae. Pliny the Younger, from his (5) <u>vantage point</u> across the bay in Naples, observed the (6) <u>A.D. 79</u> eruption of Mount Vesuvius. Winds (7) <u>carried</u> a tall (8) <u>column</u> of ash and dust (9) <u>directly</u> over Pompeii. Pumice, ash, and dust caused (10) <u>complete</u> darkness. The next stage of the eruption (11) <u>brought</u> hot, rocky avalanches and (12) <u>then</u> mudflows. The (13) <u>glowing</u> avalanches advanced (14) <u>slowly</u>, (15) <u>until</u> they surged toward Herculaneum and then (16) <u>again</u> toward Pompeii. The dark cloud covered the entire area and dropped (17) <u>ash</u> on the surrounding landscape. (18) <u>Hot</u> ashes and cinders showered (19) <u>down</u> for days. (20) <u>Furthermore</u>, the deep coverings preserved (21) <u>these</u> towns (22) <u>for</u> modern archaeologists. Digs and excavations (23) <u>have unearthed</u> historical information about first-century (24) <u>Italian</u> life and (25) <u>about</u> the volcanic eruption.

> **Exercise 60** **Writing Application** Write a paragraph about the Earth, using at least three prepositional phrases, three conjunctions, two interjections, three adverbs, and three adjectives. Underline all nouns once, underline all verbs twice, and circle all prepositions.

Standardized Test Preparation Workshop

Analogies

Analogy questions test your ability to determine a relationship between a given pair of words and to identify a similar relationship between the words in the second pair.

The words in the correct answer choice will usually, but not always, be the same parts of speech combination (nouns, pronouns, verbs, adjectives, or adverbs) as the original pair. To answer correctly, find the more specific relationship between the words.

Types of word relationships include:

- *Antonyms*, such as *infuriate : please*
- *Part-Whole* or *Whole-Part*, such as *vest : buttons*
- *Definitional/ Synonyms*, such as *tacit : unspoken*
- *Cause-Effect* or *Effect-Cause*, such as *deceit : mistrust*
- *Functional Relationship*, such as *needle : knitting*
- *Relationship of Degrees*, such as *rivulet : torrent*

Test Tip

Sometimes the relationship between two words is multiple. Always probe beneath the first relationship you recognize to see if there is a less obvious but more important secondary relationship.

Sample Test Item

Directions: The question below consists of a related pair of words, followed by five pairs of words labeled *A* through *E*. Select the pair that *best* expresses a relationship similar to that expressed in the original pair.

CRUMB : BREAD ::

    (A) ounce : unit

    (B) splinter : wood

    (C) water : bucket

    (D) twine : rope

    (E) cream : butter

Answer and Explanation

The correct answer is *B.* A crumb is a tiny, broken off bit of a piece of bread. In the same way, a splinter is a tiny, broken off bit of a piece of wood.

▶ **Practice 1** **Directions:** Each question below consists of a related pair of words or phrases, followed by five pairs of word or phrases labeled *A* through *E*. Select the pair that best expresses a relationship similar to that expressed in the original pair.

1. SUBMERGE : WATER ::
   (A) parch : soil
   (B) bury : earth
   (C) suffocate : air
   (D) disperse : gas
   (E) extinguish : fire

2. TACIT : WORDS ::
   (A) visible : scenes
   (B) inevitable : facts
   (C) colorful : hues
   (D) suspicious : clues
   (E) unanimous : disagreements

3. DEFECTOR : CAUSE ::
   (A) counterfeit : money
   (B) deserter : army
   (C) critic : book
   (D) advertiser : sale
   (E) intruder : meeting

4. COMPATRIOTS : COUNTRY ::
   (A) transients : home
   (B) kinsfolk : family
   (C) competitors : team
   (D) performers : audience
   (E) figureheads : government

▶ **Practice 2** **Directions:** Each question below consists of a related pair of words or phrases, followed by five pairs of words or phrases labeled *A* through *E*. Select the pair that best expresses a relationship similar to that expressed in the original pair.

1. UNFETTER : PINIONED ::
   (A) recite : practiced
   (B) sully : impure
   (C) enlighten : ignorant
   (D) revere : unrecognized
   (E) adore : cordial

2. CHIEF : HIERARCHY ::
   (A) office : rank
   (B) platoon : army
   (C) president : term
   (D) lawyer : court
   (E) summit : mountain

3. SHOVE : NUDGE ::
   (A) vex : mutter
   (B) calm : quell
   (C) teach : lecture
   (D) push : fight
   (E) stare : glance

4. BARLEY : GRAIN ::
   (A) yeast : bread
   (B) pine : tree
   (C) vine : fruit
   (D) knot : rope
   (E) twig : nest

Basic Sentence Parts

When words combine to form a sentence, they can convey great meaning. As sentences increase in complexity and sophistication, they take on even greater meaning.

In many ways, words are like ants. An ant, though an extraordinary creature in itself, is still limited in size and strength. However, ants are social creatures. They live in colonies inhabited by thousands of other ants and share the workload of the entire colony. They combine their efforts, each ant carrying out a specific task, to produce more work as a whole than any individual ant could accomplish alone in a lifetime. Like ants, words work together to form limitless possibilities.

This chapter will focus on how words are combined to form sentences and to convey meaning.

▲ **Critical Viewing**
In two complete sentences, explain what these ants could be doing.
[Speculate]

Diagnostic Test

Directions: Write all answers on a separate sheet of paper.

Skill Check A. Copy the following sentences, drawing a vertical line between the subject and the complete predicate.

1. Ants are very closely related to wasps.
2. They have similar body structures.
3. Their antennae are jointed in the middle.
4. Like wasps, some ant species have a functional sting for the defense of their colony.
5. Because of their physical similarities, both wasps and ants belong to the Hymenoptera order of insect classification.

Skill Check B. Write each sentence, underlining the subject once and the verb twice. Include in parentheses any word that is understood.

6. There is a nest of fire ants in our basement.
7. In every corner of the basement crawled the busy ants.
8. Have you ever been bitten by a fire ant?
9. In case of a bite, apply alcohol.
10. Please, get me my antihistamine.

Skill Check C. Identify the complement(s) in each sentence as *direct object, indirect object, objective complement, predicate nominative,* or *predicate adjective.*

11. Ants improve the environment.
12. Some ants give their prey vicious bites.
13. Scientists call ants social creatures.
14. Ants are foragers and builders.
15. Ants appear ugly, but most are harmless.

Skill Check D. Write each sentence, underlining the subject once, underlining the verb twice, and circling each complement.

16. I gave my brother an ant farm for his birthday.
17. Ants are members of the Formicidae family.
18. Some ants construct nests in mounds of soil.
19. One often sees the mounds in sidewalk cracks.
20. Ant colonies include workers, males, and a queen.
21. Small, younger workers are nurse ants.
22. Some workers feed other ants honeydew, a substance secreted by other insects.
23. Farmers find some ants useful.
24. In a house, however, ants are a nuisance.
25. Ants are highly intelligent.

Subjects and Predicates

A sentence is a group of words that expresses meaning. In English, every sentence has two essential parts, a *complete subject* and a *complete predicate*. Being aware of these parts can help you avoid letting the order of your words get in the way of your ideas.

▶**KEY CONCEPT** A **sentence** is a group of words with two main parts: a complete subject and a complete predicate. Together, these parts express a complete thought. ■

The complete subject contains the noun, pronoun, or group of words acting as a noun, plus their modifiers, that tells *who* or *what* the sentence is about. The complete predicate consists of the verb or verb phrase, plus any modifiers and complements, that tells what the complete subject *does* or *is*.

Complete Subjects	Complete Predicates
Critters	creep.
A bell-clanging streetcar	moved through the intersection.
Wood or cellulose	is a delicious meal for a termite.
The candidate's pragmatic approach to fiscal problems	impressed the voters attending the rally last Thursday.

In some sentences, a portion of the predicate may precede the complete subject.

                    COMPLETE   COMPLETE SUBJ   PREDICATE
EXAMPLE: At midnight, the multitude of spiders spun webs.

▶**Exercise 1** Recognizing Complete Subjects and Complete Predicates Copy the following paragraph, drawing a vertical line between each complete subject and complete predicate. Some sentences may require more than one line.

EXAMPLE: Suddenly, | the trilling of the cicadas | filled the room.

(1) Cicadas adapt well to their surroundings. (2) From tropical to temperate regions, they survive in a wide range of climates. (3) In the United States, cicadas are most abundant in the East and Midwest. (4) Some cicada species are known as locusts or harvest flies. (5) These species are neither true locusts nor flies.

Theme: Insects
• •
In this section, you will learn about simple and complete subjects and predicates. The examples and exercises in this section are about insects.
• •
Cross-Curricular Connection: Science

▶**More Practice**
On-line
Exercise Bank
• Section 18.1
Grammar Exercise Workbook
• pp. 23–24

Simple Subjects and Predicates

When all modifiers and complements are removed from a complete subject and complete predicate, an essential word or group of words remains in each. These essential elements, called the *simple subject* and *simple predicate,* are the core around which sentences are developed.

> **KEY CONCEPTS** The **simple subject** is the essential noun, pronoun, or group of words acting as a noun that cannot be left out of the complete subject. The **simple predicate** is the essential verb or verb phrase that cannot be left out of the complete predicate. ■

The following chart shows simple subjects underlined once and simple predicates underlined twice. Notice how any remaining words either modify the simple subject and simple predicate or help to complete the meaning of the sentence.

Learn More

For a review of nouns, pronouns, and verbs, see Chapter 17.

SIMPLE SUBJECTS AND SIMPLE PREDICATES	
Complete Subjects	**Complete Predicates**
Small <u>mice</u>	<u>fit</u> nicely into coat pockets.
Many horror <u>films</u>	<u>have used</u> bugs to terrifying effect.
<u>Studies</u> of insects	<u>have</u> certainly <u>revealed</u> much about their behavior.

▼ **Critical Viewing** How is a bee's diet different from an ant's? Respond in one or more complete sentences. **[Contrast]**

Notice in the last example that the simple subject is *studies,* not *insects,* which is the object of the preposition *of.* Objects of prepositions never function as simple subjects. In this same example, notice also that the simple predicate is a verb phrase.

NOTE: In this textbook, the term *subject* will be used to refer to a simple subject and the term *verb* will be used to refer to a simple predicate.

Fragments

When either the complete subject or complete predicate is missing, the resulting group of words does not constitute a sentence. Instead, it is called a fragment, which is usually considered an error in writing.

KEY CONCEPT A fragment is a group of words that does not express a complete thought. ■

You can correct a fragment by adding the missing parts, as in the following chart.

FRAGMENTS	COMPLETE SENTENCES
People allergic to bug bites. (complete predicate missing)	People allergic to bug bites *should avoid the outdoors.* (complete predicate added)
Thrive in the rain forests. (complete subject missing)	*Tarantulas* thrive in the rain forests. (complete subject added)
From the barn. (complete subject and complete predicate missing)	*Flies* from the barn *made their way into the house.* (complete predicate and rest of complete subject added)

In conversations, fragments usually do not present a problem because repetition, tone of voice, gestures, and facial expressions help to communicate meaning. In writing, however, fragments should be avoided because the reader is alone with the words on the page and cannot go to the writer for clarification. An exception, of course, is writing that represents speech, such as the dialogue in a play or short story. Even then, fragments must be used carefully so that the reader can follow the flow of ideas.

Another exception to the rule of avoiding fragments is the occasional use of elliptical sentences.

KEY CONCEPT An elliptical sentence is one in which the missing word or words can be easily understood. ■

ELLIPTICAL SENTENCES:	Until later.
	Why such a sad face?

Journal Tip

This section contains a variety of information about insects. In your journal, note some of the facts that interest you; review them later to find a topic for an essay or a report.

Exercise 2 Revising to Correct Sentence Fragments

Decide whether each item is a sentence or a fragment. If it is a sentence, write *sentence*. If it is a fragment, revise it to make it a sentence. Label the elliptical sentence.

EXAMPLE: Because of the noise from the cicadas.

ANSWER: Because of the noise from the cicadas, we could hardly have a conversation.

1. The loudest of all insects.
2. Some heard a quarter of a mile away.
3. Males produce a whirring sound.
4. Longest cycle of development of any known insect.
5. Females lay up to 600 eggs high up in trees.
6. The eggs usually hatch within six weeks.
7. Then drop to the ground.
8. The wingless young are called nymphs.
9. Work their way a few centimeters into the soil and feed on the sap of tree roots.
10. Emerge from the ground after thirteen to seventeen years, big enough to climb up the tree trunk.
11. By fastening themselves securely to tree trunks to molt their outer cases.
12. Easy to hear, but hard to find.
13. Trying to stay out of sight, move around a branch, hiding from view.
14. They live only one month.
15. Long development cycle but short life.

More Practice

On-line
Exercise Bank
• Section 18.1
Grammar Exercise
Workbook
• pp. 23–24

▼ **Critical Viewing**
Add a predicate to complete a sentence about the picture: The cicada, emerging slowly **[Relate]**

Locating Subjects and Verbs To help you check your own writing to avoid fragments, employ either of two methods for locating subjects and verbs in sentences. The first method involves locating the subject. Ask, "Which word tells what this sentence is about?" Once you have the answer—in other words, the subject— then ask, "What does the subject do?" This gives you the verb.

Some people, however, prefer to find the verb first. In this case, ask, "Which word states the action or condition in this sentence?" This question should give you the verb. Then ask, "Who or what?" before it. The resulting word or words will be the subject.

Notice how these methods are applied to the example:

EXAMPLE: Grasshoppers often feed on corn, cotton, clover, and grasses.

To find the subject first, ask, "Which word tells what this sentence is about?"

ANSWER: Grasshoppers (*Grasshoppers* is the subject.)

Then ask, "What do the grasshoppers do?"

ANSWER: feed (*Feed* is the verb.)

To find the verb first, ask, "Which word states the action or condition in the sentence?"

ANSWER: feed (*Feed* states the action and is therefore the action verb.)

Then ask, "Who or what feed?"

ANSWER: Grasshoppers (*Grasshoppers* is the subject.)

Sometimes, a sentence contains numerous modifiers, making isolation of the subject and verb difficult. Simplify these sentences by mentally crossing out adjectives, adverbs, and prepositional phrases.

EXAMPLE: The science of entomology should grow extensively in the next ten years.

~~The~~ science ~~of entomology~~ should grow ~~extensively in the next ten years.~~

With the skeletal sentence that remains, you can easily use one of the two methods just introduced to determine the subject and verb.

▲ **Critical Viewing**
What happens if large numbers of grasshoppers attack a crop? Respond in a complete sentence with several modifiers. **[Draw Conclusions]**

More Than One Subject or Verb So far, the examples in this section have contained only one subject and one verb. Sometimes, however, a sentence may contain a *compound subject* or *compound verb*.

▶**KEY CONCEPT** A **compound subject** is two or more subjects that have the same verb and are joined by a conjunction such as *and* or *or*. ■

EXAMPLES: The <u>campers</u> and <u>hikers</u> <u><u>repelled</u></u> the mosquitoes with insect spray.
<u>Flies</u>, <u>gnats</u>, or <u>bees</u> <u><u>are</u></u> always <u><u>buzzing</u></u> around the garbage can.

▶**KEY CONCEPT** A **compound verb** is two or more verbs that have the same subject and are joined by a conjunction such as *and* or *or*. ■

EXAMPLES: <u>I</u> neither <u><u>saw</u></u> them nor <u><u>heard</u></u> them.
<u>Most</u> of the bees <u><u>left</u></u> their hive and <u><u>flew</u></u> to the nearest flower patch.

Some sentences may contain both a compound subject and a compound verb.

EXAMPLE: Both my <u>father</u> and <u>brother</u> <u><u>swatted</u></u> at the fly, <u><u>missed</u></u> it, and <u><u>smacked</u></u> each other in the head.

▶**Exercise 3** **Identifying Subjects and Verbs** Copy each of the following sentences, drawing a vertical line between the complete subject and complete predicate. Then, underline each subject once and each verb twice.

EXAMPLE: The <u>state</u> with the most people | <u><u>is</u></u> California.

1. Mosquitoes inhabit most areas of the world.
2. Their nasty bites cause swelling and itching.
3. Their bites also cause many deaths each year.
4. Mosquitoes transmit a number of diseases.
5. Many viral and bacterial infections can result from mosquito bites.
6. Mosquitoes must bite and feed on blood to live.
7. The females need protein for the production of eggs.
8. Unfed females weigh only one ten-thousandth of an ounce.
9. A single bite can cause them to triple in weight.
10. Only one bite is needed for the production of seventy-five eggs.

⚙ **Grammar and Style Tip**

Compound subjects joined with *and* take the plural form of a verb. Compound subjects joined with *or* take the form of the verb that agrees with the subject closest to the verb.

▶**More Practice**

On-line
Exercise Bank
• Section 18.1
Grammar Exercise
Workbook
• pp. 25–26

▶ **Exercise 4** Locating Compound Subjects and Compound **Verbs** Write the parts of each compound subject and compound verb. Notice that some sentences may have both.

EXAMPLE: The babies kicked their feet and gurgled.
ANSWER: kicked   gurgled

1. Beetles and other insects are studied by entomologists.
2. Entomologists examine insect anatomy and study insect behavior.
3. The study of insects was practiced as early as the fourth century B.C. but did not develop into an organized science until the seventeenth century A.D.
4. In recent years, medical research and agricultural planning have driven entomology further into the scientific mainstream and made it the largest branch of zoology.
5 Rain forests, swamps, and other delicate ecosystems are being explored for their exotic insect species.

More Practice

On-line Exercise Bank
• Section 18.1
Grammar Exercise Workbook
• pp. 23–24

GRAMMAR IN LITERATURE

from **A Mild Attack of Locusts**
Doris Lessing

In the following passage, the compound verbs are italicized and highlighted in blue.

A tree down the slope *leaned* over and *settled* heavily to the ground. Through the hail of insects a man came running. More tea, more water was needed. She supplied them. She *kept* the fires stoked and *filled* the cans with liquid, and then it was four in the afternoon, and the locusts had been pouring across overhead for a couple of hours. Up came old Stephen again, crunching locusts underfoot with every step, locusts clinging all over him; he *was cursing* and *swearing, banging* with his old hat at the air. At the doorway he *stopped* briefly, hastily pulling at the clinging insects and throwing them off, then he *plunged* into the locust-free livingroom.

▼ **Critical Viewing** Using a compound verb, describe your likely reaction to encountering a swarm of locusts, such as the one in this photograph. **[Relate]**

Section 18.1 *Section Review*

GRAMMAR EXERCISES 5–10

▶ Exercise 5 Recognizing Complete Subjects and Predicates Copy the following paragraph, drawing a vertical line between each complete subject and complete predicate. Then, underline each subject once and each verb twice.

(1) *Locust* is the common name of a number of jumping insects. (2) However, true locusts are migratory grasshoppers. (3) Farmers revile them. (4) True locusts swarm in great numbers. (5) In a brief span of time, they can destroy vast expanses of crops.

▶ Exercise 6 Revising to Eliminate Fragments Revise this paragraph, eliminating the fragments. Then, underline each subject once and each verb twice.

Mosquitoes in most areas of the world. Their nasty bites! Cause swelling and itching. The buzzing of mosquitoes in a darkened room annoying. More than mere irritants, also cause many deaths each year. In people with allergies or because of disease. Some viral and bacterial infections from mosquito bites. Including malaria.

▶ Exercise 7 Locating Compound Subjects and Compound Verbs Write the parts of each compound subject and compound verb.

1. Termites live in tropical countries but also inhabit temperate regions of the Americas and Europe.
2. A colony has anywhere from one hundred to one million termites and possesses a rigid caste structure.
3. The king and queen, the soldiers, and the workers perform specialized roles for the good of the colony.
4. The workers provide for the nest, tend to the queen's eggs, and feed the other members of the colony.
5. The soldiers grow huge heads and are equipped for the protection and defense of the colony.

▶ Exercise 8 Find It in Your Reading Reread the excerpt from Doris Lessing's "A Mild Attack of Locusts" on the preceding page. Then, on your paper, list at least six simple subjects you find in the excerpt. Of those you find, how many are nouns and how many are pronouns?

▶ Exercise 9 Find It in Your Writing Review a piece of work from your writing portfolio. Revise at least four sentences by adding either compound subjects, compound verbs, or both. Notice the effect the revision has on your writing.

▶ Exercise 10 Writing Application In Czech author Franz Kafka's story *The Metamorphosis*, the protagonist awakens one morning to find that he has been transformed into a giant cockroach. Imagine that you awake one morning to find that you are transformed into a giant insect. Write a brief description of the experience from the moment of your discovery. Use complete sentences to convey the experience clearly and meaningfully.

Hard-to-Find Subjects

The position of a subject in relation to its verb may vary according to the function of the sentence. Some subjects, therefore, are more difficult to find than others.

Subjects in Declarative Sentences In most declarative sentences, the subject precedes the verb. This subject-verb order is the normal pattern for declarative sentences. There are, however, two exceptions: sentences beginning with *there* or *here* and sentences that are inverted for emphasis.

When *there* or *here* begins a declarative sentence, it is often erroneously identified as the subject.

▶**KEY CONCEPT** The subject of a sentence is never *there* or *here*. ■

There and *here* usually serve as adverbs that modify the verb by explaining *where*. The most effective technique for making the subjects visible in these kinds of sentences is to rearrange the sentence in your mind so that *there* or *here* comes after the verb. If *there* sounds awkward after the verb, it is an *expletive*, a device used merely to get the sentence started. In this case, simply drop *there* from the sentence when you rearrange it.

Sentences Beginning With *There* or *Here*	Sentences Rearranged With Subject Before Verb
There <u>are</u> my subway <u>tokens</u>.	My subway <u>tokens</u> <u>are</u> there.
Here <u>is</u> your <u>ticket</u> to the Bedford Falls station.	Your <u>ticket</u> to the Bedford Falls station <u>is</u> here.
There <u>was</u> <u>room</u> to sit down.	<u>Room</u> to sit down <u>was</u> there.

Occasionally, a sentence beginning with *there* or *here* may be in normal word order, with the subject coming before the verb.

EXAMPLES: Here <u>you</u> <u>are</u> at last!
There <u>it</u> <u>goes</u>, out of the station.

Theme: Train Travel
In this section, you will learn to locate hard-to-find subjects. The examples and exercises are about train travel.
Cross-Curricular Connection: Social Studies

▷ **KEY CONCEPT** In some declarative sentences, the subject follows the verb. ■

Often, prepositional phrases begin such inverted sentences. Mentally shifting the words at the beginning of the sentence to the middle or to the end makes the subject easier to detect.

Sentences Inverted for Emphasis	Sentences Rephrased With Subject Before Verb
Deep into the cavernous tunnel <u>went</u> the <u>subway</u> crew.	The subway <u>crew</u> <u>went</u> deep into the cavernous tunnel.
Around my head <u>buzzed</u> the most persistent <u>fly</u>.	The most persistent <u>fly</u> <u>buzzed</u> around my head.

Subjects in Interrogative Sentences Many interrogative sentences follow the usual subject-verb order, making the subject easy to identify.

EXAMPLE: Which train <u>lines</u> <u>are traveled</u> the most?

Almost as often, however, an inversion occurs, changing the subject's location within the sentence.

▷ **KEY CONCEPT** In interrogative sentences, the subject often follows the verb. ■

Inverted interrogative sentences will commonly begin with a verb, a helping verb, or one of the following words: *how, what, when, where, which, who, whose,* or *why*. When looking for the subject in these sentences, mentally change the interrogative sentence into a declarative sentence, as in the following examples.

Questions	Rephrased as Statements
<u>Is</u> the <u>coffee</u> ready?	The <u>coffee</u> <u>is</u> ready.
<u>Will</u> <u>you</u> <u>prepare</u> the monthly train schedule?	<u>You</u> <u>will prepare</u> the monthly train schedule.
<u>Should</u> this <u>line</u> <u>be read</u> now?	This <u>line</u> <u>should be read</u> now.

▼ **Critical Viewing** The gloved hand on the right belongs to a person hired to help Tokyo commuters squeeze into the subway car. Will this "shover" succeed? Use *there is* or *there are* in your response. **[Judge]**

Hard-to-Find Subjects • **421**

Subjects in Imperative Sentences Subjects in imperative sentences are usually implied, not specifically stated.

▶**KEY CONCEPT** In imperative sentences, the subject is understood to be *you*. ■

In the following chart, the left side shows imperative sentences in which the subjects are implied. The right side shows the positions where the understood subjects logically occur.

Imperative Sentences	With Understood *You* Added
Wait for the conductor, please.	[You] wait for the conductor, please.
In an earthquake, crawl under a sturdy table.	In an earthquake, [you] crawl under a sturdy table.
Carolyn, take the A-train to Park Slope.	Carolyn, [you] take the A-train to Park Slope.

In the last example, the person addressed is named. However, *Carolyn*, a noun of direct address, is not the subject of the sentence. The subject is still understood to be *you*.

Subjects in Exclamatory Sentences In exclamatory sentences, subjects may come after verbs or be missing entirely.

▶**KEY CONCEPT** In an exclamatory sentence, the subject may come after the verb or may be understood. ■

The same technique employed to find subjects in interrogative sentences can be used to find the subject in many exclamatory sentences.

EXAMPLES: What could I have done! (I could have done what.)
Can this be real! (This can be real.)

Some exclamatory sentences may be so elliptical that both the subject *and* the verb are implied. For such sentences as these, common sense and context serve as your best guides for determining the unstated subject and verb.

Exclamatory Sentences	With Understood Parts Added
Quickly!	[You come here] quickly!
Air!	[I need] air!

GRAMMAR IN
LITERATURE

from **The Train from Rhodesia**
Nadine Gordimer

In the following passage, the imperative sentences spoken by the woman are italicized in blue. The understood subject is you.

. . .*Oh leave it*—she said. The young man stopped. Don't you want it? he said, keeping his face closed to the boy. *No, never mind,* she said, *leave it.* The old native kept his head on one side, looking at them sideways, holding the lion. Three-and-six, he murmured, as old people repeat things to themselves.

The young woman drew her head in. She went into the coupé and sat down. Out of the window, on the other side, there was nothing; sand and bush; a thorn tree. Back through the open doorway, past the figure of her husband in the corridor, there was the station . . .

▲ **Critical Viewing**
Describe the state of these train passengers. Answer using an inverted sentence beginning with a prepositional phrase, such as "In repose . . . " [Relate]

▶ **Exercise 11** **Locating Hard-to-Find Subjects** Write the subject and verb in each sentence. Include in parentheses any words that are understood or implied. Underline each subject once and each verb twice.

EXAMPLE: Here is my report.

ANSWER: report <u>is</u>

1. Where is the train schedule?
2. On the counter lay the schedule.
3. There beside the schedule is your train pass.
4. To the station walked the sleepy commuters.
5. There are thousands of them taking the train to the city every day.
6. Does your father commute to work by train?
7. No!
8. Where does he work?
9. Are the conductors adequately prepared in case of an emergency?
10. After work, take the train home.

▶ **More Practice**

On-line
Exercise Bank
• Section 18.2
Grammar Exercise
Workbook
• pp. 27–28

Hands-on Grammar

Dual-Direction Subject Locator

Make and use a Dual-Direction Subject Locater to reinforce your ability to locate subjects in sentences where the subject and verb are inverted. Use a sheet of 6 1/2" x 8 1/2" paper and fold in each side edge 1 3/4", leaving a space of 1 1/2" in the middle. Next, draw 11 lines across the folds at 1/2" intervals. Then, open the folds and finish drawing the lines on the inside from crease to crease. Now, print 8 of the following verbs down the middle section:

SITS	RUN	ARE	PLAYED	FLIES	DROVE
CAME	GOES	DANCED	SLEEPS	SHOUTED	FELL

Next, on each line on the outside of the left fold, write a prepositional phrase, a question word (*who, what, where,* etc.), the word *there,* or the word *here.* On the right fold, write a subject that makes sense with the words on the left and the verb. Examples: ***Here SITS my loyal dog. Finally, at night CAME the storm.*** Cut on the lines as far as the fold on each side, creating a double "fringe." Under each piece of fringe on the left, write the subject from the outside right piece of fringe. Under each piece of fringe on the right, write the words from the outside left piece of fringe. (See illustration.)

Finally, with a partner or alone, practice reading your inverted sentences and the same sentences in normal word order underneath. Notice what happens to the subjects.

Find It in Your Reading Poets often use inverted word order to maintain rhythm or rhyme in their poems. Find examples of inverted word order in a poem; then, restate the sentence in subject-verb order.

Find It in Your Writing Add interest to a piece of your own writing by revising some sentences to invert the word order.

Section Review

GRAMMAR EXERCISES 12–17

 Exercise 12 Identifying Subjects and Verbs in Interrogative Sentences
Write the subject and verb in each sentence. Include in parentheses any words that are understood or implied. Underline each subject once and each verb twice.

1. Will we take a train across the country?
2. Where are we going?
3. Have you packed your bags?
4. Did you remember to take your toothbrush?
5. How much will the train cost?
6. Where are some maps of the route?
7. Will we have a sleeping car?
8. How will we eat?
9. Will we see the majestic scenery of the American countryside?
10. Having fun?

Exercise 13 Revising to Invert Subjects and Verbs Revise each sentence, inverting the word order according to the instructions given in parentheses.

1. A family of four was in line for tickets. (Begin with a prepositional phrase.)
2. They will have to buy tickets for the children. (Ask a question.)
3. Will you please pay quickly? (Turn into an imperative.)
4. Ten more people are in line. (Begin with *There*.)
5. We must wait for the train [for what length of time]. (Ask a question.)
6. The express train is pulling into the station now. (Begin with *There*)
7. The porter is helping them with their luggage. (Ask a question.)
8. The children jump into the train first. (Begin with a prepositional phrase.)
9. This is the right car. (Ask a question.)
10. Our seats are here. (Begin with *Here*.)

Exercise 14 Revising to Form Imperative Sentences Revise these sentences, turning each one into an imperative.

1. Hey, can we go now?
2. I wish you wouldn't walk quite so fast.
3. I want you to put that down now.
4. You turn left here to reach the station.
5. Would you please pick me up at noon?
6. If you leave early, you'll arrive before the crowds.
7. You shouldn't wait to buy your ticket.
8. I ask that you write to me soon.
9. You need to get the form signed if you want to attend.
10. We can all go together and have fun!

Exercise 15 Find It in Your Reading Reread the excerpt from Nadine Gordimer's "The Train from Rhodesia" on page 423. Identify the interrogative sentence and its subject.

Exercise 16 Find It in Your Writing Revise a piece of written dialogue to include at least one interrogative, one exclamatory, and one imperative sentence. Notice how changing the sentences affects the presentation of your characters and the tone of the dialogue.

Exercise 17 Writing Application Consider the different types of jobs associated with trains, such as conductor, engineer, stationmaster, and track maintenance crew. Write a brief essay detailing which job you think would be the best and why. Use each of the four sentence functions in your essay.

Complements

Some sentences are complete with just a subject and a verb or with a subject, verb, and modifiers, as in *The crowd cheered.*

The meaning of many sentences, however, depends on additional words to finish the idea begun by the subject and verb. For example, *The satellite continually sends . . .* is confusing and incomplete, even though it has a subject and verb. To complete the meaning of the predicate parts of those sentences, a writer must add *complements.*

▶ **KEY CONCEPT** A **complement** is a word or group of words that completes the meaning of the predicate of a sentence. ■

There are five different kinds of complements in English: *direct objects, indirect objects, objective complements, predicate nominatives,* and *predicate adjectives.* The first three occur in sentences with transitive action verbs, whereas the last two, often grouped together as *subject complements,* are found only with linking verbs. (See Chapter 17 for more information about action and linking verbs.)

Direct Objects

Direct objects, the most common of the five types of complements, complete the meaning of action verbs by telling *who* or *what* receives the action.

▶ **KEY CONCEPT** A **direct object** is a noun, pronoun, or group of words acting as a noun that receives the action of a transitive verb. ■

EXAMPLES:
                                  DO
              I visited the Air and Space Museum.

                                     DO
              Mud and leaves clogged the gutters.

To determine the direct object of a sentence, ask *Whom?* or *What?* after an action verb. If the sentence offers no answer, the action verb is intransitive and there is no direct object in the sentence.

EXAMPLES:
              The curator of the museum led the tour. (Led *what? Answer:* tour)
              The satellite spun beyond the atmosphere. (Spun *what? Answer:* none; the verb is intransitive)

▲ **Critical Viewing** What are some of the things this astronaut might be seeing as he maneuvers this massive satellite? Use direct objects in your answer. **[Draw Conclusions]**

▶**KEY CONCEPT** In some inverted questions, the direct object may appear before the verb. Rephrase such questions as statements in normal word order to locate the direct objects. ■

	DO
INVERTED QUESTION:	Which rocket <u>did</u> they <u>launch</u>?

	DO
REWORDED AS A STATEMENT:	They <u>did launch</u> which rocket?

Keep alert for sentences with more than one direct object, known as a *compound direct object*. If a sentence contains a compound direct object, asking *Whom?* or *What?* after the action verb will yield two or more answers.

<table>
<tr><td></td><td colspan="2">DO   DO</td></tr>
<tr><td>EXAMPLES:</td><td colspan="2">The <u>astronaut</u> <u>wore</u> a helmet and a spacesuit.</td></tr>
</table>

                                    DO
NASA's <u>programs</u> <u>have included</u> the Mercury, the
   DO   DO
Gemini, and the Apollo during the last forty years.

In the last example, *years* is the object of the preposition *during*. The object of a preposition is never a direct object.

▶**Exercise 18** **Recognizing Direct Objects** Read the paragraph below, and then write the direct objects in each sentence, including all parts of any compound direct objects.

EXAMPLE: Often, space shuttle astronauts conduct scientific experiments.

ANSWER: experiments

(1) In 1958, the United States Congress created the National Aeronautics and Space Administration (NASA). (2) The National Aeronautics and Space Act established the organization. (3) NASA plans, directs, and conducts all non-military U.S. space activity. (4) The President appoints a civilian administrator to the organization. (5) The U.S. Senate, however, must approve the President's selection. (6) NASA coordinates all research and study of the cosmos. (7) Then, it disseminates the results of the research. (8) Under the President's guidance, NASA also develops cooperative space programs with other countries. (9) With the advent of the space shuttle program, NASA increasingly began work on military projects, despite its original mandate as a civilian agency. (10) Because of the 1986 *Challenger* shuttle disaster, however, the military expanded its own separate fleet of rockets.

✓ Spelling Tip

NASA is an acronym that stands for the National **A**eronautics and **S**pace **A**dministration. When an acronym is three or more letters, it is usually written without periods after each letter.

▶**More Practice**

On-line Exercise Bank
• Section 18.3
Grammar Exercise Workbook
• pp. 29–30

Indirect Objects

Indirect objects are found in sentences with direct objects.

▶ KEY CONCEPT An **indirect object** is a noun or pronoun that appears with a direct object and names the person or thing that something is given to or done for. ■

Indirect objects are common with such verbs as *ask, bring, buy, give, lend, make, promise, show, teach, tell,* and *write.*

EXAMPLES:

    IO   DO
NASA gave the astronauts a course correction.

                IO   DO
The satellite sent the television stations its signal.

Like direct objects, indirect objects can be compound.

EXAMPLE:

      IO   IO   DO
I showed my mom and dad the NASA poster.

To locate an indirect object, first be sure the sentence contains a direct object. Then, ask one of these questions after the verb and direct object: *To or for whom?* or *To or for what?*

EXAMPLES:

          IO   DO
The teacher taught our class astrophysics.
(Taught astrophysics *to whom? Answer:* class)

      IO   DO
We made the couch a slipcover.
(Made slipcover *for what? Answer:* couch)

To avoid confusing an indirect object with a direct object, always remember to ask the right questions in the correct order. First, ask *Whom?* or *What?* after the verb to find the direct object. If the sentence contains a direct object, then ask *To or for whom?* or *To or for what?* after the verb and direct object to find the indirect object.

EXAMPLE:

       IO   DO
Pat gave Doug a model space shuttle. (Gave
what? Answer: shuttle) (Gave shuttle *to whom?
Answer:* Doug)

Remember also that an indirect object almost always sits squarely between the verb and direct object. In a sentence in normal word order, it will never follow the direct object nor will it ever be the object of the preposition *to* or *for.*

EXAMPLES:

             DO   OBJ OF PREP
NASA sent the poster to me.

       IO   DO
NASA sent me the poster.

Internet Tip

Most search engines on the Internet recognize common acronyms such as NASA and NATO. However, initiating a second search using the spelled-out version of an organization's abbreviated name sometimes generates more or different results.

▶ **Exercise 19** **Recognizing Indirect Objects** Write the underlined words in each sentence, and identify each as a *direct object, indirect object,* or *object of a preposition.*

EXAMPLE: Frank gave his <u>friends</u> rock <u>samples</u> from the moon.

ANSWER: friends (indirect object) samples (direct object)

1. NASA designed the <u>space shuttle</u> for human and cargo <u>transport</u>.
2. Congress granted <u>NASA</u> <u>funds</u> for the spacecraft in the 1970's.
3. A reusable spacecraft, the space shuttle gave <u>scientists</u> a way to study the effects of repeated space exposure.
4. Because of the shuttle's reusability, the program marked a major <u>departure</u> from previous space <u>programs</u>.
5. After ten years of preparation, NASA presented the <u>country</u> its first <u>shuttle</u> in 1981.
6. NASA now keeps four <u>shuttles</u> in <u>operation</u>.
7. In response to NASA's <u>shuttles,</u> the Soviet Union started a shuttle <u>program</u> themselves.
8. However, a scarcity of funds halted the <u>program</u> in 1993.
9. At first, NASA's space shuttle deployed <u>satellites</u> into <u>orbit</u>.
10. As the program matured, the space shuttle retrieved ailing <u>satellites</u> for <u>repair</u>.

▶ **Exercise 20** **Writing Sentences With Indirect Objects** Write sentences with indirect objects using the verbs given below. Then, underline each indirect object, and draw a circle around the direct object.

EXAMPLE: wrote

ANSWER: I wrote <u>NASA</u> a letter.

1. promise
2. gave
3. told
4. lend
5. will show

More Practice

On-line
Exercise Bank
• Section 18.3
Grammar Exercise
Workbook
• pp. 29–30

▶ **Critical Viewing**
What role does the rocket play in the shuttle launch? Use an indirect object in your response. **[Interpret]**

Objective Complements

Whereas an indirect object almost always comes before a direct object, an *objective complement* almost always follows a direct object. As its name implies, the objective complement "complements," or adds to the meaning of, the direct object.

> **KEY CONCEPT** An objective complement is an adjective or noun that appears with a direct object and describes or renames it. ∎

A sentence containing an objective complement may at first glance seem to have two direct objects. Identifying objective complements is simplified when you know they occur only with such verbs as *appoint, call, consider, declare, elect, judge, label, make, name, select,* or *think.*

EXAMPLES:

  DO   OC

The <u>directors</u> of the launch <u>declared</u> it successful.

  DO   OC

The <u>President</u> <u>appointed</u> him NASA administrator.

Like other sentence parts, objective complements can be compound.

  DO   OC

EXAMPLE: I <u>called</u> Dave a very talented swimmer and a

  OC

brilliant astronaut.

> **Exercise 21** Revising to Add Objective Complements

Revise each sentence, adding an objective complement of the type indicated.

EXAMPLE: The committee judged that entry (<u>noun</u>).
    The committee judged that entry the winner.

1. NASA named one space shuttle (noun).
2. It considered the early missions (adjective).
3. The President appoints a scientist (noun) of NASA.
4. Florida considers Cape Kennedy (noun).
5. Many children find spacecraft (adjective).
6. NASA's research has made space less (adjective) and (adjective).
7. Scientists consider one another (adjective) and (adjective).
8. NASA's work has made the U.S. space program (noun).
9. In fact, scientists generally consider NASA's research (adjective).
10. New advancements from NASA's research have made life on Earth (adjective).

► **More Practice**

On-line
Exercise Bank
• Section 18.3
Grammar Exercise
Workbook
• pp. 31–32

GRAMMAR IN LITERATURE

from **We'll Never Conquer Space**

Arthur C. Clarke

Notice how the author has used several subject complements (predicate nominatives and predicate adjectives) in the passage.

To our ancestors, the vastness of the earth was a dominant *fact* controlling their thoughts and lives. In all earlier ages than ours, the world was *wide* indeed, and no man could ever see more than a tiny fraction of its immensity. A few hundred miles—a thousand, at the most—was *infinity*. Only a lifetime ago, parents waved farewell to their emigrating children in the virtual certainty that they would never meet again.

▲ **Critical Viewing**
Using subject complements, describe some of the features of this satellite. **[Analyze]**

Subject Complements

Linking verbs require *subject complements* to complete their meaning.

▶ **KEY CONCEPT** A **subject complement** is a noun, pronoun, or adjective that appears with a linking verb and tells something about the subject. ■

Predicate Nominatives The subject and the predicate nominative refer to the same person, place, or thing.

▶ **KEY CONCEPT** A **predicate nominative** is a noun or pronoun that appears with a linking verb and renames, identifies, or explains the subject. ■

The last example has a compound predicate nominative.

EXAMPLES:
                     PN
Ann Pace <u>became</u> a scientist for NASA.

          PN
The <u>winner</u> <u>is</u> you.

             PN   PN
<u>John Glenn</u> <u>is</u> a politician and former astronaut.

Predicate Adjectives As the name indicates, a predicate adjective is not a noun or a pronoun but an adjective.

> **KEY CONCEPT** A **predicate adjective** is an adjective that appears with a linking verb and describes the subject of the sentence. ∎

A predicate adjective refers to the subject by describing it in much the same way any adjective modifies a noun or pronoun.

EXAMPLES:
                  PA
       Your reasoning seems logical.

                 PA   PA
       The launch sounded loud and thunderous.

> **Exercise 22** Identifying Subject Complements Write the subject complement or complements in each sentence. Then, identify each as a *predicate nominative* or *predicate adjective*.

EXAMPLE: Jean should become a successful college student.
ANSWER: student (predicate nominative)

1. After a high-school course in astronomy, I became an avid stargazer.
2. The heavens appeared distant yet inviting.
3. My interest grew more intense in college.
4. Following a series of difficult advanced astronomy courses, I remained fervent in my passion for the heavens.
5. With enough credits, I had become an astronomy major.
6. Graduate school looked good to me after graduation.
7. With my degree, I will be a candidate for a post at NASA.
8. NASA's requirements are strict and demanding.
9. A future with NASA appears challenging but exciting.
10. Working with NASA is a dream of mine.

> **Exercise 23** Writing Sentences With Subject Complements Write sentences with the verbs and types of subject complements indicated. Then, underline each subject complement.

EXAMPLE: was (predicate pronoun)
ANSWER: The first shuttle captain was he.

1. become (predicate noun)
2. grow (predicate adjective)
3. felt (predicate adjective)
4. will be (predicate noun)
5. is (predicate pronoun)

More Practice

On-line
Exercise Bank
• Section 18.3
Grammar Exercise
Workbook
• pp. 31–32

Section 18.3 · Section Review

GRAMMAR EXERCISES 24–29

Exercise 24 **Recognizing Direct Objects and Indirect Objects** Write the underlined words in each sentence, and identify each as a *direct object, indirect object,* or *object of a preposition.*

1. The Russians designed their space station *Mir* for long-term space habitation.
2. They launched the station into orbit on February 20, 1986.
3. Russian spacecraft and American space shuttles bring crew members instant fame.
4. Through the *Salyut* series, the Russians developed the technology for *Mir.*
5. The series gave the Russians valuable information about living in space.

Exercise 25 **Identifying Objective Complements** Write the objective complement(s) in each of the following sentences. Then, identify them as *nouns* or *adjectives.*

1. NASA named the first American space station Skylab.
2. NASA considers its astronauts hard-working.
3. For each mission, the administration appoints astronauts crew members.
4. Most people think an astronaut's training impossible.
5. The difficult training makes astronauts tough and alert.
6. The astronaut must consider the hardships of the job necessary.
7. Astronauts consider space an adventure.
8. NASA has made astronauts heroes.
9. NASA has declared satellites a priority.
10. Communications and industry have made the continual development of satellites vital.

Exercise 26 **Supplying Subject Complements** Complete each sentence with an appropriate subject complement. Then, identify each as a *predicate nominative* or *predicate adjective.*

1. Satellites have become ___?___ of modern life.
2. Circling beyond the atmosphere, satellites seem ___?___ than they are.
3. They are ___?___ for virtually all communication.
4. Since 1962, satellites have become ___?___ in the telephone and television industries.
5. Satellites appear ___?___ for voice, data, and image transfer.

Exercise 27 **Find It in Your Reading** Identify the subject complements in the following passage from Arthur C. Clarke's "We'll Never Conquer Space."

. . .For it seems as certain as anything can be that no signal—still less any material object—can ever travel faster than light. The velocity of light is the ultimate speed limit, being part of the very structure of space and time.

Exercise 28 **Find It in Your Writing** Review one of your lab reports for a science class, and underline each direct object.

Exercise 29 **Writing Application** Write a brief story about space travel. Underline any complements you use.

GRAMMAR EXERCISES 30–36

▶ **Exercise 30** Identifying Complete Subjects and Predicates Copy each of the following sentences, drawing a vertical line between the complete subject and complete predicate. Then, underline each subject once and each verb twice.

1. The Canadian province of Alberta is rich in natural beauty.
2. Nothing proves this more than Banff National Park.
3. Banff is located in the southwestern part of the province.
4. Canada's oldest national park, it was formally established in 1885.
5. Famous for its spectacular scenery, glaciers, hot springs, and lakes, Banff is nestled in the Rocky Mountains.
6. Perfect for exploration, the mountains provide a spectacular environment for outdoor recreation.
7. Its pristine lakes, mountainous terrain, and intricate network of trails make it suitable as both a summer and winter resort.
8. Wildlife such as elk, cougar, and bighorn sheep populate Banff.
9. With an area of more than 2,500 square miles, Banff is Canada's eleventh largest nature preserve.
10. Nature lovers of all kinds should find Banff a fulfilling destination.

▶ **Exercise 31** Identifying Hard-to-Find Subjects Copy the following sentences, underlining each subject once and each verb twice. Include in parentheses any words that are understood or implied.

1. There are dozens of national parks in the United States.
2. Deep into the cavern trekked the brave spelunkers.

3. Are you planning to visit Howe Caverns this summer?
4. Wait for your guide, please.
5. Help!
6. Here are our backpacks.
7. In the event of a storm, find shelter immediately.
8. Over the rapids surged a group of white-water rafters.
9. Was Yellowstone worth the trip?
10. Hammer the tent stakes securely into the ground.

▶ **Exercise 32** Recognizing Sentence Parts Label each of the underlined sentence parts *subject, verb, direct object, indirect object, objective complement, predicate nominative,* or *predicate adjective.*

1. The Gir National Park and Lion Sanctuary <u>is</u> in western India.
2. It was declared a forest <u>reserve</u> in 1913, a wildlife <u>sanctuary</u> in 1965, and a national <u>park</u> in 1975.
3. The lion <u>sanctuary</u> occupies 445 square <u>miles</u> in the Kathiawar Peninsula.
4. Within that area, the national park <u>comprises</u> 100 square miles.
5. This conservation area is <u>one</u> of the largest in India.
6. The region's climate is <u>hot</u> and <u>arid</u>.
7. The area's scrublike vegetation includes teak <u>trees</u> and thorn <u>forests</u>.
8. In 1948, the local ruler, the nawab of Junagadh, gave the endangered Asiatic <u>lions</u> a larger <u>area</u> in which to roam.
9. Later agricultural considerations made the <u>area</u> <u>smaller</u>.
10. Despite the shrinking preserve lands, conservation <u>efforts</u> took effect about fifty years later.

11. From a low of about 20 Asiatic lions in the area, 300 lions now <u>roam</u> the sanctuary.
12. Unfortunately, the growing numbers of lions <u>present</u> difficulties for the park authorities.
13. The sanctuary is not <u>large</u> enough to accommodate them, and some <u>have moved</u> beyond the park.
14. The park and sanctuary are also <u>home</u> to many other animals.
15. These include <u>antelope</u> and several <u>species</u> of reptiles.

> **Exercise 33** **Writing Sentences With Complements** On your paper, write sentences following the instructions given below.

1. Use *mountain* as a direct object.
2. Use *campers* as an indirect object.
3. Use *brisk* as a predicate adjective.
4. Use *campsite* as a predicate noun.
5. Use *adventure* as an objective complement.

> **Exercise 34** **Revision Practice** On a separate sheet of paper, revise the following paragraph. Where appropriate, combine sentences, using compound subjects and predicates. Eliminate fragments.

Many African countries are working to protect elephants. Many preservation groups are also trying to protect elephants. Although elephants can sometimes be dangerous to people. People have turned out to be much more dangerous to elephants. Loggers have eliminated elephant habitats. Farmers have done the same. Hunters have killed elephants for their valuable ivory tusks. Elephants now in danger of extinction. Some nations have banned any trade in ivory. In addition, they have discouraged poaching by helping communities to profit from tourism. Many countries have set aside parklands and preserves to protect elephants. They also protect other endangered species. Hoping for success.

> **Exercise 35** **Writing Application**

Imagine that you are a reporter writing about the activities of an environmental conservation club in your community. Craft a feature-length story (about 200 words) describing the club's projects and their overall effect. Edit and proofread your work, and as you revise, make sure you have used a variety of sentence patterns.

> **Exercise 36** **CUMULATIVE REVIEW**

Parts of Speech and Basic Sentence Parts On your paper, write the part of speech of each underlined word, including those that are boldfaced. Then, revise the passage, changing each underlined word to a more precise word in the same part of speech. Finally, underline the subject once and the verb twice in each sentence, and circle elliptical sentences.

Every <u>February</u>, the Mahoney family gathers at Lake Tahoe to ski. <u>Among</u> the family <u>members</u>, some are <u>great</u> skiers, <u>some</u> are <u>good</u>, and two <u>are</u> <u>forever</u> on the beginners' slope. No matter. The object of the <u>trip</u> is to have fun, and, *boy*, what fun they have!

Renting cabins <u>near</u> the <u>pretty</u> lake, the family rises <u>every</u> clear, <u>nice</u> morning to a view of <u>rich</u> blue water, forests of <u>tall</u> pines and cedars, and the <u>great</u> Sierra Nevada <u>and</u> Carson range of <u>granite</u> mountains covered with <u>bright</u> snow. After a <u>big</u> breakfast, <u>everyone</u> <u>goes</u> to the <u>slopes</u>. <u>Some</u> days, the sun <u>is</u> <u>so</u> warm <u>that</u> the skiers wear <u>only</u> sweaters.

In the afternoon, the <u>tired</u> <u>adults</u> and <u>children</u> <u>go</u> to the lodge to <u>have</u> <u>hot</u> chocolate and warm <u>themselves</u> <u>by</u> the fire. Often, the teenagers <u>go</u> to Emerald Bay, where some take photographs of this <u>very</u> <u>lovely</u> natural <u>place</u>. Well-read cousin Daniel Mahoney <u>admires</u> the view and <u>quotes</u> <u>Mark Twain</u>, <u>who</u> described Lake Tahoe as "a noble <u>sheet</u> of blue water . . . it must <u>surely</u> be the <u>fairest</u> picture the <u>whole</u> earth affords." What a life!

Standardized Test Preparation Workshop

Recognizing Appropriate Sentence Construction

Knowing how to use the basic parts of a sentence correctly is the foundation of good writing. Standardized tests measure your ability to identify a complete sentence. Every sentence must contain a subject—the *who* or *what* that performs the action—and a verb—the action the subject is performing—to express a complete thought. If one of these parts is missing, you have an incomplete sentence, or a fragment.

When answering these test questions, check each group of words for a subject and verb. Then, determine whether the group of words expresses a complete thought. Finally, choose the group of words that contains all of the elements of a complete sentence to replace any sentence fragments.

The following questions will give you practice with the format used for testing your knowledge of basic sentence parts.

> **Test Tip**
>
> Remember that a verb can either follow or come before its subject. Also, a form of *be* can be the main verb of a sentence, but it does not express action; instead, it links words together.

Sample Test Item	Answer and Explanation
Directions: Choose the letter of the best way to write each underlined section. If the underlined section needs no change, choose "Correct as is." The guests were given birdseed. To throw at (1) the bride and groom. Instead of rice. **1** **A** The guests were given birdseed. They were supposed to throw it at the bride and groom. It was instead of rice. **B** The guests were given birdseed to throw at the bride and groom instead of rice. **C** To throw at the bride and groom, the guests were given birdseed and not rice. **D** Correct as is	The correct answer is *B.* This answer choice smoothly combines the two fragments with the sentence that precedes them and successfully integrates all the information into a complete thought. Choice *A,* on the other hand, eliminates the fragments but makes three choppy sentences. Choice *C* contains a misplaced modifier that changes the meaning of the sentence.

Practice 1 **Directions:** Choose the letter of the best way to write each underlined section. If the underlined section needs no change, choose "Correct as is."

A century ago. A family boarded an emi-
(1)
grant ship. Sailed from Ireland. The ship
(2)
was bound for America. And was

rickety. The O'Connells were a strong
(3)
bunch, Eight in all, the youngest named

Connor.

1 A A century ago, a family boarded an emigrant ship. It sailed from Ireland.

B A century ago. A family boarded an emigrant ship that sailed from Ireland.

C A century ago. when a family boarded an emigrant ship, it sailed from Ireland.

D Correct as is

2 F The ship was bound for America, and the ship was rickety.

G The ship, bound for America, was a rickety ship.

H The rickety ship was bound for America.

J Correct as is

3 A The O'Connells were a strong, bunch. There were eight in all. The youngest was named Connor.

B The O'Connells were a strong bunch, eight in all. The youngest was named Connor.

C There were eight strong O'Connells in all, the youngest was named Connor.

D Correct as is

Practice 2 **Directions:** Choose the letter of the best way to write each underlined section. If the underlined section needs no change, choose "Correct as is."

The sound system. It was all set up. It
(1)
was ready to go. Rafik tested the bass levels
(2)
one more time. Nothing like a lot of bass.

Gets people dancing. He closed his eyes
(3)
and saw the dance floor. Packed with people.

1 A The sound system was all set up. And ready to go.

B The sound system was all set up and ready to go.

C The sound system, was all set up, and it was ready to go.

D Correct as is

2 F Rafik tested the bass levels one more time. There is nothing like a lot of bass to get people dancing.

G Rafik tested the bass levels one more time. Nothing like a lot of bass to get people dancing.

H Rafik tested the bass levels one more time, and nothing like a lot of bass got people dancing.

J Correct as is

3 A He closed his eyes, and there he saw the dance floor packed with people.

B He closed his eyes and saw the dance floor. It was packed with people.

C He closed his eyes and saw the dance floor packed with people.

D Correct as is

Phrases and *Clauses*

Previous chapters have discussed the essential materials at a writer's command: the parts of speech and the basic English sentence patterns. This chapter will describe additional elements—phrases and clauses—that writers can use to expand these basic patterns and to achieve richer communication.

Phrases and clauses function in sentences in much the same way as passageways in a cave. The various chambers are connected by passageways, which expand the overall size and scope of the cave. At the same time, they also add to the detail and beauty of the cave.

In this chapter, you will learn how phrases and clauses add meaning to sentences and make a writer's work more interesting and informative.

▲ **Critical Viewing** Use the phrase "through the archway" in a sentence about this picture. What other phrases could you use to describe the features of the cave? **[Describe]**

Diagnostic Test

Directions: Write all answers on a separate sheet of paper.

Skill Check A. List prepositional phrases or appositives in each of the following sentences. Label each prepositional phrase *adjective* or *adverb,* and identify the word each appositive modifies.

1. Many of the world's caves have been discovered by accident.
2. Carlsbad Caverns, a series of caves in the American Southwest, was discovered by a cowboy who noticed a large swarm of bats.
3. While looking for a stray goat, two men in Jordan stumbled upon a very important cave near the Dead Sea.
4. Another famous cave, Lascaux, was discovered by four French teenagers who were looking for an underground passage.
5. Altamira, a town in Spain, was made famous by a five-year-old girl's discovery of prehistoric paintings on a cave's ceiling.

Skill Check B. Identify the verbal or verbal phrase in each of the following sentences. Tell whether each one is an *infinitive,* a *gerund,* a *participle,* or a *nominative absolute.*

6. The fascinating story of the cave paintings at Altamira, Spain, begins in 1879.
7. The cave having been discovered years earlier, Don Marcelino de Sautuola was searching for artifacts on the cave floor.
8. De Sautuola brought his young daughter along to help him.
9. Digging in the dirt tired her, so she lay down on the ground.
10. She looked up and saw the ancient paintings staring back at her.

Skill Check C. In each of the following sentences, identify the subordinate clause, and then tell whether it is an *adjective,* an *adverb,* a *noun,* or an *elliptical clause.*

11. In 1901, a cowboy named Jim White, who worked on a ranch in New Mexico, stumbled upon Carlsbad Caverns.
12. On a warm summer day, White was riding across the desert when he noticed an enormous dark cloud billowing out of the ground.
13. Whatever was causing the cloud puzzled the young cowboy.
14. In fact, the "cloud" that White saw was actually an enormous swarm of bats, and they were coming from a large cave.
15. This cave proved to be one of the largest in the country.

Skill Check D. Identify each of the following sentences as *simple, compound, complex,* or *compound-complex.*

16. In 1940, four French teenaged boys made a startling discovery.
17. The boys, who were from the small town of Montignac, were exploring a dark, deep hole near a dead tree.
18. The boys were looking for an underground passage.
19. They cleared the ground around the opening and then ventured into the hole.
20. The boys, who had an oil lamp with them, squeezed into the tight opening, and they soon discovered the prehistoric paintings that have made the cave famous.

Prepositional Phrases and Appositives

When one-word adjectives and adverbs cannot convey all of the details and relationships that a writer needs to express, the writer can use a *phrase* to express the precise idea.

> **KEY CONCEPT** A **phrase** is a group of words that functions in a sentence as a part of speech. ∎

Two common types of phrases that add to the meaning of sentences are *prepositional phrases* and *appositive phrases*.

Prepositional Phrases

As shown in Section 17.4, prepositional phrases contain a preposition and a noun or pronoun called the object of the preposition. The object may have modifiers and be compound.

EXAMPLES:

PREP   OBJ OF PREP
on the ancient limestone floor

PREP   OBJ OF PREP   OBJ OF PREP
beside the underground stream and rocks

Prepositional phrases function as either adjectives or adverbs.

Adjective Phrases Like adjectives, adjective phrases modify nouns and pronouns.

> **KEY CONCEPT** An **adjective phrase** is a prepositional phrase that modifies a noun or pronoun by stating *what kind* or *which one*. ∎

Adjective phrases can modify any sentence part that is acting as a noun.

EXAMPLES:

S

An etching *of a cave bear* was found. (*What kind* of etching?)

DO

I have a fear *of the dark.* (*What kind* of fear?)

IO

I sent my friend *in Iowa* a picture. (*Which* friend?)

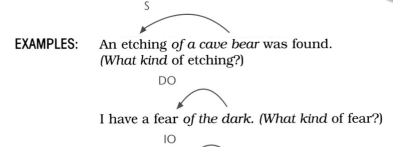

Adverb Phrases Like adverbs, adverb phrases modify verbs, adjectives, and other adverbs.

KEY CONCEPT An **adverb phrase** is a prepositional phrase that modifies a verb, an adjective, or an adverb by pointing out *where, when, in what way,* or *to what extent.* ■

When modifying a verb, an adverb phrase may come before or after the modified word.

MODIFYING
A VERB:
In Mammoth Cave National Park, you can tour the caves. (Can tour *where?*)

Except for one section, the cave had been mapped. (Was mapped *to what extent?*)

MODIFYING
AN ADJECTIVE:
I am angry *beyond belief.* (Angry *to what extent?*)

MODIFYING
AN ADVERB:
The shovel bit well *into the earth.* (Well *where?*)

As with adjective phrases, more than one adverb phrase can modify the same word.

EXAMPLE:
Before breakfast, the smell of bacon drifted *into our campsite.* (Drifted *when?* Drifted *where?*)

Exercise 1 Identifying Adjective and Adverb Phrases Write the prepositional phrases in the following sentences. Then, identify each prepositional phrase as *adjective* or *adverb.*

EXAMPLE:
Have you ever been to the cave?
to the cave (adverb)

1. Caves occurring in nature can be formed in different ways.
2. Caves formed by the long-term effect of acidic water are called solution caves.
3. Most of these caves are formed from limestone, which dissolves easily in slightly acidic water.
4. In certain geographic areas, water tends to absorb large amounts of carbon dioxide and other acidic compounds.
5. Over time, this acidic ground water eventually eats away at the rock, leaving an underground chamber, or cave.

More Practice

Language Lab
CD-ROM
• Recognizing and Using
  Phrases lesson
On-line
Exercise Bank
• Section 19.1
Grammar Exercise
Workbook
• pp. 33–34

Appositives and Appositive Phrases

To *appose* means "to place near or next to." Appositives and appositive phrases are words placed next to nouns and pronouns to provide additional information.

Appositives When you name something and then immediately rename it to give further information, you are using an appositive.

> **KEY CONCEPT** An **appositive** is a noun or pronoun placed next to another noun or pronoun in order to identify, rename, or explain it. ∎

EXAMPLES: My dog, *a pointer*, stood silently outside the cave.

She did not care for his hobby, *spelunking.*

These examples show appositives set off by commas. Dashes and colons can also be used to set off appositives. Punctuation is used to set off an appositive only when the appositive contains *nonessential* (or *nonrestrictive)* material—that is, material that can be removed from the sentence without altering its meaning. If the material is *essential* (or *restrictive)*, no commas are used.

EXAMPLE: My friend *Marilyn* enjoyed the tour of the cavern.

Appositive Phrases When an appositive is accompanied by one or more modifiers, it becomes a phrase.

> **KEY CONCEPT** An **appositive phrase** is a noun or pronoun with modifiers placed next to a noun or pronoun in order to add information and details. ∎

One-word adjectives, adjective phrases, or other groups of words acting as adjectives can modify an appositive.

EXAMPLE: The explorer, *a daring scientist*, braved the dark recesses of the cave.

 Internet Tip

Specific information about most large caves, such as Mammoth Cave National Park or Luray Caverns, can be found on numerous Web sites.

▶ **KEY CONCEPT** Appositives and appositive phrases can modify or rename any sentence part that is acting as a noun. ■

WITH A SUBJECT:
My jacket, *a windbreaker*, keeps me perfectly warm in the cool, damp cave.

WITH A DIRECT OBJECT:
I bought a book, *an atlas of famous caves.*

WITH AN INDIRECT OBJECT:
The man gave his fellow caving enthusiast, *his friend for ten years,* a brand-new flashlight.

WITH AN OBJECTIVE COMPLEMENT:
I called my friend Caruso, *the name of a famous operatic tenor,* because he likes to sing in the caves.

WITH A PREDICATE NOMINATIVE:
She is an archaeologist, *a historic explorer.*

WITH THE OBJECT OF A PREPOSITION:
In a shady area, *a small cave in the side of the hill,* I ate my lunch.

Appositives and appositive phrases can be compound.

EXAMPLE:
The family—*Mr. Trapp, his wife, and his children*—spent their vacation at Mammoth Cave in Kentucky.

Use appositives and appositive phrases to tighten your writing. Often, two sentences can be combined by turning the information in one sentence into an appositive.

TWO SENTENCES:
Tarantulas were hiding in the cave. Tarantulas are large, hairy spiders.

SENTENCE WITH APPOSITIVE PHRASE:
Tarantulas—*large, hairy spiders*—were hiding in the cave.

▼ **Critical Viewing** How can appositives and appositive phrases help a writer describe a single element in a larger scene, such as this cave entrance set in the mountainside? **[Connect]**

> **Exercise 2** Identifying Appositives and Appositive Phrases
Write each appositive or appositive phrase.

EXAMPLE: The tour guide, a very knowledgeable fellow, explained the history of the cave.

a very knowledgeable fellow

1. Caves, natural subterranean cavities, have many unique characteristics.
2. Calcium carbonate, a chemical compound, leaches from rock to form structures found only in caves.
3. Speleothems, the scientific name for these structures, form after the cave itself has developed.
4. Stalactites, hanging formations on the roof of a cave, are formed when water rich in calcium carbonate drips through cracks in the rock above.
5. Stalagmites, formations on the ground, are formed when this mineral-rich water drips to the floor of the cave.

> **Exercise 3** Combining Sentences With Appositives and Appositive Phrases Combine each pair of sentences by turning one into an appositive or appositive phrase.

EXAMPLE: Washington, D.C., is fascinating. It is our capital.
Washington, D.C., our capital, is fascinating.

1. Carlsbad Caverns is located in southeast New Mexico. It is a national park.
2. Carlsbad Caverns is very interesting. It contains one of the largest caves in the world.
3. Jim White explored the caves in the 1890's. He was a cowboy.
4. A group of scientists first explored the caves in 1924. They were members of the National Geographic Society.
5. Today, tourists flock to Carlsbad Caverns. It is a beautiful vacation spot with much to see.
6. The Big Room is the largest chamber in the cave. It is 1,800 feet long and 1,100 feet wide.
7. It is home to the Giant Dome. The Giant Dome is a massive column of rock 16 feet thick and 62 feet high.
8. The temperature in the cave rarely varies. It is a constant 56° F.
9. The fee to enter the cave is relatively inexpensive. It is only six dollars.
10. Call the park's phone number to make reservations for a special tour. The park has a toll-free number.

More Practice

Language Lab
CD-ROM
• Recognizing and Using Phrases lesson
On-line
Exercise Bank
• Section 19.1
Grammar Exercise Workbook
• pp. 35–36

Learn More

To learn more about properly punctuating appositives and appositive phrases, refer to Sections 27.2 and 27.5.

Section
19.1

Section Review

GRAMMAR EXERCISES 4–9

Exercise 4 Identifying Adjective and Adverb Phrases Write the prepositional phrases in the following sentences. Then, identify each prepositional phrase as *adjective* or *adverb*.

1. For some 32,000 years, people have been drawing on cave walls.
2. The first example of cave art was discovered in a Spanish cave in 1879.
3. At first, people did not believe that the realistic pictures of animals could have been drawn by prehistoric peoples.
4. It was only after the discovery of art in caves that had been sealed off for thousands of years that skeptics were disproved.
5. Today, more than 230 caves are known to contain examples of cave art.

Exercise 5 Identifying Appositive Phrases On your paper, write each appositive phrase you find in the following sentences and the word it identifies.

1. The Ice Cave near Grants, a small town in western New Mexico, attracts thousands of tourists each year.
2. The temperature in the cave never gets above 32º F, the freezing point of water.
3. As rainwater and snow melt seep into the cave, its floor—a solid block of ice 20 feet deep—continues to thicken.
4. The unique green tint of the ice, the result of Arctic algae trapped within, often fascinates tourists.
5. Pueblo Indians, who explored the cave hundreds of years ago, gave it a special name—"Winter Lake."

Exercise 6 Combining Sentences by Using Prepositional Phrases and Appositive Phrases Combine each group of sentences by turning one or more into a prepositional phrase or an appositive phrase.

1. Bats live throughout the United States. Caves are home to many of them.
2. Their seclusion makes them seem more mysterious. Caves are where they are secluded. People wonder about them.
3. Two main groups of bats exist in the world. The two main groups are Megachiroptera and Microchiroptera.
4. While most "megabats" have excellent eyesight, "microbats" rely on echolocation to find their way. Echolocation is a form of natural sonar.
5. The smallest bat weighs about two grams. Its size resembles a bumblebee's. Its weight is less than a dime's.

Exercise 7 Find It in Your Reading Reread the first paragraph on page 438. Locate and identify the two appositives in the paragraph. Hint: Neither is punctuated with commas.

Exercise 8 Find It in Your Writing Revise sentences in one of your social studies essays by using appositives and appositive phrases to combine sentences.

Exercise 9 Writing Application Compose a descriptive passage of an outdoor scene. Use adjective and adverb phrases to characterize and locate the scene you have chosen.

Verbals and Verbal Phrases

> **KEY CONCEPT** A **verbal** is a word derived from a verb but used as a noun, an adjective, or an adverb. ■

Like verbs, verbals may be modified by adverbs and adverb phrases or have complements. A verbal with modifiers or a complement is called a *verbal phrase*.

Participles and Participial Phrases

Many adjectives are actually verbals known as *participles.*

> **KEY CONCEPT** A **participle** is a form of a verb that can act as an adjective. ■

EXAMPLES: A *devastating* fire swept through the valley.
A *frightened* doe bounded into the woods.

Forms of Participles Participles come in three forms: *present participles*, *past participles*, and *perfect participles.*

Kinds of Participles	Forms	Examples
Present Participle	Ends in *-ing*	The *burning* embers fell to the ground. The water shone with *glimmering* phosphorescence.
Past Participle	Usually ends in *-ed*; sometimes *-t*, *-en*, or another irregular ending	The *scorched* forest eventually regenerated itself. The *exhausted* firefighter didn't hear the alarm.
Perfect Participle	Includes *having* or *having been* before a past participle	*Having tested the smoke detector,* I replaced its cover. *Having been asked*, he gave his opinion.

Participles precede or follow the words they modify, answering *Which one?* or *What kind?* as do one-word adjectives.

A verb has a subject and expresses the main action; a participle acting as an adjective describes a noun or pronoun.

In this section, you will learn to recognize participals, gerunds, infinitives, and various verbal phrases. The examples and exercises are about fires and firefighters.

Cross-Curricular Connection: Social Studies

Functioning as a Verb	Functioning as a Participle
The firefighter's muscles are *aching*.	The firefighter rubbed her *aching* muscles.
The firefighters *respected* their chief.	The *respected chief* had the firefighters' support.

Participial Phrases The addition of modifiers and complements to a participle produces a *participial phrase*.

▶ **KEY CONCEPT** A **participial phrase** is a participle modified by an adverb or adverb phrase or accompanied by a complement. The entire phrase acts as an adjective. ■

The following examples show different modifiers and complements that a participial phrase can have.

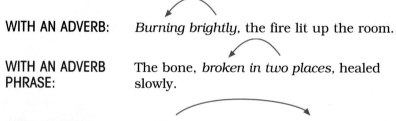

WITH AN ADVERB:	*Burning brightly*, the fire lit up the room.
WITH AN ADVERB PHRASE:	The bone, *broken in two places*, healed slowly.
WITH A DIRECT OBJECT:	*Holding the high-pressure hose*, I struggled to stand still.

A comma usually sets off a participial phrase at the beginning of a sentence. Within the sentence, however, a participial phrase is set off by commas only if it is *nonessential* to the sentence.

The sentence on the left side of the chart below would still make sense even if the participial phrase were removed. The phrase in the sentence on the right is necessary to identify the specific man being discussed.

Nonessential Participial Phrase	Essential Participial Phrase
Mr. Sharp, *driving that fire engine*, is well trained.	The man *driving that fire engine* is well trained.

🕮 Learn More

Refer to Section 27.2 for more information about punctuating participial phrases.

▶ **KEY CONCEPT** Participial phrases can be used to combine the information in two sentences into one sentence. ■

TWO SENTENCES: The fire marshal's speech expressed her opinion about several important issues. It convinced many people to vote for her.

COMBINED SENTENCE: The fire marshal's speech, convincing many people to vote for her, expressed her opinions about several important issues.

The fire marshal's speech, expressing her opinions about several important issues, convinced many people to vote for her.

Nominative Absolutes Sometimes, participles occur in phrases that are grammatically separate from the rest of the sentence. These phrases, called *nominative absolutes,* can show time, reason, or circumstance.

▶ **KEY CONCEPT** A **nominative absolute** is a noun or pronoun followed by a participle or participial phrase that functions independently of the rest of the sentence. ■

The following examples show nominative absolutes.

TIME: *Precious minutes having been lost,* I decided to call the fire department.

REASON: *My stomach growling with hunger,* I made a sandwich.

CIRCUMSTANCE: Many cadets missed final exams, *the flu epidemic having struck at the end of the semester.*

The participle *being* is sometimes understood rather than expressed in some nominative absolutes.

EXAMPLE: *The camera [being] out of film,* we stopped taking pictures of the forest fire.

Do not mistake a nominative absolute for the main subject and verb in a sentence. As a phrase, a nominative absolute cannot stand independently as a complete sentence.

▲ **Critical Viewing** Write a sentence introduced by a nominative absolute to explain how this fire may have started. **[Analyze]**

> **Exercise 10** Recognizing Participles and Participial
> **Phrases** Write the participle or participial phrase in each sentence. Then, label it *present, past,* or *perfect.*

> EXAMPLE: Led by the captain, the firefighters ran to the
> building.
> Led by the captain (past)

1. Besieged by drought for several months, the city of Chicago was ripe for a major fire in the fall of 1871.
2. On September 30,1871, the Burlington Warehouse burned down, causing $600,000 damage.
3. A few days later, a devastating fire destroyed four city blocks.
4. Having battled both of these blazes, the firefighters were exhausted.
5. The exhausted firefighters were unprepared for another fire.
6. Additionally, the beleaguered fire department had lost several pieces of badly needed equipment.
7. Mrs. O'Leary's cow was once blamed for accidentally starting the Great Chicago Fire on October 8, having knocked over a lantern in the barn at 8:30 P.M.
8. Once started, the fire was carried by high winds throughout the city.
9. Spreading quickly, the fire soon ravaged the west side of Chicago.
10. After three days, the raging fire eventually burned itself out.

> **Exercise 11** Revising Sentences by Using Participial
> **Phrases** Revise the following sentences by changing the underlined verb into a participial phrase.

> EXAMPLE: The town <u>elected</u> a fire chief, and he is a fearless
> leader.
> The fire chief elected by the town is a fearless
> leader.

1. On the morning of April 18, 1906, a massive earthquake <u>rocked</u> San Francisco and destroyed much of the city.
2. The earthquake <u>lasted</u> approximately one minute but caused extensive damage.
3. Gas mains, stoves, and fireplaces were soon <u>initiating</u> fires all across the city, and these fires contributed to a larger blaze.
4. More than fifty small fires <u>contributed</u> to the larger blaze and resulted in the Great San Francisco Fire.
5. The firemen <u>responded</u> to the numerous fires, but they were hampered by broken water mains and high winds.

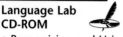

More Practice

Language Lab
CD-ROM
• Recognizing and Using
Phrases lesson
On-line
Exercise Bank
• Section 19.2
Grammar Exercise
Workbook
• pp. 37–38

Verbals and Verbal Phrases • **449**

▶ **Exercise 12** **Recognizing Nominative Absolutes** Write each sentence, underlining the subject once, underlining the verb twice, and circling the nominative absolute.

EXAMPLE: (Lightning having struck the dry forest,) a <u>fire</u> <u><u>swept</u></u> through twenty acres.

1. The freighter *Grandcamp* having docked at Texas City, Texas, workers were loading its cargo on April 16, 1947.
2. The ship having transported a cargo of ammonium nitrate, an onboard fire caused a tremendous explosion.
3. Most townspeople having been far enough away, casualties in the town were kept to a minimum.
4. The blast having damaged much of the town, people were evacuated because of the prospect of a second explosion.
5. Most people having left, a second explosion did not cause many casualties.
6. The dock engulfed in flames, the ship *High Flyer* eventually exploded early the next morning.
7. The city's fire department having been destroyed in the first explosion, many buildings could not be saved.
8. The blast having originated on the outskirts of the town, the fires were not as destructive as those in Chicago or San Francisco.
9. Nearly six hundred people having died, the town was in a state of shock.
10. The fire on the *Grandcamp* having been caused by careless actions, the event could easily have been prevented.

▶ **Critical Viewing** Create participial phrases from the verbs *burn*, *watch*, and *exhaust* in sentences to describe this picture. **[Connect]**

Gerunds and Gerund Phrases

Verbs ending in *-ing* can be used as nouns called *gerunds*.

▶ **KEY CONCEPT** A **gerund** is a form of a verb that acts as a noun. ■

EXAMPLES: *Training* is the fire department's favorite activity.
             Climbing is an important part of the job.

The Function of Gerunds in Sentences By themselves, gerunds function in sentences like any other nouns.

SOME USES OF GERUNDS IN SENTENCES	
As a Subject	*Firefighting* is often dangerous.
As a Direct Object	A successful firefighter must enjoy *firefighting*.
As an Indirect Object	He gives *studying* all of his attention.
As a Predicate Nominative	Her favorite pastime is *reading*.
As an Object of a Preposition	Check the smoke detector before *leaving*.
As an Appositive	One field, *engineering*, has made great advances in fire safety.

To avoid confusing verbs, participles, and gerunds—which all can end in *-ing*—check the word's use in the sentence.

VERB PHRASE: My friends *are fighting* the fire.
PARTICIPLE: A *fighting* spirit permeated the fire station.
GERUND: *Firefighting* tires me out.

Note About *Gerunds and Possessive Pronouns:* Only the possessive form of a personal pronoun is appropriate before a gerund.

INCORRECT: *Them* risking their lives is heroic.
CORRECT: *Their* risking their lives is heroic.

Gerund Phrases A gerund with modifiers or a complement is called a *gerund phrase.*

> **KEY CONCEPT** A **gerund phrase** is a gerund with modifiers or a complement, all acting together as a noun. ■

In the following chart, notice the variety of different kinds of modifiers and complements that a gerund phrase can contain.

GERUND PHRASES	
With Adjectives	*His loud, persistent snoring* disrupted the entire fire station.
With an Adjective Phrase	*Worrying about the next fire* prevented the captain from sleeping.
With an Adverb	I contacted the fire department by *dialing quickly.*
With an Adverb Phrase	*Fishing from the pier* is permitted.
With a Direct Object	*Battling arson* grows more expensive each year.
With Indirect and Direct Objects	The teacher suggested *writing the firemen a letter.*

> **Exercise 13** Identifying Gerunds and Gerund Phrases
Write the gerund or gerund phrase in each sentence. Then, identify its function in the sentence.

EXAMPLE: Taking this shortcut will save firefighters time.
           Taking this shortcut (subject)

1. Fighting fires is a dangerous profession that requires courage and dedication.
2. The job of the fire department is protecting buildings and people from the ravages of a fire.
3. Arriving at a fire within a few minutes is the goal of the fire department.
4. Risking their lives is a regular part of firefighters' jobs.
5. They completely extinguish the flames before leaving.
6. Handling a fire hose is difficult because the water is under such high pressure.
7. An important part of a firefighter's job is rescuing people.
8. Firefighters are often seen ascending ladders.
9. The showering of water from the high-pressure hoses is impressive to see.
10. After the fire is extinguished, salvaging property becomes the main focus of the firefighters.

More Practice

**Language Lab
CD-ROM**
• Recognizing and Using Phrases lesson
**On-line
Exercise Bank**
• Section 19.2
**Grammar Exercise
Workbook**
• pp. 39–40

Infinitives and Infinitive Phrases

Infinitives, the third type of verbal, can function as three parts of speech.

> **KEY CONCEPT** An *infinitive* is a form of a verb that generally appears with the word *to* and acts as a noun, an adjective, or an adverb. ∎

EXAMPLES: The firefighter would like *to sleep*.
The instructor gave them an assignment *to do*.

Forms of Infinitives There are two kinds of infinitives— *present infinitives* and *perfect infinitives*.

Kinds of Infinitives	Forms	Examples
Present Infinitive	*To* plus the base form of a verb	I like *to debate. To concede* is *to lose.*
Perfect Infinitive	*To have* or *to have been* plus a past participle	I would have liked *to have gone. To have been mentioned* would have sufficed.

Do not mistake prepositional phrases for infinitives. In an infinitive, a verb follows the word *to*. In a prepositional phrase beginning with the word *to*, a noun or pronoun follows the word *to*.

INFINITIVES: to fight, to have excelled
PREPOSITIONAL   to them, to a
PHRASES: friend

Sometimes infinitives do not include the word *to*. After the verbs *dare, hear, help, let, make, please, see*, and *watch*, the *to* will usually be understood rather than stated.

EXAMPLES: The student helped *extinguish* the fire. No one dared *rush* into the blazing building.

▼ **Critical Viewing** Use infinitives and infinitive phrases formed from the verbs *battle* and *rage* in a sentence to describe the scene below. **[Connect]**

Infinitive Phrases When you add modifiers, complements, or subjects to an infinitive, an infinitive becomes an *infinitive phrase.*

▶ **KEY CONCEPT** An **infinitive phrase** is an infinitive with modifiers, a complement, or a subject, all acting together as a single part of speech. ■

WITH AN ADVERB:	The firefighters at the scene needed *to act quickly.*
WITH AN ADVERB PHRASE:	They hoped *to finish within a few minutes.*
WITH A COMPLEMENT:	They tried *to confine the blaze.*
WITH A SUBJECT AND COMPLEMENT:	The firefighters asked *the crowd to leave the area.*

The Function of Infinitives in Sentences The flexibility of infinitives enables them to be used in almost any capacity. Note in the chart below that infinitives, like gerunds, often function as nouns. Unlike gerunds, however, infinitives can also act as adjectives or adverbs in sentences.

INFINITIVES AND INFINITIVE PHRASES USED AS NOUNS AND MODIFIERS	
As a Subject	*To play with matches* is wrong.
As a Direct Object	The fire inspector decided *to leave the scene.*
As a Predicate Nominative	Our best protection against a fire was *to have been prepared.*
As an Object of a Preposition	I was about *to speak.*
As an Appositive	The fire department's intention, *to save the house,* intensified quickly.
As an Adjective	The fireman gave us some safety advice *to follow.*
As an Adverb	Fires are hard *to contain.*

 **Internet Tip**

Most city and county fire departments have their own Web sites. To learn more about firefighting, search for the site of a fire department in your city or in a city near your home.

GRAMMAR IN
LITERATURE

from *The Diary*
Samuel Pepys

Participial phrases in this diary excerpt are highlighted in blue italics, infinitive phrases are in red, and gerund phrases are in green.

. . . *My meeting dead corpses* of the plague, *carried to be buried* close to me at noonday through the city in Fanchurch Street. *To see a person* sick of the sores, *carried close by me* by Grace church in a hackney coach. *My finding the Angell Tavern* at the lower end of Tower Hill, *shut up*, and more than that . . .

▶ **Exercise 14** **Identifying Infinitives and Infinitive Phrases**
Write each infinitive or infinitive phrase. Then, label its part of speech *noun, adjective,* or *adverb.* If the infinitive or infinitive phrase is used as a noun, further identify its function as a *subject, direct object, predicate nominative, object of a preposition,* or *appositive.*

EXAMPLE: We tried for two hours to start the campfire.
              to start the campfire (noun, direct object)

1. Here are the facts to understand about the tragic fire at Peshtigo, Wisconsin, in 1871.
2. The hot, arid summer had managed to drain the surrounding forest of any moisture.
3. Just one day before the fire, the local newspaper chose to declare, "Without rain, a conflagration may ensue."
4. Initially, it was difficult to perceive the fire as a threat, but it soon developed into an all-consuming blaze.
5. To make matters worse, a strong wind propelled the fire through the forest with great speed.
6. The town's only fire engine was called to stop the flames.
7. The firemen were quick to realize that they could not save the town.
8. To save their own lives, the firemen fled to the river.
9. To return to the ashes of the town was difficult for the citizens of Peshtigo.
10. A memorial was built to honor the men and women who perished.

▶ **More Practice**

Language Lab CD-ROM
• Recognizing and Using Phrases lesson
On-line Exercise Bank
• Section 19.2
Grammar Exercise Workbook
• pp. 39–40

Hands-on Grammar

Verbal-Phrase Folds

One way to write sentences that are longer and more varied is to use verbal phrases in your writing. Often, you can change part of the predicate of one sentence into a participial, gerund, or infinitive phrase that you can incorporate into a second sentence. To practice this sentence-combining technique, try the following activity.

Cut out a series of long, thin strips of paper. On one strip, write the following pair of sentences: *He was climbing the rock face. He fell and broke his leg.* Bend under the first two words of the first sentence to form a combined sentence that starts with a participle: *Climbing the steep rock face, he fell and broke his leg.* On the strip, correct the capitalization and punctuation as needed.

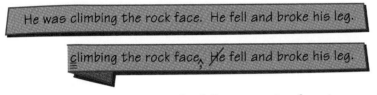

Complete a second strip with the following pair of sentences: *He was losing his grip on the rocks. That led to his accident.* Bend under the first two words of the first sentence and fold the paper over to cover the word *That* at the beginning of the second sentence. The result is a combined sentence that starts with a gerund phrase: *Losing his grip on the rocks led to his accident.*

Use the following sentences to create more verbal phrase folds. Some sentences can be folded in more than one way. For each folded strip, identify the type of verbal phrase you have formed and its function in the new sentence.

He hoped to reach the top of the rock wall. That was his goal.
Alice was frightened of heights. Alice wouldn't attempt the climb.
Cheryl had her own secret method. She was keeping her eyes shut.
Sal was exhausted by the effort. Sal almost gave up.
Sal was determined. Sal wanted to reach the top of the rock face.

Find It in Your Reading Find examples of sentences in a short story or novel that contain verbal phrases. For each one you find, identify the type of phrase and its function in the sentence.

Find It in Your Writing Review a piece of writing from your portfolio. Combine at least two pairs of sentences using phrases.

Section 19.2 Section Review

GRAMMAR EXERCISES 15–19

Exercise 15 Identifying Verbals and Verbal Phrases Identify the underlined verbals in the following sentences as either a *gerund phrase*, an *infinitive phrase*, a *participle*, a *participial phrase*, or a *nominative absolute*. Identify the way each gerund or infinitive functions in the sentence.

1. The movie having ended, my friend and I walked to our homes.
2. On the way, I noticed a burning smell.
3. Originating above an old, empty warehouse was a cloud of smoke.
4. As we got closer to the building, I could see smoke billowing from the top floor.
5. My friend ran to the nearest pay phone to call the fire department.
6. Soon after he returned, we could hear the blaring sirens of the fire engines.
7. By now, sparks could be seen falling to the ground.
8. Two brightly painted fire engines came to a stop in front of the building.
9. The firefighters knew exactly how to handle the situation.
10. Several immediately began unraveling the long hoses.
11. Another one ran to open the nearby fire hydrant.
12. Dousing the fire with water immediately reduced the level of the blaze.
13. The ladder truck having been moved into position, one person climbed up to the top floor of the building.
14. Wielding an axe, she shattered the windows so the others could douse the flames with water from the hoses.
15. Witnessing the firefighters' skills made us feel more secure.

Exercise 16 Revising Sentences by Using Verbal Phrases On your paper, rewrite each sentence that follows using the directions in parentheses.

1. A fire damaged and destroyed much of London in 1666. (Change *damaged* to a present participle.)
2. The fire started in a bakery, and the smell of burnt bread soon filled the air. (Change the first clause into a nominative absolute.)
3. Londoners who lived nearby saw the blaze. The sight frightened them. (Change *frightened* into a participle.)
4. London's citizens were unprepared to battle the fire. They stood by helplessly. (Combine by using a participial phrase.)
5. We discovered that very few people died in the fire. That was amazing. (Combine with an infinitive subject.)

Exercise 17 Find It in Your Reading Identify the verbals and verbal phrases in this passage from Samuel Pepys's diary.

. . . [T]o see how the streets and the highways are crowded with people running and riding, and the getting of carts at any rate to fetch away things.

Exercise 18 Find It in Your Writing Review a piece of writing from your portfolio. Identify at least two gerunds or gerund phrases. If you have not used any gerunds, challenge yourself to include at least two.

Exercise 19 Writing Application Write a newspaper article describing a fire or other tragedy. Use several types of verbal phrases to make your writing more interesting and descriptive.

Clauses

Clauses, like phrases, are groups of related words, but unlike phrases, they have a subject and a verb.

> ▶**KEY CONCEPT** A **clause** is a group of words with its own subject and verb. ■

There are two basic kinds of clauses: *independent* and *subordinate* clauses.

> ▶**KEY CONCEPT** An **independent clause** has a subject and a verb and can stand by itself as a complete sentence. ■

All complete sentences must contain at least one independent clause; additional independent or subordinate clauses may be added. *The flag will be lowered at sundown* is an independent clause. *I bought a flag, but I didn't have a flag pole* is one independent clause added to another. *The flagpole was barren after the banner was removed* is an example of an independent clause followed by a subordinate clause. Though *after the banner was removed* contains a subject *(banner)* and a verb *(was removed)*, the clause cannot stand alone.

> ▶**KEY CONCEPT** A **subordinate clause** cannot stand by itself as a complete sentence; it is only part of a sentence. ■

Subordinate clauses can add important details to sentences and show relationships between ideas. Within sentences, subordinate clauses act as either adjectives, adverbs, or nouns.

Theme: Flags

In this section, you will learn to recognize adjective, adverb, and noun clauses. The examples and exercises are about flags.

Cross-Curricular Connection: Social Studies

▼ **Critical Viewing** What fact about this flag could be set off in a nonessential adjective clause? Write a sentence that includes that clause. **[Analyze]**

Adjective Clauses

Adjective clauses modify nouns or pronouns in ways often not possible with one-word adjectives or adjective phrases.

KEY CONCEPT An **adjective clause** is a subordinate clause that modifies a noun or pronoun. ■

An adjective clause appears after the noun or pronoun it modifies. It usually begins with a relative pronoun *(that, which, who, whom,* or *whose)* or with a relative adverb (such as *before, since, when, where,* or *why).*

EXAMPLES: The flag, *which was created in 1847,* is striped.

There was a time *when the flag had only thirteen stars.*

Essential and Nonessential Adjective Clauses

Adjectives clauses are punctuated according to whether they add *essential* or *nonessential* information to a sentence.

KEY CONCEPTS An adjective clause that is not essential to the basic meaning of a sentence is set off by commas. An essential clause is not set off. ■

The following chart demonstrates the difference between nonessential and essential clauses.

Nonessential Adjective Clauses	Essential Adjective Clauses
The tattered flag, which inspired Francis Scott Key, was on display at the museum.	The tattered flag that inspired Francis Scott Key was on display at the museum.

You can often combine two sentences into one by using either a nonessential or an essential adjective clause.

TWO SENTENCES: "The Star-Spangled Banner" is a patriotic song about the American flag. It became the national anthem in 1931.

ADJECTIVE CLAUSE: "The Star-Spangled Banner," which became the national anthem in 1931, is a patriotic song about the American flag.

Learn More

For more information about punctuating adjective clauses, see Chapter 27.

Introductory Words in Adjective Clauses *Relative pronouns* and *relative adverbs* not only begin adjective clauses but also function within the subordinate clause.

> ►**KEY CONCEPT** **Relative pronouns** connect adjective clauses to the words they modify and act as subjects, direct objects, objects of prepositions, or adjectives in the clauses. ■

Relative pronouns act as an introduction to the clause and as a subject, direct object, object of a preposition, or adjective *within* the clause. The role of the relative pronoun can be determined by isolating the adjective clause from the rest of the sentence and then by identifying its subject and verb. Because adjective clauses are sometimes in inverted order, you may need to rearrange the words mentally.

THE USES OF RELATIVE PRONOUNS WITHIN ADJECTIVE CLAUSES	
As a Subject	*Sentence:* The flag *that was just lowered* is the Italian flag. *Clause:* <u>that</u> <u>was</u> just <u>lowered</u>
As a Direct Object	*Sentence:* Someone scratched the flagpole *that I recently painted.* *Reworded clause:* <u>I</u> recently <u>painted</u> that ^{DO}
As the Object of a Preposition	*Sentence:* This is the flag designer *of whom I have spoken.* *Reworded clause:* <u>I</u> <u>have spoken</u> of whom ^{OBJ OF PREP}
As an Adjective	*Sentence:* I have a friend *whose grandfather raised the flag at San Juan Hill.* *Clause:* whose <u>grandfather</u> <u>raised</u> the flag at San Juan Hill

Note About *Understood Relative Pronouns:* In some adjective clauses, the relative pronoun may be understood.

EXAMPLE: The flag *[that] I own* is from the War of 1812.

▶ **KEY CONCEPT** **Relative adverbs** function only as adverbs within clauses. ■

THE USE OF RELATIVE ADVERBS WITHIN ADJECTIVE CLAUSES	
As an Adverb	*Sentence:* The spot *where we stood* afforded us an excellent view of the flag. *Reworded clause:* we stood where

▶ **Exercise 20** **Identifying Adjective Clauses** Write each adjective clause, underlining its subject once and its verb twice. Then, circle the relative pronoun or relative adverb and identify its function in the clause.

EXAMPLE: I salute the same flag that my forefathers saluted.
(that) my forefathers saluted (direct object)

1. A flag is a piece of fabric that functions as a symbol.
2. Historians know surprisingly little about the first flags that ancient peoples used.
3. The first place where flags are known to have been used was China.
4. The Chinese, who made flags from silk, began using them more than 3,000 years ago.
5. Roman flags, which developed at a later date, were called *vexilla*.

▶ **Exercise 21** **Punctuating Adjective Clauses** On your paper, underline each adjective clause and add commas if necessary.

EXAMPLE: We wrote to Ms. Gomez who was our instructor.
We wrote to Ms. Gomez, who was our instructor.

1. The flag of the United States which is often called the Stars and Stripes originated during the Revolutionary War.
2. Congress passed a resolution on June 14, 1777, that prescribed the official design of the new flag.
3. The flag's design consisted of thirteen stars and stripes which represented the thirteen colonies.
4. Historians who study flags are unable to determine the first flag's creator.
5. According to popular legend, Betsy Ross who was a seamstress made the first American flag.

▶ **More Practice**

Language Lab CD-ROM
• Varying Sentence Structure lesson
On-line Exercise Bank
• Section 19.3
Grammar Exercise Workbook
• pp. 41–42

Adverb Clauses

An *adverb clause* functions in a sentence in much the same way one-word adverbs and adverb phrases do.

▶ **KEY CONCEPT** An **adverb clause** is a subordinate clause that modifies a verb, an adjective, an adverb, or a verbal. It does this by pointing out *where, when, in what way, to what extent, under what condition,* or *why.* ■

An adverb clause begins with a subordinating conjunction and contains a subject and a verb, although they are not the main subject and verb in the sentence. This kind of subordinate clause may modify any word that an adverb can.

ADVERB CLAUSES

Modified Words	Examples
Verb	We saluted *because the flag had been raised.*
Adjective	The veteran appeared proud *as he saluted the flag.*
Adverb	The flag ceremony ended sooner *than we expected.*
Participle	The flag, flapping in the wind *as I attempted to do my studies,* made concentration impossible.
Gerund	I relax by sitting under the flagpole *after I study.*
Infinitive	I wanted to visit the museum *while "The Star-Spangled Banner" was still being displayed.*

🕐 Learn More

Refer to Section 17.4 for a list of subordinating conjunctions.

Adverb clauses can be used to combine two sentences into one and to show relationships between ideas.

TWO SENTENCES:	The design was used by the king. It was added to the flag in 1924.
COMBINED:	The design was used by the king before it was added to the flag in 1924.

▶ **KEY CONCEPT** Some adverb clauses beginning with *as* or *than* are **elliptical**. The verb or both the subject and the verb in the clause are understood but not stated. ■

VERB UNDERSTOOD: I recognized as many flags *as he* [*did*].

SUBJECT AND
VERB UNDERSTOOD: The UN building has more flags *than* [*it has*] *rooms*.

▶ **Exercise 22** **Identifying Adverb Clauses** Write the adverb clause in each sentence. Then, indicate whether it modifies a *verb*, an *adjective*, an *adverb*, or a *verbal*.

EXAMPLE: Although rain had been predicted, the flag was still raised.
Although rain had been predicted (verb)

1. There are specific rules to know before you display the American flag.
2. Although the flag should always be raised quickly, it should be lowered slowly.
3. The flag is generally raised after the sun has risen.
4. It should be lowered when the sun sets.
5. The flag should be flown every day unless it is raining.
6. The American flag should be displayed on the right-hand side of any other flags if it is carried in a procession.
7. Marchers, parading while they hold the American flag, may also carry it in front of the procession.
8. A public building, such as a courthouse, should display the flag once the building has been occupied.
9. The flag is often flown prominently wherever U.S. troops are stationed.
10. Folding the flag into a small triangular-shaped bundle is appropriate unless it is being displayed.

▶ **Exercise 23** **Recognizing Elliptical Clauses** Write each elliptical adverb clause, showing understood words in parentheses.

EXAMPLE: I enjoyed making this banner more than that one.
than (I did) that one

1. Not all flags are the same shape as the American flag.
2. However, there are more rectangular national flags than square national flags.
3. The width of most of these flags is usually longer than the height.
4. Horizontal stripes are as common to national flags as vertical stripes.
5. Some national flags contain more colors than others.

▶ **More Practice**

Language Lab CD-ROM
• Varying Sentence Structure lesson
On-line Exercise Bank
• Section 19.3
Grammar Exercise Workbook
• pp. 43–44

Learn More

Refer to Section 22.2 for rules about the correct use of pronouns in elliptical clauses.

Noun Clauses

The *noun clause* is the third kind of subordinate clause.

▶ **KEY CONCEPT** A **noun clause** is a subordinate clause that acts as a noun in a sentence. ∎

As the following chart shows, a noun clause can perform any function in a sentence that any other kind of noun can.

USES OF NOUN CLAUSES IN SENTENCES

Functions in Sentences	Examples
Subject	*Whatever information you need* can be found in this book.
Direct Object	The soldiers carried *whichever flag belonged to their country.*
Indirect Object	The group sent *whoever requested information* a brochure about the history of flags.
Predicate Nominative	To change the design of the ensign is *what I would like.*
Object of a Preposition	I will cut the banner to *whatever length you desire.*

Noun clauses frequently begin with *that, which, who, whom,* or *whose,* the same words that can begin adjective clauses. Other words that can begin noun clauses are *how, if, what, whatever, when, where, whether, whichever, whoever,* or *whomever.* Besides serving to introduce a noun clause, these words sometimes serve a function within the clause as well.

▼ **Critical Viewing** Use the noun clause "what a red dragon looks like" in a sentence about the flag of Wales. **[Apply]**

SOME USES OF INTRODUCTORY WORDS IN NOUN CLAUSES

Functions in Clauses	Examples
Adjective	She could not decide *which Scandinavian flag was her favorite.*
Adverb	I do not know *when the flag pole was painted.*
Subject	*Whoever recognizes the American flag* should treat it with respect.
Direct Object	*Whatever my supervisor advised,* I did.
No Function	The historian said *that the flag was two hundred years old.*

Grammar and Style Tip

With noun clauses, you can also try substituting the words *fact, it, thing,* or *you* for the clause. If the sentence retains its smoothness, the clause is probably a noun clause. I knew *the flag was waving.* I knew *it.*

When the word *that* has no function within the clause except to introduce it, it is often omitted.

EXAMPLE: We remembered [*that*] *you wanted to raise the flag in the morning.*

Because some of the words that introduce noun clauses also introduce adjective and adverb clauses, do not let the introductory word be your only guide to determining the type of clause. Always check the function of the clause in the sentence.

▶ **Exercise 24** **Identifying Noun Clauses** Write each noun clause. Then, identify the function of each noun clause as *subject, direct object, indirect object, predicate nominative, object of a preposition,* or *appositive.*

EXAMPLE: A symbolic flag is what everyone wants.
                  what everyone wants (predicate nominative)

1. A ship at sea traditionally flies whichever flag represents its country of origin.
2. Specific guidelines often govern how flags should be displayed on ships.
3. Whichever national flag is flown at the front of a ship is called the jack.
4. An ensign is what the national flag is called on the rear of a ship.
5. As a courtesy, most ships usually fly the national flag of whichever country they are visiting.

▶ **More Practice**

Language Lab CD-ROM
• Varying Sentence Structure lesson
On-line Exercise Bank
• Section 19.3
Grammar Exercise Workbook
• pp. 45–46

GRAMMAR IN
LITERATURE

from **The Distant Past**
William Trevor

The author has included several noun clauses (in blue italics) that serve as direct objects in the passage.

The Middletons, privately, often considered *that they led a strange life*. Alone in their two beds at night they now and again wondered *why they hadn't just sold Carraveagh forty-eight years ago* when their father had died—*why had the tie been so strong* and *why had they in perversity encouraged it?*

Exercise 25 **Combining Sentences With Subordinate Clauses** Combine each pair of sentences by using a subordinate clause. You may need to change or rearrange words or make other minor changes. Underline the subordinate clause and label it *adjective*, *adverb*, or *noun*.

1. Flags have been used to signal messages at sea. They have been used since ancient times.
2. Signal flags were used before radio was invented. It was one way for ships to communicate.
3. In the fifth century B.C., Greeks were using signal flags. These flags communicated attack plans.
4. There is one thing researchers don't completely understand. They don't understand the way these flags were used.
5. The Italian city-states had ships roaming the Mediterranean Sea. By the Middle Ages, they had developed a more sophisticated system of signaling.
6. In 1369, the British created a new flag. The flag was used only as a signal flag.
7. The admiral used the flag. With this flag, he summoned his officers to his ship.
8. The British created the first true code of flag signals. This fact is widely held to be an accurate statement.
9. In 1812, Sir Home Popham created a system of flags. The system represented all twenty-six letters and each numeral.
10. The first international signal flag code was recognized by most nations. It was introduced after the twentieth century had begun.

Section Review

GRAMMAR EXERCISES 26–31

Exercise 26 **Identifying Adjective and Adverb Clauses** Write each adjective or adverb clause, underlining its subject once and its verb twice. If a clause is elliptical, add the understood words in parentheses.

1. The flag that the British fly today is called the Union Jack.
2. This flag, which incorporates the flags of England, Scotland, and Ireland, has been in use since 1801.
3. Ireland's tricolor flag has been flown almost fifty years less than the Union Jack.
4. When the Irish rose against England, the tricolor became a symbol of unity and national pride in Ireland.
5. Wales is the only U.K. member that is not represented on the Union Jack.

Exercise 27 **Identifying Noun Clauses** Write each noun clause. Then, identify the function of each noun clause as *subject, direct object, indirect object, predicate nominative,* or *object of a preposition.*

1. That the Dutch flag is the first modern national flag is an accepted fact.
2. The flag commemorates when the Dutch rebelled against the Spanish in 1568.
3. Who created the flag is not known.
4. The flag of red, white, and blue stripes is what vexillologists call a tricolor flag.
5. For nearly 500 years, the tricolor flag has functioned as the national flag for whoever lives in the Netherlands.

Exercise 28 **Revising Sentences by Using Subordinate Clauses** Rewrite the following pairs of sentences by converting one sentence into the type of clause indicated in parentheses.

1. An army indicates its intention to surrender. It waves a white flag. (adverb)
2. A flag is flown upside down. It is a signal of distress. (noun)
3. Some groups fly flags upside down. They want to indicate a political protest. (adverb)
4. The Mexican flag is a tricolor flag. It has a strip of white between green and red bands. (adjective)
5. The person salutes the flag. The person should stand at attention. (noun)

Exercise 29 **Find It in Your Reading** Identify an adjective clause and an adverb clause in this passage from "The Distant Past." What word does each clause modify?

But as the town increased its prosperity, Carraveagh continued its decline. The Middletons were in their middle sixties now and were reconciled to a life that became more uncomfortable with every passing year.

Exercise 30 **Find It in Your Writing** Look through your portfolio for a paragraph that consists mostly of short sentences. Challenge yourself to combine some sentences by using subordinate clauses.

Exercise 31 **Writing Application** Write a short biography of a friend or family member. Add details and provide characterization by making use of each type of phrase and clause discussed in this chapter. Check your work carefully to ensure that you have used phrases and clauses correctly.

Sentences Classified by Structure

Sentences may be classified according to the kind and number of clauses they contain.

The Four Structures of Sentences

Different combinations of independent and subordinate clauses form four basic sentence structures. You should try to use all four types of sentences in your writing.

▶ **KEY CONCEPTS** A **simple sentence** consists of a single independent clause. A simple sentence can still have a compound subject or compound verb. ■

A **compound sentence** consists of two or more independent clauses joined by a comma and a coordinating conjunction or by a semicolon. ■

A **complex sentence** consists of one independent clause and one or more subordinate clauses. ■

A **compound-complex sentence** consists of two or more independent clauses and one or more subordinate clauses. ■

Study the examples of each type of sentence structure in the chart on page 469. Notice that simple sentences can contain compound subjects, compound verbs, or both. Notice also that a subordinate clause may fall between the parts of an independent clause or even within an independent clause.

As you can see in the examples of complex sentences, independent clauses in complex sentences are often called *main clauses* to distinguish them from subordinate clauses. The subject and verb of a main clause are often respectively called the *subject of the sentence* and the *main verb* to distinguish them from the other subjects and verbs that appear in the sentence.

Theme: Royal Symbols

In this section, you will learn to classify sentences according to their structure. The examples and exercises are about royal symbols, such as crowns, sceptres, and thrones.

Cross-Curricular Connection: Social Studies

▶ **Critical Viewing** What simple symbol of royalty does this king display? What complex ideas does that royal symbol convey? **[Analyze]**

Henry III

FOUR STRUCTURES OF SENTENCES

Simple Sentences	The <u>king</u> <u>ruled</u> for forty years. Either the firstborn <u>son</u> or the firstborn <u>daughter</u> <u>will become</u> the new ruler.
Compound Sentences	The <u>duke</u> <u>was</u> courageous on the battlefield, so the <u>king</u> <u>rewarded</u> him. The <u>prince</u> <u>was</u> unfit to rule; nevertheless, <u>he</u> <u>became</u> king upon his father's death.

Complex Sentences	SUBORDINATE CLAUSE
	Although the <u>king</u> <u>had ruled</u>
	                       MAIN CLAUSE
	compassionately, the <u>people</u> still <u>wanted</u> to abolish the monarchy.
	
	  MAIN SUBORDINATE CLAUSE
	The <u>queen</u>, who <u>raised</u> taxes to new
	              MAIN CLAUSE
	levels, <u>was</u> no longer popular with the
	SUBORDINATE CLAUSE
	people whom <u>she</u> <u>ruled</u>.
	
	          MAIN CLAUSE SUBORDINATE CLAUSE
	The <u>people</u> <u>will do</u> whatever the <u>king</u>
	<u>says</u>.

Compound-Complex Sentences	INDEPENDENT CLAUSE
	The <u>prince</u> <u>dismissed</u> all of his advisors
	  SUBORDINATE CLAUSE
	as soon as <u>he</u> <u>became</u> king, and
	  INDEPENDENT CLAUSE
	<u>he</u> <u>began making</u> his own decisions.
	
	    SUBORDINATE CLAUSE
	When the <u>queen</u> <u>entered</u> the room,
	  INDEPENDENT CLAUSE
	<u>everyone</u> <u>bowed</u> according to custom,
	    INDEPENDENT CLAUSE
	but <u>many</u> <u>were resentful</u> of her power.

⚙ Grammar and Style Tip

Using a variety of sentence structures demonstrates a mature writing style. Varied sentence patterns make your writing richer and, therefore, more interesting to read.

Exercise 32 **Identifying the Four Structures of Sentences**
Identify each sentence as *simple, compound, complex,* or *compound-complex.*

EXAMPLE: Whenever the king makes a decision, there is no changing his mind.
complex

1. Monarchy is a form of government that is based upon the idea of a person's hereditary right to rule.
2. There are many different types of monarchical governments.
3. Some monarchs have complete control of their government, but other monarchs have very limited power.
4. Throughout the course of history, most monarchs have exercised absolute power over their subjects.
5. During the Middle Ages, this system of government spread across Europe.
6. Most of these European monarchies were ruled by one family who passed control of the country down from one generation to the next.
7. Initially, most of these governments were supported by the middle class, who prospered from the stability that a strong central government brought to the country.
8. By the end of the eighteenth century, many absolute rulers, such as Louis XVI, had become too abusive and self-centered, and several of them were overthrown by republican revolutionaries.
9. As World War I drew to a close, many European monarchies were eliminated altogether, and they were replaced by constitutional governments.
10. Today, a few countries maintain monarchs as symbols of national unity, but most have little, if any, real power.

More Practice

Language Lab CD-ROM
• Varying Sentence Structure lesson
On-line Exercise Bank
• Section 19.3
Grammar Exercise Workbook
• pp. 47–48

Learn More

To learn more about properly punctuating the various types of sentence structures, refer to Chapter 27.

▶ **Critical Viewing** Write a simple sentence describing this piece of art. Write a compound or complex sentence about the symbols of royalty shown in the painting. **[Analyze]**

Section 19.4 *Section Review*

GRAMMAR EXERCISES 33–38

▶ **Exercise 33** **Identifying the Four Structures of Sentences** Identify each of the following sentences as *simple, compound, complex,* or *compound-complex.*

1. Elizabeth I was the daughter of Henry VIII, the king of England, and his second wife, Anne Boleyn.
2. Elizabeth was born in 1533, and she spent the better part of her childhood away from London.
3. Shortly before the death of her father in 1547, Elizabeth returned to the court in London, where Henry's sixth wife, Katherine Parr, took care of her.
4. Elizabeth's two siblings, Edward VI and Mary I, ruled England for the next eleven years.
5. During her short reign, Mary suspected that Elizabeth, who was her half sister, had supported a revolt against the throne; consequently, Mary had Elizabeth imprisoned.

▶ **Exercise 34** **Forming Complex Sentences** Add a subordinate clause to each of the following sentences to form a complex sentence.

1. The country is ruled by a queen.
2. The queen is respected by her subjects.
3. She has ruled the country for ten years.
4. The monarch has initiated many excellent policies.
5. She is a generous and thoughtful ruler.

▶ **Exercise 35** **Forming Compound-Complex Sentences** Add a subordinate clause to each of the following sentences to form a compound-complex sentence.

1. The king of England ruled over a large empire in the 1700's, and America was a part of that empire.

2. The American colonies wanted to form an independent nation, but the king wanted them to remain a part of his empire.
3. The king would not change his position, nor would the colonies alter theirs.
4. In 1776, the colonies revolted against the king's authority, so he sent soldiers to stop their independence movement.
5. Ultimately, the colonies were victorious over the king, and he was forced to admit defeat.

▶ **Exercise 36** **Find It in Your Reading** Read the following advice to a monarch from Sir Thomas More's *Utopia.* Identify whether the sentence is *compound, complex,* or *compound-complex.*

> He ought to shake off either his sloth or his pride, for the people's hatred and scorn arise from these faults in him.

▶ **Exercise 37** **Find It in Your Writing** Review a social studies essay from your writing portfolio. Evaluate the ratio of simple sentences to compound, complex, and compound-complex sentences. If you have mostly simple sentences, decide which sentences could be combined or expanded into other types.

▶ **Exercise 38** **Writing Application** Rewrite some or all of the social studies essay you reviewed in Find It in Your Writing. Revise and combine sentences to form compound, complex, and compound-complex sentences.

Chapter 19 · Chapter Review

GRAMMAR EXERCISES 39–46

Exercise 39 Identifying Adjective and Adverb Phrases Write the prepositional phrases in the following sentences. Then, identify each prepositional phrase as *adjective* or *adverb*.

(1) Snow leopards live in the isolated area high in the mountains of northern India. (2) They are most common on the north side of the Himalayan mountain range. (3) This habitat contains numbers of high mountains, vast snowfields, glaciers, and cliffs. (4) This territory is so vast and wide that humans rarely will glimpse a snow leopard in the wild. (5) During the summer, they have been spotted in the mountains when they run above the timberline.

Exercise 40 Identifying Appositives and Appositive Phrases Write each sentence, underlining the appositive or appositive phrase. Then, draw an arrow to the noun for which it provides extra information.

1. The ounce, another name for the snow leopard, is a member of the cat family.
2. Hair cushions, a protection against the bitter environment, are located on its paws.
3. The furry tail, a device used by the snow leopard to keep its balance on rocky terrain, is about three feet long.
4. The thick, furry coat protects the snow leopard from extreme weather conditions—bitter cold in winter and scorching heat in summer.
5. It has camouflaging marks: black rosettes and small spots.

Exercise 41 Recognizing Verbal Phrases On your paper, identify the underlined phrase in each sentence below as a *participial phrase*, a *nominative absolute*, a *gerund phrase*, or an *infinitive phrase*.

1. To find information about cougars, you can also look up *puma, catamount,* or *mountain lion.*
2. Outweighing the lynx and the bobcat, jaguars are the biggest wildcats in North America.
3. They can grow to weigh up to 250 pounds.
4. Running long distances after prey can tire out a cougar.
5. It being easier to hide and hunt deer, cougars roam in hills and forests.
6. Cougars can swim but prefer jumping across water to avoid getting wet.
7. Once thriving throughout the United States, cougars now live mainly in the West.
8. Hunting cougars became very popular in the 1800's.
9. By 1900, most cougars formerly living in the East and Midwest had been killed.
10. The existence of the cougar being threatened, several organizations have created Internet alerts.

Exercise 42 Identifying Subordinate Clauses On your paper, write the subordinate clause in each sentence and identify it as *adjective, adverb,* or *noun.* If it is an *elliptical clause*, place parentheses around the understood words.

1. Sand cats are smaller than most species of wildcats.
2. They live in sand dunes located in the Sahara and African deserts.

3. Their coloring, which is sandy-yellow or yellowish-gray, blends in well with their surroundings.
4. They hunt for whatever prey is available, including small rodents, lizards, small snakes, and insects.
5. Occasionally, they supplement their diet when they catch hares and birds.

▶ **Exercise 43** **Combining Simple Sentences to Form the Four Structures of Sentences** Combine the simple sentences in each item to form the type of sentence indicated in parentheses.

1. The caracal is also known as the Persian lynx. It is native to Africa and Asia. (complex)
2. Caracals prey on rodents, birds, and small antelope. In India and Iran, they are sometimes trained to keep areas pest-free. (complex).
3. They have speed and agility. They are accomplished hunters. (simple)
4. Caracals have been known to chase birds. The birds flocked together on the ground. They have even been known to attack eagles. (compound-complex)
5. A caracal's coat is reddish-brown with a white belly. There are tufts of black hair on the tips of its ears. (compound)

▶ **Exercise 44** **Revising Sentences by Using Phrases and Clauses** Rewrite the following sentences so that they include the types of phrases or clauses indicated in parentheses.

1. Several private and governmental efforts have been enacted. Their aim is saving species that are threatened. (infinitive phrase)
2. The Endangered Species Act was passed in 1973. It provided steps for the conservation of ecosystems containing endangered species. (adjective clause, gerund phrase)

3. The Endangered Species Act also banned the importation and trade of any product made from an endangered animal. (compound infinitive phrase)
4. Two other nations have joined with the United States in agreements that protect migratory birds. These nations are Canada and Mexico. (appositive phrase)
5. The Convention on International Trade in Endangered Species of Wild Flora and Fauna (CITES) has become the center of international conservation efforts. It was ratified by the United States and fifty-one other nations in 1973. (participial phrase)

▶ **Exercise 45** **Revision Practice: Using Phrases and Clauses** On a separate sheet of paper, revise the following paragraph, combining sentences as appropriate. You may need to change or rearrange words and make other minor changes. Identify the structure of each sentence in your final revision.

A park ranger has many duties. He or she patrols the park, maintains park grounds, and enforces park rules. A park ranger often lives in the park. The park is the place the park ranger works. Rangers face some dangers. This is the reason some people don't want the job. Rangers are often alone. They live in the wilderness. Sometimes they need supplies or help. They use the radio to call for supplies or help.

▶ **Exercise 46** **Writing Application** Write a short description of a park or natural area near your home. Include two simple sentences, one complex sentence, one compound sentence, and one compound-complex sentence in your description.

Standardized Test Preparation Workshop

Recognizing Appropriate Sentence Construction

Knowledge of grammar is tested on standardized tests. Questions that measure your ability to use phrases and clauses show your understanding of basic sentence construction and style. When faced with these types of questions, first read the entire passage to get an idea of the author's purpose. Focus on the underlined group of words, and note any ways they can be combined without changing the meaning. Then, choose a rewrite that uses a phrase or clause to combine similar ideas without changing the meaning of the author's message.

The following will give you practice with the format of questions that test rules of standard grammar.

Sample Test Item	Answer and Explanation
Directions: Read the passage, and choose the letter of the best way to write the underlined sentences. New England is known for its beautiful (1) foliage. There is no sight more breathtaking than New England in the autumn.	
A There is no sight more breathtaking than the foliage for which New England is known. **B** New England is known for breathtaking foliage, and there nothing is more beautiful than New England in the autumn. **C** There is no sight more breathtaking than New England's beautiful autumn foliage. **D** New England is known for its beautiful foliage, and it's breathtaking.	The correct answer is *C*. This is the best rewrite of the two sentences because it combines related ideas in a direct way without changing the meaning of the original sentence or changing the author's intent.

Practice 1 **Directions:** Read the passage, and choose the letter of the best way to write the underlined sentences.

Reggie's father taught him to box. He was
(1)
a former pro boxer. Reggie was only six

years old. Reggie had great speed and
(2)
agility. He was so young. He caught on to

the sport quickly.

1 A Reggie's father was a pro boxer, and he taught Reggie to box, and Reggie was only six years old.

B Reggie's father, a former pro boxer, taught Reggie to box at the age of six.

C When Reggie was only six years old, his father taught him how to box, and he was a former pro boxer.

D Being a former pro boxer, Reggie learned how to box from his father when he was only six.

2 F Reggie caught on to the sport quickly because he was so young and his speed and agility were so great.

G Reggie had great speed and agility because he was so young; therefore, he caught on to the sport quickly.

H Reggie had great speed and agility for someone who was so young, and he caught on to the sport quickly.

J Being young, Reggie caught onto the sport quickly because of his great speed and agility.

Practice 2 **Directions:** Read the passage, and choose the letter of the best way to rewrite the underlined sentences.

It was morning. It was the day after the
(1)
school dance. Marianne had danced for
(2)
hours. She had danced the jitterbug. Her

feet felt as if they would fall off. She woke
(3)
up. She was exhausted. She was happy.

1 A It was in the morning, and it was the day after the school dance.

B It was after the school dance.

C The next morning, it was the day after the school dance.

D It was the morning after the school dance.

2 F Marianne had danced for hours, doing the jitterbug until her feet felt as if they would fall off.

G Marianne had danced for hours, and she did the jitterbug until her feet felt as if they would fall off.

H Dancing the jitterbug, Marianne had danced for hours when her feet felt as if they would fall off.

J Marianne danced the jitterbug until her feet felt as if they would fall off for hours.

3 A She woke up and she was exhausted and she was happy.

B She woke up when she was exhausted she was happy.

C She woke up exhausted but happy.

D She, exhausted, woke up happy.

Cumulative Review

GRAMMAR

> **Exercise A** **Recognizing the Part of Speech and Function of Words in Sentences** Identify the part of speech of each underlined word in the following sentences. Indicate the function in the sentence or clause of any underlined noun or pronoun, whether an underlined verb is action or linking, what word any adjective or adverb modifies, and whether any conjunction is coordinating, subordinate, correlative, or a conjunctive adverb.

1. Egyptian <u>history</u> has been divided into three <u>periods</u>, the Old, <u>Middle</u>, and New kingdoms.
2. Manetho, a <u>Ptolemaic</u> priest, organized the country's rulers into 30 dynasties, <u>which</u> <u>roughly</u> corresponded to different ruling families.
3. The Old Kingdom <u>spanned</u> five <u>centuries</u>, from 2755–2255 B.C., <u>and</u> was centered at the city of Memphis.
4. From <u>this</u> capital, monarchs <u>exercised</u> absolute power over the people.
5. The <u>Step Pyramid</u>, built by the ruler Zoser, still <u>gives</u> <u>Egyptians</u> pride <u>today</u>.
6. King Snefru was an <u>early</u> warrior <u>king</u>; through his military campaigns, he brought <u>prosperity</u> to the kingdom.
7. <u>It</u> was <u>his</u> son, Khufu, also known as Cheops, <u>who</u> built the Great Pyramid at Giza.
8. Yes, one of Khufu's sons, Redjedef, <u>reportedly</u> introduced a religion centered around the sun god Ra.
9. <u>These</u> <u>are</u> men who ruled during the 4th Dynasty, <u>when</u> Egypt reached a cultural zenith <u>not only</u> in architecture and engineering, <u>but also</u> in sculpture, painting, <u>astronomy</u>, and surgery.
10. Astronomers created a <u>solar</u> calendar based on a year with 365 days; <u>furthermore</u>, physicians <u>demonstrated</u> broad knowledge of the body's circulatory system.

> **Exercise B** **Recognizing Basic Sentence Parts** Identify the simple subject and simple predicate in each sentence. Then, identify the word underlined in the sentence as *direct object, indirect object, objective complement, object of a preposition, predicate nominative,* or *predicate adjective.*

1. Starting the Middle Kingdom, Mentuhotep unified the <u>kingdoms</u> and ruled for more than fifty years.
2. Amenemhet I established a capital near <u>Memphis</u> and favored national unity.
3. He considered Amon, a Theban god, the principal <u>deity</u> for the people.
4. There was literature at the time that was <u>propaganda</u> in support of the king.
5. Amenemhet named his son, Sesostris I, <u>co-regent</u> in the twentieth year of his reign.
6. He then built his <u>people</u> fortresses and established trade with foreign lands.
7. Architecture, art, and jewelry designs of the period were <u>graceful and delicate</u>.
8. However, succeeding rulers were weak and <u>ineffective</u>.
9. The Hyksos people challenged and eventually took control of the middle and northern <u>portions</u> of the country.
10. The Hyksos were later conquered by forces of Ahmose I, who reunited <u>Egypt</u>.

> **Exercise C** **Identifying Phrases and Clauses** Identify the underlined group of words in each of the following sentences as a phrase or a clause. Tell whether each phrase is a *gerund phrase, prepositional phrase, appositive phrase, infinitive phrase,* or *participial phrase.* Tell whether each

clause is an *independent clause, adjective clause, adverb clause,* or *noun clause.*

1. Unifying Egypt was the first step Ahmose I took to begin the New Kingdom.
2. His rule featured a revived balance of power; in addition, it saw an increasingly important role for women.
3. Hatshepsut, a royal princess and the wife of Thutmose II, governed as regent, and she then crowned herself king.
4. Although he had ruled with his mother, Thutmose III attempted to remove her image and name from Egyptian records and monuments.
5. Growing in strength, forces of the Hittite states later threatened the kingdom of Thutmose IV.
6. The 19th Dynasty began with Ramses I, who had earlier commanded the army.
7. When Ramses died after only two years on the throne, his son, Seti I, replaced him.
8. As the next several centuries went by, power usually passed to whoever was the eldest son of the royal family.
9. Ramses II was more interested in establishing peace with the Hittites than his predecessors were.
10. His son, Merneptah, fought whoever invaded the area, and in the thirteenth century B.C., he worked on extending the empire he had inherited.

> **Exercise D** Revision Practice: **Combining Sentences to Vary Structure**

Combine the sentences in each item to form the type of sentence indicated in parentheses.

1. Merneptah ruled a large empire. His successors were unable to preserve it. (complex)
2. Ramses III won several key victories. Royal power was beginning to decline. (compound)

3. Priests and nobles began dividing the country into sections. Royal power weakened. Egypt soon became the target of numerous invasions. (compound-complex)
4. A series of rulers controlled Egypt for the next 700 years. Many of these rulers were from outside nations. (simple)
5. In 332 B.C., Alexander the Great conquered Egypt. He was from Macedonia. (complex)

> **Exercise E** Revising a Paragraph

Write the paragraph below on a separate sheet of paper. Revise by using phrases and clauses to vary sentence length and structure. You may need to change or rearrange some words and make other minor changes.

Alexander died in 323 B.C. His generals divided up his empire. Ptolemy was one of the generals. He gained power over Egypt. He soon took the title of king. He founded a new dynasty. Alexandria became Egypt's capital. This happened under Ptolemy. He built a magnificent library and museum in Alexandria. This was done to spread Greek knowledge and culture. Soon, Alexandria became the cultural center. It was the center of not only Egypt. It was the center of the rest of the ancient world. Scholars from many countries came to Egypt. They were hoping to study in the library. Whoever studied in Alexandria had a responsibility. Their responsibility was to add new volumes to the library.

> **Exercise F** Writing Application

Write a description of an imaginary trip to see the Great Pyramids in Egypt or some other unusual sight. Include all four structures of sentences. Underline each simple subject once and each simple predicate twice. Circle at least three phrases and three subordinate clauses.

Effective Sentences

◄ **Critical Viewing**
What details indicate
that this is a portrait
of a powerful man?
[Analyze]

Sentences are a basic unit of communication. You use
sentences every day—to make statements, ask questions,
express emotions, give directions, or share information.
Using different types of sentences, varying the length of your
sentences, and varying their structure can give your writing
style more sophistication and help you hold a reader's attention. These techniques for writing effective sentences can help
you communicate in a clear and interesting way.

Effective sentences are the key to written communication,
just as England's monarchs were the key individuals throughout much of that nation's history.

Like a strong monarchy, whose clear decisions and swift
action helped to maintain an efficient government in England,
effective sentences are the surest, strongest means to ensure
that your ideas are understood clearly.

Diagnostic Test

Directions: Write all answers on a separate sheet of paper.

Skill Check A. Rewrite each sentence using the proper end mark. Then, identify the sentence as *declarative, interrogative, exclamatory,* or *imperative.*

1. Elizabeth II was crowned as Queen of Great Britain in 1953
2. What an amazing coronation ceremony that was
3. Look at the photographs of the wedding in this book
4. Why are so many people fascinated by the British monarchy
5. Give me your answer immediately

Skill Check B. Combine each pair of sentences to form one sentence. Try to use several different combining methods.

6. Prince Charles has the official title of Prince of Wales. He is the heir apparent to the English throne.
7. Charles graduated from Cambridge University. He is the first heir to the British crown to earn a university degree.
8. Charles served in the Royal Air Force and the Royal Navy from 1971 to 1976. He is often photographed in military uniform.
9. Charles will assume the throne after his mother dies. She may also decide to resign and turn over the crown to him.
10. Will a huge coronation ceremony be held for Charles? I wonder.

Skill Check C. Rewrite each sentence to begin with the part of speech indicated in parentheses.

11. The British Empire has undergone many changes during the reign of Elizabeth II. (preposition)
12. There has been constant turmoil in Northern Ireland, beginning in the 1950's. (participle)
13. More than forty former colonies and territories are newly independent. (adverb)
14. Britain joined the European Economic Community in 1973 as a way to improve its economic status. (infinitive)
15. Elizabeth II has overseen these changes as queen. (preposition)

Skill Check D. Identify the sentence errors below. Write *F* for fragment, *RO* for run-on, *MM* for misplaced modifier, *FP* for faulty parallelism, and *FC* for faulty coordination.

16. Windsor Castle is situated west of London, and the area became popular.
17. Windsor Castle is steeped in tradition and history, King Arthur gathered his Knights of the Round Table in the general vicinity.
18 Soon after arriving from France, a stockade was built on the site in 1070 by William the Conqueror.
19. The Round Tower, or Keep, was used as a prison in the seventeenth century, is still surrounded by a moat, and the tower is the dominant structure of Windsor Castle.
20. In 1992, Windsor Castle seriously damaged by fire and not yet restored to its former glory.

The Four Functions of a Sentence

Sentences can be classified according to what they do. The four types of sentences in English are *declarative, interrogative, imperative,* and *exclamatory.* Each type of sentence has a different purpose and is constructed in a different way. You can indicate what type of sentence you are writing by the punctuation mark you use to end the sentence.

> **KEY CONCEPT** A **declarative sentence** states an idea and ends with a period. ■

Declarative sentences are the most common type. They are used to "declare," or state facts.

DECLARATIVE: Windsor has been the surname of the British royal family since 1917.

> **KEY CONCEPT** An **interrogative sentence** asks a question and ends with a question mark. ■

Interrogative means "asking." An interrogative sentence is a question.

INTERROGATIVE: In which direction is Windsor Castle?

> **KEY CONCEPT** An **imperative sentence** gives an order or a direction and ends with either a period or an exclamation mark. ■

The word *imperative* is related to the word *emperor,* a person who gives commands. *Imperative* sentences are like emperors: They give commands. Most imperative sentences start with a verb. In this type of imperative sentence, the subject is understood to be *you.*

IMPERATIVE: Wait for me!
Turn left at the corner, and walk three blocks east.

> **KEY CONCEPT** An **exclamatory sentence** conveys strong emotion and ends with an exclamation mark. ■

To *exclaim* means to "shout out." *Exclamatory sentences* are used to "shout out" emotions, such as happiness, fear, delight, and anger.

EXCLAMATORY: The palace is on fire!
What a tiring night that was!

Theme: Rulers of England

In this section, you will learn about the four functions sentences can perform. The examples and exercises are about rulers of England.

Cross-Curricular Connection: Social Studies

▼ **Critical Viewing** King Richard I of England was known as Richard the Lion-Hearted. Write one of each type of sentence telling why, based on the picture, you think he was called that. **[Interpret]**

▶ **Exercise 1** Supplying the Appropriate End Marks Rewrite the following paragraphs, putting in the appropriate end marks. Then, identify each sentence as *declarative, interrogative, imperative,* or *exclamatory.*

Since the 1720's, England has had six kings named George What was George I's greatest drawback as British monarch He did not speak English That's unbelievable Actually, George's mother was from the German state of Hanover, and German was his most comfortable language You should look at a map of eighteenth-century Europe if you want to find where Hanover is located

What were the most significant events during the reign of his son, George II The Industrial Revolution changed manufacturing and transportation in Europe, and England extended its rule over India What an amazing time that was Have you ever heard about George III's weaknesses He had a gigantic ego and suffered from mental illness during parts of his life He dissolved the Irish Parliament in 1801 and established stronger British rule over Ireland

Is it true that George IV's extravagant spending and loose lifestyle weakened the British monarchy in the 1820's He became a very unpopular ruler who seldom left his palace Nearly eighty years passed before another George held the British throne George V's reign lasted from before World War I until just before World War II Did he do more or less than other European monarchs to help avoid war His son George VI was the father of England's current monarch, Elizabeth II

▶ **Exercise 2** Writing Sentences With Different Functions Write the type of sentence indicated about the topic that is given.
1. television (declarative)
2. television (interrogative)
3. politics (imperative)
4. politics (exclamatory)
5. trains (declarative)
6. trains (exclamatory)
7. baseball (interrogative)
8. baseball (imperative)
9. subways (declarative)
10. subways (exclamatory)

▶ **More Practice**

On-line
Exercise Bank
• Section 20.1
Grammar Exercise
Workbook
• pp. 49–50

GRAMMAR EXERCISES 3–7

▶ Exercise 3 **Identifying the Four Functions of Sentences** Label each sentence *declarative, interrogative, imperative,* or *exclamatory*. Then, write the end mark.

1. Have you ever attended the changing of the guard at Buckingham Palace
2. We thought it was fantastic
3. Imagine watching two groups of soldiers in bright red tunics and bearskin hats marching smartly together
4. The whole process takes about 45 minutes to complete
5. Make sure you bring your camera and have fast film
6. Unbelievably, the same ceremony has been followed for nearly 700 years
7. Was the ceremony of the keys at the Tower of London as interesting to watch
8. After locking the tower gates at night, the chief yeoman warder must pass by an armed guard and be recognized
9. The guard says, "Pass Queen Elizabeth's keys, and all's well"
10. What an interesting tradition that is

▶ Exercise 4 **Revising Sentences to Fit a Different Function** Rewrite each sentence to fit the function indicated in parentheses. Add the appropriate end mark.

1. You might visit Buckingham Palace when you go to England. (imperative)
2. Did George III originally buy it in 1761 as a home for his family? (declarative)
3. George IV was the one who paid a fortune to transform the house into a palace. (interrogative).
4. Did the renovation really cost nearly half a million pounds? (exclamatory)
5. It is true that George IV never got to live in the palace. (interrogative)
6. Was his niece Victoria the first royal occupant of the palace? (declarative)

7. Victoria made certain changes to the palace. (interrogative)
8. Did she add bedrooms for visitors and a nursery for her children? (declarative)
9. Was it amazing that Victoria made sure the renovation came in 50,000 pounds under budget? (exclamatory)
10. You can read more about the palace by clicking on this Web site. (imperative)

▶ Exercise 5 **Find It in Your Reading** Read this short speech from *Macbeth* by William Shakespeare. Which of the four types of sentences does it contain?

MACBETH. Bring me no more reports; let them fly all!
Till Birnam Wood remove to Dunsinane
I cannot taint with fear. What's the boy Malcolm?
Was he not born of woman? The spirits that know
All mortal consequences have pronounced me thus:
"Fear not, Macbeth; no man that's born of woman
Shall e'er have power upon thee." Then fly, false thanes,
And mingle with the English epicures.

▶ Exercise 6 **Find It in Your Writing** Look through your portfolio for examples of all four types of sentences. How does varying the types of sentences make your writing more interesting to read?

▶ Exercise 7 **Writing Application** Think of a tourist attraction you have visited. Write a paragraph for a guidebook to the attraction. Include all four types of sentences in your comments, and be sure to use appropriate end marks.

Combining Sentences

Books written for very young readers present information in short, direct sentences. While this style makes the book easy to read, it doesn't make it enjoyable or interesting to mature readers. Writing intended for mature readers should include sentences of varying lengths and complexity to produce a flow of ideas. One way to achieve sentence variety is to combine sentences—to express two or more related ideas or pieces of information in a single sentence.

EXAMPLE: We went to Scotland.
                  We saw castles.

COMBINED: We went to Scotland and saw castles.
                  We saw castles in Scotland.
                  We saw castles when we went to Scotland.

Combining Sentence Parts

Sometimes, the best way to combine ideas from several sentences into one is to join parts of the two sentences to form compound subjects, verbs, or objects.

▶ **KEY CONCEPT** Sentences can be combined by using a compound subject, a compound verb, or a compound object. ■

EXAMPLE: Maura enjoyed seeing the castles.
                  Tony enjoyed seeing the castles.

COMPOUND
SUBJECT: Maura and Tony enjoyed seeing the castles.

EXAMPLE: Latrell climbed the turret stairs.
                  Latrell saw the countryside.

COMPOUND
VERB: Latrell climbed the turret stairs and saw the countryside.

EXAMPLE: Scott visited Jolly Old England.
                  Scott visited Wales.

COMPOUND
OBJECT: Scott visited Jolly Old England and Wales.

Theme: England's History

In this section, you will learn different ways to combine sentences to make your writing more interesting. The examples and exercises are about events in the history of England.

Cross-Curricular Connection: Social Studies

▶ **Critical Viewing** How many different shapes and forms are combined in the design of this castle in Scotland? **[Analyze]**

> **Exercise 8** **Combining Sentence Parts** Combine each pair of sentences in a logical way. Identify the parts of the two sentences you have made compound as you combined them.

EXAMPLE: Frank met the queen. Freida met the queen.

ANSWER: Frank and Freida met the queen. (subject)

1. I traveled to England. My brother traveled with me.
2. We went to relax. We went to see the sights.
3. In a guidebook, we learned about the island's early occupants. We also learned how it was named.
4. In A.D. 449, Anglo-Saxons invaded the island. The Anglo-Saxons occupied its southeastern part.
5. The island was originally called "Angle-land." The island later became known as "England."

Combining Clauses

> **KEY CONCEPT** Sentences can be combined by joining two independent clauses to form a compound sentence. ■

Use a compound sentence to combine ideas that are related but independent. Join two independent clauses with a comma and a coordinating conjunction or with a semicolon. Coordinating conjunctions include *and, but, or, for, nor, yet,* and *so.*

EXAMPLE: The clouds crossed the English Channel. The rain beat down on England.

COMPOUND   The clouds crossed the English Channel, and the
SENTENCE: rain beat down on England.

> **Exercise 9** **Combining Ideas of Equal Weight** Combine the following sentences, following the directions in parentheses.
> 1. Britain had long been known to the Romans as a source of tin. The island did not come under Roman rule until 55 B.C. (comma and conjunction)
> 2. That year, Julius Caesar invaded the island. It was a fitting follow-up to his conquest of Gaul. (semicolon)
> 3. Emperor Claudius had invaded Britain in A.D. 43. His army easily conquered Celtic tribes there. (comma and conjunction)
> 4. In 122, the Romans wanted a way to defend their settlements from northern attacks. They built Hadrian's Wall near the border of Scotland. (comma and conjunction)
> 5. Under Roman rule, many new towns sprang up near Roman army camps. London developed into a prosperous port city. (comma and conjunction)

Spelling Tip

Some words are spelled differently in England than they are in America. For instance, the American word "color" is spelled "colour" in the UK. If you are not sure whether you are using the proper American spelling, check your dictionary. Most dictionaries list the British spelling.

▶ **KEY CONCEPT** Sentences can be combined by changing one of them into a subordinate clause. ■

You can combine sentences to form one complex sentence that shows the relationship between ideas. The subordinating conjunction will help readers understand the relationship. Subordinating conjunctions include *after, although, because, before, even though, if, since, until, when,* and *while.*

EXAMPLE:	We were frightened. We thought the castle was haunted.
COMBINED WITH A SUBORDINATE CLAUSE:	We were frightened because we thought the castle was haunted.

▶ **Exercise 10** Combining Sentences Using Subordinate Clauses Combine the following sentences using the subordinating conjunction indicated in parentheses.

EXAMPLE:	Julius Caesar invaded Britain. He had conquered Gaul. (after)
ANSWER:	Julius Caesar invaded Britain after he had conquered Gaul.

1. The Roman Empire began to decline in the third and fourth centuries. It was overextended. (because)
2. The Romans abandoned Britain in 410. They left behind a superb network of roads and many growing towns. (when)
3. Roman engineering was advanced for its time. Britain was able to use Roman roads for hundreds of years. (because)
4. Warriors from Ireland, Scotland, and Germany invaded Britain. The Romans left the island. (after)
5. Tribes of Britons fought hard to protect their lands. Most of the island was conquered by the invaders. (although)

▶ **Exercise 11** Combining Using Subordinate Clauses Combine the following sentences using a logical subordinating conjunction.

1. The Angles and Saxons were the most powerful of the invaders. They soon took over most of the territory.
2. The Angles and Saxons were not a united group. They divided the land into seven separate kingdoms.
3. The seven kingdoms were not Greek. Historians have given them a Greek name, the Heptarchy.
4. The Heptarchy lasted for 300 years. Raiders from Denmark invaded and conquered six of the kingdoms.
5. The Danes tried to conquer Wessex. Its king, Alfred the Great, defeated the Danes and forced them to retreat.

More Practice

On-line Exercise Bank
• Section 20.2
Grammar Exercise Workbook
• pp. 51–52

Combining Using Phrases

▶ **KEY CONCEPT** Sentences can be combined by changing one of them into a phrase. ■

Change one of the sentences into a phrase when you are combining sentences in which one of the sentences just adds detail.

EXAMPLES: The Anglo-Saxon kings feared the Jutes. The Jutes were a tribe of seafaring raiders.
The Jutes' homeland was in Denmark. Denmark was to the east.

CORRECTED The Anglo-Saxon kings feared the
SENTENCES: Jutes, a tribe of seafaring raiders.
The Jutes' homeland was in Denmark, to the east.

The Anglo-Saxon Kingdoms

▲ **Critical Viewing** Write two sentences containing phrases that describe why the British Isles could easily be invaded. **[Connect]**

▶ **Exercise 12** **Combining Using Phrases** Combine the following sentences by changing one into a phrase.

EXAMPLE: Alfred was the king of Wessex. Wessex was a region in the southwestern part of England.

ANSWER: Alfred was the king of Wessex, a region in the southwestern part of England.

1. Alfred I ruled for nearly twenty years. He ruled from A.D. 871 to 899.
2. He is known as Alfred the Great. He justly deserves that title.
3. Many English political and educational reforms began under Alfred. Alfred was the most powerful Anglo-Saxon king.
4. Alfred showed his interest in education. He built many schools.
5. He also brought in scholars to translate Latin books into Anglo-Saxon. Anglo-Saxon was the common language of his subjects.
6. Historians give credit to Alfred. Alfred established the first English naval fleet.
7. Alfred also commissioned the *Anglo-Saxon Chronicles*. This book was an extensive written history of England.
8. Scholars continued to add to the *Chronicles*. They added to the *Chronicles* for more than 250 years after Alfred's death.
9. Alfred organized his kingdom into local divisions. These divisions were known as "shires."
10. Under Alfred, English common law developed. English common law is the basis of the legal system in England and the United States.

▶ **More Practice**

Language Lab CD-ROM
• Varying Sentence Structure lesson
On-line Exercise Bank
• Section 20.2
Grammar Exercise Workbook
• pp. 51–52

Section
20.2 *Section Review*

GRAMMAR EXERCISES 13–18

Exercise 13 Combining Sentences Using Compound Subjects, Verbs, and Objects Combine each of the pairs of sentences. Revise as necessary for clarity.

1. In the mid-1200's, Edward I restored royal control. He made many reforms.
2. He limited special rights of the powerful. He limited privileges of the wealthy.
3. Edward I established English control over Wales. His son, Edward II, helped establish English control over Wales.
4. Edward II tried to conquer Scotland. He tried to make the Scots pay taxes.
5. The Scots were conquered. The Scots continued to rebel against his rule.

Exercise 14 Combining Sentences Using Clauses Combine each pair of sentences with a comma and coordinating conjunction, a semicolon, or a subordinating conjunction.

1. Edward II was a poor ruler. He was forced to give up the throne.
2. Edward III took over after his father. He proved to be more effective.
3. Edward III hoped to rule France. He sent an army across the English Channel.
4. The English developed a new weapon. They fought with the longbow.
5. The war continued for one hundred years. Its expense nearly broke England.
6. Henry VII became king in 1485. He was the first of the Tudor line.
7. He married Elizabeth of York. He wanted the support of her powerful family.
8. Henry promoted foreign trade. He hoped to increase England's wealth.
9. Henry avoided foreign wars. England enjoyed a strong government and a stable economy during his rule.
10. Henry was respected by his people. He was never really loved.

Exercise 15 Combining Sentences Using Phrases Combine the following sentences by changing one of each pair into a phrase.

1. Henry VIII was born in 1491. He was the second son of Henry VII and Elizabeth of York.
2. He became heir to the throne in 1502. This followed his brother's death.
3. Henry is known for his great appetites. The appetites were for food, hunting, and music.
4. Henry dramatically increased the size of the Royal Navy. It was increased from five to fifty-three ships.
5. He strengthened England. He made separate alliances with France and Spain.

Exercise 16 Find It in Your Reading Find three or more ideas combined in this sentence from a *London Times* article "Elizabeth II: A New Queen."

. . . She did not go to school but was taught, under the close personal direction of the Queen, by a governess, Miss Marion Crawford, who joined the household in 1933.

Exercise 17 Find It in Your Writing Look through your portfolio for a paragraph that contains several short sentences. Combine two of the short sentences to form one longer sentence.

Exercise 18 Writing Application Write a brief description of a famous world ruler. First, use only short sentences in your description. Then, rewrite it, combining some of the short sentences into longer, more interesting ones.

Varying Sentences

Vary your sentences to develop a rhythm, to achieve an effect, or to emphasize the connections between ideas.

There are several ways you can vary your sentences.

Varying Sentence Length

You have already learned that you can combine several short, choppy sentences to form a longer, more interesting, and more mature sentence. However, too many long sentences in a row can be as uninteresting to read as too many short sentences. When you want to emphasize a point or surprise a reader, insert a short, direct sentence to interrupt the flow of long sentences. Take note of the following writing sample:

EXAMPLE: The Jacobites derived their name from *Jacobus*, the Latin name for King James II of England, who was dethroned in 1688 by William of Orange during the Glorious Revolution. An unpopular king in England because of his Catholicism and autocratic ruling style, James fled to France to seek the aid of King Louis XIV. In 1690, James, along with a small body of French troops, landed in Ireland in an attempt to regain his throne. His hopes ended at the Battle of the Boyne.

Some sentences contain only one idea and can't be broken. It may be possible, however, to state the idea in a shorter sentence. Other sentences contain two or more ideas and might be shortened by breaking up the ideas.

LONGER SENTENCE: Many of James I's predecessors were able to avoid major economic problems, but James had serious economic problems.

MORE DIRECT: Unlike many of his predecessors, James I was unable to avoid major economic problems.

LONGER SENTENCE: James tried to work with Parliament to develop a plan for taxation that would be fair and reasonable, but members of Parliament rejected his efforts, and James dissolved the Parliament.

SHORTER SENTENCES: James tried to work with Parliament to develop a fair and reasonable taxation plan. Members of Parliament rejected his efforts, and James dissolved the Parliament.

Theme: England's History

In this section, you will learn how to make your writing more interesting by varying the length and beginnings of the sentences you write. The examples and exercises are about more events in the history of England.

Cross-Curricular Connection: Social Studies

Grammar and Style Tip

When revising your work to include a variety of sentence lengths and structures, make sure you do not introduce an error. Long sentences can turn into run-on sentences; inverted sentences can inadvertently contain misplaced or dangling modifiers. Proofread carefully.

▶ **Exercise 19** Revising to Vary Sentence Length In the following items, break up long sentences into two or more shorter sentences or restate long sentences more simply.

EXAMPLE: Oliver Cromwell was a man who did not have any military training, yet he was able to direct the army that had a loyalty to Parliament in many stunning victories during the English Civil War.

ANSWER: Though he had no military training, Oliver Cromwell led the army loyal to Parliament in many stunning victories during the English Civil War.

1. Oliver Cromwell came from a wealthy background and, following attendance at Cambridge University, he served his country in two ways, both as a member of Parliament and as a spokesperson for religious freedom.
2. Cromwell was a member of Parliament in 1640, and as a member of Parliament, he spoke out against King Charles and voiced disagreements with the king's policies.
3. Cromwell was a decisive leader, and he was very successful in military circles and in political circles.
4. Cromwell directed the army in the military campaigns that led to the final defeat of Charles I, and he afterward served as the chief advocate at the king's trial and execution.
5. For the next ten years, Cromwell served as chief executive, and he was a ruthless and effective leader.

More Practice

On-line
Exercise Bank
• Section 20.3
Grammar Exercise
Workbook
• pp. 53–54

GRAMMAR IN LITERATURE

from **Condition of Ireland**
The Illustrated London News

Notice how the writer has used sentences of varying length in the passage to make it more interesting to read.

The land is still there, in all its natural beauty and fertility. The sparkling Shannon, teeming with fish, still flows by their doors, and might bear to them, as the Hudson and Thames bear to the people of New York and of London, fleets of ships laden with wealth. The low grounds or *Corcasses* of Clare are celebrated for their productiveness. The country abounds in limestone: coal, iron, and lead have been found.

Varying Sentence Beginnings

Another way to create sentence variety is to avoid starting each sentence in the same way. You can start sentences with different parts of speech.

START WITH A NOUN:	Parliament's authority grew and eventually exceeded royal power.
START WITH AN ADVERB:	Eventually, Parliament's authority grew to exceed royal power.
START WITH A PARTICIPLE:	Growing over time, Parliament's authority finally exceeded royal power.
START WITH A PREPOSITIONAL PHRASE:	In time, Parliament's authority grew to exceed royal power.

▶ **Exercise 20** Revising to Vary Sentence Beginnings
Rewrite each sentence to begin with the part of speech indicated in parentheses.

1. Queen Elizabeth I came to power in 1558. (preposition)
2. Her right to the throne was challenged by her cousin Mary, Queen of Scots. (participle)
3. Adding to her problems was an attack by a fleet of Spanish ships. (article and noun)
4. The English fleet put down the attack rapidly. (adverb)
5. Elizabeth brought intelligence and keen diplomatic instincts to the problems she faced. (preposition)

Using Inverted Word Order

You can also vary sentence beginnings by reversing the traditional subject-verb order.

SUBJECT-VERB ORDER:	The queen was waiting for the attack. The royal armada sailed into the bay.
INVERTED ORDER:	Waiting for the attack was the queen. Into the bay sailed the royal armada.

▶ **Exercise 21** Revising Using Inverted Word Order Rewrite the following sentences by inverting the subject-verb order. Rearrange the rest of the words of the sentence as needed.

1. The history of British royal families is filled with fascinating stories.
2. The lives of Queens Elizabeth I, Anne, and Victoria are particularly interesting.
3. A class of students walks through the Tower of London.
4. The students talk animatedly among themselves.
5. A tour of Buckingham Palace is next on their agenda.

▲ **Critical Viewing**
Write a sentence describing how this guard marches. Then, rewrite the sentence twice. First, begin with an adverb; next, with a participle. **[Describe]**

▶ **More Practice**

On-line Exercise Bank
• Section 20.3
Grammar Exercise Workbook
• pp. 55–60

Section 20.3 *Section Review*

GRAMMAR EXERCISES 22–27

Exercise 22 **Revising Sentence Length** Rewrite the following sentences by breaking each into two sentences or writing a simpler, more direct sentence.

1. Born Alexandrina Victoria on May 24, 1819, Queen Victoria was the only daughter of Edward, Duke of Kent, fourth son of George III.
2. She became queen at the age of 18, and she succeeded her uncle, William IV.
3. She had two main advisors early in her reign, and they were her husband, Prince Albert, and the Prime Minister, Lord Melbourne.
4. Melbourne was the leader of the branch of the Whig party that later became known as the Liberal party, and he exercised a strong influence on the political thinking of the queen.
5. Victoria's marriage to Albert was an arranged marriage, but the couple loved each other very much, and she became very depressed when he died in 1861.

Exercise 23 **Revising Sentence Beginnings** Rewrite each sentence below to begin with the part of speech indicated in parentheses.

1. Victoria remained in mourning for several years following Albert's death. (participle)
2. It disturbed her to be seen in public. (infinitive)
3. Victoria remained in seclusion in the palace and allowed her son, the Prince of Wales, to represent her at most ceremonial functions. (participle)
4. She was eventually convinced to return to public life by Prime Minister Benjamin Disraeli. (adverb)
5. Victoria's popularity grew as a result of her concern for the welfare of the poor and needy. (preposition)

Exercise 24 **Inverting Sentences to Vary Beginnings** Rewrite each of the following sentences by inverting subject-verb order to be verb-subject order.

1. The Round Tower at Windsor Castle is old.
2. The Royal Family strolled through Windsor Great Park.
3. A magnificent tree-lined avenue leads to the castle grounds.
4. The Round Tower has a fascinating history.
5. The Throne Room was magnificent.

Exercise 25 **Find It in Your Reading** Notice the use of long and short sentences in this passage from "Elizabeth II: A New Queen":

Early in the New Year they set out on their public life together, and in May paid an official visit to Paris, where they were greeted with a welcome of great warmth and spontaneity. Then early in June it was announced that the Princess would soon cancel all her engagements. On November 14 her son, Prince Charles, was born.

Exercise 26 **Find It in Your Writing** Look in your portfolio for examples of long sentences. Rewrite some of the sentences to form shorter, more direct ones.

Exercise 27 **Writing Application** Write a short essay about a powerful political leader. Use both long and short sentences in your essay.

Avoiding Fragments and Run-ons

Hasty writers sometimes omit crucial words, punctuate awkwardly, or leave their thoughts unfinished, causing two common sentence errors: fragments and run-ons.

Recognizing Fragments

Although some writers use fragments purposefully for a stylistic effect, fragments are generally considered writing errors.

KEY CONCEPT Do not capitalize and punctuate phrases, subordinate clauses, or words in a series as if they were complete sentences. ■

Reading your work aloud and listening to the natural pauses and stops should help you avoid fragments. Sometimes, you can repair a fragment by connecting it to words that come before or after it.

KEY CONCEPT One way to correct a fragment is to connect it to the words in a nearby sentence. ■

PARTICIPIAL FRAGMENT:	Inspired by the grace of the dancer.
ADDED TO A NEARBY SENTENCE:	*Inspired by the grace of the dancer,* Linda saw the performance again.
PREPOSITIONAL FRAGMENT:	Before her partner.
ADDED TO A NEARBY SENTENCE:	The *ballerina* came on stage *before her partner.*

A fragment containing a pronoun and a participial phrase can often be repaired by dropping the pronoun and adding the participial phrase to a nearby sentence.

PRONOUN AND PARTICIPIAL FRAGMENT:	The one hanging in the closet.
ADDED TO NEARBY SENTENCE:	I wore the leotard *hanging in the closet.*

Sometimes, you may need to add missing sentence parts. Remember that every complete sentence must have both a subject and a verb and express a complete thought. Check to see that each of your sentences contains all of the parts necessary to be complete.

Theme: Ballet

In this section, you will learn how to avoid two problems that can make your sentences incorrect or hard to understand. The examples and exercises are about ballet and ballet dancers.

Cross-Curricular Connection: Performing Arts

🖋 Spelling Tip

Two essential steps in improving your spelling are proofreading carefully and using a dictionary. To catch misspelled words, try proofreading your draft backward, word by word. Use a dictionary to confirm the spelling of unfamiliar words.

▶ **KEY CONCEPT** Another way to correct a fragment is to add any missing sentence part that is needed to make the fragment a complete sentence. ■

One typical fragment error involves writing a noun phrase (a noun with its modifiers) as if it were a sentence. However, a noun phrase will need a verb if it is to be used as a subject. If the noun phrase is to be used as a complement, an object of a preposition, or an appositive, it will need both a subject and a verb.

NOUN FRAGMENT:	The troupe of lively young dancers.
COMPLETED SENTENCES:	The troupe of lively young dancers moved across the stage. We excitedly watched the troupe of lively young dancers.

Notice what missing sentence parts must be added to the following types of phrase fragments to make them complete.

NOUN FRAGMENT WITH PARTICIPIAL PHRASE:	The food eaten by us.
COMPLETED SENTENCE:	The food was eaten by us.
VERB FRAGMENT:	Will be at the rehearsal today.
COMPLETED SENTENCE:	I will be at the rehearsal today.
PREPOSITIONAL FRAGMENT:	In the hall closet.
COMPLETED SENTENCE:	I put the toe shoes in the hall closet.
PARTICIPIAL FRAGMENT:	Found under the desk.
COMPLETED SENTENCES:	The dance books found under the desk were mine. The dance books were found under the desk.
GERUND FRAGMENT:	Teaching children to dance.
COMPLETED SENTENCES:	Teaching children to dance can be rewarding. She enjoys teaching children to dance.
INFINITIVE FRAGMENT:	To see the new ballet.
COMPLETED SENTENCES:	To see the new ballet is my goal. I expect to see the new ballet.

⚙ Grammar ⚙ and Style Tip

Sentence fragments are easier to identify when they appear out of context than when they appear with related sentences. Read each of your sentences individually, aloud if necessary, to isolate fragments.

▶ **KEY CONCEPT** You may need to attach a subordinate clause to an independent clause to correct a fragment. ■

A subordinate clause contains a subject and a verb but does not express a complete thought. Therefore, it cannot stand alone as a sentence. Link the subordinate clause to an independent clause to make the sentence complete.

ADJECTIVE CLAUSE FRAGMENT:	Which was being performed outdoors.
COMPLETED SENTENCE:	I enjoyed watching the dance rehearsal, *which was being performed outdoors.*
ADVERB CLAUSE FRAGMENT:	After she practiced the new dance routine.
COMPLETED SENTENCE:	*After she practiced the new dance routine*, she was ready for the show.
NOUN CLAUSE FRAGMENT:	Whatever ballet we see in this theater.
COMPLETED SENTENCE:	We always enjoy *whatever ballet we see in this theater.*

A fragment does not always contain a small number of words. If a series of words seems long enough to be a sentence, you still need to make sure that it contains a subject and a verb and expresses a complete thought. It may be a long fragment masquerading as a sentence.

▶ **KEY CONCEPT** Some series fragments may look long enough to be sentences, but they may still not express a complete thought. ■

SERIES FRAGMENT:	After reading Steinbeck's novel, with its probing look at poverty and greed, in the style so typical of this master storyteller.
COMPLETED SENTENCE:	After reading Steinbeck's novel, with its probing look at poverty and greed, in the style so typical of this master storyteller, I was able to prepare an interesting oral presentation.

Grammar and Style Tip

Do not confuse verbals and verbs! Fragments are often verbal phrases; make sure that you can differentiate between verbal phrases and verbs. Review Chapter 17 if you need extra help.

▶ **Exercise 28** **Identifying and Correcting Fragments** If an item contains only complete sentences, write *correct*. If the item contains a fragment, rewrite it to make a complete sentence.

EXAMPLE: Pleased by the applause of the audience. The ballerina danced an encore.

ANSWER: Pleased by the applause of the audience, the ballerina danced an encore.

1. An ice-skating champion at the age of ten. Nina Ananiashvili was encouraged to study in Moscow.
2. She studied dance at the Moscow Ballet School. From which she graduated in 1981.
3. To win a Gold Medal at the age of seventeen in an international competition, she had to work very hard.
4. After she graduated from the Moscow Ballet School, Nina fulfilled her dream of joining the Bolshoi Ballet.
5. Miss Ananiashvili has danced in the United States. With the New York City Ballet.
6. She made her debut with the Boston Ballet. In a performance of *Swan Lake.*
7. She has danced with troupes all over the world. Making the audience gasp in Finland, awing her peers in Portugal, and earning great respect in England.
8. Her debut with the Royal Ballet in *The Nutcracker.*
9. Such a great honor to be named a People's Artist of the Georgia Republic.
10. The first Russian ballerina to appear in a United States production of George Balanchine's *Apollo.*

More Practice

Language Lab CD-ROM
• Sentence Errors: Fragments and Run-on Sentences lesson
On-line Exercise Bank
• Section 20.4
Grammar Exercise Workbook
• pp. 61–62

◀ **Critical Viewing** Write a fragment describing these dancers. Then, correct your fragment by making it into a complete sentence. **[Describe]**

Avoiding Run-on Sentences

A run-on sentence is two or more sentences capitalized and punctuated as if they were one.

> **KEY CONCEPT** Use punctuation and conjunctions to join or separate parts of a run-on sentence correctly. ∎

There are two kinds of run-ons: *fused sentences*, which are two or more sentences joined with no punctuation, and *comma splices*, which have two or more sentences separated only by commas rather than by commas and conjunctions.

FUSED SENTENCE: The dancers practiced every day they were soon the best in the state.

COMMA SPLICE: Only one package arrived in the mail, the other items never came.

As with fragments, proofreading or reading your work aloud will usually help you spot run-ons. Once found, they can be corrected by adding punctuation and conjunctions or by rewording the sentences. Four ways to correct run-ons are described below.

FOUR WAYS TO CORRECT RUN-ONS	
With End Marks and Capitals	
Run-on: The dance was in full swing in the gym people crowded together.	*Sentence:* The dance was in full swing. In the gym, people crowded together.
With Commas and Conjunctions	
Run-on: The wrapping paper needed cutting we could not locate the scissors.	*Sentence:* The wrapping paper needed cutting, but we could not locate the scissors.
With Semicolons	
Run-on: Our city has many cultural activities, for example it hosts the National Ballet.	*Sentence:* Our city has many cultural activities; for example, it hosts the National Ballet.
By Rewriting	
Run-on: The horse show began late, someone had misplaced the registration forms.	*Sentence:* The horse show began late because someone had misplaced the registration forms. (Changed to complex sentence)
Run-on: We replaced the sparkplugs, the filter was also bad.	*Sentence:* We replaced the sparkplugs and the filter. (Changed to simple sentence with compound direct object)

Exercise 29 Revising to Eliminate Run-on Sentences If a sentence is a run-on, correct it. Use each of the four methods for correcting run-ons at least once. If it is correct as written, write *correct*.

EXAMPLE: I want to study dance it is a beautiful art form.

ANSWER: I want to study dance, a beautiful art form.

1. Ballet as an art form began in Italy in the 1400's, this was during the Renaissance.
2. Many Italian dukes were successful businessmen they were willing to spend some of the money they earned to support the arts.
3. Each duke wanted to outdo the others, they sponsored elaborate song-and-dance performances.
4. Ballet moved from Italy to France Catherine de Medici, a Florence noblewoman, brought ballet with her when she became Queen of France in 1547.
5. Some people consider French King Louis XIV to be the father of modern ballet, he ruled in the seventeenth century.
6. Louis founded the *Academie Royale de Musique et de Danse* in 1661 it trained musicians and dancers to perform for the royal court.
7. In the mid-nineteenth century, the ballet centers of the world shifted from Paris and Milan, they moved to St. Petersburg and Moscow in Russia.
8. Marius Petipa, a Frenchman, Christian Johansson, a Swede, and Enrico Cecchetti, an Italian, developed a new style of ballet in Russia.
9. These three men worked with generations of Russian dancers the dancers developed the most precise techniques in the world.
10. Two of the world's most famous dancers began their careers in St. Petersburg, they were Anna Pavlova and Vaslav Nijinsky.

▲ **Critical Viewing**
In what ways does writing correct sentences relate to dancing ballet routines correctly? **[Compare]**

> **More Practice**
> **Language Lab CD-ROM**
> • Sentence Errors: Fragments and Run-on Sentences lesson
> **On-line Exercise Bank**
> • Section 20.4
> **Grammar Exercise Workbook**
> • pp. 63–64

Avoiding Fragments and Run-ons • **497**

Exercise 30 Revising to Eliminate Fragments and Run-ons

Rewrite the two paragraphs below, correcting all fragments and run-ons. You may combine items and add or delete words to revise the paragraphs.

Toe dancing was developed in the early nineteenth century it did not become widely used until the 1830's. When Swedish-Italian ballerina Marie Taglioni demonstrated its potential for poetic effect. Also known as *pointe* work, Almost exclusively used by women, although male dancers may use it as well.

The term *line* in ballet refers to the configuration of the dancer's body. Whether it is in motion or at rest. Good line is partly a matter of physique a dancer is born with a certain physical stature, Can also be developed and enhanced by training. In ballet, the arms, legs, head, and torso expected to work together in harmony. Large movements of a whole limb are preferred. Over small isolated movements of individual body parts. Ballet is often described in terms of moving upward and outward, ideally, the dancer's limbs should appear to extend into infinity. Ballet dancers will carry out many movements and poses. During a performance. Jumps and turns an important part of a ballet as well and add to its excitement. All of these movements take years to learn, they require extensive practice. With all of its intricate moves and romantic expressions, a beautiful art form.

More Practice

Language Lab CD-ROM
• Sentence Errors: Fragments and Run-on Sentences lesson

On-line Exercise Bank
• Section 20.4

Grammar Exercise Workbook
• pp. 61–64

▼ **Critical Viewing** Correct the following fragment by adding an independent clause: *as they extend their arms.* **[Apply]**

Hands-on Grammar

Fragment Completion

Practice correcting sentence fragments by doing this activity.

First, cut twelve pieces of paper approximately 3" x 2 ¹/₂" each. On six of the pieces, write the following fragments:

with his hand in the cookie jar
the one waiting nearby
the food eaten by us
on the kitchen table
a hurricane with fierce winds and rain
angered by the injustice of the remark

On the other six pieces of paper, write the following:

she argued with her friend
the forecaster predicted
I put the groceries
was prepared by my aunt
the child was caught
was the bus downtown

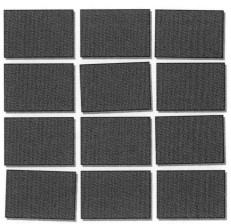

Then, shuffle the pieces of paper around and arrange them face down, as shown in the drawing. Take turns with a classmate trying to match a fragment from the first group with something from the second group that will complete it and make sense. The first person turns over two pieces of paper. If they work together, the person removes them and tries two more. If they do not work together, it is the next person's turn. Continue like this until all fragments have been completed.

Find It in Your Reading Fragments do not normally occur in formal writing. However, they often do appear in the dialogue of a story. Look through a story you have read, and identify six fragments. Write completions for the fragments.

Find It in Your Writing Review some writing from your portfolio to see if you have used sentence fragments. If you find any, correct them by making them complete sentences.

GRAMMAR EXERCISES 31–35

▶ **Exercise 31** Proofreading to **Eliminate Fragments** Read the following paragraph. Rewrite any sentences that are fragments.

George Balanchine, a Russian-born American choreographer, one of the foremost choreographers in the history of ballet. The son of a composer, Balanchine, born in Saint Petersburg, Russia. In 1925, while touring Europe with his small ballet company, he joined the Diaghilev Company as a choreographer. In 1933, Balanchine moved to New York City. Where he co-founded the School of American Ballet and the American Ballet Company. He also helped create the New York City Ballet, which performed new, exciting versions of *The Nutcracker* and *Don Quixote.*

▶ **Exercise 32** Identifying and **Correcting Run-on Sentences** Correct the following run-ons. Try to use each of the four methods described in the chart on page 496.

1. The Bolshoi Ballet is one of the oldest Russian ballet companies, it is famous for its dramatic performances of classic ballets.
2. The Bolshoi Ballet began with classes given at a Moscow orphanage, the classes were held in the 1770's.
3. The Petrovsky Theatre Ballet gave its first performance in 1776 it became the Bolshoi Ballet in 1825.
4. In the 1950's, the company began to tour the world, it entertained and impressed audiences around the globe.
5. The two dancers Rudolf Nureyev and Margot Fonteyn became celebrities, they were featured on magazine covers worldwide.

▶ **Exercise 33** Revising to Eliminate **Sentence Errors** Rewrite the paragraph below, correcting all fragments and run-ons as needed.

Ballet consists of five numbered positions of the feet. Which form the basis of almost all ballet steps. Corresponding positions exist for the arms. Which should generally be held with gently curved elbows. All of the movements of the dancer's limbs flow from the body's vertical axis, all of the dancer's body parts must be correctly aligned. Ballet dancers must often resist gravity, they jump and twist in difficult but graceful positions. Ballet possesses many such steps it even includes those that require the dancers, while in midair, to turn, beat their legs or feet together, or change their leg position. Steps for male and female dancers different. Neither easier than the other. Require constant practice and repetition.

▶ **Exercise 34** Find It in Your **Writing** Look through your portfolio to see if you have used fragments or run-ons in any compositions. Rewrite the incorrect sentences, and explain how you corrected your errors.

▶ **Exercise 35** Writing Application Write a brief narrative about a live performance you once saw. Write complete sentences that use varied structures to relate information about the performance. Be sure to include details about the performance, the performer(s), and perhaps even the audience.

Section 20.5 *Misplaced and Dangling Modifiers*

Careful writers put modifiers as close as possible to the words they modify. When modifiers are misplaced or left dangling in a sentence, the result is often silly, illogical, or confusing. This section will show you methods for correcting misplaced and dangling modifiers.

Recognizing Misplaced Modifiers

A *misplaced modifier* is placed too far from the modified word and appears to modify the wrong word or words.

▷ **KEY CONCEPT** A *misplaced modifier* seems to modify the wrong word in the sentence. ■

Any modifying phrase or clause can be misplaced.

MISPLACED MODIFIERS:	The man fell over a rock *running across the bridge.*
	We heard the telephone ring *while watching television.*
CORRECTED SENTENCES:	The man *running across the bridge fell* over a rock.
	While watching television, we heard the telephone ring.

A vague modifier appears to modify two words.

VAGUE MODIFIER:	She heard *upon her arrival* that Lee had resigned.

The phrase *upon her arrival* could modify either the verb *heard* or the verb *had resigned.* Move the phrase so that it clearly modifies one part of the sentence or the other.

CORRECTED SENTENCE:	*Upon her arrival,* she heard that Lee had resigned.

Grammar and Style Tip

As a rule, related words should be kept together in a sentence. Place limiting modifiers such as *only, almost, nearly, even,* and *just* in front of the words they modify.

Recognizing Dangling Modifiers

With *dangling modifiers*, the word that should be modified is missing completely from the sentence.

> **KEY CONCEPT** A *dangling modifier* seems to modify the wrong word or no word at all because the word it should modify has been omitted from the sentence. ■

Dangling participial phrases are corrected by adding missing words and making other needed changes. In the following example, an *engineer* did the measuring, not the *span over the river.*

DANGLING PARTICIPIAL PHRASE:	Measuring carefully, the span over the river was closed accurately.
CORRECTED SENTENCE:	Measuring carefully, the engineer accurately closed the span over the river.

Dangling infinitive phrases and elliptical clauses can be corrected in the same way. The problem will generally be with the verb rather than with the noun or pronoun. However, you will usually need to change a noun or pronoun as well as the verb.

DANGLING INFINITIVE CLAUSE:	To cross the river, the bridge toll must be paid.
CORRECTED SENTENCE:	To cross the river, you must pay the bridge toll.
DANGLING ELLIPTICAL CLAUSE:	While sailing under the bridge, a school of porpoises was sighted.
CORRECTED SENTENCE:	While sailing under the bridge, we sighted a school of porpoises.

A dangling adverb clause may also occur when the antecedent of a pronoun is not clear.

DANGLING ADVERB CLAUSE:	*When she was ninety years old*, Mrs. Smith's granddaughter planned a picnic near the bridge.
CORRECTED SENTENCE:	*When Mrs. Smith was ninety years old*, her granddaughter planned a picnic near the bridge.

⚙ Grammar and Style Tip

If you are unsure of the construction of your sentence, a good way to check for errors is to read the sentence aloud. This is particularly true with misplaced and dangling modifiers, which usually sound ridiculous when read aloud.

▶ **Critical Viewing** Write a sentence with a misplaced modifier describing the bridge over the water in the photograph. How can you correct the misplaced modifier? **[Describe]**

Exercise 36 Identifying and Correcting Misplaced

Modifiers Rewrite each sentence, putting the misplaced modifiers closer to the words they should modify.

EXAMPLE: Spanning San Francisco Bay, we saw the great bridge.

ANSWER: We saw the great bridge spanning San Francisco Bay.

1. The George Washington Bridge is a two-level suspension toll bridge for vehicular traffic rising 212 feet above the water.
2. For pedestrians and cyclists, the upper level carries eight lanes for motor-vehicle traffic and two footpaths.
3. The Brooklyn Bridge connects the boroughs of Brooklyn and Manhattan, once the longest suspension bridge in the world.
4. Both the George Washington Bridge and the Brooklyn Bridge for tourists and residents are landmarks.
5. These bridges are major thoroughfares into and out of New York City centrally located.

Exercise 37 Identifying and Correcting Dangling

Modifiers If a sentence contains a dangling modifier, rewrite it using one of the techniques described in this section. If a sentence is correct, write *correct*.

EXAMPLE: Having finally finished the drawings, the hour was late.

ANSWER: Having finally finished the drawings, the engineer realized how late it was.

1. Born and educated in Germany, America became John Augustus Roebling's home in 1831.
2. A pioneer in the construction of suspension bridges, steel cables were Roebling's innovation.
3. America's oldest existing suspension aqueduct, John Roebling constructed it at Laxawaxen, Pennsylvania.
4. Spanning 1,595 feet across New York's East River, Roebling designed the Brooklyn Bridge.
5. Before his death, the plans for the Brooklyn Bridge were well received.

More Practice

Language Lab CD-ROM
• Sentence Errors: Misplaced Modifiers lesson
On-line Exercise Bank
• Section 20.5
Grammar Exercise Workbook
• pp. 65–66

Section Review

GRAMMAR EXERCISES 38–42

▶ **Exercise 38** Identifying and Correcting Misplaced Modifiers Write each sentence, correcting all misplaced modifiers. If the sentence is correct, write *correct.*

1. Stretching logs, ropes, or cables across a narrow valley or stream, the earliest bridges were built by ancient peoples.
2. An outgrowth of these elementary forms, engineers still design single-span bridges.
3. About 2200 B.C., historians think the first arch bridges were designed by the Babylonians.
4. For the earliest arch bridges upon which a roadway was built, stone blocks were wedged together to form an arch.
5. Still surviving to this day, the Romans built many stone arch bridges.
6. Timber-trestle bridges were also built by the Romans that did not survive.
7. The Pont du Gard in Nimes, France, is a surviving example of a Roman aqueduct, which has three tiers of arches rising 155 feet above the Gard River.
8. Consisting of two sections, cantilever bridges can span long distances joined together in the middle.
9. Suspension bridges can span even longer distances using a system of towers and cables.
10. Stretching back to medieval times, drawbridges also have a long history.

▶ **Exercise 39** Identifying and Correcting Dangling Modifiers Rewrite the following sentences, correcting any dangling modifiers by supplying missing words or ideas.

1. To get from the Lower Peninsula of Michigan to the Upper Peninsula, a bridge was needed.
2. While reading about the building of the Brooklyn Bridge, a plan was conceived by Michigan business people.
3. After hearing arguments for more than sixty years, a law to fund the new bridge was finally approved.
4. Building the bridge, nearly a million tons of concrete was used.
5. Overcoming many obstacles related to water and weather, the giant bridge took three years to build.

▶ **Exercise 40** Writing Effective Sentences Fill in each blank with the kind of phrase or clause indicated. Be careful to avoid using any misplaced or dangling modifiers.

1. After paying the toll, (independent clause).
2. (Infinitive) Brooklyn from Staten Island, cross the Verrazzano Bridge.
3. (Participial phrase), Roger caught sight of a sailboat.
4. Most bridges are designed (prepositional phrase).
5. After (gerund phrase), Rosa became an architect.

▶ **Exercise 41** Find It in Your Writing Look through your portfolio to see if you have written any misplaced or dangling modifiers. Rewrite the sentences correctly, and explain the changes you have made.

▶ **Exercise 42** Writing Application Find out the history of a building, road, or bridge near your home. Write a brief description of the structure's history. Proofread your writing carefully to be certain that you have not used any modifiers incorrectly.

Section 20.6 *Faulty Parallelism*

Good writers try to present a series of ideas in similar grammatical structures so that they will read smoothly. If one element in a series is not parallel with the others, the result may be jarring and its meaning may be unclear.

Recognizing the Correct Use of Parallelism

To present a series of ideas of equal importance, you should use parallel grammatical structures.

▶ **KEY CONCEPT** *Parallelism* involves presenting equal ideas in words, phrases, or clauses of similar types. ■

Parallel grammatical structures may be two or more words of the same part of speech, two or more phrases of the same type, two or more clauses of the same type, or even two or more sentences of the same type.

PARALLEL WORDS: The surfer looked *strong, fit,* and *agile.*

PARALLEL PHRASES: The greatest feeling I know is *to ride a giant wave flawlessly* and *to have all my friends watch me enviously.*

PARALLEL CLAUSES: The surfboard *that you recommended* and *that my brother wants* is on sale.

PARALLEL SENTENCES: *It couldn't be, of course. It could never, never be.*
—Dorothy Parker

Examine the following paragraph, which begins *A Tale of Two Cities* by Charles Dickens, a novel about the French Revolution. Notice how the parallel structures set up vivid contrasts.

EXAMPLE: It was the best of times, it was the worst of times, it was the age of wisdom, it was the age of foolishness, it was the epoch of belief, it was the epoch of incredulity, it was the season of Light, it was the season of Darkness, it was the spring of hope, it was the winter of despair, we had everything before us, we had nothing before us, we were all going direct to Heaven, we were all going direct the other way—in short, the period was so far like the present period, that some of its noisiest authorities insisted on its being received, for good or for evil, in the superlative degree of comparison only.

Theme: Surfing

In this section, you will learn how to place equal ideas in sentences so that they are balanced correctly. The examples and exercises are about surfing and surfboards.

Cross-Curricular Connection: Physical Education

▼ **Critical Viewing** Think of three equal adjectives or phrases that you might use in a sentence describing this surfer or his actions. **[Analyze]**

Faulty Parallelism • 505

> **Exercise 43** **Recognizing Parallel Structures** Write the parallel structures in the following sentences. Then, identify each as *words, phrases, clauses,* or *sentences.*

EXAMPLE: They leaped to their feet, sprinted toward the water, and jumped onto their boards.

ANSWER: leaped to their feet, sprinted toward the water, jumped onto their boards (phrases)

1. People can surf with their bodies or on their surfboards.
2. Lying, kneeling, or standing on a surfboard requires practice.
3. Because it can be enjoyed in many areas and because it is inexpensive, surfing is a very popular sport.
4. Surfing requires no formal training, but it requires practice.
5. Riding waves takes skill, stamina, and agility.

Correcting Faulty Parallelism

Faulty parallelism occurs when a writer uses unequal grammatical structures to express related ideas.

> **KEY CONCEPT** Correct a sentence containing faulty parallelism by rewriting it so that each parallel idea is expressed in the same grammatical structure. ∎

Faulty parallelism can involve words, phrases, and clauses in a series or in comparisons.

Nonparallel Words, Phrases, and Clauses in a Series

Always check a series of ideas in your writing for parallelism. If, for example, you begin a series with a prepositional phrase, make all the items in the series prepositional phrases.

The chart at the top of the next page presents some nonparallel structures and shows how they can be rephrased to restore smoothness and clarity to the sentence. Notice how coordinating conjunctions (such as *and, but, or*) often connect the items in a series and can signal you to check the connected items for parallelism.

Another potential problem to note involves correlative conjunctions, such as *both . . . and* or *not only . . . but also.* Though these conjunctions connect two related items, writers sometimes misplace or split the first part of the conjunction. The result is faulty parallelism.

NONPARALLEL: Our lifeguard not only won the local surfing championship but also the state title.

PARALLEL: Our lifeguard won not only the local surfing championship but also the state title.

More Practice

On-line
Exercise Bank
• Section 20.5
Grammar Exercise
Workbook
• pp. 67–68

CORRECTING FAULTY PARALLELISM IN A SERIES

Nonparallel Structures	Corrected Sentences
GERUND GERUND *Planning, drafting,* and NOUN *revision* are three steps in the writing process.	GERUND GERUND *Planning, drafting,* and GERUND *revising* are three steps in the writing process.
INFIN I could not wait *to try my* PHRASE INFIN *new surfboard, to catch* PHRASE PART PHRASE *some waves,* and *visiting the* beach.	INFIN I could not wait *to try my* PHRASE INFIN *new surfboard, to catch* PHRASE INFIN *some waves,* and *to visit the* PHRASE beach.
NOUN Some people feel *that surfing* CLAUSE *is not a sport,* but *it* INDEP CLAUSE *requires athleticism.*	NOUN Some experts feel *that surfing* CLAUSE *is not a sport* but NOUN CLAUSE *that it requires athleticism.*

Nonparallel Words, Phrases, and Clauses in Comparisons

As the old saying goes, you cannot compare apples with oranges. In writing comparisons, you generally should compare a phrase with the same type of phrase and a clause with the same type of clause. Furthermore, you should make sure your ideas themselves, as well as the structures you use to express them, are logically parallel.

CORRECTING FAULTY PARALLELISM IN COMPARISONS

Nonparallel Structures	Correlated Sentences
NOUN Most people prefer *corn* to GERUND PHRASE *eating Brussels sprouts.*	NOUN Most people prefer *corn* to NOUN *Brussels sprouts.*
PREP PHRASE I left my job *at 7:00 P.M.* PART rather than *stopping work* PHRASE *at 5:00 P.M.*	PREP PHRASE I left my job *at 7:00 P.M.* PREP rather than *at the usual* PHRASE *5:00 P.M.*
S PREP PHRASE *I* delight *in foggy days* as S much as sunny *days* delight DO other *people.*	S PREP PHRASE *I* delight *in foggy days* as S much as other *people* delight PREP PHRASE *in sunny days.*

✹ Grammar and Style Tip

You may want to use parallel structure for emphasis, for emotional effect, or for humor. An unexpected item at the end of a series can have a significant impact. Consider James Thurber's take on a familiar proverb: "Early to bed and early to rise makes a man healthy, wealthy, and dead."

Exercise 44 **Correcting Faulty Parallelism** Rewrite each sentence to correct the faulty parallelism.

EXAMPLE: On the beach, they not only play volleyball but also soccer.

ANSWER: On the beach, they play not only soccer but also volleyball.

1. Surfboards are made of a plastic foam core that is shaped by hand and then a shell of fiberglass and resin covers it.
2. Individual surfboards vary in length, width, and how much they weigh.
3. Top professional surfers use shortboards; longboards are usually used by amateur surfers.
4. Compared to shortboards, longboards are three feet longer, three inches wider, and they weigh twice as much.
5. The bottom of a surfboard has fins to provide stability and for enhancing performance.
6. Most surfers use longboards for recreation rather than competing with them.
7. In competition, surfers are judged on the size of the wave, the distance of the ride, and how difficult their maneuvers are.
8. Surfing competitions not only can take place at the shore but also in artificial indoor wavepools.
9. Paddling out to waves and to catch a wave, a surfer prepares for competition.
10. Turning sharply, gaining momentum, and to gently ride are a few surfing maneuvers.

More Practice

On-line
Exercise Bank
• Section 20.5
Grammar Exercise
Workbook
• pp. 67–68

▼ **Critical Viewing**
Write a short poem in the style of "The Seafarer," describing in parallel structure the ocean waves in this photograph. **[Connect]**

GRAMMAR IN
LITERATURE

from **The Seafarer**
Translated by Burton Raffel

Notice how the writer of this very old Anglo-Saxon poem has placed several series of items in parallel structure.

This tale is true, and mine. It tells
How the sea took me, swept me back
And forth in sorrow and fear and pain,
Showed me suffering in a hundred ships,
In a thousand ports, and in me. . . .

Section 20.6 Section Review

GRAMMAR EXERCISES 45–49

Exercise 45 **Recognizing Parallel Structures** Write the parallel structures in the following sentences. Then, identify each as *words*, *phrases*, *clauses*, or *sentences*.

1. Duke Kahanamoku surfed fast. He swam fast. He sailed fast.
2. Duke Kahanamoku, who broke a world record in freestyle swimming in 1912 and who was a talented surfer, popularized surfing in Hawaii.
3. Kahanamoku promoted, popularized, and expanded the sport of surfing.
4. Kahanamoku is credited with inventing windsurfing and perfecting wakesurfing.
5. Teaching water safety, swimming to break records, and acting in movies, Kahanamoku traveled all over the world.

Exercise 46 **Revising to Eliminate Faulty Parallelism** Rewrite each sentence to correct any nonparallel structures.

1. In the 1950's, some people said surfers were illiterate, lazy, and they were not responsible.
2. Surfing in the California sun had a bad image. A better image was working in an office.
3. By the 1960's, however, surfing became more popular, and more respect was given to surfers.
4. A counterculture emerged that admired, emulated, and was promoting the surfing lifestyle.
5. This lifestyle was easygoing, youth centered, and loved to have fun.
6. Popular music in the 1960's was about cars, love, and they sang about surfing.
7. Watching surfing movies, singing surfing songs, and to have a tan were very popular.
8. Bands that sang surfing songs and they looked like surfers grew famous.
9. Young people on the West Coast, in the Midwest, and who lived in the East all listened to surfing songs on the radio.
10. The surfing look was featured in television ads. To have a lifestyle of a surfer was considered admirable.

Exercise 47 **Find It in Your Reading** Notice parallel structures in these lines from the poem "The Seafarer":

But there isn't a man on earth so proud, / So born to greatness, so bold with his youth, / Grown so brave, or so graced by God, / That he feels no fear as the sails unfurl, / Wondering what Fate has willed and will do.

Exercise 48 **Find It in Your Writing** Look through your portfolio for sentences in which you have presented a series of two or more related ideas. Correct any sentences with faulty parallelism.

Exercise 49 **Writing Application** Follow the instructions in parentheses to expand each sentence, making sure the new sentences contain parallel structures.

1. Riding the wave, Mandy was thrilled. (Add another participial phrase.)
2. I surfed in Hawaii last spring. (Add another independent clause.)
3. The surfer caught a wave. (Add three adjectives.)
4. I love surfing. (Compare surfing to something else.)
5. Before wiping out, Ted rode on top of the wave. (Add two more verbs with prepositional phrases.)

Faulty Coordination

When two or more independent clauses of unequal importance are joined by *and*, the result is *faulty coordination.*

Recognizing Faulty Coordination

To *coordinate* means to "place side by side in equal rank." Two independent clauses that are joined by the coordinating conjunction *and*, therefore, should have equal rank.

▶ **KEY CONCEPT** Use *and* or other coordinating conjunctions only to connect ideas of equal importance. ■

The following example shows ideas of equal importance joined by the conjunction *and*.

CORRECT COORDINATION: Otis designed an airplane, and Oliver built it.

Sometimes, however, writers carelessly use *and* to join independent clauses that either should not be joined or should be joined in another way so that the real relationship between the clauses will be clear. The faulty coordination puts all the ideas on the same level of importance, even though logically they should not be.

FAULTY COORDINATION: Production of aircraft accelerated in World War II, *and* aircraft became a decisive factor in the war.

I didn't do well, *and* the race was very easy.

The dog looked ferocious, *and* it was snarling and snapping at me.

Occasionally, writers will also string together so many ideas with *and's* that the reader is left breathless.

STRINGY SENTENCE: The plane that flew over the field did a few dips and turns, *and* the people on the ground craned their necks to watch, *and* everyone laughed and cheered, *and* then the pilot made one more circle of the field and landed, *and* he walked toward us, *and* everyone cheered even louder.

▲ **Critical Viewing** In a sentence that describes these planes, use a coordinating conjunction to connect ideas of equal importance. **[Describe]**

Theme: World War II Planes

In this section, you will learn how to place unrelated ideas properly in sentences. The examples and exercises are about World War II fighter planes.

Cross-Curricular Connection: Social Studies

More Practice

On-line
Exercise Bank
• Section 20.7
Grammar Exercise Workbook
• pp. 69–70

Exercise 50 **Identifying Faulty Coordination** For the sentences in which *and* is used improperly, write *faulty.* For the sentences in which *and* is used properly, write correct.

EXAMPLE: He builds model airplanes, and he displays them in shows.

ANSWER: correct

1. When World War II began, private airlines expanded their facilities and trained thousands of students, and these new pilots became the backbone of the army, navy, and marine air operation.
2. Aircraft designed for personal use were refitted for military use, and civilian pilots were trained for military duty.
3. Important advances were made in the development of planes for bombing and combat, and small aircraft were produced rapidly.
4. American military aircraft were in action on all fronts, and the number of people employed in the American aviation industry totaled 450,000.
5. At the end of the war, airplane production reached an all-time high, and air warfare increased in intensity.

Correcting Faulty Coordination

Faulty coordination can be corrected in the following ways:

KEY CONCEPT One way to correct faulty coordination is to put unrelated ideas into separate sentences. ■

When faulty coordination occurs in a sentence in which the independent clauses are not closely related, separate the clauses and omit the coordinating conjunction.

FAULTY COORDINATION: Production of aircraft accelerated in World War II, *and* aircraft became a decisive factor in the war.

CORRECTED SENTENCES: Production of aircraft accelerated in World War II. Aircraft became a decisive factor in the war.

▲ **Critical Viewing** Identify four details you would include in a description of this airplane. In your description, avoid a stringy sentence and faulty coordination. **[Analyze]**

▶ **KEY CONCEPT** You can correct faulty coordination by putting less important ideas into subordinate clauses or phrases. ■

If one independent clause is less important or subordinate to the other, turn it into a subordinate clause.

FAULTY
COORDINATION: I didn't do well, *and* the race was very easy.

CORRECTED
SENTENCE: I didn't do well, even though the race was very easy.

You can also reduce a less important idea to a phrase—that is, change the compound sentence into a simple sentence.

FAULTY
COORDINATION: The dog looked ferocious, *and* it was snarling and snapping at me.

CORRECTED
SENTENCE: Snarling and snapping at me, the dog looked ferocious.

Stringy sentences should be broken up and revised using any of the three methods just described. Experiment with a few possibilities before making a choice. Following is one way that the stringy sentence presented earlier can be revised.

REVISION OF
A STRINGY
SENTENCE: The plane that flew over the field did a few dips and turns. Craning their necks to watch, the people on the ground laughed and cheered. The pilot made one more circle of the field and landed. Everyone cheered even louder when he walked toward us.

▶ **Exercise 51** Correcting Faulty Coordination Rewrite each sentence, correcting the faulty coordination.

1. High-speed offense bombers were developed during the 1930's, and America's long-range Boeing B-17 Flying Fortress was also developed.
2. Between 1935 and 1936, Great Britain and Germany developed prototypes of more advanced fighters, and these fighters included the Hawker Hurricane, Supermarine Spitfire, and the Messerschmitt Bf 109.
3. The German Luftwaffe (air force) defeated the Polish Air Force and bombed major Polish cities, and World War II began in 1939.
4. Denmark, Norway, Holland, Belgium, and France were defeated by Germany's troops in 1940, and the troops were helped largely through air support.
5. The Battle of Britain was a turning point in World War II, and Britain's Royal Air Force defeated Germany's Luftwaffe.

⚙ Grammar and Style Tip

Stringy sentences are connected not only by *and; so* is also often overused as a connector. Be careful not to turn a series of sentences that are causally related into a stringy sentence with too many *so's.*

▶ **More Practice**

On-line
Exercise Bank
• Section 20.7
Grammar Exercise
Workbook
• pp. 69–70

Section Review

GRAMMAR EXERCISES 52–56

Exercise 52 **Recognizing Faulty Coordination** For the sentences in which *and* is used improperly, write *faulty.* For the sentences in which *and* is used properly, write *correct.*

1. The *Spirit of St. Louis* was the plane that Charles Lindbergh used to fly nonstop from New York to Paris, and it is on display at the Smithsonian Institution in Washington, D.C.
2. The plane was built by the Ryan Aeronautical Company of San Diego, and it was specially built for the transatlantic flight.
3. Lindbergh had been an airmail pilot for a corporation, and he was born in Detroit.
4. After his historic nonstop flight, Lindbergh flew the *Spirit of St. Louis* on "goodwill" tours, and he flew 22,000 miles.
5. In 1927, Lindbergh published a book entitled *We*, and it was about his transatlantic flight.

Exercise 53 **Revising to Eliminate Faulty Coordination** Rewrite each sentence, correcting the faulty coordination.

1. The Boeing B-17 Flying Fortress is one of the most famous airplanes ever built, and the prototype first flew on July 28, 1935.
2. Few B-17's were in service when the U.S. entered World War II, and production quickly accelerated.
3. The Flying Fortress served in every World War II combat zone, and bombing German industrial targets in daylight was its claim to fame.
4. Germany's main air weapon early in the war was the Messerschmitt Bf 109, and that plane was used to bomb London during the Battle of Britain.

5. The British Spitfire prevailed over the Bf 109 at the Battle of Britain, and it was faster and lighter.

Exercise 54 **Combining Sentences Effectively** Combine each pair of sentences, avoiding faulty coordination.

1. The Me 262 was the world's first operational turbojet aircraft. It was much faster than conventional aircraft.
2. There were delays in production of the Me 262. Development problems, Allied bombings, and cautious Luftwaffe leadership contributed.
3. In July 1944, an Me 262 became the first fighter jet used in combat. It attacked a British reconnaissance plane flying over Munich.
4. More than 1,400 Me 262's were produced. Fewer than 300 saw combat.
5. Many of the German jets were destroyed by Allied bombing raids. The jets were still on the ground.

Exercise 55 **Find It in Your Writing** Look through your portfolio to see if you have written any "stringy" sentences that contain too many *and*'s or *so*'s. Rewrite the sentences using some of the techniques described in this section.

Exercise 56 **Writing Application** Imagine that you are a newspaper reporter who has been assigned to cover a local air show. Describe the planes that are on display, the stunts that the pilots perform, and the general atmosphere of the show. Remember to vary your sentence structure, and be sure to use proper coordination.

GRAMMAR EXERCISES 57–63

▶ **Exercise 57** Writing the Four Types of Sentences Rewrite each sentence to fit the function indicated in parentheses. Add the appropriate end marks to the rewritten sentences.

1. The ancient Greeks were the first civilization to experiment with flying machines (interrogative)
2. Did they conduct their first experiments around 400 B.C. (declarative)
3. The Chinese invented kites at around the same time (interrogative)
4. Can you imagine how it felt to be the first kite flyer (imperative)
5. Making a machine fly must have been so exciting (exclamatory)

▶ **Exercise 58** Revising to Combine and Vary Sentence Length Rewrite this paragraph, combining some short sentences and leaving others short for emphasis.

Try this experiment. Get a long, thin strip of paper, and put the paper in a book. Insert about two inches of the paper between the pages of the book. Hold the book right up in front of your mouth. The paper should hang over the side of the book farthest from you. Blow gently over the top of the paper, and see what happens. You do this experiment correctly. The paper will be pushed upward, or lifted. You have demonstrated a principle. The principle was formulated by an eighteenth-century Swiss scholar. The scholar was named Daniel Bernoulli. Bernoulli's principle explains why flight is possible. The pressure in a moving stream of air is less than the pressure in the surrounding air. The air pressure under the paper was greater than the pressure above it. The paper was pushed upward into the moving air.

▶ **Exercise 59** Revising to Eliminate Fragments and Run-ons Rewrite this paragraph, correcting any fragments or run-ons.

If the Wright brothers were the fathers of the airplane. Sir George Cayley was its grandfather. Lived and worked during the beginning of the nineteenth century. Cayley studied many different theories of flight, he carefully examined Leonardo da Vinci's wing-flapping ornithopter. He measured birds' muscles and wing patterns he also studied human muscle activity and he determined that people could not strap on wings and be able to fly as birds did. Cayley suggested that airplanes needed a fixed-wing design, they also should have a self-contained system for propelling the craft, and a tail to help control it. The only engines available in Cayley's time were steam engines these were too heavy to permit the plane to get off the ground. Using Cayley's theories and the new technological developments. The Wright brothers were able to build a self-propelled plane that could carry a man into the air. And bring him back down safely.

▶ **Exercise 60** Revising to Correct Modifiers Rewrite the following sentences, correcting any misplaced or dangling modifiers.

1. Sailing gracefully, the first manned balloon flight took place with two aviators in Paris in November 1783.
2. Invented by the Montgolfier brothers, two French adventurers sailed a hot-air balloon for twenty-two minutes.
3. Inspired by watching wood chips float over a fire, the idea of a hot-air balloon was first conceived.
4. The Montgolfiers believed that forcing

air into a lightweight bag heated by a coal stove would cause the bag to rise.

5. Testing materials, many experiments were conducted by the Montgolfiers.
6. Showing off their invention in Paris in 1783, King Louis XVI was impressed.
7. The two pilots reached an altitude over the rooftops of Paris of 500 feet.
8. Watching the men sail over their fields, fear was felt by many French farmers.
9. A Frenchman and an American teamed up over the English Channel in 1785 to make the first international flight.
10. The first hot-air-balloon flight took place in North America in 1793.

▶ Exercise 61 Proofreading to Correct Errors in Sentence Structure

Correct any errors in parallelism or coordination in the following sentences.

1. At first, people who believed humans could fly were considered fools, madmen, or those who dreamed.
2. Otto Lilienthal brought respectability to flight invention, and he was a well-respected engineer.
3. Lilienthal once said: "To invent an airplane is nothing, to build one is something, but flying is everything."
4. Lilienthal's flying machines were hang-gliders, and you can see similar craft in use today.
5. Lilienthal built 18 gliders, flew 2,500 successful glider flights, and he wrote a book about his experiments.
6. Some of Lilienthal's gliders had one level of wings, and two levels of wings were on some of the others.
7. The Wright brothers read Lilienthal's book, and they made the first successful airplane flight in 1903.
8. Lilienthal inspired the Wrights, and he was courageous and thoughtful.
9. Lilienthal died in a glider accident, and his work was carried on by the Wrights.
10. Today, Lilienthal is honored as a technician, for being a scientist, and a pioneer.

▶ Exercise 62 Revising Sentences

Rewrite the following paragraph, combining or revising sentences and correcting any errors in sentence structure.

Amelia Earhart saw her first airplane at the Iowa State Fair, and it was in 1909, and she was twelve years old, and she was not impressed. It was not until eleven years later. That she took her first plane ride. She was up in the air only for a few minutes, and she knew she wanted to become a pilot. Adventurous and headstrong, a plane was purchased by her a few weeks later. Earhart had several accidents, her instructor doubted her talents as a pilot. She kept practicing soon she was breaking altitude records for women fliers. In 1928, Earhart part of a three-person crew that flew across the Atlantic. As the first woman to make a transatlantic flight. She became a celebrity. She was asked to give lectures, written up in newspapers, and people cheered for her everywhere she went. After flying solo from Hawaii to California in 1935, President Roosevelt honored her. He praised her for proving that to men aviation is not limited. Earhart began making plans for a round-the-world flight, she undertook the flight in 1937, and there was a disappearance over the Pacific. Neither body nor plane ever found.

▶ Exercise 63 Writing Application

Imagine that you are one of the first people to fly a balloon, a glider, or an airplane. Write a narrative of your first flight. Try to vary the length of your sentences, and include at least two examples of parallel structure. Proofread your narration carefully to make sure that you have no fragments, run-ons, or misplaced modifiers.

Standardized Test Preparation Workshop

Recognizing Appropriate Sentence Construction

Standardized tests will measure your ability to write by providing a written passage with numbered sentences. You will be asked to read the passage and to choose from several possible revisions of each sentence. The following tips for writing effective sentences should help you.

- **Avoid choppy sentences** by using a variety of simple, compound, complex, and compound-complex sentences.

- **Correct run-on sentences** by inserting a comma and coordinating conjunction, by inserting a semicolon, or by making one or two distinct, properly punctuated sentences.

- **Correct misplaced modifiers** by placing adverbs and adjectives as close as possible to the words they modify.

- **Varying the beginnings** of your sentences by starting some sentences with adverbs, some with prepositional phrases, some with verbs or verbal phrases, and some with subordinate clauses.

Sample Test Item	Answer and Explanation
Directions: Read the passage, and choose the best rewrite of each numbered sentence. (1) Susan Williams-Ellis founded Portmeirion Pottery in 1960 since then she and her family have designed many different patterns.	
1 A Susan Williams-Ellis founded Portmeirion Pottery. In 1960, since then she and her family have designed many different patterns. **B** Susan Williams-Ellis was the founder of Portmeirion Pottery in 1960. She designed many different patterns. **C** Since founding Portmeirion Pottery in 1960, Susan Williams-Ellis and her family have designed many different patterns. **D** Correct as is	Choice *A* breaks the passage at an illogical point, and choice *B* slightly changes the meaning of the passage. In the correct choice, *C*, the run-on passage is rewritten as a grammatically correct sentence.

> **Practice 1** **Directions:** Read the following passage. Choose the best rewrite in the questions that follow.

(1) Resistant strains of bacteria develop. (2) If a prescribed antibiotic fails to kill all the bacteria in an infection. (3) Experts fear that these resistant strains are becoming stronger and stronger the overuse of antibiotics can be blamed for this serious danger. (4) Bacterial infections are being seen by doctors that do not respond to traditional antibiotics. (5) Although much research is being done to formulate stronger antibiotics, experts fear that future strains of bacteria will continue to develop. (6) Future bacteria may be deadly. (7) Future bacteria will almost surely develop faster. (8) Than the antibiotics needed to combat them.

1 Which of the following is the best rewrite of passages 1 and 2?

  A Resistant strains of bacteria develop; if a prescribed antibiotic fails to kill all the bacteria in an infection.

  B Resistant strains of bacteria develop if a prescribed antibiotic fails to kill all the bacteria in an infection.

  C Strains of bacteria develop if an antibiotic fails to kill all an infection.

  D Correct as is

2 Which of the following is the best rewrite of passage 3?

  F Experts fear these stronger resistant strains can be blamed for this serious danger.

  G The strong overuse of antibiotics can be blamed for the fear of experts.

  H Experts fear that these resistant strains are becoming stronger and stronger. The overuse of antibiotics can be blamed for this serious danger.

  J Correct as is

3 Which of the following is the best rewrite of passage 4?

  A Doctors are seeing bacterial infections that do not respond to traditional antibiotics.

  B Bacterial infections are being seen by doctors. Bacterial infections that do not respond to traditional antibiotics.

  C Bacterial infections are being seen that do not respond to traditional antibiotics by doctors.

  D Correct as is

4 Which of the following is the best rewrite of passage 5?

  F Although much research is being done to create stronger antibiotics, experts fear the developing future strains of bacteria.

  G Experts who are doing much research fear developing future bacteria.

  H Experts fear that future strains of bacteria; although much research is being done to create stronger antibiotics, will continue to develop.

  J Correct as is

5 Which of the following is the best rewrite of passages 6, 7, and 8?

  A Future bacteria may be deadly; future bacteria will almost surely develop faster than the antibiotics needed to combat them.

  B Future bacteria will almost surely develop faster than the antibiotics needed to combat them.

  C Future bacteria may be deadly, because they will almost surely develop faster than the antibiotics needed to combat them.

  D Correct as is

Verb Usage

▲ **Critical Viewing**
A solid understanding of architectural principles was necessary to build the Taj Mahal. In what way is a solid understanding of verbs necessary for clear communication? **[Relate]**

Monuments have long served to remind us of people and events of importance. Throughout history, monuments have been erected to commemorate great battles, to celebrate various religions, and to honor myriad heroes. Although various cultures have built many different types of monuments—pyramids, statues, museums, and churches—the rules regarding construction methods have developed in a remarkably similar way by every civilization.

In the same way, the rules concerning the use of verbs and verb tenses have been developed to allow for more effective communication. Like the individual building blocks that form the foundation of even the largest monument, the rules concerning verb usage form a basic support structure that enables you to communicate effectively.

A solid understanding of verbs and their uses is necessary in order to speak and write well. Generally, native speakers of English tend to use correct verb forms automatically when they speak, but many grammatical situations are tricky.

In this chapter, you will study how verbs are formed and how they show time. You will also learn how verbs express facts, commands, and wishes or possibilities, as well as how verbs indicate whether subjects perform or receive actions.

Diagnostic Test

Directions: Write all answers on a separate sheet of paper.

Skill Check A. Identify the tense of the italicized verbs, and tell whether the form is *basic, progressive,* or *emphatic.*

1. Gary *did travel* to many sports arenas during his vacation.
2. Some arenas *have been* tourist attractions for many decades.
3. At this very moment, people *are visiting* famous sports arenas.
4. Many communities *have been trying* to build new arenas.
5. Someday, these arenas *will serve* as monuments to our society's fascination with sports.

Skill Check B. On your paper, form the tenses listed using the pronouns in parentheses as their subjects.

6. past progressive of *borrow* (*we*)
7. past perfect of *sing* (*they*)
8. present progressive of *acknowledge* (*it*)
9. future perfect of *investigate* (*you*)
10. future perfect progressive of *hope* (*I*)

Skill Check C. For each sentence, write the verbs and their tenses, and tell whether the sentence describes simultaneous or sequential events.

11. We know that people have always enjoyed seeing monuments.
12. We learned that the White House was completed in 1800.
13. It has been called the President's House.
14. Now that I have learned about this famous building, I will add the information to my knowledge of our nation's history.
15. By the time this class ends, we will have learned a lot about famous buildings in the nation's capital.

Skill Check D. Rewrite the following sentences, changing the verbs to the subjunctive mood as necessary.

16. If I was to travel back in time, I would go to the early 1930's.
17. Then, as if I was a citizen of the period, I could witness the construction of the National Archives Building in Washington, D.C.
18. If the National Archives Building was damaged by a fire, many of the nation's most famous documents might be destroyed.
19. I would prefer that these famous documents are protected from all possible damage.
20. It is crucial that the heritage of our nation is preserved for the sake of posterity.

Skill Check E. On your paper, identify whether the verbs in the following sentences are in the active or passive voice.

21. Many people have visited the Library of Congress.
22. The Library of Congress was founded by Thomas Jefferson.
23. Numerous books are held in storage by the Library of Congress.
24. Over the years, much information has been provided by the Library of Congress to scholars.
25. In 2000, the Library of Congress celebrated its bicentennial.

Verb Tenses

Besides expressing actions or conditions, verbs have different *tenses* to indicate when the action or condition occurred.

> **KEY CONCEPT** A **tense** is the form of a verb that shows the time of an action or a condition. ■

The Six Verb Tenses

There are six tenses that indicate when an action or a condition of a verb is, was, or will be in effect. Each of these six tenses has at least two forms:

> **KEY CONCEPT** Each tense has a basic and a progressive form. ■

The chart that follows shows the *basic* forms of the six tenses:

THE BASIC FORMS OF THE SIX TENSES	
Present	I visit the Statue of Liberty.
Past	I visited Ellis Island last Sunday.
Future	I will visit the Washington Monument next week.
Present Perfect	I have visited the children at the hospital for almost a year now.
Past Perfect	I had visited my grandmother on weekends until this past month.
Future Perfect	I will have visited my aunt once a week for a year by the end of May.

> **Exercise 1** Writing Sentences in All Six Tenses Write six sentences on the subject of a monument or an important building in your town. Use a different verb tense in each sentence, and indicate the tense.

EXAMPLE: The Veterans' Memorial *has stood* in the middle of town for more than fifty years. (present perfect)

Notice in the next chart that all of the progressive forms end in *-ing.*

THE PROGRESSIVE FORMS OF THE SIX TENSES

Present Progressive	I *am drawing* right now.
Past Progressive	I *was drawing* when you called.
Future Progressive	I *will be drawing* all weekend.
Present Perfect Progressive	I *have been drawing* more than usual lately.
Past Perfect Progressive	I *had been drawing* apples until the art teacher suggested that I draw boats.
Future Perfect Progressive	I *will have been drawing* in my spare time for two years by the end of this month.

There is also a third form, the *emphatic,* which exists only for the present and past tenses. The present emphatic is formed with the helping verbs *do* or *does,* depending on the subject. The past emphatic is formed with *did.*

THE EMPHATIC FORMS OF THE PRESENT AND THE PAST

Present Emphatic	I *do exercise* more frequently than you.
Past Emphatic	I *did exercise* last night to burn more calories.

Exercise 2 Recognizing Verb Tenses and Their Forms
Identify the tense of each verb. Identify its form as well, if the form is not basic.

EXAMPLE: We *have been learning* about monuments.
ANSWER: present perfect progressive

1. We traveled for nearly two days.
2. Jerry has viewed the pyramids at Giza.
3. In fact, my mother did visit the Valley of the Kings.
4. The Egyptians had been building tombs and temples along the Nile River thousands of years ago.
5. The obelisk will have been standing for 4,000 years by the early part of this century.

More Practice

Language Lab CD-ROM
• Correct and Effective Use of Verbs lesson
On-line Exercise Bank
• Section 21.1
Grammar Exercise Workbook
• pp. 71–72

The Four Principal Parts of Verbs

Every verb in the English language has four *principal parts* from which all of the tenses are formed.

> **KEY CONCEPT** A verb has four principal parts: the *present*, the *present participle*, the *past*, and the *past participle*. ∎

The chart below shows the principal parts of two verbs:

THE FOUR PRINCIPAL PARTS			
Present	**Present Participle**	**Past**	**Past Participle**
talk	talking	talked	talked
draw	drawing	drew	drawn

The first principal part is used for the basic forms of the present and future tenses, as well as for the emphatic forms. The present tense is formed by adding an *-s* or *-es* when the subject is *he, she, it*, or a singular noun. The future tense is formed with the helping verb *will* (*I will talk, Mary will draw*). The present emphatic is formed with the helping verbs *do* or *does* (*I do talk, Mary does draw*). The past emphatic is formed with the helping verb *did* (*I did talk, Mary did draw*).

The second principal part is used with various helping verbs for all six of the progressive forms (*I am talking, Mary was drawing*, and so on).

The third principal part is used to form the past tense (*I talked, Mary drew*).

The fourth principal part, with helping verbs, is used for the basic forms of the perfect tenses (*I have talked, Mary had drawn*, and so on).

▼ **Critical Viewing** A memorial such as this one is built to honor something or someone from the past. What types of written works serve the same purpose? What tense or tenses would predominate in such works? **[Connect]**

> **Exercise 3** Recognizing **Principal Parts** Underline and identify the principal part used to form each verb in Exercise 2.

EXAMPLE: We have been <u>learning</u> about movements.

ANSWER: present participle

Jefferson Memorial, Washington, D.C.

Regular and Irregular Verbs

The way the past and past participle of a verb are formed determines whether the verb is classified as *regular* or *irregular.*

Regular Verbs The majority of verbs are regular; their past and past participles are formed according to a predictable pattern.

> **KEY CONCEPT** A **regular verb** is one for which the past and past participle are formed by adding *-ed* or *-d* to the present form. ■

The chart that follows shows the principal parts of three regular verbs. Pay particular attention to the spelling. Notice that a final consonant is sometimes doubled to form the present participle (*stopping*), as well as the past and past participle (*stopped*). A final *e* may also be dropped to form the present participle (*managing*).

PRINCIPAL PARTS OF REGULAR VERBS			
Present	**Present Participle**	**Past**	**Past Participle**
contend	contending	contended	(have) contended
manage	managing	managed	(have) managed
stop	stopping	stopped	(have) stopped

Irregular Verbs Although most verbs are regular, many of the most common verbs are irregular.

> **KEY CONCEPT** An **irregular verb** is one whose past and past participle are not formed by adding *-ed* or *-d* to the present form. ■

The charts that follow group a number of irregular verbs according to common characteristics. It is important to master the principal parts of irregular verbs to avoid usage problems. One common problem is using a principal part that is non-standard.

INCORRECT:	They *knowed* about the Jefferson Memorial.
CORRECT:	They *knew* about the Jefferson Memorial.

A second problem is confusing the past and past participle when they are different.

INCORRECT:	She *done* the right thing.
CORRECT:	She *did* the right thing.

Learn More

To review basic information about verbs and verb phrases, turn to Chapter 17.

IRREGULAR VERBS WITH THE SAME PAST AND PAST PARTICIPLE

Present	Present Participle	Past	Past Participle
bind	binding	bound	(have) bound
bring	bringing	brought	(have) brought
build	building	built	(have) built
buy	buying	bought	(have) bought
catch	catching	caught	(have) caught
cling	clinging	clung	(have) clung
creep	creeping	crept	(have) crept
fight	fighting	fought	(have) fought
find	finding	found	(have) found
fling	flinging	flung	(have) flung
get	getting	got	(have) got or (have) gotten
grind	grinding	ground	(have) ground
hang	hanging	hung	(have) hung
hold	holding	held	(have) held
keep	keeping	kept	(have) kept
lay	laying	laid	(have) laid
lead	leading	led	(have) led
leave	leaving	left	(have) left
lend	lending	lent	(have) lent
lose	losing	lost	(have) lost
pay	paying	paid	(have) paid
say	saying	said	(have) said
seek	seeking	sought	(have) sought
sell	selling	sold	(have) sold
send	sending	sent	(have) sent
shine	shining	shone or shined	(have) shone or (have) shined
sit	sitting	sat	(have) sat
sleep	sleeping	slept	(have) slept
spend	spending	spent	(have) spent
spin	spinning	spun	(have) spun
stand	standing	stood	(have) stood
stick	sticking	stuck	(have) stuck
sting	stinging	stung	(have) stung
strike	striking	struck	(have) struck
swing	swinging	swung	(have) swung
teach	teaching	taught	(have) taught
win	winning	won	(have) won
wind	winding	wound	(have) wound
wring	wringing	wrung	(have) wrung

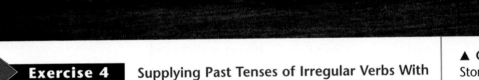

> **Exercise 4** **Supplying Past Tenses of Irregular Verbs With the Same Past and Past Participles** Supply the verb and tense indicated to complete each sentence.

EXAMPLE: We (get—past) our map and headed for Stonehenge.
ANSWER: We got our map and headed for Stonehenge.

1. This ancient monument of huge stones (stand—present perfect) on Salisbury Plain in Wiltshire, England, for 4,000 years.
2. Over hundreds of years, investigators (seek—present perfect) to learn the origins of Stonehenge.
3. Theories about who (build—past) it have included the Druids, Greeks, Phoenicians, and Atlantians.
4. Investigators (find—present perfect) that it was constructed in stages from 2000 to 1500 B.C.
5. Some believe that the ancient population (hold—past perfect) ceremonies of worship at Stonehenge.
6. Others (say—present perfect) that it was used to observe astronomical phenomena.
7. Stonehenge certainly (catch—past) our imagination.
8. We (spend—past perfect) only three days in England before we went to visit it.
9. We (leave—past) with a feeling that we had had a close encounter with ancient history.
10. As time goes on, we wonder what people from the past (teach—future perfect) us.

▲ **Critical Viewing** Stonehenge is a great tourist attraction. What makes this and other remnants of the past so intriguing? In your response, use the perfect tense of at least one irregular verb from the chart on page 524. **[Draw Conclusions]**

> **More Practice**

Language Lab CD-ROM
• Correct and Effective Use of Verbs lesson
On-line Exercise Bank
• Section 21.1
Grammar Exercise Workbook
• pp. 73–74

IRREGULAR VERBS THAT CHANGE IN OTHER WAYS

Present	Present Participle	Past	Past Participle
arise	arising	arose	(have) arisen
bear	bearing	bore	(have) borne
beat	beating	beat	(have) beaten or (have) beat
become	becoming	became	(have) become
begin	beginning	began	(have) begun
bite	biting	bit	(have) bitten
blow	blowing	blew	(have) blown
break	breaking	broke	(have) broken
choose	choosing	chose	(have) chosen
come	coming	came	(have) come
do	doing	did	(have) done
draw	drawing	drew	(have) drawn
drink	drinking	drank	(have) drunk
drive	driving	drove	(have) driven
eat	eating	ate	(have) eaten
fall	falling	fell	(have) fallen
fly	flying	flew	(have) flown
forget	forgetting	forgot	(have) forgotten or forgot
freeze	freezing	froze	(have) frozen
give	giving	gave	(have) given
go	going	went	(have) gone
grow	growing	grew	(have) grown
know	knowing	knew	(have) known
lie	lying	lay	(have) lain
ride	riding	rode	(have) ridden
ring	ringing	rang	(have) rung
rise	rising	rose	(have) risen
run	running	ran	(have) run
see	seeing	saw	(have) seen
shake	shaking	shook	(have) shaken
shrink	shrinking	shrank	(have) shrunk
sing	singing	sang	(have) sung
sink	sinking	sank	(have) sunk
slay	slaying	slew	(have) slain
speak	speaking	spoke	(have) spoken
spring	springing	sprang	(have) sprung
steal	stealing	stole	(have) stolen
stride	striding	strode	(have) stridden
strive	striving	strove	(have) striven
swear	swearing	swore	(have) sworn
swim	swimming	swam	(have) swum
take	taking	took	(have) taken
tear	tearing	tore	(have) torn
throw	throwing	threw	(have) thrown
wear	wearing	wore	(have) worn
weave	weaving	wove	(have) woven or (have) wove
write	writing	wrote	(have) written

 **Internet Tip**

You can use the present participle of verbs to find information about activities that may interest you. For instance, to find information about Ellis Island, you can type "visiting Ellis Island" in the query field of your search engine.

▶ **Exercise 5** Learning the Principal Parts of Irregular Verbs
Write the present participle, the past, and the past participle
of each verb.

EXAMPLE: become

ANSWER: becoming   became   become

1. feel
2. teach
3. lead
4. bring
5. win
6. pay
7. hold
8. strike
9. choose
10. bear

More Practice

**Language Lab
CD-ROM**
• Correct and Effective
  Use of Verbs lesson
**On-line
Exercise Bank**
• Section 21.1
**Grammar Exercise
Workbook**
• pp. 73–74

▶ **Exercise 6** Using the Correct Forms of Irregular Verbs On
your paper, write the form of the verb indicated in parentheses.

1. People throughout the world (build—present perfect progressive) monuments for thousands of years.
2. Remarkably, people of ancient civilizations (build—past)
   some of the world's most impressive monuments before
   the advent of industrial machinery.
3. From around 221 B.C. to 214 B.C., the Chinese emperor
   Shih Huang-ti (oversee—past) the construction of walls to
   connect a single wall about 1,650 miles long.
4. Since its construction, the Great Wall of China (be—present perfect) one of the world's largest constructions.
5. By the year 2800, people (stand—future perfect) upon the
   Great Wall of China for about 3,000 years.
6. Stonehenge is another famous monument that
   (leave—present perfect) visitors with a strong impression
   for many years.
7. No one who has visited the
   monument (forget—future
   progressive) its mysterious
   beauty.
8. Scholars (set—present perfect progressive) forth theories about Stonehenge's original function for decades.
9. By the time we arrived in
   Athens, our friends already
   (spend—past perfect) many
   hours viewing the Parthenon.
10. This majestic monument
    (stand—present perfect pro-
    gressive) atop the Acropolis
    for nearly 2,500 years.

▼ **Critical Viewing**
Although millions of
people visit the Great
Wall of China every
year, this photograph
shows a solitary person
on the wall. What
effect might the pho-
tographer have hoped
to achieve by doing
so? Use at least one
irregular verb in your
response. **[Analyze]**

▶ **Exercise 7** Supplying the Correct Forms of Regular and Irregular Verbs Write the appropriate past or past participle for each verb in parentheses.

EXAMPLE: The development of new and stronger materials (bring) about vast improvements in building construction.

ANSWER: brought

1. Monuments have often (function) as reminders of an important cause or a famous historical figure.
2. The efforts of a group of ordinary people (be) instrumental in the building of a famous American monument.
3. In 1833, concerned citizens (form) the Washington National Monument Society to raise funds for a memorial to George Washington.
4. These people (want) to be sure that future generations would remember the "father" of their country.
5. In 1848, the United States Congress (authorize) the building of the Washington Monument in Washington, D.C.
6. The American architect Robert Mills had initially (design) the monument, but other architects reconceived it.
7. The Civil War (delay) the completion of the monument until 1884.
8. Since its completion, it has (stand) out as a distinct landmark in Washington, D.C.
9. The monument, which is covered on the outside by marble, has also (become) an irreplaceable part of Washington, D.C.'s, skyline.
10. Not surprisingly, thousands of visitors have (pay) the monument a visit since it was opened to the public in 1888.

More Practice

Language Lab
CD-ROM
• Correct and Effective Use of Verbs lesson
On-line
Exercise Bank
• Section 21.1
Grammar Exercise Workbook
• pp. 73–74

▶ **Critical Viewing** The Washington Monument evokes images of an American leader. Similarly, how can the tense of a verb evoke a certain time period in the mind of a reader? **[Relate]**

Verb Conjugation

The *conjugation* of a verb presents all its different forms.

> **KEY CONCEPT** A **conjugation** is a complete list of the singular and plural forms of a verb in a particular tense. ■

The singular forms of a verb correspond to the singular personal pronouns (*I, you, he, she, it*), and the plural forms correspond to the plural personal pronouns (*we, you, they*).

The chart that follows conjugates the irregular verb *to go*. To conjugate a verb, you need the principal parts: the present (*go*), the past participle (*going*), the past (*went*), and the past participle (*gone*). You also need various helping verbs, such as *has, have, or will.*

The chart below conjugates the verb *to go* in its basic forms. Notice that only three principal parts—the present, the past, and the past participle—are used to conjugate all six of the basic forms.

CONJUGATION OF THE BASIC FORMS OF *GO*		
Present	Singular	Plural
First Person	I go	we go
Second Person	you go	you go
Third Person	he, she, it goes	they go
Past		
First Person	I went	we went
Second Person	you went	you went
Third Person	he, she, it went	they went
Future		
First Person	I will go	we will go
Second Person	you will go	you will go
Third Person	he, she, it will go	they will go
Present Perfect		
First Person	I have gone	we have gone
Second Person	you have gone	you have gone
Third Person	he, she, it has gone	they have gone
Past Perfect		
First Person	I had gone	we had gone
Second Person	you had gone	you had gone
Third Person	he, she, it had gone	they had gone
Future Perfect		
First Person	I will have gone	we will have gone
Second Person	you will have gone	you will have gone
Third Person	he, she, it will have gone	they will have gone

Speaking and Listening Tip

People often misuse the past participle of *go*. For example, instead of saying, "I should've gone," they say, "I should've went." To accustom yourself to hearing and using the correct past participle of *go*, team up with a classmate and take turns making up sentences using the perfect tenses in the third column of this chart.

GRAMMAR IN LITERATURE

from **An Arundel Tomb**

Philip Larkin

Notice how the poet has used verbs in different tenses to show events in present, past, and future time.

Time *has transfigured* them into
Untruth. The stone fidelity
They hardly *meant has come* to be
Their final blazon, and to prove
Our almost-instinct almost true:
What *will survive* of us *is* love.

Note About *Be*: The present participle of *be* is *being*. The past participle is *been*. The present and the past depend on the subject and tense of the verb.

PRESENT:	I *am*	we *are*
	you *are*	you *are*
	he, she, it *is*	they *are*
PAST:	I *was*	we *were*
	you *were*	you *were*
	he, she, it *was*	they *were*
FUTURE:	I *will be*	we *will be*
	you *will be*	you *will be*
	he, she, it *will be*	they *will be*

▶ **Exercise 8** **Supplying Conjugated Forms** Complete these sentences with forms of the conjugation of the verb *swim*.
1. Who ___?___? We ___?___. (present tense)
2. You ___?___ yesterday, right? No, they ___?___ yesterday. (past tense)
3. They ___?___ again tomorrow, too, and you ___?___ with them, right? (future tense)
4. You ___?___ with the team on Fridays. (present perfect tense)
5. It ___?___ ___?___ in several meets before the new coach arrived. (past perfect tense)

▶ **Exercise 9** **Conjugating Verbs** Conjugate the verbs below in their basic, progressive, and emphatic forms.
1. bring   3. leave   5. stay
2. believe   4. stride

More Practice

Language Lab
CD-ROM
• Correct and Effective
Use of Verbs lesson
On-line
Exercise Bank
• Section 21.1
Grammar Exercise
Workbook
• pp. 73–76

Section 21.1 *Section Review*

GRAMMAR EXERCISES 10–17

Exercise 10 Identifying Verb Tenses and Their Forms Identify the tense of each verb. Identify its form as well if the form is not basic.

1. Angkor Wat has been one of the most famous Hindu temples in Southeast Asia for more than 800 years.
2. The temple stands sixty meters tall.
3. The people of central Cambodia built Angkor Wat in the twelfth century.
4. Earlier, Cambodians had practiced their religion in smaller temples.
5. People in Southeast Asia have been practicing Buddhism for centuries.

Exercise 11 Identifying Principal Parts and Tenses Identify the principal part used to form each verb; then identify the tense.

1. One of England's most famous attractions *is* the Tower of London.
2. The Tower of London was *built* over many years.
3. After its construction, royal families did *use* the tower as a royal residence.
4. Today, the tower has been *converted* into a museum.
5. Architecture experts will be *restoring* parts of the tower in the future.

Exercise 12 Writing Sentences With Irregular Verbs Write sentences using the verbs in the tenses and forms indicated.

1. read (past perfect)
2. take (future perfect)
3. catch (past emphatic)
4. sit (present perfect)
5. do (future perfect progressive)

Exercise 13 Supplying the Correct Forms of Verbs Write the form of the italicized verb indicated in parentheses.

1. Arlington National Cemetery *be* (present perfect) one of northern Virginia's most popular attractions for decades.
2. Next year, around four million people *visit* (future) Arlington.
3. The cemetery *occupy* (present emphatic) more than 600 acres.
4. Until recently, most of the cemetery *be* (past perfect) devoted to the graves of soldiers who died in combat.
5. In 1932, the government *dedicate* (past) the Tomb of the Unknown Soldier, now the Tomb of the Unknowns.

Exercise 14 Conjugating Verbs On your paper, conjugate these verbs:

1. sing   2. forget

Exercise 15 Find It in Your Reading Reread the excerpt from "An Arundel Tomb" on page 530. Write down the tense of at least three of the verbs.

Exercise 16 Find It in Your Writing Look through your portfolio for a paragraph written in the present tense. Rewrite it first in the past tense and then in the future tense.

Exercise 17 Writing Application Imagine that you are a sportswriter. Write a prediction of how the local team will fare this season. Use at least three of the following verb forms: *past emphatic, present emphatic, present progressive, future progressive, future perfect progressive.*

Section 21.2

The Correct Use of Tenses

The basic, progressive, and emphatic forms of the six tenses show time within one of three general categories: present, past, and future. This section will explain how each verb form has a specific use that distinguishes it from the other forms.

Theme: World Monuments

In this section, you will learn the many uses of verb tenses and forms. The examples and exercises in this section tell more about great monuments around the world.

Cross-Curricular Connection: Social Studies

Present, Past, and Future Time

Good usage depends on an understanding of how each form works within its general category of time to express meaning.

Uses of Tense in Present Time Three different forms can be used to express present time.

KEY CONCEPT The three forms of the present tense show present actions or conditions as well as various continuing actions or conditions. ■

The chart below gives an example of each of these forms:

FORMS EXPRESSING PRESENT TIME	
Present:	I weld.
Present Progressive:	I am welding.
Present Emphatic:	I do weld.

The main uses of the basic form of the present tense are shown in the chart below:

FORMS EXPRESSING PRESENT TIME	
Present action:	The shopper *strolls* down the aisle.
Present condition:	My head *is* aching.
Regularly occurring action:	They frequently *drive* to Maine.
Regularly occurring condition:	This road *is* slippery in winter.
Constant action:	Fish *breathe* through gills.
Constant condition:	Human beings *are* primates.

The present may also be used to express historical events. This use of the present, called the *historical present*, is occasionally used in narration to make past actions or conditions come to life.

THE HISTORICAL PRESENT

Past action expressed in historical present:
In the late 1800's, thousands of immigrants pass through Ellis Island before starting their lives anew in the U.S.

Past condition expressed in historical present:
The exodus of middle-class people from the cities in the 1960's is one of the factors in the decline of urban areas.

The *critical present* is most often used to discuss deceased authors and their literary achievements.

THE CRITICAL PRESENT

Action expressed in critical present:
Dame Agatha Christie writes with a skill that makes her stories classics.

Condition expressed in critical present:
In addition to his novels, Thomas Hardy is the author of several volumes of poetry.

The *present progressive* is used to show a continuing action or condition of a long or short duration.

USES OF THE PRESENT PROGRESSIVE

Long continuing action:	I *am working* at the visitors' center this summer.
Short continuing action:	I *am watering* the plants.
Continuing condition:	Julio *is being* very helpful.

USES OF THE PRESENT EMPHATIC

Emphasizing a statement:	I *do intend* to meet her at the airport.
Denying a contrary assertion:	No, he *does* not *have* the answer.
Asking a question:	*Do* you *guide* people to the pyramids?
Making a sentence negative:	She *does* not *have* our blessing.

Uses of Tense in Past Time There are seven verb forms that express past actions or conditions.

> **KEY CONCEPT** The seven forms that express past time show actions and conditions beginning in the past. ∎

FORMS EXPRESSING PAST TIME	
Past	I drew.
Present Perfect	I have drawn.
Past Perfect	I had drawn.
Past Progressive	I was drawing.
Present Perfect Progressive	I have been drawing.
Past Perfect Progressive	I had been drawing.
Past Emphatic	I did draw.

The uses of the most common form, the past, are shown in the next chart:

USES OF THE PAST	
Completed action:	They halted work on the new bridge.
Completed condition:	Several apartments were empty.

Notice in the chart above that the time of the action or the condition could be changed from indefinite to definite if such words as *last week* or *yesterday* were added to the sentences.

The *present perfect* always expresses indefinite time. Use it to show action or conditions continuing from the past to the present.

USES OF THE PRESENT PERFECT	
Completed action: (indefinite time)	They have befriended us.
Completed condition: (indefinite time)	I have been here before.
Action continuing to present:	It has rained intermittently for two days now.
Condition continuing to present:	I have felt sluggish all day.

The *past perfect* expresses a past action that took place before another.

USES OF THE PAST PERFECT

Action completed before another past action:
Perhaps the nomadic hunters had drawn on the ground before they drew on the cave walls.

Condition completed before another past condition:
Rhoda had been a photographer until she became ill.

These charts show the past progressive and emphatic forms.

USES OF THE PROGRESSIVE FORMS THAT EXPRESS PAST TIME	
Past Progressive	**Long continuing action in the past:** She *was going* to China that year. **Short continuing action in the past:** I *was talking* to Mary when you tried to call. **Continuous condition in the past:** I *was being* honest when I said I was sorry about the incident.
Present Perfect Progressive	**Action continuing to the present:** Edith *has been visiting* more monuments this summer.
Past Perfect Progressive	**Continuing action interrupted by another:** He *had been dreaming* of victory until reality interrupted his dreams.

📖 Journal Tip

The past perfect and past progressive forms often serve as intriguing beginnings to a story. For example, "It had been raining all morning when Jillian first noticed the stranger. . . . " In your journal, jot down several similar sentences. Perhaps one of them will inspire an idea for a short story.

USES OF THE PAST EMPHATIC

Emphasizing a statement:
The cactus *did grow* without any water.

Denying a contrary assertion:
But I *did hike* to the ancient ruins!

Asking a question:
When *did* the United States *recognize* Vietnam?

Making a sentence negative:
He *did* not *appreciate* her hard work.

▶**KEY CONCEPT** The four forms that express future time show future actions or conditions. ■

FORMS EXPRESSING FUTURE TIME	
Future	I will walk.
Future Perfect	I will have walked.
Future Progressive	I will be walking.
Future Perfect Progressive	I will have been walking.

USES OF THE FUTURE AND THE FUTURE PERFECT	
Future	**Future action:** I *will jog* in the morning. **Future condition:** I *will be* late for the meeting.
Future Perfect	**Future action completed before another:** I *will have run* a mile by the time you arrive. **Future condition completed before another:** The orchestra *will have been* on tour for a month before the new concert season begins.

Notice in the next chart that the *future progressive* and the *future perfect progressive* express only future actions.

USES OF THE PROGRESSIVE FORMS THAT EXPRESS FUTURE TIME	
Future Progressive	**Continuing future action:** Rita *will be studying* all weekend.
Future Perfect Progressive	**Continuing future action completed before another:** Sharon *will have been preparing* for ten years before she embarks on her trip around the world.

Note About *Expressing Future Time With the Present Tense:* The basic form of the *present* and the *present progressive* are often used with other words to express future time.

EXAMPLES: The new store *opens* next weekend.
             That family *is leaving* next month for Hawaii.

▶ **Exercise 18** Identifying the Uses of Tense in Present and Past Time Identify the use of the verb in each sentence, using the labels in the charts on pages 532–535.

1. The sphinx is a creature found in Greek and Egyptian mythology.
2. Greeks envision the sphinx as a monster with the head of a woman, the body of a lion, and the wings of a bird.
3. For Egyptians, sphinxes are statues that represent rulers.
4. Egypt is a country in northeast Africa.
5. People from around the world often visit Egypt's many sphinxes.
6. Around 2500 B.C., the ancient Egyptians built the Great Sphinx of Giza.
7. That sphinx stands more than 60 feet high.
8. At this very moment, many people may be visiting sphinxes.
9. The ancient Greek historian Herodotus writes eloquently about Egypt.
10. Do you like the sphinxes of Egypt?

▲ **Critical Viewing** How does this sphinx compare to present-day monuments? Use a different form of a present-tense verb in each sentence. **[Compare and Contrast]**

▶ **Exercise 19** Using Tense in Past Time Write the indicated form of each verb in parentheses.

1. Many people (believe—present perfect) that pyramids are found only in Egypt.
2. In fact, ancient peoples (erect—past) their own pyramids throughout Central America thousands of years ago.
3. The Mayas (build—past) their earliest pyramid in Central America between 600 and 400 B.C.
4. The Mayas (construct—past progressive) four-sided pyramids with flat platforms on the top while ancient Egyptians were building pyramids with four sides that met at a point on the top.
5. Unlike the ancient Egyptians, the Mayas (use—past emphatic) their pyramids as ceremonial platforms.
6. The Mayas (perform—past progressive) elaborate ceremonies on their pyramids when ancient Egyptians were using their pyramids as burial tombs.
7. The Mayas (thrive—past perfect progressive) for many centuries before the arrival of Europeans.
8. People (travel—present perfect) to Mexico to visit these sites for many years.
9. Archaeologists (wonder—present perfect progressive) for a long time just how the Mayas were able to build such formidable structures.
10. (see—past emphatic asking a question) you a Mayan pyramid during your trip to Mexico last year?

▶ **More Practice**

Language Lab CD-ROM
• Correct and Effective Use of Verbs lesson
On-line Exercise Bank
• Section 21.1
Grammar Exercise Workbook
• pp. 77–78

The Correct Use of Tenses • 537

GRAMMAR IN
LITERATURE

from The Canterbury Tales: The Prologue
Geoffrey Chaucer

The verbs highlighted in blue type show the translator's use of the past tense.

A *Doctor* too *emerged* as we *proceeded*;
No one alive could talk as well as he *did*
On points of medicine and of surgery,
For, being grounded in astronomy,
He *watched* his patient's favorable star
And, by his Natural Magic, knew what are
The lucky hours and planetary degrees
For making charms and magic effigies.
The cause of every malady you'd got
He *knew*, and whether dry, cold, moist or hot;
He *knew* their seat, their humor and condition.
He *was* a perfect practicing physician.
These causes being known for what they *were*,
He *gave* the man his medicine then and there.

> **Exercise 20** **Using Tense in Future Time** Write the verb in parentheses in the tense indicated.

1. Downtown, a sign indicates the dedication of the new skyscraper that (take—express future time with present tense) place next year.
2. Everywhere one goes these days, the rate of new construction (increase—express future time with present progressive) rapidly.
3. Improvements in construction materials and methods (continue—future) to change the landscape of modern cities for many years.
4. Architects and city planners (plan—future progressive) great changes for cities like Tokyo, New York, and Chicago in the near future.
5. Towering skyscrapers (serve—future) as monuments to the immense impact of both technology and increased urbanization on the lives of ordinary people worldwide.

> **More Practice**

Language Lab CD-ROM
• Correct and Effective Use of Verbs lesson
On-line Exercise Bank
• Section 21.1
Grammar Exercise Workbook
• pp. 77–78

Sequence of Tenses

A sentence with more than one verb must be consistent in its time sequence.

▶ **KEY CONCEPT** When showing a sequence of events, do not shift tenses unnecessarily. ■

It is, however, sometimes necessary to shift tenses, especially when a sentence is complex or compound-complex. The tense of the main verb often determines the tense of the subordinate verb. Moreover, the form of a participle or infinitive often depends on the tense of the main verb in the sentence.

Verbs in Subordinate Clauses It is frequently necessary to look at the tense of the main verb in a sentence before deciding the tense of the verb in the subordinate clause.

▶ **KEY CONCEPT** The tense of a verb in a subordinate clause should follow logically from the tense of the main verb. ■

As you study the combinations of tenses in the charts that follow, notice that the choice of tenses affects the logical relationship between the events being expressed. Some combinations indicate that the events are *simultaneous*—meaning that they occur at the same time. Other combinations indicate that the events are *sequential*—meaning that one event occurs before or after the other.

▼ **Critical Viewing** Mt. Rushmore honors presidents from different time periods. How can you use verbs to show different time periods within a single sentence? **[Analyze]**

SEQUENCE OF TENSES

Main Verb in Present		
Main Verb	Subordinate Verb	Meaning
I understand. . .	PRESENT that he *writes* novels. PRESENT PROG that he *is writing* a novel. PRESENT EMPH that he *does write* novels.	Simultaneous events: All events occur in present time.
I understand. . .	PAST that he *wrote* a novel. PRESENT PERF that he *has written* a novel. PAST PERF that he *had written* a novel. PAST PROG that he *was writing* a novel. PRESENT PERF PROG that he *has been writing* a novel. PAST PERF PROG that he *had been writing* a novel. PAST EMP that he *did write* a novel.	Sequential events: The writing comes before the understanding.
I understand . . .	FUTURE that he *will write* a novel. FUTURE PERF that he *will have written* a novel. FUTURE PROG that he *will be writing* a novel. FUTURE PERF PROG that he *will have been writing* a novel.	Sequential events: The understanding comes before the writing.
Main Verb in Past		
I understood. . .	PAST that he *wrote* a novel. PAST PROG that he *was writing* a novel. PAST EMP that he *did write* a novel.	Simultaneous events: All events take place in past time.
I understood. . .	PAST PERF that he *had written* a novel. PAST PERF PROG that he *had been writing* a novel.	Sequential events: The writing came before the understanding.

Grammar and Style Tip

When relating the events of a story, generally try to keep your verbs consistently in either past or present tenses to avoid confusing your reader.

Main Verb in Future		
I will understand. . .	PRESENT if he *writes* a novel. PRESENT PROG if he *is writing* a novel. PRESENT EMPH if he *does write* a novel.	Simultaneous events: All events take place in future time.
I will understand. . .	PAST if he *wrote* a novel. PRESENT PERF if he *has written* a novel. PRESENT PERF PROG if he *has been writing* a novel. PAST EMP if he *did write* a novel.	Sequential events: The writing comes before the understanding.

Time Sequence With Participles and Infinitives

Frequently, the form of a participle or infinitive determines whether the events are simultaneous or sequential. Participles can be present *(seeing)*, past *(seen)*, or perfect *(having seen)*. Infinitives can be present *(to see)* or perfect *(to have seen)*.

▶ **KEY CONCEPTS** The form of a participle or an infinitive should set up a logical time sequence in relation to a verb in the same clause or sentence. ■

To show simultaneous events, you will generally need to use the present participle or the present infinitive, whether the main verb is present, past, or future.

SIMULTANEOUS EVENTS	
In Present Time	PRESENT PRESENT *Seeing* the results, she *laughs.* PRESENT PRESENT He *needs to confirm* the results.
In Past Time	PRESENT PAST *Seeing* the results, she *laughed.* PAST PRESENT He *needed to confirm* the results.
In Future Time	PRESENT FUTURE *Seeing* the results, she *will laugh.* FUTURE PRESENT He *will need to confirm* the results.

SEQUENTIAL EVENTS	
In Present Time	PERFECT PRESENT PROG *Having seen* the results, she *is laughing.* (The seeing comes before the laughing.) PRESENT PERFECT He *is* fortunate *to have worked* with you. (The working comes before the being fortunate.)
In Past Time	PERFECT PAST *Having seen* the results, *she laughed.* (The seeing came before the laughing.) PAST PERFECT He *was* fortunate *to have worked* with you. (The working came before the being fortunate.)
Spanning Past and Future Time	PERFECT FUTURE *Having seen* her work, I *will recommend* her. (The seeing comes before the recommending.) FUTURE PERFECT He *will be* fortunate *to have worked* with you. (The working comes before the being fortunate.)

▼ **Critical Viewing**
Scientists used clues to determine that these Easter Island statues were carved between A.D. 1000 and 1600. In addition to verbs, what clues can you look for in a sentence to determine the time period to which it refers? **[Connect]**

To show sequential events, you will generally need to use the perfect form of the participle and infinitive, regardless of the tense of the main verb.

▶ **Exercise 21** Using the Correct Forms of Subordinate Verbs, Participles, and Infinitives Rewrite each sentence, following the instructions in parentheses.

EXAMPLE: The architect was sad he had planned so poorly. (Change *had planned* to a perfect infinitive.)

ANSWER: The architect was sad to have planned so poorly.

1. Many scholars have attempted deciphering the mystery of the large stone monuments on Easter Island. (Change *deciphering* to a present infinitive.)
2. Having seen the stone statues, many visitors are overcome by awe. (Change *having seen* to a present participle).
3. Many visitors feel fortunate to see these stone monuments. (Change *to see* to a perfect infinitive.)
4. Archaeologists have tried finding out just who made these magnificent statues. (Change *finding* to present infinitive.)
5. The statues seem to be carved between A.D. 1000 and 1600. (Change *to be* to a perfect infinitive.)

Exercise 22 **Supplying Correct Verb Tenses** Supply the correct form of the verb indicated to complete each sentence.

1. Joan of Arc is a patron saint of France who (lead) the resistance to the English invasion of France in the Hundred Years War.
2. Joan was born around 1412 and (grow) up on her father's tenant farm.
3. By the time she was thirteen, she already (begin) to believe that her mission was to save France from the English.
4. She (be) still remembered today for her success at the 1429 battle of Orleans, where she led French troops in a miraculous defeat of the English.
5. There is little doubt that French people always (consider) Joan of Arc a great heroine of France.

Exercise 23 **Revising to Correct Errors in Tense** Revise the following sentences, correcting unnecessary shifts in tense. If the tense does not shift, write *correct*.

1. Mount Saint Helens is an active volcano, which *will have been lying* in southwest Washington.
2. Before erupting in 1857, the volcano *have* not *been erupting* for more than 100 years.
3. Not surprisingly, most people *have* not *expected* it to erupt ever again.
4. To the people who used Mount Saint Helens for recreation, it *will have been* simply a pristine mountain.
5. However, on May 18, 1980, the volcano *has erupted* with extreme force, surprising nearby residents.
6. A cloud of ash and gases *had shot up* around 12 miles into the sky.
7. The eruption *comes* as a surprise and *resulted* in great destruction.
8. The eruption *was destroying* much animal and plant life in an area of some 230 square miles.
9. In 1982, the U.S. government *established* the National Volcanic Monument there.
10. Today, the volcano *will be continuing* to have small eruptions.

More Practice
Language Lab
CD-ROM
• Correct and Effective
  Use of Verbs lesson
On-line
Exercise Bank
• Section 21.2
Grammar Exercise
Workbook
• pp. 79–80

Modifiers That Help Clarify Tense

The time expressed by a verb can often be clarified by adverbs such as *always* or *frequently* and phrases such as *last week* or *now and then.*

▶ **KEY CONCEPTS** Use modifiers when they can help clarify tense. ■

EXAMPLES: We read about great monuments *every weekend.*
My brother practices singing *once a week.*

▶ **Exercise 24** Using Modifiers to Improve Meaning
Rewrite each sentence by adding a modifier that indicates time. (*Note:* There are no right or wrong modifiers, but all sentences must make sense once rewritten.)

1. Millions of people travel to Washington, D.C., to visit the city's many famous monuments.
2. Thousands of tourists visit the Washington Monument, the Lincoln Memorial, the Jefferson Memorial, and the Franklin D. Roosevelt Memorial.
3. People take photographs at these and other famous sites in our nation's capital.
4. There are often long lines for tickets to tour the White House.
5. The United States flag is raised outside all memorials and government office buildings.
6. Because we're studying United States history, our class is visiting Washington, D.C.
7. Many of the monuments remind us of the contributions of men who served as president.
8. Other monuments commemorate the sacrifices of men and women who have served during wars.
9. In addition to the monuments and memorials, there are special celebrations.
10. There was an important celebration to honor foreign dignitaries who had come to see the monuments.

▶ **Critical Viewing** Using a modifier to clarify tense, speculate on the number of visitors to the Lincoln Memorial. **[Speculate]**

More Practice

Language Lab CD-ROM
• Correct and Effective Use of Verbs lesson
On-line Exercise Bank
• Section 21.2
Grammar Exercise Workbook
• pp. 79–80

Hands-on Grammar

Two-Way Modifier Slide

Make and use a Two-Way Modifier Slide to see how modifiers clarify the time expressed by a verb. To begin, fold a piece of lined notebook paper in half the long way, and then unfold it. Next, fold the right side of the paper in half to the crease, cut in 1 1/4" on every third line, and unfold. You should have 12 2 1/2" slits. At the top of the left side of the paper, print the title "Present and Past Tenses." Turn the paper over, and print "Future Tenses" at the top of the right side. Then, cut a 2 1/4" x 8 1/2" strip of colored paper, and draw 16 lines across it at 1/2" intervals on both sides. Now, on one side of the strip, write modifiers that would clarify present or past tense verbs: *today, every day, this year, on Monday, last week, yesterday, before dinner,* and so on.

On the other side, write modifiers that would clarify future tense verbs: *tomorrow, next week, in an hour, in 2030, after lunch,* and so on. (Some modifiers will serve all purposes.) Then, weave the strip through the slits, making sure that the "present and past" modifiers face the appropriate head to the left. Finally, on the notebook paper lines parallel to the modifiers, write short sentences using present and past tense verbs on one side and future

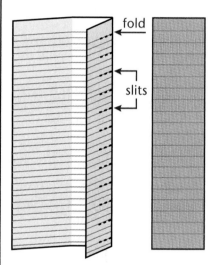

tense verbs on the other. Now, slide the strip of paper through the slits, seeing how many ways the meaning of a sentence can change by adding a modifier. On the "future" side, the modifiers will begin the sentences. Note that not every modifier will work with every sentence.

Find It in Your Reading Look through a recent news article, and note how modifiers are used to clarify the time of the events.

Find It in Your Writing See if you can used modifiers to clarify the times of events in an essay or

Present and Past Tenses	
	Today
Alex is working	This year
Mia made lunch	Yesterday
We play tennis	on Monday

GRAMMAR EXERCISES 25–35

> **Exercise 25** Identifying the Uses of Tense in Present Time Referring to the charts on pages 532–533, identify the use of the verb in each sentence.

1. Pyramids are among the most impressive monuments in the world.
2. Some pyramids in Egypt stand more than 400 feet tall.
3. People are visiting Egyptian pyramids at this very moment.
4. There is a famous group of pyramids near Cairo, Egypt.
5. The Egyptologist Samuel Mercer writes in great detail about the artifacts found in these pyramids.

> **Exercise 26** Supplying Verbs in Past Time On your paper, write the indicated form of each verb in parentheses.

1. From A.D. 532 to 537, during the reign of Emperor Justinian I, thousands of workers (labor—past) to build Hagia Sophia.
2. These workers (complete—past progressive) Hagia Sophia in the Turkish city of Istanbul, which was once known as Constantinople.
3. Hagia Sophia, also known as the Church of Holy Wisdom, (is—present perfect) one of the most famous structures of the Byzantine Empire for nearly 1,500 years.
4. Prior to the completion of the majestic church, worshippers of the Orthodox Christian faith in Constantinople (worship—past perfect progressive) in smaller churches.
5. Hagia Sophia's large size and rich history (establish—present perfect) it as one of the world's most impressive monuments.

> **Exercise 27** Supplying Verbs in Future Time Rewrite each sentence, changing each underlined verb as indicated in parentheses.

1. It is inevitable that the landscape of cities and entire nations changes (future) with the passage of time.
2. By the next century, people establish (future perfect) dozens of monuments.
3. It is likely that people of the future use (future progressive) different materials to create monuments.
4. It is possible that they choose (future) different types of events and people to honor.
5. By the time the next generation is grown, they admire (future perfect progressive) for years the monuments that don't even exist now.

> **Exercise 28** Identifying the Time Sequence in Sentences With More Than One Verb Identify whether the time sequence of events described by the two verbs in each sentence is sequential or simultaneous. If it is sequential, identify which event occurs before the other.

1. Before it became a federal prison, Alcatraz Island served as the site of a military prison from 1868 to 1933.
2. The prison finally closed in 1963, and the island now lures thousands of tourists to its grounds each year.
3. At the time it was a prison, reformers demanded that government officials improve conditions.
4. Soon it will have been forty years since the prison closed.
5. Although it was left empty for many years, the island became a part of the Golden Gate National Recreation Area in 1972.

Exercise 29 Using the Correct Forms of Subordinate Verbs, Participles, and Infinitives On your paper, rewrite the sentences, following the instructions in parentheses.

1. People have long needed reminding themselves of their place in history. (Replace *reminding* with a present infinitive.)
2. Ancient people are known for building structures commemorating important events. (Change *for building* to a perfect infinitive.)
3. Having wanted to show their power, rulers built monuments for themselves. (Change *having wanted* to a present participle.)
4. Creating these monuments often involved the mobilization of thousands of workers. (Change *the mobilization of* to a present participle.)
5. These people worked hard creating astonishingly huge structures. (Change *creating* to a present infinitive.)

Exercise 30 Revising to Correct Errors in Tense Revise these sentences, correcting unnecessary shifts in tense.

1. Monuments provide information and are serving as guideposts in research.
2. Monuments often had been commemorating heroic deeds and people.
3. In ancient times, people built structures that were reminding them of their stories.
4. Monuments had been serving a similar function today.
5. Early this century, entire historic battlefields are being designated as monuments in the United States.

Exercise 31 Revising to Add Modifiers to Enhance Meaning Revise each sentence, adding a modifier to indicate time.

1. Ellis Island was the headquarters of the immigrant processing center.
2. Around twelve million immigrants passed through Ellis Island.
3. Back then, thousands of people from all over the world came to New York.
4. Due to increased use of U.S. Consulates abroad, the United States Immigration Service closed the center.
5. The immigration station on the island was turned into a museum.

Exercise 32 Writing Sentences With Correct Verb Tenses In the tenses given, write sentences on the topic of monuments or tourist attractions,

1. past and past perfect
2. present perfect and past
3. present and future progressive
4. past progressive and past
5. present and future perfect progressive

Exercise 33 Find It in Your Reading Reread the excerpt from "The Canterbury Tales" on page 538. List the verbs that would change if the speaker and doctor were with you now relating the story.

Exercise 34 Find It in Your Writing Looking through your portfolio, find any sentences with more than one verb and check to see that the verbs are correctly sequenced. Rewrite any sentences not consistent in their time sequence.

Exercise 35 Writing Application Write a paragraph about something interesting a friend of yours did. Use at least five verbs in the past tense, and use verbs to show sequential events at least once.

The Subjunctive Mood

There are three *moods,* or ways in which a verb can express an action or condition: indicative, imperative, and subjunctive. The *indicative* mood, the most common, is used to make factual statements ("Karl *is* helpful.") and to ask questions ("*Is* Karl helpful?"). The *imperative* mood is limited to sentences that give orders or directions ("*Be* helpful."). This section will focus on the correct uses of the subjunctive mood.

The Correct Use of the Subjunctive Mood

There are two important differences between verbs in the subjunctive mood and those in the indicative mood. First, in the present tense, third-person singular verbs in the subjunctive mood do not have the usual *-s* or *-es* ending. Second, the subjunctive mood of *be* in the present tense is *be* and in the past tense it is *were,* regardless of the subject.

Indicative Mood	Subjunctive Mood
He *listens* to me.	I suggest that he *listen* to me.
They *are* ready.	He insists that they *be* ready.
She *was* impatient.	If she *were* impatient, she would not be suited for this work.

There are two general uses of the subjunctive mood:

KEY CONCEPT Use the subjunctive mood (1) in clauses beginning with *if* or *that* to express an idea contrary to fact or (2) in clauses beginning with *that* to express a request, a demand, or a proposal. ■

To use the subjunctive mood correctly, you must remember to check the *if* and *that* clauses in your sentences.

Expressing Ideas Contrary to Fact Ideas contrary to fact are commonly expressed as wishes or conditions. Using the subjunctive mood in these situations helps to show that the idea expressed is not now true and may never be true.

EXAMPLES: He wishes that the climate *were* more mild.
He talks about meteorology as if he *were* an expert.

Internet Tip

You can use the Internet to look up weather forecasts. Use key words like *weather report* and *regional weather* in the query field of your search engine.

KEY CONCEPT Not all *if* clauses take a subjunctive verb. If the idea expressed may be true, an indicative form is used.

EXAMPLES: I said that *if* the weather was bad, we'd leave early, so let's go.
You'd know *if* a storm was coming *if* you looked up and saw black clouds.

This use of the indicative in *if* clauses suggests that the ideas expressed could or should be.

Expressing Requests, Demands, and Proposals Most verbs that request, demand, or propose are often followed by a noun clause beginning with *that,* containing a verb in the subjunctive mood.

REQUEST: She requests that we *be* on time for the trip.
DEMAND: It is required that each student *wear* a uniform.
PROPOSAL: He proposed that a motion *be* made to adjourn.

Exercise 36 Using the Subjunctive Mood Rewrite each sentence, changing the verb to the subjunctive mood as necessary. Write *correct* if no change is needed.

EXAMPLE: She wished that she *was* famous.
ANSWER: She wished that she *were* famous.

1. Most people hope that the weather stays pleasant, particularly while they are on vacation.
2. It is proposed that one consults weather forecasts to learn what the weather will be before planning outdoor activities.
3. We suggest that a person heeds the advice of a capable meteorologist.
4. If the future was evident to all, people would have no need for weather forecasts.
5. On the other hand, if it was easier to predict the weather, people would be able to prepare better for extreme weather events like hurricanes, blizzards, and hailstorms.

▼ **Critical Viewing** If you could have a career in weather, what type of "weather person" would you be? Respond using the subjunctive mood. **[Connect]**

More Practice

Language Lab
CD-ROM
• Correct and Effective Use of Verbs lesson
On-line
Exercise Bank
• Section 21.3
Grammar Exercise Workbook
• pp. 81–82

Auxiliary Verbs That Help Express the Subjunctive Mood

Because certain helping verbs suggest conditions contrary to fact, they can often be used in place of the subjunctive mood.

> **KEY CONCEPT** *Could, would,* or *should* can be used to help a verb express the subjunctive mood. ■

The sentences on the left in the chart below have the usual subjunctive form of the verb *be*: *were*. The sentences on the right have been reworded with *could, would,* and *should*.

THE SUBJUNCTIVE MOOD EXPRESSED THROUGH AUXILIARY VERBS	
If the future were clear, we'd act decisively.	If the future <u>could</u> be clear, we'd act decisively.
If someone were to escort her, she would go.	If someone <u>would</u> escort her, she would go.
If you were to move, would you write to me?	If you <u>should</u> move, would you write to me?

> **Exercise 37** Using Auxiliary Verbs to Express the Subjunctive Mood On your paper, rewrite these sentences, replacing the subjunctive verb form with one using an auxiliary.
> 1. If I were able to get the car out of the snowbank, we wouldn't be in this predicament.
> 2. Last winter, John said that he would come and help any time if I were to call him.
> 3. You know, if this weather were to warm up a bit, some of this snow might melt.
> 4. However, if you were to pick up that shovel over there, maybe together we could clear the car.
> 5. I see that you would be happier if I were able to lend a hand.

▶ **Critical Viewing** Using verbs such as *suggest, require, request, propose,* write three sentences that explain how people can protect themselves from a dangerous weather event such as a hurricane. For example: "It is required that people evacuate coastal areas." **[Relate]**

Section
21.3 *Section Review*

GRAMMAR EXERCISES 38–42

▶ **Exercise 38** **Revising to Correct the Mood of Verbs** Rewrite the following sentences, changing verbs to the subjunctive mood as necessary.

1. Even with the emergence of meteorology as a rigorous science, many people still view weather forecasting as if it was a matter of luck or chance.
2. Prior to modern weather forecasting methods, people often recommended that folk methods are used to predict the weather.
3. Predicting weather was an important activity for sailors, since a sea voyage could be disastrous if there was a typhoon.
4. If bad weather was coming, my uncle would know it by the aches in his bones.
5. Actually, today there is a new science called biometeorology, and some scientists now propose that these aches and pains are acknowledged as weather predictors.

▶ **Exercise 39** **Using Auxiliary Verbs to Express the Subjunctive Mood** On your paper, rewrite each of the following sentences using an auxiliary verb to express the subjunctive mood.

1. It is hoped that information about weather and climate be utilized to prepare for trips overseas.
2. For example, a trip to the South Pacific would be less pleasant if a traveler were there during the typhoon season.
3. Most people wish they were able to be spared from disastrous weather calamities like tornadoes and droughts.

4. If you were aware of the weather at your destination, you would have an easier time deciding what to pack.
5. Of course, if you were to study meteorology, you might want to pick a destination with extreme weather.

▶ **Exercise 40** **Find It in Your Reading** Scan a few newspaper or magazine articles, looking for uses (or abuses) of the subjunctive mood. The subjunctive mood is sometimes misused or forgotten when writers are in a hurry. Try to find at least one instance where this mood was used correctly and another where it should have been used but wasn't.

▶ **Exercise 41** **Find It in Your Writing** Look through your writing portfolio to find places where you used the subjunctive mood. If you find any instances where you should have used it but didn't, correct the sentence. If you can find no example, rewrite a paragraph (or create a new one) using at least one instance of the subjunctive mood.

▶ **Exercise 42** **Writing Application** Imagine that you are a meteorologist reporting for your local newspaper. Write a weather forecast for the next five days. Make sure to use the following phrases with a corresponding verb in the subjunctive mood.

1. suggests that
2. seems as if
3. that people be
4. It is recommended that

Voice

This section discusses a characteristic of verbs called *voice*.

> **KEY CONCEPT** **Voice** is the form of a verb that shows whether the subject is performing the action. ■

In English, there are two voices: *active* and *passive*. Only action verbs can indicate the active voice; linking verbs cannot.

Active and Passive Voice

If the subject of a verb performs the action, the verb is *active*; if the subject receives the action, the verb is *passive*.

Active Voice Any action verb can be in the active voice. The action verb may be transitive (that is, it may have a direct object) or intransitive (without a direct object).

> **KEY CONCEPT** A verb is active if its subject performs the action. ■

In both examples below, the subject performs the action. In the first example, the verb *telephoned* is transitive; *team* is the direct object, which receives the action. In the second example, the verb *gathered* is intransitive; it has no direct object.

| ACTIVE VOICE: | The captain *telephoned* the team. |
| | Telegraph messages *gathered* on the desk. |

Passive Voice Most action verbs can also be passive.

> **KEY CONCEPT** A verb is passive if its action is performed upon the subject. ■

In the following examples, the subjects are the receivers of the action. The first example names the performer, the captain, as the object of the preposition *by* instead of the subject. In the second example, no performer of the action is mentioned.

| PASSIVE VOICE: | The team *was telephoned* by the captain. |
| | The telegraph messages *were gathered* into neat piles. |

**Theme:
The Telephone**

In this section, you will learn the forms and uses of the active and passive voices. The examples and exercises in this section are about the telephone.

**Cross-Curricular Connection:
Social Studies**

▲ **Critical Viewing**
In what ways has technology changed the way we use telephones in recent years, and how have our lives changed as a result? **[Analyze, Cause and Effect]**

▶ **KEY CONCEPT** A passive verb is always a verb phrase made from a form of *be* plus the past participle of a verb. The tense of the helping verb *be* determines the tense of a passive verb. ■

The chart below provides a short conjugation in the passive voice of the verb *believe* in the three moods. Notice in the chart that there are only two progressive forms and no emphatic form.

THE VERB *BELIEVE* IN THE PASSIVE VOICE	
Present Indicative	he is believed
Past Indicative	he was believed
Future Indicative	he will be believed
Present Perfect Indicative	he has been believed
Past Perfect Indicative	he had been believed
Future Perfect Indicative	he will have been believed
Present Progressive Indicative	he is being believed
Past Progressive Indicative	he was being believed
Present Imperative	(you) be believed
Present Subjunctive	(if) he be believed
Past Subjunctive	(if) he were believed

▶ **Exercise 43** **Distinguishing Between the Active and Passive Voice** Identify each verb as *active* or *passive.*

1. The telephone makes communication easier.
2. Convenience and efficiency have been delivered by the telephone.
3. The telephone affects life today in many ways.
4. This great device was invented by Alexander Graham Bell more than 100 years ago.
5. In 1876, Bell patented his invention with the United States government.
6. In 1854, the principles behind the transmission of human speech by electronic means had been developed by Charles Bourseul of France.
7. In 1878, the world's first commercial telephone company was opened by entrepreneurs in New Haven, Connecticut.
8. In 1915, a telephone link between New York City and San Francisco was established by engineers.
9. In 1955, engineers placed the first transatlantic telephone cable between Newfoundland, Canada, and Scotland.
10. In the near future, more advances in telephone technology will be made by scientists.

▶ **More Practice**
Language Lab CD-ROM
• Strengthening Sentences lesson
On-line Exercise Bank
• Section 21.4
Grammar Exercise Workbook
• pp. 83–84

> **Exercise 44** Forming the Tenses of Passive Verbs On your paper, conjugate each verb in the passive voice, using the first eight entries in the chart on page 553 as your model.
> 1. confirm (with *it*)
> 2. praise (with *you*)
> 3. prove (with *they*)
> 4. select (with *I*)

Using Active and Passive Voice

As soon as you can distinguish between the active and passive voice, you can use this knowledge to improve your own writing. Most good writers prefer the active voice to the passive voice.

> **KEY CONCEPT** Use the active voice whenever possible. ■

The active voice is usually more direct and economical. The first sentence below is shorter and more direct than the second.

ACTIVE VOICE: Finally, Debbie *repaired* the telephone.

PASSIVE VOICE: Finally, the telephone *was repaired* by Debbie.

The passive voice has two important uses in English:

> **KEY CONCEPTS** Use the passive voice to emphasize the *receiver* of an action rather than the *performer* of an action. Use the passive voice to point out the receiver of an action whenever the performer is not important or not easily identified. ■

RECEIVER EMPHASIZED: Lori *was mystified* by the new computer program.

PERFORMER UNKNOWN: A telegram *was tacked* to the front door.

PERFORMER UNIMPORTANT: The potholes on our street *will be repaired* soon.

> **Exercise 45** Using the Active Voice On your paper, rewrite each of the six sentences in Exercise 43 that have verbs in the passive voice. Change or add words as necessary in order to put each verb in the active voice.

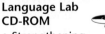

> **More Practice**
>
> **Language Lab CD-ROM**
> • Strengthening Sentences lesson
> **On-line Exercise Bank**
> • Section 21.4
> **Grammar Exercise Workbook**
> • pp. 83–84

GRAMMAR IN LITERATURE

from **Meditation 17**
John Donne

Notice the use of active voice verbs (in blue) and passive voice verbs (in red) in the passage.

. . . when one man *dies*, one chapter *is* not *torn* out of the book, but *translated* into a better language; and every chapter must be so translated; God *employs* several trans-lators; some pieces *are translated* by age, some by sickness, some by war, some by justice; but God's hand is in every translation, and his hand *shall bind* up all our scattered leaves again for that library where every book *shall lie* open to one another.

▶ **Exercise 46** **Revising to Correct Unnecessary Use of the Passive Voice** Rewrite the following sentences, changing the passive voice to active when passive is used. If active voice is used, write *active*.
1. Before the inventions of the telephone and the telegraph, people communicated primarily by mail.
2. In the mid-1800's, a daring attempt to improve mail delivery in the western part of the United States was made by a group of brave people.
3. From April 1860 to October 1861, mail was delivered from Missouri to California by the pony express.
4. Mail sent from Missouri was delivered to Sacramento, California, by the pony express in ten days.
5. Boats ferried mail from Sacramento to San Francisco.

▼ **Critical Viewing** Car phones can be a help and a danger. Explain instances of both, using the active voice and then the passive voice. **[Evaluate]**

Section Review

GRAMMAR EXERCISES 47–52

Exercise 47 Distinguishing Between the Active and Passive Voice On your paper, identify each verb in the following sentences as *active* or *passive*.

1. In 1837, the electric telegraph was invented by the American inventor Samuel F.B. Morse.
2. In 1844, Morse's telegraph was used to send the world's first telegram.
3. The electric telegraph was eventually supplanted by wireless radio-wave transmission and the telephone.
4. In wireless transmission, electromagnetic waves are sent over the airwaves by a system of transmitters.
5. Guglielmo Marconi, an Italian engineer, perfected this radio technology.

Exercise 48 Conjugating Verbs in the Passive Voice On your paper, conjugate each of the following verbs in the passive voice, using the tenses and pronouns given.

1. analyze (present; it, me)
2. spare (past; he, you)
3. show (future; it, them)
4. promote (past perfect; we, him)
5. applaud (future progressive; they, us)

Exercise 49 Using the Active and Passive Voice On your paper, change each sentence in active voice to passive voice and change each sentence in passive voice to active voice.

1. Long ago, people wrote messages on clay tablets or animal hides.
2. Around A.D. 105, papermaking was developed by the Chinese.

3. Paper was introduced to Europe by Moors more than 1,000 years later.
4. Then, in the fifteenth century, a great breakthrough was made in printing by Johann Gutenberg, a German printer.
5. Gutenberg utilized movable type to print books.

Exercise 50 Find It in Your Reading Reread the excerpt from John Donne's "Meditation 17" on page 555. In small groups, discuss the use of active and passive voice. Why is the use of the passive voice effective in a work like this? How does it add to the meaning? In what types of writing would it be less effective?

Exercise 51 Find It in Your Writing Looking through your portfolio, examine your use of passive and active voice. Are there sentences that could be made stronger by switching them to the active voice? Try to find at least one example of each voice, and either explain why the voice used is appropriate or rewrite the sentence to change the voice.

Exercise 52 Writing Application Imagine that you are on your way to an awards show to accept an award for something you have invented. Write an acceptance speech, thanking the people who have supported you over the years. Be sure to use verbs effectively in both the passive voice and the active voice in your speech.

Chapter **21**

Chapter Review

GRAMMAR EXERCISES 53–64

▶ **Exercise 53** Recognizing Verb Tenses and Their Forms On your paper, identify the tense of each italicized verb, and tell whether the form is *basic, progressive,* or *emphatic.*

1. Television *has played* a significant role in the lives of Americans for more than fifty years.
2. In 1927, Philo T. Farnsworth, an American engineer, *developed* the basic elements of an all-electronic television system.
3. It's true that Farnsworth *did invent* the dissector tube, which makes television transmission and reception possible.
4. Farnsworth *had been working* for many years to perfect his invention.
5. By the postwar years, television *was supplanting* radio as the primary source of entertainment in most homes.
6. Just as people *had gathered* around the radio, people began to gather around the television set.
7. In 1955, around 63 percent of American households *owned* a television set.
8. By 1960, that figure *had increased* to around 85 percent.
9. It is likely that future inventors *will be looking* to Farnsworth for inspiration.
10. By the year 2027, people *will have been using* Farnsworth's invention for 100 years.

▶ **Exercise 54** Supplying the Correct Forms of Irregular Verbs On your paper, write the appropriate past or past participle for each verb in parentheses.

1. Around 1500, a German locksmith's invention of the mainspring (bring) about a new timepiece—the watch.
2. The first watches, about 5 inches across and 3 inches deep, were not (wear)—they were carried in the hand.
3. Like clocks of the period, these watches (strike) the hour.
4. However, the owner never (know) the exact time because early watches had only an hour hand.
5. By 1675, the English had (begin) the custom of having a special vest pocket made for their watches.

▶ **Exercise 55** Conjugating Verbs Conjugate the verbs below in their basic, progressive, and emphatic forms in the tenses indicated.

1. plan (present)   2. go (past)

▶ **Exercise 56** Using Tense in Past, Present, and Future Time Write the tense indicated for each verb in parentheses.

1. Before the invention of the hearing aid, people who could not hear well (have—past) few options for improving their hearing.
2. Those who (seek—past perfect) a way to help those with hearing loss were delighted when the hearing aid was invented.
3. Indeed, the hearing aid (change—past emphatic) the way many people deal with hearing loss.
4. For many decades, the simple device (amplify—present perfect progressive) sounds for people who cannot hear well.

5. The hearing aid (make—present perfect) it possible for people with partial to nearly full hearing loss to experience sounds again.
6. Moreover, it (do—present emphatic) so in an unobtrusive way.
7. With incredible ingenuity, engineers (manage—present perfect) to squeeze together the components of a public-address system into a device that fits neatly in or around a person's ear.
8. Thousands of people (hear—present progressive) better because of this wonderful device.
9. Scientists (make—future progressive) additional improvements in aiding those with hearing loss in the future.
10. By the next century, the hearing aid (help—future perfect) millions of people around the world.

▶ **Exercise 57** **Recognizing and Correcting a Sequence of Events** On your paper, identify whether the events described by the verbs in the following sentences describe simultaneous or sequential events. If the events are sequential, identify which action occurred first and which event occurred second.

1. In the 1960's, the U.S. Department of Defense began to search for ways to connect computers to a single network.
2. Recognizing the impressive progress of university research, the U.S. Department of Defense funded research at many university computer science departments.
3. Many of these researchers expected to build a functioning computer network before the 1970's.
4. By the late 1960's, a functioning computer network was built after researchers had experimented greatly.
5. If these researchers had worked less diligently, the Internet would have been developed at a later time.

▶ **Exercise 58** **Using Modifiers to Improve Meaning** On your paper, rewrite the following sentences by adding adverbs or adverb phrases that indicate time.

1. The U.S. Postal Service (USPS) handles millions of pieces of mail every day.
2. The federal postal system, which was created in 1789 by the U.S. Congress, has undergone numerous changes.
3. Mail was carried by stagecoach.
4. To connect people worldwide, the USPS uses airmail.
5. The USPS will make more changes to improve efficiency and service.

▶ **Exercise 59** **Revising to Correct the Mood of Verbs** On your paper, rewrite the following sentences by changing verbs to the subjunctive mood as necessary.

1. Some people talk as if it was only young people using the Internet, but the fastest growing segment of users is people over fifty.
2. This growing segment demands that the Internet meets the needs and interests of an older population.
3. One woman who is sixty said she wished she was a Web site developer.
4. Today, if she was to teach a class, many would be interested in learning what she knows.
5. If someone was developing Web sites, you could be sure that he or she was familiar with the Internet.

▶ **Exercise 60** **Subjunctive and Auxiliary Verbs** Rewrite these sentences using auxiliary verbs to express the subjunctive mood.

1. Many people wish it were easier to learn a foreign language.

2. If such study were encouraged more, perhaps more people would try.
3. If you were to study another language, which would you choose?
4. It might be easier if you were to have a friend learn with you.
5. Imagine what fun you could have if you were able to speak another language fluently!

▶ **Exercise 61** **Using the Active and Passive Voice** Identify the voice of these sentences. Then, rewrite each, changing the active voice to the passive and changing the passive voice to the active.

1. A blind French teenager, Louis Braille, invented an ingenious writing and printing system for the blind.
2. At a school in Paris, Braille was taught by nuns to read by touching raised letters on a page.
3. However, Braille could not distinguish between letters like *O* and *Q*.
4. A better method was developed by Braille to allow blind people to read more easily.
5. In the Braille system, clusters of raised dots are utilized to represent letters, numerals, and punctuation marks.

▶ **Exercise 62** **Revising to Correct Verb Usage** Rewrite the following sentences to correct all improper verb usage.

1. The facsimile transmission process, commonly known as the fax, is transmitting printed material through telephone cables.
2. Prior to the 1980's, people will use facsimile machines primarily for the transmission of news photographs.
3. Everyone said, "If it was faster, more people would use it."

4. With improvements in transmission speed and a decline in cost, the fax machine becomes a staple of businesses in the 1980's.
5. By the 1980's, large businesses routinely have send and receive hundreds of faxes in a typical day.

▶ **Exercise 63** **Writing Application** Imagine that you are an advice columnist for a newspaper. Write a response to a person who has requested your advice about studying for exams. Be sure to use the active voice and the passive voice, as well as the subjunctive mood.

▶ **Exercise 64** **CUMULATIVE REVIEW Verb Usage and Writing Effective Sentences** Revise the following paragraph, correcting errors in verb usage and in sentence structure. Make changes as needed to improve the flow of the sentences.

Computers increasingly part of the communication equation. E-mail and the Internet are important communication tools, but the use of computers is going in so many new directions, that sometimes it's hard to keep up with the latest developments, which have occurred continually. Computers are reading printed matter out loud for those who cannot see using a scanner. Spoken words are being translated by them into characters on a screen for those who cannot hear. Even now, computers can be used like televisions, they can also transmit live video. Some people propose that a computer handles even more complex communication tasks.

Standardized Test Preparation Workshop

Standard English Usage: Using Verbs

Your knowledge of verb usage is often measured on standardized tests. Your ability to determine the correct tense of a verb (present, present perfect, past, past perfect, future, or future perfect or their progressive forms) or the correct mood (indicative or subjunctive) is tested when you must choose a verb or verb phrase to complete a sentence. When choosing a verb, first read the sentence silently to yourself and determine when it is taking place. Then, choose a verb that indicates the same time or tense of the sentence.

The following test items will give you practice with the format of questions that test verb usage.

Test Tip

Look for consistent verb tenses within a passage. If different tenses are used, be sure the sequence makes sense.

Sample Test Items	Answers and Explanations

Directions: Read the passage, and choose the letter of the word or group of words that belongs in each space.
 	
My brother Mark __(1)__ the baseball team since he __(2)__ high school four years ago.
 	
1 A dominates
  B will dominate
  C had dominated
  D has dominated
	The correct answer is *D*. The word *since* at the beginning of the second clause gives a clue that the action is one that began in the past and is continuing in the present; therefore, the present perfect tense is needed.

2 F started
  G had started
  H will have started
  J was starting
	The correct answer is *F, started.* Because the event began and ended in the past, the past tense is used. Answer *G* and *J* are also past tense forms; however, *G* (the past perfect) would be used to indicate an action that preceded another past action, and *J* (past progressive) indicates a continuing action in the past.

▶ **Practice 1** **Directions:** Read the following passage. Choose the letter of the verb or verb phrase that belongs in each space.

Yesterday, the baseball game almost __(1)__ place on time. The league __(2)__ it to start at 3:00 P.M. However, it __(3)__ raining at 11:00, and at 1:00 it __(4)__ down. We __(5)__ to ourselves, "We __(6)__ to play this game."

1 A doesn't take
  B hasn't taken
  C wasn't taking
  D didn't take

2 F had scheduled
  G was scheduling
  H has scheduled
  J had been scheduling

3 A begins
  B began
  C has begun
  D is beginning

4 F will still have been coming
  G still came
  H has still come
  J was still coming

5 A were thinking
  B had been thinking
  C will think
  D will have been thinking

6 F will never have gotten
  G have never gotten
  H will never get
  J were never getting

▶ **Practice 2** **Directions:** Read the following passage. Choose the letter of the verb or verb phrase that belongs in each space.

Tomorrow afternoon, we __(1)__ the second-round tournament game. I __(2)__ for it all week. As a result, I __(3)__ in top condition. The coach said that if I __(4)__ smart, I __(5)__ to bed early tonight. I certainly __(6)__ his advice.

1 A play
  B would play
  C were to play
  D will have been playing

2 F had practiced
  G have been practicing
  H will practice
  J was practicing

3 A will have been
  B had been
  C have been
  D am

4 F was
  G were
  H had been
  J will be

5 A would go
  B will go
  C may go
  D am going

6 F took
  G take
  H have taken
  J will take

22 *Pronoun Usage*

At one time in the English language, the form of both nouns and pronouns was changed according to their use in a sentence. For example, the form that a noun would have as a subject was different from the form it would have as a direct object. Today, the form of a noun is changed only to show possession. There are a variety of forms that indicate how pronouns are used, however.

In this chapter, you will study the various forms of pronouns and the rules that govern their use.

▲ **Critical Viewing** Imagine that you are one of the travelers in the picture. Write a caption for the photo that includes at least three pronouns. **[Analyze]**

Diagnostic Test

Directions: Write all answers on a separate sheet of paper.

Skill Check A. Write the pronoun, and tell whether its case is *nominative*, *objective*, or *possessive*.

1. our atlas
2. sent the map to him
3. dedicated it to the benefactor
4. We consulted the map.
5. your best student

Skill Check B. Identify the case of each underlined pronoun in the following sentences, and tell how it is used in the sentence.

6. My aunt is studying to be a cartographer.
7. She is very interested in maps.
8. The professors at her school have been teaching cartography for several decades.
9. Drawing maps gives her pleasure.
10. The two most diligent students in the class are she and her best friend.
11. They hope that they will earn scholarships.
12. They can use their knowledge to make interesting new maps.
13. They gave me maps to study, too.
14. My aunt bought an atlas for me as a birthday present.
15. Studying the atlas has helped me to get A's on geography tests.

Skill Check C. Write the correct pronoun in parentheses, and identify its function in the sentence or clause.

16. (Who, Whom) gave you the directions to the cartography school?
17. (Who, Whom) are we expecting?
18. Do you know (who, whom) made the first map of your town?
19. From (who, whom) have you received the correct directions?
20. (Who, Whom) will they hire at their school?

Skill Check D. Choose the correct pronoun in parentheses. Then, write any words or phrases that are understood to be included in the sentences.

21. I was less skilled in reading maps than (she, her).
22. The cartography student was as dedicated to making maps as (we, us).
23. The physical features of the Great Lakes were as familiar to the mapmaker as to (I, me)
24. No living cartographer is as famous as (she, her).
25. This collection of maps from ancient Egypt is more important to the students from Cairo than to (we, us).

Case

The only parts of speech that have *case* are nouns and pronouns.

> **KEY CONCEPT** **Case** is the form of a noun or a pronoun that indicates its use in a sentence. ■

The Three Cases

Both nouns and pronouns have three cases, each of which has its own distinctive uses.

> **KEY CONCEPT** The three cases of a noun or pronoun are the *nominative*, the *objective*, and the *possessive*. ■

The uses of the three cases are explained in the following chart.

Case	Use in Sentence
Nominative	Subject of a Verb, Predicate Nominative, or Nominative Absolute
Objective	Direct Object, Indirect Object, Object of a Preposition, Object of a Verbal, or Subject of an Infinitive
Possessive	To Show Ownership

Nouns generally pose no difficulty because their form is changed only to show possession.

NOMINATIVE: The *map* had been hidden for years.
OBJECTIVE: We tried to find the *map.*
POSSESSIVE: The *map's* location could not be determined.

In the first sentence, *map* is nominative because it is the subject of the verb. In the second sentence, *map* is objective because it is the object of the infinitive *to find.* The form changes only in the possessive case when an *'s* is added.

Notice in the chart on the next page that personal pronouns often have different forms for all three cases. The pronoun that you use depends upon its function in a sentence.

Theme: Maps
· · · · · · · · · · · · · · · ·
In this section, you will learn about the three cases of pronouns and their uses. The examples and exercises in this section are about ancient and modern maps.
· · · · · · · · · · · · · · · ·
Cross-Curricular Connection: Social Studies

Nominative	Objective	Possessive
I	me	my, mine
you	you	your, yours
he, she, it	him, her, it	his, her, hers, its
we	us	our, ours
they	them	their, theirs

Exercise 1 **Identifying Case** Write the case of each underlined pronoun. Then, indicate its use in the sentence.

EXAMPLE: The letter was addressed to <u>me</u>.
objective (object of a preposition)

1. Travelers often carry maps and study <u>them</u>.
2. <u>We</u> have been making maps to represent the physical world for thousands of years.
3. Around 1000 B.C., the ancient Babylonians drew circular disks on clay tablets to represent <u>their</u> world.
4. <u>They</u> were among the first mapmakers in history.
5. Around A.D.150, the Greek scientist Ptolemy helped to make advances in mapmaking for <u>his</u> contemporaries.
6. They came to <u>him</u> for information about the natural world.
7. Another important mapmaker of the past was the Muslim scholar Al-Idrisi, who advanced the work of <u>his</u> predecessors.
8. It was <u>he</u> who made one of the first maps of the world.
9. He made many advances in cartography, and later mapmakers admired <u>him</u>.
10. Despite developments in mapmaking, <u>it</u> did not become an exact science until several centuries later.

More Practice

Language Lab CD-ROM
• Nouns and Pronouns lesson
On-line Exercise Bank
• Section 22.1
Grammar Exercise Workbook
• pp. 85–86

▶ **Critical Viewing** What do the different symbols on the map represent? How is the purpose that the symbols serve similar to that served by pronouns? **[Connect]**

The Nominative Case

The nominative case is used when a personal pronoun acts in one of three ways:

KEY CONCEPT Use the **nominative case** for the subject of a verb, for a predicate nominative, and for the pronoun in a nominative absolute. ■

These uses are illustrated in the chart below.

NOMINATIVE PRONOUNS	
As the Subject of a Verb	*I* will consult the map while *she* asks for directions.
As a Predicate Nominative	The finalists were *he* and *she*.
In a Nominative Absolute	*She* having finished the meal, the waiter cleared her table.

You have learned a lot about subjects and predicate nominatives. The third use of nominative case pronouns is a little more unusual. A *nominative absolute* consists of a noun or nominative pronoun followed by a participial phrase. It functions independently from the rest of the sentence.

EXAMPLE: We having opened our textbooks, the geography teacher pointed out the map on page 435.

Nominative Pronouns in Compounds When you use a pronoun in a compound subject or predicate nominative, check the case by mentally removing the other part of the compound or by mentally inverting the sentence.

COMPOUND SUBJECT: The teacher and *I* inspected the map.
(*I* inspected the map.)
His father and *he* sailed the boat.
(*He* sailed the boat.)

COMPOUND PREDICATE NOMINATIVE: The fastest sailors were Jody and *he*.
(Jody and *he* were the fastest sailors.)
The surveyors were Lin and *I*.
(Lin and *I* were the surveyors.)

Nominative Pronouns With Appositives When an appositive follows a pronoun used as a subject or predicate nominative, the pronoun should stay in the nominative case.

SUBJECT: *We* mapmakers are using more technology.

PREDICATE NOMINATIVE: The programmers were *we* seniors.

 **Internet Tip**

The designation ".gov" as part of a Web address lets you know that the Web site is a part of a government organization. Official Web sites of local, state, and federal governments all have the ".gov" designation as part of their addresses.

> **Exercise 2** Choosing Pronouns in the Nominative Case

Choose the pronoun in the nominative case to complete each sentence. Then, write the use of the pronoun.

1. (We, Us) cartographers have been traveling to remote regions for many years.
2. Two veteran explorers and (I, me) traveled to a remote region of the Amazon River to map it.
3. The participants on that trip were they and (I, me).
4. Their understanding of the world was greater than mine, (they, them) having traveled throughout the world.
5. The most inexperienced traveler was (I, me).

> **Exercise 3** Using Pronouns in the Nominative Case Write a nominative pronoun to complete each sentence. Then, write the use of the pronoun.

1. ___?___ students have been admiring the contributions of cartographers since the beginning of civilization.
2. My classmates and ___?___ learned that prehistoric maps may date to around 6200 B.C.
3. ___?___ were amazed to l earn that numerous advances in mapmaking have been made.
4. ___?___ having made many advances in mapmaking, people celebrated their achievements.
5. It was ___?___ who developed latitude and longitude grids to indicate exact locations on the surface of Earth.

> **Exercise 4** Revising Sentences With Pronouns in the Nominative Case Revise these sentences where necessary, correcting errors in pronoun usage. Write *correct* if no revision is needed.

1. Latitude is a system of imaginary lines placed east to west around Earth; it allows you to measure how far a particular location is from the equator.
2. Longitude lines are placed north to south from the North Pole to the South Pole; them help you measure distances east to west or west to east.
3. After several attempts, Joanne and me determined the exact location of the source of the Amazon River.
4. Early cartographers made improvements that were passed on by they to later generations.
5. The Egyptians developed useful mapmaking techniques; some of the best early cartographers were they.

> **More Practice**

Language Lab CD-ROM
• Nouns and Pronouns lesson
On-line Exercise Bank
• Section 22.1
Grammar Exercise Workbook
• pp. 87–88

▼ **Critical Viewing**
Use several pronouns to answer the question: What do the lines that cross this map show? **[Identify]**

The Objective Case

Objective pronouns are used for any kind of object in a sentence as well as for the subject of an infinitive.

KEY CONCEPT Use the **objective case** for the object of any verb, preposition, or verbal or for the subject of an infinitive. ∎

The chart below illustrates the uses of objective pronouns.

OBJECTIVE PRONOUNS	
Direct Object	A piece of plaster hit *him* on the head.
Indirect Object	My uncle sent *me* a lace fan from Hong Kong.
Object of Preposition	Three very tall men sat in front of *us* in the movie theater.
Object of Participle	The sharks following *them* were very hungry.
Object of Gerund	Meeting *you* will be a great pleasure.
Object of Infinitive	I am obligated to help *her* move this Saturday.
Subject of Infinitive	The firm wanted *her* to work the graveyard shift.

Objective Pronouns in Compounds As with the nominative case, errors with objective pronouns most often occur in compounds. To check yourself, mentally remove the other part of the compound.

EXAMPLES: Cracking ice floes alarmed Burt and *him.*
(Cracking ice floes alarmed *him.)*
Sally drew Laurie and me a map to her house.
(Sally drew *me* a map.)

Take special care to use the objective case after the preposition *between.*

INCORRECT: This argument is just between you and *I.*
CORRECT: This argument is just between you and *me.*

Objective Pronouns With Appositives

When a pronoun used as an object or as the subject of an infinitive is followed by an appositive, remember to use the objective case.

EXAMPLES: The mapmaking quiz intimidated *us* students.
She brought *us* amazed nieces a pet iguana from her trip to Central America.
The guide asked *us* stragglers to hurry.

▷ **Exercise 5** Choosing Pronouns in the Objective Case
Choose the pronoun in the objective case to complete each sentence. Then, write the use of the pronoun.
1. Aerial photographs have aided (we, us) cartographers.
2. Taking (I, me) up in the bad weather worried the pilot.
3. We asked (he, him) to fly over the uncharted area.
4. The dangers hovering over (we, us) travelers were great.
5. I informed (he, him) that I needed to take aerial photographs for my sister.

▷ **Exercise 6** Using Pronouns in the Objective Case Complete these sentences by adding objective pronouns.
1. I was determined to take __?__ on the next flight.
2. Asking __?__ to fly with me on a mapping expedition would not be easy.
3. The problem stopping __?__ was a fear of crashing.
4. She remembered that during our last trip, an unexpected air pocket had given __?__ and __?__ a scare.
5. Still, I think that she secretly wanted __?__ to invite her to join the flight

▼ **Critical Viewing**
If you were in a plane looking down on this landscape, how would you describe the experience? What pronouns would you use? [Describe]

▷ **Exercise 7** Revising a Paragraph With Pronouns in the Objective Case Correct the errors in pronoun usage. Write *correct* if no change is needed.

(1) In school today, my geography teacher showed we several topographical maps. (2) She asked Charlayne and me to point out some of the features on the maps. (3) Examining they carefully, we were able to point out such features as hills, valleys, lakes, and streams. (4) Helping us was a key located at the bottom of each map. (5) We students in the geography class will be expected to create a topographical map of our county.

▷ **More Practice**

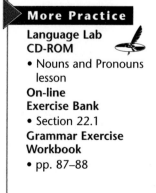

Language Lab CD-ROM
• Nouns and Pronouns lesson
On-line Exercise Bank
• Section 22.1
Grammar Exercise Workbook
• pp. 87–88

The Possessive Case

Although errors are less common in the possessive case than they are in the other two cases, you should take care to use the possessive case before gerunds. A *gerund* is a verbal form ending in *-ing* that is used as a noun.

▶ **KEY CONCEPT** Use the possessive case before gerunds. ■

EXAMPLES: *Your* tracing of the map was sloppy.
We objected to *his* insinuating that we were lazy.
Ms. Malin insists on *our* attending her slide presentation.

Another mistake to avoid is using an apostrophe with possessive pronouns, which already show ownership. Spellings such as *her's, our's, their's,* and *your's* are incorrect. In addition, do not confuse a possessive pronoun with a contraction that sounds almost the same. *It's* (with an apostrophe) is the contraction for *it is* or *it has*. *Its* (without the apostrophe) is a possessive pronoun that means "belonging to it." *You're* is a contraction of *you are*; the possessive form of *you* is *your*.

POSSESSIVE PRONOUNS: The map had served *its* purpose.
The students displayed *their* maps.

CONTRACTIONS: *It's* not likely that we will become lost.
You're the only ones who refused to consult the map.

▼ **Critical Viewing** Describe this map using pronouns in at least two different cases. **[Describe]**

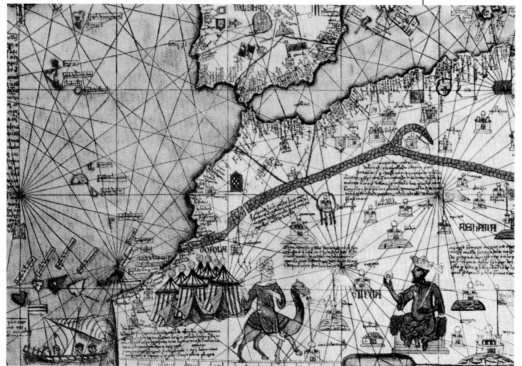

GRAMMAR IN
LITERATURE

from **The Canterbury Tales: The Nun's Priest's Tale**
Geoffrey Chaucer

Notice how the poet has used pronouns in all three cases in the passage. Which of the pronouns in blue type are in the nominative, objective, or possessive case?

"This man as *he* lay sleeping, *it* would seem,
Just before dawn had an astounding dream.
He thought a man was standing by *his* bed
Commanding *him* to wait, and thus *he* said:
'If *you* set sail tomorrow as *you* intend
You will be drowned. *My* tale is at an end.'"

Exercise 8 **Using Pronouns in the Possessive Case** Choose the correct word in each set of parentheses.
1. If (your, you're) looking for an interesting world map, you should consult this book.
2. The history of mapmaking is filled with (it's, its) share of innovators.
3. These innovators used (they're, their) talents to improve existing maps and to create new maps.
4. (Their, Them) experimenting with new mapmaking techniques helped to change the way people viewed the world.
5. Gerardus Mercator was profiled in (your, you're) geography book.

Exercise 9 **Revising Sentences With Pronouns in the Possessive Case** Revise these sentences where necessary to correct errors in pronoun usage. Write *correct* if no revision is needed.
1. Mercator, who lived in the 1500's, sought to improve the maps of he's era.
2. He is known for his' unique system of drawing maps over grids of lines.
3. This type of map became popular because its easy to use.
4. Ms. Lassiter supervised us posting of the class maps on the school Web site.
5. Her specifying dates for completing each part of the assignment forced us to stay on schedule.

More Practice

Language Lab
CD-ROM
• Nouns and Pronouns lesson
On-line
Exercise Bank
• Section 22.1
Grammar Exercise
Workbook
• pp. 89–90

Hands-on Grammar

Pronoun Sentence Slide

To help you see how the use of a pronoun in a sentence determines its case, complete the following activity. Fold a sheet of paper in half lengthwise. Make several cuts, approximately 2 inches apart, from the fold to the open edge. Do not cut all the way to the open edge.

Next, cut from index cards or construction paper pronoun slides. For each pronoun, cut one card as shown. On one side of the card, write the nominative case. On the other side, write the objective case.

Unfold the paper, and write a sentence along each cut. Use a proper noun at each end of the sentence—in some sentences, have the second proper noun be the subject of a clause; in others, the object. Both nouns should be the same number and gender. Use the pronoun slide to cover and replace the noun acting as the subject. Then, slide the pronoun to the other end of the sentence to replace the object. Flip the card to show the objective case.

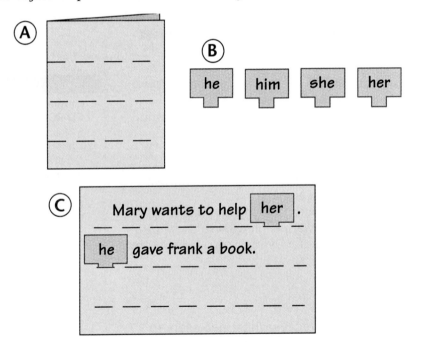

Find It in Your Reading Prepare additional slide sheets to do this activity with sentences from a short story or novel you are currently reading.

Find It in Your Writing Choose from your portfolio a piece of writing in which you use many pronouns. Revise sentences to eliminate any errors in pronoun usage.

Section Review

GRAMMAR EXERCISES 10–15

Exercise 10 Identifying Case
Write the case of each underlined pronoun. Then, write its use.

1. I saw a time-zone map in <u>my</u> planner.
2. This map shows <u>me</u> what time it is in different parts of the world.
3. <u>We</u> having brought up the subject, our teacher discussed time zones.
4. <u>Our</u> asking her prompted an interesting discussion.
5. She started by providing some background information for <u>us</u> students.
6. In 1884, an international conference proposed <u>its</u> system for twenty-four time zones.
7. Look in the mid-Pacific Ocean, and <u>you</u> can locate the International Date Line.
8. This line was <u>their</u> marker for where each day began.
9. As travelers go eastward, the system requires <u>them</u> to adjust their watches forward.
10. The first people on our plane to adjust their watches were Helene and <u>she</u>.

Exercise 11 Using Pronouns
Choose the correct pronoun to complete each sentence. Then, identify its use.

1. Most cities with public transit systems provide maps for (we, us) riders.
2. Bus and subway maps help (we, us) to plan the easiest and fastest routes.
3. To assist riders, maps also show (they, them) where to make bus transfers.
4. Mapmakers hope (we, us) will consult their maps more frequently.
5. However, reading (they, them) is often difficult and confusing.

Exercise 12 Correcting Errors in Pronoun Usage Revise the following sentences as necessary to correct errors in pronoun usage. Write *correct* if no revision is needed.

1. Us requesting better maps may lead to improvements.
2. The Transit Authority asked Jill and me to serve on a riders' council.
3. Between her and I, we came up with twelve suggestions.
4. The only people to challenge our suggestions were them.
5. In the end, the Transit Authority was grateful for we help.

Exercise 13 Find It in Your Reading In these lines from *The Canterbury Tales*, label at least two pronouns in each case and tell how each is used. Then, rewrite the lines, changing the male pronouns to female pronouns.

"He woke and told his friend what had
  occurred
And begged him that the journey be
  deferred
At least a day, implored him not to start.
But his companion, lying there apart,
Began to laugh and treat him to derision.
'I'm not afraid,' he said, 'of any vision, . . .'"

Exercise 14 Find It in Your Writing In your portfolio, find two examples of pronouns in each of the three cases. Check to make sure each is used correctly. Then, write down each pronoun, its case, and its use in the sentence.

Exercise 15 Writing Application
Write a short letter describing a real or imaginary adventure you had that involved following a map. Be sure to describe the adventure using pronouns in all three cases. Circle each pronoun in your letter.

Special Problems With Pronouns

Choosing the correct form of a pronoun is not always a matter of choosing the form that sounds correct. For example, would it be correct to say, "John is smarter than *me*"? Though the sentence may sound right to you, it is incorrect because an objective pronoun has been used when a nominative one is needed. Several words are understood in the sentence, which reads, in full, "John is smarter than I (am)."

This section will discuss two special pronoun problems: the proper uses of *who* and *whom* and the use of pronouns in clauses where some words are omitted but understood.

Using *Who* and *Whom* Correctly

In order to decide when to use *who* or *whom* and the related forms *whoever* and *whomever*, you need to know how the pronoun is used in a sentence and what case is appropriate.

▶ **KEY CONCEPT** *Who* is used for the subjective case. *Whom* is used for the objective case. ■

The chart below shows the forms and uses of these pronouns.

CASE	PRONOUNS	USE IN SENTENCES
Nominative	who, whoever	Subject of a Verb Predicate Nominative
Objective	whom, whomever	Direct Object Object of a Verbal Object of a Preposition Subject of an Infinitive
Possessive	whose, whosever	To Show Ownership

Note About *Whose*: Do not confuse the possessive pronoun *whose* with the contraction *who's*, which means "who is" or "who has."

POSSESSIVE PRONOUN: *Whose* umbrella is this?

CONTRACTION: *Who's* taken my umbrella?

The nominative and objective cases are the real source of problems. Get into the habit of analyzing the structure of your sentences when you use these pronouns. There are two kinds of sentences in which these pronouns can appear: direct questions and complex sentences.

Theme: Whales

In this section, you will learn how to determine which pronouns to use in certain problem situations. The examples and exercises are about types of whales.

Cross-Curricular Connection: Science

Technology Tip

Because a computer spell-check feature may not discern between *whose* and *who's,* remember that *whose* is possessive and *who's* means "who is."

In Direct Questions *Who* is the correct form when the pronoun is the subject of a simple question. *Whom* is the correct form when the pronoun is the direct object, object of a verbal, or object of a preposition. A question in the normal subject-verb order will always correctly begin with *who*.

EXAMPLE: *Who* wants a free ticket to the whaling museum?

A question in inverted order will never correctly begin with *who*. To see if you should use *whom* instead of *who*, reword the question as a statement. If you change the order of the words, you often find that you need to use *whom*.

EXAMPLES: *Whom* were you discussing?
(You were discussing *whom*.)
Whom did you take with you?
(You did take *whom* with you.)

In Complex Sentences Choosing the correct case of *who* and *whom* is easier if you remember that the pronoun's use within the subordinate clause determines its case.

EXAMPLE: They screened *whoever* applied for the scholarship.

In the example above, the pronoun appears to be the direct object of *screened*. A closer look at the pronoun's position, however, reveals that it is the subject of the subordinate clause *whoever applied for the scholarship*. Thus, the nominative form *whoever* is correct. The entire subordinate clause is the direct object of the sentence.

Follow these steps to see if the case of a pronoun in a subordinate clause is correct. First, isolate the subordinate clause. (If the complex sentence is a question, rearrange it in normal subject-verb order.) Second, if the subordinate clause itself is inverted, rearrange the words in their usual order. Finally, determine the pronoun's use within the subordinate clause.

EXAMPLE: *Who*, may I ask, has seen a whale?
Reworded sentence: I may ask *who* has seen a whale.
Use of pronoun: subject of the verb *has seen*

EXAMPLE: Is the tall man the one *whom* they selected to captain the ship?
Reworded clause: They selected *whom* to captain the ship.
Use of pronoun: object of *selected*

▼ **Critical Viewing**
Pose several questions about this whale show, using either *who* or *whom* in each question. **[Analyze]**

More Practice

Language Lab CD-ROM
• Nouns and Pronouns lesson

On-line Exercise Bank
• Section 22.2

Grammar Exercise Workbook
• pp. 91–92

Exercise 16 Using *Who* and *Whom* Correctly in Questions
On your paper, write the correct pronoun in each sentence.
1. (Who, Whom) would like to learn about whales?
2. (Who, Whom) is hoping to go on the whaling expedition?
3. From (who, whom) did you borrow the book about whales?
4. (Who, Whom) did you contact for information?
5. (Who, Whom) told you that a whale's heart rate slows when it dives to the depths of the ocean?

Exercise 17 Using *Who* and *Whom* Correctly in Clauses
On your paper, write the subordinate clause in each sentence. Then, indicate how the form of *who* or *whom* is used.
1. Do you know who wrote the book *Moby-Dick*?
2. It is about a sea captain who is obsessed with killing a giant sperm whale.
3. That sea captain is not the only person for whom killing whales is a goal.
4. Many whalers whom we have met hunt whales for money.
5. They sell parts of the whales they catch to whoever offers them a good price.

Exercise 18 Revising to Correct Errors in the Use of *Who* and *Whom* Revise the following sentences as necessary to correct errors in pronoun usage. Write *correct* if no revision is needed.
1. With who are you doing the assignment?
2. Whom has been the whale's most threatening predator?
3. Whom should we ask about efforts to save whales?
4. By who were the pictures of whales taken?
5. The world's leading expert on whales is whom?
6. Whalers are opposed by those whom want to help preserve whales and conserve the environment.
7. Whoever I ask insists that whales are highly intelligent and communicative.
8. An oceanographer whom I interviewed described the song of the humpback whale.
9. The scientist is working with a navy team who are studying whale communication.
10. Team members, who are based in Hawaii, made recordings of whale songs.

▼ **Critical Viewing** Describe your feelings about whale hunters and those opposed to them. Use *who* in one sentence and *whom* in another. **[Analyze]**

GRAMMAR IN
LITERATURE

from **Paradise Lost**
John Milton

John Milton published the first edition of Paradise Lost *in 1667, not long after England had endured eighteen years of war and several changes of government. In his epic, Milton seems to have his nation's strife in mind as he offers a poetic explanation for the suffering and unhappiness in the world. Notice in this excerpt how Milton has used* whom *rather than* who *in the passage. How is* whom *used?*

Titanian, or Earthborn, that warred on Jove,
Briareos or Typhon, *whom* the den
By ancient Tarsus held, or that sea beast
Leviathan, which God of all his works
Created hugest that swim the ocean stream: . . .

Pronouns in Elliptical Clauses

An *elliptical clause* is one in which some words are omitted but still understood. Errors in pronoun usage can easily be made when an elliptical clause that begins with *than* or *as* is used in making a comparison.

▶ **KEY CONCEPT** In elliptical clauses beginning with *than* or *as,* use the form of the pronoun that you would use if the clause were fully stated. ■

The case of the pronoun depends on whether the omitted words belong after or before the pronoun. The omitted words in the examples below are supplied in brackets.

WORDS LEFT OUT
AFTER PRONOUN: Ray is as dedicated as *he.*
                 Ray is as dedicated as he [is].

WORDS LEFT OUT
BEFORE PRONOUN: You gave Lewis more than *me.*
                  You gave Lewis more than [you gave] me.

Mentally add the missing words. If they come after the pronoun, choose a nominative pronoun. If they come before the pronoun, choose an objective pronoun.

CHOOSING A PRONOUN IN ELLIPTICAL CLAUSES

1. Consider the choices of pronouns: nominative or objective.
2. Mentally complete the elliptical clause.
3. Base your choice on what you find.

As you can see in the examples below, the case of the pronoun can sometimes change the entire meaning of the sentence.

NOMINATIVE PRONOUN:	He liked whales more than *I.*
	He liked whales more than I [did].
OBJECTIVE PRONOUN:	He liked whales more than *me.*
	He liked whales more than
	[he liked] me.

▶ **Exercise 19** **Identifying the Correct Pronoun in Elliptical Clauses** Rewrite each sentence, choosing one of the pronouns in parentheses and completing the elliptical clause.

EXAMPLE: She wrote a better report on whales than (I, me)
ANSWER: She wrote a better report on whales than I did.

1. Your science teacher can help you learn more about whales than (I, me).
2. The need to preserve whales is more pressing to them than (she, her).
3. Studying whales can actually help us learn more about us than (they, them).
4. In many ways, whales behave as (we, us) human beings.
5. Whales can be as nurturing as (we, us).

▶ **Exercise 20** **Supplying Correct Pronouns in Elliptical Clauses** Complete each sentence by supplying the appropriate nominative or objective pronoun.

1. Whales are as well suited to their surroundings as ___?___ to ours.
2. Because they rely more on their hearing than ___?___ humans, whales can navigate through dark waters.
3. Whales can move in the dark better than you or ___?___ because they use sound to navigate.
4. The biologist cares more about whales than ___?___.
5. Whales are less interesting to me than ___?___.

More Practice

Language Lab
CD-ROM
• Nouns and Pronouns
  lesson
On-line
Exercise Bank
• Section 22.2
Grammar Exercise
Workbook
• pp. 91–92

Section Review

GRAMMAR EXERCISES 21–27

> **Exercise 21** Using *Who* and *Whom* in Questions Write the pronoun that completes each question.

1. To (who, whom) did you send the article about the history of whaling?
2. (Who, Whom) told you about the whaling museum in Massachusetts?
3. With (who, whom) are you sitting on the class trip to the museum?
4. The most interested visitors to the museum were (who, whom)?
5. (Who, Whom) did the teacher ask to narrate our slides of the trip?

> **Exercise 22** Using *Who* and *Whom* in Clauses Complete each sentence by choosing the correct pronoun.

1. We aren't sure (who, whom) first wrote about whales and their social habits.
2. Anyone (who, whom) likes science will enjoy learning about whales.
3. That's the oceanographer (who, whom) they visited in the Arctic.
4. He is the one (who, whom), I heard, had been studying beluga whales.
5. Those are the scientists (who, whom) have been studying white whales.

> **Exercise 23** Using Pronouns in Elliptical Clauses Complete each sentence by choosing the correct pronoun.

1. Whalers of the 1800's were more skilled with boats than (we, us).
2. The average whaler was a better sailor than you and (I, me).
3. Sailing was a more vital skill to them than to (we, us).
4. Most people today know far less about whales than (they, them).
5. No one enjoyed *Moby-Dick* more than (I, me).

> **Exercise 24** Revising to Correct Special Problems With Pronouns Revise this passage, correcting errors in pronoun usage.

Whom would be interested in going on a whale-watching trip? I know that no one is more interested in the trip than me. The people who went on an earlier trip had a great time. Based on what they told me, I think that whomever isn't going is crazy.

> **Exercise 25** Find It in Your Reading How are *who* and *whom* used in this passage from *Paradise Lost*?

. . . Be it so, since he
Who now is sovereign can dispose and
    bid
What shall be right: farthest from him is
    best,
Whom reason hath equaled, force hath
    made supreme
Above his equals.

> **Exercise 26** Find It in Your Writing Look through your portfolio, and identify five sentences or questions in which you have used *who* or *whom*. Make sure you used the pronouns correctly.

> **Exercise 27** Writing Application Imagine that you are interviewing a nineteenth-century whaling captain. Write five to ten questions and answers from your interview. Use *who, whom, whoever,* and *whomever* at least once. Include at least one elliptical clause.

Chapter Review

GRAMMAR EXERCISES 28–37

▶ **Exercise 28** **Identifying Cases of Pronouns** On your paper, write the case of each underlined pronoun. Then, write its use.

1. My brother bought <u>his</u> friend expensive perfume made with ambergris.
2. He thought she would be thrilled to receive <u>it</u>.
3. Instead, <u>she</u> became extremely upset.
4. She could not believe that <u>he</u> would purchase something made from a whale.
5. My brother should have realized that he had insulted his friend, <u>she</u> having worked for years to protect whales.
6. The impact of his blunder hit <u>him</u> two days later.
7. She sent <u>him</u> a brochure from a conservation organization.
8. Attached was a letter from <u>her</u> that explained her concerns about animals.
9. The brochure writers noted <u>their</u> worries about the future of some whales.
10. It is <u>they</u>, the brochure warns, that may become extinct someday.

▶ **Exercise 29** **Using Pronouns Correctly** On your paper, write the appropriate pronoun in the following sentences. Then, write its use.

1. (We, Us) humans have been hunting whales for hundreds of years.
2. In the nineteenth century, whalers hunted (them, they) for oil and whalebone.
3. Because the whales were heavily hunted, (they, them) soon disappeared from many ocean areas.
4. Their diminishing numbers alarmed (we, us) environmentalists.
5. (They, Them) having noticed the problem, other people decided to help.

▶ **Exercise 30** **Revising to Correct Errors in Pronoun Usage** Revise these sentences as necessary to correct errors in pronoun usage. Write *correct* if no revision is needed.

1. The people most concerned with improving conditions are us.
2. Have we spoken with you and her about the Endangered Species Act?
3. You being interested is certain to enhance our work.
4. The beneficiaries of today's conservation efforts will be you and me.
5. What would the impact of a world without these magnificent creatures be on we human beings?

▶ **Exercise 31** **Adding Possessive Pronouns or Contractions to Sentences** On your paper, rewrite each sentence, supplying a possessive pronoun or a contraction to fill the blank.

1. The whale's large size makes ___?___ movements relatively easy to follow in captivity.
2. However, their size helps scientists only slightly when ___?___ studying whales in the vast oceans of the world.
3. Whales are fascinating to study because of ___?___ large brains.
4. ___?___ probably wondering just how large a whale's brain is.
5. The brain of an average adult blue whale weighs up to twenty pounds, or more than six times the weight of ___?___ brain.

▶ **Exercise 32** **Using *Who* and *Whom* Correctly** Write the correct pronoun from each set of parentheses in the following sentences.

1. (Who, Whom) is reading the book on beluga whales?
2. (Who, whom) did you ask?
3. With (who, whom) are you working on the whale project?
4. To (who, whom) should we direct our questions about the life span of the beluga whale?
5. The best person to letter the posters is (who, whom)?

Exercise 33 Identifying Subordinate Clauses in Sentences On your paper, write the subordinate clause in each sentence. Then, write how the form of *who* is used in the clause.

1. We are not sure who will be coming to the marine biology exhibit.
2. We have invited only people whom we greatly admire.
3. Most of the guests are oceanographers who have accomplished great things in their field.
4. They are certain to impress whomever they meet.
5. After the exhibit, we will interview whoever has time to answer questions.

Exercise 34 Using Pronouns in Elliptical Clauses On your paper, write two versions of each elliptical sentence— one for each pronoun in parentheses. Include the words that are understood in each version.

1. My brother Rodrigo likes whales more than (I, me).
2. Sometimes, I suspect that he would enjoy living with whales more than (we, us).
3. He does spend more time with books about whales than (we, us).
4. He told me that whales can communicate more clearly with each other than (we, us).
5. My annoying sister says Rodrigo looks more similar to a whale than (we, us).

Exercise 35 Revising to Correct All Types of Errors in Pronoun Usage Copy the paragraph below on a separate sheet of paper. Revise by correcting errors in pronoun usage.

The ocean has long captured the imagination of we writers. Two prominent novelists for who the sea was important were Herman Melville and Ernest Hemingway. Hemingway's fisherman in *The Old Man and the Sea* is memorable; no character is more touching than him. Hemingway was familiar with whoever he was writing about, him having lived and fished in Cuba for many years. In *Moby-Dick*, Melville's sea captain's struggle is both with himself and with a giant whale who is called Moby-Dick.

Exercise 36 Writing Application Write a paragraph about an animal that interests you. Use pronouns in all three cases in your paragraph, and include either *who* or *whom* in at least one sentence. Underline the pronouns you use.

Exercise 37 CUMULATIVE REVIEW Effective Sentence, Verb, and Pronoun Usage Rewrite the following paragraph, correcting any errors in verb and pronoun usage.

(1) My aunt and uncle took they're last vacation on a freighter. (2) They boarded the boat in San Diego, sailed to Hawaii, and then continue on to Japan. (3) Over three months. (4) The trip was exciting it was also hard work. (5) The captain expected they to help the crew load and unload cargo. (6) My uncle even assist with the cooking. (7) My aunt wanted to learn how to tie knots she did. (8) She has teached me how to tie knots, too. (9) Brought me many gifts. (10) If I was older, I'd be able to go on a trip like there's.

Standardized Test Preparation Workshop

Pronoun Usage

Standardized tests measure your knowledge of the rules of standard grammar, such as correct pronoun usage. Questions test your ability to use the three cases of personal pronouns correctly. When answering these questions, determine what type of pronoun is needed in the sentence—nominative case pronouns are used as subjects or predicate pronouns; objective case pronouns are used as direct objects, indirect objects, or objects of prepositions; and possessive case pronouns are used to show ownership.

The following test item will give you practice with the format of questions that test your knowledge of pronoun usage.

Test Tip

A possessive pronoun will never have an apostrophe or change form. The possessor in the sentence always determines possessive case pronouns.

Sample Test Items

Directions: Read the passage, and choose the letter of the word or group of words that belongs in each space.

Lou and ___(1)___ tried out for the lead role in our school play. I automatically assumed the role would be ___(2)___ .

1 A I
   B me
   C her
   D us

2 F my
   G mine
   H ours
   J him

Answers and Explanations

The correct answer is *A*. Because the pronoun is part of a compound subject, a nominative case pronoun is the correct choice. Therefore, the pronoun *I* best completes the compound subject.

The correct answer is *G*. Because the sentence shows ownership, a possessive case pronoun is the correct choice. Therefore, the pronoun *mine* best completes the sentence.

▶ **Practice 1** **Directions:** Read the passage, and choose the letter of the word or group of words that belongs in each space.

The director, Mr. King, said it wasn't an easy decision for ___(1)___ to make. I thought I'd get it, but he chose Lou, ___(2)___ also deserved it. ___(3)___ had more acting experience than I did. I got the role of understudy, and as the rehearsals progressed, ___(4)___ director was pleased. He said he felt confident that either of ___(5)___ could play the lead well.

1 **A** us
   B he
   C me
   D him

2 **F** whom
   G who
   H they
   J we

3 **A** They
   B Him
   C He
   D I

4 **F** its
   G her
   H their
   J our

5 **A** us
   B whom
   C our
   D they

▶ **Practice 2** **Directions:** Read the passage, and choose the letter of the word or group of words that belongs in each space.

On opening night, Mr. King gave a gift to both Lou and ___(1)___ . Lou said it was one of the nicest things anyone had ever done for ___(2)___ . One night, Lou was out with the flu, so ___(3)___ had to replace him. I've never been so nervous in all ___(4)___ life. But the audience loved it. ___(5)___ applause lasted through two curtain calls!

1 **A** me
   B she
   C I
   D her

2 **F** them
   G him
   H us
   J he

3 **A** they
   B I
   C we
   D me

4 **F** our
   G their
   H his
   J my

5 **A** Her
   B Its
   C Their
   D Our

Agreement

When the ancient Egyptian pyramids were constructed, each stone had to fit perfectly into the next. Similarly, when you write a sentence, you need to make sure that all of the words fit together just right. For the words in a sentence to fit together properly, the subject and verb must agree, and any pronouns and antecedents must also agree. In this chapter, you will review the rules of agreement and see how to apply these rules to your writing.

▲ **Critical Viewing**
Think of a sentence that gives historical information about this pyramid. What are the subject and verb of your sentence? How do they agree in number? **[Classify, Distinguish]**

Diagnostic Test

Directions: Write all answers on a separate sheet of paper.

Skill Check A. Choose the verb in parentheses that agrees with the subject in each sentence.

1. The pyramids at Giza (is, are) among the most famous attractions in the world.
2. The Sphinx and the Great Pyramid (is, are) located at Giza.
3. Over the centuries, the pyramids (has, have) experienced decay and abuse.
4. The forces of nature (has, have) been difficult to control.
5. Desert winds and the hot sun (erodes, erode) the pyramids.
6. While nature is one enemy, another (is, are) people.
7. For centuries, grave robbers (has, have) stolen treasures from the pyramids.
8. The Turks, who invaded Egypt in the early 1500's, (was, were) responsible for using the Sphinx for target practice.
9. Tourists to Egypt, who (arrives, arrive) by the thousands, are also responsible for causing damage.
10. Neither signs nor a guard (deters, deter) tourists from climbing the pyramids.
11. Not all tourists who (enters, enter) a pyramid show respect for the site.
12. (There's, There are) other issues affecting the preservation of the pyramids.
13. What (has, have) been the impact of air and noise pollution?
14. Experts on the environment (agrees, agree) that pollution from vehicles and vibrations from traffic are eroding the pyramids.
15. A joint committee of Egyptian government leaders, scientists, and archaeologists (is, are) trying to remedy the problems.

Skill Check B. Choose the correct pronoun in each sentence.

16. The government has (its, their) problem of reducing pollution.
17. The joint committee offered (its, their) own suggestions, too.
18. According to the new plan, most people must make (its, their) trips to the pyramids in electric buses.
19. The tourist who tries to take (his or her, their) car to a pyramid site will be turned back.
20. This plan met with the approval of my father and (me, myself).

Skill Check C. Rewrite the following sentences, correcting the vague, ambiguous, or distant pronoun references.

21. If tourists visit Egypt, you should certainly tour the pyramids.
22. The Sphinx stands near the Great Pyramid, and it is impressive.
23. Our tour guide told us about the ancient pharaohs and about the building of the pyramids, which impressed me.
24. On the news, it talked about the flooding of the Nile.
25. Dams have been built on the river, and they hope they will ease the flooding problem.

Subject and Verb Agreement

Recognizing the Number of Nouns, Pronouns, and Verbs

In grammar, *number* indicates whether a word is singular or plural. Only three parts of speech have different forms to indicate number: nouns, pronouns, and verbs.

Recognizing the number of most nouns is seldom a problem. The plural of most nouns is formed by adding -*s* or -*es*. Some, such as *mouse* or *ox*, form their plurals irregularly: *mice, oxen.*

Many pronouns have different forms to indicate their number. The chart below shows the different forms of personal pronouns in the case used for subjects.

PERSONAL PRONOUNS		
Singular	**Plural**	**Singular or Plural**
I he, she, it	we they	you

The grammatical number of verbs is sometimes more difficult to determine. The form of many verbs can be either singular or plural, depending on the number of the subject.

SINGULAR: She *sees.*   She has *seen.*

PLURAL: We *see.*   We *have seen.*

The verb *be* in the present tense has special forms to agree with singular subjects. The pronoun *I* has its own singular form of *be.* So do *he, she, it,* and singular nouns.

ALWAYS SINGULAR: I *am.*   He *is.*

All singular subjects except *you* share the same past tense verb form of *be.*

ALWAYS SINGULAR: I *was.*   He *was.*

The chart on the next page shows those verb forms that are always singular and those that can be singular or plural, depending on the subject.

In this section, you will learn how to recognize and correct errors in subject-verb agreement. The examples and exercises are about the pyramids of ancient Egypt.

Cross-Curricular Connection: Social Studies

VERBS	
Always Singular	**Singular or Plural**
(he, Jane) sees (he, Jane) has seen (I) am (he, Jane) is (I, he, Jane) was	(I, you, we, they) see (I, you, we, they) have seen (you, we, they) are (you, we, they) were

More Practice

**Language Lab
CD-ROM**
• Subject-Verb
  Agreement lesson
**On-line
Exercise Bank**
• Section 23.1
**Grammar Exercise
Workbook**
• pp. 93–94

A verb form will always be singular if it has had an -s or -es added to it or if it includes the words *has, am, is,* or *was.* The number of any other verb depends on its subject.

Exercise 1 **Determining the Number of Nouns, Pronouns, and Verbs** Identify each item as *singular, plural,* or *both.*

EXAMPLE: explodes
ANSWER: singular

1. pyramid
2. digs (verb)
3. am
4. pharaohs
5. you
6. builds
7. is
8. they
9. construct (verb)
10. mummies
11. tomb
12. are
13. bricks
14. will be
15. purifies
16. capstone
17. has fallen
18. was carving
19. have
20. measured

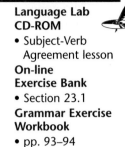

▶ **Critical Viewing** Use the words *rocks* and *statue* in a sentence about this photograph. What verbs did you use? **[Connect]**

Singular and Plural Subjects

Two general rules of subject and verb agreement cover all of the more specific rules:

KEY CONCEPTS (1) A singular subject must have a singular verb. (2) A plural subject must have a plural verb. ∎

In the following examples, subjects are underlined once; verbs, twice.

SINGULAR SUBJECT AND VERB:	The archaeologist works in Egypt. She was being mysterious about the dig's location.
PLURAL SUBJECT AND VERB:	These archaeologists work in Egypt. They were being mysterious about the dig's location.

Exercise 2 Making Subjects Agree With Their Verbs
Choose the verb in parentheses that agrees with the subject of each sentence.
1. A pyramid (is, are) a four-sided structure.
2. Its triangular walls (meets, meet) in a point at the top.
3. Egypt's Giza Plateau (is, are) the site of the best-known pyramids.
4. Nearly two million tourists (comes, come) to see the pyramids at Giza each year.
5. The Giza pyramids (demonstrates, demonstrate) the best examples of ancient Egyptian pyramid building.

▼ **Critical Viewing** Write two sentences about this photograph: one that includes a singular subject and verb and one with a plural subject and verb. [Connect, Identify]

Exercise 3 Proofreading for **Agreement Errors** Revise this passage, correcting errors in subject-verb agreement. If there are no errors, write *correct*.

(1) Laborers was employed to build the Giza pyramids more than four thousand years ago. (2) The three largest of the Giza Plateau pyramids rises hundreds of feet above the plain. (3) The pharaohs Khufu, his son Khafre, and his grandson Menkaure is buried in these pyramids. (4) Khufu was Egypt's ruler from approximately 2550 B.C. to 2525 B.C. (5) He chose the site at Giza because it were close to the royal city of Memphis.

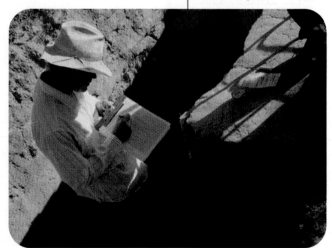

Intervening Phrases and Clauses

When a sentence contains a phrase or clause that separates the subject from its verb, simply ignore the intervening group of words when you check for agreement.

▶ **KEY CONCEPT** A phrase or clause that interrupts a subject and its verb does not affect subject-verb agreement. ■

In the first example below, the singular subject *discovery* agrees with the singular verb *interests* despite the intervening prepositional phrase that contains a plural noun. In the second example, the plural subject *archaeologists* agrees with the plural verb *require* despite the intervening clause.

EXAMPLES: The <u>discovery</u> of mummies <u>interests</u> many people.
The <u>archaeologists</u>, whose work is nearly complete, <u>require</u> a bit more funding.

Intervening parenthetical expressions—such as those beginning with *as well as, in addition to, in spite of,* or *including*—also have no effect on the agreement of the subject and its verb.

EXAMPLE: Your <u>information</u>, in addition to the data gathered by those working at the site, <u>is helping</u> to solve the mystery surrounding the pyramid.

▶ **Exercise 4** **Making Separated Subjects and Verbs Agree**
Choose the verb that agrees with the subject of each sentence.
1. The Egyptian pyramids, many of which are found at the Giza Plateau, (are, is) an example of precise planning.
2. A chief architect, along with many assistants, (was, were) usually in charge of planning and design.
3. Imhotep, one of ancient Egypt's greatest architects, (was, were) responsible for pioneering the pyramid form.
4. Remarkably, the sides of an Egyptian pyramid, no matter where it is located, (is, are) almost perfectly equal.
5. Today's engineers, accustomed to modern technology, (considers, consider) Egyptian tools to be somewhat crude.

▶ **Exercise 5** **Proofreading for Errors in Agreement** Revise this passage, correcting errors in subject and verb agreement. If there are no errors, write *correct.*
(1) An ancient Egyptian stonecutter, working with copper and dolerite tools, were especially skillful. (2) Dolerite, as well as other hard stones, was used by workers to chip away at limestone and granite. (3) One of the most difficult tasks facing pyramid builders were moving stones. (4) A fact that people have a hard time believing is that the ancient Egyptians did not use the wheel. (5) Instead, workers, laboring under the hot Egyptian sun, was pulling cut stones on giant sleds.

💡 Spelling Tip

Remember not to confuse *were* and *we're. Were* is the past principal form of *to be. We're* is a contraction meaning "we are."

▶ **More Practice**

Language Lab CD-ROM
• Subject-Verb Agreement lesson
On-line Exercise Bank
• Section 23.1
Grammar Exercise Workbook
• pp. 93–94

Relative Pronouns as Subjects

When *who, which,* or *that* acts as a subject of a subordinate clause, its verb will be singular or plural depending on the number of the antecedent.

> **KEY CONCEPT** The antecedent of a relative pronoun determines its agreement with a verb. ■

In the first example below, the antecedent of *who* is *one;* therefore, the singular verb *has* is used. In the second example, the antecedent of *who* is *archaeologists;* therefore, the plural verb *have* is used

EXAMPLES: Chuck is *the only one* of those archaeologists who has prior experience working in Egypt.

Chuck is only *one of several archaeologists* who have prior experience working in Egypt.

GRAMMAR IN
LITERATURE

from Don Juan
George Gordon, Lord Byron

Notice that the plural subject hopes *agrees with the plural verb* are *in the first line, and the singular noun* pinch *agrees with the singular verb* remains *in the last line.*

What are the hopes of man? Old Egypt's King
    Cheops erected the first pyramid
And largest, thinking it was just the thing
    To keep his memory whole, and mummy hid:
But somebody or other rummaging
    Burglariously broke his coffin's lid:
Let not a monument give you or me hopes,
    Since not a pinch of dust remains of Cheops.

▶ **Exercise 6** **Making Relative Pronouns Agree With Their Verbs** Choose the verb in parentheses that agrees with the subject of each subordinate clause.

1. The Great Sphinx of Giza, which (is, are) located near the Great Pyramid, seems to stand on guard.
2. Those who (has, have) studied the Sphinx estimate that it was built about the same time as the pyramids of Giza.
3. How the Sphinx was carved from a single giant block of limestone is a mystery that (continues, continue) to puzzle archaeologists.
4. The name *Sphinx* was given to the statue by the Greeks, who (was, were) associating it with a monster from an ancient Greek myth.
5. The Sphinx was also the subject of attacks by invading soldiers of Turkey and France, who (was, were) trying out their weapons on the sculpture.

▶ **Exercise 7** **Proofreading for Agreement Errors** Revise this passage, correcting errors in subject-verb agreement. If there are no errors, write *correct*.

(1) Long exposure to sand and wind has worn down the face that adorns the Great Sphinx. (2) In addition, the shifting desert sands, which has covered the Sphinx nearly to its neck, need to be cleared from the Sphinx from time to time.

(3) The Great Sphinx is not the only statue of its kind that exist in Egypt. (4) There are other statues similar to the Great Sphinx that has rams' heads or hawks' heads set on animal-like bodies. (5) Ram-headed sphinxes line the main avenue near the Great Temple of Amon-Re, which are located in southern Egypt.

More Practice

Language Lab CD-ROM
• Subject-Verb Agreement lesson
On-line Exercise Bank
• Section 23.1
Grammar Exercise Workbook
• pp. 93–94

◀ **Critical Viewing** How does seeing this photograph of the Great Sphinx add to what you learned in Exercises 6 and 7? **[Analyze]**

Compound Subjects

Different rules of agreement apply when the words *or, nor,* or *and* are used to join two or more subjects:

Singular Subjects Joined by *or* or *nor*

When two singular subjects are joined by *or* or *nor,* use a singular verb.

KEY CONCEPT Two or more singular subjects joined by *or* or *nor* must have a singular verb. ■

EXAMPLE: Either the Step Pyramid *or* the Bent Pyramid is open to tourists.

Plural Subjects Joined by *or* or *nor*

A compound consisting of two plural subjects requires a plural verb.

KEY CONCEPT Two or more plural subjects joined by *or* or *nor* must have a plural verb. ■

EXAMPLE: Neither the pyramids at Giza *nor* the pyramids at Dahshur have escaped the ravages of weather.

Subjects of Mixed Number Joined by *or* or *nor*

If a compound subject consists of a singular subject and a plural subject, determining the number of the verb is more difficult.

KEY CONCEPT If one or more singular subjects are joined to one or more plural subjects by *or* or *nor,* the subject closest to the verb determines agreement. ■

EXAMPLES: Either a lantern *or* candles are used to see into the pyramid's burial chamber.
Either candles *or* a lantern is used to see into the pyramid's burial chamber.
Neither the candles *nor* the lantern was very helpful.

Subjects Joined by *and*

A single rule applies to most situations in which *and* joins two or more subjects.

▶ **KEY CONCEPTS** A compound subject joined by *and* is generally plural and must have a plural verb. ■

Whether the parts of the compound subject are all singular, all plural, or mixed in number, the conjunction *and* usually acts as a plus sign and indicates the need for a plural verb.

EXAMPLES: A <u>lantern</u> *and* a <u>candle</u> <u>are used</u> to see into the pyramid's burial chamber.

<u>Candles</u> *and* <u>lanterns</u> <u>are used</u> to see into the pyramid's burial chamber.

<u>Candles</u> *and* a <u>lantern</u> <u>are used</u> to see into the pyramid's burial chamber.

Exceptions occur when the parts of the compound subject equal one thing or when the word *each* or *every* is used before a compound subject. Each of these situations requires a singular verb.

EXAMPLES: <u>Bread and butter</u> <u>was</u> all the workers were fed.
Every <u>chart and diagram</u> <u>was</u> precise.

▶ **Exercise 8** **Making Compound Subjects Agree With Their Verbs** Choose the verb in parentheses that agrees with the subject in each sentence.

1. Either Saqquarah or Giza (is, are) a good place to study pyramid-building techniques.
2. The burial grounds and the step pyramid at Saqquarah (fascinates, fascinate) me.
3. Archaeologists and historians (has, have) found *mastabas*, or royal tombs, at Saqquarah 's burial grounds.
4. Mud or stones (is, are) used to build a mastaba.
5. The mastaba and the pyramids (protects, protect) bodies buried below ground.
6. In a mastaba, weapons or food (was, were) stored in the above-ground chambers.
7. I doubt that macaroni and cheese (was, were) among the dishes stored for a pharaoh.
8. Either the pharaoh or other members of the royal family (lies, lie) in the mastaba's underground chambers.
9. The size and complexity of the mastaba (varies, vary) depending on the importance of the pharaoh buried inside.
10. Grave robbers or dishonest guards (was, were) responsible for stealing treasures from many mastabas.

▶ **More Practice**

Language Lab CD-ROM
• Subject-Verb Agreement lesson
On-line Exercise Bank
• Section 23.1
Grammar Exercise Workbook
• pp. 95–96

Using Confusing Subjects

Certain confusing subjects require special attention.

Hard-to-Find Subjects

If a subject comes after its verb, you must still make sure they agree in number.

> **KEY CONCEPT** A subject that comes after its verb must still agree with it in number. ■

If a subject comes after its verb, the sentence is said to be inverted. Check the agreement of the subject and verb by mentally putting the sentence in the usual subject-verb order.

EXAMPLES: Under the mummy's bandages <u>was</u> a <u>pendant</u>.
(A pendant was under the mummy's bandages.)

Which pyramid <u>is</u> <u>he</u> visiting?
(He does visit which pyramid.)

There <u>are</u> no more <u>pharaohs</u> in Egypt.
(No more pharaohs are in Egypt.)

Note About *There's* and *Here's:* A common mistake is the misuse of *there's* and *here's,* contractions for *there is* and *here is.* They cannot be used with plural subjects.

INCORRECT: Here's <u>Ann</u> and <u>Tanya</u> now, both ready to leave for Egypt as soon as possible.

CORRECT: Here <u>are</u> <u>Ann</u> and <u>Tanya</u> now, both ready to leave for Egypt as soon as possible.

Subjects of Linking Verbs

Another agreement problem involves linking verbs and predicate nominatives—words that rename the subject. Do not be confused by the number of the predicate nominative. Make sure the verb agrees in number with the subject.

> **KEY CONCEPT** A linking verb must agree with its subject, regardless of the number of its predicate nominative. ■

EXAMPLES: Religious <u>beliefs</u> <u>were</u> the motivation for the ancient Egyptians to build pyramids.

(The <u>motivation</u> for the ancient Egyptians to build pyramids <u>was</u> religious beliefs.)

Speaking and Listening Tip

Avoid using *there's* and *here's* for plural subjects in your speaking as well as in your writing.

Collective Nouns

Collective nouns—words such as *jury, family,* or *committee*—name groups of persons or things. They may be either singular or plural, depending on their use in the sentence.

▶ **KEY CONCEPTS** A collective noun takes a singular verb when the group it names acts as a single unit. A collective noun takes a plural verb when the group it names act as individuals with different points of view. ■

SINGULAR: The <u>team</u> of archaeologists <u>has made</u> a discovery.
The royal <u>family</u> <u>is buried</u> under the pyramid.

PLURAL: The <u>team</u> of archaeologists <u>are quarreling</u>.
The royal <u>family</u> <u>are debating</u> the tomb's location.

One collective noun, *number,* deserves special attention. When used with *the, number* is always singular; when used with *a, number* is always plural.

SINGULAR: *The* <u>number</u> of digs in Egypt <u>has been</u> increasing.
PLURAL: *A* <u>number</u> of digs <u>have unearthed</u> ancient artifacts.

Nouns That Look Like Plurals

Nouns that look plural but are actually singular can also cause agreement problems.

▶ **KEY CONCEPT** Nouns that are plural in form but singular in meaning agree with singular verbs. ■

Some of these nouns name branches of knowledge: *acoustics, aesthetics, civics, economics, gymnastics, mathematics, physics, politics,* and *social studies.* Others are singular in meaning because, like collective nouns, they name singular units: *confetti, macaroni, measles, molasses, news, rickets,* and so on.

SINGULAR: <u>Mathematics</u> <u>is</u> my most difficult subject.
<u>Measles</u> <u>threatens</u> unborn babies.

Some of these words are especially tricky. When *ethics* and *politics,* for example, name characteristics or qualities rather than branches of knowledge, their meanings are plural. Also, such words as *eyeglasses, pliers, scissors,* and *trousers* generally take plural verbs although they name single items.

PLURAL: Nina's <u>ethics</u> <u>change</u> to fit any occasion.
Jack's <u>politics</u> <u>were</u> not our concern.
The <u>scissors</u> <u>are</u> in the sewing box.

Technology Tip

A grammar check feature in a word-processing program can help you find errors in subject-verb agreement. However, using a grammar checker is not a substitute for proofreading your work carefully.

Indefinite Pronouns

Some indefinite pronouns are always singular, including those that end in *-one* (*anyone, everyone, someone*), those that end in *-body* (*anybody, everybody, somebody*), and those that imply one (*each, either*). Others are always plural: *both, few, many, others,* and *several.*

> **KEY CONCEPTS** Singular indefinite pronouns take singular verbs. Plural indefinite pronouns take plural verbs. ■

ALWAYS SINGULAR: Almost everyone is interested in his report on Egyptian pyramids.
Everybody is expected to hear him speak.
Neither of the pyramids has been pillaged by thieves.

ALWAYS PLURAL: Both of these tombs are thousands of years old.
Many in the class excel in Egyptian history.
Others overlook the difficulties of studying ancient history.

Some indefinite pronouns can be either singular or plural, depending on the antecedent.

> **KEY CONCEPT** The pronouns *all, any, more, most, none,* and *some* usually take a singular verb if the antecedent is singular and a plural verb if the antecedent is plural. ■

In the first example below, the antecedent of *most* is *pyramid,* a singular noun, so *most* is singular. In the second, the antecedent of *most* is *chambers,* a plural noun, so *most* is plural.

SINGULAR: Most of the pyramid was explored.
PLURAL: Most of the inner chambers have been examined.

Titles

The titles of books and other works of art can be misleading if they sound plural or consist of many words.

> **KEY CONCEPT** A title is singular and must have a singular verb. ■

EXAMPLES: *Dr. Jekyll and Mr. Hyde* is a psychological thriller.
The Bunner Sisters is a novel by Edith Wharton.

Amounts and Measurements

▶ **KEY CONCEPT** A noun expressing an amount or measurement is usually singular and requires a singular verb. ■

In the first two examples below—a single sum and a part of a whole—the subjects agree with singular verbs. In the third example, *half* refers to many individual items, so it is plural.

EXAMPLES: Twenty-five cents <u>buys</u> an Egyptian postcard.

Three fourths of that nation <u>is impoverished.</u>

<u>Half</u> of the brochures <u>were mailed</u> yesterday.

▶ **More Practice**

Language Lab CD-ROM
• Subject-Verb Agreement lesson
On-line Exercise Bank
• Section 23.1
Grammar Exercise Workbook
• pp. 97–98

▶ **Exercise 9** **Making Confusing Subjects Agree With Their Verbs** Choose the correct verb to complete each sentence.

1. On which side of the Nile (does, do) the pyramids lie?
2. Just beyond the Nile's west bank (is, are) the pyramids.
3. (There's, There are) reasons the pyramids were built on the west side of the Nile.
4. Everybody (knows, know) that the sun sets in the west.
5. All of the ancient Egyptians (was, were) convinced that the West was the Realm of the Dead.

▶ **Exercise 10** **Proofreading for Agreement With Confusing Subjects** Revise this passage, correcting errors in agreement. If there are no errors, write *correct.*

(1) Most archaeologists knows about Egyptian methods of mummification, (2) yet no original accounts of the process of mummification exists today. (3) Each of the steps have been determined by examining physical evidence. (4) A deceased member of a royal family were sure to be mummified. (5) A team of priests was assigned to mummify a dead pharaoh. (6) Placed inside the wrappings of a mummy were charms and jewels.

(7) Here is some facts about the pyramids. (8) The *Arabian Nights* mention the Great Pyramid of Khufu. (9) About 480 feet are the height of the Great Pyramid. (10) None of the tours of the pyramids leave after 8:30.

▼ **Critical Viewing** Write two sentences about this photograph. Begin one with *both* and the other with *each*. What is the number of the verb in each sentence? **[Connect, Identify]**

Section Review

GRAMMAR EXERCISES 11–20

▶ **Exercise 11** Determining Number of Nouns, Pronouns, and Verbs Identify the subject and verb in each sentence as singular or plural.

1. The pyramids were built as monuments to house the pharaohs' tombs.
2. Pictures on the wall of a tomb describe events in the lives of the pharaohs.
3. According to some archaeologists, the Great Pyramid was built in 23 years.
4. Peasant farmers were the majority of unskilled laborers building a pyramid.
5. Each was usually paid in cloth and food.

▶ **Exercise 12** Making Subjects and Verbs Agree Choose the verb that agrees with the subject of each sentence.

1. Scribes, or people who knew how to read and write, (was, were) very important to pyramid builders.
2. A scribe (writes, write) a list that includes the amount and sizes of stones needed to build the pyramid.
3. Jobs as scribe (was, were) in demand.
4. Every worker, both skilled and unskilled, (was, were) valued.
5. The quarrymen (was, were) among the strongest workers who labored to build the pyramids.
6. Limestone (was, were) quarried for many pyramids built in the Nile valley.
7. The best quality stone (was, were) available on the east bank of the Nile.
8. To quarry the best stone, tunnels (was, were) dug into the face of cliffs.
9. Workers, who labored deep in the quarry, (cuts, cut) the blocks that would be used for the pyramid.
10. Each worker who labored in the quarry (was, were) an important part of the team.

▶ **Exercise 13** Proofreading for Agreement Errors Revise these paragraphs, correcting errors in agreement. If there are no errors, write *correct*.

(1) Boats, which crossed the Nile regularly, was used to transport the stones from the quarry to the pyramid site. (2) After reaching one of the pyramid sites, each boat were unloaded. (3) The blocks of limestone were chiseled smooth. (4) The paving stones was the first group to be laid. (5) The casing stones, which was to form the outer walls, had to be cut perfectly.

(6) Historians who has studied the pyramids are not exactly sure how the Egyptians built the structures. (7) Most believes that the Egyptians built ramps to haul the stones up to each level. (8) One historian performed an experiment that was quite clever. (9) He were able to re-create the ramps thought to be used by pyramid makers and asked his staff to haul stones up the ramps. (10) The staff concluded that the best way to haul stones up a ramp were to lubricate the ramp with liquid.

▶ **Exercise 14** Making Compound Subjects Agree With Their Verbs Choose the verb in parentheses that agrees with the subject of the sentence.

1. The architect and his surveyors (was, were) expected to carefully examine the location of the pyramid.
2. Next, the pharaoh or his chief advisor (was, were) called to approve the site.
3. After their approval, prayers and animal sacrifices (was, were) offered by priests to the gods.
4. Leveling the site and laying the foundations (was, were) the next major tasks.

5. A channel or trench system (was, were) dug to help level the site.
6. A mortuary temple and a causeway (was, were) also constructed.
7. Neither the skilled nor unskilled workers (was, were) usually slaves.
8. Instead, either an unemployed laborer or a farmer (was, were) usually added to a construction gang.
9. Accidents and injury (was, were) common during the construction process.
10. Both my sister and my brother (enjoys, enjoy) learning about the pyramids.

Exercise 15 Proofreading for Agreement Errors With Compound Subjects
Revise this paragraph, correcting errors in agreement.

Limestone or granite were the typical stone used to build pyramids. Prayers and incense was presented by priests when the capstone was placed atop the pyramid. After the capstone was positioned, grinding and polishing the surface was the next steps. Tunneling and creating burial chambers was done while the pyramid was being built.

Exercise 16 Making Confusing Subjects Agree With Their Verbs
Choose the verb in parentheses that agrees with the subject of the sentence.

1. This gang of workers (is, are) responsible for maintaining the supply ramps that surround the pyramid.
2. The gang (is, are) unable to agree on how to complete the work.
3. (There's, There are) several ways to proceed.
4. At least half of the pyramid's stones (was, were) from the mines at Tura.
5. Everyone (agrees, agree) that thousands of laborers were needed to build a pyramid.

Exercise 17 Proofreading for Agreement Errors With Confusing Subjects
Revise this paragraph, correcting errors in agreement.

The exact number of workers who constructed a pyramid are unknown. No matter how many workers it took, all of the experts concludes that it was a monumental task. Only after years of planning and construction were a pyramid completed. *The Pyramids of Giza* by Tim McNeese explain many of these details.

Exercise 18 Find It in Your Reading
Identify the subjects and verbs in these lines from Byron's "Don Juan." Identify each as singular or plural.

What is the end of fame? 'tis but to fill
    A certain portion of uncertain paper:
Some liken it to climbing up a hill,
    Whose summit, like all hills, is lost in
        vapor;
For this men write, speak, preach, and
    heroes kill,
    And bards burn what they call their
        "midnight taper," . . .

Exercise 19 Find It in Your Writing
Review a piece of writing from your portfolio to find examples of at least four of the agreement rules in this chapter. Check to see that you have applied the rules correctly.

Exercise 20 Writing Application
Write a summary of what you know about the pyramids of Egypt. After you have completed the paragraph, underline the subject of each sentence once and the verb twice. Tell whether each subject and verb is singular or plural, and make sure that they agree in number.

Pronoun and Antecedent Agreement

Like a subject and its verb, a pronoun and its antecedent must agree. An antecedent is the word or group of words for which the pronoun stands.

Agreement Between Personal Pronouns and Antecedents

While a subject and verb must agree only in number, a personal pronoun and its antecedent must agree in three ways:

KEY CONCEPT A personal pronoun must agree with its antecedent in number, person, and gender. ■

The *number* of a pronoun indicates whether it is singular or plural. *Person* refers to a pronoun's ability to indicate either the person speaking (first person); the person spoken to (second person); or the person, place, or thing spoken about (third person). *Gender* is the characteristic of nouns and pronouns that indicates whether the word is *masculine* (referring to males); *feminine* (referring to females); or *neuter* (referring to neither males nor females).

The only pronouns that indicate gender are third-person singular personal pronouns.

GENDER OF THIRD-PERSON SINGULAR PRONOUNS

Masculine	Feminine	Neuter
he, him, his	she, her, hers	it, its

Theme: Medieval Times

In this section, you will learn how to make sure that pronouns agree in number, case, and gender with their antecedents. The examples and exercises are about castles in medieval times.

Cross-Curricular Connection: Social Studies

▼ **Critical Viewing** What personal pronouns might you use in writing about this British castle? **[Connect]**

In the example below, the pronoun *her* agrees with the antecedent *Queen* in number (both are singular), in person (both are third person), and in gender (both are feminine).

EXAMPLE: The *Queen* of England has opened some of *her* castles to the public.

Agreement in Number

When an antecedent is compound, making the pronoun agree can be a problem. There are three rules to keep in mind to determine the number of compound antecedents.

> **KEY CONCEPT** Use a singular personal pronoun with two or more singular antecedents joined by *or* or *nor.* ■

EXAMPLE: Either Craig *or* Todd will bring *his* model of a castle to class.

> **KEY CONCEPT** Use a plural personal pronoun with two or more antecedents joined by *and.* ■

EXAMPLE: Melissa *and* I are studying for *our* examinations in medieval history.

An exception occurs when a distinction must be made between individual and joint ownership. If individual ownership is intended, use a singular pronoun to refer to a compound antecedent. If joint ownership is intended, use a plural pronoun.

SINGULAR: *Sir Thomas* and *Lady Cecily* practiced playing *her lyre.*
(Lady Cecily owns the lyre.)

PLURAL: *Sir Thomas* and *Lady Cecily* practiced playing *their lyre.*
(Both Thomas and Cecily own the lyre.)

SINGULAR: Neither my *brother* nor my *father* let me ride *his* horse in the jousting tournament.
(The brother and father each own a horse.)

PLURAL: Neither my *brother* nor my *father* let me ride *their* horse in the jousting tournament.
(The brother and father own the same horse.)

The third rule applies to compound antecedents whose parts are mixed in number.

> **KEY CONCEPT** Use a plural personal pronoun if any part of a compound antecedent joined by *or* or *nor* is plural. ■

PLURAL: When the *princesses* or the *queen* comes home, offer *them* refreshments.

Agreement in Person and Gender

Try to avoid shifts in person or gender of pronouns.

> **KEY CONCEPT** As part of pronoun-antecedent agreement, take care not to shift either person or gender. ■

SHIFT IN PERSON: *Mike* is planning to visit Windsor Castle so *you* can see how royalty lives.

CORRECT: *Mike* is planning to visit Windsor Castle so *he* can see how royalty lives.

SHIFT IN GENDER: The *horse* threw *its* head back and stood on *his* hind legs.

CORRECT: The *horse* threw *its* head back and stood on *its* hind legs.

Generic Masculine Pronouns

Traditionally, a masculine pronoun has been used to refer to a singular antecedent whose gender is unknown. Such use is called *generic* because it applies to both masculine and feminine genders. Although using the generic masculine pronoun is still acceptable, many writers prefer to use *his or her* or to rephrase the sentence.

> **KEY CONCEPT** When gender is not specified, use *his or her* or rewrite the sentence. ■

EXAMPLES: Each *student* found a useful Web site on which to research *his or her* report on castles.
Each *student* found a useful Web site on which to research the report on castles.
Students found useful Web sites on which to research *their* reports on castles.

> **Exercise 21** **Making Personal Pronouns Agree With Their Antecedents** Write an appropriate personal pronoun to complete each sentence.

1. A castle was both fortress and home to a lord and ___?___ family.
2. A huge wall and a moat surrounded the castle to protect ___?___ from invaders.
3. A lord and lady usually had a huge great room in which ___?___ entertained hundreds of guests.
4. Neither a woman nor a young girl living in the castle was permitted to spend ___?___ days in a frivolous manner.
5. Either a queen or noblewomen were accustomed to servants attending to most of ___?___ needs.

▶ **More Practice**

Language Lab CD-ROM
• Nouns and Pronouns lesson
On-line Exercise Bank
• Section 23.2
Grammar Exercise Workbook
• pp. 99–100

▶ **Exercise 22** Revising to Eliminate Shifts in Person and
Gender Rewrite each sentence, correcting the unnecessary
shift in person or gender. In some instances, you may need to
change only a pronoun, while in others you may want to
rephrase the sentence.

EXAMPLE: The ideal castle was a self-sufficient village that
             met all of their residents' needs.

ANSWER: The ideal castle was a self-sufficient village that
             met all of its residents' needs.

1. Each lord had to provide their king or queen with soldiers,
   called knights.
2. In exchange, the ruler gave their loyal nobles an estate.
3. The nobles built his castles on
   these grants of land.
4. Nobles would usually encourage
   their followers to develop villages on his land.
5. A lord had the right to demand
   that peasants living on an
   estate pay them in work, rents,
   and taxes.
6. Peasants farmed plots of land
   around the castle, paying the
   lord with a portion of the produce he grew.
7. Some peasants, called serfs,
   were agricultural workers who
   were tied to a lord's land and
   bound to serve it for life.
8. A village resident would often
   use their special skills to serve
   as a blacksmith, herbalist,
   cook, seamstress, or musician.
9. Inside the walls of a great castle, a lord or lady could find
   everything you wanted.
10. Villagers' sons might hope to
    use his intelligence to become a
    page and then a knight.

▶ **Critical Viewing** How does this
photograph add to the information
provided in Exercises 21 and 22?
[Analyze]

Agreement With Indefinite Pronouns

When an indefinite pronoun—such as *each, one,* or *several*—is the antecedent of a personal pronoun, both pronouns must agree. Errors are rare when both pronouns are plural.

KEY CONCEPT Use a plural personal pronoun when the antecedent is a plural indefinite pronoun. ■

EXAMPLE: *All* of the knights left *their* weapons outside.

A similar rule applies when both pronouns are singular.

KEY CONCEPT Use a singular personal pronoun when the antecedent is a singular indefinite pronoun. ■

As in subject-verb agreement, an intervening phrase or clause does not affect agreement in number between a personal pronoun and its antecedent.

EXAMPLES: *Either* of the horses will perform in battle for *its* knight. (*Either* is a singular antecedent.)
One of the noblewomen volunteered *her* time to nurse the sick. (*One* is a singular antecedent.)

If other words in the sentence do not indicate gender, use *he or she, him or her, his or her,* or rephrase the sentence.

EXAMPLES: *Each* of the villagers gave *his or her* opinion to the lord of the estate.
All of the villagers gave *their* opinions to the lord of the estate.

For indefinite pronouns that can be either singular or plural (*all, any, more, most, none,* and *some*), agreement depends on the number of the antecedent. In the first example below, the antecedent of *some* is *estate,* a singular noun. In the second example, the antecedent of *some* is *pages,* a plural noun.

EXAMPLES: *Some* of the estate had lost *its* value.
Some of the pages disliked *their* jobs.

Sometimes, strict grammatical agreement may be illogical. In these situations, you should let the meaning of the sentence determine the number of the personal pronoun.

ILLOGICAL: Because *neither* of the windows would budge, we had to leave *it* open.

CORRECT: Because *neither* of the windows would budge, we had to leave *them* open.

Exercise 23 Making Personal Pronouns Agree With **Indefinite Pronouns** Choose the correct pronoun in parentheses for each sentence.

1. Each of the castles had (its, their) own army of knights.
2. Many of the knights were vassals who received (its, their) plots of land by pledging loyalty and service to the lord.
3. All of the dukes selected the best knights to join (his, their) armies.
4. Most of the knights began (his, their) careers as pages.
5. Some of the pages started (his, their) service at eight years of age.
6. Most learned to read while (he, they) lived in the castle.
7. All of the pages served (his, their) knights with dignity.
8. Not one of the boys took (his, their) duties lightly.
9. Most of the knights had to become accustomed to wearing (his, their) heavy suits of armor.
10. All of the horses were carefully trained by the knights who owned (it, them).

More Practice

Language Lab
CD-ROM
• Nouns and Pronouns
  lesson
**On-line
Exercise Bank**
• Section 23.2
**Grammar Exercise
Workbook**
• pp. 101–102

Exercise 24 Proofreading for Errors in Agreement **With Indefinite Pronouns** Revise the two paragraphs, correcting agreement errors.

(1) Before knights engaged in battle, each raised their weapon in unison with the others. (2) In a battle, when every one of the knights charges at once, he has a better chance of defeating the enemy. (3) In addition to knights, each of the lords used foot-soldiers in their army. (4) None of the knights or the foot-soldiers could win battles on his own. (5) Only the best of the foot-soldiers could use his cross-bows effectively. (6) Each of the knights looked out for their fellow soldiers.

(7) Each of a knight's family members often visited the castle of their lord. (8) Each of a knight's daughters hoped they would be wed to a wealthy and sophisticated husband. (9) Every one of the children was expected to abide by their parents' wishes. (10) Only a few of the children ever traveled far from her village.

▶ **Critical Viewing** What indefinite pronouns and personal pronouns might you use in two sentences describing this knight? **[Analyze, Identify]**

Agreement With Reflexive Pronouns

Reflexive pronouns end in *-self* or *-selves* and are used correctly only when they refer to a word appearing earlier in the same sentence.

EXAMPLE: A *knight* who wins every battle should refrain from congratulating *himself.*

KEY CONCEPT A reflexive pronoun must agree with an antecedent that is clearly stated. ■

Do not use a reflexive pronoun if a personal pronoun can logically be used instead. In the example below, *myself* has no antecedent. The personal pronoun *me* should be used instead.

INCORRECT: The hard work was done by Leslie and *myself.*
CORRECT: The hard work was done by Leslie and *me.*

Exercise 25 Supplying Correct Pronouns On your paper, write a reflexive or personal pronoun to fill each blank.
1. My family and ___?___ decided to tour an English castle this summer.
2. My parents said we had to agree among ___?___ which castle we wanted to visit.
3. At first, I wasn't sure which castle I would prefer ___?___.
4. However, after ___?___ saw pictures of Rochester Castle near London, I knew that would be my choice.
5. My sister arrived at the same choice ___?___.

Exercise 26 Proofreading to Correct Errors in the Use of Reflexive Pronouns Rewrite each sentence, correcting the misused reflexive pronoun. If a sentence is correct, write *correct.*
1. Ann and myself learned that castle building in Europe began in earnest after William the Conqueror invaded England in 1066.
2. William built castles to defend the territory recently conquered by his armies and himself.
3. The only person who could have conquered and unified England was himself.
4. May Sarah and I study for the history test with yourself?
5. Who besides herself has ever visited a castle?

More Practice

Language Lab
CD-ROM
• Nouns and Pronouns lesson
On-line
Exercise Bank
• Section 23.2
Grammar Exercise Workbook
• pp. 101–102

Section Review

GRAMMAR EXERCISES 27–33

> **Exercise 27** Supplying Personal
**Pronouns That Agree With Their
Antecedents** Write an appropriate personal pronoun to complete each sentence.

1. Nobles built castles to protect __?__ lives and property from enemies.
2. A castle's moat also served to protect __?__ from attack.
3. Attackers staged sieges against __?__ enemies.
4. A knight fought bravely to defend __?__ lord's castle.
5. A noblewoman might assist __?__ husband in defending the castle.

> **Exercise 28** Avoiding Shifts in
Person and Gender Choose the correct pronoun in parentheses for each sentence.

1. Each of the estates had (its, their) own routine.
2. A peasant's wife or daughter might plant (her, their) garden in early spring.
3. In August, everyone joined the harvest so that (he or she, they) would not go hungry.
4. During September, peasants picked grapes near (its, their) lord's castle.
5. Each of the animals relied on (its, their) owners to cut hay in September.

> **Exercise 29** Making Personal
**Pronouns Agree With Indefinite
Pronouns** Choose the correct pronoun in parentheses to complete each sentence.

1. Some of the nobles had several castles under (his, their) control.
2. Each of the castles had a large staff to see to (its, their) upkeep.
3. Every one of the lords served (his, their) peasants by acting as judges of disputes.
4. Each of the noblewomen learned to run a household from (her, their) mother.

5. Neither of the sexes had much choice in (his or her, their) future spouses.

> **Exercise 30** Using Reflexive
Pronouns Correctly Rewrite any sentence that contains an incorrectly used reflexive pronoun. Write *correct* if a sentence is correct.

1. A noble relied on his wife, his clerks, and himself to run the castle.
2. The lord's wife looked after matters that were important to herself.
3. The lord and herself would make plans.
4. Clerks and himself handled accounts.
5. Together, themselves managed the estate efficiently.

> **Exercise 31** Find It in Your
Reading Identify the pronouns and antecedents in these lines from Thomas Gray's "Elegy Written in a Country Churchyard," and explain why they agree.

No children run to lisp their sire's return,
  Or climb his knees the envied kiss to
    share.

> **Exercise 32** Find It in Your
Writing Go through your portfolio to find examples of personal and indefinite pronouns. Draw an arrow from each pronoun to its antecedent, and check that they agree in number, gender, and case.

> **Exercise 33** Writing Application
Write a paragraph about people who live in an unusual place. Describe their daily routine. Use several personal and indefinite pronouns, and check for agreement.

Special Problems With Pronoun Agreement

Pronouns whose antecedents are vague, ambiguous, or too distant can cloud the meaning of a sentence. This section will show you how to avoid these special problems or how to correct them in your writing.

Vague Pronoun References

For the meaning of a sentence to be clear, the antecedent of any pronoun needs to be clearly stated or understood.

> **KEY CONCEPT** A pronoun requires an antecedent that is either stated or clearly understood. ■

Antecedents for *Which, This, That,* and *These*

The pronouns *which, this, that,* and *these* can cause confusion if their antecedents are unclear or too general.

> **KEY CONCEPT** The pronouns *which, this, that,* and *these* should not be used to refer to a vague or overly general idea. ■

In the following sentence, it is impossible to point to exactly what the pronoun *this* stands for.

VAGUE REFERENCE: During his trip to Kenya, Mr. Winter climbed Mount Kenya, toured Nairobi, and visited a coffee plantation. *This* made his trip exciting.

"*This* what?" a reader might ask. The answer is not stated nor is it clearly understood. You can correct such vague, overly general references by turning the pronoun into an adjective that modifies a specific noun or by revising the sentence to eliminate the vague pronoun.

CORRECT: During his trip to Kenya, Mr. Winter climbed Mount Kenya, toured Nairobi, and visited a coffee plantation. This variety of activities made his trip exciting.

Climbing Mount Kenya, touring Nairobi, and visiting a coffee plantation all made Mr. Winter's trip to Kenya exciting.

Antecedents for *It, They,* and *You*

The personal pronouns *it, they,* and *you* can also confuse readers if the antecedents are not stated clearly.

▶ **KEY CONCEPT** The personal pronouns *it, they,* and *you* should not be used with vague antecedents. ■

Errors with these pronouns can be corrected either by replacing the pronoun with a specific noun or rewriting the sentence to eliminate the imprecise pronoun.

In the example below, the pronoun *it* has no clearly stated antecedent. The pronoun should be replaced with a precise noun or the sentence should be rephrased in order to eliminate the pronoun altogether.

VAGUE REFERENCE:	When I rode on a *matatu* in Nairobi, *it* traveled on the left side of the road.
CORRECT:	When I rode on a *matatu* in Nairobi, the minibus traveled on the left side of the road.
	The *matatu* I rode on in Nairobi traveled on the left side of the road.

In the next example, the pronoun *they* is used without an accurate antecedent.

VAGUE REFERENCE:	When we arrived in Mombasa, they described the port city's long history.
CORRECT:	When we arrived in Mombasa, the tour guide described the port city's long history.

A somewhat different problem occurs when the personal pronoun *you* is misused. The use of *you* is valid only when it refers directly to the reader or listener.

VAGUE REFERENCE:	The gathering was so somber *you* dared not speak.
CORRECT:	The gathering was so somber *one* dared not speak.
VAGUE REFERENCE:	Before homes had modern plumbing, *you* had to pump water from a well.
CORRECT:	Before homes had modern plumbing, *people* had to pump water from a well.

Note About *It*: In a number of idiomatic expressions, *it* is used correctly without an antecedent. In phrases such as "*It* is dark," "*It* is time," and "*It* is raining," the idiomatic use of *it* is accepted as standard English.

▶ **Exercise 34** **Revising Vague Pronoun References** Rewrite the sentences below, correcting the vague pronouns.

EXAMPLE: I visited areas where they live in *shambas*.

ANSWER: I visited areas where the people live in *shambas*.

1. English and Swahili, which I cannot speak, are familiar languages in Kenya.
2. The Portuguese and, later, the British controlled Kenya at different times. They granted Kenya independence in 1963.
3. To appreciate the beauty of Kenya, you have to go there.
4. Kenya contains reserves of gold, silver, and gemstones. This is very valuable.
5. In Kenya, there is much open land. It has fourteen vast national parks.
6. Kenya is divided into almost equal parts by the equator. They have different climates.
7. Roughly 11 percent of Kenya's land is suitable for agriculture. They grow crops on one third of that territory.
8. The northern region has several deserts. This is hot and dry.
9. In recent years, many rural Kenyans have moved to Nairobi and Mombasa. This has led to overcrowding.
10. Though only about 4 percent of Kenya's land is arable, you can grow almost every basic foodstuff there.
11. Kenya has forests containing teak and forests containing baobab trees. These are found in the lowlands.
12. Kenya has two main rivers, the Tana and the Galana. It also contains a small portion of Lake Victoria.
13. Kenya is famous for wildlife. They have giraffes and lions.
14. Kenya also has elephants and rhinoceroses that have been threatened by hunters.
15. Kenya abounds in birds and reptiles. This attracts many zoologists to the country.
16. The southern part of Kenya has three distinct climactic regions: humid, tropical, and temperate. This leads to a wide variety of plant and animal life.
17. Native Kenyans belong to more than thirty different ethnic groups. They almost all have a different language.
18. Many tourists visit Kenya's parks that want to see wildlife.
19. Kenya is a member of the Commonwealth of Nations, which has a modified parliamentary form of government.
20. The giraffe has a long neck and is a herbivore. That means it eats plants.

▲ **Critical Viewing** Write two sentences describing these elephants. Use a pronoun in the second sentence. **[Describe]**

Ambiguous Pronoun References

A pronoun is *ambiguous* if it can refer to more than one possible antecedent.

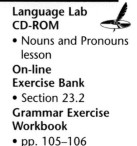

More Practice

Language Lab CD-ROM
• Nouns and Pronouns lesson
On-line Exercise Bank
• Section 23.2
Grammar Exercise Workbook
• pp. 105–106

Personal Pronouns With Two or More Antecedents

A personal pronoun's antecedent should be unmistakable.

▶ **KEY CONCEPT** A personal pronoun should always be tied to a single, obvious antecedent. ■

In the example below, the pronoun *he* is confusing because it can refer to either *Sam* or *Steve.*

AMBIGUOUS REFERENCE: Sam reminded Steve that *he* had some remarkable photos of Kenya.

CORRECT: Sam reminded Steve that Steve had some remarkable photos of Kenya.
In talking with Steve, Sam said that he himself had some remarkable photos of Kenya.

Ambiguous Repetition of Personal Pronouns

Sometimes, repetition of the same pronoun within a sentence can create confusion.

▶ **KEY CONCEPT** Do not repeat a personal pronoun in a sentence if it can refer each time to a different antecedent. ■

In the example below, the second use of *she* is unclear. The sentence needs to be rephrased to clarify the meaning.

AMBIGUOUS REPETITION: Janet shouted to Kelly when *she* saw that *she* was about to be splashed by a bus.

CORRECT: Janet shouted to Kelly when *she* saw that *Kelly* was about to be splashed by a bus.
Janet shouted to Kelly when *Janet* saw that *she herself* was about to be splashed by a bus.

More Practice

**Language Lab
CD-ROM**
• Nouns and Pronouns
  lesson
**On-line
Exercise Bank**
• Section 23.2
**Grammar Exercise
Workbook**
• pp. 105–106

▶ **Exercise 35** Revising Sentences With Ambiguous
Pronoun References Rewrite the following sentences, correcting the ambiguous pronoun references.

1. Sarita told Denise that she had gotten an *A* on her geography project on Kenya.
2. When Denise read her report to Anna, she seemed very
   interested.
3. The report mentioned key facts about Kenya's climate,
   landforms, and population, and they were well covered.
4. Denise noted that Lake Victoria and Lake Turkana are
   both in Kenya, but it doesn't contain all of them.
5. The temperature in Nairobi is different from the temperature on the coast, but it is still quite warm.
6. The coastal region is much smaller than the plains area. It
   is more densely populated.
7. There are both Christians and Muslims in Kenya. Many of
   them are Roman Catholics.
8. Only Mount Kilimanjaro in Tanzania is higher than Mount
   Kenya. Its peak is more than 17,000 feet above sea level.
9. Coffee as well as tea grows abundantly in the highland
   region. It is one of Kenya's chief exports.
10. Sarita and Denise promised to help Cathy and Liz with
    their project, but they never got started.

Avoid Distant Pronoun References

A pronoun that is too far away from its antecedent can also
confuse a reader.

▶ **KEY CONCEPT** A personal pronoun should always be
close enough to its antecedent to prevent confusion. ■

A distant pronoun reference can be corrected by moving the
pronoun closer to its antecedent or by changing the pronoun
to a noun.

DISTANT REFERENCE:	Two chickens moved about in the doorway. On the porch, an old rocker creaked slightly back and forth. *They* pecked aimlessly at the floor.
CORRECT:	As the two chickens moved about in the doorway, *they* pecked aimlessly at the floor. On the porch, an old rocker creaked slightly back and forth.
	Two chickens moved about in the doorway. On the porch, an old rocker creaked slightly back and forth. The *chickens* pecked aimlessly at the floor.

▶ **Exercise 36** Correcting Distant Pronoun References

Rewrite the following sentences, correcting the distant pronoun references.

1. The Great Rift Valley is found in the west of Kenya, while the south of the country is heavily forested. It is defined by steep cliffs.

2. Volcanic mountain chains are formed to the west of the plateau that rises gradually from the coast and covers most of the country. Their principal peak is Mount Kenya.

3. The population of Kenya has a majority of Africans of different ethnic groups. There are also Europeans, Asians, and Arabs. Some of its largest ethnic groups are the Kikuyu, Luhya, and Kamba.

4. Nairobi is home to the National Museums of Kenya, the Kenya National Archives, and the McMillan Memorial Library, which houses a large collection of Africana. It is the capital of Kenya.

5. Kenya's exports total around $1 billion per year. The exports go principally to Uganda, England, Germany, Rwanda, and Pakistan. Its largest cash crop is tea.

6. Mombasa is the chief port of Kenya, a country that has little river transportation. It serves Uganda and Ethiopia as well as Kenya.

7. Kenya has four universities, as well as an extensive system of grade schools for younger children. Close to 40,000 students were enrolled in them in the early 1990's.

8. Bantu- and Arabic-speaking peoples lived together for centuries on the Kenyan coast. Many of the Arabs were traders who came originally from northern Africa. Eventually, they formed a hybrid language, Swahili.

9. A region of plains covers about three fourths of Kenya. The northern part of this region is hot and dry. It is the country's largest and least-populated area.

10. There are vast tracts of savanna, or grasslands, in Kenya. The country has a wide variety of wildlife. It supports elephants, rhinoceroses, giraffes, lions, and other big cats.

▼ **Critical Viewing** Describe this scene in downtown Nairobi with a pair of sentences that contain the pronoun *they* and a clear antecedent. **[Connect]**

Hands-on Grammar

Vague-Pronoun Cutouts

Complete the following activity to practice eliminating vague pronoun references. Work with a group of classmates to come up with a series of sentences that contain vague pronoun references. Write each sentence on a separate strip of paper. Place the vague pronoun in the lower left corner, as shown in the example.

Exchange your sentences with those of another group. Then, work with your group to correct the vague pronoun references by replacing each pronoun with an appropriate noun. Cut out the vague pronoun, and tape on a piece of paper containing the noun that is replacing the pronoun. Share your answers with the group that originated the sentences.

> When the team arrived at the competition, they told them that their game would be the next day.

> When the team arrived at the competition, officials told them that their game would the next day.

To get started, use the following sentences:
When we arrived at the zoo, they told us it was closed.
This book is so interesting you can't put it down.
The book is in my bag; it is very heavy.

Find It in Your Reading Sometimes, articles appearing in publications contain vague pronoun references. Look through a newspaper, and find any examples you can. Use these examples as part of your activity.

Find It in Your Writing Go through your portfolio in search of vague pronoun references. Use any you find as sample sentences for this activity. Revise your writing to eliminate the vague pronoun references.

Section 23.3

Section Review

GRAMMAR EXERCISES 37–42

Exercise 37 Revising to Eliminate
Vague Pronoun References Rewrite the
following sentences, correcting vague pronoun references.

1. I heard they have elephants in Kenya.
2. In the savanna, you have to be careful
   of wild animals.
3. The tour guide told us that the Great
   Rift Valley is more than 2,000 miles
   long and more than 400 miles wide.
   That impressed us.
4. Kenya attracts more than one-half million tourists annually, mostly to its
   national parks. They may also visit its
   Indian Ocean beaches.
5. Kenyan radio and television stations
   broadcast programs in English and
   show African- and Asian-language programs. This is because of the many
   languages spoken in the country.

Exercise 38 Revising to Correct
Ambiguous and Vague Pronouns
Rewrite the following paragraph, rephrasing and combining sentences to eliminate
ambiguous and vague pronouns.

(1) Nairobi is Kenya's capital, and it is
also its largest city. (2) Nairobi is now more
populous than the city of Chicago. (3) It
has grown very rapidly in recent years.
(4) Many of Nairobi's residents used to live
in rural villages. (5) They were very poor.
(6) Life in Nairobi is much more hectic
than in the rural villages. (7) This has had
an impact on many of the new residents.
(8) They spend weekdays working in
Nairobi, and then they often return to their
villages on the weekend to see friends and
family. (9) They are happy to see them
again. (10) It can be a difficult and confusing lifestyle.

Exercise 39 Revising Distant
Pronoun References Rewrite each sentence, correcting the distant pronouns.

1. Kenya has more than 30 million people, and its rate of growth is very fast.
   Most of them live in rural areas.
2. Kenya's tourist industry centers around
   popular beaches and national parks. It
   has been growing steadily.
3. Agricultural products are also an
   important part of the economy, which
   include coffee, tea, and pineapples.
4. Most roads in Kenya are unpaved.
   Because very few people drive cars, they
   have not caused much inconvenience.
5. Kenya has two major cities. The rest of
   the country is primarily rural. They
   are Nairobi and Mombasa.

Exercise 40 Find It in Your
Reading Identify the pronouns and
their antecedents in this excerpt from "No
Witchcraft for Sale" by Doris Lessing.

. . . Teddy had been on his scooter, and
had come to a rest with his foot on the
side of a big tub of plants. A tree-snake,
hanging by its tail from the roof, had
spat full into his eyes.

Exercise 41 Find It in Your
Writing Review a piece of narrative
writing from your portfolio. Find all of the
pronouns you've used, and identify their
antecedents. Revise any pronouns that
don't have clear antecedents.

Exercise 42 Writing Application
Write a description of an interesting
place you have visited. Check that all of
your pronouns have clear antecedents.

GRAMMAR EXERCISES 43–51

Exercise 43 Making Subjects Agree With Their Verbs Choose the verb in parentheses that agrees with the subject of each sentence.

1. Kenya's largest ethnic group, the Kikuyu, (comprises, comprise) about 16 percent of the country's population.
2. Family and tradition (is, are) very important to Kikuyu culture.
3. Traditionally, a young man of one of the Kikuyu tribes (undergoes, undergo) an adulthood ceremony at age eighteen.
4. There (is, are) three things the young man must do: have his ears pierced, his head shaved, and his face marked with white earth.
5. A young woman, who does not undergo the same ceremonies as a man, (faces, face) several challenging tests of endurance.

Exercise 44 Revising Sentences to Make Compound Subjects Agree With Their Verbs Rewrite any sentence that contains a subject-verb agreement error. Write *correct* if a sentence is correct.

1. Either Kenya or Tanzania provide excellent opportunities to view animals living naturally on the savanna.
2. Both the flora and fauna of Kenya seems to flourish in its national park reserves.
3. Neither a tourist nor a Kenyan citizen are permitted to hunt within a reserve.
4. Park rangers and officials of the government attempts to regulate poaching, the illegal killing of protected animals.
5. The high value of both tusks and skins tempts poachers to act against the law.

Exercise 45 Making Confusing Subjects Agree With Their Verbs Chose the verb in parentheses that agrees with the subject of each sentence.

1. One of Kenya's top priorities (is, are) to educate its people.
2. Which of the government's tasks (is, are) more important than this one?
3. Many in a village (balances, balance) schoolwork with their farming chores.
4. Swahili and English are both spoken throughout Kenya. Each (is, are) taught to Kenyan students.
5. Experts have noted at least eighty different languages spoken in Kenya, and the number (keeps, keep) going up.

Exercise 46 Supplying Personal Pronouns That Agree With Their Antecedents Write an appropriate personal pronoun to complete each sentence.

1. The people of Kenya enjoy traditional dancing, singing, and storytelling when __?__ have free time.
2. A Kenyan dancer or singer might perform __?__ act for tourists at a hotel.
3. Good storytellers not only entertained, but also educated with __?__ stories.
4. When my family and __?__ visited Kenya, we agreed that __?__ favorite entertainment was Kenyan music.
5. Neither Kenyan music nor Tanzanian music has found __?__ niche in the United States.

Exercise 47 Revising to Use Reflexive Pronouns Correctly Rewrite any of the following sentences that contain a misused reflexive pronoun. Write *correct* if a sentence is correct.

1. My brother and myself are planning a trip to Kenya.
2. My brother planned our visit to the Meru Game Reserve himself.
3. Who besides yourself can join our trip?
4. Sara and themselves may join ourselves.
5. The person who has the best itinerary for Kenya is herself.

Exercise 48 **Correcting Pronoun References** Rewrite the sentences below correcting the vague, ambiguous, or distant pronoun references.

1. Soccer in Kenya is a very popular sport that you play as a child or an adult.
2. Schools, towns, and companies sponsor soccer teams in Kenya much as they do in the United States.
3. Kenya's national soccer team competes in the Pan-African Games and in World Cup matches. However, these seem to be dominated by teams from west and central Africa.
4. It is difficult for young Kenyans to receive good athletic instruction and coaching, for few schools have athletic programs to train them.
5. Many of Kenya's athletes have received coaching and education at American universities. This has helped them succeed.

Exercise 49 **Using All the Rules of Agreement** Revise the following passage, correcting all errors in agreement. Underline each correction.

(1) Between A.D. 700 and 900, the coast between Kenya and Tanzania were settled by Arab traders. (2) Wars in their homelands prompted them to move to east Africa. (3) For several centuries, the Arabs faced no competition for trade with tribes in the interior of the country, and this helped them prosper. (4) During the fifteenth century, however, ships from Portugal were finding their way to east Africa. (5) It meant that things were bound to change. (6) The Portuguese established trading centers and built forts, several of which you can still see today. (7) They were intent on controlling the east African coast. (8) Each of the groups were trying to monopolize trade in the area. (9) The Arabs finally succeeded in overthrowing the Portuguese during the early 1700's. (10) Soon, however, they were joined by groups from England, France, and Germany, who was interested in expanding its trade and colonization.

Exercise 50 **Writing Application** Write a brief essay comparing people or places in another country with what you know about Kenya. Proofread your essay carefully for errors in subject-verb or pronoun agreement.

Exercise 51 **CUMULATIVE REVIEW** **Verb and Pronoun Usage and Agreement** Revise the following sentences, correcting all errors in verb usage, pronoun usage, and agreement. If a sentence has no errors, write *correct*.

1. In 1963, Jomo Kenyatta become the first president of independent Kenya.
2. It's no coincidence that his last name contain "Kenya."
3. He changed its name after he begin to participate in national politics.
4. Early on, Kenyatta seen the need for his country to be independent.
5. A book about Kenyan tribal life was written by him in the 1930's.
6. He described how life would be if Kenya was independent.
7. Kenyatta represented his country at political meetings in England.
8. He spoke eloquently and explains their people's point of view well.
9. At one time, the British accuse Kenyatta of inciting riots and throwed them in jail.
10. He was released in 1961 and lead his party to victory in Kenya's first election.

Standardized Test Preparation Workshop

Standard English Usage: Agreement

Many standardized tests call on you to demonstrate your knowledge of the rules of agreement. For example, some tests contain sections in which you are asked to identify the part of a sentence that contains an error. Often, the errors are problems with agreement. In other tests, you will be called on to identify the best way to rewrite a sentence or a passage. In some cases, the revision will involve correcting agreement errors. Below are samples of these two formats, along with the answers and an explanation of the answers.

> **Test Tip**
>
> Read each sentence completely before choosing the correct answer. This process will ensure that you consider all options.

Sample Test Items

Directions: Identify which of the underlined words and phrases in the following sentence contains an error.

Neither Brendan nor Claudia are interested in
(A)   (B)   (C)
traveling to Boston for the reunion.
(D)
No error
(E)

Directions: Choose the revised version of the following sentence that eliminates all errors in grammar, usage, and mechanics.

Neither Brendan nor Claudia are interested in traveling to Boston for the reunion.

A Neither Brendan nor Claudia is interested in traveling to Boston for the reunion.

B Both Brendan and Claudia is interested in traveling to Boston for the reunion.

C Neither Brendan and Claudia are interested in traveling to Boston for the reunion.

D Brendan or Claudia are not interested in traveling to Boston for the reunion.

Answers and Explanations

The correct answer is C—*are interested*. The subject, *Brendan nor Claudia,* is a compound subject made up of two singular subjects joined by *or* or *nor*. Such a subject takes a singular verb; in this case, *is*.

The correct answer is *A*. The subject, *Brendan nor Claudia,* is a compound subject made up of two singular subjects joined by *or* or *nor*. Such a subject takes a singular verb; in this case, *is*.

▶ **Practice 1** **Directions:** Identify which of the underlined words and phrases in each of the following sentences contains an error.

1. Our environment are full of natural
   (A)   (B)   (C)(D)
   resources. No error.
          (E)

2. Because water evaporate into the air
   (A)   (B)
   and falls as rain, snow, hail, and
      (C)
   sleet, it is considered a recyclable
       (D)
   resource. No error.
         (E)

3. Plants and animals are considered
   (A)   (B)
   renewable resources because they
             (C)
   can be used up if they are not
            (D)
   replaced. No error.
        (E)

4. Some timber companies has helped
     (A)   (B)
   keep up a steady supply of renewable
       (C)
   resources by planting new trees to
      (D)
   replace the ones they cut. No error.
                (E)

5. When nonrenewable resources like
   (A)   (B)
   minerals, natural gas, and oil

   is used up, they cannot be replaced.
   (C)   (D)
   No error.
   (E)

▶ **Practice 2** **Directions:** Choose the revised version of each numbered sentence that eliminates all errors in grammar, usage, and mechanics.

1 Because aluminum cans and plastic bottles are made of nonrenewable resources, city recycling programs is often eager to recycle them.

  A Because aluminum cans and plastic bottles are made of nonrenewable resources, city recycling programs are often eager to recycle them.

  B Because aluminum cans and plastic bottles is made of nonrenewable resources, city recycling programs is often eager to recycle them.

  C Because aluminum cans and plastic bottles was made of nonrenewable resources, city recycling programs is often eager to recycle them.

  D Because aluminum cans and plastic bottles are made of nonrenewable resources, city recycling programs was often eager to recycle them.

2 People has always been dependent on water. Although it is a recyclable resource, we need to conserve it as much as possible.

  E People have always been dependent on water. Although it are a recyclable resource, we need to conserve it as much as possible.

  F People have always been dependent on water. Although it is a recyclable resource, we need to conserve it as much as possible.

  G People have always been dependent on water. Although it is a recyclable resource, we needs to conserve it as much as possible.

  H People has always been dependent on water. Although it are a recyclable resource, we need to conserve it as much as possible.

Using Modifiers

You have probably noticed that you must sometimes change the form of adjectives and adverbs, especially in comparisons. You might say, for example, "Sir Percival traveled *farther* than Sir Gawain, but Sir Hector traveled the *farthest* of them all." The form of the adjective depends on whether two things or more than two things are being compared.

This chapter will show you how to form various adjectives and adverbs and how to avoid some specific errors that often occur in comparisons.

▲ **Critical Viewing**
"Who is the fairest of them all?" Compare the gowns of the ladies in this photo-graph. **[Describe]**

Diagnostic Test

Directions: Write all answers on a separate sheet of paper.

Skill Check A. Write the comparative and superlative degrees of the following modifiers.

1. strong
2. valiantly
3. enduring
4. generous
5. safe

Skill Check B. Identify the degree of each underlined modifier as *positive, comparative,* or *superlative.*

6. The earliest knights were usually of <u>noble</u> birth.
7. As armor grew <u>more sophisticated</u>, it also became <u>more expensive</u>.
8. Because of the expense involved, <u>fewer</u> noblemen wanted to become knights.
9. A knight's battle armor was usually <u>less shiny</u> than is popularly imagined.
10. After armor became expensive, nobles <u>most commonly</u> relied on hired men-at-arms for defense purposes.

Skill Check C. Choose the correct comparative or superlative modifier in each sentence.

11. Tournaments were (more/most) popular in the twelfth century than they were in the thirteenth.
12. Because of the expense involved, knighthood became restricted to only the (wealthier/wealthiest) noblemen.
13. Decorative armor was (heavier/heaviest) than battle armor.
14. Today's armor weighs (less/least) than medieval armor.
15. Mobility was the (better/best) attribute a suit of armor could have.

Skill Check D. Write the correct form of the modifier in parentheses to complete each sentence.

16. In England, the coronation of a king or queen is (ceremonious) than the dubbing of a knight.
17. Today, a person of (little) noble birth than royalty can be dubbed a knight in recognition of personal merit or service to society.
18. The (good) recent examples of such pageantry are the British royal weddings.
19. The (bad) aspect of such ceremonies is the expense involved.
20. You would travel a long distance to go to England to witness such pageantry, but the ceremony takes you even (far) back in history.

Skill Check E. Rewrite the following sentences to make the comparisons logical.

21. The shield is older than any protective device.
22. Bad weather could be fatal to a tournament.
23. Medieval armor was much heavier than today.
24. The helmet is a more enduring piece of armor than any.
25. Kings were of nobler birth than anyone.

Degrees of Comparison

In the English language, there are three *degrees*, or forms, of most adjectives and adverbs that are used in comparisons.

Recognizing Degrees of Comparison

In order to write effective comparisons, you first need to know the three degrees.

KEY CONCEPT The three degrees of comparison are the *positive*, the *comparative*, and the *superlative*. ■

In the following chart, both adjectives and adverbs are shown in each of the three degrees. Notice the three different ways that the words change form: (1) with *-er* and *-est*, (2) with *more* and *most*, and (3) with entirely different words.

DEGREES OF ADJECTIVES		
Positive	**Comparative**	**Superlative**
slow	slower	slowest
disagreeable	more disagreeable	most disagreeable
good	better	best
DEGREES OF ADVERBS		
slowly	more slowly	most slowly
disagreeably	more disagreeably	most disagreeably
well	better	best

Exercise 1 Recognizing Positive, Comparative, and Superlative Degrees Identify the degree of each underlined modifier.

EXAMPLE: Armor was <u>most commonly</u> made of metal.
ANSWER: superlative

1. *Armor* is the name given to any <u>protective</u> body equipment.
2. The <u>oldest</u> protective device is the shield.
3. Medieval knights are <u>most frequently</u> shown wearing armor.
4. Tournament armor was <u>heavier</u> than battle armor.
5. It was also <u>more highly</u> decorated.

Theme: Knights

In this section, you will learn how to form the comparative and superlative degrees of adjectives and adverbs. The examples and exercises in this section are about knights and armor.

Cross-Curricular Connection: Social Studies

More Practice

On-line Exercise Bank
• Section 24.1
Grammar Exercise Workbook
• pp. 107–108

Regular Forms

Like verbs, adjectives and adverbs can be either regular or irregular. The number of syllables in regular modifiers determines how their degrees form.

KEY CONCEPT Use *-er* or *more* to form the comparative degree and *-est* or *most* to form the superlative degree of most one- and two-syllable modifiers. ■

EXAMPLES:

smart	smarter	smartest
funny	funnier	funniest
brisk	more brisk	most brisk
spiteful	more spiteful	most spiteful

KEY CONCEPT All adverbs that end in *-ly* form their comparative and superlative degrees with *more* and *most* regardless of the number of syllables. ■

EXAMPLES:

curtly	more curtly	most curtly
shrewdly	more shrewdly	most shrewdly

KEY CONCEPT Use *more* and *most* to form the comparative and superlative degrees of all modifiers with three or more syllables. ■

EXAMPLES:

beautiful	more beautiful	most beautiful
generous	more generous	most generous

Note About *Comparisons* With *Less and* Least: *Less* and *least* can be used to form another version of the comparative and superlative degrees of most modifiers.

EXAMPLES:

soft	less soft	least soft
appetizing	less appetizing	least appetizing

Exercise 2 **Forming Regular Comparative and Superlative Degrees** Write the comparative and the superlative forms of each modifier.

EXAMPLE: wise

ANSWER: wiser, wisest

1. strong
2. protective
3. durable
4. acceptable
5. heavy
6. classical
7. modified
8. resistant
9. convenient
10. festive

Grammar and Style Tip

Choosing vivid, descriptive modifiers to compare people, places, things, and ideas can enhance your writing and make it more interesting.

Spelling Tip

When comparing two things, add the suffix *-er* or the word *more,* but never add both together.

Irregular Forms

Because several adjectives and adverbs form their comparative and superlative degrees in unpredictable ways, it is necessary to memorize them.

KEY CONCEPT The irregular comparative and superlative forms of certain adjectives and adverbs must be memorized. ■

As you read the following chart, separate the irregular modifiers that cause problems for you from the ones you already use correctly. Then, study and memorize those that cause problems for you. Notice that some modifiers differ only in the positive degree. *Bad, badly,* and *ill,* for example, all have the same comparative and superlative forms (*worse, worst*).

Spelling Tip

When comparing three or more things, add the suffix *-est* or the word *most,* but never add both together.

IRREGULAR MODIFIERS		
Positive	**Comparative**	**Superlative**
bad	worse	worst
badly	worse	worst
far (distance)	farther	farthest
far (extent)	further	furthest
good	better	best
ill	worse	worst
late	later	last *or* latest
little (amount)	less	least
many	more	most
much	more	most
well	better	best

Note About *Bad* and *Badly:* *Bad* is an adjective; *badly* is an adverb. *Bad* cannot be used as an adverb after an action verb.

EXAMPLES:
ADVERB
The children behaved *badly.*

ADJECTIVE
The children felt *bad* about it.

Note About *Good* and *Well:* *Good* is an adjective; *well* can be used as an adjective or an adverb. *Good* cannot be used as an adverb after an action verb.

EXAMPLES:
ADJECTIVE
The children felt *good* about it.

ADVERB
The children behaved *well.*

ADJECTIVE
The children did not feel *well* after eating candy.

More Practice

On-line
Exercise Bank
• Section 24.1
Grammar Exercise
Workbook
• pp. 109–110

▶ **Exercise 3** Forming Irregular Comparative and
Superlative Degrees Write the appropriate form of the underlined modifier to complete each sentence.

EXAMPLE: Battle armor did not cost too <u>much</u> money, but
            tournament armor cost ___?___ .

ANSWER: more

1. <u>Some</u> knights fought without armor, but many ___?___
   knights wore armor.
2. When a knight was in full armor, <u>little</u> of his body and
   even ___?___ of his face showed.
3. Wealthy knights wore <u>good</u> suits of armor, but they wore
   their ___?___ armor to a tournament.
4. Knights traveled <u>far</u> in their homeland, but those who
   went to the Crusades traveled ___?___ .
5. When a boy became a page, he had <u>far</u> to go to become a
   squire but even ___?___ to become a knight.
6. A wound from a sword was <u>bad</u>, but a wound from a
   bullet was ___?___ .
7. A battle had <u>some</u> ceremony, but a tournament had
   much ___?___ ceremony.
8. Medieval armor was a <u>good</u> protective device, but
   today's armor is ___?___ and lighter.
9. Tournament armor was designed to allow <u>some</u>
   mobility, but safety was the ___?___ important
   concern.
10 Tournament armor was a <u>little</u> cumbersome,
   but battle armor had to be ___?___ so.

▶ **Exercise 4** Writing Sentences With
Comparative and Superlative Degrees Write
a sentence for each of the following.
1. secretive (comparative)
2. good (superlative)
3. well (comparative)
4. jocular (comparative)
5. malicious (superlative)
6. likely (comparative)
7. funny (superlative)
8. badly (superlative)
9. calmly (comparative)
10. heroic (superlative)

▼ **Critical Viewing**
Compare the armor
worn by this knight with
the safety gear worn by
people on skateboards
or rollerblades. Use the
comparative and superla-
tive degrees in your
sentences. [**Compare
and Contrast**]

Degrees of Comparison • **625**

Hands-on Grammar

Irregular-Modifier Pocket Fold

Practice using irregular comparative and superlative forms of modifiers with a pocket fold. Take a 6 1/2"-inch-square sheet of paper, and fold in the corners so that they meet in the middle. Turn the paper over, and again fold in the corners. Then, crease the paper by folding it in half and in half again. You will have a small square. Unfold only the small square, and lay the paper flat so that four square sections are facing upward. Write the positive degree of a different irregular modifier on each of the four squares. (See example A.)

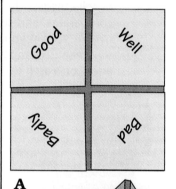

A

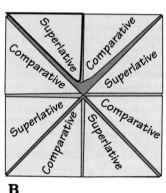

B

Next, turn the paper over, and on each of the eight triangular sections, write *comparative* or *superlative.* (See example B.) Then, lift up each triangle, and write underneath it the corresponding forms of the comparative or superlative on the back of the square. Each modifier will have two forms.

Finally, refold the square so that the positives are on the outside.

Place your thumbs and index fingers in each of the four slots formed by the small squares, and pinch them together. You should be able to open and close the square in two directions, exposing either the comparative or the superlative form each time. (See example C.)

C

With a partner, take turns choosing a modifier from the other's pocket fold. After opening and closing the square in different directions four or five times, each person must give the form of the modifier indicated on the triangle. Check your answers by lifting up the triangle.

Find It in Your Reading Read two or three paragraphs of a story or article, and see how many comparative and superlative forms you recognize.

Find It in Your Writing Review the use of modifiers in a piece of your writing, and make sure that you used and formed the modifiers

Section 24.1 Section Review

GRAMMAR EXERCISES 5–10

Exercise 5 Recognizing Positive, Comparative, and Superlative Degrees
Identify the degree of each underlined modifier.

1. <u>Knightly</u> behavior was regulated by a code of conduct known as chivalry.
2. Tournaments involved <u>much</u> pageantry.
3. Pageantry is <u>difficult</u> to define.
4. It is one of the <u>most ritualistic</u> features of any society.
5. Early pageants were religious in origin, but that aspect is <u>less emphasized</u> now.

Exercise 6 Supplying the Comparative and Superlative Degrees
Write the appropriate comparative or superlative degree of the modifier in parentheses.

1. Becoming a knight involved (much) ceremony in the thirteenth century than it did in the twelfth.
2. In the twelfth century, a squire became a knight when his abilities were recognized by another knight, but in the thirteenth century, he was dubbed by someone of (noble) birth.
3. A good suit of armor weighed around 65 pounds, but carrying a lance, sword, and shield made the load (heavy).
4. Interlinked iron rings known as mail was the (common) armor.
5. It was useful against a sword blow, but (little) so against the point of a lance or an arrow.

Exercise 7 Revising to Eliminate Errors in Comparisons Revise the following paragraph, correcting any errors in comparison you find.

In his own lifetime, Geoffrey Chaucer was considered one of the most greatest English poets. His more wider read work, *The Canterbury Tales*, is a story told by pilgrims on the way to the cathedral of Canterbury. In medieval Christianity, pilgrimages were considered well things to do. Some pilgrims would travel as far as Rome, and some would travel even further. *The Canterbury Tales* is written in Middle English, which is more easier to read than Old English but not as easy as modern English.

Exercise 8 Find It in Your Reading
Identify the comparatives and superlatives in this passage from *Sir Gawain and the Green Knight*, which was translated by Marie Borroff.

That no host under heaven is hardier of will, / Nor better brothers-in-arms where battle is joined; / I am the weakest, well I know, and of wit feeblest; / And the loss of my life would be least of any; . . .

Exercise 9 Find It in Your Writing
Review a poem from your writing portfolio, and locate the positive, comparative, and superlative modifiers. Check for correct usage. Could adding or intensifying modifiers improve your work?

Exercise 10 Writing Application
Write a comparison-and-contrast essay using positive, comparative, and superlative forms of appropriate modifiers. Check your work for correct usage.

Making Clear Comparisons

In this section, you will learn the proper uses of the comparative and superlative degrees and how to avoid making illogical comparisons.

Using Comparative and Superlative Degrees

One basic rule that has two parts covers the correct use of comparative and superlative forms:

▶ **KEY CONCEPT** Use the comparative degree to compare two persons, places, or things. Use the superlative degree to compare three or more persons, places, or things. ■

As the following examples illustrate, the number of items being compared is often indicated in the context of the sentence.

COMPARATIVE: Orange will be *more conspicuous* than blue.
                I am *less talented* than Sheila.

SUPERLATIVE: Orange is the *most conspicuous* color of all.
           I am the *least talented* person for this work.

Note About *Double Comparisons*: A *double comparison* is a usage error caused by using both *-er* and *more* or both *-est* and *most* to form a regular modifier. A double comparison can also be created by adding any of these endings to an irregular modifier.

INCORRECT: This is the *most happiest* day of my life.
          My cold is *worser* today than it was yesterday.

CORRECT: This is the *happiest* day of my life.
        My cold is *worse* today than it was yesterday.

GRAMMAR IN LITERATURE

from **Song**

John Donne

In this love poem, the poet uses a superlative form to refer to his love. In the second line, he uses a comparative form.

Sweetest love, I do not go, / For weariness of thee,
Nor in hope the world can show / A *fitter* love for me;

 **Internet Tip**

To find out more about skyscrapers, use search words like *skyscraper, construction,* and *architecture.* You can even learn what massive buildings are planned for the future!

Exercise 11 Supplying the Comparative and Superlative **Degrees** Write the appropriate comparative or superlative degree of the modifier in parentheses.

EXAMPLE: Winston is the (funny) student in our class.
ANSWER: funniest

1. The world's (old) skyscrapers were built in Chicago.
2. They were much (small) than modern buildings.
3. Many were demolished to make room for (new) structures.
4. Unlike today's skyscrapers, the (early) structures were built of solid masonry construction.
5. It was discovered that using a steel skeleton would make possible the construction of (high) buildings.
6. A steel skeleton is (well) able to bear the load of the walls and floors than masonry alone.
7. The antennae added to the Empire State Building make it (tall) now than when it was first built.
8. Is the (tall) building in the United States still the Sears Tower in Chicago?
9. Which is the (high) building in the world?
10. One of the (important) design concerns is the type of air currents that will be hitting the top of the building.

Exercise 12 Using the Comparative and Superlative Degrees Correctly Choose the correct comparative or superlative form in each sentence.

1. The (taller/tallest) buildings in the world are skyscrapers.
2. They can be found in (more/most) big cities.
3. The (earlier/earliest) skyscrapers were built in the United States.
4. Today's skyscrapers are much (higher/highest) than those early versions.
5. The invention of the electric elevator made it (more feasible/most feasible) to design taller buildings.

▶ **Critical Viewing** The Sears Tower in Chicago is the tallest building in the United States. Compare the Sears Tower with a tall building in a city near you. Use comparatives and superlatives in your sentences.
[Compare and Contrast]

More Practice

On-line
Exercise Bank
• Section 24.2
Grammar Exercise Workbook
• pp. 111–112

Logical Comparisons

In order to write logical comparisons, you must make sure that you do not unintentionally compare unrelated items or compare something with itself.

▶**KEY CONCEPT** Make sure that your sentences compare only items of a similar kind. ■

In the following unbalanced examples, the sentences illogically compare dissimilar things: *Message* cannot be compared with *postcard*, and *plants* in a greenhouse cannot be compared with an entire *greenhouse*.

UNBALANCED:	A *message* conveyed by telephone is more private than a *postcard*.
CORRECT:	A *message* conveyed by telephone is more private than *one* written on a postcard.
UNBALANCED:	The *plants* in this greenhouse are fresher than the *greenhouse* down the road.
BALANCED:	The *plants* in this greenhouse are fresher than *those* in the greenhouse down the road.

***Other* and *Else* in Comparisons** Another kind of illogical comparison results when something is unintentionally compared with itself.

▶**KEY CONCEPT** When comparing one of a group with the rest of the group, make sure that your sentence contains the word *other* or the word *else*. ■

In the first example below, the *Grand Canyon*, which is one of the national parks, cannot be compared with all national parks. Adding *other* excludes the Grand Canyon from the rest of the national parks. In the second example, *Corey* cannot be compared to all the members on the team because *Corey* is one of those people. Adding *else* separates *Corey* from the rest of the group.

ILLOGICAL:	We thought the Grand Canyon was *more beautiful than any* national park we visited.
LOGICAL:	We thought the Grand Canyon was *more beautiful than any other* national park we visited.
ILLOGICAL:	Corey runs *faster than anyone* on the team.
LOGICAL:	Corey runs *faster than anyone else* on the team.

▷ **Exercise 13** **Making Balanced Comparisons** Rewrite each sentence, correcting the unbalanced comparison.

EXAMPLE: Shelly's voice is better than Ted.
ANSWER: Shelly's voice is better than Ted's.

1. There are more floors in the World Trade Center than the Empire State Building.
2. The shape of the Petronas Towers in Malaysia is different from the World Trade Center.
3. Skyscrapers are taller now than the beginning of the last century.
4. The tallest building in Paris is smaller than New York.
5. Building a skyscraper is harder than a house.

▷ **Exercise 14** **Revising Sentences Using *Other* and *Else* in Comparisons** Rewrite each sentence, correcting the illogical comparison.

1. The Petronas Towers in Kuala Lumpur are taller than almost any building.
2. Builders in California are more concerned about earth-quakes than builders anywhere in the United States.
3. The United States has more skyscrapers than any country.
4. Tall buildings were being built in the United States earlier than they were anywhere.
5. The Paris skyline is more beautiful than that of any city.
6. By the turn of the century, steel was more abundant than at any time.
7. Tokyo may have more plans for extremely high buildings than any city.
8. In 1990, Chicago had the tallest building of any city.
9. In 1913, the Woolworth Building was taller than any building.
10. Because of the large numbers of people living and working in skyscrapers, safety is more important than almost anything.

▷ **Exercise 15** **Writing Sentences With Logical Comparisons** Write a sentence comparing the given items in a logical way.

1. skyscrapers of New York and Chicago
2. dogs and cats
3. inches and centimeters
4. your town with all others
5. chocolate with all other candy

▷ **More Practice**

On-line Exercise Bank
• Section 24.2
Grammar Exercise Workbook
• pp. 113–114

Absolute Modifiers

A few modifiers cannot be used in comparisons because they are *absolute* in meaning; that is, their meanings are entirely contained in the positive degree. If, for example, one vase is *priceless*, another vase cannot be *more priceless*.

> **KEY CONCEPT** Avoid using absolute modifiers illogically in comparisons. ■

Among the most common absolute modifiers are the words *dead, entirely, eternal, fatal, final, identical, infinite, mortal, opposite, perfect,* and *unique*. Rather than use words such as these in comparisons, try to find similar words whose meanings are not absolute.

ILLOGICAL: This truth is *more eternal* than any other.
LOGICAL :   This truth is *more enduring* than any other.
ILLOGICAL: Your thesis is *more unique* than anyone else's.
LOGICAL: Your thesis is *more original* than anyone else's.

> **Exercise 16** Avoiding Absolute Modifiers in Comparisons

Rewrite each sentence, correcting the illogical comparison.
1. The top of the World Trade Center is more perfect than the top of the Empire State Building.
2. The Empire State Building was most unique when first built.
3. It is more identical to the Chrysler Building than to any other building.
4. He was more overwhelmed by the view from the Eiffel Tower than he was by the view from the Sears Tower.
5. For the most utmost in safety, tall buildings are required to have protected stairways as a means of escape.
6. The design of the Hancock Building in Boston is said by some to be more eternal than that of the Art Institute.
7. The architectural plans for the new music center are more final than they were last month.
8. He is more finished with the drawings of the building's facade than he was last week.
9. The view from the observation deck is the most infinite.
10. The houses of Frank Lloyd Wright are more immortal than any others.

Grammar and Style Tip

An absolute modifier can never be more or less absolute than it is already. Never add the suffix *-er* or *-est* or the words *more* and *most* to words like *unique* or *impossible*.

More Practice

On-line Exercise Bank
• Section 24.2
Grammar Exercise Workbook
• pp. 115–116

Section Review

GRAMMAR EXERCISES 17–22

▶ **Exercise 17** Supplying the
Comparative and Superlative Degrees
Write the appropriate comparative or
superlative degree of the modifier in
parentheses.

1. Skyscrapers are subject to (some) rigorous building standards than smaller
   structures are.
2. Before the use of steel frames, buildings were (small) than they are now.
3. It seems as though there is a competition to see who can build the (high)
   building.
4. Is Hong Kong's Central Plaza (far) away
   than the Eiffel Tower?
5. I wonder which building receives the
   (some) visitors each year?

▶ **Exercise 18** **Revising Sentences
to Make Logical Comparisons** Revise
each sentence, correcting the illogical
comparison.

1. Singapore's new bank building was
   completed sooner than Toronto.
2. It is harder to climb stairs than an
   escalator.
3. Do more people work at the World
   Trade Center than your office?
4. Are there more skyscrapers in New
   York than Paris?
5. The skyscrapers in New York are nearer than Tokyo.
6. Which building is taller than any?
7. Do more people go to the Sears Tower
   than anywhere in Chicago?
8. In 1930, the Empire State Building
   was taller than any building.
9. Is the Eiffel Tower taller than any
   Parisian structure?
10. He will design a larger building than
    anyone.

▶ **Exercise 19** Revising to Avoid
Absolute Modifiers in Comparisons
Rewrite each sentence, correcting the illog-
ical comparison.

1. Skyscrapers are the most eternal
   feature of a city's skyline.
2. Buildings are more infinitely higher
   today than they were in the 1930's.
3. Skyscrapers are given the most complete inspection before they open.
4. The skyscraper is the most unique
   form of architecture.
5. Use of substandard materials could be
   more fatal to a building's occupants.

▶ **Exercise 20** Find It in Your
Reading Identify the superlative forms
of modifiers that appear in the following
excerpt from "Here Is New York" by E. B.
White.

New York is nothing like Paris; it is nothing like London; and it is not Spokane
multiplied by sixty, or Detroit multiplied
by four. It is by all odds the loftiest of
cities. It even managed to reach the highest point in the sky at the lowest moment
of the Depression.

▶ **Exercise 21** Find It in Your
Writing Review a story that you have
written. Are comparative modifiers used correctly? Revise your work to add comparative
modifiers.

▶ **Exercise 22** Writing Application
Write a description of a fictional character from one of your reading assignments.
Challenge yourself to use adjectives and
adverbs logically and in every degree of
comparison.

GRAMMAR EXERCISES 23–30

Exercise 23 Recognizing Positive, Comparative, and Superlative Degrees
Identify the degree of each underlined modifier.

1. Elevators travel <u>faster</u> now than ever before.
2. They travel so fast it makes some people feel <u>ill</u>.
3. Other people are <u>more afraid</u> of the confined space.
4. This fear is <u>most commonly</u> known as claustrophobia.
5. There are people whose <u>greatest</u> fear is of heights.

Exercise 24 Forming Regular Comparative and Superlative Degrees
Write the comparative and superlative forms of each modifier.

1. fearfully
2. regular
3. expensive
4. durable
5. decisive
6. uneasy
7. dangerous
8. windy
9. slyly
10. innovative

Exercise 25 Forming Irregular Comparative and Superlative Degrees
Write the correct form of the underlined modifier to complete each sentence.

1. Masonry construction gives <u>good</u> support, but in comparison, a steel frame gives the ___?___ .
2. The Eiffel Tower is <u>far</u> away, but the Petronas Towers are even ___?___ .
3. High-rise building technology has advanced very <u>far</u>, and it appears it will go even ___?___ .
4. He felt <u>ill</u> in the elevator but ___?___ when he reached the top.

5. There are <u>some</u> skyscrapers in Paris but ___?___ in New York.
6. Many Parisians feel <u>bad</u> about demolishing old buildings but even ___?___ about building skyscrapers.
7. Some say the tall buildings of Montparnasse are <u>bad</u>-looking, but others believe the Pompidou Center is the ___?___ -looking building in Paris.
8. Not all Parisians think <u>well</u> of the new tall buildings; they believe the city was ___?___ as it was.
9. The Sacre Coeur cathedral has <u>some</u> renown, but the ___?___ famous Paris landmark of all is the Eiffel Tower.
10. London is <u>far</u> away; is Paris even ___?___ ?

Exercise 26 Using the Comparative and Superlative Degrees Correctly Choose the correct comparative or superlative form in each sentence.

1. Which city has the (more/most) skyscrapers?
2. There are (better/best) construction methods today than there were in 1920.
3. Is Paris the (prettier/prettiest) city you have ever seen?
4. The buildings seem (cleaner/cleanest) there than anywhere else.
5. One of the city's (less/least) familiar ordinances requires regular cleaning of buildings.
6. Parisians are (prouder/proudest) of their city than inhabitants of almost any other city.
7. It has some of the (more/most) beautiful buildings in the world.
8. The Notre Dame cathedral is one of the (finer/finest) examples of French Gothic architecture.

9. The cornerstone was laid in 1163, and the building was finally completed more than 30 years (later/latest).
10. Notre Dame is (older/oldest) than another famous Parisian church: Sacre Coeur.

6. Its history is older than New York.
7. After World War II, the alteration of the London skyline was most permanent.
8. London lost more buildings to wartime damage than Paris.
9. It suffered more wartime damage than any English city.
10. There have been more monarchs crowned at Westminster Abbey than buried.

▶ **Exercise 27** Supplying the **Comparative and Superlative Degrees** Write the appropriate degree of the modifier in parentheses.

1. Skyscrapers rise to (great) heights now than ever before.
2. Some people think being on top of a skyscraper is the (scary) thing that could happen to them.
3. Phobias are usually (irrational) than other fears.
4. He is (afraid) of heights than of anything else.
5. Which do you think is (bad)—claustrophobia or acrophobia?
6. Doctors sometimes can help people handle their fears (well) than people can handle them by themselves.
7. What was the (bad) fright you have ever had?
8. Arachnophobia is my (big) fear.
9. There are probably (few) spiders on top of a skyscraper than there are on the ground.
10. She is (little) afraid of heights than he is.

▶ **Exercise 28** Revising Sentences **to Make Comparisons Clear** Revise each sentence, making sure that the comparisons are clear.

1. There are more tall buildings in London than Dublin.
2. London's skyscrapers are smaller than New York.
3. Do you like London better than anywhere?
4. Westminster Abbey is one of England's most perfect examples of Gothic architecture.
5. Is London larger than any city?

▶ **Exercise 29** Writing Sentences **With Comparatives** Write at least two comparative sentences for each set of facts.

1. Largest States:
   Texas, 261,914 square miles
   Alaska, 570,374 square miles
   California, 155,973 square miles
2. Smallest States:
   Rhode Island, 1,045 square miles
   Delaware, 1,982 square miles
   Connecticut, 4,845 square miles
3. Largest Cities:
   Los Angeles, CA, population: 3,485,398
   New York, NY, population: 7,322,564
   Chicago, IL, population: 2,783,726
4. Highest Recorded Temperatures:
   California, 134 degrees Fahrenheit
   Arizona, 128 degrees Fahrenheit
   Nevada, 125 degrees Fahrenheit
   New Mexico, 122 degrees Fahrenheit
5. Lowest Recorded Temperatures:
   Alaska, -80 degrees Fahrenheit
   Montana, -70 degrees Fahrenheit
   Utah, -69 degrees Fahrenheit

▶ **Exercise 30** Writing Application Write a brief comparison in which you compare an actor or actress with several others. Make sure that you use modifiers correctly.

Standardized Test Preparation Workshop

Standard English Usage: Modifiers

Standardized test questions often measure your ability to use modifiers correctly. Use the following strategies to help you determine which form to use in a sentence:

- If no comparison is being made, use the positive form of the modifier.
- If one thing or action is compared to another thing or action, use the comparative form of the modifier—ending in *-er* or preceded by *more.*
- If one thing or action is being compared to more than one other thing or action, use the superlative form of the modifier—ending in *-est* or preceded by *most.*
- Be aware that some modifiers, such as *good, bad, much,* and *many,* have irregular forms.

Sample Test Items	Answers and Explanations
Directions: Read the passage, and choose the word or group of words that belongs in each space. Jamaica has always been one of the __(1)__ tourist destinations in the Caribbean. True, the beaches are beautiful, but the __(2)__ culture is also a main attraction.	

1 A popularest
   B popular
   C mostest popular
   D most popular
	The correct answer for item 1 is *D, most popular.* Because Jamaica is being compared to multiple tourist destinations, the superlative form should be used.

2 F diverser
   G most diverse
   H more diverse
   J diverse
	The correct answer for item 2 is *J, diverse.* Because no comparison is being made, the positive form of the modifier is used.

▶ **Practice 1** **Directions:** Read the passage, and choose the word or group of words that belongs in each space.

Jamaica has an abundant musical history, even compared to __(1)__ countries. Although some forms of music from the island are known __(2)__ than others, the __(3)__ known music is called reggae. Even people with the __(4)__ bit of knowledge about Jamaican music have heard of Bob Marley. Marley is considered one of the __(5)__ Jamaican musicians in the history of the island.

1 A many large
  B many larger
  C more large
  D largest

2 F good
  G better
  H best
  J more better

3 A good
  B better
  C best
  D more better

4 F less
  G little
  H least
  J littler

5 A most important
  B importantest
  C importanter
  D important

▶ **Practice 2** **Directions:** Read the passage, and choose the word or group of words that belongs in each space.

Jamaican music didn't begin with reggae. Nothing could be __(1)__ from the truth. There were __(2)__ forms of Jamaican music that influenced reggae. Mento, one of the first recorded Jamaican sounds, may be the __(3)__ of all of them. To an untrained ear, it resembles music from Trinidad called calypso. But mento was __(4)__ by Jamaican folk music than by calypso. Today, the popularity of Jamaican music is growing __(5)__ than ever.

1 A more far
  B furthest
  C further
  D furthier

2 F old
  G more old
  H older
  J more older

3 A least known
  B lesser known
  C lesser
  D least

4 F influenced
  G mostly influenced
  H most influenced
  J more influenced

5 A most fast
  B faster
  C fastest
  D more fast

Chapter 25

Miscellaneous Problems in Usage

For centuries, the moon's luminous presence in the night sky has fascinated Earth's inhabitants and encouraged the study of our nearest neighbor. Today, we have developed technology that has allowed us to learn much about the moon. Just as we have striven to bring the moon into focus, we must strive to bring clarity and precision to our writing.

Many small problems that can spoil the clarity of speaking or writing do not fall into any of the broad categories of usage that were covered in preceding chapters. Some of these problems involve distinctions between standard and nonstandard usage. Others involve similar spellings or meanings. The next two sections will help you improve your mastery of certain details that contribute to effective speaking and writing.

▲ **Critical Viewing**
Write a sentence explaining how the moon influences some people's behavior. Use either *affect* or *effect* correctly in your sentence. **[Analyze]**

Diagnostic Test

Directions: Write all answers on a separate sheet of paper.

Skill Check A. Choose the word in parentheses that best completes each sentence.

1. Because early civilizations didn't know (nothing, anything) about the moon, they devised their own theories.
2. Without a single visit to the moon, they hadn't (no, any) facts.
3. The absence of facts, however, (won't, will) hardly stop people from devising explanations for the unknown.
4. There (is, isn't) no end to people's fascination with the moon.
5. These days, astronauts can visit the moon, but they can't stay for (any, no) length of time.

Skill Check B. Indicate whether or not each of these sentences uses understatement.

6. Once, people thought the shapes on the surface of the moon looked like cheese.
7. That's not to say that there weren't other explanations for the shapes.
8. Some people thought creatures lived on the moon.
9. They didn't believe there wasn't anybody else in the universe.
10. It seems there wasn't anyone who didn't have some theory.

Skill Check C. Choose the word in parentheses that correctly completes each sentence.

11. Sometimes, people's beliefs about the moon (affected, effected) the way they lived their lives.
12. Myths about the moon are (a, an) universal tie among cultures.
13. Some people tried to (adapt, adopt) their theories to fit the scientific facts they learned.
14. Philosophers and kings also stated (they're, their) theories.
15. Musicians have been fascinated with the moon, (too, to).
16. There is agreement (among, between) music lovers that "Blue Moon" is one of the best songs written about the moon.
17. (Beside, Besides) inspiring songs, the moon has also motivated writers to compose stories and poems.
18. Since the first person landed on the moon in 1969, scientists have made (further, farther) discoveries.
19. Scientists in many nations often share information with (each other, one another).
20. With today's technology, scientists (may, can) communicate more easily than ever before.
21. Someday, space travel may (bring, take) tourists to the moon.
22. Plans for lunar vacations will most likely take (awhile, a while).
23. After all, the moon is much (farther, further) than any earthly holiday spot.
24. New studies about the moon (proceed, precede) at a steady rate.
25. Many of us are (all ready, already) for a trip to the moon!

Negative Sentences

In today's English, a clause usually needs just one negative word to convey a negative idea. More than one negative word can be redundant and confusing.

Recognizing Double Negatives

A clause containing two negative words when only one is needed is said to contain a *double negative.*

▶ **KEY CONCEPT** Do not write sentences with double negatives. ■

The following chart provides examples of double negatives and the two ways of correcting each double negative.

CORRECTING DOUBLE NEGATIVES	
Double Negatives	**Corrections**
The moon *doesn't never* produce its own light.	The moon *never* produces its own light. The moon *doesn't ever* produce its own light.
You *can't* grow *nothing* on the moon.	You *can't* grow *anything* on the moon. You can grow *nothing* on the moon.
I *didn't* know *nothing* about the moon.	I knew *nothing* about the moon. I *didn't* know *anything* about the moon.

Sentences containing more than one clause can correctly contain more than one negative word. Each clause, however, should contain no more than one negative word.

EXAMPLE: Because the moon *doesn't* revolve around the sun, it *isn't* considered a planet.

▶ **Exercise 1** Avoiding Double Negatives Choose the word in parentheses that makes each sentence negative without forming a double negative.
1. There aren't (no, any) life forms on the moon.
2. The atmosphere (isn't, is) no good for Earth organisms.
3. Nobody (can't, can) breathe on the moon.
4. There (is, isn't) no free-moving water there.
5. Nothing (can, can't) live on the moon.

Theme: The Moon

In this section, you will learn the proper way to write sentences that express negatives. The examples and exercises are about the moon.

Cross-Curricular Connection: Science

💡 **Spelling Tip**

Most helping verbs can be made negative by adding *n't,* but watch out for some exceptions, such as *am, may, might, shall,* and *will.*

▶ **More Practice**

Language Lab CD-ROM
• Problems With Modifiers lesson
On-line Exercise Bank
• Section 25.1
Grammar Exercise Workbook
• pp. 117–118

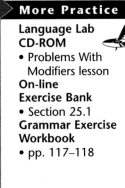

Forming Negative Sentences Correctly

A negative sentence can be formed correctly in one of three ways:

Using One Negative Word The most common way to form a negative sentence is to use a single negative word, such as *never, no, nobody, nothing, nowhere, not,* or the contraction *n't* added to a helping verb.

▶ **KEY CONCEPT** Do not use two negative words in the same clause. ■

DOUBLE NEGATIVE: The moon *doesn't* have *no* satellites of its own.

CORRECT: The moon has *no* satellites of its own.
The moon *doesn't* have any satellites of its own.

Using *But* in a Negative Sense *But* used negatively means *only* and should not be used with another negative word.

▶ **KEY CONCEPT** Do not use *but* in its negative sense with another negative. ■

DOUBLE NEGATIVE: Earth hasn't but one moon.
CORRECT: The Earth has *but* one moon.
The Earth has *only* one moon.

Using *Barely, Hardly,* and *Scarcely* Each of these words also makes a sentence negative.

▶ **KEY CONCEPT** Do not use *barely, hardly,* or *scarcely* with another negative. ■

DOUBLE NEGATIVE: We *haven't barely* begun our hands-on study of the moon.

CORRECT: We have *barely* begun our hands-on study of the moon.

DOUBLE NEGATIVE: The moon *isn't hardly* as big as the sun.
CORRECT: The moon is *hardly* as big as the sun.
DOUBLE NEGATIVE: Earth *hasn't scarcely* as many moons as Jupiter.

CORRECT: Earth has *scarcely* as many moons as Jupiter.

Technology Tip

In formal writing, it is better to write out the negative than to use a contraction. On your computer, use the search feature to find *n't* and change it to *not.* Be careful with the words *can't* and *won't.*

▼ **Critical Viewing** Write two sentences about the moon in this picture, using *isn't* in one sentence and *doesn't* in the other. Watch out for double negatives. **[Analyze]**

▶ **Exercise 2** **Correcting Double Negatives** Eliminate the error in each of the following phrases, and expand the corrected phrase into a sentence of your own.

1. can't see but half
2. nobody can't see
3. doesn't look nothing like
4. can't barely make out
5. isn't hardly devoid
6. don't appear nowhere
7. aren't but the most numerous
8. don't hardly appear
9. aren't scarcely found
10. aren't no seas

▶ **Exercise 3** **Revising Sentences to Avoid Double Negatives** Revise each of the sentences, eliminating any problems with negatives.

1. There isn't no celestial body closer to Earth than the moon.
2. At first, nobody knew nothing concrete about the moon.
3. People didn't have no idea how to get there.
4. With only primitive technology, early humans couldn't get nowhere close to it.
5. Ancient admirers of the moon couldn't see nothing except what they could see with their eyes.
6. Renaissance observers hadn't but a telescope to aid them.
7. No one had no idea what to expect when the manned spacecraft went to the moon.
8. The first close-range photographs didn't hardly stop further lunar exploration.
9. Once airborne, the first astronauts to land on the moon couldn't scarcely stop for directions.
10. The moon wasn't but the first extraterrestrial body visited by humans.

▼ **Critical Viewing** Write a sentence describing how the Earth seems from the moon. Use the word *hardly* or *barely* in your sentence without creating a double negative. **[Connect]**

Using Understatement

Occasionally, a speaker or writer may want to imply a positive idea without actually stating it. This indirect method is called *understatement*. Understatement may be used to minimize the importance of an idea or, conversely, to emphasize its importance.

KEY CONCEPT Understatement can be achieved by using a negative word and a word with a negative prefix. ■

EXAMPLES: The study of the moon is *hardly* an *uninteresting* subject.
The moon's light *isn't* completely *unromantic*.

Exercise 4 Revising Sentences to Create Understatement
Rewrite each sentence so that it achieves understatement.
1. The phases of the moon are interesting.
2. The sliver after a new moon is recognizable.
3. The waxing of the moon from new to full is graceful.
4. The light of the full moon is inviting.
5. Many people who are intelligent have lost their hearts in the light of the full moon.
6. They find their love is requited.
7. A blue moon, the second full moon in one calendar month, seldom occurs.
8. A harvest moon rises soon after sunset and is appreciated by farmers.
9. They are pleased with the extra hours of light.
10. The waning of the moon can be a sad occasion.

Exercise 5 Writing Negative Sentences Use each item in a negative sentence of your own. Proofread carefully to make sure you have not created a double negative.
1. hardly deserved
2. no one had walked
3. wasn't upsetting
4. never wore
5. can't carry
6. barely finished
7. but one choice
8. scarcely upset
9. nobody can imagine
10. never cared

Grammar and Style Tip

You can use negatives to add emphasis to an idea by accomplishing the opposite of understatement. For example, "She is definitely *not* a friend of mine."

More Practice
Language Lab
CD-ROM
• Problems With Modifiers lesson
On-line
Exercise Bank
• Section 25.1
Grammar Exercise Workbook
• pp. 119–120

Hands-on Grammar

Unpuzzling Double Negatives

When you want to convey a negative idea, you should use only one negative adverb in a clause. Putting two negative words together leads to a confusing error called a *double negative*. To help you remember which words you can and cannot put together in a clause, try the following activity:

Make several squares out of paper or index cards. Cut each square into two interlocking L shapes (see diagram).

On the left *L*, write a negative word or a verb connected to a negative word (*hardly, doesn't, wasn't*). On the right (upside down) *L*, write a positive word that creates a phrase with the negative word (*any, anybody, ever*). Flip each square over. This time, write a positive word or verb on the left (*has, almost, was*) and a negative word on the right to create a phrase (*no, nobody, never*).

Mix and match the negative and positive L's. If you try to put two negatives together, you will not be able to complete the puzzle and form a square.

Put your puzzles into an envelope, and store them in your notebook. You can refer to the puzzles to help you avoid forming double negatives in your writing.

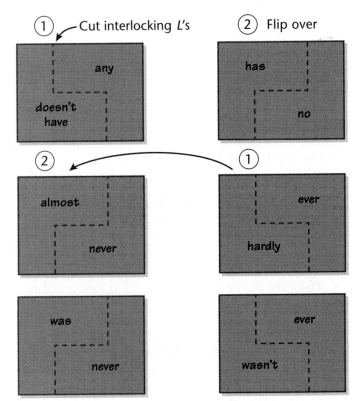

Find It in Your Reading Search a short story, newspaper article, or textbook chapter for negative words. Use your puzzle pieces to explore which words can and can't be used with the negative word. Discuss with a partner how each of the words you can use might affect the meaning of the sentence in which the negative word was originally used.

Find It in Your Writing Choose a piece of writing from your portfolio. Proofread it for double negatives. Identify any negative words you have used correctly.

Section Review

GRAMMAR EXERCISES 6–10

> **Exercise 6** **Proofreading to Avoid Double Negatives** Rewrite any sentence that contains a double negative. If a sentence is correct, write *correct.*

1. A complete eclipse isn't hardly a common experience.
2. There aren't but two kinds of eclipses involving Earth and the moon.
3. A lunar eclipse can't occur if the moon isn't completely in Earth's shadow.
4. If the moon is nowhere near Earth's shadow, it won't be obscured.
5. Lunar eclipses don't never occur when the moon isn't anywhere near the umbra.
6. Yes, a complete lunar eclipse doesn't last but two hours.
7. The sun is so bright it seems as if nothing couldn't block out its light.
8. The moon doesn't scarcely seem big enough for the job.
9. You shouldn't watch any solar eclipses without protective eyewear.
10. Eclipses aren't hardly random occurrences.

> **Exercise 7** **Revising to Eliminate Double Negatives** Revise each sentence to eliminate the double negatives.

1. There aren't but two types of tide that occur daily: high tide and low tide.
2. The flow of Earth's tides isn't never left to its own devices.
3. They don't never occur without a little help from the moon and the sun.
4. The sun isn't nowhere near as close to Earth as the moon is.
5. Therefore, the sun's gravitational pull isn't scarcely as strong as the moon's.
6. Ordinarily, high tide isn't never as high as at spring tide, when the moon, sun, and Earth form a straight line and the moon and sun work together on the tides.

7. When the moon and sun form right angles with Earth, there aren't no spring tides.
8. During those neap tides, high tide isn't hardly considered all that high.
9. There aren't but two high tides and two low tides a day.
10. Nothing else doesn't consistently exert such powers on Earth's tides.

> **Exercise 8** **Find It in Your Reading**
Read the following excerpt from "We'll Never Conquer Space" by Arthur C. Clarke. Identify the negative word in the sentence. Then, identify the word that should be changed to a negative word if the original negative word were replaced with *a.*

. . . For it seems as certain as anything can be that no signal—still less any material object—can ever travel faster than light.

> **Exercise 9** **Find It in Your Writing**
Choose a piece of persuasive writing from your portfolio. Identify the negative sentences you have used. If you cannot find examples, add a sentence to elaborate on your position or show your opposition.

> **Exercise 10** **Writing Application**
Use each item in a correctly worded negative sentence of your own.

1. couldn't ask
2. was hardly ready
3. had but one reason
4. could never go
5. hadn't any

Common Usage Problems

(1) a, an The article *a* is used before consonant sounds; *an,* before vowel sounds. Words beginning with *h, o,* or *u* may have either a consonant sound or a vowel sound.

EXAMPLES: a *h*ighwayman (*h* sound)
a *o*ne-day excursion (*w* sound)
a *u*tensil (*y* sound)
an *h*onest peddler (no *h* sound)
an *o*men (*o* sound)
an *u*rchin (*u* sound)

(2) accept, except *Accept,* a verb, means "to receive." *Except,* a preposition, means "leaving out" or "other than."

VERB: I *accept* your offer to teach me about archaic careers.
PREPOSITION: All the apprentices, *except* the youngest, learned the new techniques.

(3) adapt, adopt *Adapt,* a verb, means "to change." *Adopt,* also a verb, means "to take as one's own."

EXAMPLES: Some craftsmen *adapt* new technologies to produce old-looking items.
Purists prefer to *adopt* the old methods instead.

(4) affect, effect *Affect* is almost always a verb meaning "to influence." *Effect,* usually a noun, means "result." Occasionally, *effect* is a verb meaning "to bring about" or "to cause."

EXAMPLES: The success of a country's privateers could *affect* the outcome of a war.
He suffered no ill *effects* from traveling.
The Declaration of Paris *effected* a change in the status of privateers.

(5) aggravate *Aggravate* means "to make worse." Avoid using this word to mean "to annoy."

LESS ACCEPTABLE: The success of the privateers *aggravated* their enemies.
PREFERRED: Their successes *aggravated* the strained relationship.

(6) ain't *Ain't,* originally a contraction of *am not,* is no longer considered acceptable standard English.

NONSTANDARD: Privateers who work for the government *ain't* pirates.
CORRECT: Privateers who work for the government *aren't* pirates.

Theme: Unusual Occupations Past and Present

In this section, you will learn to recognize and avoid many common usage problems in your writing. The examples and exercises are about unusual occupations from the past and present.

Cross-Curricular Connection: Social Studies

(7) all ready, already *All ready* is an expression that functions as an adjective and means "ready." *Already* is an adverb meaning "by or before this time" or "even now."

ADJECTIVE: Many sea captains were *all ready* to try their fortunes as pirates.

ADVERB: Many privateers were *already* pirates when their sovereigns granted them legitimacy.

(8) all right, alright *Alright* is a nonstandard spelling.

NONSTANDARD: The escapades of Sir Francis Drake were *alright* with his sovereign, Queen Elizabeth I.

CORRECT: The escapades of Sir Francis Drake were *all right* with his sovereign, Queen Elizabeth I.

(9) all together, altogether *All together* means "all at once." *Altogether* means "completely" or "in all."

EXAMPLES: The crew decided to mutiny *all together*.
The captain was *altogether* mistaken.

(10) among, between *Among* and *between* are both prepositions. *Among* always implies three or more. *Between* is generally used with just two items.

EXAMPLES: There is a code *among* pirates and privateers.
The pay rate for each voyage was determined *between* the crew's leader and the captain.

▼ **Critical Viewing**
If you were writing about preparing to board this ship, would you use *all ready* or *already* in your sentence? **[Distinguish]**

> **Exercise 11** Avoiding Usage Problems Choose the word or expression that most correctly completes each sentence.
> 1. The sailor (ain't, hasn't) come home since last winter.
> 2. He knew what (effect, affect) his absence would have.
> 3. His wife has (all ready, already) prepared for a reunion.
> 4. Howard considered himself (an, a) honorable peddler.
> 5. Sometimes, his customers would not (accept, except) his prices.
> 6. It (aggravated, annoyed) him to lose money.
> 7. He was good at (adapting, adopting) to the moods around him.
> 8. Do you feel (all right, alright)?
> 9. The sailor left the ship (altogether, all together).
> 10. The three men shared the costs (among, between) them.

> **More Practice**
>
> **Language Lab CD-ROM**
> • Using Precise Language lesson
> **On-line Exercise Bank**
> • Section 25.2
> **Grammar Exercise Workbook**
> • pp. 121–122

(11) anxious *Anxious* means "worried," "uneasy," or "fearful." Do not use it as a substitute for *eager.*

AMBIGUOUS: Privateers were *anxious* to make their fortune.

CLEAR: Privateers were *eager* to make their fortune.
Privateers were always *anxious* about safety.

(12) anyone, any one, everyone, every one *Anyone* and *everyone* mean "any person" and "every person." *Any one* means "any single person (or thing)," and *every one* means "every single person (or thing)."

EXAMPLES: *Anyone* could become a pirate.
Any one of those pirates could be a privateer.

(13) anyway, anywhere, everywhere, nowhere, somewhere These adverbs should never end in *-s.*

NONSTANDARD: Merchants learned that they weren't safe *anywheres* on the high seas.

CORRECT: Merchants learned that they weren't safe *anywhere* on the high seas.

(14) as Do not use this conjunction to mean "because" or "since."

LESS ACCEPTABLE: Privateering grew *as* each European country wanted control.

PREFERRED: Privateering grew *because* each European country wanted control.

(15) as to *As to* is awkward. Replace it with *about.*

NONSTANDARD: There are many theories *as to* why people turned to piracy.

CORRECT: There are many theories *about* why people turned to piracy.

(16) at Do not use *at* after *where.* Simply eliminate *at.*

NONSTANDARD: Only he knows *where* the plunder is hidden *at.*

CORRECT: Only he knows *where* the plunder is hidden.

(17) at about Avoid using *at* with *about.* Simply eliminate *at* or *about.*

LESS ACCEPTABLE: The golden age of European piracy was over *at about* the end of the 1720's.

PREFERRED: The golden age of European piracy was over *at* the end of the 1720's. (or *by*)

Technology Tip

Keep a list of words you sometimes misuse. When you work in a word-processing program, do a search for each word on your list. Correct any misuses. Soon, you will start to notice the problem words as you are using them and can correct yourself while drafting.

(18) awful, awfully *Awful* is used informally to mean "extremely bad." *Awfully* is used informally to mean "very." Both modifiers are overused and should be replaced with more descriptive words. In formal writing, *awful* should be used only to mean "inspiring fear."

INFORMAL:	The Spanish fleet suffered many *awful* losses to the British privateers.
BETTER:	The Spanish fleet suffered many *catastrophic* losses to the British privateers.
INFORMAL:	Pirates are depicted as *awfully* fierce.
BETTER:	Pirates are depicted as *savage* and *bloodthirsty*.
FORMAL:	Many feared the great pirates because of their *awful* reputations.

(19) awhile, a while *Awhile* is an adverb that means "for a short time." *A while* (an article and a noun) means "a period of time." The term is usually used after the preposition *for*.

ADVERB:	A sea voyage could last *awhile*.
NOUN:	The ship docked in port for *a while*.

(20) beat, win *Win* means "to achieve victory in." *Beat* means "to overcome (an opponent)." Do not use *win* in place of *beat*.

NONSTANDARD:	The captain *won* the boatswain playing checkers.
CORRECT:	The captain *beat* the boatswain playing checkers.

▶ **Exercise 12** Avoiding Usage Problems Choose the correct expression to complete each sentence.
1. Lighthouses were built (somewhere, somewheres) on the coast to guide ships around rough spots.
2. There are several theories (as to, about) the history of lighthouse use.
3. She was (eager, anxious) to take over duties as a lighthouse keeper when her father was away.
4. (Everyone, Every one) of the lighthouses sends out its own light patterns to help ships identify their locations.
5. (As, Because) the light is not visible during the day, lighthouses are painted bright colors and patterns.
6. Do you know where the lighthouse (is, is at)?
7. Most lighthouses were automated (at about, by) the 1970's.
8. A lighthouse keeper's job can be (awfully, extremely) lonely.
9. You might not see another person for (a while, awhile).
10. He (won, beat) the loneliness by listening to music.

▼ **Critical Viewing**
Make two statements expressing whether or not you would like to live in a lighthouse. In the first statement, use *a while*. In the second statement, use *awhile*. **[Distinguish]**

(21) because Do not use *because* after *the reason*. Say "The reason is . . . that" or reword the sentence.

NONSTANDARD: *The reason* privateers disappeared is *because* the countries at war signed a treaty.

CORRECT: *The reason* privateers disappeared is *that* the countries at war signed a treaty.
Privateers disappeared *because* the countries at war signed a treaty.

(22) being as, being that Avoid using either expression. Use *because* instead.

NONSTANDARD: *Being that* (or *as*) books today are mass produced, there is no longer a need for scribes.

CORRECT: *Because* books today are mass produced, there is no longer a need for scribes.

(23) beside, besides As prepositions, these two words have different meanings and cannot be interchanged. *Beside* means "at the side of" or "close to." *Besides* means "in addition to."

EXAMPLES: Illuminations appear *beside* the text.
Besides using colored paints, illuminators also used precious metals, such as gold leaf.

(24) bring, take *Bring* means "to carry from a distant place to a nearer one." *Take* means the opposite: "to carry from a near place to a more distant place."

EXAMPLES: Would you *bring* me the illuminated book?
Take the book back to the illuminator.

(25) can, may Use *can* to mean "to have the ability to." Use *may* to mean "to have permission to" or "to be possible or likely to."

ABILITY: Economics often dictates whether buyers *can* afford illuminations in their manuscripts.

PERMISSION: You *may* borrow the book.

POSSIBILITY: They *may* decide to have the manuscript illuminated at a much later date, when fortunes allow.

(26) clipped words Avoid using clipped or shortened words, such as *gym*, *phone*, and *photo*, in formal writing.

INFORMAL: *Photos* and drawings have replaced illuminations in today's books.

FORMAL: *Photographs* and drawings have replaced illuminations in today's books.

▼ **Critical Viewing** Present one reason why it might be uncomfortable to wear armor. Use either *reason* or *because* in your explanation. **[Analyze]**

(27) different from, different than *Different from* is preferred.

LESS ACCEPTABLE: Illuminations are *different than* illustrations in their techniques and materials.

PREFERRED: Illuminations are *different from* illustrations in their techniques and materials.

(28) doesn't, don't Do not use *don't* with third-person singular subjects. Use *doesn't* instead.

NONSTANDARD: A scribe *don't* need to provide illuminations.

CORRECT: A scribe *doesn't* need to provide illuminations.

(29) done *Done* is the past participle of the verb *do*. It should always follow a helping verb.

NONSTANDARD: Monastic illuminators always *done* their work in complete silence.

CORRECT: Monastic illuminators *have* always *done* their work in complete silence.

(30) due to *Due to* means "caused by" and should be used only when the words *caused by* can logically be substituted.

NONSTANDARD: The manuscript survives today *due to* its expensive illumination.

CORRECT: *Due to* the invention of the printing press, books became widely available.

▶ **Exercise 13** Recognizing Standard Usage For each pair of sentences, write the letter of the one that follows the conventions of standard English. Copy the other sentence on a separate sheet of paper, correcting the usage error.

1. (a) The first knights were not socially superior because anyone could become a knight.
   (b) The reason knighthood came to signify a noble class is because the costs of knighthood became steep.
2. (a) Beside learning the code of behavior, a knight learned how to handle small arms.
   (b) Beside the castle was a cluster of smaller buildings.
3. (a) Being as a squire was of inferior rank, he performed many tasks for the knight he served.
   (b) A squire would bring a knight his meals.
4. (a) Gaffers, or glass blowers, can make almost any shape out of glass.
   (b) Can I borrow your book?
5. (a) In the Middle Ages, the fine, thin glass of Italy was different from the heavier, darker northern glass.
   (b) Glass blowers always done their work with great care.

▶ **More Practice**

Language Lab CD-ROM
• Using Precise Language lesson
On-line Exercise Bank
• Section 25.2
Grammar Exercise Workbook
• pp. 121–122

(31) each other, one another *Each other* and *one another* are usually interchangeable. At times, however, *each other* is more logically used in reference to only two; *one another*, in reference to more than two.

EXAMPLES: They must work with *each other* (or *one another*).
The scribe and the illuminator respected *each other's* tasks.
Illuminators often shared *one another's* exemplars for specific texts.

(32) farther, further *Farther* refers to distance. *Further* means "additional" or "to a greater degree or extent."

EXAMPLES: Illuminators discovered how to make some objects appear *farther* away than others.
They made *further* discoveries and invented new perspectives in painting.

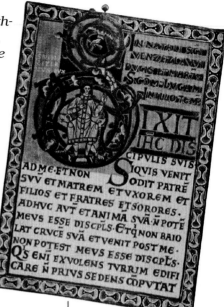

▲ **Critical Viewing**
If you wanted to note that not as many people can understand Latin today as in the past, would you use *fewer* or *less* in your sentence? **[Distinguish]**

(33) fewer, less Use *fewer* with things that can be counted. Use *less* with qualities and quantities that cannot be counted.

EXAMPLES: *fewer* commissions, *fewer* colors, *fewer* artisans
less blue paint, *less* need, *less* experience

(34) get, got, gotten These forms of the verb *get* are acceptable in standard English, but whenever possible, it is best to find a more specific word.

INFORMAL: *get* an exemplar, *got* a commission, to have *gotten* payment
BETTER: *obtain* an exemplar, *received* a commission, to have *earned* payment

(35) gone, went *Gone* is the past participle of *go* and should be used only with a helping verb. *Went* is the past tense of *go* and is never used with a helping verb.

NONSTANDARD: He *gone* to London to learn from a master illuminator.
He *could have went* to any major city.
CORRECT: He *has gone* to London to learn from a master illuminator.
He *went* to London to learn from a master illuminator.
He *could have gone* to any major city.

**Technology Tip**

When you're in a word-processing application and want to find a more specific word to replace *get*, highlight the word and then click on the thesaurus feature.

(36) good, lovely, nice Whenever possible, replace these weak and overused words with a more specific adjective.

WEAK: *good* description, *lovely* painting, *nice* taste
BETTER: *clear* description, *exotic* painting, *refined* taste

(37) in, into *In* refers to position. *Into* suggests motion.

POSITION: How many illuminations are *in* the typical prayerbook?

MOTION: How many illuminations did an artist put *into* the typical prayerbook?

(38) irregardless Avoid this word. Use *regardless*.

(39) kind of, sort of Do not use *kind of* or *sort of* to mean "rather" or "somewhat."

(40) lay, lie *Lay* means "to put or set (something) down." Its principal parts—*lay, laying, laid,* and *laid*—are usually followed by a direct object. *Lie* means "to recline." Its principal parts—*lie, lying, lay,* and *lain*—are never followed by a direct object.

LAY: *Lay* your tools on the table.
        They *are laying* their tools down for the evening.
        He *laid* the manuscript in its carrying pouch.
        She had *laid* the book away for safe keeping.

LIE: The monks may *lie* down for their evening's rest.
        The exemplars are *lying* on the desk over there.
        The monk *lay* down after a difficult day of close handwork.
        The old manuscript has *lain* in our attic for decades.

▶ **Exercise 14** **Revising to Eliminate Usage Problems** Write each sentence on a separate sheet of paper. Revise to eliminate any usage problems, informal usage, or overused words. If a sentence is correct, write *correct as is.*

1. A cooper and a blacksmith must work with one another to produce barrels.
2. Barrels were needed to store a ship's provisions. They were further necessary for containing the whale oil.
3. Because the barrels were made before the voyage began, a cooper had less steps to assemble them.
4. Highwaymen got money from travelers.
5. Good stories about highwaymen survive today.
6. The character Robin Hood appeared into several movies.
7. Many people consider Robin Hood to be heroic.
8. Irregardless of his motives, he was in the eyes of the sheriff a criminal.
9. It seems as if he could never lay down and take a rest.
10. I gone to the library to find that book.

(41) learn, teach *Learn* means "to acquire knowledge." *Teach* means "to give knowledge to."

EXAMPLES: It is difficult to *learn* that skill.
              Originally, a master craftsman would *teach* you.

(42) leave, let *Leave* means "to allow to remain." *Let* means "to permit."

NONSTANDARD: *Leave* it go!
CORRECT: *Let* it go!

(43) like *Like* is a preposition and should not be used in place of the conjunction *as* to join two clauses.

NONSTANDARD: A smart apprentice was valued *like* a prized possession is valued.
CORRECT: A smart apprentice was valued *as* a prized possession is valued.
                 A smart apprentice was valued *like* a prized possession.

(44) loose, lose *Loose* is usually an adjective or part of such idioms as *cut loose, turn loose,* or *break loose. Lose* is always a verb, generally meaning "to miss from one's possession."

EXAMPLES: The ropemaker cut *loose* the excess hemp.
              An artisan did not want to *lose* a good apprentice.

(45) maybe, may be *Maybe* is an adverb meaning "perhaps." *May be* is a helping verb and a verb.

ADVERB: *Maybe* this apprentice will be promoted to journeyman.
VERB: Choosing an apprentice *may be* a personal matter.

(46) of Do not use *of* after a helping verb such as *should, would, could,* or *must.* Use *have* instead. Do not use *of* after *outside, inside, off,* and *atop.* Simply eliminate it.

NONSTANDARD: By now, he should *of* known the proper steps for making a barrel.
CORRECT: By now, he should *have* known the proper steps for making a barrel.

(47) OK, O.K., okay In informal writing, *OK, O.K.,* and *okay* are acceptably used to mean "all right." Do not use either the abbreviations or *okay* in formal writing, however.

INFORMAL: The Romans thought gladiator competitions were *okay.*
FORMAL: The Romans thought gladiator competitions were acceptable forms of entertainment.

> **More Practice**
> **Language Lab CD-ROM**
> • Using Precise Language lesson
> **On-line Exercise Bank**
> • Section 25.2
> **Grammar Exercise Workbook**
> • pp. 121–122

(48) only *Only* should be placed in front of the word it logically modifies.

EXAMPLES: *Only* they used nets as weapons. (No one else used a net as a weapon.)
They used *only* nets and a small trident as weapons. (They used no other weapons.)

(49) ought Never use *ought* with *have* or *had.* Simply eliminate *have* or *had.*

NONSTANDARD: Some think that chivalry *had ought* to be practiced today.

CORRECT: Some think that chivalry *ought* to be practiced today.

(50) outside of Do not use this expression to mean "besides" or "except."

NONSTANDARD: No one remembers the names of any gladiators *outside of* Spartacus.

CORRECT: No one remembers the names of any gladiators *except* Spartacus.

▷ **Exercise 15** **Revising Sentences to Eliminate Usage Problems** Write each sentence on a separate sheet of paper. Revise to eliminate any usage problems, informal usage, or overused words. If a sentence is correct, write *correct as is.*
1. In the past, blacksmiths must of enjoyed respect.
2. Jim's parents think he maybe good at metalworking.
3. Jim was learned the skills by a master.
4. The shop becomes hot like a sauna.
5. The instructor wouldn't let Jim try to shape a horseshoe.
6. When he banged it with a hammer, it was so lose it fell.
7. The king thought the jester's performance was witty.
8. He only felt the jester lacked a costume.
9. He had ought to be better prepared.
10. No one outside of the jester could have spoken to the king in such a way.

▼ **Critical Viewing** Write a sentence discussing something a blacksmith ought to know. Consult usage problem 49 (ought) before you write your sentence. **[Make a Judgment]**

(51) plurals that do not end in -s The plurals of certain nouns from Greek and Latin are formed as they were in their original language. Words such as *criteria, media,* and *phenomena* are plural and should not be treated as if they were singular (*criterion, medium, phenomenon*).

INCORRECT: The modern *media* has romanticized the story of Spartacus.

CORRECT: The modern *media* have romanticized the story of Spartacus.

(52) precede, proceed *Precede* means "to go before." *Proceed* means "to move or go forward."

EXAMPLES: The gladiator had been trained carefully *preceding* his first fight.
His victory means that he can *proceed* to the next contest.

(53) principal, principle As an adjective, *principal* means "most important" or "chief." As a noun, it means "a person who has controlling authority." *Principle*, always a noun, means "a fundamental law."

ADJECTIVE: The *principal* goal of a gladiator was to stay alive.

NOUN: The *principal* of the gladiator school was responsible for the fighters' physical health.

NOUN: Fighting was not against the Romans' *principles*.

(54) real *Real* means "authentic." The use of *real* to mean "very" or "really" should be avoided in formal writing.

INFORMAL: The crowd was *real* disappointed with the outcome.

FORMAL: The crowd was *sorely* disappointed with the outcome.

(55) says *Says* should not be used as a substitute for *said*.

NONSTANDARD: Afterward, the emperor *says* to the crowd, "Let the games begin!"

CORRECT: Afterward, the emperor *said* to the crowd, "Let the games begin!"

(56) than, then *Than* is used in comparisons. Do not confuse it with the adverb *then*, which usually refers to time.

EXAMPLES: He is stronger *than* his opponent.
First, he learned to handle a sword; *then*, he began to compete.

💡 Spelling Tip

When trying to decide which word you need, remember this useful hint: *Principal* is spelled p-a-l; the princi*pal* of your school can be a "pal."

(57) that, which, who *That* and *which* refer to things; *who* refers to people.

EXAMPLES: He dropped the sword *that* was his only weapon.
Spartacus was a slave *who* incited a rebellion of gladiators.
The rebellion, *which* ended in defeat for Spartacus, lasted for two years.

(58) their, there, they're *Their,* a possessive pronoun, always modifies a noun. *There* can be used either as an expletive at the beginning of a sentence or as an adverb. *They're* is a contraction for *they are.*

PRONOUN: Spectators in the Colosseum cheered for *their* favorite gladiators.

EXPLETIVE: *There* is no doubt who is the winner.

ADVERB: *There* are the winners in that large open area.

CONTRACTION: *They're* waiting for their next competitions to begin.

(59) to, too, two *To,* a preposition, begins a prepositional phrase. It may also be connected to a verb to form an infinitive. *Too,* an adverb, modifies verbs, adjectives, or other adverbs. *Two* is a number and can be used as an adjective or a noun.

PREPOSITION: *to* the Colosseum, *to* the school
INFINITIVE: *to* fight, *to* win
ADVERB: *too* slowly, *too* sweet
NUMBER: *two* blows, *two* victories

(60) when, where Do not use *when* or *where* directly after a linking verb. Do not use *where* as a substitute for *that* or *which.*

NONSTANDARD: After his tenth victory was *when* the poets began to sing his praises.
A ludi is *where* gladiators were trained for fighting.
The museum is a place *where* we like to visit.

CORRECT: After his tenth victory, the poets began to sing his praises.
A ludi is a school *where* gladiators were trained for fighting.
The museum is a place *that* we like to visit.

▶ **Exercise 16** **Recognizing Standard Usage** For each pair of sentences, write the letter of the one that follows the conventions of standard English. Revise the other sentence, correcting the usage error.

1. (a) With his timely remarks, the jester preceded to make himself one of the king's favorites.
   (b) Each joke was preceded by a jingle of bells.
2. (a) In time, Will became the king's principal advisor.
   (b) Lying is against his principals.
3. (a) After the performance, the emperor says to the jester that he did a good job.
   (b) Everyone says that he is very funny.
4. (a) She had grown up in a culture that was real interested in oral poetry.
   (b) The festival included a real *griot*—a traditional storyteller.
5. (a) She'd rather hear poetry then stories.
   (b) First, we heard stories. Then, we heard poems.
6. (a) The knights' tournament was canceled due to bad weather.
   (b) The loyal page stood valiently beside his knight.
7. (a) Carvers that produced signposts and shop signs were essential to a town's economy.
   (b) The signs that identified places were both decorative and functional.
8. (a) The bakery was a place where a person could buy bread.
   (b) Do you know where we can buy some bread?
9. (a) Paul carved the ornate fence bordering the post office over there.
   (b) The townspeople are very proud of there post office.
10. (a) He made the statue of Justice for the courthouse, to.
    (b) Many people came to the unveiling.

▼ **Critical Viewing** Think of two sentences to describe ideas in this picture: one containing *then* and one containing *than*. Consult usage problem 56 *(than, then)* before you write. **[Distinguish]**

▶ **Exercise 17** **Revising a Passage to Eliminate Usage Problems** On a separate sheet of paper, revise the following paragraph to eliminate awkward or problematic usage.

Even before the telegraph, there was all ready one means of long-distance communication. The semaphore method, using lights or signals, proceeded the telegraph. The telegraph, however, was more efficient, and it leave people send longer messages over greater distances. At first, there were many speculations about the future of the telegraph. It soon became the principle means of sending information over great distances.

Section
25.2

Section Review

GRAMMAR EXERCISES 18–23

▶ **Exercise 18** Supplying the
Correct Article Write each phrase on
your paper, supplying *a* or *an* in the blank.

1. ___?___ archaic career
2. ___?___ useful skill
3. ___?___ honorific title
4. ___?___ old cobbler
5. ___?___ onetime matchmaker

▶ **Exercise 19** Proofreading to
Correct Usage Errors Rewrite any sentence below that contains a usage error. If a sentence is correct, write *correct.*

1. Before the twentieth century, their was no refrigeration.
2. Because people didn't have fridges, they used icehouses and iceboxes to keep food cold.
3. A need for preserved food proceeded the demand for ice.
4. Previous methods of preservation were different from the process of keeping the food cold.
5. There are many theories as to what was the best method of preserving food before the use of ice became so widespread.
6. Outside of using ice, people could preserve their food by smoking, drying, salting, or canning it.
7. Some food, however, doesn't taste as fresh or appetizing after salting and drying.
8. Being that ice was in such demand, a profitable industry sprang up.
9. Icemen were hired to bring ice from frozen ponds, lakes, and rivers to towns and cities.
10. The reason they gathered ice from frozen bodies of water is because they had no means of producing their own ice yet.

▶ **Exercise 20** Revising a Paragraph
to Eliminate Usage Problems Rewrite the following paragraph, correcting any errors in usage.

Since ancient times, weavers done much of the work for making cloth. Weaving is a craft that has been around for quite awhile. Almost anywheres you go, you will find examples of looms and woven cloth. The hand loom was first used in China and the Middle East, and than it was used in Europe as well. The principals of weaving haven't changed much for thousands of years. A pick is used to push the yarn against the fabric that has all ready been woven. The reason this is done is because the fabric has to be evenly knit. While weaving is still very popular, you will find less weavers around today then in the past.

▶ **Exercise 21** Find It in Your
Reading Review a newspaper article to find examples of correct usage of *there, their; lose, loose; then, than;* and *fewer, less.*

▶ **Exercise 22** Find It in Your
Writing Choose one piece of writing in your portfolio. Proofread it carefully for the usage problems discussed in this chapter. Identify examples of correct usage. Correct any usage errors that you find.

▶ **Exercise 23** Writing Application
Use each word below in a sentence. Be sure your sentence reflects the right meaning.

1. done
2. adapt
3. gone
4. into
5. bring

GRAMMAR EXERCISES 24–31

Exercise 24 Supplying Words to Correctly Form Negative Sentences

Rewrite each sentence below on your paper, filling the blank with a word that does not form a double negative.

1. Some old careers didn't last __?__ great length of time at all.
2. Other careers will probably not __?__ fade away.
3. Because we need food, we can't survive without __?__ farmers.
4. A farmer 200 years ago didn't have __?__ of the large farm machinery used today.
5. No one __?__ deny that the methods of farming have changed.

Exercise 25 Avoiding Double Negatives Choose the word in parentheses that makes each sentence negative without creating a double negative.

1. Without technology, we wouldn't have (some, none) of the jobs we have today.
2. For example, electricians weren't (never, ever) needed until we learned how to harness electricity.
3. The world didn't have (no, any) need for electricians until the twentieth century.
4. Even after we learned how to use electricity, not everyone (could, couldn't) afford it.
5. Before long, it seemed as if there wasn't (nowhere, anywhere) in the United States that didn't have electric lights.

Exercise 26 Revising Sentences to Correct Double Negatives Rewrite each sentence on your paper, correcting the double negative.

1. Medicine is one profession that hardly never stays the same.
2. Medical research isn't never standing still, and much progress has been made during the hundreds of years that medicine has been practiced.
3. Not all the changes haven't been of a medical nature.
4. Other advances have included preventing people from practicing medicine who didn't know nothing about it.
5. Oftentimes in the Old West, for example, if there weren't no doctors nowhere nearby, a barber might perform surgical procedures.

Exercise 27 Revising Sentences to Achieve Understatement Rewrite each sentence to achieve understatement.

1. Transportation is a changing area of technology.
2. Airplanes are a convenient way to travel.
3. Airlines hire competent pilots to fly their planes.
4. Pilots are trained before they are allowed to fly solo.
5. There are many air-travel-related jobs a pilot can handle.

Exercise 28 Avoiding Usage Problems Choose the correct expression to complete each sentence.

1. As a profession, the practice of law has been around for (awhile, a while).
2. To become a lawyer, one must first study for many years and (than, then) take a qualifying examination.
3. Attorneys and solicitors represent and act for (their, there) clients in such matters as drawing up wills, settling property, or working out details of contracts.
4. Oftentimes, two opposing counsels will

discuss the details of a particular case with (one another, each other).

5. They may come to an agreement rather than to (proceed, precede) to a trial.

Exercise 29 Proofreading to Correct Usage Problems

Rewrite each sentence, correcting the errors in usage.

1. The reason Ansel Adams is famous is because he is a great photographer.
2. His principle focus was the American West.
3. Few photographers outside of Adams have received such acclaim.
4. Some say his talent lays in him choosing the right subjects.
5. Adams had first went to Yosemite National Park in 1916, where many believe he was inspired by the beauty he saw there.
6. Perhaps what he saw was different than anything he had seen before.
7. Surely, his works have learned others about the glory of the western landscape.
8. Sally always brings at least two cameras with her whenever she goes out.
9. She has many feelings as to what components are needed for a good picture.
10. Early evening is when the light is ideal for outdoor shots.
11. When shooting in the early evening, she must work quickly before she looses the light.
12. Her photos have appeared in numerous art exhibitions.
13. Outside of the work of Ansel Adams, we've never seen such moving nature photography.
14. Everyone of the spectators at her last show agreed with us.
15. Many people couldn't hardly believe how nice her pictures were.

Exercise 30 Revising to Eliminate Usage Problems

On a separate sheet of paper, rewrite the following paragraph. Revise to eliminate errors in usage. You may rearrange words or make other minor changes if necessary.

(1)There are many different genres of writing today, and one person can use a number of them. (2)The two principle types of fiction writers are novelists and short-story writers. (3)The to types are most obviously different than one another in length. (4)Since there are no boundaries to the imagination, fiction writers may find it difficult to invent a good plot. (5)A reporter, however, all ready has the story. (6)Once she gets the information, she only needs to write it down in an interesting and coherent form. (7)A critic, being as his job is to review recent art productions and current trends, often relies on knowledge and taste. (8)Critics hope that their opinions will effect the way consumers spend they're money. (9)Their opinions often aggravate the artist they are reviewing, especially when they write less then enthusiastic or awful comments about the work. (10)Sometimes, it is difficult to remember that one critic don't represent everyone.

Exercise 31 Writing Application

Write five pairs of sentences about jobs you may pursue in the future. In each sentence, use one of the two words correctly to illustrate the difference in meaning.

1. among, between
2. can, may
3. all ready, already
4. learn, teach
5. they're, there

Standardized Test Preparation Workshop

Recognizing Standard English Usage

Your mastery of standard English usage is frequently evaluated on standardized tests. Some test items focus on choosing the correct word to fill in a blank; others may test your ability to avoid or correct double negatives.

The following questions will give you practice with a format that is used to assess your understanding of standard English usage.

Sample Test Item

Directions: Read the sentence, and choose the word or group of words that belongs in each space. Mark the letter for your answer.

No one ___(1)___ Joe could answer the question about the movie.

1 **A** accept

   B except

   C accepted

   D exception

Answer and Explanation

The correct answer is *B*. The word *except* completes the sentence according to the conventions of standard English usage and makes sense in the sentence. *Except* means "other than," whereas *accept* means "to take what is offered."

> **Practice 1** **Directions:** Read the passage, and choose the word or group of words that belongs in each space.

The movie was produced __(1)__ the book was written. For once, the director didn't __(2)__ change the __(3)__ the author told the story. The main character, Jerry, is lost __(4)__ far from his home, and he has lost his memory. During the movie, Jerry wanders __(5)__ away from his starting point and the truth of his identity.

1 A like
   B as
   C as to
   D similar to

2 F substantially
   G but
   H hardly
   J scarcely

3 A way
   B ways
   C anyway
   D anyways

4 F anywheres
   G somewheres
   H somewhere
   J nowhere

5 A further
   B farther
   C less
   D fewer

.

> **Practice 2** **Directions:** Read the passage, and choose the word or group of words that belongs in each space.

__(1)__ being lost and losing his memory, Jerry becomes involved in a spy ring. I can't imagine what else could have __(2)__ wrong for him! Finally, he learns about his true identity after seeing himself on a flyer posted in a store window. After he reads __(3)__ flyer, Jerry discovers he is __(4)__ than an hour from his home. The movie ends with Jerry embracing his wife and children. It was a great book and a great movie, __(5)__ .

1 A Besides
   B Besides that
   C Being that
   D Beside

2 F gone
   G goed
   H go
   J went

3 A that there
   B this here
   C their
   D that

4 F fewer
   G closer
   H more
   J less

5 A to
   B too
   C two
   D there

Cumulative Review

USAGE

Exercise A Writing Effective Sentences Rewrite the following sentences according to the instructions in parentheses.

1. Homer wrote the *Iliad*. The *Odyssey* was written by Homer, describing the interactions between gods and mortals. (Combine by creating a compound direct object and an infinitive phrase.)
2. To appreciate the *Iliad*, the stories of the Trojan War must be understood. (Correct the dangling modifier.)
3. Using the conflict between Agamemnon and Achilles as the background, the *Iliad*. (Correct the sentence fragment and begin with a noun.)
4. Achilles leaves the battle; the Greeks proceed to suffer many setbacks against the Trojans. (Correct the faulty coordination; start with a subordinate clause.)
5. When his friend Patroclus leads the troops in his place he is slain and Achilles turns on Hector. (Create a compound verb and correct the run-on.)
6. He both wanted to be expressing his sadness and to take revenge. (Correct the faulty parallelism.)
7. Achilles after fighting his son met with King Priam. (Correct the misplaced modifier and the ambiguous reference.)
8. They felt sad similarly. Achilles and Priam had both faced a tragedy. (Combine with a compound subject and start the sentence with an adverb.)
9. The characters in the *Iliad* deal with emotions, facing dilemmas, and they fight a war. They are Achilles, Agamemnon, and Priam. (Combine sentences with an appositive phrase and correct faulty parallelism.)
10. The *Odyssey* has different themes, which scholars believe may have been written by a person other than Homer. (Correct the misplaced modifier.)

Exercise B Making Words Agree Choose the correct word or groups of words that makes each sentence correct.

1. The *Odyssey* (describe, describes) the travels of Odysseus after (his, its) time in the Trojan War.
2. Odysseus fought for the Greeks, and (he, they) is credited with the idea for the Trojan horse.
3. Some in Ithaca (was, were) courting his wife, Penelope, in his absence.
4. Each wanted her for (his, their) wife.
5. Either Penelope or the dog (recognize, recognizes) Odysseus first.

Exercise C Using Pronouns, Verbs, and Modifiers Choose the correct word or group of words that makes each sentence correct.

1. The (great, greatest) importance of the mythological Greek gods is demonstrated by their presence in all stories, including Homer's epic poems.
2. Zeus is king of the gods (who, whom) lived on Mount Olympus, the (higher, highest) point in all of Greece.
3. He is (more, most) powerful than the other gods.
4. This year, we (learned, are learning) about several of the Greek gods.
5. Poseidon, who rules the sea and all its creatures, (spend, spends) (most, more) of his time in his sea kingdom than on Olympus.
6. Anyone who (had swum, had swam) in the sea honored Poseidon.
7. Poseidon ruled the Nereids and Tritons, lesser sea gods. It is (they, them) who carried out his orders.
8. Demeter was (more, most) associated with the Earth and agriculture than (any other gods, other gods were.)

9. Hestia is not as well known. However, the goddess of the hearth and the home is (she, her).
10. Homemakers in ancient Greece would have given (she, her) special honors.

> **Exercise D** Proofreading Sentences to Correct Miscellaneous Problems in Usage Rewrite the following sentences, correcting negative sentences and other common usage problems.

1. Athena was more important then many other goddesses in Greek mythology.
2. There wasn't hardly anything that she wasn't involved with.
3. Because she was loyal too the people of the city of Athens, they built her major temple, the Parthenon, there.
4. One of the reasons Athena was so popular is because she was Zeus' favorite child.
5. Irregardless of the other gods, Athena was a strong supporter of the Greeks during the Trojan War.
6. However, after the Greeks disregarded her wishes concerning the prophet Cassandra, Athena wasn't going to do nothing for them.
7. Then, Athena gave fewer support to Greek ships returning from that war.
8. The storms she and Poseidon sent gave the sailors a farther challenge.
9. Athena was awful useful as the goddess of wisdom, industry, and the arts.
10. Between her gifts to men were the flute and the instructions for building ships and taming animals.

> **Exercise E** Revising a Passage to Eliminate Usage Errors On a separate sheet of paper, copy the following paragraph. Revise to eliminate all errors. You may need to rearrange words or make other minor changes.

(1)The Graces, the three goddesses of joy, charm, and beauty, was daughters of Zeus. (2)They are most often treated as a group than as individuals. (3)They're tasks included bringing joy to both gods and mortals, and she presided over dances, dinners, and other social events. (4)In art, they are usually represented as three young maidens. (5)Together with the Muses, they sung and danced. (6)The Muses was a group of nine goddesses, also daughters of Zeus. (7)They were each associated with but one particular art. (8)Clio, for example have been associated with history, and Melpomene with tragedy. (9)On Olympus, they sat closer to the throne of Zeus, where they sang of his greatness. (10)The Muses were kind of a group that was worshiped all over Greece, but more at Helicon and Pieria than anywhere.

> **Exercise F** Writing Application
Write a summary of a myth or legend with which you are familiar. Make your writing interesting by varying your sentence lengths and structures. Try to avoid sentence errors and the common usage problems that you have studied. Be sure that the words in your sentences follow the rules of agreement and that your modifiers are used correctly. Then, list your verbs and verb phrases, identifying their tense. Make a list of your pronouns, and label the cases of each.

Capitalization

When you're writing an e-mail message and you want to express strong emotion or emphasize a word, you can do so by typing in capital letters. Showing emotion by using capital letters is one of the most recently developed uses of capitals. Throughout the history of the English language, many rules have been developed for using capital letters to indicate changes of thought, to highlight certain types of words, and to serve a variety of other purposes. In this chapter, you will review the rules of capitalization to help you apply them to your writing.

▲ **Critical Viewing**
In what ways would you use capital letters in a written description of this waterfall? **[Describe]**

Diagnostic Test

Directions: Write all answers on a separate sheet of paper.

Skill Check A. Label each of the underlined words *proper noun* or *proper adjective*.

1. <u>italian</u> language
2. the state of <u>arizona</u>
3. an <u>english</u> accent
4. <u>russian</u>-born playwright
5. ex-senator <u>harris</u>

Skill Check B. Copy the following sentences. Add capitals where needed.

6. the highest uninterrupted cataract in the world is called angel falls, which is located in southeastern venezuela.
7. it was named for an american aviator, james c. angel, in 1937.
8. on the río churún, it descends around 3,000 feet from the guiana highlands.
9. another famous waterfall, victoria falls, can be found in south central africa.
10. this waterfall, on the zambezi river, straddles the border of zimbabwe and zambia.
11. the zambezi is more than a mile wide at this point and falls about 350 feet into the gorge below.
12. there is also an impressive waterfall to be found in north america, on the border of new york state and ontario, canada.
13. it is called niagara falls, and it is on the niagara river.
14. there are two branches that make up niagara falls: one located on the american side and one on the canadian side.
15. the canadian falls, also known as the horseshoe falls, carries about nine times more water than the american falls.

Skill Check C. Copy the following sentences. Add capitals where needed.

16. uncle louis was an engineer on the wisconsin central railroad until he retired on memorial day 1962.
17. on super bowl sunday, more pretzels and potato chips are eaten in the united states than anywhere else in the world.
18. when joe was a senior, he was a member of the brunswick high school chess club.
19. grandma and i took aunt martha's children to the bronx zoo to see the special exhibit of the himalayan snow leopards.
20. the allegheny and monongahela rivers come together in pittsburgh, pennsylvania, to form the ohio river.

Using Capitals for First Words

Capitalization signals the beginning of a sentence or points out certain words within a sentence.

Theme: Natural Wonders

In this section, you will learn about capitalization. The examples and exercises in this lesson are about natural wonders.

Cross-Curricular Connection: Science

▶**KEY CONCEPT** Capitalize the first word in declarative, interrogative, imperative, and exclamatory sentences. ■

DECLARATIVE:	The mountain was tall and forbidding.
INTERROGATIVE:	Where is the highest peak in the world?
IMPERATIVE:	Take your camera with you.
EXCLAMATORY:	What a breathtaking view!

▶**KEY CONCEPT** Capitalize the first word in interjections and incomplete questions. ■

INTERJECTIONS:	Oh! Marvelous!
INCOMPLETE QUESTIONS:	Why not? When?

▶**KEY CONCEPT** Capitalize the first word in a quotation if the quotation is a complete sentence. ■

EXAMPLES: "The water rushes to the edge of the falls," the tour guide said. "Its force could crush a person."

"As the water crashes to the bottom of the falls," he said, "a thick spray of mist is flung up."

After seeing the Grand Canyon, Theodore Roosevelt said that "the ages have been at work upon it and man cannot improve it."

The first example shows a quotation that consists of two sentences. Notice that the first word of each sentence is capitalized.

The second example consists of one sentence that is interrupted by a "he said/she said" expression. Only the first word of the sentence that has been interrupted is capitalized.

The last example contains a portion of a quotation that is not a complete sentence. When only a portion of a sentence is quoted, do not capitalize the first word unless it is the first word of the sentence in which it is used.

▶ **KEY CONCEPT** Capitalize the first word after a colon if the word begins a complete sentence. ■

COMPLETE SENTENCE: In 1866, David Livingstone set out to attempt something never before accomplished: He led an expedition to discover the source of the Nile.

LIST OF WORDS OR PHRASES: Previous to this, Livingstone had explored much of Africa: the Kalahari Desert, the Zambezi River, Lake Ngami, and Victoria Falls.

Poetry should always be written as the poet intended it to be. In most poetry, the first word in each line is capitalized, even if it does not begin a new sentence.

▶ **KEY CONCEPT** Capitalize the first word in each line of traditional poetry. ■

EXAMPLE: Tyger! Tyger! burning bright,
In the forests of the night,
What immortal hand or eye
Could frame thy fearful symmetry?

—William Blake

▶ **KEY CONCEPT** Capitalize the first word after a colon in a formal resolution that states the subject of debates, legislative decisions, and acts. ■

EXAMPLE: Resolved: That the Senior Class hold an exhibit of its work on natural wonders.

▶ **Exercise 1** **Capitalizing First Words** Copy each of the following items, capitalizing the appropriate words.
1. the falls at Niagara were formed about 12,000 years ago.
2. since that time, erosion has taken its toll: the waterfall has been pushed about seven miles upstream.
3. "a man who has never looked on Niagara," said Lord Macauley, "has but a faint idea of a cataract."
4. it is fortunate for humankind that more people did not listen to the poet Tennyson: "surely, surely, slumber is more sweet than toil."
5. instead, many great explorers went in search of nature's wonders among what Shakespeare called the "thorns and dangers of this world."

▲ **Critical Viewing**
How would you compare Victoria Falls (pictured here) with Niagara Falls (shown on page 666)? **[Compare and Contrast]**

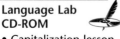

▶ **More Practice**
Language Lab
CD-ROM
• Capitalization lesson
On-line
Exercise Bank
• Section 26
Grammar Exercise
Workbook
• pp. 123–124

Using Capitals for Proper Nouns

Nouns, as you know, name people, places, and things. They are classified as either *common* or *proper*.

COMMON NOUNS: river, mountain, prairie, lake, sea, hill, valley

Proper nouns—which name specific examples of people, places, or things—require capitalization.

▶**KEY CONCEPT** Capitalize all proper nouns. ■

PROPER NOUNS: Henry, Sir Edmund Hillary, the White House, Cincinnati, H.M.S. *Beagle, National Geographic*

As you can see from the preceding examples, there are several categories of proper nouns.

▶**KEY CONCEPT** Capitalize each part of a person's full name. ■

EXAMPLES: Roald Amundsen, T. S. Eliot, Francis Drake

Surnames sometimes consist of several parts. Capitalize both parts of surnames beginning with *Mc, O',* or *St.*

EXAMPLES: McCarthy   O'Donovan   St. James

The proper names of animals should also be capitalized.

EXAMPLES: Lassie, a dog   Velvet, a horse

Proper nouns referring to particular places must also be capitalized. Articles are not usually capitalized.

▶**KEY CONCEPT** Capitalize geographical and place names. ■

EXAMPLES: Hillside Road, Dallas, Putnam County, Arizona, British Columbia, Australia, the Alps, Kalahari Desert, Fiji Islands, the Southwest, Amazon River, Angel Falls, Coral Sea, Saturn, Halley's Comet, the Alamo, the Pentagon, the Oval Office, Room 14, Laboratory C

Note About *Capitalizing Directions:* Words indicating direction can be used in two ways: to name a section of a country and to give travel directions. These words are capitalized only when they refer to a section of a country.

EXAMPLES: Urban areas of the *Northeast* face many problems. We traveled two miles *west* and one mile *south.*

▷ **KEY CONCEPT** Capitalize the names of specific events and periods of time. ■

SPECIAL EVENTS AND TIMES	
Historical Events	the Louisiana Purchase, the Battle of Waterloo, the Russian Revolution
Historic and Geographic Periods	the Renaissance, the Bronze Age, the Mesozoic Era, the Ice Age
Documents	the Magna Carta, the Declaration of Independence
Days and Months	Tuesday, Fridays, July 20, the third week in April
Holidays and Religious Days	Easter, Father's Day, Memorial Day, Hanuka, Christmas
Special Events	the World's Fair, the Super Bowl, the Montreux International Jazz Festival

Most dictionaries and encyclopedias include lists of historic events and periods that require capitalization.

Note About *the Seasons:* Do not capitalize any reference to the seasons.

EXAMPLE: The winds were so cold during the winter that we thought we were at the North Pole.

▷ **KEY CONCEPT** Capitalize abbreviations of titles before and after names. ■

EXAMPLES: Mr. Green
Mrs. Bellamy
Mr. Paige
Arthur Romano, Ph.D

Although *Miss* is not an abbreviation, it is capitalized when used with a name.

▼ **Critical Viewing** This photograph shows the Arctic Ocean. What are some of the ways in which you would use capital letters in a research report about the Arctic region? **[Connect]**

▶**KEY CONCEPT** Capitalize the names of various organizations, government bodies, political parties, races, nationalities, languages, and religious references. ■

VARIOUS GROUPS	
Clubs	Kennedy High School Stamp Club, Rotary, New York Athletic Club
Organizations	the Salvation Army, American Medical Association
Institutions	National Museum of Art, the Boston Symphony, Johns Hopkins Hospital
Schools	Adlai E. Stevenson High School, Stanford University
Businesses	Allied Chemical Corporation, Prentice-Hall Canada, Inc.
Government Bodies	the Senate, the House of Lords, Nuclear Regulatory Commission, Army of the Potomac
Political Parties	Republican party, Liberal party, the Democrats
Nationalities	American, Canadian, Mexican, German, Israeli, Chinese, Mexican
Languages	English, Spanish, Polish, Swahili
Religious References	*Christianity:* God, the Lord, the Father, the Holy Spirit, the Bible, the New Testament, the Savior *Judaism:* God, the Lord, the Prophets, the Torah, the Talmud *Islam:* Allah, the Prophets, the Koran, Mohammed, Muslims *Hinduism:* Brahma, the Bhagavad-Gita, the Vedas *Buddhism:* the Buddha, Mahayana, Hinayana

Note About *Religious References:* When you use pronouns to refer to the Judeo-Christian deity, they should always be capitalized.

EXAMPLE: I prayed for *His* help.

When referring to ancient mythology, you should not capitalize the word *god* or *goddess.* The names of the gods and goddesses, however, are capitalized.

EXAMPLES: the *gods* of ancient Greece
the Roman *god* Mars

KEY CONCEPT Capitalize names of awards; names of specific types of air, sea, space, and land craft; and brand names. ■

AWARDS: Nobel Peace Prize, the Pulitzer Prize, Phi Beta Kappa, the Medal of Honor

SPECIFIC CRAFTS: Boeing 747, the U.S.S. *Kearsarge, Apollo V,* Ford Mustang

BRAND NAMES: Aunt Molly's Crackers, John's Elixir

Exercise 2 **Capitalizing Proper Nouns** Write the following sentences, adding the missing capitals.

EXAMPLE: st. louis, missouri, is subject to turbulent weather in the summer partly because of its proximity to the mississippi river and the missouri river.

St. Louis, Missouri, is subject to turbulent weather in the summer partly because of its proximity to the Mississippi River and the Missouri River.

1. i watched the knights of columbus march in the memorial day parade.
2. nat fein won the pulitzer prize for photography for his picture of babe ruth entitled *the babe bows out.*
3. the author of the declaration of independence was thomas jefferson.
4. the roman god jupiter is synonymous with the greek god zeus.
5. lassen volcanic national park was the home of the only active volcano in the northwestern region of the united states until mount saint helens erupted in 1980.

More Practice

Language Lab
CD-ROM
• Capitalization lesson
On-line
Exercise Bank
• Section 26
Grammar Exercise
Workbook
• pp. 123–124

> **Exercise 3** Proofreading to Correct Errors in Capitalization of First Words and Proper Nouns Revise this passage, adding and eliminating capitals as necessary.

The Colorado river flows through the Grand canyon. A particularly spectacular section of the Canyon is preserved as the Grand Canyon national park.

The first europeans to see the grand canyon were a group of spaniards led by francisco vásquez de coronado. the group left mexico, then known as new spain, in february of 1540. Some surveys and maps were made in the early 1800's, but the civil war interrupted the work. After the war, an american named John Wesley Powell studied the region and wrote geology reports. Powell became the first person to travel the full length of the Colorado river.

Though the erosion of the grand canyon began about Six Million Years Ago, the rocks in its walls are older than that. there are about thirteen layers of rock deposited in different geological periods: the permian, mississippian, devonian, and cambrian periods. Oldest of all are the precambrian period rocks on the bottom of the grand canyon: they are from half a billion to two billion years old.

▲ Critical Viewing What proper adjectives might you use in writing about the Grand Canyon? **[Connect]**

Using Capitals for Proper Adjectives

A proper adjective is an adjective formed from a proper noun or a proper noun used as an adjective. Most proper adjectives require capitalization.

> **KEY CONCEPT** Capitalize most proper adjectives. ■

PROPER ADJECTIVES FROM PROPER NOUNS:	American, Elizabethan, biblical, Chinese
PROPER NOUNS AS ADJECTIVES:	a Chicago accent, a March day, a Eugene O'Neill play

Some proper adjectives that once were capitalized have become such a common part of the language that they are no longer capitalized.

> **KEY CONCEPT** Do not capitalize certain frequently used proper adjectives. ■

EXAMPLES: bowie knife, china cabinet, french toast, afghan blanket, napoleon pastry, quixotic quest

▶ **KEY CONCEPT** Capitalize a brand name used as an adjective, but do not capitalize the common noun it modifies. ■

EXAMPLES: Everlasting refrigerator, Big Guy jeans

▶ **KEY CONCEPT** Do not capitalize a common noun used with two proper adjectives. ■

Compare the examples in the following chart. Notice in each case that a common noun used with two or more proper adjectives is not capitalized.

Compound Proper Noun	Two Proper Adjectives With Common Noun
Volstead Act	Volstead and Payne-Aldrich acts
Main Street	Main, Welch, and Macopin streets
Mississippi River	Mississippi and Missouri rivers

▶ **KEY CONCEPT** Do not capitalize prefixes attached to proper adjectives unless the prefix refers to a nationality. ■

EXAMPLES: pro-English   Franco-Prussian War

Notice that the prefix in the example on the left is not capitalized. The prefix in the example on the right is capitalized because it refers to a nationality.

▶ **KEY CONCEPT** In a hyphenated adjective, capitalize only the proper adjective. ■

EXAMPLE: Swedish-speaking immigrant

▶ **Exercise 4** Capitalizing Proper Adjectives and Nouns
Copy each of the following items, making the necessary corrections in capitalization.

1. niagara falls
2. russo-chinese border
3. house of lords
4. nile river delta
5. bay of fundy
6. the democratic party
7. lake titicaca
8. northwest new york
9. european explorers
10. anti-british protesters
11. the magna carta
12. dutch colonizers
13. henry m. stanley
14. anglo-american journalist
15. native american
16. rocky mountains
17. chitambo, zambia
18. irish accent
19. british and french Empires
20. nepalese-speaking guides

▶ **More Practice**

Language Lab
CD-ROM
• Capitalization lesson
On-line
Exercise Bank
• Section 26
Grammar Exercise
Workbook
• pp. 123–124

Using Capitals for Titles

Capitalize a person's title when it is used with the person's name or when it is used as a name.

▶KEY CONCEPT Capitalize titles of people and titles of works. ■

WITH A PROPER NAME:	Yesterday, Governor Wilson addressed the state legislature.
AS A NAME:	Mrs. Alvarez is on the phone, Doctor.
IN A GENERAL REFERENCE:	Have you ever met the mayor of our city?

TITLES OF PEOPLE	
Commonly Used Titles	Sir, Madam, Doctor, Professor, Father, Reverend, Rabbi, Sister, Archbishop, Sergeant, Governor, Senator, Ambassador
Abbreviated Titles	*Before names:* Mr., Mrs., Dr., Prof. *After names:* Jr., Sr., Ph.D., Esq.
Compound Titles	Commander in Chief, Vice President, Secretary of Defense, Lieutenant Governor
Titles With Prefixes or Suffixes	Mayor-elect Ross, ex-Senator Norman

▶KEY CONCEPT Capitalize the titles of certain high government officials even when the titles are not used with a proper name or in direct address. ■

Titles that are always capitalized include those of the current President, Vice President, and Chief Justice of the Supreme Court of the United States, as well as that of the Queen of England.

EXAMPLE: The Chief Justice was appointed by the President.

As a sign of respect, you may also capitalize other titles used without names.

▶ **KEY CONCEPT** Capitalize titles showing family relationships when they are used with a name or as a name. ■

WITH THE PERSON'S
NAME: Aunt Liz speaks two languages.
IN DIRECT ADDRESS: I'm glad you're coming to lunch, Grandma.
REFERRING TO A
SPECIFIC PERSON: Will Grandfather come with us on our trip to Africa?

▶ **KEY CONCEPT** Capitalize the titles and subtitles of works of literature, art, and media and of various publications. ■

Capitalize the first word and all other key words in the titles of books, periodicals, poems, stories, plays, television programs, paintings, and other works of art.

BOOK: *Profiles in Courage*
MOVIE: *The Great Train Robbery*
MAGAZINE: *Life*
PLAY: *The Tragedy of Macbeth*

▶ **KEY CONCEPT** Capitalize titles of courses when they are language courses or when they are followed by a number. ■

WITH CAPITALS: Spanish, Sociology 1, English 2
WITHOUT CAPITALS: biology, zoology, home economics

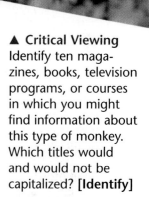

▲ **Critical Viewing** Identify ten magazines, books, television programs, or courses in which you might find information about this type of monkey. Which titles would and would not be capitalized? **[Identify]**

▶ **Exercise 5** **Capitalizing Titles of People and Things** Copy the following sentences, capitalizing the titles correctly. Underline any words that should be printed in italics.
1. After his successful assault on Mount Everest, mr. Edmund Hillary was knighted by the queen of england.
2. The leader of the expedition, colonel John Hunt, was made a life peer and took the title of baron.
3. The television station the discovery channel shows many programs about nature.
4. Before his famous encounter with doctor Livingstone, mr. Stanley had gone on an expedition in the American West led by general Winfield Scott Hancock.
5. When no one had heard from dr. Livingstone for several years, mr. James Gordon Bennet, jr., told Stanley, who worked for him at the new york herald, to go to Africa to find him.

More Practice
Language Lab CD-ROM
• Capitalization lesson
On-line Exercise Bank
• Section 26
Grammar Exercise Workbook
• pp. 125–126

Using Capitals in Letters

Capitalization is also required in parts of personal letters and business letters.

> **KEY CONCEPT** Capitalize the first word and all nouns in letter salutations and the first word in letter closings. ■

SALUTATIONS: Dear Eric,   Dear Sirs:
CLOSINGS: With love,   Yours truly,

> **Exercise 6** **Using Capitals in a Business Letter** Copy the following letter, adding and removing capital letters as appropriate.

▲ **Critical Viewing** Do you think that the student who wrote the letter to the left would be interested in traveling to Antarctica (shown here)? On what do you base your answer? **[Speculate]**

                                        23 spur avenue
                                 north Salem, New York
                                       august 29, 20--

mr. daniel lucey
Far Horizons Travel, incorporated
232 sherman avenue
new york, new york 10063

dear mr. lucey,

   I am a Student at state university, where i am working on my ph.d. i have an opportunity to do some travel and research in my area of interest. i plan to travel first to australia in the wake of captain james cook. while there, I wish to explore the Great Barrier reef off the Coast of queensland. i also wish to visit uluru national park in the northern territory to examine the world's largest Monolith, formerly known as Ayers rock.
   i recently read in national geographic magazine that your agency specializes in the kind of adventure tour that i am seeking and that you offer flights over the antarctic. i wish to trace the route of sir ernest shackleton and his ship the endurance. i would like to see south Georgia, the weddell sea, the south Sandwich Islands, and elephant island in the south shetlands. i am hoping that you can assist in planning my itinerary, as well as advise me on climatic conditions. i look forward to hearing your suggestions.

                                        sincerely,
                                        Jerry Coughlan

> **More Practice**
>
> Language Lab
> CD-ROM
> • Capitalization lesson
> On-line
> Exercise Bank
> • Section 26
> Grammar Exercise
> Workbook
> • pp. 125–126

▶ **Exercise 7** **Using All the Rules of Capitalization** Write the words that should be capitalized, and underline anything that should be printed in italics.

1. today, the memorial to david livingstone is found near the place where he was born, by the river clyde in scotland.
2. though never finding the source of the nile river, he was among the first europeans to discover lake ngami and victoria falls.
3. the nile river is the longest river in the world.
4. its major source is lake victoria, and it flows north through uganda, the sudan, and egypt to the mediterranean sea.
5. the ruvyironza river, one of the upper branches of the kagera in tanzania, is regarded as the ultimate source of the nile.
6. different sections of the nile are known by different names: the victoria nile, the blue nile, and the white nile.
7. other explorers have written accounts of their travels: in 1895, major john wesley powell published a book entitled canyons of the colorado.
8. the grand canyon was so awe-inspiring that powell said later, "the wonders of the grand canyon cannot be adequately represented in symbols of speech, nor by speech itself."
9. natural wonders are not seen only above ground.
10. australia boasts an amazing underwater attraction called the great barrier reef.

▲ **Critical Viewing** What capitalization rules might you use in describing this underwater scene from Australia's Great Barrier Reef? [Describe]

▶ **Exercise 8** **Applying Capitalization Rules to Writing** Write a few paragraphs describing an interesting or beautiful location you have seen or visited. Include each of the following items, correctly capitalized.

1. name of the main attraction
2. proper adjective that describes this attraction
3. name of the place where the attraction is located
4. name of someone who suggested that you visit it
5. date you saw or visited it
6. name of the person who discovered or built it
7. nationalities of other visitors
8. date it was discovered or built
9. name of the organization that administers the site
10. your first reactions to the site put into words
11. names of any famous visitors
12. name of another place you would like to see
13. language spoken in the country the site is in
14. historical event associated with the place
15. sentence that contains a colon

Internet Tip

To learn more about natural wonders and explorers, use search words like *discovery, exploration,* and *nature.* Use proper nouns, such as *Mount Everest,* to be more specific.

Exercise 9 Proofreading to Correct All Types of Capitalization Errors Revise these two paragraphs, adding and removing capitals as necessary.

Another natural phenomenon that erupts is a geyser. they release steam and hot water instead of Lava and ash. Most known geysers are found in only three countries: the united states, new zealand, and iceland. a famous geyser in the united states is old faithful. It is in Yellowstone national park in the state of wyoming. Old faithful erupts at intervals of 33 to 120 minutes: it expels from 3,700 to 8,400 gallons of water per eruption.

Four types of Glaciers include the alpine, piedmont, icecap, and continental. a Glacier is a large mass of ice formed where the rate of snowfall is greater than the rate of melting. alpine glaciers, such as those found on Mount rainier in washington, are found worldwide on high Mountain ranges. the hubbard Glacier in alaska is one of the longest alpine Glaciers in the world. piedmont Glaciers, which result from glaciers flowing together in a valley, are particularly common in alaska. The largest piedmont glacier in the world is the malaspina glacier in alaska. An example of a continental Glacier is the glacial blanket that covers almost the entire surface of greenland. it is similar to the one that covers the antarctic continent, which has an area of 5 million square miles. Icebergs are formed when chunks of these Glaciers break off near the sea.

Exercise 10 Writing Application Write a sentence for each numbered item that includes the type of word or words specified. Use capitals as needed.

1. name of a business
2. title
3. name of a country and city
4. language
5. quotation
6. name of a celestial body
7. specific date
8. name of a land craft, sea craft, spacecraft, or aircraft
9. street or road name
10. person's name

More Practice

Language Lab CD-ROM
• Capitalization lesson
On-line Exercise Bank
• Section 26
Grammar Exercise Workbook
• pp. 123–126

▲ **Critical Viewing** How would you describe this glacier? How would you use capitals in your description? **[Describe]**

Hands-on Grammar

Memo Mania

In the business world, there is another way in which capitalization is used: It is used in memorandums to emphasize key points. For example, to stress the importance of a looming deadline, a manager might write a sentence spelling out the implications of missing the deadline and type the entire sentence in capital letters.

Work with a group of classmates to experiment with the impact of presenting various sentences in capital letters. Type one or more imaginary memoranda about situations at a workplace. If you can't come up with any ideas, use the sample below. Then, retype the memo or memos in capital letters. Cut each of the sentences into strips.

Then, experiment with pasting the capitalized sentences over the corresponding sentences in the original memo. Discuss how emphasizing different sentences affects the overall impact of the memo. Share your findings with classmates.

TO: Development Staff
FR: Arthur Singer
Re: Schedule

I have been notified that the development schedule has slipped. However, it is essential that we meet our April deadline for product delivery. To move the process forward, all decisions about specifications must be finalized. In addition, staff members must come up with solutions for cutting time out of the schedule. Suggestions should be submitted to me no later than next Thursday. Once we have decided how to streamline the schedule, we must see to it that all interim deadlines are met. No additional slippage will be tolerated.

NO ADDITIONAL SLIPPAGE WILL BE TOLERATED.

SUGGESTIONS SHOULD BE SUBMITTED TO ME NO LATER THAN THURSDAY.

Find It in Your Reading The technique of capitalizing words and sentences for emphasis is also used in e-mail messages. For a week, track the use of capitalization in e-mail messages that you read.

Find It in Your Writing If you have any samples of business writing in your portfolio, review them to see if any sentences should be capitalized for emphasis.

Chapter Review

GRAMMAR EXERCISES 11–18

▶ **Exercise 11** **Capitalizing Proper Adjectives** Correctly capitalize each of the following.

1. scottish-born
2. norwegian explorer
3. shackleton's ship
4. anti-british
5. siamese cat

▶ **Exercise 12** **Capitalizing First Words** On a separate sheet of paper, capitalize words in the following sentences, as needed.

1. in the 1840's, Antarctica's status as a continent was confirmed.
2. three separate expeditions sailed along enough coast to realize that Antarctica was, in fact, a continental landmass.
3. many expeditions visited Antarctica between the late nineteenth and early twentieth centuries.
4. after Robert Peary reached the North Pole, Roald Amundsen decided to go south "just as swiftly as the news had spread through the cables."
5. in 1911, he became the first man to reach the South Pole.
6. in the 1920's, people began to fly over Antarctica: an American and a Norwegian became the first to fly over the Antarctic continent in 1929.
7. during the winter, Antarctica doubles in size because of all the sea ice that forms at its edges.
8. "i could not doubt now that the *Endurance* was confined for the winter," wrote Shackleton. "the seals were disappearing and the birds were leaving us."
9. "we must wait for the spring," he continued, "which may bring us better fortune."

10. though Shackleton and his men did not reach the South Pole, they all survived the loss of the *Endurance* and a long trek to South Georgia and rescue.

▶ **Exercise 13** **Capitalizing Proper Nouns** On a separate sheet of paper, write the words in the following sentences that should be capitalized.

1. Many volcanoes, such as mount etna and mount vesuvius, are born on the sea floor.
2. These volcanoes are both located in italy: vesuvius is near naples, and etna is in sicily.
3. Some volcanoes are more active than others: stromboli, in the lipari islands near sicily, has been continually active since ancient times.
4. Other constantly active volcanoes are found in an area called the ring of fire that encircles the pacific ocean.
5. Some volcanoes, like vesuvius, are moderately active and then become dormant for months or years.
6. An eruption that follows a long period of inactivity is usually violent, as was the case with mount saint helens in washington.
7. It erupted after a 123-year period of dormancy; in the philippines, mount pinatubo erupted after six quiet centuries.
8. Volcanic eruptions trigger mudflows that are extremely dangerous; the one caused by the eruption of nevada del ruiz in colombia claimed more than 25,000 lives in 1985.
9. In indonesia in 1883, the volcano krakatoa erupted with so much energy that ash was reportedly flung to a height of 17 miles.
10. The summit of mount saint helens was

blown off when it erupted in 1980, and the eruption of krakatoa destroyed most of the island on which it was located.

Exercise 14 Proofreading Sentences to Correct Capitalization of Proper Nouns and Adjectives Revise these sentences, adding capitals as necessary. Underline any words that should be printed in italics.

1. The motion picture industry has evolved dramatically since the days of the lumière brothers, edwin s. porter, and d. w. griffith.
2. Early films were controlled and limited by the motion picture patents company until americans and europeans formed independent production companies.
3. The star of *queen elizabeth* was sarah bernhardt, the french actress who was to achieve worldwide fame.
4. The most influential filmmaker of the early silent era was d. w. griffith, who in 1908, at the biograph studio in new york city, began to refine his craft.
5. It was griffith who trained such future stars as mary pickford, lionel barry- more, and lillian gish.

Exercise 15 Writing Sentences With Capitals Write a sentence about each of the following. Follow the rules for capitalization.

1. great vacation spot
2. governor of your state
3. battle of World War II
4. national park
5. piece of music
6. work of art
7. largest city in your state
8. museum you have visited
9. your birthplace
10. famous government building

Exercise 16 Proofreading to Correct the Use of Capitals in Letters Copy the following letter onto a separate sheet of paper. Use capitals where needed.

1401 smith street
sanderville, texas 11101

march 26, 20--

chamber of commerce
fort lauderdale, florida

to whom it may concern:

i am preparing a brochure for my english class in which i would like to describe the attractions of the fort lauderdale area. please send me the tourism package that you distribute to travel agents. i asked for one at my local travel agency, jet travel, inc., but they have been out of brochures since the thanksgiving break. i would appreciate any materials you can send me.

with thanks,

carly meyer

Exercise 17 Proofreading for All Types of Errors in Capitalization Revise the following paragraph, correcting errors in capitalization.

The name of mount Everest in tibetan is *chomo lungma*, which means "goddess-mother." its name in english is in honor of sir George everest, who was surveyor-general of india from 1830 to 1843. he first recorded the location and height of the Mountain in 1841.

Exercise 18 Writing Application Write a paragraph about a voyage of discovery. Include important names, dates, and places. When you are finished, under-line each capitalized word. Give the reason for each capitalization.

Standardized Test Preparation Workshop

Proofreading

Standardized tests will often measure your understanding of the rules of capitalization. You will be given a passage to proofread and identify the types of errors, including capitalization, spelling, and punctuation. The following sample items will help you practice proofreading for errors.

Test Tip

Remember that errors in capitalization can be words that should be capitalized but are not, as well as words that are capitalized when they shouldn't be.

Sample Test Item

Directions: Read the passage, and decide which type of error, if any, appears in each underlined section.

One of my favorite Poets is Emily Dickinson.
(1)
My Mother gave me a copy of her complete
(2)
works on my birthday.

1 A Spelling error

   B Capitalization error

   C Punctuation error

   D No error

2 F Spelling error

   G Capitalization error

   H Punctuation error

   J No error

Answers and Explanations

The correct answer for item 1 is *B.* The common noun *poets* should not be capitalized.

The correct answer for item 2 is *G.* Titles showing family relationships, such as *mother*, are not capitalized when they are preceded by a possessive pronoun, such as *my*.

Practice 1

Directions: Read the passage, and decide which type of error, if any, appears in each underlined section.

Last thursday, the entire team went out for
    (1)
Italian Food after the game. Our Eagles
    (2)
trounced the other Team. Next week,
    (3)
maybe coach Hay will join us, but only if
    (4)
we are buying!
    (5)

1 A Spelling error
   B Capitalization error
   C Punctuation error
   D No error

2 F Spelling error
   G Capitalization error
   H Punctuation error
   J No error

3 A Spelling error
   B Capitalization error
   C Punctuation error
   D No error

4 F Spelling error
   G Capitalization error
   H Punctuation error
   J No error

5 A Spelling error
   B Capitalization error
   C Punctuation error
   D No error

Practice 2

Directions: Read the passage, and decide which type of error, if any, appears in the underlined section.

I was born in sewickley, Pennsylvania,
(1)
in October 1962. My Parents, Tom and
 (2)   (3)
Nancy, brought me home to a brand new
        (4)
three-bedroom house in Suburbia.
(5)

1 A Spelling error
   B Capitalization error
   C Punctuation error
   D No error

2 F Spelling error
   G Capitalization error
   H Punctuation error
   J No error

3 A Spelling error
   B Capitalization error
   C Punctuation error
   D No error

4 F Spelling error
   G Capitalization error
   H Punctuation error
   J No error

5 A Spelling error
   B Capitalization error
   C Punctuation error
   D No error

Punctuation

Neuschwanstein Castle

Punctuation marks help to make a written work easier to understand by helping to organize and clarify the ideas in each sentence.

To understand the rules of punctuation and to punctuate your writing correctly, you must have a thorough knowledge of the elements of sentence structure. You should be able to recognize an appositive, a participial phrase, items in a series, and a complex or compound sentence. Each of these elements—and many others—is punctuated in a specific way.

In this chapter on punctuation, you will learn the major rules of punctuation that are so important to effective writing.

▲ **Critical Viewing** Neuschwanstein Castle in Bavaria, Germany, looks like a fairy-tale castle. Write several lines of dialogue about this castle, and punctuate them correctly. **[Describe]**

Diagnostic Test

Directions: Write all answers on a separate sheet of paper.

Skill Check A. Write the following sentences, using proper end marks to punctuate them.

1. Germany is a country in central Europe
2. Is France to the west of Germany
3. Yes, they share a border that has been a source of conflict
4. The Maginot line was a series of fortifications that the French built on that border for protection
5. Imagine their alarm when it proved utterly useless

Skill Check B. Use commas to punctuate these sentences.

6. Germany is large and it contains many beautiful cities.
7. Berlin Munich Bonn Frankfurt and Stuttgart are some of its principal cities.
8. The capital is Berlin which was famous for the wall that divided the city during the Cold War.
9. At that time in Germany's history Bonn served as the capital of West Germany the noncommunist nation that encompassed more than half of German territory.
10. The reunification of Germany however ended those divisions and the German economy became much stronger.

Skill Check C. Add colons and semicolons to these sentences.

11. Industry is the backbone of the German economy some of the world's largest corporations are based in that country.
12. Economic success has come with a price industrial pollution.
13. That pollution is particularly acute in Germany's major rivers the Rhine, the Danube, and the Elbe.
14. Most of Germany's woodlands have been harmed by acid rain in fact, the famed Black Forest has suffered extensive damage.
15. The largest cities in Germany are as follows Berlin, Bonn, Hamburg, and Munich.

Skill Check D. Punctuate the following sentences properly using quotation marks, underlining, dashes, and parentheses where necessary.

16. It was in Berlin that U.S. President John F. Kennedy uttered his now famous line: Ich bin ein Berliner!
17. Did you know that in some translations, that means, I am a jelly doughnut? my friend asked.
18. I responded, That shows how important it is to avoid grammatical errors; my friend nodded in agreement.
19. Germany now plays a central role along with France, Great Britain, and several other countries in the stability of Europe.
20. Few nations have had such a profound effect on the world a fact we must never forget.

End Marks

End marks include the period, the question mark, and the exclamation mark. They are used mainly to conclude sentences. The period and the question mark are also used in several special situations.

Using End Marks

To conclude sentences correctly, you must know whether to use a period, a question mark, or an exclamation mark. First, look at the rules governing the use of the period.

Period The period is the end mark used most often.

▶ **KEY CONCEPT** Use a period to end a declarative sentence, a mild imperative, and an indirect question. ■

A declarative sentence is a statement of fact or opinion. An imperative sentence gives a command or a direction. (Imperative sentences often begin with a verb.) An indirect question restates a question within a declarative sentence.

STATEMENT OF FACT:	Herman Hesse was a famous German writer.
STATEMENT OF OPINION:	I enjoyed many of his works.
COMMAND:	Finish your reading before you go out.
DIRECTION:	Turn left at the second traffic light.
INDIRECT QUESTION:	I asked him where he had learned to ski.

▶ **Exercise 1** Writing Declarative and Imperative Sentences
Follow each of the directions to write a declarative or imperative sentence, and punctuate it correctly.

EXAMPLE:	command about reading
ANSWER:	Read your assignment.

1. statement of fact about Germany
2. direction for finding Berlin on a map
3. indirect question about a German author
4. statement of opinion about German food
5. command about studying for a social studies test

Theme: Germany

In this section, you will learn when to use periods, question marks, and exclamation marks. Most of the examples and exercises in this section are about Germany.

**Cross-Curricular Connection:
Social Studies**

▶ **More Practice**

**On-line
Exercise Bank**
• Section 27.1
**Grammar Exercise
Workbook**
• pp. 127–128

Brandenburg Gate, Germany

Question Mark Direct questions, often in inverted word order, require a question mark at the end.

KEY CONCEPT Use a question mark to end an interrogative sentence, an incomplete question, or a statement intended as a question. ■

INTERROGATIVE SENTENCES:	Have you visited Germany?
	Which country will you visit next?
INCOMPLETE QUESTIONS:	Why? How much?
STATEMENTS INTENDED AS QUESTIONS:	This clock runs on batteries?
	We're going to have spaghetti?

Statements intended as questions should not be used too often. It is often better to rephrase them as direct questions.

STATEMENT INTENDED AS A QUESTION:	You agree?
REPHRASED AS A DIRECT QUESTION:	Do you agree?

Exclamation Mark An exclamation mark is intended for emphasis. It calls attention to an exclamatory sentence, an imperative sentence, or an interjection. Exclamation marks should be used sparingly. Reserve them for those situations in which you want to indicate strong emotion in a dramatic way.

▲ Critical Viewing
Write three questions about the Brandenburg Gate in Berlin, Germany. Make sure you punctuate your questions correctly. **[Analyze]**

27.1

▶ **KEY CONCEPT** Use an exclamation mark to end an exclamatory sentence, a forceful imperative sentence, or an interjection expressing strong emotion. ■

EXCLAMATORY SENTENCES: His admission of guilt shocked us!
                        That sunset is magnificent!

IMPERATIVE SENTENCES: Never try that trick again!
                        Come here quickly!

An interjection can be used with either a comma or an exclamation mark. An exclamation mark increases the emphasis.

WITH A COMMA: Oh, she is usually on time.
WITH AN EXCLAMATION MARK: Oh! I am amazed!

▶ **Exercise 2** Using End Marks Copy each item, and punctuate it correctly.

1. Linda thinks that nearly all Germans are literate
2. Impressed with the German education system, she asked the professor where he had studied for his degree
3. He mentioned Heidelberg University, the foremost institution in the country
4. The most difficult school before the university level is called the gymnasium
5. Wow The gymnasium has an intense academic program

Other Uses of End Marks

▶ **KEY CONCEPT** Use a period to end most abbreviations. ■

ABBREVIATIONS FOR TITLES:	Dr. Sr. Mrs. Mr. Gov. Maj. Rev. Prof. Lt.
ABBREVIATIONS FOR PLACE NAMES:	Ave. Bldg. Blvd. Mt. Dr. Jct. St. Ter. Rd. Pk.
ABBREVIATIONS FOR TIME AND DATES:	Sun. Dec. sec. min. hr. wk. yr. mo. Sat. A.M. P.M.
ABBREVIATIONS FOR MEASUREMENTS:	in. ft. yd. mi. tsp. tbsp. gal. pt. oz. lb. F.
ABBREVIATIONS WITHOUT PERIODS:	mm cm m km mg g kg L C

▶ **More Practice**

**On-line
Exercise Bank**
• Section 27.1
**Grammar Exercise
Workbook**
• pp. 127–128

🔵 **Learn More**

For a full list of abbreviations and the words for which they stand, see pages 902–905.

690 • Punctuation

KEY CONCEPT When an abbreviation ending with a period is placed at the end of a sentence, do not add another period as an end mark. If an end mark other than a period is required, however, you must add the end mark. ■

INCORRECT: The speaker will be Adam Martin, Jr..
CORRECT: The speaker will be Adam Martin, Jr.

INCORRECT: Is the speaker Adam Martin, Jr.
CORRECT: Is the speaker Adam Martin, Jr.?

The following chart lists some abbreviations.

ABBREVIATIONS WITH AND WITHOUT END MARKS			
anon.	anonymous	mgr.	manager
approx.	approximately	misc.	miscellaneous
assoc.	association	mph	miles per hour
A.W.O.L.	absent without leave	myth.	mythology or mythological
C.O.D.	cash on delivery	No.	number
dept.	department	pg.	page
doz.	dozen(s)	pkg.	package
ea.	each	poet.	poetical, poetry
EDT	Eastern Daylight Time	POW	prisoner of war
EST	Eastern Standard Time	pp.	pages
FM	frequency modulation	pub.	published, publisher
gov. or govt.	government	pvt.	private
Gr.	Greek	recd.	received
ht.	height	rpm	revolutions per minute
incl.	including	R.S.V.P.	please reply
intro.	introduction	sp.	spelling
ital	italics	SRO	standing room only
kt.	karat or carat	SST	Supersonic transport
meas.	measure	vol.	volume
mfg.	manufacturing	wt.	weight

Internet Tip

When choosing a user name for the Internet, don't put any periods in the name. Periods have special signifi-cance to computers as they communicate with each other over the Internet, and a bad user name (one with periods) can cause all kinds of trouble for you, such as lost e-mail.

▶ **KEY CONCEPT** Use a period after numbers and letters in outlines. ■

EXAMPLE: I. Maintaining your pet's health
          A. Diet
               1. For a puppy
               2. For a mature dog
          B. Exercise

▶ **Exercise 3** **Using End Marks in Other Situations** On a separate sheet of paper, add the necessary end marks to the following.

1. A package arrived COD from Munich today
2. Prof Schmidt sent books about German philosophers
3. The names of Hegel and Kant who are giants in that field are familiar to any Ph D candidate
4. I checked with Mr George Frasier, Jr, in the German Studies Dept at the U of Wisconsin, in Madison, Wisconsin, but he was unsure of Hegel's date of birth
5. He suggested the year AD 1725

▶ **Exercise 4** **Using End Marks Correctly in Your Own Writing** Write a paragraph about a famous German writer or scientist. Correctly use each type of end mark.

More Practice

On-line
Exercise Bank
• Section 27.1
Grammar Exercise
Workbook
• pp. 127–128

GRAMMAR IN LITERATURE

from The Rocking-Horse Winner
D. H. Lawrence

In this dialogue, the author has used a variety of punctuation. There are three questions. There is one exclamation. "Don't you stop till you get there" is an imperative sentence. The remaining sentences are declarative.

"Where did you get to?" asked his mother.

"Where I wanted to go to," he flared back at her.

"That's right, son!" said Uncle Oscar. "Don't you stop till you get there. What's the horse's name?"

"He doesn't have a name," said the boy.

"Gets on without all right?" asked the uncle.

Section Review

GRAMMAR EXERCISES 5–11

Exercise 5 Using End Marks On a separate sheet of paper, add the proper end marks to these sentences.

1. Schooling in Germany is compulsory and free for those aged 6 to 18
2. Children are given extensive tests after primary school, around the age of 10
3. What is the purpose of those tests
4. He asked if we had heard that many students are also musically talented
5. Do you know that the concert halls in Dresden attract large audiences

Exercise 6 Using End Marks in Special Situations On a separate sheet of paper, add end marks to these sentences.

1. I had nearly sixty dollars—$58 25, to be precise—that I wanted to convert to German marks
2. The US Treasury office in Boston, MA, gave me the shocking news: The mark effectively doesn't exist anymore
3. I asked Prof Martin, who has a PhD in economics, how that could be
4. Dr Martin explained that Germany is one of several member countries of the European Union (EU) that have agreed to use a single new currency, the euro
5. As of 12 PM today, a euro was worth $1 041, just over a dollar

Exercise 7 Using All Types of End Marks Rewrite the following items, adding end marks as needed.

1. Two of Germany's many music festivals are the Wagner Festival and the Bach Festival
2. Many believe that there was nothing—preludes, operas, concertos, sonatas—that Mozart could not compose or play

3. Oh I had no idea that Mozart was Austrian, not German
4. Who can top Brahms and Mendelssohn, two great composers
5. Did all these great classical composers really emerge from one country Why

Exercise 8 Revising to Add Correct End Marks Revise the following letter, adding or revising end marks as necessary.

(1) 45 Blazewood Dr
(2) Uniondale, NY. 11553
(3) Mon, Jan 3, 2010
(4) Dear Mr Kohl:
(5) Wow. Thanks for the tickets to Bayreuth! (6) I'm sorry about that late phone call the other night; I forgot that 7:00 PM in New York is 1:00 AM in Germany (7) At least now I know how to pronounce *Wagner* properly? (8) That's "VAHGner," right
(9) Sincerely,
(10) Lincoln Townes, Jr

Exercise 9 Find It in Your Reading Skim through a magazine article, and highlight at least three uses of each type of end mark. Explain each example.

Exercise 10 Find It in Your Writing Choose a piece of writing from your portfolio. Revise one of the paragraphs so that it includes question marks and exclamation marks as well as periods.

Exercise 11 Writing Application Write a letter like the one above. Use every type of end mark at least once.

Commas

This section presents the rules governing the use of commas. To use commas correctly, you must have a thorough knowledge of sentence structure. Studying this section can help you master the rules governing the use of commas and, at the same time, serve as a review of some basic elements of sentence structure.

Using Commas With Compound Sentences

A single independent clause expresses a complete thought and often stands alone as a simple sentence. Two independent clauses, correctly joined and punctuated, form a compound sentence. The conjunctions used to connect independent clauses are called *coordinating conjunctions.* The seven coordinating conjunctions are *and, but, for, nor, or, so,* and *yet.*

 **KEY CONCEPT** Use a comma before the conjunction to separate two or more independent clauses in a compound sentence. ■

EXAMPLES: My cousin is getting married this summer, but I won't be able to attend the wedding.

The Newport Jazz Festival draws a big crowd every year, and this year won't be any different.

Remember to use both a comma and a coordinating conjunction in a compound sentence. Using only a comma would result in a run-on sentence.

Notice also that the ideas in both independent clauses in each of the preceding examples are related. Do not construct a compound sentence from two unrelated clauses.

Finally, do not confuse a compound sentence with a simple sentence that has a compound verb.

SIMPLE SENTENCE
WITH A COMPOUND VERB: John bought them a blender and waited to have it gift wrapped.

COMPOUND SENTENCE: John bought them a blender, and he waited to have it gift wrapped.

**Theme:
Celebrations**
In this section, you will learn about the many uses of the comma. Most of the examples and exercises in this section are about different kinds of celebrations and milestones.

**Cross-Curricular Connection:
Social Studies**

> **Exercise 12** Using Commas to Separate Independent

Clauses Copy each of the following sentences, adding commas as needed.

EXAMPLE: I wanted to go to my cousin's wedding in Denver but plane tickets cost too much.

ANSWER: I wanted to go to my cousin's wedding in Denver, but plane tickets cost too much.

1. The wedding was on January 12 and that is a popular time to go to Denver.
2. People fly into Denver and drive to ski resorts from there.
3. I enjoy going to weddings for there is always great food and good dancing music.
4. My father doesn't usually dance but at a wedding he might.
5. I was invited to the wedding so I will have to send a wedding present.
6. I don't know my cousin's bride very well so I don't know what to send.
7. Money is always a good present but it seems too impersonal for my cousin.
8. My mother usually sends towels but I don't know what color their bathroom is.
9. Art is very personal yet I think I know my cousin well enough to choose art for him.
10. I will go to the mall today and I will browse in the art store.

> **Exercise 13** Proofreading to Correct the Use of Commas

Revise the following paragraph, adding and deleting commas as necessary.

(1) Celebrations are the familial, or communal sharing of an event. (2) Many celebrations are based on traditional customs and many of those customs involve rites of passage. (3) Birthdays and "sweet-sixteen" parties celebrate a new phase in the life of a person and new responsibilities, and attitudes are expected. (4) In many cultures, sweet-sixteen parties are elaborate and some families consider them as formal as a wedding. (5) Marriage and death are two other life phases, that are celebrated in different ways around the world.

> **More Practice**

**Language Lab
CD-ROM**
• Commas lesson
**On-line
Exercise Bank**
• Section 27.2
**Grammar Exercise
Workbook**
• pp. 129–134

Using Commas With Series and Adjectives

Series A series consists of three or more words, phrases, or subordinate clauses of a similar kind.

▶ **KEY CONCEPT** Use commas to separate three or more words, phrases, or clauses in a series. ■

WORDS IN A SERIES:	Venice, Rio, and Trinidad have notable carnivals.
	Her costume was exotic, exciting, and original.
PHRASES IN A SERIES:	The groom was fidgeting at first, then chewing his lip, and finally sweating profusely.
	It's important to drink plenty of fluids before the day arrives, during the event, and immediately afterward.
SUBORDINATE CLAUSES IN A SERIES:	The newspapers reported that the weather was flawless, that the dinner was impeccable, and that the band played remarkably well.

Notice that the number of commas in each of the preceding series is one fewer than the number of items in the series. If there are three items in a series, two commas are used; if there are four items in a series, three commas are used; and so on.

◀ **Critical Viewing** Describe what you see in this picture of the Carnival in Brazil. Use commas in a series in at least one place in your description. **[Describe]**

When conjunctions are used to separate all of the items in a series, no commas are needed.

EXAMPLE: We saw fireworks and streamers and confetti.

You should also avoid placing commas before items, such as *salt and pepper,* that are paired so often that they are thought of as one item.

EXAMPLE: The best man, bride and groom, and maid of honor sat together.

Coordinate Adjectives Sometimes, two or more adjectives are used together. Follow the rules below.

> **KEY CONCEPT** Use commas to separate *coordinate adjectives, or* adjectives of equal rank. ■

COORDINATE ADJECTIVES: a tasteless, boring affair
a raucous, festive, thrilling occasion

An adjective is equal in rank to another if the word *and* can be inserted between them without changing the meaning of the sentence. Another way to test whether or not adjectives are coordinate is to reverse their order. If the sentence still sounds correct, they are of equal rank.

If you cannot place the word *and* between adjectives or reverse their order without changing the meaning of the sentence, they are called *cumulative adjectives.*

> **KEY CONCEPT** Do not use a comma between cumulative adjectives. ■

CUMULATIVE ADJECTIVES: a new dinner jacket
many unusual guests

> **Exercise 14** Supplying Commas to Separate Items in a Series Copy each of the following sentences, inserting commas to separate items as needed.
> 1. The bride's mother was making up the list of invitations arranging for the delivery of flowers and making place-cards for the reception.
> 2. The groom's mother was arranging for the rehearsal the rehearsal dinner and accommodations for the guests.
> 3. The bride and groom were responsible for the dinner menu the reception the music and gifts for the bridal party.
> 4. They were hoping to arrange a truly tasteful lovely wedding.
> 5. Getting married buying a house and having children are some of the most stressful things in life.

> **More Practice**
> Language Lab
> CD-ROM
> • Commas lesson
> On-line
> Exercise Bank
> • Section 27.2
> Grammar Exercise
> Workbook
> • pp. 129–134

◄ **Critical Viewing**
Which of the
paragraphs in the
exercise below
does this photo-
graph illustrate?
Explain. **[Connect]**

▶ **Exercise 15** Proofreading to Correct Errors in the Use of
Commas to Separate Items in a Series Revise the following,
adding or deleting commas as necessary.

Because of the agricultural nature of previous centuries,
large families were common welcome, and necessary. Children
were needed for the farm chores of milking feeding animals
sowing and harvesting.

Today, parents worry whether the new baby is healthy
whether its needs are provided for and whether its future
happiness is secure. New parents both feed and dress the
baby—often nervously. As time passes, they become more
confident and the tasks that once took hours are quickly
performed.

For monarchs, producing children is a necessary means
of continuing, the line maintaining authority and receiving the
country's financial stipends. Announcements of royal births
are still cause for the hoisting of castle flags cannon or rifle
salutes and a national day of celebration.

Births are celebrated, and commemorated throughout the
world in a variety of ways. In Denmark, families celebrate
births with a festive noisy party and a traditional dance.
Selecting godparents to help guide nurture and protect the
child is a common practice in various countries. In most cultures, the baby is introduced to the community in a celebration such as a presentation ceremony a bris or a christening.

▶ **More Practice**

**Language Lab
CD-ROM**
• Commas lesson
**On-line
Exercise Bank**
• Section 27.2
**Grammar Exercise
Workbook**
• pp. 129–134

Using Commas After Introductory Material

Most introductory material is set off with a comma.

▶ **KEY CONCEPT** Use a comma after an introductory word, phrase, or clause. ■

INTRODUCTORY WORDS:	Yes, we do expect to hear from them soon. No, there has been no response. Well, I was definitely surprised by her question.
NOUNS OF DIRECT ADDRESS:	Joe, will you attend?
INTRODUCTORY ADVERBS:	Hurriedly, they gathered up their equipment. Patiently, the children's mother explained it to them again.
PARTICIPIAL PHRASES:	Moving quickly, she averted a potential social disaster. Marching next to each other in the parade, we introduced ourselves and started to chat.
PREPOSITIONAL PHRASES:	In the shade of the maple tree, a family spread a picnic cloth. After the lengthy festivities, we were all exhausted.
INFINITIVE PHRASES:	To choose the right gift, I consulted the bridal registry. To finish my speech on time, I will have to cut some remarks.
ADVERBIAL CLAUSES:	When she asked for a permit for the fair, she was sure it would be denied. If you compete in marathons, you may be interested in this one.

Only one comma should be used after two prepositional phrases or a compound participial or infinitive phrase.

EXAMPLES: In the pocket of his vest, he found the ring.

Lost in the crowd and overwhelmed by the confusion, the children asked the policeman for help.

It is not absolutely necessary to set off short prepositional phrases. However, you may find that a comma is needed with a two- or three-word phrase in order to avoid confusion.

CLEAR: In the evening we ate dinner at the reception.
CONFUSING: In the rain drops stained the fine tablecloths.
CLEAR: In the rain, drops stained the fine tablecloths.

Exercise 16 Using Commas to Set Off Introductory Material Copy each sentence that needs commas, adding them as necessary. If a sentence needs no commas, write *correct.*

1. Without a doubt entering into adulthood is one of the most difficult steps of life.
2. In many Middle Eastern, Native American, and African societies very specific ceremonies welcome teenage boys and girls into adulthood.
3. These rituals and ceremonies include being taught by selected elders.
4. Traditionally customs and beliefs held sacred by the community are taught to the young people.
5. In some cases boys and girls are secluded for months to concentrate exclusively on matters of growing up.
6. After this intensive training the young people prove their worthiness by demonstrating their maturity.
7. Yes some even undergo dangerous physical endurance tests, such as surviving a night out in the deep woods.
8. To prove their merit other young people must flawlessly recite or perform traditional oral and written works of the culture.
9. In some ways these are similar to such religious rites of passage as bar and bat mitzvahs, first communion, and confirmation.
10. Though not quite the same a secular equivalent might be high-school or college final exams.

More Practice

Language Lab
CD-ROM
• Commas lesson
On-line
Exercise Bank
• Section 27.2
Grammar Exercise
Workbook
• pp. 129–134

▶ **Critical Viewing** Using introductory phrases, describe what the people in this picture are celebrating. **[Infer]**

KEY CONCEPT Use commas to set off parenthetical expressions—words or phrases that interrupt the flow of a sentence. ■

Parenthetical expressions may come at the end of a sentence or in the middle. When a parenthetical expression appears in the middle of a sentence, two commas are needed to set it off from the rest of the sentence.

NOUNS OF DIRECT ADDRESS:	Will you have lunch with us, Ted? I wonder, Mr. Green, where they'll go for their honeymoon.
CONJUNCTIVE ADVERBS:	Someone else had already bought them a toaster, however. We could not, therefore, buy one.
COMMON EXPRESSIONS:	I listened to the teacher's explanation as carefully as anyone else, I think.
CONTRASTING EXPRESSIONS:	Tom is seventeen, not eighteen. Lisa's personality, not her beauty, won Bill's heart.

Appositives, participial phrases, and adjective clauses can be either essential or nonessential. (The terms *restrictive* and *nonrestrictive* are also used to refer to these two kinds of materials.) Essential material, which is necessary to the meaning of a sentence, is not set off with commas.

ESSENTIAL APPOSITIVE:	The singer *Diana Ross* is also an actress.
ESSENTIAL PARTICIPIAL PHRASE:	The woman *buying the tomatoes* is my mother.
ESSENTIAL ADJECTIVE CLAUSE:	The report *that the committee will consider today* was prepared by members of the first-aid squad.

The preceding examples illustrate three kinds of essential elements. In the first example, the appositive *Diana Ross* identifies the specific singer. In the next example, the participial phrase *buying the tomatoes* identifies the specific woman. In the last example, the adjective clause *that the committee will consider today* identifies the specific report. Because they limit, or restrict, identification to the person or thing described in the appositive, participial phrase, or adjective clause, these items are all essential. They cannot be removed without changing the meaning of the sentence, so they require no commas.

Nonessential elements also provide information, but that information is not essential to the meaning of the sentence. Because nonessential elements do not alter the meaning and are not necessary for purposes of identification, they require commas to set them off.

KEY CONCEPT Use commas to set off nonessential expressions. ■

NONESSENTIAL APPOSITIVE:	Diana Ross, *the singer,* is also an actress.
NONESSENTIAL PARTICIPIAL PHRASE:	My mother, *buying the tomatoes,* is an excellent cook.
NONESSENTIAL ADJECTIVE CLAUSE:	The first-aid squad's report, *which the committee will consider today,* took six months to prepare.

The nonessential elements in the preceding examples are interesting, but they are not necessary to the main ideas in the sentences. *Diana Ross, my mother,* and *the first-aid squad's report* clearly identify the items *being discussed.* The nonessential elements, therefore, are set off with commas.

Exercise 17 **Setting Off Parenthetical Expressions** Copy these sentences, inserting commas to set off nonessential parenthetical expressions. If the sentence is correct as is, write *correct.*

EXAMPLE: You look best I think in bright colors.
ANSWER: You look best, I think, in bright colors.

1. Festivals and feasts without a doubt are favorite forms of celebration.
2. They are community or national celebrations involving the careful not haphazard planning of events.
3. People don't realize that festivals in fact don't just happen; they are usually organized by civic and cultural groups.
4. Feasts and festivals in most cases honor some special event that occurred in the history of the town or nation.
5. Heroic individuals however are sometimes the subject of these celebrations; Zapata is one such Mexican hero.
6. Historical and cultural aspects of a nation are celebrated.
7. Traditions such as baking bread in earthen clay ovens as practiced centuries ago are usually included in festivals.
8. Costumes many of them homemade are often the most fascinating part of festivals such as the Carnival in Venice.
9. These traditional feasts and festivals originated one would think with the ancient festivities at harvest time.
10. Some festivals such as the Carnival in Trinidad include the selection of the King and Queen of Calypso.

More Practice

Language Lab
CD-ROM
• Commas lesson
On-line
Exercise Bank
• Section 27.2
Grammar Exercise
Workbook
• pp. 129–134

GRAMMAR IN LITERATURE

from **The Rocking-Horse Winner**
D. H. Lawrence

In the first sentence, the author has used commas to separate items in a series. In the second sentence, the author has used commas to set off a participial phrase.

Daffodil came in first, Lancelot second, Mirza third. The child, flushed and with eyes blazing, was curiously serene.

▶ **Exercise 18** Distinguishing Between Essential and Nonessential Material Add commas to the following sentences where necessary.

1. Festivals the world over serve many beneficial purposes.
2. The Italian navigator Christopher Columbus is credited with bringing knowledge of the Americas to Europeans.
3. The American holiday that bears his name acknowledges his contributions to exploration.
4. The Balloon Fiesta which is held in Albuquerque is widely attended.
5. Local celebrations that boost the morale of a town by honoring local successes are usually well attended.
6. Patriot's Day which is observed in Massachusetts combines the celebration of local heroes with the sponsorship of the Boston Marathon.
7. Judging which festival is best is difficult because there are so many types of them.
8. Independence celebrations which note release from control by another country build national pride.
9. In places like ancient Athens where women's freedoms were severely restricted festivals were an opportunity for female citizens to relax and to release tensions for a day.
10. These days, women like Margaret Thatcher the former British prime minister lead their governments and are celebrated in their own right.

Using Commas in Other Ways

Geographical Names Geographical names that have more than one part require commas.

▶ **KEY CONCEPT** When a geographical name is made up of two or more parts, use a comma after each item. ■

EXAMPLES: My cousin who lives in Dallas, Texas, is cutting the ribbon for the grand opening.

They're going to Kouchibouguac, New Brunswick, Canada, for their honeymoon.

Dates Dates that have more than one part require commas.

▶ **KEY CONCEPT** When a date is made up of two or more parts, use a comma after each item. ■

EXAMPLES: The wedding took place on June 16, 1985, and their son was born on June 16, 1986.

Friday, August 23, was the first day of the fair.

Titles After a Name Whenever you use a title after the name of a person or a company, add commas.

▶ **KEY CONCEPT** When a name is followed by one or more titles, use a comma after the name and after each title. ■

EXAMPLE: Susan Martini, Ph.D., announces her engagement to Bob Taormina, M.D.

⊙ Technology Tip

If you are a writer who uses too many commas, you can use the "Find" or "Search" function under the "Edit" to find all the commas in your document. This way, you can focus solely on them and decide whether they are really required.

▼ **Critical Viewing** How is the Boston Marathon a fitting celebration of Patriot's Day in Massachusetts? Use nonessential elements in your response. **[Connect]**

Addresses Commas are also necessary in addresses.

▶ **KEY CONCEPT** Use a comma after each item in an address made up of two or more parts. ■

EXAMPLE: Send an invitation to Mrs. Robert Brooks, 145 River Road, Jacksonville, Florida 32211.

Commas are placed after the name, street, and city in the preceding example. Instead of inserting a comma between the state and the ZIP Code, extra space is left between them.

Most commas in an address are unnecessary when stacked in a letter or on an envelope or package. A comma is still required, however, between the city and the state.

EXAMPLE: Mrs. Robert Brooks
             145 River Road
             Jacksonville, Florida 32211

Salutations and Closings Commas are also needed in other parts of letters.

▶ **KEY CONCEPT** Use a comma after the salutation in a personal letter and after the closing in all letters. ■

SALUTATIONS: Dear Emily,   Dear Uncle Frank,   My dear Jane,
CLOSINGS: Yours truly,   Sincerely,   Your friend,

▲ **Critical Viewing**
For what kind of celebrations are candles used? Why do you think we use candles? Make sure you punctuate your response correctly. **[Speculate]**

Large Numbers Commas make large numbers easier to read.

> **KEY CONCEPT** With numbers of more than three digits, use a comma after every third digit from the right. ∎

EXAMPLES: 3,823 students
205,000 gallons
2,674,970 tons

Do not use commas in ZIP Codes, telephone numbers, page numbers, serial numbers, years, or house numbers.

ZIP CODE:	07632
TELEPHONE NUMBER:	(805) 555-6224
PAGE NUMBER:	1258
SERIAL NUMBER:	602 988 6768
HOUSE NUMBER:	18436
YEAR:	2004

Elliptical Sentences In elliptical sentences, words that are understood are left out. Commas make these sentences easier to read.

> **KEY CONCEPT** Use a comma to indicate the words left out of an elliptical sentence. ∎

EXAMPLE: Alan celebrates his birthday solemnly; Fred, casually.

The words *celebrates his birthday* have been omitted from the second clause of the elliptical sentence. The comma has been inserted in their place, however, so the meaning is still clear.

Grammar and Style Tip

Elliptical sentences require parallel construction between clauses to be easily understood; if the two clauses aren't exactly the same in construction, do not use an elliptical sentence for that idea.

▶ **Critical Viewing** What can you conclude about the address pictured here based on the details in the photograph? **[Infer]**

Direct Quotations Another use of commas is to indicate where direct quotations begin and end.

▷ **KEY CONCEPT** Use commas to set off a direct quotation from the rest of the sentence. ∎

EXAMPLES: "You came home late," commented James's mother.

He said, "The wedding rehearsal ran longer than expected."

"I hope," James's mother said, "the best man doesn't forget the ring."

Misuses of Commas You have now seen many rules governing the use of commas. Studying these rules will help you use commas correctly. Knowing the rules will also help you avoid using unnecessary commas. Because commas appear so frequently in writing, some people are tempted to use them where no commas are required. Be sure you know the reason that you are inserting commas each time you use them.

MISUSED WITH AN ADJECTIVE AND NOUN:	After a dance, I enjoy a cool, refreshing, drink.
CORRECT:	After a dance, I enjoy a cool, refreshing drink.
MISUSED WITH A COMPOUND SUBJECT:	After the election, my friend Nancy, and her sister Julia, were invited to the inaugural ball.
CORRECT:	After the election, my friend Nancy and her sister Julia were invited to the inaugural ball.
MISUSED WITH A COMPOUND VERB:	The groom looked deep into her eyes, and spoke from his heart.
CORRECT:	The groom looked deep into her eyes and spoke from his heart.
MISUSED WITH A COMPOUND OBJECT:	She chose a dress with long sleeves, and a train.
CORRECT:	She chose a dress with long sleeves and a train.
MISUSED WITH PHRASES:	Reading the invitation, and wondering who sent it, Brian did not hear the phone ringing.
CORRECT:	Reading the invitation and wondering who sent it, Brian did not hear the phone ringing.

MISUSED WITH CLAUSES:	He discussed what elements are crucial to a successful office party, and which caterers are most reliable.
CORRECT:	He discussed what elements are crucial to a successful office party and which caterers are most reliable.

Exercise 19 Using Commas in Geographical Names, Dates, Titles, Addresses, Large Numbers, Elliptical Sentences, and Direct Quotations Revise the following passage, inserting the necessary commas.

Thanksgiving was first celebrated on November 26 1789. Today it is meant to be a reenactment of the Pilgrim survival in Plymouth Massachusetts. Turkey is the traditional meal served in remembrance of the four wild turkeys that were the main source of food for the entire settlement at Plymouth in 1621.

Holiday observances not only honor survivors but also honor the dead. On November 1 Mexicans clean and decorate cemeteries in respect for those who have died. Since May 30 1868 Memorial Day has been set aside in the United States to honor war heroes. National celebrations often center on the birthdays of deceased heroes: United States citizens celebrate George Washington; South Americans Simon Bolivar. The fallen civil rights leader Martin Luther King Jr. who said "Free at last, free at last, thank God almighty, we're free at last" is honored on his birthday.

National celebrations can be fun-filled too such as Oktoberfest which has been held in Germany since October 17 1810 in honor of the wedding of Louis I King of Bavaria.

More Practice

Language Lab
CD-ROM
• Commas lesson
On-line
Exercise Bank
• Section 27.2
Grammar Exercise
Workbook
• pp. 129–134

▼ **Critical Viewing** How does this photograph relate to the information in the exercise above? **[Connect]**

▶ **Exercise 20** **Using Commas in a Letter** Add the missing information and necessary commas to complete this letter.

Your address (Make one up if you wish.)
February 12 20--
Dear Martha

Thanks for the invitation to your wedding on August 14 2010. I am sending a gift as soon as I can to your apartment at 255 Great Lane Eden New York. Martha I forgot to tell you that I did a research paper on marriage and weddings and I read it at the club last month. Are you and Jim "the Brain" going to have an engagement party? If so are you going to have it in Chicago Illinois? I'll call you after six at the dorm on Friday June 20.

Your friend always
Your name

▶ **Exercise 21** **Writing a Paragraph Using Commas for Various Purposes** Write a paragraph in which you use commas for at least five of the purposes explained in this section.

▶ **Exercise 22** **Using Commas Correctly in Your Writing** Write ten original sentences following each direction below.
1. Write a compound sentence about a birthday celebration.
2. Write a sentence listing four presents you received at a birthday or other celebration.
3. Write a sentence using the introductory phrase "In some cases."
4. Write a sentence using the introductory word "Yes."
5. Write a sentence using the introductory phrase "Moving quickly."
6. Write a sentence using the parenthetical phrase "in fact."
7. Write a sentence about a national holiday using the parenthetical phrase "although I tried."
8. Write a sentence describing an actor or singer at a celebration or holiday concert using "talented" and "attractive."
9. List the dates of birth of two friends. Begin with: "(Name) was born on. . . ."
10. Write a sentence about yourself. Within the sentence, show two academic or other titles that you would like to have after your name.

GRAMMAR EXERCISES 23–30

> **Exercise 23** Punctuating Simple and Compound Sentences, Introductory Elements, and Items in a Series Revise the following paragraphs, adding commas where necessary.

(1) Marriage has existed since ancient times and as a social contract it reflects the customs of its society. (2) In almost all cultures marriage is preceded by a betrothal period during which gifts are exchanged and families get to know each other. (3) In Western nations such as the United States Canada England and Italy an engagement ring is given to the prospective bride the families of the betrothed visit each other and engagement parties are held. (4) In Eastern societies—Japan India and China for example—families spend the engagement period socializing and negotiating business matters such as a dowry. (5) Families also discuss future living arrangements the right time for the wedding and other important matters that will affect the marriage. (6) Usually an outside consultant of some kind is present at the planning. (7) Wedding ceremonies of most cultures are filled with symbols and rituals of fertility prosperity and long-lasting union. (8) In certain cultures the couple actually ties a knot and in some African-based wedding rituals the couple "jumps the broom." (9) In all societies health fortune and prosperity are wished along with the presentation of gifts to the marrying couple. (10) Depending on the culture gifts vary widely from pigs or cattle to blenders or silverware and they are given before the wedding or on the actual day of the ceremony.

> **Exercise 24** Punctuating Items in a Series, in Coordinate Adjectives, and After Introductory Material Revise this paragraph, adding commas as necessary.

(1) Today most marriages are romantic free-will marriages. (2) However in Middle Eastern Asian and African families arranged marriages still exist. (3) Although many arranged marriages are the result of regional tradition they also occur in aristocratic groups of all cultures as a means of maintaining societal status and financial solvency. (4) It is believed that an arranged marriage guarantees a long-lasting union happy healthy children and family stability. (5) The professional marriage arranger objectively studies the two people and therefore logic good sense and a dispassionate perspective prevail in approving the match.

> **Exercise 25** Setting Off Introductory Elements, Parenthetical Expressions, and Nonessential Material Revise these sentences, adding commas as necessary.

1. In Western societies such as Europe and the Americas weddings are often seen as a private matter between the two people not a public event.
2. However in non-Western societies such as Asia, Africa, and the Middle East weddings are seen as a family and community event.
3. Wedding preparations vary considerably; for example traditional East Indian brides have their hands tattooed in ornate, intricate designs whereas Western brides usually wear white.
4. Throughout the world brides are usually veiled.
5. Obviously a groom seeing his veiled bride for the first time as is sometimes the case in an arranged marriage can be in for a surprise.

Exercise 26 Punctuating Introductory and Nonessential Material

Revise these sentences, adding commas where necessary.

1. In recent times the color white which represents innocence and purity has been the color of choice for wedding dresses in the West.
2. Traditional East Indian wedding attire which is quite different from Western equivalents bursts with color.
3. Asian wedding dresses of red silk embroidered with gold thread dazzle the eye.
4. In Western weddings the bride wears a certain gown for the ceremony and changes during the reception into her "going-away" or honeymoon dress.
5. In Asian weddings the bride will occasionally disappear and then reappear each time in a stunning new outfit.

Exercise 27 Proofreading for the Correct Use of Commas

Revise these paragraphs, adding and deleting commas where necessary.

Weddings are usually at least, several hours long and often a full day from dawn to dusk consisting of ceremonial rites and feasting is typical in some cultures. Without question the reception is the most costly part of a wedding. It is a ritual in which the bride, and groom are introduced to society for the first time as man and wife. It is also a time when friends and family welcoming new members into their circle extend their best wishes and hopes for the young couple. Merriment, and a good time are the object of the reception.

Regardless of how simple, or how ornate weddings are they are the favorite celebrations of many people. The wedding celebration is seen as a time of hope for a better future.

Exercise 28 Find It in Your Reading

Read through one of your favorite magazines, and find at least one example each of ten of the rules in this section.

Exercise 29 Find It in Your Writing

Review a sample from your portfolio, finding examples of different uses of commas. Then, use commas to combine four pairs of sentences to form compound sentences.

Exercise 30 Writing Application

Write an original sentence for each of the following:

1. A compound sentence about what the perfect graduation party would be like.
2. A sentence listing some of the things you'd like to do after graduation.
3. A sentence about a famous actress, describing what awards ceremonies she might attend and in which capacity.
4. A sentence beginning, "In any case."
5. A brief letter inviting someone with an impressive title to a royal wedding.

Semicolons and Colons

This section presents rules governing the use of semicolons (;) and colons (:). Semicolons can help you establish a relationship between independent clauses. They can also help you avoid confusion in sentences with other internal punctuation. Colons can be used as introductory devices to point ahead to additional information as well as in other special situations.

Using Semicolons

Semicolons establish relationships between independent clauses that are closely related in thought and structure.

▶ **KEY CONCEPT** Use a semicolon to join independent clauses that are not already joined by the conjunction *and, but, for, nor, or, so,* or *yet.* ∎

The most common way to join independent clauses is by using a coordinate conjunction and a comma.

EXAMPLE: We explored the attic together, and we were amazed at all the useless junk we found there.

When no coordinating conjunction is used, however, closely related independent clauses can be joined with a semicolon.

EXAMPLE: We explored the attic together; we were amazed at all the useless junk we found there.

Sometimes, the second independent clause may begin with a conjunctive adverb or a transitional expression. Conjunctive adverbs include such words as *also, furthermore, accordingly, besides, consequently, however, instead, otherwise, similarly, therefore,* and *indeed.* Transitional expressions include *as a result, first, second, at this time, for instance, for example, in fact, on the other hand, that is, in conclusion,* and *finally.*

▶ **Critical Viewing** This scuba diver may be searching for treasure. Imagine and describe the treasure that can be found in the ocean. Use independent clauses and semicolons in your response. **[Speculate]**

◀ **Critical Viewing**
What type of discovery has this scuba diver made? **[Speculate]**

KEY CONCEPT Use a semicolon to join independent clauses separated by either a conjunctive adverb or a transitional expression. ■

CONJUNCTIVE ADVERB: We visited curio shops in eight counties in only two days; *consequently,* we had no time for sightseeing.

TRANSITIONAL EXPRESSION: She never found the shipwreck; *in fact,* she really had no interest in scuba diving.

In the first example, the conjunctive adverb *consequently* is set off by a semicolon and a comma. A comma follows it because it is an introductory expression.

In the second example, the transitional expression is *in fact*. It, too, is set off by a semicolon and a comma.

KEY CONCEPT Use semicolons to avoid confusion when independent clauses or items in a series already contain commas. ■

INDEPENDENT CLAUSES: The city, supposedly filled with gold, was a fable; and the hungry, tired explorers would only find it in their dreams.

ITEMS IN A SERIES: I was convinced that we had won when I heard the music of the band playing our victory march; the jubilant players clapping and shouting; and the roar of spectators rising to their feet.

In the last example, semicolons are used instead of commas to separate the three major parts of the series. Commas are used within each of the major parts to set off nonessential participial phrases. You should also consider the use of semicolons when items in a series contain nonessential appositives or adjective clauses.

⚙ **Grammar** ⚙ **and Style Tip**

You can add more variety to your writing by alternating the use of compound sentences joined by commas and conjunctions with sentences containing independent clauses joined by a semicolon.

> **Exercise 31** **Using Semicolons** Revise the following paragraphs, adding semicolons where necessary.

A treasure is something held in high value an antique is a piece of furniture or decorative object that is a hundred years old or older. Opinions have changed in recent years consequently, items that are only fifty years old are now considered antiques.

Every country has its antiques and treasures however, many such objects are universally acclaimed. Treasures often cross boundaries in fact, vigorous discussions have been held between countries in regard to ownership of valued objects. Conflicts can arise if a crew seeks ownership after spending months, sometimes years, to discover a treasure and if the host country is poor, proud, or seeks international recognition. Now, agreements are made before large amounts of time, money, and energy have been spent on diving expeditions, land excavations, or art restorations and before expectations are raised unrealistically. Cautionary measures are taken nevertheless, things aren't always smooth between host and "discoverers."

At one time, there was a dispute over Leonardo da Vinci's *The Last Supper* between Italian government officials claiming authority over the work the international art community trying to protect a priceless painting and the restoration team seeking greater autonomy in their efforts. Almost all of these conflicts are resolved rancorous arguing would serve no purpose, since the objective of both parties is to preserve a treasure. In the end, most recovered treasures are preserved or restored for people of all cultures to enjoy.

More Practice

Language Lab CD-ROM
• Semicolons, Colons, and Quotation Marks lesson

On-line Exercise Bank
• Section 27.3

Grammar Exercise Workbook
• pp. 135–136

◀ **Critical Viewing** Why do some coins become worth more than their "face" value? **[Speculate]**

Using Colons

Colons are used in several situations. Primarily, colons serve as introductory devices.

▶ **KEY CONCEPT** Use a colon before a list of items following an independent clause. ■

EXAMPLES: As part of our assignment, we had to interview a group of experts: an economist, a scientist, and a business manager.
His travels took him to a number of continents: Africa, Australia, Asia, and South America.

Notice that each list above follows an independent clause. If terms such as *a group of experts* or *a number of continents* were not used, colons would not be appropriate because there would no longer be independent clauses preceding the lists.

EXAMPLES: As part of our assignment, we had to interview an economist, a scientist, and a business manager.
His travels took him to Africa, Australia, Asia, and South America.

Sometimes, an independent clause preceding a list ends in a phrase such as *the following* or *the following items.* These phrases should signal the use of a colon to introduce the list.
Colons also introduce certain kinds of quotations.

▶ **KEY CONCEPT** Use a colon to introduce a quotation that is formal or lengthy or a quotation that does not contain a "he said /she said" expression or tag line. ■

EXAMPLE: Oliver Wendell Holmes, Jr., wrote this about freedom: "It is only through free debate and free exchange of ideas that government remains responsive to the will of the people and peaceful change is effected."

Dialogue or a casual remark should be introduced by a comma even if it is lengthy. Use the colon if the quotation is formal or has no tag line.
A colon may also be used to introduce a sentence that explains the sentence that precedes it.

🖳 **Internet Tip**

Most World Wide Web addresses (URLs) use a colon in the beginning section. Avoid colons in other parts of the URL because they could render the address unreadable by certain systems. A full Web address might read as follows:
http://www.your website.com

KEY CONCEPT Use a colon to introduce a sentence that summarizes or explains the sentence before it. ∎

EXAMPLE: His explanation for being late was believable:
He had had a flat tire on the way.

Notice that the complete sentence introduced by the colon starts with a capital letter.

KEY CONCEPT Use a colon to introduce a formal appositive that follows an independent clause. ∎

EXAMPLE: I had finally decided on a career: nursing.

The colon is a stronger punctuation mark than a comma. Using the colon gives more emphasis to the appositive it introduces.

KEY CONCEPT Use a colon in a number of special writing situations. ∎

The chart below shows colons used in special writing situations. Study the examples carefully.

SPECIAL SITUATIONS REQUIRING COLONS	
Numerals Giving the Time	1:30 A.M. 9:15 P.M.
References to Periodicals (Volume Number:Page Number)	*Scientific American* 74:12 *Sports Illustrated* 53:15
Biblical References (Chapter Number:Verse Number)	1 Corinthians 13:13
Subtitles for Books and Magazines	*A Field Guide to the Birds: Eastern Land and Water Birds*
Salutations in Business Letters	Dear Mrs. Gordon: Dear Sir:
Labels Used to Signal Important Ideas	**Danger:** High-voltage wires

▶ **Exercise 32** **Using Colons** Revise the following letter, adding colons where appropriate.

　　Dear Ms. Richards

　　Thank you for the information you sent me. However, instead of biochemistry, I have chosen another major archaeology. I'm fascinated by a number of things about the field travel, ancient cultures, and the strange customs of other times and places. For example, the ancient Egyptians filled tombs with gold objects and precious jewelry, which makes sense in light of their religion They believed in a rich afterlife. Especially notable was the tomb of Tutankhamen, which was described as follows "Everything was gold. Gold! Gold! Everywhere!" Stories like this, retold in *National Geographic* 181 54, offer insight as to why I find the prospect of a dig so exciting. Also, I have a personal explanation for this career choice Several of my ancestors were archaeologists. I'd love to explain further, but I have a flight to a Peruvian site at 6 15 P.M., and if I don't leave now, I'll miss the flight.

▶ **Exercise 33** **Using Semicolons and Colons** Revise the following paragraph, adding semicolons and colons where appropriate.

　　Treasures found in tombs include a variety of items amulets shaped like real animals, fanciful creatures, and plant-life brooches made of gold and silver and necklaces and headdresses studded with precious jewels. An abundance of jewelry was made for funeral ceremonies and tombs on the other hand, the living also enjoyed displays of finery on a daily basis. This love of finery was especially true of nobility for example, Empress Theodora of Italy wore a dress that was stiff with gold and inlaid with jewels diamonds, emeralds, and rubies. To complete this show of wealth, the dress was worn with stunning jewelry a neckpiece made of emeralds set in gold. Many special jewels are world treasures the Hope diamond, the Phoenix jewel, and the Canning jewel. Intricate designs displaying fine craftsmanship clever mechanics, boxes within boxes, and exquisite jewel settings creating stunning arrangements are the hallmarks of some famous jewelry makers. Collections of jeweled treasures are in many museums the Hermitage in Russia, the British Museum in London, and the Vienna Treasury are just a few. The Smithsonian in Washington, D.C., houses an extensive collection of jewels from a variety of Asian countries, including China, Japan, and Burma. Silver and gold are employed abundantly in Asian jewelry many pieces are in filigree, lacy metalwork. Ivory ornaments are important Japanese treasures nevertheless, the most precious material in Japan is jade.

More Practice

Language Lab CD-ROM
• Semicolons, Colons, and Quotation Marks lesson
On-line Exercise Bank
• Section 27.3
Grammar Exercise Workbook
• pp. 135–136

Hands-on Grammar

Punctuation Circles

1. On the next page is a piece of writing from which the punctuation has been removed. Photocopy the passage or retype it (without punctuation) using a word-processing program. Use a large font size—18 or 20 points. Print out the complete passage.
2. Obtain different-colored self-sticking dots at an office-supply store.
3. Read the selection aloud. Following the chart below, place the different-colored self-sticking dots in places where you feel punctuation is needed based on the sound of your reading.
4. Compare your punctuated version with those of some other students. What did you punctuate differently? Why? What did you punctuate the same? Why?

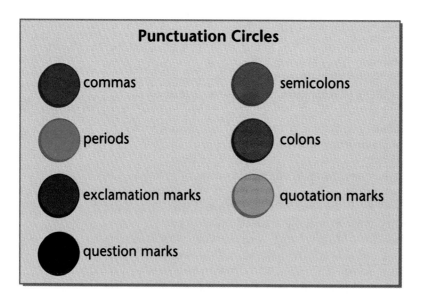

Punctuation Circles

commas   semicolons

periods   colons

exclamation marks   quotation marks

question marks

Find It in Your Reading Try the above activity with a piece of writing from your portfolio. Eliminate the punctuation, and complete the steps above. How does your color-coded version compare with the original?

Find It in Your Writing Select an article from a newsmagazine. Choose a passage that especially interests you. Then, follow the steps outlined above.

Hands-on Grammar

today the average American can expect to live about 76 years only 100 years ago life expectancy was less than 48 years in the seventeenth century life expectancy was about 30 to 35 years improvements in disease prevention and treatment general medical care diet exercise environmental conditions and other factors have continued to increase the length of time people can expect to live moreover not only has the average life expectancy increased but the average Americans general health and the resultant quality of life has improved as well the average American can now expect to be vigorous and active throughout most of his or her life

GRAMMAR EXERCISES 34–41

▶ **Exercise 34** **Using Semicolons**
Revise these sentences, adding semicolons where necessary.

1. Materials of all types are used in jewelry semiprecious stones, feathers, leather, and metal are common.
2. Rituals are a vital part of Native American cultures as a result, special jewelry was made of turquoise, shells, and silver beads for these ceremonies.
3. Masks, pendants, and feather headdresses are prevalent in Native American work consequently, the Museum of the American Indian has a large collection of these treasures.
4. Many outsiders, drawn by rumors of the native peoples' exotic treasures, tried to plunder relics legends persist—some fact-based, some fanciful—about explorers finding statuettes encrusted with rubies and emeralds.
5. These items were of monetary value to the explorers however, to the tribes they were spiritual symbols.
6. Gold represented the sun in fact, the sun is considered a god in many cultures.
7. But the sun isn't the only thing that shines encrusted in decorative metals, women in traditional East Indian garb shine as well.
8. They may wear earrings, flashing in the sunlight sport nose rings, gleaming from their nostrils and don bracelets and anklets, jangling as they move.
9. Men in ancient Persia also wore a rich array of jewelry for example, pearls and rubies adorned their turbans, sashes, and silk slippers.
10. At times, Chinese and Japanese empresses could barely move their elaborate headdresses were heavy with jewels and precious metals.

▶ **Exercise 35** **Using Colons** Add colons to the following sentences.

1. Museums exhibit many royal headdresses the British royal crown, tiaras, diamond-studded veils, and so on.
2. Books of African art invariably show the Benin treasures bronzes, pendants, earrings, and statuettes.
3. A book entitled *Art Treasures Jeweled Objects of the World* shows the gem-studded umbrellas of Ethiopia.
4. Nonetheless, treasures are best viewed at the museum with perhaps the greatest jewelry display the Smithsonian Institution.
5. A prominently displayed sign there warns, "Attention Do not lean on the display window!"

▶ **Exercise 36** **Revising a Letter With Semicolons and Colons** Revise the following letter, adding or deleting semicolons and colons where necessary.

Dear Mr. Newssance

Our government is filing suit to stop the publication of your book *Relics The Bounty From Smuggling.* Our legal action won't stop there we are also filing to recover the artifacts you took six vases; and dozens of jewels. The sign at the excavation site reads "Warning Trespassers will be prosecuted." The damage you have done, disturbing a research project in progress, is irreparable. Our Minister of Culture observes; "That Newssance absconded with some of our greatest treasures is reprehensible that he has flaunted his crimes is astonishing." He concludes with the most apt summary to date "There is only one word for this man thief." Ours is a proud culture, spanning millennia a proud nation,

standing firmly on the side of justice.
Rest assured You will be brought to
justice.

▶ **Exercise 37** Revising Sentences
With Semicolons and Colons Rewrite
the following sentences, inserting the necessary punctuation.

1. The world is full of treasures not all of
   them are of the precious stone variety.
2. Literary treasures abound Herman
   Melville's *Moby-Dick*, Gabriel García
   Marquez's *Cien Años de Soledad*, and
   so on.
3. However, in the English language, the
   works of one writer are held above all
   others William Shakespeare.
4. Great works have been penned by
   other English-language writers, too
   from the poems of Walt Whitman to
   the plays of Tennessee Williams, a
   store of words awaits those who would
   explore them.
5. Other creative endeavors yield their
   own gems the paintings of Leonardo
   da Vinci and the sculptures of
   Michelangelo in the fine arts the
   operas of Verdi in the performing arts
   and the music of Wolfgang Amadeus
   Mozart and Scott Joplin.
6. In cinema, noted treasures include
   Citizen Kane, revered for its ground-
   breaking techniques *The Wizard of Oz*,
   popular for bringing a children's classic to life through the use of color film
   and *Schindler's List*, for its moving
   examination of the Holocaust.
7. Of course, not everyone agrees on
   what constitutes a gem *Star Wars,
   Episode IV A New Hope* is one movie-
   goer's breakthrough, another's
   pablum.
8. Controversy over many films still rages
   however, quality is more apparent with
   the perspective of time.
9. That may explain why television's
   treasures are so hard to identify the
   medium is still too young.

10. Other precious things exist beyond the
    scope of human creation the natural
    world offers treasures of its own.

▶ **Exercise 38** Writing Sentences
With Semicolons and Colons Complete
each sentence. Then, add to or revise the
sentence by following the instructions.
Use colons and semicolons as needed.

1. My favorite dinner has ___?___ as its
   main course.
   Write a sentence with a colon pointing
   to a list.
2. The most annoying habit is ___?___ .
   Write a sentence with a colon pointing
   to a formal appositive.
3. My favorite sport is ___?___ .
   Write a sentence using semicolons to
   separate a series of items that contain
   internal punctuation.
4. I have a hard time studying when
   ___?___ is on television.
   Write a sentence containing a semicolon and a conjunctive adverb.
5. If I could see any musician perform, I
   would see ___?___ .
   Write a sentence with a semicolon joining two contrasting clauses.

▶ **Exercise 39** Find It in Your
Reading In a newspaper, find an example of each use of semicolons and colons.

▶ **Exercise 40** Find It in Your
Writing Revise a piece of your writing
to add three semicolons and two colons.

▶ **Exercise 41** Writing Application
Demonstrate your knowledge of semicolons and colons by writing a brief essay
containing each of the following:
   two independent clauses
   items in a series
   a list after an independent clause
   a quotation within a quotation

Quotation Marks and Underlining

Using direct quotations in your writing can enliven short stories and other works of fiction. Direct quotations, the actual words of a character, provide readers much information about a character, both from what he or she says and from the way he or she speaks.

Direct quotations can also be used to support or refute ideas and arguments in nonfiction. You can quote an expert in a particular field to help prove a point you are trying to make.

Using Quotation Marks for Direct Quotations

There are two ways in which you can cite a person's ideas: through direct quotations and through indirect quotations.

▶ **KEY CONCEPTS** A **direct quotation** represents a person's exact speech or thoughts and is enclosed in quotation marks (" "). An **indirect quotation** reports only the general meaning of what a person said or thought and does not require quotation marks. ■

DIRECT QUOTATION:	"When I learn to ride," said the student, "I'll use the bridle path every day."
INDIRECT QUOTATION:	The student said that when she learns to ride, she plans to use the bridle path every day.

Both types of quotations are acceptable when you write. Using a direct quotation whenever possible, however, generally results in more interesting and convincing writing.

To enclose a sentence that is an uninterrupted direct quotation, place double quotation marks around the quotation.

EXAMPLE:	"One can live in the shadow of an idea without grasping it."—Elizabeth Bowen

Notice that this quotation begins with a capital letter. The same is true of every complete sentence of quoted material.

You may also quote just part of a sentence directly. When a phrase or a fragment is quoted, enclose the quoted words in quotation marks just as you would a full sentence. Capitalize the first word of the quote, however, only when it falls at the beginning of the sentence you are writing or when it is a proper noun or a proper adjective that would be capitalized in any case.

Theme: Horses

In this section, you will learn about the many uses of quotation marks and underlining. Most of the examples and exercises in this section are about horses.

Cross-Curricular Connection: Science

EXAMPLES: In one of his essays, George Mistry calls the stables near his home "the source of an almost profound stench."

"The source of an almost profound stench" is how Mistry refers to the stables near his home.

Many direct quotations contain not only the actual words of a speaker but also words identifying the speaker. These identifying words or phrases are called conversational tags. They include such expressions as *she asked, they replied, my father explained,* and *Jenny shrieked.* Conversational tags are never enclosed in quotation marks.

Conversational tags may appear in various positions in relation to direct quotations.

▶ **KEY CONCEPT** Use a comma after short introductory expressions that precede direct quotations. ■

EXAMPLE: My mother warned, "If you get a horse, you'll be responsible for taking care of it."

If the introductory conversational tag is very long or formal in tone, set it off with a colon instead of a comma.

EXAMPLES: Bert rose to his feet: "I'd like to announce the winner of the event."
At the end of the meeting, Marge spoke of her dreams: "I hope to advance the cause of women jockeys everywhere."

▶ **Critical Viewing** Write a brief dialogue in which the woman shown here describes riding a horse to someone who's never ridden one. **[Describe]**

Conversational tags may also act as concluding expressions.

▶ **KEY CONCEPT** Use a comma, question mark, or exclamation mark after a direct quotation followed by a concluding expression. ■

EXAMPLE: "If you get a horse, you'll be responsible for taking care of it," my mother warned.

In addition, you may use a conversational tag to interrupt the words of a direct quotation.

▶ **KEY CONCEPT** Use a comma after part of a quoted sentence followed by an interrupting conversational tag. Use another comma after the tag. Use two sets of quotation marks to enclose the quotation. ■

EXAMPLE: "If you get a horse," my mother warned, "you'll be responsible for taking care of it."

Sometimes, a conversational tag interrupts a quotation several sentences in length.

▶ **KEY CONCEPT** Use a comma, question mark, or exclamation mark after a quoted sentence that comes before an interrupting conversational tag. Use a period after the tag. ■

EXAMPLE: "You own a horse now," warned my mother. "You are responsible for taking care of it."

▶ **Exercise 42** Revising With Quotation Marks and Capitalization Revise the following passage, breaking it into paragraphs and adding necessary punctuation and capitalization.

During a lecture, a speaker stated that horses have existed since the Eocene epoch. She remarked fossils indicate that a leaf-browsing mammal about the size of a fox was the precursor to the horse. Descendants of this species developed high-crowned teeth, she continued. This allowed them to graze on grass instead of browsing on leaves. She told us how this animal developed over the centuries. The scientific name for the present-day domestic horse is *Equus caballus,* she said. An expert on the Q & A panel chimed in A marked characteristic of the modern horse is one single toe on each of its four feet. He informed us that earlier species had four toes on the forefeet and three on the hind feet! Both male and female horses can reproduce from the age of two, another panelist explained, but breeding is delayed until they are three. The gestation period for horses is about eleven months, a panelist added. The handout from the museum suggested that we do further research on horses.

▶ **More Practice**

Language Lab
CD-ROM
• Semicolons, Colons, and Quotation Marks lesson
On-line
Exercise Bank
• Section 27.4
Grammar Exercise
Workbook
• pp. 135–142

Using Other Punctuation Marks With Quotation Marks

Quotation marks are used with commas, semicolons, colons, and all the end marks. The location of the quotation marks in relation to the different punctuation marks varies. Below are rules to help you place the punctuation marks correctly.

> **KEY CONCEPT** Always place a comma or a period inside the final quotation mark. ■

EXAMPLES: "Secretariat was a great horse," sighed Mother.

Marge said, "We're all ready to ride now."

The rule for the use of semicolons and colons with quotation marks is just the opposite.

> **KEY CONCEPT** Always place a semicolon or colon outside the final quotation mark. ■

EXAMPLES: We were just informed about his "earth-shaking discovery"; we are all pleased.

The panelists gave her ideas their "strong endorsement": Most of them promised to spread her theory of equine development.

▼ **Critical Viewing** Write a brief dialogue about the horses pictured here. Include both a colon and a semicolon. **[Describe]**

◀ **Critical Viewing**
This is a statue of
King Richard III of
England. What can
you tell about the
time in which he
lived based on the
statue? **[Analyze]**

▶ **KEY CONCEPT** Place a question mark or an exclamation
mark inside the final quotation mark if the end mark is part of
the quotation. ■

EXAMPLES: Larry wondered, "How could such a fast stallion
              lose the race?"

              King Richard shouted, "My kingdom for a horse!"

    The question mark and exclamation mark in these exam-
ples are placed inside the final quotation mark because they
apply only to the quoted portion of each sentence.

▶ **KEY CONCEPT** Place a question mark or an exclamation
mark outside the final quotation mark if the end mark is not
part of the quotation. ■

EXAMPLES: Did the officer say, "I'll be back soon"?

              We were shocked when he said, "Yes"!

> **Exercise 43** **Using Other Punctuation Marks Correctly With Quotations** Revise this passage, adding the necessary punctuation.

My friend sounded bored when he broke the news: Horses came to the Americas by way of Egypt. He stated that Syrian invaders were able to conquer Egypt in the seventeenth century B.C. because of their new weapon: horse-drawn chariots.

These Egyptian horses were the predecessors of the highly prized, fast Arabian breed, explains a book that he lent me. The book further explains, Europeans had slower, heavier horses, but these horses were powerful. According to the book's author, an idea was born: Arabian stallions should be brought into England and France to breed with mares of the sturdier stock. He writes: Introduced into various parts of Europe, these horses, along with the purebred Arabians, were brought to the Americas by the Spanish conquistadors; in this manner, the Arabian bloodline made the leap across the Atlantic.

I asked my friend, Why did Cortés and others abandon their horses?

Who said anything about their being abandoned? my friend sighed in exasperation, adding, The men, being tired, lost, and demoralized in unknown territory, simply lost many of their horses.

I asked, Did these horses become, as my friend put it, the galloping, gorgeous wild horses of western North America?

Precisely! my friend replied.

More Practice

Language Lab CD-ROM
• Semicolons, Colons, and Quotation Marks lesson
On-line Exercise Bank
• Section 27.4
Grammar Exercise Workbook
• pp. 135–142

GRAMMAR IN LITERATURE

from **The Lagoon**
Joseph Conrad

In this excerpt of dialogue, the first quotation is a question. The question mark is inside the quotation marks. In the last sentence, the exclamation mark is also inside the quotation marks.

"Has she been long ill?" asked the traveler.

"I have not slept for five nights," answered the Malay, in a deliberate tone. "At first she heard voices calling her from the water and struggled against me who held her. But since the sun of today rose she hears nothing—she hears not me. She sees nothing. She sees not me—me!"

Using Quotation Marks in Special Situations

Dialogue and Long Quotations Dialogue—spoken words of characters—is one of the best ways to move the action forward in a story. When writing dialogue, rules must be followed so that readers can keep track of who is speaking.

▶ **KEY CONCEPT** When writing dialogue, begin a new paragraph with each change of speaker. ■

Look at this example from *The Pearl* by John Steinbeck.

EXAMPLE: The wind drove off the clouds and skimmed the sky clean and drifted the sand of the country like snow.

Then Juan Tomas, when the evening approached, talked long with his brother. "Where will you go?"

"To the north," said Kino. "I have heard that there are cities in the north."

"Avoid the shore," said Juan Tomas. "They are making a party to search the shore. The men in the city will look for you. Do you still have the pearl?"

"I have it," said Kino. "And I will keep it. I might have given it as a gift, but now it is my misfortune and my life and I will keep it."

A different rule is followed when a writer uses several consecutive paragraphs of material quoted from the same person.

▶ **KEY CONCEPT** For quotations longer than a paragraph, put quotation marks at the beginning of each paragraph and at the end of the final paragraph. ■

EXAMPLE: John McPhee has written an essay about a canoe trip down the St. John River in northern Maine. He introduces his readers to the river in the following way: "We have been out here four days now and rain has been falling three. The rain appears to be ending. Breaks of blue are opening in the sky. Sunlight is coming through, and a wind is rising.

"I was not prepared for the St. John River, did not anticipate its size. I saw it as a narrow trail flowing north, twisting through the balsam and spruce—a small and intimate forest river, something like the Allagash, . . ."

💡 Spelling Tip

When writing dialogue, you may deliberately misspell words in order to show a character's particular style of pronunciation, such as a regional accent, but be sure to use correct spelling in the rest of the work.

Ellipsis Marks and Single Quotation Marks Ellipsis marks (. . .) are used when you want to present only part of a long quotation.

▶ **KEY CONCEPT** Use three ellipsis marks in a quotation to indicate that words have been omitted. ■

The examples below show how to use ellipsis marks at the beginning, in the middle, and at the end of a quotation.

AN ENTIRE QUOTATION:	"The Black River, which cuts a winding course through southern Missouri's rugged Ozark highlands, lends its name to an area of great natural beauty. Within this expanse are old mines and quarries to explore, fast-running waters to canoe, and wooded trails to ride." 　　　　　　　—Suzanne Charle
ELLIPSIS AT THE BEGINNING:	Suzanne Charle described the Black River area in Missouri as having ". . . old mines and quarries to explore, fast-running waters to canoe, and wooded trails to ride."
ELLIPSIS IN THE MIDDLE:	Suzanne Charle wrote, "The Black River . . . lends its name to an area of great natural beauty. Within this expanse are old mines and quarries to explore, fast-running waters to canoe, and wooded trails to ride."
ELLIPSIS AT THE END:	Suzanne Charle wrote, "The Black River, which cuts a winding course through southern Missouri's rugged Ozark highlands, lends its name to an area of great natural beauty. . . ."

Notice in the last example that when a period falls right before an omitted portion of the quotation, it is added along with the ellipsis marks to conclude the sentence.

Another special situation involving quotation marks occurs when a writer wishes to include one quotation within another.

◉ Technology Tip

In some word-processing programs, you may select preferences for curved or straight quotation marks. When using curved marks, make sure your marks are curving in the correct direction—toward the type, whether they are opening or closing quotation marks.

▼ **Critical Viewing** What can you conclude about Missouri's Ozark highlands based on this photograph? **[Analyze]**

Ozark Mountains, Missouri

▶ **KEY CONCEPT** Use single quotation marks for a quotation within a quotation. ■

EXAMPLES: "I will always remember my grandmother quoting Shelley, 'If winter comes, can spring be far behind?'" Michael commented.

"The doctor said, 'Good news!'" she explained.

Rephrase most sentences with one quotation within another to include the same information in a less complicated way.

▶ **Exercise 44** **Punctuating With Ellipsis Marks and Single Quotation Marks** Copy each of the following sentences, inserting double quotation marks or single quotation marks as required.

1. The brochure described the ranch as having . . . large tracts of land; many horses of different types, including several Shetlands; and a well-informed ranch foreman.
2. The brochure also stated, This ranch in Montana . . . is known for western hospitality and knowledge of horses.
3. In a letter to me, my friend Alan wrote, The ranch was once owned by J.R. Blackwell and has been kept up to his high standards. . . .
4. Alan continued, The Wild Horse Ranch, filled with these beautiful animals . . . truly lives up to its name. . . .
5. I plan to join you there to see, as Galway said, mane blowing free, magnificence racing in the wind, Alan's letter concluded.
6. The foreman said, You are in luck regarding your reservations at the ranch, Alan informed me.
7. Luck, indeed! Alan huffed indignantly, adding, I told that foreman, You're lucky to have our patronage!
8. I told Alan, Try to remember what your mother is always saying: Don't let your temper gallop away like a wild stallion, son.
9. My friend Beth reminded me, Alan has always had a temper, as his own mother puts it, like a wild stallion; are you sure you want to go to Montana with him?
10. But the next morning, I heeded Horace Greeley's advice: Go West, young man. Go West!

▶ **Exercise 45** **Writing Original Dialogue** Write one page of original dialogue between two people on a horseback ride. Include a few lines of description wherever necessary. Enclose the lines of dialogue in quotation marks. Include enough conversational tags so that there will be no confusion about the speaker.

More Practice

Language Lab CD-ROM
• Semicolons, Colons, and Quotation Marks lesson

On-line Exercise Bank
• Section 27.4

Grammar Exercise Workbook
• pp. 137–142

Using Underlining and Quotation Marks

Several methods are used to indicate different types of titles in various situations. These methods include italics, underlining, and quotation marks. Books, magazines, and other printed material are set in *italics,* a slanted typeface that indicates some types of titles. In handwritten or typed material, underlining would be used for those titles. Other titles require quotation marks.

KEY CONCEPT Underline the titles of long written works; of publications that are published as a single work; of plays, movies, and television series; and of other works of art. ■

BOOK: <u>To Kill a Mockingbird</u> is a modern classic.
PLAY: He starred in <u>Long Day's Journey Into Night</u>.
MAGAZINE: I read <u>Newsweek</u> to keep up with current events.
NEWSPAPER: She agreed with the story in the <u>Los Angeles Times</u>.
MUSICAL: She went to see <u>Peter Pan</u>.
PAINTING: I saw Chagall's painting <u>The Green Violinist</u>.

The portion of a newspaper title that should be underlined will vary from newspaper to newspaper. <u>The New York Times</u> should always be fully capitalized and underlined. Other papers, however, can usually be treated in one of two ways: the <u>Los Angeles Times</u> or the Los Angeles <u>Times</u>.

KEY CONCEPT Underline names of individual air, sea, space, and land craft. ■

EXAMPLE: I wonder if Columbus had horses aboard the <u>Santa Maria</u>.

KEY CONCEPT Underlining is also used for foreign words and phrases not yet accepted into English. ■

EXAMPLES: The voyage was so rough that they suffered from <u>mal de mer</u> constantly.
Her <u>sturm und drang</u> manner was shocking to those of us who had expected a milder response.

Many foreign words and phrases are used so often by English-speaking people that they are now considered part of the language. Although these words may often retain their foreign pronunciation, they are no longer underlined or italicized.

NOT UNDERLINED: chili, amour, milieu, lasagne, plaza, gestalt, raconteur, teriyaki, andante, sauna

Consult a dictionary that includes foreign words and phrases if you are in doubt about whether a particular word or phrase should be underlined.

KEY CONCEPT Underline numbers, symbols, letters, and words used as names for themselves. ■

EXAMPLES: Her i's and her l's look too much alike.
Is that an 8 or a 6?
Avoid sprinkling your speech with you know.

KEY CONCEPT Underline words that you wish to stress. ■

EXAMPLE: What a ridiculous situation!

In most cases, you should indicate emphasis not by underlining but by choosing and arranging your words with care. Reserve underlining for use only in special instances.

KEY CONCEPT Use quotation marks to enclose the titles of short written works, episodes in a television series, songs, and parts of long musical compositions or collections. ■

EXAMPLES: "Edward, Edward" and "Lord Randall" are two familiar English ballads.
Winifred Welles's essay "The Attic" describes her as a child exploring her grandfather's attic.
Read Chapter 1, "Dialogue and Action," in Understanding Drama.
"The Tell-Tale Heart" is an effective horror tale.
One of the most loved songs of the American people is Woody Guthrie's "This Land Is Your Land."

Titles That Do Not Use Underlining or Quotation Marks

Religious works require neither underlining nor quotation marks.

▶ **KEY CONCEPT** Do not underline or place in quotation marks the name of scriptures, such as the Bible, the Torah, and the Koran, or their books, divisions, or versions. ■

EXAMPLE: She recited the Twenty-third Psalm.

Other titles needing neither underlining nor quotation marks include various kinds of government documents.

▶ **KEY CONCEPT** Do not underline or place in quotation marks the titles of government charters, alliances, treaties, acts, statutes, or reports. ■

EXAMPLE: The Versailles Treaty officially ended World War I.

▶ **Exercise 46** **Proofreading for Underlining and Quotation Marks** Revise this passage, adding necessary punctuation.

Horse and Rider magazine, in the ranch library, lists all the equestrian activities: rodeos, harness racing, steeplechase competitions, and so on. One thing we learned from an article entitled Horsemanship 101 was never, ever mount a horse with your right foot first; if you do, you will be facing backward.

Before reaching the ranch, I explored the equestrian theme; I rented the movie National Velvet on video and read the book Black Beauty as we crossed the Atlantic aboard the Queen Elizabeth II. I also amused myself on deck by painting a portrait of a horse I call Mare of the Sea—a pun, because the English word mare refers to a female horse, although in Latin, mare means "sea."

The ranch foreman told us that he learned about a bridle bit from a series of articles in Ranch Animal. Then, in a column he read called Know Your Horse, the writer explained that there is a wide gap in the mouth of a horse between the canine and premolars, where the metal bit is designed to fit. The foreman also confessed that in those early days, he had a motorcycle, but traveling that way lacked a certain je ne sais quoi compared to horseback riding.

From Horsemanship, we learned that an ungelded male horse is called a colt until his fifth year; from then on, he is referred to as a stallion. A female horse is called a filly up to her fifth year; then she is referred to as a mare, according to Horseman's Catalog. My favorite book about horses is called Everything You Ever Wanted to Know About Horses.

▶ **More Practice**

Language Lab
CD-ROM
• Semicolons, Colons, and Quotation Marks lesson
On-line
Exercise Bank
• Section 27.4
Grammar Exercise
Workbook
• pp. 137–142

Section Review

GRAMMAR EXERCISES 47–53

Exercise 47 **Enclosing Direct Quotations in Quotation Marks** Copy each sentence, and supply the correct quotations marks or underlining if needed. If the sentence is correct, write *correct.*

1. Every Friday at the ranch, we would have some form of entertainment just to relax, the manager said.
2. Hank told me, We saw a movie starring Nathan Lane last year. He was also the lead in A Funny Thing Happened on the Way to the Forum on Broadway, he added excitedly.
3. Of course, Ashley quipped, in the musical Oklahoma!, everybody rides a horse.
4. One of the songs sung by Curly, the hero, is about a horse-drawn surrey, she added with a smile.
5. The first line of that song—When I take you out in a surrey . . . —sets a cheerful tone, she volunteered teasingly.

Exercise 48 **Using Other Punctuation Marks Correctly With Quotations, Dialogue, and Ellipsis Marks** Copy each sentence, and supply the correct quotation marks or underlining if needed.

1. According to the visiting artist, There probably isn't a home in Britain that doesn't have a picture or a painting of a horse; however, I already knew that the English were great equestrians.
2. There are many portraits, he continued, depicting members of royal families with their beloved steeds.
3. Any on horseback? Hank muttered.
4. In fact, the artist continued, legend has it that because of Charles II of England, who was an avid horseman, the term sport of kings came into the language.

5. Tennyson writes: . . . Into the valley of Death rode the six hundred. . . .

Exercise 49 **Underlining and Quotation Marks** Copy each sentence, and supply the correct quotation marks or underlining if needed.

1. A journalist from National Geographic recently wrote, Arabian horsemen are the most highly regarded.
2. Their abilities are unmatched, she concluded, commenting on their cavalrylike horsemanship.
3. At one of our Friday night shows at the ranch, we watched Cavalry, an installment of the Channel 72 series Warfare, about the fierce and destructive nature of cavalry units.
4. Mike started a conversation about horse racing: I'd like to see the big races, such as Royal Ascot in England, the Kentucky Derby, and the Belmont Stakes.
5. I'm interested in the famous horses that emerge from these events, Beth said, most of whom are discussed in The Horseman's Catalog.
6. Among these sportly champions, as the foreman calls them, Beth continued, were Citation, Secretariat, Bold Ruler, and Native Dancer.
7. However, in books from Towers (1922) to present-day editions of The Horseman's Catalog, the most revered horse is the American colt Man O' War.
8. Man O' War set track records for speed and was defeated only once in 21 races! Beth exclaimed.
9. There were many stories about Man O' War in newspaper columns of that time, the foreman interjected, such as Town Talk.

10. Bob started reading aloud from Grayson's Encyclopedia: Racing horses are a breed unto themselves . . . called thoroughbreds.

11. The foreman told us that Native Americans have a long history with the wild horses that roam the plains.

12. Appaloosas and palominos had to be captured first and then tamed, added the foreman, before they could become part of a valuable herd.

13. Lippizaners are another example of a powerful horse; they were originally imperial carriage horses, stated a pamphlet from the local riding school.

14. The pamphlet, Horses Around the World, continued: Lippizaners are trained at the Spanish Riding School in Vienna to execute extremely intricate and difficult movements.

15. Many of these movements are done in unison with other Lippizaners inside a covered circle and, often, with a rider. I was reading that very same pamphlet just a moment ago, Beth explained after quoting verbatim.

Exercise 50 Applying All the Rules Governing the Use of Quotation Marks and Underlining Copy the following sentences, using quotation marks or underlining as necessary.

1. The professor began the lecture by saying, Horses belong to a group of animals called ungulates.

2. This term, he continued, comes from the Latin word ungula, meaning hoof.

3. I was shocked when the professor so matter-of-factly said, Both the horse and the elephant are ungulates!

4. According to The Audubon Field Guide to African Mammals, there are no wild horses on that continent.

5. Of course, zebras live there, Wilfredo interjected, and they're closely related; however, as my brother says, Close, but not close enough!

6. In fact, both horses and zebras belong to the same genus: Equus.

7. The zebra's well-known black-and-white stripe pattern serves to make it hard for a predator to pick a single target; in a herd of hundreds of moving zebras, the professor chuckled, a lion can get really confused!

8. Tragically, the quagga (Equus quagga) of southern Africa is extinct.

9. The New York Times reported, however, that quagga genes may exist in the gene pool of closely related zebras.

10. The professor concluded, If so, might it not one day be possible to restore that species to the Earth?

Exercise 51 Find It in Your Reading Find a passage in one of your favorite novels that illustrates the rules of punctuating dialogue. Write a brief explanation of each rule that the passage shows.

Exercise 52 Find It in Your Writing Choose one story and one research report from your portfolio. Find at least two indirect quotations in each, and rework them into direct quotations. Make sure that you follow the rules for punctuating direct quotations.

Exercise 53 Writing Application Write a brief passage of dialogue involving two or three people discussing their pets or some other topic about animals. Use quotation marks correctly where appropriate. Include titles of works—books, movies, art, and so on—in the conversation.

Dashes, Parentheses, and Brackets

Although they are used infrequently, you should be familiar with the use of dashes (—), parentheses (( )), and brackets ([ ]) and be able to use them when necessary.

Using Dashes

The dash is a strong, dramatic punctuation mark. It has specific uses and should not be used as a substitute for a comma, a semicolon, or parentheses. Overuse of the dash diminishes its effectiveness. Consider the proper uses of the dash in the Key Concepts below.

▶ **KEY CONCEPT** Use dashes to indicate an abrupt change of thought, a dramatic interrupting idea, or a summary statement. ■

EXAMPLES: The tornado struck at dusk—to this day, survivors remember which houses were leveled.
It was a dilapidated wreck—it should have been condemned—but she bought it anyway.
The foundation, the roof, and the plumbing—every aspect of the house was in good condition.

The following chart shows the three basic uses of the dash.

USES OF THE DASH	
To indicate an abrupt change of thought	The article doesn't provide enough information on Japan—by the way, did you find it in the school library?
To set off interrupting ideas dramatically	The pagoda was built—you may find this hard to believe—in one month. The pagoda was built—where did they get the money?—in one month.
To set off a summary statement	A good scholastic record and good political connections—if you have these, you may be able to get a job in a congressional office.

Words such as *all*, *these*, *those*, *this*, and *that* will often be found at or near the beginning of a summary sentence preceded by a dash.

Theme: Houses

In this section, you will learn about the many uses of dashes, parentheses, and brackets. Most of the examples and exercises are about types of houses.

Cross-Curricular Connection: Social Studies

Technology Tip

Don't let your word-processing program put spaces around dashes; there should never be a space between the dash and the two phrases that it connects.

▶ **KEY CONCEPT** Use dashes to set off a nonessential appositive or modifier when it is long, when it is already punctuated, or when you want to be dramatic. ■

APPOSITIVE: The cause of the damage to the porch and the roof—a rare species of termite—went undiscovered for years.

MODIFIER: The home-improvement book editor—bored with writing about cement, joists, and grout—quit the next day.

Dashes may be used to set off one other special type of sentence interrupter—the parenthetical expression.

▶ **KEY CONCEPT** Use dashes to set off a parenthetical expression when it is long, already punctuated, or especially dramatic. ■

EXAMPLE: Yesterday we visited a castle—could you imagine living in such a place?—set on a small body of water out in the country.

▼ **Critical Viewing** What types of people do you imagine would have lived in a "house" like this one? **[Speculate]**

▶ **Exercise 54** **Revising a Paragraph With Dashes** Revise the following paragraph, adding dashes where necessary.

Houses range from remote tropical huts one scarcely can believe how simple they can be to elaborate stone castles. To serve as a dwelling place, provide shelter from weather, and provide protection from adversaries these are the three basic functions of a house. In rural areas the pampas of Argentina is a good example people and animals once shared the same housing quarters. Now, animals except those that are pets are kept outside in separate areas. Houses today unless the unit is very small include areas for storage, work, rest, and entertainment. The basic home is there really one type that can be considered basic? gives way to endless variations among tribal groups on every continent. Extended groups of Melanesians gregarious, socially active, as well as community-oriented share one large home with communal areas for cooking and relaxing. The custom of some Native Americans clustering housing in family-related groups has largely been supplanted by urban ways. The Dogons of Sudan as well as Zambian tribes build family dwellings so that they join with other houses. Houses built in this way in the United States in Queens, New York, for example are called semi-attached houses.

More Practice

On-line Exercise Bank
• Section 27.5
Grammar Exercise Workbook
• pp. 143–148

GRAMMAR IN LITERATURE

from **The Lagoon**
Joseph Conrad

In this passage, the author uses dashes for dramatic reasons. The first dash is used to set off and burns. *The author also uses dashes to indicate that someone is going to speak and say something dramatic.*

"She breathes," said Arsat in a low voice, anticipating the expected question. "She breathes and burns as if with a great fire. She speaks not; she hears not—and burns!"

He paused for a moment, then asked in a quiet, incurious tone—

"Tuan . . . will she die?"

The white man moved his shoulders uneasily, and muttered in a hesitating manner—

"If such is her fate."

◄ **Critical Viewing**
How would you
describe this
Victorian house?
[Describe]

▶ **Exercise 55** **Revising Sentences With Dashes** Revise
the following sentences, adding one or two dashes where
necessary.

1. Victorian houses my favorite type of house are often painted in colors such as plum or pink.
2. They often have very fancy trim work some people call it
   gingerbread.
3. Cape May a town filled with Victorian houses is in New
   Jersey.
4. There is a house in Cape May called the Pink House,
   which is covered with gingerbread the gingerbread is
   unique to that house.
5. I read somewhere I'm not sure where that gingerbread
   trim was different on each house.
6. Some people not me particularly prefer a Cape Cod style
   house.
7. A Cape Cod house my mother doesn't agree looks like a
   box with a pointed roof.
8. They are actually much larger inside than they look from
   the outside usually three bedrooms.
9. Cape Cod houses are often sided in cedar that is allowed
   to weather to a natural gray good if you don't like house-
   painting.
10. I plan to own a Victorian house someday which means I'd
    better learn to paint!

Using Parentheses

Parentheses are occasionally used to set off material within a sentence. Commas are the appropriate punctuation marks to use for this purpose in most cases, especially when the material is short and closely related in meaning to the rest of the sentence. Parentheses, on the other hand, are appropriate in some circumstances.

KEY CONCEPT Use parentheses to set off asides and explanations only when the material is not essential or when it consists of one or more sentences. ■

EXAMPLES: The task of cleaning the mansion (as she learned within the month) was far greater than she had believed.

Turn-of-the-century wealth (two of the more famous fortunes are those of the Rockefeller and Frick families) spawned estate homes of incredible opulence.

Parentheses are the strongest separators that writers can use. Although material enclosed in parentheses is not essential to the meaning of the sentence, a writer indicates that the material is important and calls attention to it by using parentheses.

Using Parentheses With Other Punctuation Marks

Four rules govern parentheses used with other marks:

KEY CONCEPT When a phrase or declarative sentence interrupts another sentence, do not use an initial capital letter or end mark inside the parentheses. ■

EXAMPLE: Bill Frazier finally sold his vacation home (we used to love to visit) to a young couple.

KEY CONCEPT When a question or exclamation interrupts another sentence, use both an initial capital letter and an end mark inside the parentheses. ■

EXAMPLES: Joseph Allen (Didn't he once star in the television show *Homes for Tomorrow*?) has had a string of personal difficulties.

Uncle Bruce (He is a fabulous decorator!) chose our window treatments.

▶ **KEY CONCEPT** When you place a sentence in parentheses between two other sentences, use both an initial capital letter and an end mark inside the parentheses. ■

EXAMPLE: Newport is known for its incredible mansions. (See the Vanderbilt home as an example.) These wild excesses of wealth are staggering to behold.

▶ **KEY CONCEPT** In a sentence that includes parentheses, place any punctuation belonging to the main sentence after the parenthesis. ■

EXAMPLE: The town council approved the construction (after some deliberation), and they explained the new zoning laws to the public (with some doubts about how the changes would be received).

Special Uses of Parentheses Parentheses are also used to set off numerical explanations such as dates of a person's birth and death and numbers and letters marking a series.

EXAMPLES: Frank Lloyd Wright (1867–1959) was an innovative American architect.

His phone number is (303) 555-4211.

Her research will take her to (1) Portugal, (2) Canada, and (3) Romania.

▼ **Critical Viewing** How does this grass hut differ from most of the houses you are used to seeing? Use parentheses at least once in making your comparison. **[Compare]**

▶ **Exercise 56** Enclosing Material in Parentheses Copy the
following items, adding parentheses and capital letters where
needed.

More Practice

On-line
Exercise Bank
• Section 27.5
Grammar Exercise
Workbook
• pp. 143–148

EXAMPLE: Cockroaches how I detest them! invaded our
home.

ANSWER: Cockroaches (How I detest them!) invaded our
home.

1. In the United States, semi-attached housing was used to bring affordable homes to a rising middle class, not for communal purposes unlike the Dogon and Zambians.
2. Another feature of the Dogon and Zambian housing tradition their devotion to communal principles that must be admired is that homes are built close to the civic center.
3. This tradition can also be seen in places such as in the Caribbean, where a strong African influence endures persisting in other areas such as music and religion as well.
4. You can go into any village in Tobago a small Caribbean island situated to the north of Venezuela, lying at the far southern end of the Caribbean chain and find sections of about four or five houses occupied by one family unit.
5. Mediterranean and Latin American families though from disparate areas also seem to follow this tradition.
6. The Dogon-Zambian style of home building creates a fascinating geometric appearance as can be discerned in aerial photographs, like a beehive.
7. Accustomed to the solitary life of the Arctic, the Inuit can live in relative isolation, compared to the cultural traditions of the Dogon and Zambians. Inuit housing reflects that.
8. Today, the Inuit also known, less accurately, as Eskimos live in modern homes, with a walrus skin or sealskin covering used the way one might use shingles.
9. On occasions when the family must go on a long journey for example, on an ice-fishing expedition, an igloo is built.
10. These snow houses rarely seen in Greenland and unknown in Alaska! were once the permanent winter homes of the Inuit in eastern Canada.

Using Brackets

Brackets are used to enclose a word or phrase added by a writer to the words of another.

> **KEY CONCEPT** Use brackets to enclose words you insert in quotations when quoting someone else. ■

EXAMPLES:　Cooper noted: "And with [*ET*'s] success, 'Phone home' is certain to become one of the most oft-repeated phrases of the year [1982]."

Lady Caroline Lamb wrote of Byron, "[He is] mad, bad, and dangerous to know."

The Latin expression *sic* (meaning "thus") is sometimes enclosed in brackets to show that the author of the quoted material has misspelled or mispronounced a word or phrase.

EXAMPLE:　Michaelson, citing Dorothy's signature line from *The Wizard of Oz*, wrote, "Theirs [sic] no place like home."

> **Exercise 57** **Enclosing Material in Brackets** Insert brackets and *sic* where needed. Added words are underlined.

EXAMPLE:　"These houses are all picture-prefect."

ANSWER:　"These houses are all picture-prefect [sic]."

1. According to an expert on nomadic tribes, "Homes of nomads all have one feature in common: They must be potable."
2. "Whether they were in the plains of the American Wild West 1890's or are living today on the tranquil plains of Tibet, the ability to pack up quickly <u>if necessary</u> and efficiently is paramount," he claims.
3. A rival expert on nomadic tribes expresses a different view: "To suggest that portability is the only share characteristic of the dwelling structures of nomads is pure poppycock."
4. "The cone-shaped teepee of the Plains Indians is an example; it is made of animal hide stretched around poles <u>arranged in a tripod</u>, used as a framework," she continues.
5. "At any given moment, the pegs holding the skins securely to the ground could be removed and the entire skin structure rolled up to become a lightweigt bundle with three poles."

Spelling Tip

Sic is used only when there is an error in a work from which you are quoting. You cannot use it after misspellings in your own work!

GRAMMAR EXERCISES 58–63

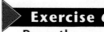 **Exercise 58** Using Dashes Copy the following sentences, inserting dashes where needed.

1. Home for some people in the world is in the most literal sense a castle.
2. Manors, palaces, marbled halls, gold fixtures these are the amenities of daily life for them.
3. Sometimes, these homes are so big have you been to the White House? it takes a day to see the whole place.
4. The White House perhaps the most exclusive estate in the world is made of white sandstone from Virginia.
5. Probably the most exciting rooms at the White House as if there could be any rooms there that aren't exciting! are the state rooms where balls, receptions, and dinners are held.

Exercise 59 Enclosing Material in Parentheses and Brackets Insert parentheses or brackets as appropriate, using capital letters where necessary. Added material is underlined.

1. A palace as you can imagine is a larger and more ornate version of a mansion.
2. "Buckingham Palace, the official residence of the British royal family, has a vast number of rooms 600 in total and is known for its beautiful garden grounds, a well-manicured 50 acres."
3. The palace was purchased for the royal family by George III 1738–1820.
4. Many formerly residential palaces have long since been converted to other uses no doubt because of the enormous expense of their upkeep, such as ballet institutes, art museums, and libraries.
5. The Alhambra in Granada, Spain, it is a beautiful structure! is still as alive and vibrant as it was centuries ago.

Exercise 60 Using Dashes, Parentheses, and Brackets Punctuate the following sentences.

1. Studios, efficiency apartments, one-room flats no matter the euphemism, there's no concealing that affordable Manhattan apartments are small.
2. For example, Richard insisted on a home that 1 was in a safe neighborhood; 2 got lots of sunlight he's fond of his plants; and 3 wouldn't send him into bankruptcy.
3. The apartment he found was tiny it fit the bill but couldn't fit his bed but he took it anyway.
4. After he signed the lease you wouldn't believe how much of his income would be paying for the roof over his head! he felt outraged by what he was paying.
5. He wrote, "Now I know why they call these apartments a 'flat': That's the only way anything fits into them, and they leave you flat broke!"

Exercise 61 Find It in Your Reading Skim through a reference book about architecture. Find at least two examples of dashes, parentheses, or brackets.

Exercise 62 Find It in Your Writing Review a piece of research writing to find at least one place where you can use information in brackets to clarify a quotation.

Exercise 63 Writing Application Write a paragraph about your home or someone else's. Use dashes, parentheses, and brackets—each at least once.

Hyphens and Apostrophes

Section 27.6

As a writer, you must know the rules governing the use of hyphens and apostrophes. Although the rules are not difficult, you must carefully study them and the examples that illustrate them to avoid making mistakes.

Using Hyphens

Hyphens are used to join some words and to divide others. The hyphen (-) resembles the dash (—) but is shorter. In your handwriting, make your hyphens about half the length of your dashes. In typewriting, one hyphen mark is used for a hyphen and two hyphen marks are used for a dash.

Writers use hyphens with numbers, word parts, and words.

With Numbers Hyphens are used to join compound numbers.

▶ **KEY CONCEPT** Use a hyphen when writing out the compound numbers *twenty-one* through *ninety-nine*. ■

EXAMPLES: twenty-eight ounces
              fifty-five apartments

With Fractions Fractions used as adjectives are also hyphenated.

▶ **KEY CONCEPT** Use a hyphen with fractions used as adjectives. A fraction used as a noun is not hyphenated. ■

EXAMPLES: seven-tenths full
              three-quarters finished

              One fourth of the members
              were present.

▶ **Critical Viewing** How can you determine fractions of an inch using a tape measure? **[Analyze]**

**Theme:
The Ordinary
and the Unusual**

In this section, you will learn about the many uses of hyphens and apostrophes. Most of the examples and exercises are about ordinary objects and animals as well as some unusual places, things, or ideas.

**Cross-Curricular
Connection:
Social Studies**

With Word Parts In some circumstances, a hyphen is used after a prefix.

> **KEY CONCEPT** Use a hyphen after a prefix that is followed by a proper noun or a proper adjective. ■

EXAMPLES: pre-Renaissance
mid-February
un-American

Prefixes that may be used before proper nouns or proper adjectives are *ante-, anti-, mid-, post-, pre-, pro-,* and *un-.*

> **KEY CONCEPT** Use a hyphen in words with the prefixes *all-, ex-, self-,* and words with the suffix *-elect.* ■

EXAMPLES: all-powerful
ex-jockey
self-made
mayor-elect

With Compound Words Some compound words are also joined with hyphens.

> **KEY CONCEPT** Use a hyphen to connect two or more words that are used as one word unless the dictionary gives a contrary spelling. ■

Although some compound words are written as one word and others are written as two words, many compound words are joined with hyphens. Always consult your dictionary if you are in doubt about the spelling of a compound word.

EXAMPLES: sister-in-law
tractor-trailer
six-year-old

▲ **Critical Viewing** What hyphenated word could you use to describe this truck? **[Connect]**

 **Learn More**

For additional information about using hyphens, see Chapter 29: "Vocabulary and Spelling."

▶**KEY CONCEPT** Use a hyphen to connect a compound modifier that comes before a noun unless it includes a word ending in -*ly* or is a compound proper adjective or compound proper noun acting as an adjective. ■

EXAMPLES WITH HYPHENS:	a well-made pair of jeans the bright-eyed children an up-to-date decision
EXAMPLES WITHOUT HYPHENS:	widely distributed information East European languages Red River valley

When compound modifiers follow a noun, they generally do not require the use of hyphens.

EXAMPLE: The jeans were well made.

If your dictionary lists a word as hyphenated, however, it should always be hyphenated.

EXAMPLE: The news was up-to-date.

For Clarity Sometimes, a word or group of words might be misread if a hyphen were not used.

▶**KEY CONCEPT** Use a hyphen within a word when a combination of letters might otherwise be confusing. ■

EXAMPLES:	semi-illiterate re-press (to press again)

▶**KEY CONCEPT** Use a hyphen between words to keep readers from combining them erroneously. ■

INCORRECT:	the special delivery-man
CORRECT:	the special-delivery man

Dividing Words at the End of a Line Although you should try to avoid dividing a word at the end of a line, if a word must be broken, use a hyphen to show the division.

▶**KEY CONCEPT** If a word must be divided at the end of a line, always divide it between syllables. ■

EXAMPLE:	The lonely children had been sending let- ters describing their adventures at camp.

💡 Spelling Tip

Generally, words that contain double letters are divided between the double letters, as in *run-ner.* Check a dictionary if you are unsure of where to break a word.

▶**KEY CONCEPT** Do not divide a word so that a single letter or the letters -*ed* stand alone. ■

INCORRECT:	a-bout	scream-ed	toast-y
CORRECT:	about	screamed	toasty

▶**KEY CONCEPT** Avoid dividing proper nouns and proper adjectives. ■

INCORRECT:	Fe-licia	Amer-ican
CORRECT:	Felicia	American

▶**KEY CONCEPT** Divide a hyphenated word only after the hyphen. ■

INCORRECT: We are going with my sister and my bro-
ther-in-law.

CORRECT: We are going with my sister and my brother-
in-law.

▶ **Exercise 64** Using Hyphens to Join Words Add hyphens as needed. Write *correct* if none are required.

1. third largest country
2. mountain rimmed area
3. self imposed isolation
4. large scale project
5. flat topped mountains
6. estimated population
7. west east direction
8. non Chinese speaking
9. mineral rich country
10. ten year plan

▶ **Exercise 65** Using Hyphens at the Ends of Lines If a word is broken correctly, write *correct*. If not, rewrite it.

EXAMPLE: cur-ed
ANSWER: cured

1. enterp-rise
2. Bei-jing
3. pan-da
4. populat-ion
5. politi-cal
6. Chi-nese
7. cult-ure
8. mon-soon
9. state-own-ed
10. tour-ism

Grammar and Style Tip

When writing, avoid placing a broken or hyphenated word at the end of a page.

▶ **More Practice**

On-line
Exercise Bank
• Section 27.6
Grammar Exercise
Workbook
• pp. 147–148

Using Apostrophes

Apostrophes are used to form possessives, contractions, and a few special plurals.

Forming Possessives The following rules tell you how to show possession with various types of nouns.

▶ **KEY CONCEPT** Add an apostrophe and an -s to show the possessive case of most singular nouns. ■

EXAMPLES: the wallet of the woman   the woman's wallet
            the collar of the dog   the dog's collar
            the lines of the actress   the actress's lines

For classical references ending in -s, only an apostrophe is used.

EXAMPLES: Confucius' teachings
            Tacitus' history

The possessive case of plural nouns follows two rules:

▶ **KEY CONCEPT** Add an apostrophe to show the possessive case of plural nouns ending in -s or -es. ■

EXAMPLES: the barking of the dogs
            the dogs' barking
            the color of the leaves
            the leaves' color

▶ **KEY CONCEPT** Add an apostrophe and an -s to show the possessive case of plural nouns that do not end in -s or -es. ■

EXAMPLES: the books of the women
            the women's books
            the grazing lands of oxen
            the oxen's grazing lands

▶ **Critical Viewing** Write a sentence describing this photograph, using the possessive form of the word *dog*. **[Connect]**

▶ **KEY CONCEPT** Add an apostrophe and an *s* (or just an apostrophe if the word is a plural ending in *s*) to the last word of a compound noun to form the possessive. ■

NAMES OF BUSINESSES AND ORGANIZATIONS:	the Salvation Army's headquarters the Department of the Interior's budget the Johnson Associates' clients
TITLES OF RULERS AND LEADERS:	Catherine the Great's victories Louis XVI's palace the chairman of the board's desk
HYPHENATED COMPOUND NOUNS USED TO DESCRIBE PEOPLE:	my sister-in-law's car the secretary-treasurer's idea the nurse-practitioner's patient

▶ **KEY CONCEPT** To form possessives involving time, amounts, or the word *sake,* use an apostrophe and an *-s* or just an apostrophe if the possessive is plural. ■

TIME:	a month's vacation three days' vacation a half-hour's time
AMOUNT:	one quarter's worth two cents' worth
SAKE:	for Marjorie's sake for goodness' sake

▶ **Critical Viewing** How much time does it take for you to do your homework on an average day? Respond using a time phrase with an apostrophe. **[Connect]**

When you make words possessive, you should also indicate the difference between something owned jointly by two or more people and something owned by individuals.

KEY CONCEPT To show joint ownership, make the final noun possessive. To show individual ownership, make each noun possessive. ■

JOINT OWNERSHIP: I always enjoyed Bob and Ray's radio show.

INDIVIDUAL OWNERSHIP: Liz's and Meg's coats are hanging here.

Use the owner's complete name before the apostrophe to form the possessive case.

INCORRECT SINGULAR: Jame's idea
CORRECT SINGULAR: James's idea
INCORRECT PLURAL: two girl's books
CORRECT PLURAL: two girls' books

Forming the possessives of pronouns requires two rules:

KEY CONCEPT Use an apostrophe and an -s with indefinite pronouns to show possession. ■

EXAMPLES: everyone's time   one another's friends
            somebody's umbrella   each other's homework

Notice in two of the examples that you add an apostrophe and an -s only to the last word of a two-word indefinite pronoun to form the possessive.

GRAMMAR IN LITERATURE

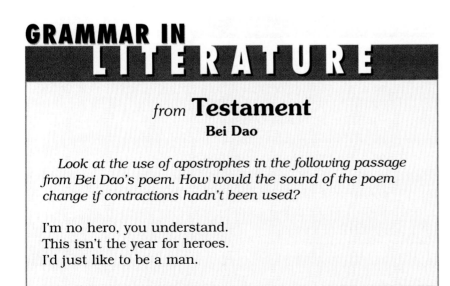

from **Testament**
Bei Dao

Look at the use of apostrophes in the following passage from Bei Dao's poem. How would the sound of the poem change if contractions hadn't been used?

I'm no hero, you understand.
This isn't the year for heroes.
I'd just like to be a man.

> **KEY CONCEPT** Do not use an apostrophe with the possessive forms of personal pronouns. ∎

The possessive forms of personal pronouns already show ownership. Pronouns in this form should be left just as they are to show possession.

EXAMPLES: his jazz records
our house
her blue sweater
its tires
their party
whose paper

Be careful not to confuse the contractions *who's*, *it's*, and *they're* with possessive pronouns. They are contractions for *who is*, *it is* or *it has*, and *they are*. Remember also that *whose*, *its*, and *their* show possession.

PRONOUNS: *Whose* homework is this?
Its tires were all flat.
Their dinner is ready.

CONTRACTIONS: *Who's* at the door?
It's going to rain.
They're going to the beach.

Forming Contractions Another important use of the apostrophe is in forming contractions. One general rule covers all the different types of contractions:

> **KEY CONCEPT** Use an apostrophe in a contraction to indicate the position of the missing letter or letters. ∎

APOSTROPHES INDICATING MISSING LETTERS				
VERB AND *NOT:*	cannot	can't	are not	aren't
	could not	couldn't	will not	won't
PRONOUN AND *WILL:*	he will	he'll	I will	I'll
	you will	you'll	we will	we'll
	she will	she'll	they will	they'll
PRONOUN AND *WOULD:*	she would	she'd	I would	I'd
	he would	he'd	we would	we'd
	you would	you'd	they would	they'd
PRONOUN OR NOUN AND THE VERB *BE:*	you are	you're	I am	I'm
	she is	she's	Jane is	Jane's
	they are	they're		

Notice that one of these contractions changes letters as well as drops them. *Will not* becomes *won't* in contracted form.

Contractions with verbs should be used mainly in informal writing and in dialogue. The same is true for another type of contraction, one for years.

EXAMPLES: the class of '04
                      the depression of '29

Still another type of contraction is found in poetry.

EXAMPLES: e'en (for even)
                      o'er (for over)

Other contractions represent the abbreviated form of *of the* and *the* as they are written in several different languages.

EXAMPLES: O'Hare   o'clock
                      d'Lorenzo   *l'Abbé*

These letters are most often combined with surnames.

A final use of contractions is for representing individual speaking styles in dialogue. As noted above, you will often want to use contractions with verbs in dialogue. You may also want to approximate a regional dialect or a foreign accent, which may include unusual pronunciations of words or omitted letters.

EXAMPLES: "Hi, ol' buddy. How you been feelin'?"
                      "Don' you be afoolin' me."

Avoid overusing the apostrophe with contractions even in dialogue. Overuse reduces the effectiveness of the apostrophe.

Using Apostrophes for Special Plurals The following rule presents four other situations in which apostrophes are used:

▶ **KEY CONCEPT** Use an apostrophe and an *-s* to write the plurals of numbers, symbols, letters, and words used to name themselves. ■

EXAMPLES: during the 1860's
                      m's and *n*'s
                      your *2*'s and *3*'s
                      no *if*'s or *maybe*'s
                      three *?*'s in a row

Grammar and Style Tip

In formal writing, it is always best to avoid contractions. Write the words out in full.

> **Exercise 66** **Using Apostrophes** Rewrite each of the following items, following the instructions in parentheses.

1. the written language of the country (Use the possessive case.)
2. who is (Write the contracted form.)
3. the dialects of the regions (Use the possessive case.)
4. the efforts of the government (Use the possessive case.)
5. the country's climate (Use a possessive pronoun for *country's.*)
6. the topography of the regions (Use the possessive case.)
7. the languages of the minorities (Use the possessive case.)
8. the religion of the people (Use a possessive pronoun for *people.*)
9. the diversity of the fauna and flora (Use the possessive case.)
10. will not (Write the contracted form.)
11. 15 (Write the plural form.)
12. the home of the panda (Use a possessive pronoun for *panda.*)
13. Southeast China is home to whom? (Rewrite, using a possessive pronoun instead of *to whom.*)
14. the importance of Confucius (Use the possessive case.)
15. the variety of the dialects (Use the possessive case.)
16. the dialects of the Han and non-Han people (Use the possessive case.)
17. 1940 (Write the plural form.)
18. they are (Write the contracted form.)
19. the mineral deposits of China (Use the possessive case.)
20. the borders of China and Russia (Use the possessive case.)

> **Exercise 67** **Using the Rules for Hyphens and Apostrophes in Original Sentences** Choose ten different rules from this section. Then, write sentences of your own that illustrate each of the rules you have chosen.

More Practice

On-line
Exercise Bank
• Section 27.6
Grammar Exercise
Workbook
• pp. 149–150

Section 27.6

Section Review

GRAMMAR EXERCISES 68–71

Exercise 68 Using Hyphens to Join Words If an item does not need hyphenating, write *correct*. If it does, add one.

1. pro isolationist policies
2. one fifth of the world's population
3. Sino Russian border
4. geographically diverse regions
5. life size figures
6. thirty first floor
7. ex Senator
8. well intentioned advice
9. South American history
10. pro American

Exercise 69 Using Hyphens at the Ends of Lines If a word is broken correctly, write *correct*. If not, rewrite it.

1. Budd-hist
2. tradit-ion
3. dy-nasty
4. nam-ed
5. communic-ation
6. sis-ter-in-law
7. partici-pation
8. Span-ish
9. excitem-ent
10. frisk-y

Exercise 70 Using Apostrophes to Show the Possessive Case Choose the correct word in parentheses to complete the following sentences.

1. Confucius was one of (China's, Chinas') most influential figures.
2. Despite his (families, family's) poverty, he received a fine education.
3. After mourning his (mother's, mothers) death, he began to travel and teach.
4. Confucius deplored his (societies, society's) vices and urged a return to ancient values.

5. He believed that (ruler's, rulers') lives must be exemplary if their states were to prosper.
6. He was born in the state of Lu (now Shandong), and, at age 51, was elected that (state's, states') minister of crime.
7. His (administrations', administration's) policies were successful.
8. Lu became so powerful that a neighboring ruler contrived to secure (Confucius', Confucius's) dismissal.
9. Confucius was venerated both during and after his life, and his (philosophys's, philosophy's) principles were practical and ethical.
10. His (teachings', teaching's) influence on the Chinese nation has been profound.

Exercise 71 Using Apostrophes Correctly With Pronouns Rewrite the following sentences, choosing the correct form from the choices in parentheses.

1. The population of China is larger than (any other country's, any other countries).
2. (It's, Its) the third largest country in the world in area.
3. (It's, Its) recorded history dates from around 3500 B.C.
4. The regional climates of China are similar to those of the United States, but (they're, their) weather patterns usually have greater contrasts.
5. The giant panda, (who's, whose) only home is southwestern China, feeds on certain bamboo shoots.
6. China was one of the first countries to enact environmental legislation, and (its, it's) chief concerns are deforestation and erosion.
7. Close to ten million people call Shanghai (they're, their) home.

Section Review Exercises cont'd.

8. (Education and literacy's, Education's and literacy's) growths are of primary concern to the Chinese government.
9. Confucius dedicated (his, he's) life to the betterment of the people.
10. The Chinese language is quite different from (ours, our's).

▶ **Exercise 72** Using Apostrophes in Contractions and Special Situations Add an apostrophe to the following items to form contractions or plurals.

1. they are
2. *B*
3. 1900
4. but
5. he would

▶ **Exercise 73** Proofreading for All the Rules for Apostrophes Revise the following sentences, using apostrophes to form contractions, possessive nouns, and possessive pronouns where appropriate.

1. Ive learned a lot of interesting things in my social studies class, but now that were studying Chinas history and culture, Im really interested.
2. For much of it's history, China had little to do with the rest of the world.
3. The Great Wall of China is a symbol of Chinas desire to keep the world at a distance.
4. China took it's name from the Qing dynasty.
5. The Chinese trace they're ancestry to the Han dynasty.
6. I enjoy reading Confucius's teachings.
7. He taught about everyones duties and responsibilities.
8. Confucius' ideas helped Chinas government run smoothly for year's.
9. Itd take a months vacation to tour just a small part of China.
10. My sister's-in-law's family went to China during the 60s.

▶ **Exercise 74** Writing Sentences With Possessives and Contractions Write sentences with possessives and contractions requiring apostrophes, following the instructions.

1. Describe the speaking voice of a family member, using his or her name.
2. Tell about something they would do but you would not. Use contractions.
3. Ask a question to find out who owns the earrings you found. Use the possessive of an indefinite pronoun.
4. Write instructions for your friend to meet you at the mall at a specific time. Write out the time.
5. Compare the hairstyles of two friends. Use their names.

▶ **Exercise 75** Find It in Your Reading Look through a section of an atlas about a country that interests you. Find examples of at least five different uses of hyphens and apostrophes.

▶ **Exercise 76** Find It in Your Writing Proofread a piece from your portfolio one more time to correct any errors in the use of hyphens and apostrophes.

▶ **Exercise 77** Writing Application Write a few paragraphs about a country that interests you. Use hyphens and apostrophes in at least five different ways.

Chapter Review

GRAMMAR EXERCISES 78–86

Exercise 78 **Using End Marks**
Copy each of the following items, correcting the punctuation where necessary.

1. The subcontinent of India was its own island continent until about 5,000 BC, though perhaps that date is incorrect
2. It is bordered by significant territories, though it is an entire peninsula unto itself
3. China lies to the north and Bangladesh to its east
4. Are you aware that India is bordered on the west by Pakistan
5. These two areas have been engaged in disagreements for many years
6. Never try to intercede in that territorial dispute
7. Go north and start on an upward trek to find the Himalayas
8. This mountain range extends 1,500 miles across India
9. The Himalayas, which include Mt Everest—the tallest mountain in the world, measuring over 29,000 ft at its highest elevation—are astonishing
10. Sir Edmund Hillary, in addition to earning a PhD degree, has also received the honor of Officer of the Order of the British Empire for his work in the Himalayas

Exercise 79 **Using All the Rules for Commas** Revise the following paragraph, inserting commas as necessary.

(1) Receiving abundant rainfall India's verdant and vast land teems with a variety of animal life. (2) Miles of impenetrable jungle create a safe haven and the hills and mountains also provide protection. (3) Tigers panthers and cheetahs inhabit many sections of the forests. (4) Other members of the cat family such as the snow leopard roam the slopes of the Himalayas. (5) Elephants can be found on the broad fertile plains though these elephants are a different species from those found in Africa. (6) It may seem strange that there are wolves in the Himalayan area. (7) A pair was seen on August 24 1997 west of the Kashi Hills Deccan Plateau. (8) Venomous reptiles including cobras saltwater snakes and vipers are widespread in India. (9) Pythons though a nuisance to small cattle and humans when hungry keep down the rodent population. (10) Crocodiles not to be confused with alligators are also prevalent in the estuaries of India's rivers.

Exercise 80 **Using Colons and Semicolons** Use colons and semicolons to punctuate the following items correctly.

1. Throughout history, India has been a prize to be won even Alexander the Great led an expedition into India.
2. The Macedonian influence on India was negligible politically in contrast, the art, sculpture, and science of Greece did have an effect on Indian culture.
3. Leaders of the Mughal Empire controlled the trade routes in fact, it was through their connection that Europeans became aware of India.
4. To European monarchs eager to expand, one thing was clear A new route to the Far East could not be overlooked.
5. India became the object of a fierce struggle between three European countries Portugal, the Netherlands, and Great Britain. To find new treasures and stake out new lands before their rivals could lay a claim, these nations sent forth men who would become the great explorers in history Christopher Columbus, Amerigo Vespucci, and Vasco da Gama.

► **Exercise 81** **Using Quotations and Underlining** Use quotation marks and underlining to punctuate the following sentences. Quoted fragments are underlined.

1. John Assam lives in India, so we should call him for information, said Brian.
2. John exclaimed over the speaker-phone, Bombay has a vast population: over 8,225,000!
3. The population density is about 762 per square mile, he continued.
4. Brian's sister Janet warned, We'd better go to New Delhi, because even though it's the capital, it's not as populous.
5. That's a good idea, Brian said, hastening to add that New Delhi and Delhi are two different cities.
6. Janet was eager to see a range of saris because she regards this traditional Indian women's garb as even more gorgeous than the <u>enchanting</u>, shimmering gown I wore the night of the junior prom.
7. Brian, who prefers more conservative clothes, claimed the gown was <u>too bright</u>.
8. John was eager to cut short any sibling bickering: While I can still get a word in edgewise, I should mention I have to go to a wedding; maybe you two would like to come with me?
9. He felt that attending the wedding might <u>broaden our horizons</u>.
10. I'd love to attend said Janet I think we'll enjoy the event.

► **Exercise 82** **Using Dashes, Parentheses, Brackets, Hyphens, and Apostrophes** Add the necessary punctuation to each sentence. Added material is underlined.

1. One of Indias assets a varied population is also a drawback.
2. Culture, ethnicity, religion, class all these divisions still exist in India.
3. Major religious groups in India, for example, include 1 Hindus; 2 Muslims; and 3 Buddhists, to name just a few.
4. Though many groups have assimilated and have lived together for centuries, India's leadership still has a difficult task in forming a unified country <u>see</u> recent articles on Sikh separatism.
5. Many well intentioned social programs there are thousands of programs in India! are unsuccessful because of language differences and social taboos.
6. Distances between villages and lack of adequate transportation maintaining roads in extreme weather conditions can be difficult are hindrances to the implementation of many programs.
7. The greatest challenges <u>Smith's assertion is verified by a recent World Bank report</u> are in the two areas that most affect children: health programs and education.
8. Mary Sanderson 1942–1992, like Mother Theresa, devoted her entire life to helping those in need.
9. Overall life expectancy grew to 60 years by 2000 an improvement over 1944, when i was 32 years old.
10. Sadly, infant mortality a great tragedy in any country is still high in India.

Exercise 83 **Proofreading for Punctuation** Revise the following passage, adding the necessary punctuation.

The most widely practiced religion in India is Hinduism which is a polytheistic religion. Central to Hindu belief is a supreme triad formed by three deities Brahma the father of the gods and humankind and the creator of the universe Vishnu the god of love and Siva or Shiva the god of the cosmic dance. An interesting contrast can be drawn between Hindu deities and Greek gods Greek gods always looked and acted more or less human albeit with some incredible tricks up their sleeves Hindu gods sometimes take on some very nonhuman attributes. For example Brahmas wife Sarasvati grew out of his side. Can you think of any similar stories from other cultures Vishnu a god of light and love and the enemy of darkness is described as having dark blue skin. The last of the triad Siva is perhaps the most complicated god of all in some myths he acts as protector but in others as destroyer. A blue throat, a third eye in his forehead, anywhere from two to who knows how many arms are just a few of the physical attributes that reflect Sivas complexity. To be sure with all those extra arms Siva can do a lot of pointing. Hindu gods and goddesses are worshiped in many forms and appear in all sorts of guises indeed the concept of gods who reincarnate through the centuries in several human forms called avatars is an important key to understanding Hinduism

Exercise 84 **Proofreading Paragraphs for Punctuation** Rewrite the following paragraphs, adding the necessary punctuation.

Various powers have ruled the nation of Burma in its long embattled history From 1885 Britain ruled Burma as a province of India another of its territories By the 1920's when George Orwell author of the short story Shooting an Elephant served in Burma as a police officer Burmese protests against British rule were growing stronger

In 1937 Britain granted Burma some rights to self government However in 1942 Japan occupied the country which they ruled until 1945 At the end of World War II Britain resumed control of Burma Finally in 1948 Burma gained independence

Exercise 85 **Writing and Punctuating Original Sentences** Choose a subject with which you are familiar. It might be a person you know, a sport you play, a restaurant you like, or a topic you're studying in one of your classes. Then, write sentences, following the directions below.

1. Describe three features of your subject using commas in a series.
2. Write something you like about your subject using your subject as a possessive noun.
3. Quote something that someone else has said about your subject inserting a remark or clarification of your own inside the quotation.
4. Complete a sentence that begins, "These two things are good (or bad) about [your subject]."
5. Describe one thing that may affect your subject in the future; add a contrary or explanatory comment in the middle or at the end of the sentence.

Exercise 86 **Writing Application** Write a description of one of your favorite places. Correctly use each type of punctuation at least once.

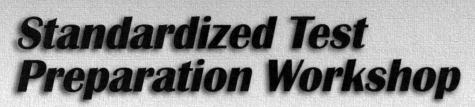

Standardized Test Preparation Workshop

Proofreading

Standardized tests often include items that test your knowledge of punctuation rules. Most often, this testing involves proofreading written passages for errors in punctuation.

The following sample items will give you practice with identifying punctuation errors.

Test Tip

When you choose the item that you think contains an error, correct the error on scrap paper. If you cannot identify how the item should be corrected, see if another section contains an error.

Sample Test Items

Directions: Choose the best way to write each underlined section. If the underlined section needs no change, mark the choice "Correct as is."

(1) "Look" she called, "up there"!

(2) The science teacher directed the students parents and other guests to look at the migrating birds.

1 A "Look she called, "up there."

   B "Look," she called, "up there!"

   C "Look"! she called "up there."

   D Correct as is

2 F The science teacher directed the students: parents: and other guests to look at the migrating birds.

   G The science teacher directed, the students parents and other guests, to look at the migrating birds.

   H The science teacher directed the students, parents, and other guests to look at the migrating birds.

   J Correct as is

Answers and Explanations

The correct answer for item 1 is *B*. As a part of the direct quotation, the exclamation mark belongs before the quotation mark. All other punctuation in this passage is correct.

The correct answer for item 2 is *H*. The series *students, parents, and other guests* requires commas to separate each element.

Practice **Directions:** Choose the best way to write each underlined section. If the underlined section needs no change, mark the choice "Correct as is."

(1) Last call for flight 1233 to Washington D.C announced the ticket agent, (2) "The 345 PM. flight to Washington D.C. will be leaving the gate immediately"! (3) Mr. Solomon his wife and their three children ran down the stairs to the small plane? (4) Thank goodness we made it exclaimed Dr. Solomon, (5) "I was afraid we would miss the AMA Convention in Washington." (6) Mr Solomon settled into his seat his wife reviewed her notes for her presentation at the conference

1 A "Last call for flight 1233 to Washington D.C" announced the ticket agent,
B "Last call for flight 1233 to Washington D.C" announced the ticket agent.
C "Last call for flight 1233 to Washington, D.C.," announced the ticket agent.
D Correct as is

2 F "The 3:45 P.M. flight to Washington, D.C., will be leaving the gate immediately!"
G "The 345 P.M. flight to Washington D.C. will be leaving the gate immediately"!
H "The 345 PM flight to Washington D.C. will be leaving the gate immediately!"
J Correct as is

3 A Mr. Solomon, his wife, and their three children, ran down the stairs to the small plane.
B Mr. Solomon, his wife, and their three children ran down the stairs to the small plane.
C Mr. Solomon; his wife; and their three children ran down the stairs to the small plane.
D Correct as is

4 F "Thank goodness we made it." exclaimed Dr. Solomon,
G "Thank goodness we made it"! exclaimed Dr. Solomon.
H "Thank goodness we made it!" exclaimed Dr. Solomon.
J Correct as is

5 A "I, was afraid we would miss the AMA Convention, in Washington."
B "I was afraid we would miss the A.M.A. Convention in Washington."
C I was afraid "we would miss the AMA Convention in Washington."
D Correct as is

6 F Mr. Solomon settled into his seat! his wife reviewed her notes for her presentation at the conference.
G Mr. Solomon settled into his seat; his wife reviewed her notes for her presentation at the conference.
H Mr Solomon settled into his seat, his wife reviewed her notes for her presentation at the conference?
J Correct as is

Cumulative Review

MECHANICS

Exercise A **Using Capitalization**

Copy all the items in the following sentences that require capitalization, adding the missing capitals.

1. william shakespeare was born in 1564 in stratford-upon-avon, warwickshire, a part of england.
2. at a young age, he was married to anne hathaway, and they had two daughters.
3. it is rumored that he was forced from stratford after he was caught hunting sir thomas lucy's deer.
4. seeking success as an actor and a playwright, shakespeare arrived in london in 1588.
5. the publication of two poems, "venus and adonis" and "the rape of lucrece," as well as a compilation of his sonnets, established shakespeare's reputation.
6. with the patronage of henry wriothesley, third earl of southampton, shakespeare continued to write in the renaissance style.
7. he had arrangements allowing him to share in the profits of his acting company, known as the lord chamberlain's men and later known as the king's men.
8. shakespeare is associated with two theaters, the globe theater and the blackfriars.
9. his plays were frequently performed for both queen elizabeth I and king james I.
10. however, a performance of his play about king richard III almost caused shakespeare to fall out of favor with elizabeth.
11. after almost twenty years in london, which is when he wrote his 38 plays, shakespeare moved back to stratford.
12. by 1608, he had moved his family to a house called new place and had become a prominent local citizen.
13. after his death in 1616, shakespeare was buried in the stratford church.
14. his many plays, from *julius caesar* to *romeo and juliet* to *the life of king henry the fifth*, have become the most widely known and highly quoted works.
15. his earliest works are about english kings henry IV and richard III.

Exercise B **Using End Marks, Commas, Semicolons, and Colons**

Write the following sentences, inserting end marks, commas, semicolons, and colons where necessary.

1. The years up to AD 1594 form Shakespeare's first period of writing
2. This period is the time he wrote his first historical plays *The First Part of King Henry the Sixth The Second Part of King Henry the Sixth The Third Part of King Henry the Sixth* and *The Tragedy of King Richard the Third*
3. Was he influenced by the Roman playwright Seneca
4. Yes Seneca's influence can be seen particularly in the bloody tragic scenes in Shakespeare's early plays
5. During this time period Shakespeare wrote a wide range of comedies their styles vary from farcical to satirical
6. The first *The Comedy of Errors* written in 1592 imitates the farcical improbable style of classic Roman comedies by using the motif of mistaken identity
7. Wow Did you realize that *Love's Labour's Lost* was written in such a different style
8. Satirizing the noble pursuit of knowledge before romance this play is concerned with revealing the pretensions of society in fact it also mocks the writing of other contemporary playwrights

9. In particular the dialogue seems to invoke the works of one English novelist at the time John Lyly

10. Do the plays *The Taming of the Shrew* *The Two Gentlemen of Verona* and *Titus Andronicus* fall into this time period

Exercise C Using All the Rules of Punctuation

Write the following sentences, inserting end marks, commas, semicolons, colons, quotation marks, underlining, dashes, brackets, parentheses, hyphens, and apostrophes where necessary. Quotations are underlined.

1. The play that I saw on Apr 13 1994 Twelfth Night was one of Shakespeares most charming love stories

2. Is that the play that features the strong minded character Beatrice however Im not sure Was she in Much Ado About Nothing 1599

3. In Twelfth Night the two pairs of lovers encounter obstacles they are also confronted with an entire cast of amusing characters

4. Feste who is also known as Fool and is the jester to Olivia has a similar role to Puck in A Midsummer Night's Dream 1595 They speak to the audience

5. Festes first aside is this <u>Wit, an't be thy will, put me into good fooling</u> sic

6. Malvolio whose name literally means ill wisher in Latin reveals on lines 80 86 that he is not concerned with his mistress Olivias happiness

7. <u>But that's all one, our play is done, And we'll strive to please you every day</u> sings Feste to end Twelfth Night

8. Have you ever seen Shakespeares plays As You Like It or The Merry Wives of Windsor

9. Besides writing comedies Shakespeare wrote some tragedies The tone of the writing is so different from his comedies during this period

10. Gosh I found Romeo and Juliet very sad the family feuds and the misunderstandings are frustrating.

Exercise D Using Capitalization and Punctuation

Write the following dialogue, inserting the proper capitalization, punctuation, and indentation.

1. what plays fall into shakespeares third period of writing are those the years from 1600 1608 ken asked

2. well said emma there is othello which is about a general in the venetian army and his jealousy

3. is that the play with iago oh yes i remember his wife is desdemona

4. right emma continued have you heard of the play king lear it is about one of britains early rulers

5. ken replied yes we read that in english class it is certainly an epic tragedy another tragedy is macbeth

6. antony and cleopatra written around 1606 is another tragedy about love the roman general mark antony falls in love with the egyptian queen cleopatra

7. i have never heard of the play coriolanus is it a tragedy or a comedy

8. when i read the introduction to coriolanus in my anthology the complete works of shakespeare it said that the play is also set in ancient rome

9. emma are you going to read hamlet before we watch the movie version of the play asked ken

10. there are so many movie versions of shakespeares plays said ken

Exercise E Writing Application

Write a brief first-person narrative that includes dialogue in which you and a friend discuss a play, movie, or show. Be sure to follow all the rules of capitalization and punctuation.

Sentence Diagraming Workshop

A pictorial representation of a sentence is called a diagram. Just as a map can help a driver understand directions, so can a diagram help you visualize a sentence's structure. This section will explain the traditional rules for diagraming the basic sentence patterns that were covered in these chapters on grammar.

Subjects, Verbs, and Modifiers

To diagram a subject and a verb, draw a horizontal line and place the subject on the left and the verb on the right of the line. Separate the two with a vertical line.

EXAMPLE: Malcolm should have volunteered.

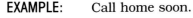

Adjectives and adverbs sit on slanted lines beneath the words they modify.

EXAMPLE: The very large bird glided surprisingly gracefully.

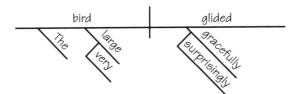

When the subject of an imperative sentence is understood to be *you*, place it in parentheses on the main line. Inverted sentences, in which the subject follows the verb, are also diagramed in the regular subject-verb order. The capital letter shows which word begins the sentence.

EXAMPLE: Call home soon.   Has Regina telephoned yet?

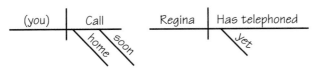

Rearrange a sentence beginning with *there* or *here* so that the subject comes first. Then, if *there* or *here* functions as an adverb, diagram it below the verb. If *there* functions as an expletive, place it on a horizontal line above the subject. Use the position of an expletive for interjections and nouns of direct address also. Diagrams illustrating these types of sentences are shown below.

EXAMPLE: There is a stranger here.   Hey, Diana, hurry up.

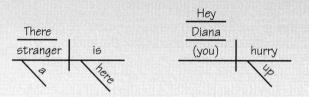

▶ **Exercise 1** **Diagraming Subjects, Verbs, and Modifers**

Correctly diagram each sentence.
1. The giant python slithered silently.
2. Her extremely high fever finally dropped.
3. Is my notebook here?
4. My, there goes one expensive automobile.
5. Leslie, do not dawdle.

Adding Conjunctions

Conjunctions are generally shown in a diagram on a dotted line between the words they connect. In the example presented below, conjunctions join both adjectives and adverbs.

EXAMPLE: The long and difficult report was read quickly but not easily.

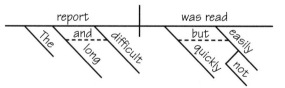

Conjunctions connecting compound subjects and compound verbs are also placed on dotted lines drawn between the words they connect. In the example on the next page, the horizontal line of the diagram is split so that each of the compound parts appears on a line of its own. Notice how correlative conjunctions and helping verbs shared by more than one verb are placed. If each part of the compound verb had its own helping verb, each helping verb would be placed on the line with its own verb.

EXAMPLE: Both you and I must pack today and move tomorrow.

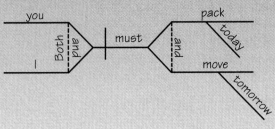

As the above example shows, modifiers in sentences that contain compound parts are carefully positioned with the individual words they modify. If a word modifies an entire compound element, as illustrated in the following example, the modifier is positioned beneath the main line of the diagram.

EXAMPLE: Yesterday, the campers and counselors swam and fished.

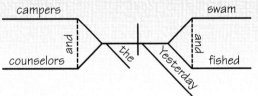

▶ **Exercise 2** **Diagraming Sentences With Conjunctions**
Correctly diagram each sentence.
1. The tiny tugboat and the gigantic cruiser steamed away.
2. The horses neighed nervously and shied away.
3. Her letter, scented and pink, arrived today.
4. Today, both Darrin and Peter have continuously memorized and rehearsed.
5. Neither Luis nor Mary has arrived yet.

Complements

Because complements complete the meaning of a verb, they are diagramed on the predicate side of the sentence. Direct objects sit on the same line as the subject and verb and are separated from the verb by a short vertical line. Indirect objects are placed on a horizontal line extending from a slanted line directly below the verb.

EXAMPLE: I sliced the cheese.   Dick bought us a wok.

An objective complement is placed right after a direct object. A short slanted line pointing toward the direct object separates it from the rest of the sentence.

EXAMPLE: The supervisor named Lee division manager.

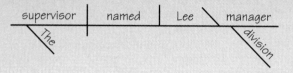

Subject complements are also placed on the main line, separated from the linking verb by a short line that slants back toward the subject and verb.

EXAMPLE: Margarita is a soprano.   The dirt road is bumpy.

Compound complements are diagramed by splitting the lines on which they appear. Conjunctions are placed on dotted lines drawn between the words they connect.

EXAMPLE: We gave our grandmother and grandfather airplane tickets and money.

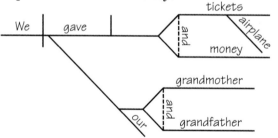

▶ **Exercise 3** **Diagraming Complements** Correctly diagram each sentence.
1. My old scrapbook held old snapshots and other mementos.
2. The group gave Kirk and Nat an elaborate map and some instructions.
3. His monthly salary was meager and inadequate.
4. My parents consider me an excellent driver.
5. Tammy is my sister and a good friend.

Prepositional Phrases

Diagram a prepositional phrase beneath the word it modifies. Place an adjective phrase beneath the noun or pronoun it modifies; place an adverb phrase beneath the verb, adjective, or adverb it modifies. Put the preposition on a slanted line and its object on a horizontal line. Place modifiers of the object beneath it on slanted lines. Diagram compound objects of the preposition just as you would other compound sentence parts.

EXAMPLE: The desk with the faulty leg is located in the first row or the second one.

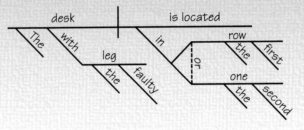

To diagram an objective phrase that modifies the object of the preposition of another prepositional phrase, study the first example below. To diagram an adverb phrase that modifies an adjective or an adverb, study the second example below.

EXAMPLES: The keys are on the table by the door.

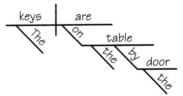

I arrived home late at night.

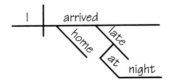

To diagram two prepositional phrases that modify the same word, use the following example as a guide.

EXAMPLE: I will meet you near the door or in the auditorium.

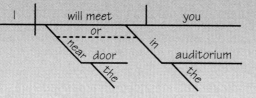

▶ **Exercise 4** Diagraming Prepositional Phrases Correctly diagram each sentence.
1. On the wall, we hung kites of every size and shape.
2. Sleepily, he pressed the alarm button on his clock.
3. Our family piled into the car and headed for the freeway.
4. My friend was sensitive to my needs and fears.
5. With ease, the mechanic changed the flat tire on our car.

Appositives and Appositive Phrases

Put an appositive in parentheses following the noun or pronoun it renames. Any modifiers go directly beneath it.

EXAMPLE: Mrs. Rebholtz, a friend of the family, will visit us.

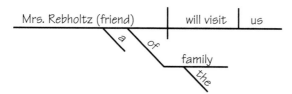

▶ **Exercise 5** Diagraming Appositive Phrases Correctly diagram each sentence.
1. My home, a small two-bedroom apartment, is convenient.
2. I gave the bride, a young woman of twenty, a handmade quilt.
3. The organization, a group of parents, wrote letters.
4. We visited Columbia, a town in Missouri.
5. Jurors should report to Judge Bean, a strict but fair guardian of the law.

Verbals and Verbal Phrases

Verbal phrases—which are constructed with participles, gerunds, and infinitives—are never diagramed on a straight line.

Participles and Participial Phrases Because a participle functions as an adjective, it is placed partly on a slanted line and partly on a horizontal line beneath the noun or pronoun it modifies. Adverbs or adverb phrases that modify the participle are placed below it. When a participle has a complement, the complement is placed in its normal position on the horizontal line with the participle, separated from it by a short vertical line.

EXAMPLE: A child selling candy came to our house.

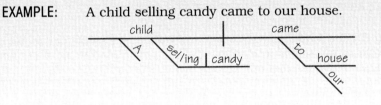

Because it is grammatically separate from the rest of the sentence, a nominative absolute is diagramed in the same way that an expletive is.

EXAMPLE: The meeting having been concluded for this month, we left.

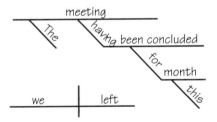

Gerunds and Gerund Phrases Gerunds can occupy any position in a diagram that a noun can. When they function as subjects, direct objects, predicate nominatives, or appositives, gerunds sit atop a pedestal on a stepped line. Modifiers and complements are diagramed in the usual way.

EXAMPLE: Fixing the garbage disposal required much time.

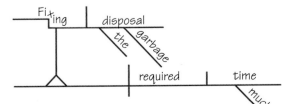

A gerund phrase functioning as an indirect object or as the object of a preposition goes on a stepped line extending from a slanted line.

EXAMPLE: We bought a small car for driving around town.

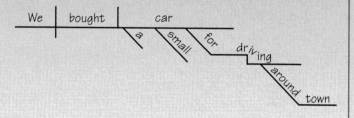

Infinitives and Infinitive Phrases An infinitive used as a noun sits on a pedestal on a line similar to, yet less complex than, the line used for a gerund. Modifiers and complements are diagramed in the usual way.

EXAMPLE: My resolution for the new year is to exercise daily.

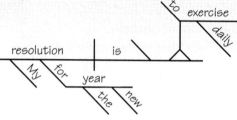

The diagram of an infinitive used as an adjective or adverb looks like the diagram of a prepositional phrase.

EXAMPLE: World War I was supposedly the war to end all wars.

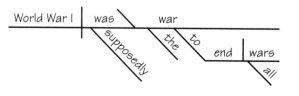

When an infinitive has an understood *to*, indicate the implied word in parentheses. If the infinitive has a subject, extend the left side of the infinitive line and place the subject there.

EXAMPLE: We heard thunder rumble during the night.

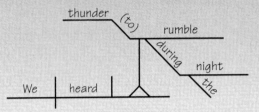

> **Exercise 6** **Diagraming Verbal Phrases** Correctly diagram each sentence.

1. The students writing feverishly in blue books ignored the entrance of the proctor.
2. Training for a major competitive event leaves an athlete little time for other activities.
3. We were asked to start with the national anthem.
4. Capitalizing on his good fortune, the man bought some property in the area.
5. She served tea tasting of herbs to her guests.
6. Help me tie this bow securely.
7. We had no desire to see that movie again.
8. Furnishing oranges and sodas was the responsibility of the team manager.
9. Learning to diagram sentences develops both manual and mental skills.
10. Her worst habit, being tardy, greatly irritated all of her teachers.

Compound, Complex, and Compound-Complex Sentences

All the sentences you have diagramed up to this point have been simple sentences. However, diagraming the other three sentence structures—compound, complex, and compound-complex—involves most of the same rules. The primary difference is that another base line is added for each additional clause.

Compound Sentences Each of the independent clauses in a compound sentence is diagramed separately. They are then joined together at the verbs by a dotted step line. The conjunction or semicolon is written on this step line.

EXAMPLE: I drove for six hours, and he slept soundly.

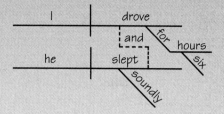

Complex Sentences Diagraming complex sentences involves knowing how to position each of the three kinds of subordinate clauses in relation to the independent clause. An adjective clause is diagramed below the main clause as if it were a separate sentence. A slanted dotted line joins the relative pronoun or relative adverb in the adjective clause to the word the clause modifies. The position of the relative pronoun varies depending on its function in the adjective clause. In the following example, the relative pronoun functions within the subordinate clause as a subject.

EXAMPLE: The car that sped around the corner had no headlights.

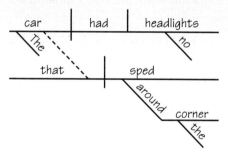

    The dotted line must be bent to connect the clauses properly when a relative pronoun acts as either an object of a preposition or as an adjective. The dotted line must also be bent when a relative adverb introduces an adjective clause.

EXAMPLE: The person to whom you spoke is president of the firm.

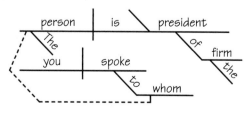

An understood relative pronoun in an adjective clause should be included in parentheses in a diagram.

EXAMPLE: I wrote the letter I owed to my friend.

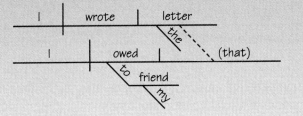

An adverb clause is diagramed with the subordinate conjunction written on the connecting line. This line should join the verb in the adverb clause to the modified verb, adjective, adverb, or verbal in the main clause.

EXAMPLE: When the speaker became ill, the lecture was canceled.

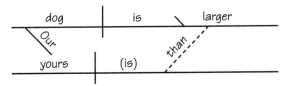

Place in parentheses any understood words in an elliptical adverb clause.

EXAMPLE: Our dog is larger than yours.

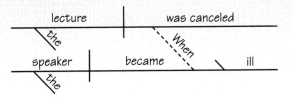

A noun clause is placed on a pedestal in the position it occupies within the sentence. The pedestal meets the noun clause at the verb. In the following example, the noun clause is acting as a direct object.

EXAMPLE: I will wear whatever is clean.

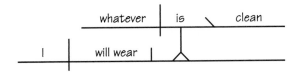

If a noun clause's introductory word has no other function than to introduce the clause, write it alongside the pedestal.

EXAMPLE: Earl said that you had a birthday.

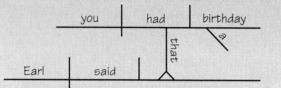

Compound-Complex Sentences To diagram compound-complex sentences, simply combine the skills you learned for diagraming compound and complex sentences.

EXAMPLE: The man who owned the shop fixed my typewriter, but he refused to charge me because the repairs were minor.

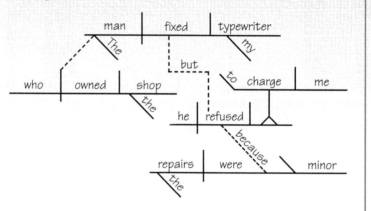

▶ **Exercise 7** Diagraming Compound, Complex, and Compound-Complex Sentences Correctly diagram each sentence.

1. I ate the sherbet quickly, but it still started to melt.
2. After we finished our errands, we had lunch.
3. We celebrated when the project was complete.
4. Salmon that are spawning know the exact river to which they must return.
5. We must mail this today, or it will not arrive on time.
6. We should stay at whatever place is cheapest; money is scarce at this time.
7. Tracy saw an automobile accident on Tuesday, and now she is driving more carefully.
8. The couple sat inside the warm house while the snow fell.
9. When he noticed a spot on his coat, he took it to the cleaners, but they were unable to remove the spot.
10. The bus that was scheduled to take us had engine problems, so the company sent us another.

3

Academic and Workplace Skills

Speaking, Listening, Viewing, and Representing

The world is in the midst of a communications explosion. Through radio, television, print, film, and the World Wide Web, information is in constant and rapid supply. Today, more than ever before, it is essential to be a strong critical listener and viewer, and it is important to be able to communicate your ideas using the latest visual media.

This chapter focuses on the viewing and listening skills needed to sift through information and to evaluate it critically. It also delves into the speaking and representing skills necessary to communicate ideas to others in this multimedia age. It provides guidance in how to be an effective oral communicator in a wide range of speaking situations—from informal group discussions and one-on-one interviews to formal public speeches—and it explores varying approaches to presenting material visually. All of these skills will be essential in both your personal and work life as you move into the future.

▲ **Critical Viewing**
What type of event do you think this news reporter is covering? How do you know? **[Analyze]**

Section 28.1

Speaking and *Listening Skills*

Developing your speaking skills will enable you to participate more effectively in class discussions, give formal presentations with greater confidence, and, in general, communicate your feelings and ideas to other people more easily. Improving your listening skills will enable you to focus your attention and identify important information when you hear it.

Speaking in a Group Discussion

A *group discussion* is an informal meeting at which people openly share ideas and observations. In school, group discussions enable you to compare your own interpretations of material with those of your classmates. In the workplace, group discussions are an excellent means for coming up with processes to improve working conditions and productivity.

KEY CONCEPT To benefit from group discussions, it is important to be an active participant, contributing your ideas and asking others questions about the ideas they contribute. ■

Thinking Before You Speak Sometimes, we may speak before we think about what we want to say, and sometimes we may want to take back what we've said. Avoid this problem in group discussions by taking a moment to think about what you're going to say before you say it. Make sure that you choose the right words to express yourself and that what you're saying will not offend any of the others.

Communicating Clearly and Effectively When you make a series of points, present them in a logical order. In addition, provide facts and examples to illustrate each point.

Asking Questions When you'd like to know more about something or an idea seems unclear, ask questions. Take care, however, to ask your questions in a polite and nonthreatening manner. Don't attack or ridicule the person you are addressing.

Making Relevant Contributions Contribute your ideas as frequently as you can, while making sure to allow others time to speak. However, avoid making contributions that stray from the topic being discussed.

Exercise 1 Holding a Group Discussion Hold a group discussion with a few classmates on an important current event.

Speaking in Public

Public speaking is the presentation of ideas, information, and points of view to an audience. Often, people feel anxious or intimidated the first few times they speak before an audience. Through practice and preparation, however, you will overcome your anxiety and become a strong presenter.

Recognizing Different Kinds of Speeches There are several different types of speeches. Each type is suited to certain occasions, audiences, and topics.

> **KEY CONCEPT** Choose the kind of speech you will give by considering your topic, your audience, and the occasion on which you will give the speech. ■

- An **informative speech** explains an idea or event or provides information about the status of something. Facts are presented in a clear, organized way. Examples of informative speeches include business presentations about a company's performance, a budget overview at a town meeting, and a review of upcoming events at a school assembly.

- A **persuasive speech** tries to convince the audience to agree with the speaker's position or to take some action. Campaign speeches by politicians are a common type of persuasive speech. In these speeches, as well as in other kinds of persuasive speeches, speakers support their opinions with examples and facts and use a variety of techniques—including repetition and appeals to emotion—to sway listeners.

- An **entertaining speech** is delivered simply to provide enjoyment to the audience. It may be included in other kinds of speeches to offer variety or emphasis. Entertaining speeches are often delivered at celebrations, such as weddings and birthday parties.

- An **extemporaneous speech** can serve any of the purposes outlined above. The key feature of this type of speech is that the speaker does not rely on a prepared manuscript. Major ideas may be outlined, but the speaker uses knowledge and skills to deliver the speech. In many cases, the speaker does not even use an outline.

> **Exercise 2** Matching Types of Speeches to Occasions
> Using the descriptions above of the kinds of speeches, give an example of an occasion, an audience, and a topic (other than those mentioned) that might determine when you would give each kind of speech. Explain each of your choices.

Learn More

Earlier chapters in this book (especially Chapters 6–11) provide information about writing for description, persuasion, and exposition. Apply those same concepts and skills to your speaking.

Preparing and Presenting a Speech The keys to a successful speech are thorough preparation and practice and a strong, confident delivery.

▶ **KEY CONCEPT** Prepare for a speech by collecting and organizing information and practicing your delivery. ■

Gather Information Thoroughly research your topic in the library, on the Internet, or by conducting interviews.

Prepare an Outline Arrange the information you gather into an outline. Divide your outline into major points and supporting details. Arrange the information in a logical sequence.

SAMPLE OUTLINE

Jane Austen's
Pride and Prejudice

A. Overview
   1. Fitzwilliam Darcy is proud and rich.
   2. Elizabeth Bennet is simple and strong-willed.
   3. Social differences complicate their relationship.

B. Aristocracy
   1. Rigid social customs
   2. Accept class divisions

C. Pride
   1. All people all fallible.
   2. Some are wise enough to admit their error.

Prepare Note Cards and Visual Aids Prepare a note card for each main point on your outline. List opening points, key details, and quotations on each card. You may also want to prepare visual aids. See pages 792–793 to learn more.

Practice Your Speech Study your outline and note cards. Then, practice your speech, using the note cards to guide you.

Deliver Your Speech Use your note cards to guide you as you deliver your speech. Make eye contact with your audience.

Use Rhetorical Strategies Repeat key words and phrases to make your points stand out. Use parallelism, the repetition of grammatical structures, to emphasize key ideas.

Use Verbal and Nonverbal Strategies Vary the tone, volume, and pace of your voice to emphasize your key points. Also, use nonverbal methods, such as hand gestures, for emphasis.

⊙ Technology Tip

On its Web site, Toastmasters International provides more tips for honing your public-speaking skills and fending off nervousness.
http://www. toastmasters.org

Evaluating a Speech You can use what you've learned about delivering a successful speech to evaluate speeches that others give.

> **KEY CONCEPT** Evaluate speeches by critically examining both content and delivery. ■

Use these questions to help guide you in making evaluations.

QUESTIONS FOR EVALUATING SPEECHES

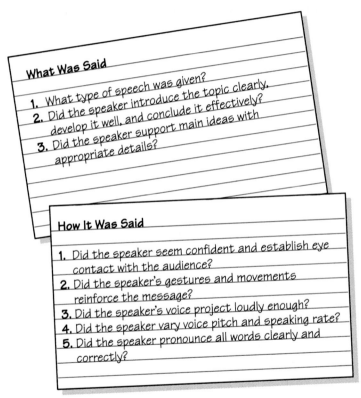

What Was Said

1. What type of speech was given?
2. Did the speaker introduce the topic clearly, develop it well, and conclude it effectively?
3. Did the speaker support main ideas with appropriate details?

How It Was Said

1. Did the speaker seem confident and establish eye contact with the audience?
2. Did the speaker's gestures and movements reinforce the message?
3. Did the speaker's voice project loudly enough?
4. Did the speaker vary voice pitch and speaking rate?
5. Did the speaker pronounce all words clearly and correctly?

> **Exercise 3** **Preparing and Giving a Speech** Prepare and deliver a speech on a current issue or topic that interests you. Follow the steps on page 781.

> **Exercise 4** **Evaluating a Speech** Using the questions above, evaluate a speech given in class. Note the speaking skills the person used effectively, and plan to use them in a speech you will give.

Listening Critically

In today's world, much of the information that people receive comes through television, radio, and other multimedia sources. For this reason, it is essential to develop the skills to critically evaluate what you hear.

KEY CONCEPT Critical listening involves the careful analysis of the purpose, accuracy, and thoroughness of spoken messages. ■

Learning the Listening Process Becoming a critical listener starts with simply learning to listen attentively. You can then go beyond comprehending *what* a person says and begin analyzing *how* it was said.

Focus Your Attention To be an effective listener, you must not only listen attentively but also focus your thoughts entirely on what the person is saying, ignoring any outside distractions.

Interpret the Information It won't be possible to remember everything a speaker says, so it is essential to identify the key points or main ideas of the message. Use the following suggestions to guide you:

1. Listen for words or phrases that are repeated or emphasized through the volume or tone of the speaker's voice.
2. Take careful note of words or phrases, such as *most important, it is essential,* and *my main point,* that signal that an idea following them is important.
3. Test your understanding by rephrasing the speaker's ideas in your own words.
4. If possible, take notes in which you record key ideas.
5. Watch for nonverbal signals—tone of voice, gestures, and facial expressions—that may alert you to important ideas.
6. Carefully follow the connections among ideas. Signal words and phrases—such as *in comparison, next, last but not least,* and *as a result*—can help you identify important connections.

Respond to the Speaker's Message After the speaker has finished, respond to what you've heard. Think about whether you agree or disagree with the speaker's thoughts and why. Connect the speaker's message to your own experiences, and consider what, if anything, you can learn from the message that you can apply to your life. Finally, ask questions about anything that especially interested you or was unclear.

Exercise 5 Using the Listening Process Apply the strategies on this page as you listen to a classroom lecture.

Using Different Types of Listening There are a number of types of listening, each appropriate for different situations. The following chart shows four types of listening and the situations for which they are most appropriate.

Types of Listening		
Type	**How to Listen**	**Situation**
Critical	Listen for facts and supporting details to understand and evaluate the speaker's message.	Informative or persuasive essays, class discussions, announcements
Empathic	Imagine yourself in the other person's position, and try to understand what he or she is thinking.	Conversations with friends or family
Appreciative	Identify and analyze aesthetic or artistic elements, such as character development, rhyme, imagery, and descriptive language.	Oral presentations of a poem or short story and dramatic performances
Reflective	Ask questions to get information, and use or reflect on the speaker's responses to form new questions.	Class or group discussions

Asking Different Types of Questions Asking questions is the best way to ensure that you have understood what a speaker has said or to delve more deeply into the speaker's topic. Following are some types of questions you might ask:

- A **question that calls for clarification** is a question that you ask to ensure that you have heard accurately what has been said. These questions might begin as follows: "What did you mean by . . .?" or "If I understand correctly, . . .?"

- A **question that calls for support** asks the speaker to back up his or her points with supporting facts and details. These questions might begin, "On what do you base . . .?"

- A **closed question** leads to a *yes* or *no* response.

- An **open-ended question** does not have a specific response but can lead to further exploration of the topic.

Evaluating Your Listening Developing strong listening skills is an ongoing process. However, improvement occurs only if you are willing to critically evaluate your own performance as a listener and find ways to improve.

Repeat or Paraphrase Key Ideas Test your understanding of a speech by repeating or restating the speaker's main points. When you use your own words to restate what you've heard, it is called **paraphrasing.** Ideally, you should share your paraphrase with the speaker and see whether he or she agrees with it.

Compare and Contrast Interpretations If you are among a group of listeners, compare your interpretation of what you've heard with other listeners' interpretations.

Use the following questions to guide your discussion:

• What was the main point or central message?
• What was the strongest argument or example?
• Do I agree with or accept the information presented or the speaker's position? Why or why not?

Check the Accuracy of the Speaker's Points If you are unsure about a point or think it sounds inaccurate, research it on the Internet or in the library.

▷ **Exercise 6** Using the Different Types of Listening and Questioning Come up with at least two specific situations in which you would use each type of listening and two specific situations in which you would ask each type of question.

▷ **Exercise 7** Tracking Your Listening Skills For one week, keep a record of your performance in listening situations. Use each of the strategies above at least once.

Viewing Skills

Visual representation is an important and effective way to communicate. Television programs, textbooks, Web sites, and works of art are common types of media that use images to add to your view of the world. In this section, you will learn how to interpret information from visual sources.

Interpreting Maps and Graphs

Any map, graph, or photograph can be a treasure chest of information. The key to the information these representations hold is your ability to interpret them.

Maps

A map can show more than the fastest route between two cities. For example, maps can identify population clusters and movement, provide demographic information for politicians and marketers, report weather patterns, clarify battle activities in war, and illustrate the geography and topography of planets.

To interpret a map, (1) determine the type and purpose of the map; (2) examine the symbols, scale, orientation, and other pertinent data (often, maps have a key that can help you decipher symbols and scale); (3) make connections between the key details of the map to written text that accompanies it.

REGIONS OF THE UNITED STATES

▲ **Critical Viewing** For what types of purposes might you use this map? Explain. **[Analyze]**

Graphs

Graphs are an excellent tool for comparing pieces of related information. Following are the main types of graphs:

Bar Graph A bar graph compares and contrasts amounts by showing differing heights or lengths of the bars. To interpret a bar graph, (1) compare and contrast the bars and (2) search the text for possible causes for the similarities and differences.

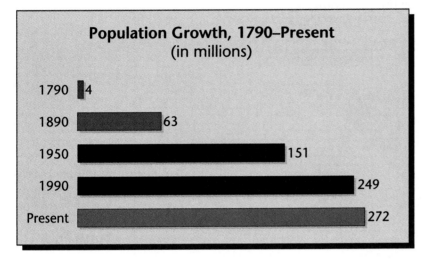

Population Growth, 1790–Present
(in millions)

1790 — 4
1890 — 63
1950 — 151
1990 — 249
Present — 272

◀ **Critical Viewing** What are some of the conclusions you can draw about population growth in the United States based on this graph? **[Analyze]**

Line Graph Line graphs illustrate changes over time. A line graph is based on two scales—one vertical and one horizontal—with each point having a value on both scales. To interpret a line graph, (1) identify patterns of change and (2) search the text for reasons for the changes.

Immigration to the United States, 1940–1990

1,200,000
1,000,000
800,000
600,000
400,000
200,000
0
1940   1950   1960   1970   1980   1990

━━━ Asia   ━━━ Americas*   ━━━ Europe

* Outside United States

◀ **Critical Viewing** What does this graph reveal about how immigration patterns have shifted over the last several decades? **[Analyze]**

Pie Graph A pie graph shows the relationship of parts to a whole. A circle, or pie, is divided into segments, each representing a percentage of the whole. The combined segments equal 100 percent. To interpret a pie graph, (1) read the title to determine what the whole (100 percent) stands for; (2) determine what each percentage represents, and relate the percentages to each other as well as to the whole; (3) relate the graph information to the text to determine the significance and possible reasons for the percentages.

AVERAGE YEARLY PRECIPITATION

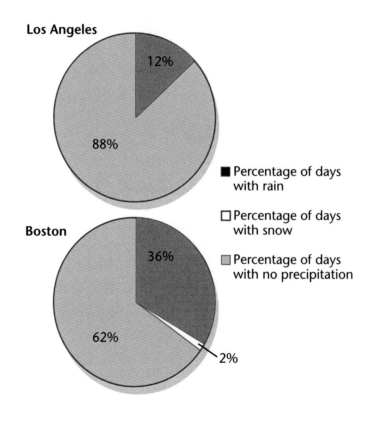

◀ **Critical Viewing** What can you tell about the differences in climate between Los Angeles and Boston based on these graphs? **[Analyze]**

Exercise 8 **Interpreting Maps and Graphs** In the library or on the Internet, find one example of each of the types of maps and graphs. Analyze each example, and write a brief explanation of the information it provides.

Viewing Information Media Critically

It is important to be a critical listener in today's media-rich world. It is perhaps even more essential to be a critical viewer. Being a critical viewer involves thinking carefully about what you see and carefully analyzing its purpose and its effectiveness. One of the first steps in becoming a critical viewer is to learn to differentiate among the various kinds of media and to understand the purposes of each.

Recognizing Kinds of Information Media In our fast-paced world, it sometimes seems that we encounter new forms of visual media almost every day. Internet Web pages, print advertisements, commercials—these are just a few of the kinds of media you'll encounter, as the chart below shows.

TODAY'S VISUAL MEDIA

Form of Media	Topic(s)	Coverage and Content	Point of View
Internet Web Pages	Unlimited	Interactive content updated regularly	Can be biased
Television News Program	Current events or news	Brief summaries illustrated by video footage	Gives objective information
Television Documentary	One topic of social interest	Story shown through narration and video footage	Often focuses on one side of an issue
Television Interview	Topics of social interest	Questions and answers	Sometimes presents opinions of interviewer
Print Advertisement and Television Commercial	Products, people, and ideas	Short message of images and slogans	Presents information to sell something or to persuade viewer

Evaluating Persuasive Techniques Much of the material presented through visual media intends to persuade. In some cases, this is immediately apparent—in commercials, for example. In other cases, it is less obvious; a news program may include persuasive segments, for instance.

> **KEY CONCEPT** Learn to identify and evaluate the use of persuasion in all visual media. ■

To identify the use of persuasion and to evaluate its effectiveness, be aware of these persuasive elements and techniques:

Facts are statements that can be verified. **Opinions** are viewpoints that cannot be verified, or proved true.

Loaded language and **loaded images** are emotional words and visuals used to stir up your feelings and persuade you to think a certain way.

Bias is a tendency to think in a certain way without considering other viewpoints.

Slogans and **repetition** are other techniques used to sway your opinions.

Evaluating Information From the Media Once you've become aware of the various persuasive techniques, use the following techniques to critically evaluate what you see:

- Distinguish between facts and opinions, and determine whether opinions are supported by facts.
- Try to avoid being swayed; instead, focus on how well the position being presented has been supported.
- Check for bias by seeing whether both sides of an issue have been addressed.
- Verify questionable information in other sources that you find in the library or on the Internet.
- Don't let slogans sway you, even though they are catchy.
- View the complete program. Develop your own views about the issues, people, and information.

> **Exercise 9** Analyzing Information Media Complete a written analysis and evaluation of a television news program or Web site. Follow the strategies above.

> **Exercise 10** Evaluating Television Commercials Write an evaluation of the effectiveness of a television commercial.

Technology Tip

Several libraries and media centers offer tips for evaluating information on their Web sites. Try these:

http://www.lib.duke. edu/libguide/ evaluating.html

http://www.cl. utoledo.edu/info/ guides/info_eval. html

Viewing Fine Art Critically

When you look at a painting, you'll discover more than just a reproduction of a person or a scene. You may also find a mood, a movement of color, an explosion of attitude, or the drama of an event. By interpreting the elements of a work of art, you can travel on imaginative and inspirational journeys.

> **KEY CONCEPT** Interpret the elements of art to understand the devices used to enrich your appreciation of it. ■

Effect of the Sun on the Water, 1905, Andre Derain, Giraudon

◀ **Critical Viewing**
What is your first impression of this painting? Why? **[Respond]**

QUESTIONS FOR INTERPRETING ARTWORK

- What is the medium? Is the work a painting, drawing, photograph, and so on?
- What scenes, shapes, images, and colors do you see?
- Are lines thick or thin, straight or curvy, solid or broken?
- Are people and objects proportional? Do they seem ordinary in size, gigantic, or tiny?
- How does the artist use light and dark tones? How do the two tones contrast with one another?
- Which parts are clearly defined? Which parts are not?
- What is the mood of the work? How do all the individual elements work together to create a feeling or an idea?

> **Exercise 11** **Interpreting Fine Art** Interpret the painting above by asking and answering the preceding questions. Write your answers, and then share and compare them with those of your classmates.

🖥 Research Tip

Many museums offer virtual tours on their Web sites. Use the World Wide Web to enhance your appreciation of art and to hone your interpretation skills.

Representing Skills

Writing is communication through words. Representing is communication through various media, such as graphic organizers, pictures, videos, and dramatic performances. As we move into the future, the ability to present your ideas through media becomes increasingly important.

Producing Graphic Organizers

Graphic organizers are useful in helping you to sort out and comprehend what you read, see, and hear; they are also a valuable tool when you present your own ideas to an audience. For instance, you may use graphic organizers in business presentations when you leave school and enter your work life.

KEY CONCEPT When you have a lot of information or technical data to comprehend or present, consider putting the information into a graphic organizer that suits the type of information. ■

Analyzing the Information Think carefully about the type of information with which you are dealing. If, for example, the information involves comparisons, you would probably want to consider using a Venn diagram. On the other hand, if you were dealing with events taking place over a period of time, you'd probably want to use a flowchart or a timeline.

Limiting the Amount of Information You Include
Graphic organizers lose their effectiveness if they present too much information. Remember that the whole point of using a graphic organizer is to present the information visually, not through words. Limit the amount of text you include in graphic organizers. Use phrases and words rather than complete sentences to indicate main ideas or details.

Exercise 12 Producing a Graphic Organizer Produce two different graphic organizers: The first should record information from a history or science textbook. The second should present information on a subject of special interest to you. The first organizer can serve as a study aid to help you prepare for a test. The second organizer can be used in a presentation.

Producing Other Visual Aids

In addition to graphic organizers, there are a variety of other visual aids that you can use in presentations.

Charts, Graphs, and Tables These are excellent tools for presenting data. For example, you might use a graph in a business presentation to show how a company's earnings have grown over time.

Maps Consider using maps in presentations discussing one or more places. For example, you might show two maps to compare and contrast the average temperatures in two different states.

Diagrams, Illustrations, and Pictures Simple line drawings, diagrams, and hand-drawn pictures can visually represent a process or specific features of something. Look at the diagram below.

▼ Critical Viewing
In what type of presentation might you use this diagram? Why? **[Connect]**

THE EARTH'S ORBIT AND THE SEASONS

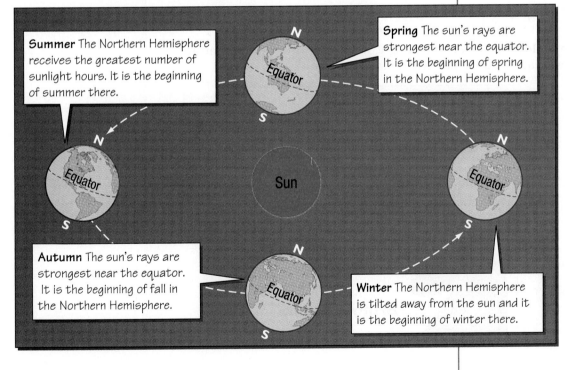

Exercise 13 Producing Visual Aids Produce two different types of visual aids listed above. Do not simply copy your examples from a book. Instead, use information gathered through research to prepare your own.

Using Formatting

You can enhance any piece of writing with the basic formatting and design features of a word-processing program or a multimedia presentation program. Formatting features include type styles and sizes, fonts, capital letters, tabs, and bullets. Design features include arrangement, balance, and color.

- **Capitals** Use capital letters in heads to call out important topics and ideas.

- **Boldface and Italics** Use boldface and italic type to add emphasis and to direct the readers' eyes to key information and ideas.

- **Fonts** Use different fonts and type sizes to distinguish heads, captions, or even sections of information. Fonts also help create a mood.

- **Numbered Lists** Use numbered lists when you are providing sequential steps in a process.

- **Bulleted Lists** Use bulleted lists for items that can be presented in any order.

- **Arrangement** Arrange your information in a way that captures and directs the readers' attention.

- **Color** Use color to highlight important information and to create a particular emotional response.

Join the Chess Club
- Learn how to
  1. open with a strong move
  2. dominate the middle
  3. finish your opponent
- Watch expert games
- Compete against other clubs

Come to our organizational meeting next Wednesday at 3:30 P.M. in the library.

Bring a friend!

> **Exercise 14** **Using Formatting to Design a Brochure** Use the tips on formatting and design to prepare a flyer or brochure that promotes recycling. When your flyer is complete, ask a classmate to evaluate your use of various formatting and design features.

Working With Multimedia

In a multimedia presentation, the presenter utilizes a combination of speech and aural and visual aids. Ideally, the different components complement each other, resulting in an interesting, engaging, multisensory experience.

KEY CONCEPT Multimedia presentations supply information through a variety of media, including text, slides, videos, music, maps, charts, and art. ■

Tips for Preparing a Multimedia Presentation

- Choose a topic, and generate an outline of what you want to communicate.

- Choose a form of media that is suited to your topic. For example, a presentation about the first moonwalk might include photographs of the astronauts and models of the spaceship, as well as music, art, and other representations of popular culture of that era. It might also contain a dramatic reading from appropriate newscasts and editorials.

- Plan the use of media you've found and created so that it is evenly spaced throughout your presentation.

- Make sure that the media you've selected is large enough and loud enough for everyone to see and hear. Photocopy and enlarge the images of small objects, or make slides of them.

- Before the presentation, check that all of your equipment works properly.

- Always have a backup plan just in case anything goes wrong with the equipment.

- Rehearse with the equipment prior to the day of your presentation.

Exercise 15 Preparing a Multimedia Presentation
Working with two or three classmates, choose a topic of interest from science, social studies, literature, or another school subject. Write an outline of the subtopics you would like to cover in an oral report, and select three types of media that will best enhance a multimedia presentation. Using the suggestions discussed in this section, prepare, practice, and present a dynamic multimedia report.

⊙ Technology Tip

There are a variety of presentation programs that can help you design multimedia presentations on a computer.

Producing a Video

Video is a powerful form of communication. Using a camera lens as your eyes, you can produce an entertaining and memorable presentation that will inform, amuse, and/or entertain your audience.

> **KEY CONCEPT** If you have access to the necessary technology, try your hand at producing a video by following the steps below. ■

Tips for Producing a Video A video can last a few seconds or several hours. Video subjects range from the sublimely ridiculous to the unflinchingly serious. Certain production steps apply to all video making:

1. **Write a shooting script.** A shooting script contains the characters' lines and dialogue. It also contains directions about camera angles, transitions, and descriptions of sets, wardrobe, and props.
2. **Prepare a storyboard** to show a clear sequence of events. A storyboard looks like a comic strip, with each important shot mapped out. Using index cards allows you to rearrange shots easily until you find the sequence that works best.
3. **Select locations for shooting**, and get any necessary permissions to use them.
4. **Cast the roles** and/or parts, and rehearse.
5. **Write a shooting schedule** that includes *who, what, when,* and *where.* Distribute the schedule to everyone involved.
6. **Film the scenes**.
7. **Edit the video** and store it in a safe place.

> **Exercise 16** Producing a Video
> Produce a ten-minute documentary about your goals after graduation. Follow the steps outlined above. Use the tips for filming to help you in development and production.

⊙ Technology Tip

This Web site gives many tips on video editing—for beginners as well as for the more experienced: **http://www. videonics.com/ Articles.html**

▶ Critical Viewing What type of video do you think these students are viewing? Why? [**Analyze**]

Performing and Interpreting

Performance art is one of the most effective and entertaining means of communicating.

▷ **KEY CONCEPT** Performers use a variety of techniques to convey the meaning of a text. ∎

Steps for Preparing an Interpretive Performance

Use the following strategies when preparing for a performance:

1. Carefully review the text. Put yourself in the place of the characters. Consider the tone of the piece, or the attitude the writer takes toward the subject.
2. Practice reading the text aloud several times. Experiment with the volume, tone, and pace of your voice to capture the mood of the piece and to emphasize key lines and ideas.
3. Memorize the text if this is called for in your presentation.
4. Add physical gestures to your performance to enhance the meaning and the mood.
5. If appropriate, find costumes, props, sets, and music to add flavor to your presentation.
6. Rehearse until you feel comfortable doing your presentation.

▷ **Exercise 17** **Performing for Your Class** Select an excerpt from a novel or a soliloquy from a play that you'd like to perform for your class. Think about the mood, tension, comic relief, and appeal of the piece you select. Decide the effect you'd like your performance to have. Then, offer your interpretation of the piece in a dramatic performance.

Reflecting on Your Speaking, Listening, Viewing and Representing

Review the concepts discussed in this chapter. Write a one-page reflection on your experiences, responding to the following questions:

- How might effective speaking and listening benefit me in the different areas of my life—school, work, hobbies, friends, and family?

- How can I use the speaking and listening strategies to improve my skills in these areas?

- What types of media are most effective in providing information?

- What did I learn from my experience of preparing and presenting my own media presentation or performance?

Standardized Test Preparation Workshop

Interpreting Graphic Aids

Some standardized tests contain questions testing your ability to gather details, draw conclusions, and interpret the information provided in maps, charts, graphs, and other graphic aids. The following sample items will help you become familiar with these types of questions.

Sample Test Items

Directions: Read the passage, and answer the questions that follow.

Before Sir Henry Bessemer developed a process to inexpensively produce steel from pig iron (the Bessemer process), industrialized nations produced only a few thousand tons of steel a year. By the end of the 1800's, steel production was measured in the millions.

Answers and Explanations

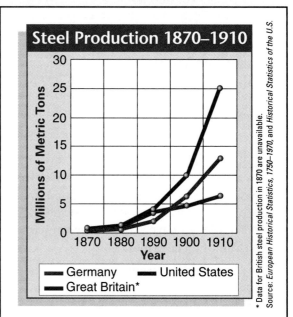

Steel Production 1870–1910

* Data for British steel production in 1870 are unavailable.
Source: European Historical Statistics, 1750–1970, and Historical Statistics of the U.S.

1 Which of the following lists countries in order of least steel produced to most steel produced in 1890?

  A United States, Germany, Great Britain
  B Germany, Great Britain, United States
  C Great Britain, United States, Germany
  D Germany, United States, Great Britain

The correct answer for item 1 is *B*. In 1890, Germany produced the least steel followed by Great Britain. The United States produced the most of the three countries.

2 How is the Bessemer process responsible for the statistics in the chart?

  F The process industrialized nations.
  G It allowed for an inexpensive and easy way to produce steel.
  H It helped provide steel producers with new minerals.
  J It had no influence over the statistics presented in the chart.

The correct answer for item 2 is *G*. Because the Bessemer process allowed for steel to be produced cheaply and quickly, countries such as Germany, Great Britain, and the United States were able to move steel production from thousands to millions of tons per year.

▶ **Practice 1** **Directions:** Read the passage, and answer the questions that follow.

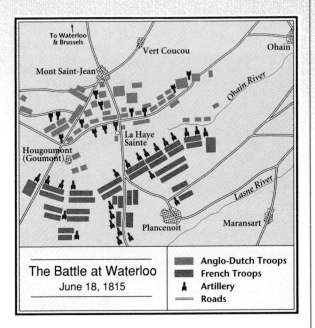

To Waterloo & Brussels

Vert Coucou

Ohain

Mont Saint-Jean

Ohain River

La Haye Sainte

Hougoumont (Goumont)

Lasne River

Plancenoit

Maransart

The Battle at Waterloo
June 18, 1815

■ Anglo-Dutch Troops
■ French Troops
♦ Artillery
═ Roads

In 1793, France declared war on Britain. Thus began a series of wars that would go on for twenty-two years, ending only when Britain and its allies defeated Napoleon at the Battle of Waterloo in 1815. A crucial moment in that battle came when one of Napoleon's officers, Marshal Ney, captured the farmhouse of La Haye Sainte. Even so, the Duke of Wellington was still able to lead British and Prussian troops to victory.

1 The British stationed most troops—
A in major cities
B along riverbanks
C around the farmhouse
D along roads

2 Where is La Haye Sainte farmhouse located in relation to the British troops?
F It is near the major artillery.
G It is located at the center of the troops.
H It is where the British leaders are residing.
J It is located near most British troops.

3 Why would it have been to France's advantage to hold the farmhouse?
A They could block the road from advancement and divide British troops.
B They could disable artillery.
C They could capture British troops.
D It meant they won the battle.

4 Which statement about the artillery is true?
F The British had more artillery than the French.
G The British artillery was more effectively placed than the French artillery.
H The French had more artillery than the British.
J The French artillery was pointed in the wrong direction.

5 What town is at the crossroads that is cut off from the French troops?
A Maransart
B Ohain
C Mont Saint-Jean
D Plancenoit

Vocabulary and Spelling

▲ Critical Viewing
What kind of communication is this girl practicing in this photograph?
[Interpret]

Developing a good vocabulary and improving your spelling skills can help you be more successful in school and in the work world. With a good vocabulary at your command, you can express yourself clearly and communicate exactly the meaning you intend, whether you are speaking or writing. In addition, any reading that you do will be accomplished more quickly and be more enjoyable. When you utilize good spelling, your written communications will be more effective and persuasive because your readers can concentrate on your ideas and information and not be distracted by mistakes.

The keys to building vocabulary and spelling skills are extensive reading and the use of proper reference sources. In addition, use whichever memory techniques suit you best.

Section 29.1
Developing Vocabulary

Listening, Discussing, and Reading

Your vocabulary is a tool that you will use throughout your life. You use words to communicate: to express yourself, to impart information, to receive information, and to persuade people. The more control you have over your vocabulary, the more effective your communication will be.

Learn Through Conversation For most people, the process of learning new vocabulary starts with hearing words and using them in conversation. This a process that begins in childhood and continues throughout your life. Most of the words you learned as a toddler you heard in conversation. You learned the meanings and pronunciations of new words by listening to family members, teachers, and friends. Then, you used the words. Keep up this process throughout your life. Listen for unfamiliar words whenever you talk to teachers or other adults, people from different backgrounds, or those whose interests and ideas are different from your own. If you don't know a word you hear, think about how it is used, ask about its meaning, or look it up in a dictionary.

Learn From Works Read Aloud Have you ever listened to a book on audiocassette or CD? If you have, then you have discovered another good way to build your vocabulary. The authors or actors reading the works will introduce you to new words and demonstrate how they are pronounced. You can use context clues from the reading to help determine a new word's meaning. You can reinforce the vocabulary-building process by reading a printed copy of the work while it is being read aloud. In that way, you can see and hear new words at the same time.

Learn From Your Reading Most important of all, keep reading. The more you read, the more new words you will encounter. Meeting the same new word several different times will help you become familiar with it. In addition, try to read a variety of materials in many different subject areas. Magazine articles or Internet pages on scientific topics will introduce you to valuable new words. So will newspaper articles about politics and current events. Read from a variety of sources to encounter a wide variety of words.

When you encounter an unfamiliar word in your reading, sometimes you may not have to use a dictionary to discover what it means. You can make inferences about its meaning by looking at the surrounding words.

Using Context

Recognizing Context Clues If you look carefully at the sentence or paragraph that contains an unfamiliar word, you can sometimes figure out its meaning by using clues from the author. These are called *context clues.*

> **KEY CONCEPT** The **context** of a word is the group of words that surround it. ∎

Figurative Language Writers often use figurative language to create "word pictures" in a reader's mind. Many times, the writers use familiar words in unfamiliar ways. You might encounter the sentence: "Janice stared at him angrily, her face a thundercloud." You know that a thundercloud comes before a storm, so you know that Janice's face is gloomy and threatening.

Idioms An idiom is an expression that takes on a special meaning different from the words in the idiom. For example, *let off steam* means to release emotion, not vapor. Use context clues to figure out the meanings of idioms. Compare unfamiliar idioms with expressions that you use to convey a similar meaning.

Technical Terms Material in your school reading, lectures, and research often includes technical words. You will find unfamiliar words and familiar words with unfamiliar meanings. For example, you know several meanings for the word *cast.* In geology, however, a *cast* is a fossil in which the space left behind in a rock by an organism has filled in, showing the same shape as the organism. Use context to determine the meaning of such words. Keep a special section of your notebook in each subject area for listing new words, along with their meanings and pronunciations. Use the glossary at the back of many textbooks to find meanings specific to a subject area.

> **Exercise 1** **Recognizing Context Clues** Use context clues to determine the meaning of each underlined word in the passage below. Check your answers in a dictionary.

Dr. Sandra Sisson, recently named Doctor of the Year, works at the Bronx Family Hospital in New York. The fifty-year-old (1) <u>laureate</u> has been chief of (2) <u>orthopedic</u> medicine for more than fifteen years. She does more than set broken bones at the hospital. The inventive doctor has (3) <u>broken new ground</u> with such (4) <u>innovations</u> as computerized (5) <u>prostheses</u>, or artificial limbs, that do more than respond to wearers' nerve impulses.

More Practice

Academic and
Workplace Skills
Activity Book
• pp. 17–18

Denotation and Connotation

Denotation is the objective meaning of a word—that to which a word refers, independent of other associations the word calls to mind. Dictionaries list the denotative meanings of words. The *connotation* of a word refers to the associations that a word calls to mind in addition to its dictionary meaning.

> **KEY CONCEPTS** The **denotation** of a word is its literal definition. Its **connotations** include the ideas, images, and feelings that are associated with the word in people's minds. ■

For example, the words *home* and *domicile* have the same dictionary meaning. However, *home* has positive connotations of warmth and security, whereas *domicile* does not.

> **Exercise 2** **Discriminating Between Denotation and Connotation** Read each pair of sentences below. For each pair, write a sentence explaining the different connotations of the underlined words. Use a dictionary to help you.

1. We have a large stone fireplace in our <u>home</u>.
   We have a large stone fireplace in our <u>residence</u>.
2. He welcomed the <u>beggar</u> into his house.
   He welcomed the <u>panhandler</u> into his house.
3. Marsha thinks that her sister is extremely <u>stubborn</u>.
   Marsha thinks that her sister is extremely <u>headstrong</u>.
4. In order to succeed in business, you must be <u>aggressive</u>.
   In order to succeed in business, you must be <u>domineering</u>.
5. Behind the diner, the dumpster is quite <u>malodorous</u>.
   Behind the diner, the dumpster is quite <u>stinky</u>.

▶ **Critical Viewing** Write two sentences describing this photograph. In one, use words with a positive connotation; in the other, put a more negative slant on it. **[Apply]**

Recognizing Related Words

You can increase your vocabulary by recognizing related words that may be similar or opposite in meaning.

KEY CONCEPT **Synonyms** are words that are similar in meaning. **Antonyms** are words that are opposite in meaning. ■

Synonyms For example, if you want to remember the meaning of *evocative*, it is easier to remember its synonym, "suggestive," than it is to memorize a long definition.

Antonyms For example, if you want to recall that *pungent* means "sharp and stimulating to the mind and senses," it would be easier to remember that its antonym is *bland*.

Finding Relationships in Analogies

Working with analogies, or word relationships, leads you to look for connections between word meanings. The way to solve analogies is to form a clear idea of the relationship between the initial pair of words. In the example below, the relationship is *part to whole*—a *rim* is a part of a *wheel*.

EXAMPLE: RIM : WHEEL ::
      a. house : apartment   c. singer : choir
      b. molecule : atom

The pair that expresses a similar relationship is choice *c*.

Other common analogy relationships include *synonym, antonym, type, defining characteristic, instrument used for a purpose, degree, sequence,* and *proximity.*

> **🖰 Research Tip**
>
> Find a standardized test-preparation book in the school library or guidance office. Practice working with the analogies included in the book.

Exercise 3 **Working With Analogies** Identify the relationship of the capitalized pair in each item below. Then, choose the lettered pair that best expresses the same relationship.
1. MALEVOLENT : KIND ::
   a. despair : sadness   c. masculine : virile
   b. famous : unknown
2. HUMOR : COMEDIAN ::
   a. finish line : runner   c. intelligence : genius
   b. lecture : teacher
3. DISLIKE : LOATHE ::
   a. agree : argue   c. tap : wallop
   b. entire : whole
4. RULER : LENGTH ::
   a. altimeter : height   c. calculator : problem
   b. race : mile
5. NEARBY : ADJOINING ::
   a. ocean : shore   c. perpendicular : parallel
   b. noisy : stentorian

> **More Practice**
>
> Academic and Workplace Skills Activity Book
> • p. 16

Studying Words Systematically

Section 29.2

Remembering Vocabulary Words

This section will introduce you to several different methods for listing and studying the new words you find in your school and personal reading. Find the method that works best for you, and follow it regularly.

▶ **KEY CONCEPT** A vocabulary notebook will help you to learn new words. You can use the notebook, flashcards, and a tape recorder to help you review. Study and review new words a few times each week. ■

Set Up a Vocabulary Notebook Keep a section in each of your subject's notebooks for vocabulary words. On the top of each page in the section, write the chapter or book title. Divide your page into three columns that cover the *words* you want to learn, hints or *bridge words* that help you remember their meanings, and their *definitions.*

▶ **Exercise 4** Setting Up a Vocabulary Notebook Select one of your current textbooks or a book you are reading for pleasure that contains new words or terms. As you read, jot down any unfamiliar words or expressions. When you have finished a chapter, look up unfamiliar words in a dictionary or the glossary (if you are studying a textbook). Record "bridge" words and the meanings of new words in your notebook. Then, write a sentence using each word.

Technology Tip

Find a short entry in an on-line encyclopedia about an unfamiliar subject. Find several related words, and prepare a categorized table for your notebook.

▶ Critical Viewing What tools might this student be using to study vocabulary words? **[Infer]**

Studying New Words

Make studying vocabulary a part of your daily activities. Set aside a regular time, such as before you begin your other assignments, to review new words. Use one or more of the following methods to review:

Using Your Notebook Use a book or your hand to cover the definition of a word, and try to remember the meaning by looking at the word and the bridge word. Then, uncover the definition and read it. You can also write sentences with your new vocabulary words. Reinforce the meaning of the word by using its definition in the sentence to give your memory an extra boost.

EXAMPLE: We thought the man was *raucous* because he was so *loud*.

Using Flashcards Use index cards to create your own vocabulary flashcards. On the front of a card, write a word you want to remember. On the back, write its definition. Flip through the cards, and try to supply the definitions, or have a friend test you. Add difficult words to your vocabulary notebook.

Using a Tape Recorder It might be easier for you to learn the definitions of new words when you hear them. If you have a tape recorder, record vocabulary words one at a time. Leave a space of about ten seconds after you record a word, and then record the definition for that word. Continue in this way with all your words. Replay the tape. Try to supply the definition of each word during the space that follows it. Repeat the exercise until you can give the definitions easily. Listen to the tape a few times each week.

Setting Goals Try to memorize new words in small groups each week, so you won't become discouraged. Take five unfamiliar words, and enter them in your notebook. Test yourself on them. Each week, add five more words.

▶ **Exercise 5** Making Flashcards or Tapes Make a set of flashcards or tapes to study the words below. Add more words from your own reading or from assigned vocabulary lists.

1. crescendo
2. scarcity
3. innocuous
4. cajole
5. odious
6. valor
7. sundry
8 intemperance
9. credulous
10. harbingers

Using Reference Aids

Two valuable resources available for building your vocabulary are a dictionary and a thesaurus. You may also have other printed and electronic resources available to help you.

KEY CONCEPT Use a dictionary to find the meaning, spelling, pronunciation, and origin of words. Use a thesaurus to find words that more precisely express your meaning. ■

Using a Dictionary It is a good idea to keep a dictionary nearby to study the pronunciation of a word, note its part of speech, and learn its different definitions or meanings. In addition, most dictionaries provide the origins of a word. Knowing a word's history can help you make associations with other words that share the origin.

Using a Thesaurus A thesaurus provides words with meanings that are the same as, or similar to, the word you are looking up. It may also provide words that reflect subtle differences in meaning. A thesaurus is helpful when you have used the same word repeatedly in your writing and need to vary your writing. You should check the definition in a dictionary to make sure that the new word gives the exact meaning you want.

Using a Synonym Finder Many word-processing programs include on-line synonym finders. While you are writing a draft, you can highlight a word for which you want to find a synonym and use the finder to check alternative words.

Using a Glossary Many textbooks contain a glossary listing terms and definitions specific to the textbook's field of study. Locate the glossary in your textbooks, and use it to help you define the new words in each book.

Using Software Like most references, dictionaries and thesauruses are available in electronic form. Some can be purchased and loaded onto your computer's hard drive, while others are available on the Internet.

Exercise 6 **Using Vocabulary Reference Aids** Look up each of the following words in the references indicated. Compare and contrast the information found in each source.
1. orbit (dictionary, science textbook glossary)
2. society (social studies textbook glossary, dictionary)
3. volatile (dictionary, thesaurus)
4. permeate (science textbook glossary, on-line thesaurus)
5. precipitous (dictionary, thesaurus)

More Practice

Academic and Workplace Skills Activity Book
• pp. 14–17

Studying Word Parts and Origins

Using Roots

The base of a word is its *root*. By learning the meaning of a root, you will have a clue to defining a whole group of related words. For example, if you know the root *puls* (or *pel)* means "drive," you have a key to the meaning of words such as *impulse, repel, propeller, expel, appellate, expulsion,* and *propulsion.*

▶**KEY CONCEPT** A **root** is the base of a word. Many roots come originally from Latin or Greek words. ■

TEN COMMON ROOTS

Root and Origin	Meaning	Examples
-chron- [Gr.]	time	chronicle
-manu- [L.]	hand	manuscript
-mono- [Gr.]	single, alone	monologue
-plic- (-pli-, -ploy-) [L.]	to fold	explicate, pliant, employer, reply
-port- [L.]	to carry	transport
-quir- (-ques-, -quis-) [L.]	to ask, say	require, request, inquisition
-sens- (-sent-, -senti-) [L.]	to feel	sensible, resent, sentiment
-tend- (-tens-, -tent-) [L.]	to stretch	pretend, tense, extent
-top- [Gr.]	place	topographer
-vad- (-vas-) [L.]	to go	pervade, evasive

▶**Exercise 7** **Finding Common Roots** Look up each pair of words in a dictionary, paying close attention to their roots. Then, write the basic meaning shared by each pair of words.
1. intercede, proceed   4. tenant, retain
2. legible, logical   5. convert, diversion
3. conscious, science

▶**Exercise 8** **Using Roots to Define Words** Using the chart to check the italicized roots, select the definition that matches the word. Check your answers in a dictionary.
1. U*top*ia   a. feelings held by many people
2. *port*able   b. operated by hand
3. com*plic*ate   c. to make difficult
4. con*sens*us   d. an imaginary place
5. *manu*al   e. capable of being carried

Using Prefixes

Many prefixes used in English come from the Latin, Greek, and the Anglo-Saxon languages.

KEY CONCEPT A **prefix** is added at the beginning of a word to change its meaning or to form a new word. ■

Learn the meanings and origins of the prefixes below. The abbreviations *L., Gr.,* and *AS.* mean *Latin, Greek,* and *Anglo-Saxon,* the languages from which the prefixes have come.

TEN COMMON PREFIXES		
Prefix and Origin	**Meaning**	**Examples**
ad- (ac-, af-, al-, ap-, as-, at-) [L.]	to, toward	*ad*here, *ac*cede, *as*pect, *at*tend
com- (co-, col-, con-, cor-) [L.]	with, together	*com*rade, *col*lapse, *con*fer, *cor*relate
epi- [Gr.]	on, upon, over	*epi*demic
hyper- [Gr.]	above, excessive	*hyper*bole
mal- [L.]	bad, wrongful	*mal*function
mis- [AS.]	wrong	*mis*trial
pre- [L.]	before	*pre*date
sub- (suc-, suf-, sup-) L.	beneath, under, below	*sub*conscious, *suc*cession, *suf*fer
syn- (syl-, sym-, sys-) [Gr.]	with, together, at the same time	*syn*thesis, *syl*lable, *sym*pathy, *sys*tem
un- [AS.]	not	*un*forgivable

Exercise 9 **Defining Words With Prefixes** Using your knowledge of prefixes, try to match each word on the left with its definition on the right. Check your answers in a dictionary.

1. unerring
2. synergy
3. subvert
4. preamble
5. malodorous

a. foul smelling
b. exact or not wrong
c. cooperative action
d. introduction
e. undermine

Exercise 10 **Defining Prefixes and Prefix Origins** Using a dictionary, write the definition of each prefix and its origin. Then, provide a word that contains each prefix. Define the words you list in a way that incorporates the meaning of the prefix.

1. *anti-*
2. *in-* (*il-, im-, ir-*)
3. *over-*
4. *super-*
5. *ob-* (*o-, oc-, of-, op-*)

More Practice

Academic and Workplace Skills Activity Book
• pp. 19–20

Using Suffixes

A suffix is added to the end of a word. It often alters the part of speech: For example, if you add the suffix *-ion* to the verb *predict*, you form the noun *prediction*.

KEY CONCEPT A **suffix** is a syllable or group of syllables added to the end of a root or word to form a new word. ■

The chart below lists suffixes, their forms, origins, meanings, and words containing each suffix. The abbreviations *L.*, *Gr.*, and *AS.* mean *Latin*, *Greek*, and *Anglo-Saxon*.

TEN COMMON SUFFIXES

Suffix and Origin	Meaning and Examples	Part of Speech
-ac (-ic) [Gr.]	characteristic of; relating to: *posaic*	noun or adjective
-al [L.]	like, suitable for: *comical*	adjective
-ary (-ery) [L.]	pertaining to, connected to: *surgery*	noun or adjective
-cy (-acy) Gr.	condition of: *hesitancy*	noun
-ish [AS.]	of, tending to: *stylish*	adjective
-ive [L.]	tending; a person who: *detective*	noun or adjective
-ize (-ise) [Gr.]	to make: *improvise*	verb
-ly [AS.]	in a certain way: *deliberately*	adjective or adverb
-tion (-ion, -sion, -ation, -ition) [L.]	the action or state of: *friction, motion*	noun
-ure [L.]	act or result of: *pleasure*	noun

Exercise 11 **Defining Suffixes** For each suffix, write its definition and origin, Use a dictionary to assist you. Then, write a word that contains each suffix.

1. -esque
2. -ism
3. -or
4. -ant (-ent)
5. -ance (-ence)

Exercise 12 **Using Suffixes to Form New Words** Add a suffix to each root to form a word that fits the definition given. Write each word with its part of speech. Check the spellings and meanings in a dictionary.

Root	Definition	Word/Part of Speech
1. *graph-*	study of handwriting	?
2. *mot-*	a reason for tending to	?
3. *cap-*	the act of seizing	?
4. *pos-*	the state of being placed	?
5. *laugh-*	causing laughter	?

◉ Technology Tip

Search for an on-line Web site that provides more information about adding suffixes to words. Find five new words, and add them and their definitions to your vocabulary notebook.

More Practice

Academic and Workplace Skills Activity Book
• pp. 19–21

Using Etymologies

Many English words have interesting histories. In fact, more than 70 percent of the words we call English are borrowed from other languages. Other English words have been added to the language in different ways. If you learn about the origins of unfamiliar words, you can determine and remember their meanings more easily. You can find a word's etymology near the beginning of its dictionary entry.

▶ **KEY CONCEPT** **Etymology** is the study of a word's history, its origin. ■

English borrows words from other languages, primarily Greek, Latin, and French.

EXAMPLES: The word *axis* comes from Latin, and the word *gelatin* comes from French.

The English language grows by giving new meaning to old words.

EXAMPLE: The word *havoc* was once an order telling an army to begin plundering.

Words can be invented, or coined, to serve new purposes.

EXAMPLE: The word *boycott* means "refusing to have any dealings with." It was coined from a man's name, Captain C. C. Boycott.

Words can be combined.

EXAMPLE: The word *dictaphone* is a combination of *dictate* and *telephone*.

Words can be shortened.

EXAMPLE: The word *bus* is short for *omnibus*.

▶ **Exercise 13** Using a Dictionary to Learn About **Etymologies** Find the etymology of each word below. Write its meaning, and explain where it originated.

1. diabolical
2. culpable
3. liberty
4. chaos
5. boomerang
6. radar
7. cardigan
8. pajama
9. canyon
10. eon

🔲 Research Tip

Find five unfamiliar words in the dictionary. Look them up in an unabridged dictionary to determine their etymology. Add the new words to your notebook.

▲ Critical Viewing Think of some other English words that use the suffix *tele-* and the root *phone.* **[Apply]**

Improving Your Spelling

Starting a Personal Spelling List

In addition to learning words you are required to study and words on which you will be tested, improve your spelling by starting a personal spelling list.

KEY CONCEPT Select words for your personal spelling list, enter them in your notebook, and study them regularly. ■

Recording Frequently Misspelled Words Make it a practice to keep a list of all the words that you regularly have trouble spelling. Review corrected tests, essays, and home-work to find your personal problem words. Add to the list words that sound the same or similar but have different spellings and meanings, such as *your/you're* or *affect/effect.*

Including Derivatives A derivative is a word that is formed from another word. Once you know how to spell a base word from which the others are formed, you can more easily spell its derivatives.

BASE WORDS: custom, guard

DERIVATIVES: customer, accustomed, guardian, guarded

Identifying Your Error Patterns Sometimes your spelling errors may follow a pattern, such as adding an extra syllable to a word (*athelete,* instead of *athlete).* Learn to identi-fy the error patterns in your misspellings. The chart below lists common error patterns. Your own error patterns may be similar to or different from these:

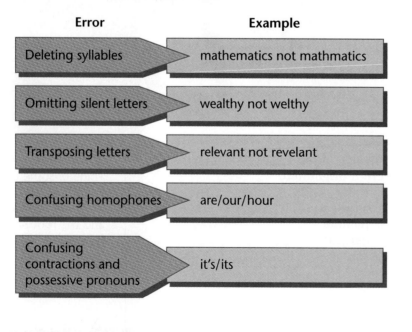

Error	Example
Deleting syllables	mathematics not mathmatics
Omitting silent letters	wealthy not welthy
Transposing letters	relevant not revelant
Confusing homophones	are/our/hour
Confusing contractions and possessive pronouns	it's/its

> **Exercise 14** **Identifying Error Patterns** Each sentence below contains one or more incorrect spellings. Identify the error pattern of the misspelled word, and write the correct spelling. Then, look over the writing you have done in the past two weeks. Circle misspelled words in your work, and try to identify your own error patterns.
> 1. A burgular climbed down the chiminey of our house.
> 2. Accept for Rob, everyone was in the living room.
> 3. The group did not condem Rob for being late.
> 4. There all waiting for him now.
> 5. We new he went to the pharmacy to get a perscription filled.

Studying Your Problem Words

Review sessions can help you to master problem words. Whether you have trouble with everyday words or words you seldom use, you can use a study system to help you. The four steps listed in the chart below will help you.

STEPS FOR REVIEWING PROBLEM WORDS
1. *Look* at each word carefully to notice the arrangement or pattern of the letters. Try to see the word in your mind.
2. *Pronounce* each syllable of the word to yourself.
3. *Write* the word and check its spelling in the dictionary.
4. *Review* your list until you can write each word correctly.

> **KEY CONCEPT** Review your personal spelling list several times each week. ■

> **Exercise 15** **Using a Dictionary for Spelling Help** Use a dictionary to answer each question below. Record your answers on your paper.
> 1. Of *affect* and *effect*, which one is usually used as a verb?
> 2. How is the pronunciation of *psychic* indicated?
> 3. Which is correct: *begginning* or *beginning*?
> 4. Which spelling is listed first: *catalogue* or *catalog*?
> 5. What is the difference in meaning between *corps* and *core*?

> **Exercise 16** **Recording Problem Words** In your notebook, record words you have misspelled in your compositions or tests. Prepare columns for misspelled words, correct spellings, and hints for remembering the correct spellings.

🔘 Research Tip

Choose five words from the dictionary that would be problem words for you. Add them to your spelling notebook, and enter the rules that apply to each one.

> **More Practice**

Academic and Workplace Skills Activity Book
• pp. 22–23

Applying Spelling Rules

In addition to studying words that give you particular trouble, you should study rules that apply to groups of words. Keep a spelling rules section in your vocabulary notebook. Write down the rules you learn in this section, and keep examples of words that follow those rules. Also, keep examples of words that are exceptions to the rules. You should look for examples in your reading and in your writing.

Spelling Changes When Adding Suffixes to Words Ending in *e*

Rule: There is no change if the suffix starts with a consonant.

Examples: settlement

Examples From My Writing:
"I felt tremendously *grateful* that no one had done anything *careless* in the glass museum."
—from "A Visit Abroad" (personal story)

Examples From My Reading:
"Turning from her own face as *precipitately* as she had gone to meet it, she went to the chest where the things were, unlocked it, threw up the lid, and knelt to search."
—from "The Demon Lover" by Elizabeth Bowen

Adding Suffixes

Adding a suffix often involves making a spelling change in the original word. Here are some rules you should learn:

> **KEY CONCEPT** Use the following rules for spelling changes when adding suffixes to words ending in *y*. ■

1. When adding a suffix to words ending in *y* preceded by a consonant, change *y* to *i* except for suffixes beginning with *i*:

mercy + -*ful* = merciful	whimsy + -*cal* = whimsical
defy + -*ance* = defiance	defy + -*ing* = *defying*
hurry + -*ing* = hurrying	dry + -*ing* = drying

2. For words ending in a *y* preceded by a vowel, make no change when adding most suffixes, with a few exceptions:

convey + -*ance* = conveyor	employ + -*ment* = employment
day + -*ly* = daily	pay + -*ed* = paid

▶ **KEY CONCEPT** Use the following rules for spelling changes when adding suffixes to words ending in *e*. ■

1. For words ending in *e*, drop the *e* when adding a suffix beginning with a vowel. Exceptions are (1) words ending in *ce* or *ge* with suffixes beginning with *a* or *o*, (2) words ending in *ee*, and (3) a few special words:

   prove + *-able* = provable   strive + *-ing* = driving
   notice + *-able* = noticeable   care + *-ing* = caring
   foresee + *-able* = foreseeable   hoe + *-ing* = hoeing
   dye + *-ing* = dyeing   be + *-ing* = being

2. For words ending in *e*, make no change when adding a suffix beginning with a consonant, with a few exceptions:

   care + *-ful* = careful   love + *-ly* = lovely
   argue + *-ment* = argument   judge + *-ment* = judgment
   true + *-ly* = truly

▶ **KEY CONCEPT** Use these rules for cases in which a final consonant may or may not change when adding a suffix. ■

1. For words ending consonant + vowel + consonant in a stressed syllable, double the final consonant when adding a suffix beginning with a vowel. The exceptions to the rules are (1) words ending in *x* or *w* and (2) words in which the stress changes after the suffix is added:

   run´ + *-y* = run´ ny   forbid´ + *-en* = forbid´ den
   box + *-ed* = boxed   draw + *-ing* = drawing
   refer´ + *-ence* = ref´ erence   confer´ + *-ence* = con´ ference

2. For words ending consonant + vowel + consonant in a unstressed syllable, make no change when adding a suffix beginning with a vowel. There are no major exceptions:

   an´ gel + *-ic* = angel´ ic   bud´ get + *-ed* = bud´ geted

▶ **Exercise 17** **Spelling Words With Suffixes** Write the correct spelling for the words below. Check your answers in a dictionary.

1. propel + *-er*
2. wrap + *-ing*
3. peace + *-ful*
4. arrive + *-ing*
5. extreme + *-ity*
6. complete + *-ly*
7. marry + *-age*
8. medal + *-ion*
9. liberal + *-ize*
10. acquit + *-al*
11. confine + *-ing*
12. repeal + *-ed*
13. compel + *-ed*
14. judge + *-ment*
15. classify + *-ed*
16. whole + *-some*
17. copy + *-er*
18. shutter + *-ed*
19. chilly + *-er*
20. suspense + *-ful*

▶ **More Practice**

Academic and Workplace Skills Activity Book
• p. 25

Adding Prefixes

> **KEY CONCEPT** When a prefix is added to a root word, the spelling of the root word remains the same. ∎

EXAMPLES: *dis-* + satisfy = dissatisfy
un- + necessary = unnecessary

> **Exercise 18** **Spelling Words With Prefixes** Form new words by combining the prefixes and root words below.
> 1. *il-* + literate
> 2. *mis-* + interpret
> 3. *re-* + engineer
> 4. *dis-* + solve
> 5. *un-* known

More Practice

Academic and
Workplace Skills
Activity Book
• pp. 24–25

Forming Plurals

The plural form of a noun means "more than one." The plural forms can be either *regular* or *irregular*.

Regular Plurals Most nouns have regular plural forms. Their plurals are formed by adding *-s* or *-es* to the singular form of the noun.

> **KEY CONCEPT** The regular plural form of most nouns is formed by adding *-s* or *-es* to the singular form. Occasionally, you may also have to change a letter or two in the word. ∎

The spelling of some regular nouns changes in the plural form. Check the rules below for examples that change slightly.

1. Words ending in *s, ss, x, z, sh,* or *ch*: Add *-es* to the base word:

   business + *-es* = businesses   walrus + *-es* = walruses
   box + *-es* = boxes   church + *-es* = churches
   waltz +*-es* = waltzes   dish + *-es* = dishes

2. Words ending in *y* or *o* preceded by a vowel: Add *-s* to the base word:

   donkey + *-s* = donkeys   guy + *-s* = guys
   radio + *-s* = radios   journey + *-s* = journeys

3. Words ending in *y* preceded by a consonant: Change the *y* to *i* and add *-es*. For most words ending in *o* preceded by a consonant, add *-es*. Musical terms ending in *o* simply add *-s*:

   colony + *-ies* = colonies   fly + *-ies* = flies
   tomato + *-es* = tomatoes   soprano + *-s* = sopranos

4. Words ending in *f* or *fe*: Change the *f* or *fe* to *v* and add *-es*. For words ending *ff*, always add *-s*:

   wolf + *-es* = wolves   dwarf + *-es* = dwarves
   life + *-es* = lives   cliff + *-s* = cliffs
   belief + *-s* = beliefs   gulf + *-s* = gulfs

Irregular Plurals Irregular plurals are not formed according to the rules on page 816. If you are unsure how to form a plural, check a dictionary. Irregular plurals are usually listed directly after the pronunciation of the word. If no plural form is given in the dictionary, simply add -s or -es to the singular form.

▶**KEY CONCEPT** Use the dictionary to look up the correct spelling of irregular plurals, and memorize them. ■

Below is a list of common irregular plurals.

IRREGULAR PLURALS		
Singular Forms	**Ways of Forming Plurals**	**Plural Forms**
ox	add -en	oxen
child	add -ren	children
tooth, mouse, woman	change one or more letters	teeth, mice, women
radius, focus, alumnus	change -us to -i	radii, foci, alumni
alumna	change -a to -ae	alumnae
crisis, emphasis	change -is to -es	crises, emphases
medium, datum, curriculum	change -um to -a	media, data, curricula
phenomenon, criterion	change -on to -a	phenomena, criteria
deer, sheep	plural form same as singular	deer, sheep
	plural form only	scissors, slacks

Note About *Plurals of Compound Words:* To form the plural of a compound word—that is, a word made up of two or more separate or hyphenated words—add -s or -es to the main noun in the compound word. For example, *rule of thumb* becomes *rules of thumb*, and *editor-in-chief* becomes *editors-in-chief*.

▶**Exercise 19** Forming Plurals Write the plural for each word. Consult a dictionary if possible.

1. radio
2. soprano
3. wife
4. fox
5. supply
6. lynx
7. chief
8. son-in-law
9. crisis
10. x-ray
11. tomato
12. waltz
13. rodeo
14. mouse
15. criterion
16. alumnus
17. gratuity
18. fantasy
19. ballerina
20. memorandum

▶**More Practice**

Academic and Workplace Skills Activity Book
• p. 24

Plurals of Compound Words Most compound nouns that are one word have regular plural forms. If one part of the compound noun is irregular, the plural form will also be irregular.

EXAMPLE: thunderstorm, thunderstorms (regular)
stepchild, stepchildren (irregular)

When you are forming the plural of a compound word written as two or more separate or hyphenated words, add *-s* or *-es* to the singular form of the word being modified by the other word.

EXAMPLE: bucket seat, bucket seats
passer-by, passers-by

> **Exercise 20** **Forming Plurals** Write the plural for each word. Consult a dictionary if necessary, and add any difficult words to your personal spelling list.

1. leaf
2. circus
3. memorandum
4. fly
5. waltz
6. pen pal
7. roof
8. lunch
9. datum
10. radio
11. alumnus
12. loaf
13. jelly
14. solo
15. mouse
16. echo
17. potato
18. salmon
19. enemy
20. attorney-at-law

Spelling *ie* and *ei* Words and Words Ending in *-cede*, *-ceed*, and *-sede*

> **KEY CONCEPTS** For *ie* and *ei* words, use the traditional rule *i* before *e* except after *c* or when sounded like *a*, as in *neighbor* or *weigh*. Memorize the exceptions. Words that end in *-cede*, *-ceed*, and *-sede* should be memorized. ■

Exceptions for *ie* words: counterfeit, either, foreign, forfeit, heifer, height, heir, leisure, neither, seismology, seize, sheik, sleight, sovereign, their, weird

Exceptions for *ei* words: ancient, conscience, efficient, financier, sufficient

Spelling Homophones

▶ **KEY CONCEPT** Homophones are words that sound alike but have different meanings and may have different spellings. ■

The following homophones sometimes cause spelling problems:

EXAMPLES:

their:	a possessive pronoun that means "belonging to them"
they're:	a contraction for "they are"
there:	a sentence starter or word meaning "in that place"
brake:	a verb meaning "slow down or stop" or a noun meaning "a device for slowing or stopping"
break:	a verb meaning "cause to come apart" or a noun meaning "a fracture"
clothes:	a plural noun meaning "wearing apparel"
close:	a verb meaning "shut"
passed:	the past tense of the verb *pass*
past:	a word meaning "time gone by" or a preposition meaning "beyond"
principal:	a noun meaning "head of a school" or an adjective meaning "main"
principle:	a noun meaning "a rule or belief"
write:	a verb meaning "put words on paper"
right:	an adjective meaning "correct"

▶ **Exercise 21** **Spelling Homophones** Select the correct word in parentheses, Check your answers in a dictionary. Add misspelled words to your personal spelling list, and review them.
1. I (past, passed) this car several times on the highway.
2. I put on the (break, brake) to slow down.
3. I wonder if (there, they're) planning to attend the meeting.
4. What is your (principal, principle) objection to the rule?
5. Would you please (write, right) it down for me?

▶ **Exercise 22** **Writing Sentences With Homophones** Write a sentence using each word in the pairs below. Check a dictionary to make sure you are using and spelling each word correctly.
1. (a) to   (b) too
2. (a) stationary   (b) stationery
3. (a) plain   (b) plane
4. (a) miner   (b) minor
5. (a) site   (b) cite

⊚ Technology Tip

Spelling checkers will not catch homophones that you have misused. Proofread all of your work, even if you have used an electronic spell checker.

▶ **More Practice**

Academic and Workplace Skills Activity Book
• p. 26

Understanding the Influence of Other Language and Cultures

Most languages have a set of rules for spelling and pronunciation that are predictable and constant. In English, however, more than 70 percent of the words are borrowed words. Along with a borrowed word comes some unique features of the spelling and pronunciation of the original language. For this reason, English uses a variety of letters to spell the same sounds.

EXAMPLE: *f* sound in puff, cough, fuel, phone

j sound in giraffe, jump, page

k sound in call, keep, pack, hike

For the same reason, English words often contain "silent letters."

EXAMPLE: silent *p* in pneumonia, psychiatrist, ptomaine

silent *k* in knowledge, knuckle, knot

silent *b* in climb, dumb, crumb

Be aware of these problem areas, and use a print or electronic dictionary to confirm the spelling of any word about which you are unsure.

▲ **Critical Viewing** Where do you think the word *giraffe* comes from? Why? **[Deduce]**

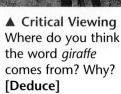

Exercise 23 Choosing the Correct Spelling On your paper, write the correct word from each group. Check your answers in a dictionary. Note the language from which each word originates.

1. -silouette   silhouette   siluette
2. -succumb   sucumm   sukkum
3. -maline   malign   malin
4. -reck   wrek   wreck
5. -exaust   exost   exhaust
6. troff   trough   trouff
7. chrome   krome   crome
8. baray   beray   beret
9. leasure   leesure   leisure
10. scheme   skeam   skeem

Proofreading

It is a good idea to get into the habit of proofreading everything you write for spelling errors. By proofreading, you can eliminate misspellings caused by hasty writing, and you will begin to pinpoint words that present problems. You should also use a dictionary, electronic spell checker, and a textbook glossary to check your spelling.

KEY CONCEPT The more you proofread, the easier it will be for you to spot your errors. Use a variety or combination of strategies. ■

- Proofread your work by slowly reading it, aloud or silently, to yourself.

- Proofread only one line at a time. Use a ruler or other device to focus on the line you are proofreading.

- Read backward, from the last word to the first. This forces you to focus only on the words themselves.

- Consult a dictionary if you suspect a word is misspelled.

- Check the spelling of proper nouns.

Exercise 24 **Proofreading for Spelling Errors** Copy and proofread the following paragraph, correcting spelling errors.

Sometimes, large numbers of people are neglected by the estableshed orgens of communication. When that happens, new media are deviced. This press of the masses might be considered elamental and emotionel. Ordnarily, the masses will probly prefer journelism that could be called "sensationel." In 1620, 1833, the 1890s, and 1920, there was a waive of sensationelizm.

More Practice

Academic and Workplace Skills Activity Book
- p. 28

Reflecting on Your Spelling and Vocabulary

Think about what you have learned in this chapter by asking yourself the following questions:

- Which of the techniques do I find the most effective for studying spelling words?

- Which do I find the most effective for studying vocabulary words?

- What do the techniques have in common? In what ways are they different?

Standardized Test Preparation Workshop

Analogies

Analogy questions on standardized tests test your vocabulary. In order to answer an analogy question correctly, you must first determine the relationship between the original pair.

When determining the relationship between words, use the parts of speech as a clue. The words in the correct answer choice will often, but not always, be the same parts of speech combination (nouns, pronouns, verbs, adjectives, or adverbs) as the original pair. Then, find a more specific relationship between the words; the following are relationship types that are most commonly tested:

- Antonyms
- Part-Whole or Whole-Part
- Definitional/Synonyms
- Cause-Effect or Effect-Cause
- Functional Relationship
- Relationship of Degrees

Test Tips

- Make sure that your choice reflects or parallels the structure in the given word pair.
- Sometimes, the relationship between two words is multiple. Always probe beneath the first relationship you recognize to see if there is a less obvious but more important secondary relationship.
- Parts of speech may be a clue. Often, but not always, the correct answer choice will be a word with the same part of speech as the given word pair.

Sample Test Item

Directions: Each question below consists of a related pair of words, followed by five pairs of words labeled *A* through *E*. Select the pair that best expresses a relationship similar to that expressed in the original pair.

CEASE-FIRE : HOSTILITIES::

(A) reckoning : probabilities

(B) truce : belligerents

(C) artillery : tanks

(D) campaign : strategies

(E) adjournment : proceedings

Answer and Explanation

The correct answer is *(E)*. The noun *adjournment* is caused by the end of proceedings, also a noun. In the original pair, the noun *cease-fire* is caused by the end of hostilities, also a noun. Answers *(B)* and *(D)* express a similar relationship to the original pair, but neither pair expresses an end to an occurrence. For example, a *truce* is not an end to *belligerents,* and a *campaign* is not an end of *strategies.* Answers *(A)* and *(C)* do not express a cause-effect relationship.

▶ **Practice 1** **Directions:** Each question below consists of a related pair of words or phrases, followed by five pairs of word or phrases labeled *A* through *E*. Select the pair that best expresses a relationship similar to that expressed in the original pair.

1 CRAVEN : COWARDLY ::
   A liberal : conservative
   B juvenile : adult
   C genuine : fake
   D feeble : fragile
   E regal : common

2 IMPERVIOUS : ACCESSIBLE ::
   A impertinent : interfering
   B articulate : eloquent
   C parched : dry
   D priceless : invaluable
   E obstinate : pliable

3 ISOLATION : LONELINESS ::
   A gloomy : murky
   B affliction : comfort
   C explanation : comprehension
   D happiness : disaster
   E impartial : partial

4 SCIENCE : ASTRONOMY ::
   A geology : physical science
   B star : planet
   C notes : music
   D chemistry : biology
   E computer language : BASIC

5 PARSIMONY : STINGINESS ::
   A falsehood : verity
   B greed : generosity
   C extraneous : relevant
   D enthusiasm : passivity
   E candor : forthrightness

6 INSOLVENT : BANKRUPT ::
   A rich : poor
   B lethargic : sluggish
   C wealthy : fortune
   D impoverished : poverty
   E serious : humorous

7 DETERIORATE : CORROSION ::
   A rain : flood
   B lecture : lesson
   C perplex : mystery
   D musician : orchestra
   E fatigue : invigoration

8 INNOCUOUS : HARMLESS ::
   A sensitive : insensitive
   B habitual : occasional
   C joyous : pleased
   D despicable : contemptible
   E social : antisocial

9 CHALK : CHALKBOARD ::
   A pen : paper
   B needle : thread
   C eraser : mistake
   D brush : paint
   E crayon : drawing

10 CANKER : DECAY ::
   A tense : fear
   B sun : moon
   C automobile : driver
   D tragedy : grief
   E destruction : earthquake

What does it mean to be a good reader? As you will learn in this chapter, effective reading means more than simply understanding the words you read. As you become a more mature thinker, it will become increasingly important to read critically and to develop the skills necessary to meaningfully evaluate the material you read. These important skills will serve you for years to come, in your schoolwork as well as in your personal reading.

▲ Critical Viewing
What type of reading do you think this student is doing? Why do you think so?
[Speculate]

Reading Methods and Tools

You will use reading skills your whole life. In college, you will read books and textbooks. On the job, you will read materials from a variety of sources, such as manuals or handbooks. Reading successfully requires that you think critically, taking in as much important information as you can.

Using Sections of Textbooks

Textbooks are organized so that you can learn the information they contain with ease and efficiency. Textbooks are divided into segments that contain reading and study aids that help you understand and remember the information.

▶ **KEY CONCEPT** Use textbook reading and study aids to help you understand and remember what you read. ■

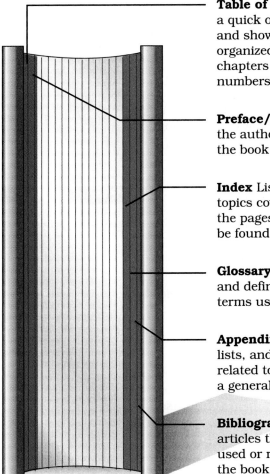

Table of Contents Provides a quick overview of the book and shows how the book is organized by listing units and chapters with their page numbers

Preface/Introduction States the author's purpose in writing the book

Index Lists alphabetically all topics covered in the book and the pages on which they can be found

Glossary Lists alphabetically and defines all specialized terms used in the book

Appendix Includes charts, lists, and other materials related to the book's subject; a general reference source

Bibliography Lists books and articles that the author has used or referred to in writing the book

Research Tip

Imagine that you will be writing a book on your favorite academic topic. Seek out books in a library or bookstore that would be most useful to you in your research. Write a bibliography, table of contents, and introduction to your imaginary book. All three of these elements should give your readers a clear sense of what the contents of your intended book will be.

Using Features of Textbooks

Textbooks have special features designed to help you find, organize, and review material.

KEY CONCEPT Use the special features of your textbook to aid your reading and studying of the material. ■

Titles, Headings, and Subheadings Printed in large, heavy type and in different sizes and colors, headings give you an idea of what the material is about. They also divide the material into sections so that you can learn it more easily. Main topics usually have larger and more prominent headings; subtopics have smaller headings.

Overviews Often, a chapter or unit will begin with an overview, an outline, or a summary of what will be covered. Use the overview to preview and review the chapter or unit.

Questions and Exercises These are often located at the end of a chapter. Review questions and exercises before you read the chapter to give you an idea of the main points to look for as you read. Afterward, answer the questions and exercises to retain the information you have read.

Pictures, Captions, and Graphics A picture can make a confusing idea clearer. Usually, next to a picture there is a caption—information describing the picture. Graphics—such as maps, charts, and diagrams—present complex information in a clear format.

Exercise 1 **Examining Two Textbooks** Select two textbooks on different subjects, and evaluate them by answering these questions:
1. How is the table of contents in each text organized (by theme, chronologically, or by some other method)?
2. If the text contains a preface, does it explain the book's purpose and give suggestions for using the book? In which of the books is the preface more helpful?
3. Which text's chapter headings can you more easily turn into questions?
4. Are the end-of-chapter questions in each text useful for study? Are the questions in one text more helpful?
5. Does each text contain an index, a glossary, an appendix, and a bibliography? How do the elements help you to use the book's material?

More Practice

Academic and Workplace Skills Activity Book
• p. 29

Using Reading Strategies

Vary Your Reading Style

By the time you are a senior in high school, you have probably established a reading style that incorporates the important reading skills: skimming, scanning, and close reading. Understanding which skill is suitable to your purpose and material is as important as understanding your learning style or style of communication.

▶ **KEY CONCEPT** Adjust your reading style whenever your purpose in reading changes. ■

Skimming involves reading a text quickly to get a general overview of its contents. You skim a book when you are previewing it or trying to get a broad idea of its meaning. Skimming is perhaps most useful to review material that you have previously read more carefully.

Scanning involves leafing through several pages at a time, paying attention to section heads and subheads and the general contents. You scan when you do research or when you are trying to locate a particular piece of information.

Close reading is just what it sounds like—reading a text closely to understand and remember its main ideas, to find relationships between ideas, and to draw conclusions. You read closely when you are studying a text and trying to make sense of and retain information.

Use Question-Answer Relationships (QARs)

Understanding how questions are written can help you answer them. There are four general types of questions. Learning to identify these types will help you answer questions more easily. You can also improve your reading skills by asking and answering these types of questions as you read:

1. **Right There** This type of question deals with answers that are right there in the text, usually in one or two sentences.

2. **Think and Search** The answer to this type of question is in the text, but you need to think about the question's answer and then search for evidence to support it.

3. **Author and You** These questions call on you to consider what the author says and connect it to what you know.

4. **On Your Own** The answers to these questions are not in the text. They require you to draw on your experiences.

Use the SQ4R Method

You can use a book's organization to your advantage by mastering the following six skills: *Survey, Question, Read, Record, Recite,* and *Review,* abbreviated as SQ4R.

KEY CONCEPT Use the SQ4R method to guide your reading and to help you recall information later. ■

Following are explanations of each step:

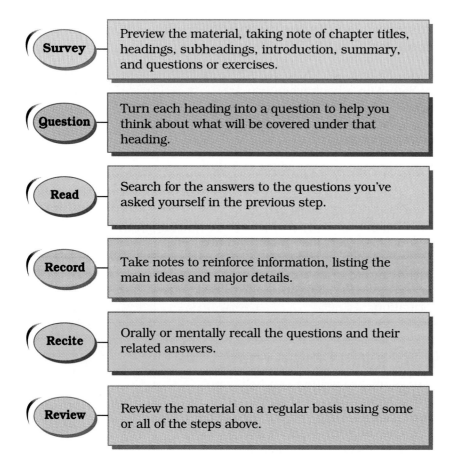

Survey — Preview the material, taking note of chapter titles, headings, subheadings, introduction, summary, and questions or exercises.

Question — Turn each heading into a question to help you think about what will be covered under that heading.

Read — Search for the answers to the questions you've asked yourself in the previous step.

Record — Take notes to reinforce information, listing the main ideas and major details.

Recite — Orally or mentally recall the questions and their related answers.

Review — Review the material on a regular basis using some or all of the steps above.

Exercise 2 **Using Reading Styles and Strategies** Choose three nonfiction books on different topics. Use the first book to help you practice varying your reading style. Start by skimming the whole book. Note what this activity reveals about the main topics. Then, scan through to find a section that especially interests you. Complete a close reading of this section, and take detailed notes. Next, choose sections from the second and third books, and apply the QAR and SQ4R strategies, respectively. Take notes as you apply the strategies.

More Practice

Academic and Workplace Skills Activity Book
• p. 30

Using Graphic Organizers

A graphic organizer is an excellent tool for summarizing and reviewing information, as well as for showing relationships between ideas. Match your choice of graphic organizer to the way in which the various parts of your subject are related.

> ▶ **KEY CONCEPT** Use graphic organizers to help you under-stand relationships between ideas in a text. ■

Analyze Comparison-and-Contrast Structure

Venn diagrams are extremely useful tools for demonstrating points of similarity and differences between two or more subjects. They can be used to analyze different characters, settings, or themes. If you have two subjects to compare, use a Venn diagram with two circles; if you have three, use one with three circles. Use the illustration below as an example.

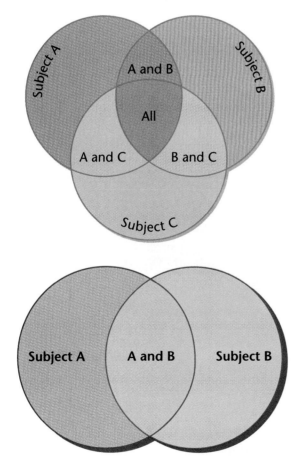

⊛ **Technology Tip**

Using a computer, see if you can design a graphic organizer like one of those that appear in this chapter.

Chart Main Points and Subtopics

Herringbone organizers can help you organize your main ideas and supporting details, show multiple causes of a complex event, or pinpoint areas for research. The sample below shows how you would use a herringbone organizer to analyze the actions that reveal a character's traits.

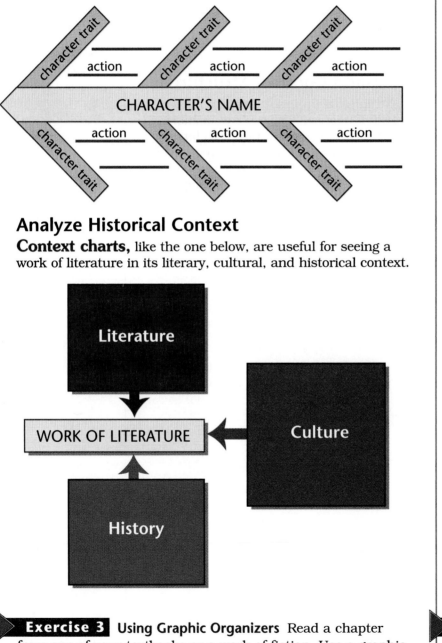

Analyze Historical Context

Context charts, like the one below, are useful for seeing a work of literature in its literary, cultural, and historical context.

▶ **Exercise 3** **Using Graphic Organizers** Read a chapter from one of your textbooks or a work of fiction. Use a graphic organizer to present the information from the text.

▶ **More Practice**

Academic and Workplace Skills Activity Book
• p. 32

Reading Nonfiction Critically

Section 30.2

Nonfiction is writing that has a basis in fact. Nonfiction provides a fine source for gathering information on just about any subject. However, just because information is published in a book or an article doesn't ensure that it is accurate. You need to read nonfiction critically, analyzing what the writer is saying and evaluating the credibility of the writer's points.

Analyzing and Evaluating Nonfiction

▶ **KEY CONCEPT** Use critical reading strategies to analyze, evaluate, and form judgments about nonfiction. ■

Make Inferences Not every point a writer makes is stated directly. It is often left up to the reader to "read between the lines" by making inferences, or drawing conclusions, based on what the writer does provide. For example, if a writer points out the major impact of a specific battle, you might infer that the battle was an important one.

Make Generalizations When you make a generalization, you piece together a related set of facts and details on one topic to make a broad statement about that topic.

Recognize the Author's Purpose or Bias It is important to recognize that every writer wants to achieve a specific purpose through writing. Sometimes, this goal involves persuading readers or telling just one side of a story. When writing to persuade, writers usually have a bias, or point of view. Watch out for language and details that suggest a bias.

Evaluate the Writer's Points or Statements Note each of the facts, statistics, and other evidence that a writer offers in support of his or her position. Evaluate whether the examples are strong ones and whether enough are presented.

Evaluate Credibility Check to see that a writer has expertise or has done thorough research in the topic being covered.

Recognize Persuasive Techniques Don't be swayed by appeals to emotion—even if the topic is one about which you have strong opinions.

Technology Tip

Treat material that you find on the Internet the same way you would treat material in a book or magazine. Read critically to evaluate it, looking for purpose and bias.

▶ **Exercise 4** **Analyzing and Evaluating Nonfiction** Design a six-column chart, labeled with the strategies above. Then, read a nonfiction article, and fill in the chart as you read.

Distinguishing Fact From Opinion

One of the single most essential skills in being an effective critical reader is the ability to distinguish fact from opinion.

KEY CONCEPT As you read, separate facts from opinions, and check to see that writers back up their opinions with facts. ■

A **fact** is the most reliable type of information because it can be verified, or proved true objectively. A fact can be verified in several ways: records searching, experimentation, and personal observation. The method you choose to determine whether or not a fact is accurate will depend on the type of statement made.

An **opinion** is a statement that cannot be proved because it is subjective; that is, influenced by personal experiences and beliefs. Opinions are most often expressed as personal feelings, judgments, or predictions. Sometimes, facts and opinions can be hard to distinguish. In persuasive writing, such as editorials and speeches, opinions are often couched in what appear to be factual statements.

When opinions are presented in a piece of nonfiction, they should be thoroughly backed up by facts. When evaluating an author's opinions, check to see that the opinions have been thoroughly supported.

▼ Critical Viewing
Why is it important for this student to distinguish fact from opinion when he is reading magazines? **[Analyze]**

Exercise 5 Analyzing Fact and Opinion Statements

Identify each statement below as *fact* or *opinion*. For each fact, list a source or method you could use to verify it. For each opinion, tell whether it could be supported by facts.
1. *Hamlet* is Shakespeare's longest play.
2. The information gathered by space-shuttle missions does not justify the high expenditures of the program.
3. Napoleon was born on the island of Corsica.
4. Children today are subject to greater stress than those in earlier times because fewer live with both natural parents.
5. Ingrid Bergman's finest role was as Ilsa in *Casablanca*.

> **More Practice**
>
> Academic and Workplace Skills Activity Book
> • p. 34

Applying Modes of Reasoning

In addition to applying critical reading strategies to the nonfiction you read, it is important to use sound critical reasoning skills, such as the following:

Inductive Reasoning This strategy proceeds from specific facts to a conclusion, or generalization, based on those facts. A valid generalization is a statement supported by evidence and holds true in a large number of cases. To determine, for example, whether apples in a basket are sweet for eating or tart for cooking, you sample many of the apples. If the apples you taste are all sweet, then you might conclude that all the apples are eating apples. Of course, when you reason inductively like this, the more evidence you have, the sounder your generalization will be.

Deductive Reasoning This strategy starts with a general statement that is assumed to be true and applies that statement to a particular case, whereas induction starts with facts and proceeds to a general statement. The purpose of deduction is to determine whether a particular case fits the general rule. A deductive argument is typically stated in a three-part formula called a *syllogism*, as shown in the following example.

SYLLOGISM: All mammals are warmblooded.
                (major premise)
                Whales are mammals.
                (minor premise)
                Therefore, whales are warmblooded.
                (conclusion)

If the premises of a syllogism are true and properly worded, the conclusion is sound, like the one above.

Examining a Syllogism When examining a syllogism, ask yourself the following three questions:

QUESTIONS FOR TESTING SYLLOGISMS
1. Is the major premise true? (Could it have been arrived at inductively through studying enough examples?)
2. Is the fact stated in the minor premise true?
3. Does the conclusion follow logically from each premise?

Research Tip

To understand the use of generalizations, research the published results of polls and surveys. Note the conclusions drawn from the results, and determine whether the generalizations are hasty or valid.

Logical Fallacies Logical fallacies are errors in logic. One type of logical fallacy is a hasty generalization, a generalization based on only a few facts or samples. Tasting only one apple and deciding that the whole basket contains sweet apples is an example of a hasty generalization.

A *non sequitur* (Latin for "it does not follow") is another type of logical fallacy in which a conclusion is drawn that does not follow from the evidence given.

NON SEQUITUR: Members of Congress are elected by the people. They make laws in Washington, D.C. They know what is best for the country.

The fact that members of Congress are elected by the people to make laws does not mean that they always know or do what is right. The conclusion does not follow from the evidence that is given.

Other Forms of Reasoning Induction and deduction are not the only forms of reasoning. There are two other forms that are used to draw valid conclusions: *cause and effect* and *analogy.*

A **cause-and-effect** sequence is one in which something is caused by one or more events that happened previously. False cause-and-effect reasoning makes a connection between two unrelated events.

An **analogy** is a comparison of two things that are alike in a number of important ways. A good analogy can promote understanding of something unfamiliar by comparing it with something familiar. A false analogy ignores obvious and important differences between the things compared.

▶ **Exercise 6** Analyzing Forms of Reasoning Identify the form of reasoning (*inductive* or *deductive, cause-and-effect, analogy*) found in each of the following statements, and explain whether it is valid or invalid.

1. It has been below freezing for three nights in a row, but the water in this pail beside the garage hasn't frozen. It must have antifreeze in it.
2. America in the 1930's was like the Roman Empire whose economic conditions brought about its collapse.
3. The Roman Empire collapsed after a period of great prosperity. We must guard against too much prosperity in this country or risk suffering a similar fate.
4. Mr. Ruiz won a million dollars in the lottery. A week later, he won two thousand dollars. His good luck the first time made him lucky again.
5. All humans are bipeds. An ostrich is a biped. An ostrich is a human.

▶ **More Practice**

Academic and Workplace Skills Activity Book
• p. 35

Analyzing and Evaluating

Evaluate the Use of Language

Critical reading demands that you be attentive to the ways writers use language to convey their thoughts. Following are some types of language usage of which you should be aware:

Denotation and Connotation When speakers or writers have a neutral attitude toward their subject and are simply interested in conveying information, they will use language in its *denotative,* or literal, sense. Speakers or writers who want to subtly influence their audience's attitude will use more *connotative* language, or words with negative or positive associations surrounding them.

DENOTATION: The team defeated its opponent.

CONNOTATION: The team soundly thrashed its opponent.

Irony Irony refers to a contrast between perception and reality; between what is said and what is actually meant. Writers use irony to highlight key points and to create humor.

EXAMPLE: The game flew by, lasting only five hours and extending into the time of night when only the worst of insomniacs are still awake.

Understatement When an idea is played down or treated casually, it is considered to be an understatement.

Inflated Language and Jargon Inflated language refers to overly scholarly or scientific language. One type of inflated language is called jargon. Jargon is the specialized vocabulary used by people in a particular field. In its place, it is useful, but jargon is often misused to impress the reader or to conceal meaning.

Euphemism A euphemism is a word or phrase used to replace words that may be considered offensive.

Slanting Slanting is the writing of a passage so that it leans toward one point of view or presents just one side of the story. Choosing words with either positive or negative connotations is one type of slanting. Another type of slanting is presenting only one side of an issue by leaving out important facts that would support another point of view. For example, a story on the negative impact of a tax increase would be slanted if it failed to mention the benefits of the increase.

▲ Critical Viewing
Write a denotative and a connotative description of what is happening in this photograph. [Interpret]

Identify the Author's Purpose

When you have finished reading a work of nonfiction, piece together all the information you have gathered about the author's purpose, the use of language, the presentation of facts and opinions, and the forms of reasoning that have been offered to draw your final conclusions about the work and its effectiveness. Consider these questions:

Criteria For Critical Reading

1. Does the author accomplish his or her purpose? Is there an honest use of language to reveal meaning, or does the author use techniques to distort meaning?

2. Does the author have something of value to say? What are the implications of the author's ideas? How are they related to other ideas?

3. Does the author have something valuable to say to you? How do the author's ideas increase your understanding or change your way of looking at things?

▶ **Exercise 7** **Making Final Judgments** Apply the questions above to the following passage:

The newcomer population of Boston has grown dramatically in recent years. The 1990 Census showed 114,547 foreign-born residents living in the Boston Metro Area—the fourteenth largest concentration in the United States. These newcomers face multiple barriers to economic self-sufficiency. Many received little or no education in their countries of origin, and their English language skills are minimal. In their home countries, they were seamstresses, farmers, shopkeepers, street vendors, military personnel—backgrounds that do not translate well to the modern American workplace. While their life experience and motivation to work are impressive, improved language and literacy skills, specialized work and cultural orientation, and job placement are critical for these individuals to access even entry-level jobs.

More Practice

Academic and Workplace Skills Activity Book
• p. 36

Reading Literary Writing

When reading fiction, turn your mind into a kind of theater, in which the mind is the stage, the actors, and the director all at the same time. Use this theater to find the relationship between the details the playwright presents and the meaning of the piece.

Analyzing and Evaluating Fiction

▶ **KEY CONCEPT** Use a variety of strategies to help you read and interpret fiction. ■

Identify With the Character or Situation When you identify with a situation in a novel or a short story, you live it with the character. You share the character's feelings and perceptions of the events. In this way, you may relate to experiences from your own life—or to experiences that you may never actually have had firsthand.

Draw Inferences By implying meanings without stating them directly, writers offer us a world in which the mind can stretch itself, finding connections wherever it looks. Fictional characters and situations don't come neatly labeled with "Villain" or "Danger"—you have to infer information from significant word choices, patterns of events, and other clues in order to understand what a writer is saying between the lines.

Question and Challenge the Text As you read, question what is going on in the text. It will help reveal secrets in the text if, as a reader, you pursue questions such as, What is happening? Why did he say that? Why is this character behaving in this way? You may not always find answers right away, but pieces of the story will start to collect around your questions, and a larger picture will take shape. Then, challenge the story: Are the characters and situations true? Do you accept the author's view of the world?

Draw Conclusions About What You Read Once you have understood and thought about the events and characters in a story, make judgments about the author's message. What general notions about human nature or the world does the author want you to carry away from the text?

Respond to the Story An important step in understanding a text is identifying your own reactions. Are you puzzled, thrilled, or scared? Is a character endearing? Disgusting? You may then judge whether your response was intended by the author, and you can analyze how the author evoked that reaction.

▼ **Critical Viewing**
What kind of a book do you suppose this student is reading? Why do you think so? **[Speculate]**

Reading Fiction

Writers of short stories and novels construct worlds that trigger our imagination and help us to learn about ourselves, other people, and the world around us. When you are familiar with the different elements of a story, you can read the story on many levels. The following reading strategies will help you peer behind the plot of a text in order to discover the ideas and messages behind the story.

Describe the Characters Being able to describe the characters in a work of fiction is an important aspect of reading. These descriptions should encompass the character's physical qualities as well as the character's personality traits. Beyond that, you should try to analyze the character's motivation—the personality traits and goals that strongly direct a character's actions. Doing this will help you understand a character more fully and possibly predict a character's behavior.

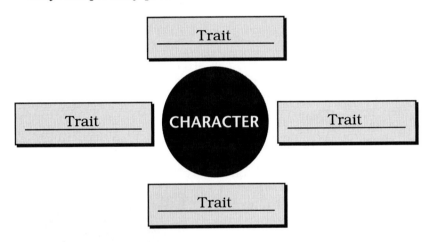

Determine the Point of View A reader must be able to answer this question: From whose vantage point is the story being told? Authors choose the point of view of a story carefully, and therefore you as the reader must pay close attention. As you begin reading, note how the story is being told: Is it a first-person narrative or is it narrated in the third-person objective? Is it limited omniscient or omniscient? Pay attention to the point of view, because it can change over the course of the novel or short story.

Unveil the Symbols Symbols are often embedded within stories. A symbol is an object, a person, a place, or some other detail that stands for something other than what it appears to be. Its literal meaning is what it appears to be in the story. Its figurative meaning is what it represents. Noticing and appreciating the symbolic meaning of an event or an object in a story shows that you are seeing beyond the plot and discovering the hidden meaning.

Analyze the Theme Understanding the theme, or main idea and truth, in a story means that you have moved from reading on a literal level to reading on a figurative one. The literal level is what happens in the story according to the plot development, and the figurative level is where the meaning lies. You can discover a story's theme by asking yourself: What does this story show me about human nature or about life? What did I learn from watching and observing these characters?

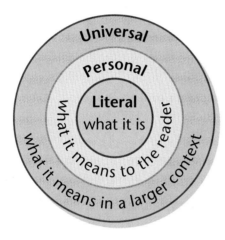

Recognize Allusions An allusion is an implied or indirect reference that is commonly found in literature. An allusion might be made to some character or situation in history or politics.

> ### Exercise 8 Reading Short Stories and Novels Read
> a short story or novel. As you read, answer the following questions:
> 1. What are the motivations behind the behavior of the main characters?
> 2. What are important symbols in the story?
> 3. What are notable themes in the story?
> 4. Have you recognized any allusions? If so, describe them.
>
> Next time you read a short story or novel, ask these same questions.

🔋 Research Tip

Using books from the library, research an allusion from a work of fiction. How does what you learn about the allusion help you see its connection to the story in which you found it?

> **More Practice**
>
> Academic and Workplace Skills Activity Book
> • pp. 37–38

Reading Drama

Plays are unique literary forms because they are written with a stage performance and an audience in mind. Unlike most works of fiction that rely heavily on narration, the story of a play is told mostly through dialogue and action and sometimes through monologues. When reading a play, you must place the text and the characters on stage.

> **KEY CONCEPT** Use the following strategies for reading drama. ■

Picture the Action in Your Mind As you read, try to picture in your mind how the play would look if it were being performed on stage. Use the stage directions, which appear in brackets, to help you envision the costumes, characters, setting, and action.

Connect the Play to Its Historical Context What is the time period and setting in which the play takes place? What are the manners, customs, and morals of the time? Look in the stage directions for information about when the play is set.

Summarize the Events Dramas are often broken into acts or scenes. These natural breaks give you an opportunity to review the action. After each scene or act, ask these questions: Who are the main characters? How are we supposed to feel about them? Have your feelings for them changed since the previous scene or act? Have any new conflicts arisen? As the play nears its end, evaluate whether the action has reached its climax and whether the conflicts have been resolved.

Recognize Dramatic Irony The audience sometimes knows more about the characters' situations than the characters know themselves. This is dramatic irony, and it is another way the playwright creates tension for the audience. For example, a prince may speak favorably about a king, while the audience knows that the prince is actually plotting to have the king murdered.

> **Exercise 9** **Reading Drama** Read the first act of a play. As you read, take notes on the strategies discussed above. List three details describing the play's historical context. Name five stage directions that you feel contributed to the play's action. What has happened in the first act? What are the tensions in the play? Describe an example of dramatic irony.

⏺ Learn More

Use a context chart like the one presented in this chapter to organize the historical context of a play you have read or are reading.

> **More Practice**

Academic and Workplace Skills Activity Book
• pp. 39–42

Reading Poetry

Written in lines and stanzas, poems are visual, but they can also be very musical when recited. When reading a poem, you must look very closely at the word choice, examine the form, and feel the rhythm. Because poetry is such a compact literary form, each word is highly significant to the overall meaning of the poem. To gain the most from poetry, use these strategies:

Read the Poem Aloud and Listen Poems were meant to be read aloud. When you read a poem, listen to its sounds and feel its rhythm. Pay attention to its tone and pace, as well as to the repetition of certain sounds. Consider how all of these attributes contribute to the mood and meaning of the poem.

Identify the Poem's Speaker Recognizing the poem's speaker will give you insight into the drama of a poem. The voice "speaking" the poem is not necessarily that of the poet, although it can be. The speaker could be a fictional character created by the poet. Using clues from the poem, decide who you think the speaker is.

Envision the Imagery Poetry often appeals to the senses. When your imagination can hear the sounds, feel the textures, and smell the aromas that are described, you will find greater enjoyment and will see how the images contribute to the poem's meaning.

Connect Structure and Meaning Poets carefully craft their poems in lines, and they often use stanzas to group their ideas. How the poet chooses to place the words in the poem often relates to the meaning in the poem. Although it may be tempting to read a poem line by line, a thought may span several lines or an entire stanza. To understand complete thoughts, read in sentences.

Paraphrase Restate the passages from the poem in your own words.

Consider the Historical Context Understanding the social, political, economic, and literary environment in which a poem was written helps you to see the poem in a more meaningful context. Research the time period in which the poem was written and the background of the poet.

Technology Tip

Find information on a poet and his or her works of poetry on the Internet. Type in the poet's name, and see what you can find. It's possible that you may discover a home page prepared by an enthusiast of the same poet or even by the poet. If you choose a contemporary poet, see if you can find an e-mail address where you could send the poet a letter.

▶ **Exercise 10** **Reading Poetry** Choose a poem from your textbook. Read the poem aloud accurately, paying close attention to the punctuation. As you read, identify the speaker, list three sensory images, and paraphrase each stanza. After you have done all of this, write a personal response to the ideas expressed in the poem.

Reading From Varied Sources

Many reading skills and strategies can be applied to just about any type of reading. However, when reading specific types of texts, such as the ones that follow, you should be aware of the key features of each. Understanding these key features will also help you understand and evaluate the works. In addition, being aware of the key features will help you to determine when it is appropriate to consult each type of text.

▲ **Critical Viewing**
What clues tell you that this cartoon communicates a message about a political conflict? **[Interpret]**

Read Newspapers

When you are looking for up-to-the-minute information on current events or when you want to know how an event was reported at the time it occurred, newspapers are probably your best source. Newspapers are one of the most objective sources of information. However, articles do at times reflect a bias or present only one side of a story—particularly feature articles. In addition, newspapers contain editorials, which by definition present a point of view on a topic.

Read Diaries, Letters, and Journals

When you are looking for a firsthand account of a historical or cultural event, you may want to consult diaries, letters, or journals. These sources let you experience what it was actually like to be a part of the events in question because they are written by people who actually lived through them. Often, you will be called on to consult these types of sources—referred to as primary sources—when you are doing research papers in school. As you read, keep in mind that each diary, letter, or journal presents events from the writer's point of view. As a result, these types of writing may reflect some bias.

Read Speeches

Like diaries, letters, and journals, speeches can provide you with a firsthand view of historical events. In addition, they are a great source for learning about the various sides of political issues. When reading a speech, keep in mind that it was originally written to be presented orally to an audience. Also, consider that a speech presents a single point of view—that of the speaker. Many speeches, such as political speeches, have a persuasive purpose. As a result, speakers often carefully choose words and details to have an intended effect.

Read Electronic Texts

Because the Internet makes them available at your fingertips, electronic texts are becoming one of the most accessible sources of information in today's world. The main type of electronic texts that you will encounter are Web pages. Some of the information on the Web is reliable and objective; some is biased or targeted toward a specific audience. When you read material on the Internet, do so with a critical eye. Determine the purpose behind the material. Often, you will discover that the material has a persuasive purpose. Look to see that any points made in a text on the Web are thoroughly supported by facts and details. Also, evaluate the credibility of the source.

▶ **Exercise 11** Reading Varied Sources Find examples of each of the sources listed in this section. Read each example carefully. Then, write a few paragraphs in which you compare and contrast these types of sources, and explain situations in which you think each would be most useful.

▶ **More Practice**

Academic and
Workplace Skills
Activity Book
• p. 43

Reflecting on Your Reading Skills

After a week of practicing your reading skills for both fiction and nonfiction works, write a paragraph about your reading skills and what you have learned about them. Focus on the areas in which you found success and on those which you need to improve. Use the following questions as guidelines for what to include in your paragraph:

• Which sections of my textbook did I find most useful?

• How has varying my reading style improved my ability to locate and remember information?

• Which steps of the SQ4R method did I find most useful? Which steps do I need to improve?

• Which graphic organizers did I use to help organize ideas?

• What materials have I recently read in which critical reading was a necessity? Which skills most helped my overall comprehension of the material?

• Which strategies for reading fiction did I find most useful? Which strategies did I find most difficult to use?

Standardized Test Preparation Workshop

Make Inferences and Predictions

In the reading sections of standardized tests, you may be asked to make inferences, or draw logical conclusions, about the characters and story you have read or about the author's purpose or point of view. Some questions require you to make a prediction, based on the material you have read. You may be asked to read part or all of a fictional story. Several multiple-choice questions will typically be followed by one or two essay questions. The essay question will ask you to respond in writing to some specific aspect of the reading.

Test Tip

Before answering essay questions, review the reading and highlight the main points. Refer to these as you draft your answer.

Sample Test Items

Directions: Read each passage. Then, answer the questions that follow the passage.

from "The Lagoon" by Joseph Conrad

The short words of the paddlers reverberated loudly between the thick and somber walls of vegetation. Darkness oozed out from between the trees, through the tangled maze of the creepers, from behind the great fantastic and unstirring leaves; the darkness, mysterious and invincible; the darkness scented and poisonous of impenetrable forests.

1   The author uses this description of the lagoon to —

    A   establish setting and character

    B   describe the water conditions

    C   explain the story's title

    D   create a mood of mystery and foreboding

In "The Lagoon," Joseph Conrad tells the story of Arsat, a man who ultimately loses his brother and his wife. How does the setting emphasize Arsat's isolation? Support your answer with details and information from the story.

Answers and Explanations

The answer for item 1 is *D*. By repeating the word *darkness* and by using vivid words and phrases like *oozed, tangled maze, mysterious and invincible,* and *scented and poisonous,* Conrad creates a dark and ominous mood.

Your answer should include a topic sentence and details from the passage that support it. The following is part of a possible response:

In "The Lagoon," Conrad uses the imagery of a tangled maze and of walls of vegetation to emphasize the theme of isolation.

> **Practice 1** **Directions:** Read each passage. Then, answer the questions that follow the passage.

from "The First Seven Years"
by Bernard Malamud

Though the attack was very mild, he lay in bed for three weeks. Miriam spoke of going for Sobel, but sick as he was Feld rose in wrath against the idea. Yet in his heart he knew there was no other way, and the first weary day back in the shop thoroughly convinced him, so that night after supper he dragged himself to Sobel's rooming house.

He toiled up the stairs, though he knew it was bad for him, and at the top knocked at the door. Sobel opened it and the shoemaker entered. The room was a small, poor one, with a single window facing the street. It contained a narrow cot, a low table and several stacks of books piled haphazardly around on the floor along the wall, which made him think how queer Sobel was, to be uneducated and read so much.

1 What does the author reveal about Sobel in the description of the room?

  A Sobel is a sloppy housekeeper.

  B Sobel enjoys entertaining in his room.

  C Sobel leads a simple life and reads many books.

  D Sobel is a highly educated man.

2 Which of the following words best describe Feld?

  F weary and defeated

  G dignified and gentlemanly

  H cheerful and jolly

  J simplistic and shallow

3 Because Feld struggles to reach Sobel, you can infer—

  A that Sobel and Feld have serious business to discuss

  B that the two men are strangers

  C that Sobel is delighted to see Feld at his door

  D that Sobel is afraid of Feld

4 Feld was in bed for three weeks because—

  A he had a mild heart attack

  B he suffered from exhaustion

  C he wants Miriam to take care of him

  D he is depressed about his relationship with Sobel

5 Predict Miriam's reaction to her father's visit to Sobel.

  F She will be angry with Feld for visiting Sobel

  G She will be sad that Feld visited Sobel

  H She will not care one way or the other

  J She will be worried that Feld wasn't strong enough to climb the stairs.

> **Practice 2** **Directions:** Answer the following question. Base your answer on "The First Seven Years" by Bernard Malamud.

How does Feld feel about going to see Sobel?

In this chapter, you will assess and develop your study, reference, and test-taking skills, making improvements that can enhance your ability to perform various tasks in a wide range of areas.

The first section of this chapter teaches you how to acquire good study skills—skills that will enable you to learn information in a college or job setting more easily. The second section discusses learning how to use the library and other reference materials, as well as how to find the information you need. A final section offers practical strategies to improve your test scores, a skill that is not only important for the aspiring scholar, for whom tests are a way of life, but is also important for those who will encounter employment tests as they enter the job market.

▲ **Critical Viewing**
How well-organized for studying do you think this student is? Explain. **[Evaluate]**

Section 31.1 *Basic Study Skills*

Acquiring good study habits can make you a more effective learner in school and at work. This section provides practice in developing a systematic approach to studying. By organizing your study time effectively, you can accomplish everything you need to do and still have leisure time.

Developing a Study Plan

The purpose of a *study plan* is to help you make the best use of the time available to you for studying and completing assignments. Your study plan should include setting up a study area, establishing a study schedule, and keeping a study notebook.

> **KEY CONCEPT** Use a study plan to manage your time for school, study, and other activities. ■

The chart below shows the necessary steps for setting up an effective study plan and its three main parts—study area, study schedule, and study notebook.

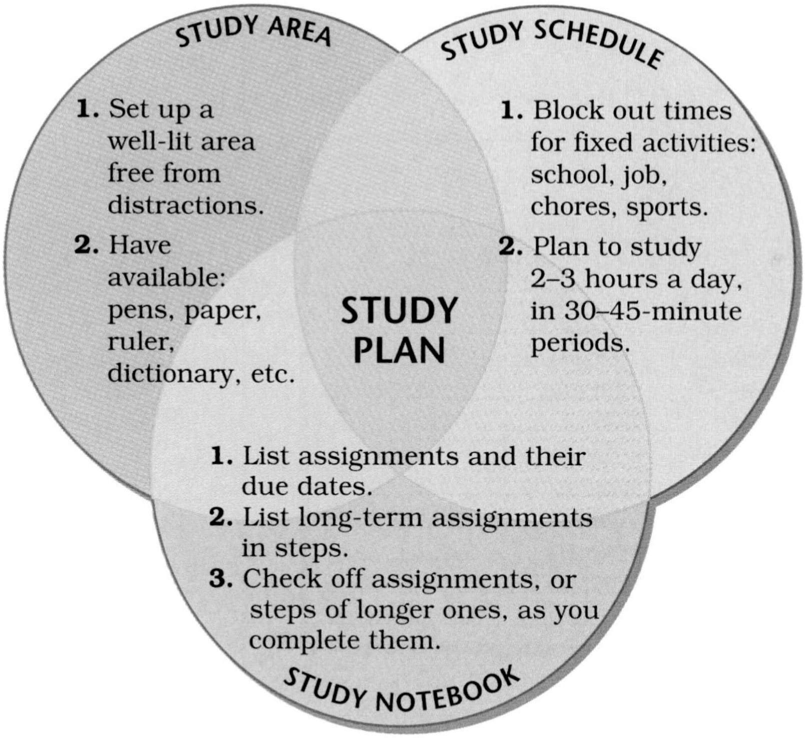

STUDY AREA

1. Set up a well-lit area free from distractions.
2. Have available: pens, paper, ruler, dictionary, etc.

STUDY SCHEDULE

1. Block out times for fixed activities: school, job, chores, sports.
2. Plan to study 2–3 hours a day, in 30–45-minute periods.

STUDY PLAN

STUDY NOTEBOOK

1. List assignments and their due dates.
2. List long-term assignments in steps.
3. Check off assignments, or steps of longer ones, as you complete them.

> **Exercise 1** Using and Evaluating Your Own Study Plan
> Develop and use a plan for one week. At the end of the week, identify which parts of your plan need improvement and revise your plan accordingly.

Taking Notes

Note-taking, if done properly, can clarify information, as well as summarize and reinforce it. For effective note-taking, keep the information you write down in a notebook that is organized, easy to follow, and up to date. Two valuable methods for taking notes are *outlines* and *summaries*.

KEY CONCEPT Keep an organized notebook in which you take notes, in outline or summary form, while listening or reading. ■

Modified Outlines A modified outline is most useful for quick note-taking from spoken or written material and for organizing ideas for questions on essay tests. When you take notes in a **modified outline form,** record each major topic as a heading when it is introduced. Use capitalization, underlining, or circling to emphasize the heading. Then, under each heading, list the important details using numbers, letters, or dashes.

The notes below, about the functions of the two hemispheres of the human brain, are in modified outline form. Notice the use of capitalization, underlining, and numbers to organize the information.

MODIFIED OUTLINE

Heading	(Left Brain	Right Brain)	Heading
Major topic	(1. Language	1. Synthesizing	Major topic
⬤	People with damage to areas of the left brain	People with damage to the right	
Included Ideas	may lose the ability to speak coherently.	brain may have difficulty recognizing familiar faces and objects.	Included Ideas

Free-form Outlines Use a free-form outline when you are taking notes from loosely structured material. Unlike other outline forms, the **free-form outline** is not written and organized from top to bottom. Instead, the main idea is placed in the center, with related information branching off from it. The following free-form outline shows notes about the same subject as the modified outline. Notice how the format is loose and only brief notes are taken.

FREE-FORM OUTLINE

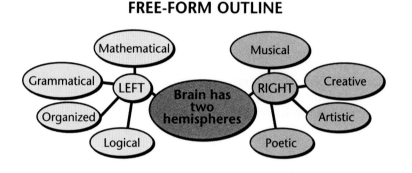

Summaries A **summary** is a brief statement or account that presents the essential information or main ideas of a reading or lecture. Writing a summary forces you to determine what the most important information is and helps you to remember this information by putting it into your own words.

Use the following suggestions to help you summarize information from your reading and listening:

- Listen or read for main ideas.

- Write main ideas in your own words.

- Shape these main ideas into sentences that express the purpose and point of view of the writer or speaker.

- Write the summary in paragraph form. The final material should be no more than one third of its original length.

> **Exercise 2** Making Modified and Free-form Outlines and Writing a Summary Read a section from one of your textbooks, and take notes on the important information. Use a modified outline form. Then, rewrite this outline as a free-form outline. As a final step, write a summary based on the information in your outlines.

Reference Skills

The growth of technology in the Information Age has made it possible for you to acquire a great deal of information on your own. Almost every form of printed reference now has its electronic equivalent, either on CD-ROM or on-line or both. Many of these works, in both printed and electronic form, are available at school or in public libraries.

Using the Library: An Overview

Most school and public libraries contain some or all of the following resources: fiction and nonfiction books, audiocassettes and videocassettes, periodicals (newspapers, magazines, and scholarly journals), reference works in printed and electronic form, and computer access to the Internet.

> **KEY CONCEPT** Use the library catalog to find valuable information about the resources that a library contains. ■

Using the Library Catalog Whether the books you seek are for pleasure or for research, your starting point is usually the *library catalog*. The catalog will show you whether a library owns a particular book. It can also help you find books by a particular author or books on a particular subject.

The library catalog will be in one of these three forms:

Card Catalog The card catalog lists books on index cards, with each book having a separate *author card* and *title card*; if the book is nonfiction, it also has at least one *subject card*. Cards are filed alphabetically in small drawers, with author cards alphabetized by last names and title cards alphabetized by the first words of the titles, excluding *A, An,* and *The.*

CARD CATALOG (AUTHOR CARD)

call number/author —— FIC/JOYCE   Joyce, James
title —— A Portrait of the Artist As a Young Man
city of publication —— Philadelphia:
publisher,/publication date —— The Word House, 1998
number of pages/size of book —— 282 p;   24 cm
subject or category —— Literature/Dublin (Ireland)

Printed Catalog This catalog lists books in printed booklets, with each book listed alphabetically by author, by title, and—if nonfiction—by subject. Often there are separate booklets for author, title, and subject listings.

PRINTED CATALOG (TITLE LISTING)		
title		author
A PORTRAIT OF THE ARTIST AS A YOUNG MAN/		James Joyce
city of publication	publisher	publication date
Philadelphia	The Word House	1998
number of pages	size of book	
282p.	24cm.	
subject		call number
Literature/Dublin (Ireland)		FIC JOYCE

Electronic Catalog This catalog lists books on a CD-ROM or in an on-line database that you access from special computer terminals in the library. You can usually find a book's catalog entry by typing in its title, key words in the title, its author's name, or for nonfiction, an appropriate subject.

Author:	Joyce, James.
Title:	A Portrait of the Artist As a Young Man.
Published:	Philadelphia: The Word House.
Description:	282p.; 24 cm.
Subject:	Literature/Dublin(Ireland).
Call No.:	FIC JOYCE
Status:	On shelf.

⊙ Technology Tip

In electronic database searches, be sure to type carefully and spell everything correctly. One wrong letter often means inaccurate results.

▶ **Exercise 3** **Using the Library Catalog** Visit your school or local library, and use the catalog to answer these questions.
1. What kind of catalogs does the library use—card, printed, or electronic? Where is it located?
2. Who wrote *War and Peace*? Is it fiction or nonfiction?
3. What are the titles, subjects, and call numbers of the books that your library carries by author George Schaller?
4. What are the titles, authors, and call numbers of three books about Japan published since 1985?
5. What are the titles and call numbers of two nonfiction books about whales that are more than 100 pages long?

Finding Books on Library Shelves By using a special method of organizing books, a library ensures that people can find specific titles. A library distinguishes between two kinds of books: *fiction* (made-up stories) and *nonfiction* (factual material), which is organized according to one of two systems—the *Dewey Decimal System* or the *Library of Congress System*. Nonfiction also includes two smaller groups that are often shelved separately: *biographies* and *reference books*.

KEY CONCEPT Fiction and nonfiction books are shelved separately in a library. Each category follows a special method of organization. ■

Fiction In most libraries, fiction books are shelved in a special section alphabetized by authors' last names. In the library catalog and on the book's spine, a work of fiction may be labeled *F* or *FIC*, followed by one or more letters of the author's last name.

Nonfiction Nonfiction books are assigned different numbers and letters. These number and letter codes, called *call numbers*, are placed on the spine of each book, and the books are arranged in number-letter order (according to the Dewey Decimal System) or letter-number order (according to the Library of Congress System) on the shelves. To find a nonfiction book, look it up in the library catalog and find out its call number; then, follow number-letter or letter-number order to locate the book on the library shelves.

The **Dewey Decimal System** can help you determine the subject of a book from its number. This classification system divides all knowledge into ten main areas numbered from 000 to 999. The chart below shows the main content areas:

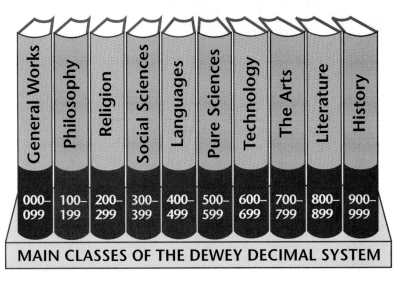

General Works	Philosophy	Religion	Social Sciences	Languages	Pure Sciences	Technology	The Arts	Literature	History
000–099	100–199	200–299	300–399	400–499	500–599	600–699	700–799	800–899	900–999

MAIN CLASSES OF THE DEWEY DECIMAL SYSTEM

The **Library of Congress System**, unlike the Dewey Decimal System, is organized letter-number, meaning that the call numbers begin with letters. The main classes are designated by a single letter; combinations of two letters designate subclasses. The letter designations are followed by a numerical notation from 1 to 9999, which can be further subdivided:

MAIN CLASS: H   Social Sciences
SUBCLASS: HA   Statistics
DIVISION: HA   Theory and Method
             29

Biographies are nonfiction books about real-life people. Most often, they are not assigned call numbers but are shelved in a special section alphabetized by the last names of their subjects (the people they are about). In the library catalog and on the book's spine, a biography may be labeled *B* or *BIO*, followed by one or more letters of the subject's last name: For example, *BIO Ein* may appear on a biography of Albert Einstein.

Reference books may also be shelved in their own special section of a library. Frequently, the sources in the library's reference section are labeled *R* or *REF*. If the book is nonfiction, a call number follows the abbreviation. Thus, if a book you look up in the card catalog has *REF* before its call number, go first to the library's reference section, and then use the call number to locate the book on the shelves in that section. Reference books are usually not allowed to circulate outside the library.

▶ **Exercise 4** Finding Books on Library Shelves

1. To find fiction by Graham Greene, would you look before or after fiction by Nadine Gordimer?
2. To find a nonfiction book with the call number 912.82N, would you look before or after a book with the call number 913.35F?
3. For a book with call number J438.4R, would you look in the reference, biography, or children's nonfiction section?
4. List these works of fiction in the order in which you would find them on the library shelves: *Clear Light of Day* by Anita Desai, *Emma* by Jane Austen, *Jude the Obscure* by Thomas Hardy, *Bleak House* by Charles Dickens, *Miguel Street* by V. S. Naipaul.
5. Arrange these call numbers in the order in which you would find them on the library shelves: 276.2M, 276.2J, 276.1L , 275.6R, 277.3S. What general subject matter would you expect to be the subject of these books?

Using Periodicals, Periodical Indexes, and the Vertical File

Periodicals are printed materials (newspapers, magazines, and journals) published daily, weekly, or at another regular interval. To search through this information, you need to use *periodical indexes* and the citations found within them. Folded maps, booklets, and pamphlets (works with a narrow focus in a small format) are found in the vertical file.

> **KEY CONCEPT** Use articles from periodicals for up-to-date information and use periodical indexes and citations to locate the articles. ∎

Periodicals Some periodicals are of general interest, while others are devoted to specialized topics. Because of their current nature, periodicals can be a valuable research aid for information that is not available in books.

Periodical Indexes and Citations To find which periodicals contain articles on a particular subject, you need to consult a *periodical index.* Issued regularly in printed or electronic form, these indexes contain *citations* that tell where and when the article was published.

SOME COMMON PERIODICAL INDEXES

- *Readers' Guide to Periodical Literature*, often referred to as the *Readers' Guide*, covers all types of periodicals
- *Art Index, Humanities Index*
- *Business Periodicals Index*

Below is a sample entry from the *Readers' Guide:*

SAMPLE *READERS' GUIDE* ENTRY

Subject heading — English language
Subheading — Spelling
Title of article — Business loves English [address, August 21, 1984] R. D. McCormick. *Vital Speeches of the Day* 51:52–4 N 1 '84
Volume; page numbers — "English" and the perils of formalism. E. D. Hirsh. *Am Sch* 53:369–79 Summ '84
Live the Mother life abroad [teaching English as a foreign language] H. Leong. il *Mother Earth News* 90:26–7 N/D '84

Illustrated — Date of issue — Title of magazine

Technology Tip

If the library computer is connected to a printer, you can generally print out a list of citations or the full text of articles for a fee. It may also be possible to download information onto a diskette that you can then use on another computer.

Research Tip

The information provided in the citation is also the information you need to list the article in a bibliography.

How to Use Periodical Indexes The citations in *printed indexes* are listed alphabetically by subject and, sometimes, also by author. These citations may include *abstracts*, or brief summaries, of the articles. In *electronic indexes*, citations are contained in a database that you can usually search by entering the subject, the author's name, or a key word or phrase in the title of the article. Some electronic indexes also provide the full text of the article cited.

Vertical Files Small printed materials, unsuitable for shelving, are arranged alphabetically by subject in a special filing filing cabinet called a *vertical file*. These materials include pamphlets, booklets, folded maps, original newspaper and magazine clippings, and photographs. The vertical file contains material of both historic interest (newspaper clippings) and current concern (pamphlets). Do not hesitate to ask the librarian whether information on the topic of your research might be found in the vertical file.

Exercise 5 **Using Periodicals, Periodical Indexes, and the Vertical File** Visit your school or local library to answer these questions.

1. Which printed periodical indexes does the library have? Which electronic indexes are available?
2. Which newspapers does the library carry? Is microfilm or microfiche available for back issues of the newspapers?
3. Give the titles of two magazines about nature and conservation that the library carries. How far back do they go? In what format are they available?
4. Using the most current issue of the *Readers' Guide*, find a citation for an article on someone you admire. Read the article in a copy of the magazine in the library, and then summarize it. (Many libraries store copies of the most current magazines and newspapers for reference use until they are bound or transferred onto microfilm.)
5. What specialized maps are available in the vertical file?

⊙ Learn More

For more on how dictionaries can help improve your vocabulary, see Chapter 29.

◀ **Critical Viewing** Why do you think pamphlets and other materials in the vertical files are kept in file cabinets such as this one? **[Deduce]**

Using Dictionaries

A *dictionary*, in either printed or electronic form, is an indispensable reference tool that contains a vast amount of information about words.

KEY CONCEPT A **dictionary** contains information about words, including spelling, definitions, pronunciation, part of speech, and origin. ■

Distinguishing Types of Dictionaries Dictionaries are compiled for different audiences and purposes: for students to use in schoolwork, for adults to use at home or at work, and for scholars to use in research. Dictionaries may come in both printed and electronic form. The following are the three main types of dictionaries.

THREE TYPES OF DICTIONARIES	
Unabridged	Exhaustive study of the English language containing over 250,000 words
Abridged	Compact editions containing listings of 55,000 to 160,000 words
Specialized	Limited to words of a particular type or field, such as foreign languages or mathematics

Exercise 6 Choosing a Dictionary Name the kind of dictionary (*unabridged*, *abridged*, or *specialized*) that would be the most appropriate for each task:
1. finding special detailed information about a word
2. finding a comprehensive definition of a legal or medical term
3. finding a word's basic meaning
4. finding the origin of a word
5. finding the translation of a foreign word

Finding Words in Printed Dictionaries A word listed in a dictionary, along with all the information about it, is called an *entry*. The *entry word* is the word defined. In printed dictionaries, entry words are arranged alphabetically. To speed your search for a word, use the following aids:

Thumb Index This series of right-hand notches allows you to thumb alphabetically through a dictionary. Each notch, labeled *A, B, C*, and so on, shows the section of entries for words that start with the letter or letters on it.

Guide Words Two large or boldfaced words at the top of each dictionary page show the first and last entry words on that page. All other entry words on that page fall alphabetically between these two guide words.

The Four-Section Approach To find words quickly, use the four-section approach, following these steps:

1. Mentally divide the dictionary into the four sections:

ABCD	MNOPQR
EFGHIJKL	STUVWXYZ

2. When you go to look up a word, decide into which section the word falls. For example, if you want to look up *homeostasis*, you know that the word falls near the middle of the second section. If, on the other hand, you want to look up *scruple*, you know that the word falls near the beginning of the last section. Flip to that section, and then complete your search using the thumb index and guide words.

Finding Words in Electronic Dictionaries In electronic dictionaries, you usually find a word's entry simply by typing the word and having the computer search the dictionary database. If you are unsure of a word's spelling, you can usually type in the first few letters and see a list of words that are similar in spelling.

> **Exercise 7** **Working With a Dictionary** Use a dictionary or your knowledge of a dictionary to answer these questions.
> 1. Which dictionary would be the most appropriate for finding detailed information of a word's history?
> 2. Which dictionary would be most appropriate for finding the translation of a word?
> 3. In your dictionary, what two guide words appear on the page with the word *declivity*?
> 4. Which entry words would appear on a page with the guide words *infective* and *infix*?
>   a. infer   b. infinite   c. inflame   d. infirmary
> 5. Which guide words would appear with the word *powder*?
>   a. powerboat/practice b. practiced/proa c. poultry/power

Understanding Dictionary Entries In a dictionary, a word and all the information about it are called an *entry*. The word itself is called an *entry word*.

MAIN ENTRY IN A DICTIONARY

Part of Speech ————
Syllabification —————
Etymology —————
Entry Word —— **cue**[1] (kyo͞o) *n.* [< *q, Q*, used in plays in 16th &
Pronunciation — 17th c. to indicate actors' entrances; prob.
Etymology —— abbrev. of some L. word (as *quando*, when, *qualis*, in what manner)] **1.** a bit of dialogue, action, or music that is a signal for an actor's entrance or speech, or for the working of
Numbered —— curtains, lights, sound effects, etc. **2.** the few
Definitions notes or bars of music directly preceding an instrumentalist's or vocalist's part and serving as a signal to begin that part **3.** anything
Usage Labels —— serving as a signal to do something **4.** [Now Rare] the role that one is assigned to play **5.** [Archaic] frame of mind; mood; temperament
Field label —— **6.** *Psychol.* a secondary stimulus that guides
Part of Speech behavior, often without entering
(2) consciousness —*vt.* **cued, cu´ing** or **cue´ing**
Inflected Forms — to give a cue to —**cue in** to add (dialogue, music, etc.) at a particular point in a script
Idiom ——

Entry Word An entry word may be a single word, a compound word (two words acting as a single word), an abbreviation, a prefix or suffix, or a person, place, or event.

Syllabification Dots, spaces, or slashes in an entry word show where that word may be divided when breaking words at the end of a line. Remember that you cannot leave a syllable of just one letter on a line by itself. Words with one syllable are never divided.

Pronunciation Appearing right after the entry word, the pronunciation uses symbols to show how to say the word and which syllable to stress. (The key to these symbols may be found along the bottom of the page or at the beginning of the dictionary.) The syllable that gets the most emphasis has a *primary stress*, usually shown by a heavy mark after the syllable. Words of more than one syllable may also have a *secondary stress*, usually shown by a shorter, lighter mark.

Part-of-Speech Label This label, an abbreviation usually given after the pronunciation, tells how a word can be used in a sentence—whether it functions as a noun, a verb, or some other part of speech.

Plurals and Inflected Forms After the part-of-speech label, dictionaries may also show the plural forms of nouns and the inflected forms of verbs—past tense and past participle—if their spelling is irregular.

Etymology The origin and history of a word are called its *etymology*. The word's etymology usually appears in brackets, parentheses, or slashes near the beginning or end of the entry. Abbreviations for languages are explained in the dictionary's key to abbreviations.

Definition and Example The *definition* is the meaning of the word. Definitions are numbered if there is more than one. Often, they include examples illustrating the uses of meanings in phrases or sentences.

Usage Labels These labels show how the word is generally used. Words labeled *Archaic* (*Arch.*), *Obsolete* (*Obs.*), *Poetic,* or *Rare* are not widely used today. Words labeled *Informal* (*Inf.*), *Colloquial* (*Colloq.*), or *Slang* are not considered part of standard English. Words labeled *Brit.* are used mainly in Britain, not in the United States.

Field Labels These labels show whether a word is used in a special way by people in a certain occupation or activity, such as *History* (*Hist.*), *Astronomy* (*Astron.*), or *Biology* (*Biol.*).

Idioms and Derived Words The end of an entry may list and define idioms, or expressions, that contain the entry word. It may also list derived words, which are formed from the entry word, along with a part-of-speech label.

▶ **Exercise 8** **Understanding Dictionary Entries** Use a dictionary to answer these questions.
1. If you have to break the word *nourish* at the end of a line, where should you put the hyphen?
2. From what language does the word *indulge* originally come? What does it mean in that language?
3. Identify two meanings of the word *incident*—one as an adjective and one as a noun.
4. What does the idiom *whistle in the dark* mean?
5. Is there an adverb and a noun derived from the word *mean*? If so, what are they?

Using Other Print References

Most libraries have a variety of useful *reference works*, resources to which you can refer for specific information.

▶ **KEY CONCEPT** Libraries offer a wide range of useful reference works in printed and electronic form. ■

Encyclopedias An encyclopedia is a collection of articles providing basic information on a great many subjects.

A *general* encyclopedia contains articles providing information on a wealth of subjects. *Specialized encyclopedias*, such as an encyclopedia of literature or of animals, cover a particular subject comprehensively, featuring articles that may be more detailed than those in a general encyclopedia.

Encyclopedia articles are arranged alphabetically by subject. People are alphabetized by their last name. Printed encyclopedias usually span several volumes, with letters printed on each spine to show which subjects a particular volume contains. Not all topics have their own article, but an alphabetical index tells you in which articles particular topics are covered. *Electronic encyclopedias* offer searches by key term.

Almanacs Almanacs are annually issued handbooks that provide lists and statistics on many subjects, including government, history, geography, weather, science, technology, and entertainment. To find a subject in a *printed almanac,* use the index. In an *electronic almanac,* use the search feature.

Atlases and Gazetteers *Atlases* and *gazetteers* contain maps and geographical information based on them. Some also show statistics about population, climates, agriculture, and so on. A *gazetteer* is a dictionary or index of place names, often including populations and sizes. In *printed atlases,* you use the *index* to find out which map shows a particular place. *Electronic map collections* offer a search feature.

Thesauruses A *thesaurus* is a specialized dictionary, arranged alphabetically or thematically, that lists *synonyms,* or words with similar meanings.

▶ **Exercise 9** **Using Other Reference Works** Use printed or electronic reference works to find answers to these questions. Indicate the type of reference you used.
1. What was Henry James's first published novel?
2. Who was the first American woman to receive a medical degree?
3. What is the highest mountain in Africa?
4. What is the capital city of Portugal?
5. What are five synonyms for the adjective *sly*?

Technology Tip

In electronic reference works, you can find information by browsing an alphabetical list or by typing in a subject or key word and having the computer search the database.

▼ **Critical Viewing** Give the names of two encyclopedia articles in which you might expect to find information about Henry James. **[Analyze]**

Using Electronic and Media References

There are more resources for research than just books. A wide range of electronic and media resources—including video collections, CD-ROMs, the Internet, and on-line subscription services—can aid you in research.

Video References Much information can be found in video format. Consult your librarian to find out about videos such as the following:

- **News programs** offer current information and insights into how people reacted to historical events as they happened.
- **Documentaries** give in-depth information on specific topics.
- **Special-interest series** provide extended, detailed coverage of many aspects of a topic—for example, the Bill Moyers series on the history of the English language provides valuable insights into how the language evolved.

CD-ROM References Reference works may appear on CD-ROM, as well as in printed form.

- **CD-ROM encyclopedias** contain the same amount of information as a complete print encyclopedia. Many CD-ROM encyclopedias also include video and audio segments. Their search function typically enables you to find information on a topic in each place it is discussed.
- **CD-ROM atlases** take the form of a database. By entering a place name or key word, you can call up relevant maps.

Electronic Databases Electronic databases are collections of data on a specific topic. They may be available on CD-ROM or over the Internet. Databases enable you to search for specific terms. These forms of data storage do not suffer from some of the limitations of traditional forms. All of the data appear in one "place"—your computer screen—rather than being spread out in different file cabinets. Computer searches can also reduce the time spent finding specific information.

Technology Tip

Although electronic reference works are valuable resources for your research, your library probably has a limited number of computer terminals for users. Ask the librarian if there is a time when there may be less demand for the computers.

Using the Internet

As you may know, the *Internet* is a global network of computers connected by telephone and cable lines. When you go *online*, or access the Internet, you can visit (call up on screen) any Web site on the network. A huge variety of information is available on these sites. Each Web site has its own address, or URL (Universal Resource Locator). It usually consists of several pages of text, graphics, and sometimes audio or video displays. Many school and public libraries offer Internet access.

KEY CONCEPT Use search engines to locate information on the Internet. ■

Locating Appropriate Web Sites Use these tips for searching the Web.

- If you know a reliable Web site and its address (URL), simply type the address into your Web browser.

- If you don't know of a particular Web site for a topic, you can use an Internet search engine to find the information. Use general search engines to search for a key term. Use other search engines to search by category. Use "metasearch engines" to find the top "hits" from other search engines.

KEY CONCEPT Always evaluate the reliability of each Internet source you use. ■

Evaluating Web Sites Almost anyone can create a Web site, but not everyone will provide reliable information. Use these tips to evaluate information you find on the Internet:

- Check the sponsor of the site. Rely more on sites established by respected publishers or organizations than on those placed by a discussion group or an individual.

- Check the credentials of the source, such as experience in the field or affiliation with a recognized organization.

- Analyze the motives of the source. Some organizations or individuals may have an interest in persuading you to form a certain opinion or to buy a certain product and may be less objective than other sources.

- Check the date when the page was last updated, to determine how up to date the information is.

- Also, consult reference librarians familiar with the Internet or Internet coverage in established library journals (such as *Booklist* and the *Library Journal*) for information on useful, reliable reference Web sites.

Technology Tip

Whenever possible, copy and paste URLs from an electronic source to the location (address) line of your browser. This common editing feature allows you to transfer URLs among word-processing programs, e-mail, and the Internet. It's easier, saves time, and there is no chance that you will type one or two letters or numbers of the URL incorrectly.

Evaluating Information on Web Sites Even a reliable Web site may contain inaccurate or misleading information. Critically examine the information you find. Look for the evidence given for important claims. As in all research, verify important information using at least one, preferably two, additional sources. Generally, print sources are preferred to electronic sources.

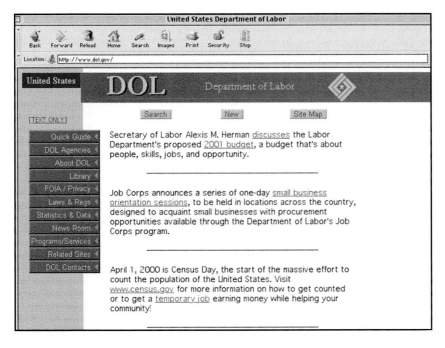

> **Exercise 10** **Using the Internet** Using a computer in your library, school computer lab, or at home, go on-line and research information to carry out the following tasks.
> 1. Find the ZIP Code for Anaheim, California.
> 2. Find the director and cast members of a contemporary film.
> 3. List the names and URLs of four Web sites that you think can help you write a history paper on the Roman Empire.
> 4. Find lyrics for a version of the ballad "John Henry." Record the name and URL of your source. Give an evaluation of the credibility of the source, explaining the reasons for your judgment.
> 5. From a reliable source, find five facts about tigers. Record your source information, and include an evaluation of its credibility, giving support for your evaluation.

Test-Taking Skills

In this section, you will learn strategies to improve your performance on objective tests.

Taking Objective Tests

Objective tests are those in which each question has a single correct answer. To prepare for such tests, carefully study the material that the test will cover. Be sure to arrive at the test on time, well rested, and with all the equipment you were told to bring—pencils, pens, books, watch, and so on.

> **KEY CONCEPT** When taking a test, organize your time, dividing it among three steps: previewing, answering, and proofreading. ■

LOOK OVER THE TEST (No more than 10% of time)

1. Skim the test to get an overview of the types of questions.
2. Decide how much time you want to spend on each section.
3. Plan to devote the most time to questions that are hardest or worth the most points.

ANSWER THE QUESTIONS (allow at least 70% of time)

1. Answer the easy questions first. Put a check next to harder questions, and come back to them later.
2. If permitted, use scratch paper to jot down your ideas.
3. Read each question at least twice before answering.
4. Supply the single best answer.
5. Answer all questions on the test unless you are told not to guess or that there is a penalty for wrong guesses.
6. Do not change your first answer without a good reason.

PROOFREAD ANSWERS (No more than 20% of time)

1. Check that you have followed directions completely.
2. Reread test questions and answers. Make sure that you have answered all of the questions.

> **Exercise 11** Taking Objective Tests Answer these questions about any objective test that you recently took.
  1. Did I study enough for the test?
  2. Did I budget enough time for the hardest questions?
  3. Did I change an answer for no convincing reason?
  4. Did I proofread carefully?
  5. What could I have done to improve my performance?

Answering Objective Questions

Although the content of objective tests varies greatly, the types of questions on these tests are fairly similar. This section will provide basic information about the different types of objective-test questions and specific strategies for answering them.

> **KEY CONCEPT** Improve your test scores by learning about the different kinds of objective-test questions and the strategies for answering them. ∎

True-or-False Questions True-or-false questions ask you to identify whether or not a statement is accurate.

- If a statement seems true, be sure that the entire statement is true.
- Pay special attention to the word *not*, which often changes the whole meaning of a statement.
- Take note of the generalizing words *all, always, never, no, none,* and *only.* They often make a statement false.
- Take note of the qualifying words *generally, much, many, most, often, sometimes,* and *usually.* They often make a statement true.

Fill-in Questions A fill-in question asks you to supply an answer in your own words. The answer may complete a statement, or it may simply answer a question.

- Read the question or incomplete statement carefully.
- If you are completing a statement, look for context clues that may signal the answer. Pay special attention if the word *an* appears right before the missing word. This indicates that the missing word begins with a vowel sound.
- If you are answering a question using interrogative words such as *Who? What? How much?* or *What kind?* replace these words with your answer and make a statement out of the question. Check to make sure this statement makes sense.

Learn More

For tips and practice in responding to essay questions, see Chapter 15, "Writing for Assessment."

Multiple-Choice Questions This kind of question asks you to choose from four or five possible responses.

- Try answering the question before reading the choices. If your answer matches one of the choices, select that choice.

- Eliminate any obviously incorrect answers. If you are allowed to write on the test paper, cross them out.

- Change a question to a statement by inserting your answer. See whether the statement makes sense.

Matching Questions Matching questions require that you match items in one group with items in another.

- Count the items in each group to see whether any will be left over.

- Read all the items before you start matching.

- Match the items you know first, and then match the others. If you can write on the paper, cross out items as you use them.

▶ **Exercise 12** **Understanding Objective Questions** Using a subject you are studying in one of your classes, prepare an objective test on the material. Write five true-or-false questions, five matching questions, five multiple-choice questions, and five fill-in questions. Exchange papers with another student, and take that student's test, writing your answers on a separate sheet of paper. Exchange again and grade the test.

Analogies An *analogy* is a special type of multiple-choice question that often appears on vocabulary and reading tests. Analogy items usually provide a pair of words and ask you to choose another pair that expresses a similar relationship.

PECAN : NUT ::
a. apple : fruit
b. house : domestic
c. instrument : piano
d. orange : peel

   In the preceding example, the answer is *a*. The relationship between the pairs of words is *kind*. A pecan is a *kind* of nut, and an apple is a *kind* of fruit. Notice that the sequence of the words matters: a piano is a kind of instrument, but the relationship is given in reverse order. Review the common analogy relationships in the chart:

▼ **Critical Viewing** Why is wearing a watch to a test, as this student has, a good idea? **[Apply]**

Common Analogy Relationships

Relationship	Example
Quality	disturbance : riot
Lack of a quality	shyness : congeniality
Degree (greater or lesser)	shout : speak
Part to whole	leg : chair
Kind	carrot : vegetable
Sequence	student : graduate
Proximity	sidewalk : street
Instrumental relations	stethoscope : doctor

▶ **Exercise 13** **Answering Analogies** For each item, choose the letter of the pair of words that expresses the relationship most like the relationship expressed by the words in capital letters. Also, indicate the type of relationship.

1. IMPOVERISHED : AFFLUENT ::
   a. poor : honest
   b. depleted : enriched
   c. rich : wealth
   d. hungry : thin

2. ARCHIPELAGO : ISLAND ::
   a. constellation : star
   b. symphony : orchestra
   c. mountain : hill
   d. leaf : tree

3. GUITAR : PICK ::
   a. bow : violin
   b. clarinet : reed
   c. drum : drumsticks
   d. conductor : baton

4. ARROW : ARCHER ::
   a. needle : tailor
   b. choir : organ
   c. actor : stage
   c. dessert : chef

5. AVARICE : GREED ::
   a. extravagant : frugal
   b. valor : cowardice
   c. candor : honesty
   d. charity : piety

▲ Critical Viewing
Come up with an analogy for the subject of this picture. [**Analyze**]

Performing on Standardized Tests

In addition to the tests you take for particular classes, you will also take standardized tests, often used to evaluate your readiness for the next level of education. These include state tests, high-school exit exams, and college board tests, such as the SAT and the ACT. The following tips will help you to perform well on standardized tests:

Tips for Taking Standardized Tests

1. **Get plenty of sleep the night before**.
2. **Eat a healthy meal beforehand**.
3. **Build confidence with thorough preparation.** Confidence is one of the keys to success on standardized tests. To build your confidence, begin preparing for the test weeks or even months beforehand. Use sample tests available in books, on the Internet, or from your teacher.
4. **Arrive prepared for the test.** Determine which supplies—pencils, paper, calculator, and so on—you need or are allowed to use for the test, and bring them with you.
5. **Fill in bubble sheets carefully.** If you skip an item on the test, make sure that you skip the corresponding row on the bubble sheet. To make sure you have filled in the sheet properly, check it over before you turn in your test.
6. **Budget your time.** Determine how much time you have for each section and how many questions each contains. Then, calculate how much time you can allow for each question. Skip questions you can't answer, so that you don't run out of time to complete the test.

▶ Critical Viewing
What is some advice you might offer to this student to help her on the standardized test she is taking? **[Speculate]**

Types of Standardized Tests

Familiarize yourself with the format of any test you are preparing to take. Following are a few important standardized tests for college-bound students:

PSAT The PSAT is the preliminary SAT (see the description below). Given nationwide, it is designed to provide students with the opportunity to practice for the SAT. PSAT results also determine which students are eligible for National Merit Scholarships.

The PSAT has the same format as the SAT with the following exceptions: (1) The PSAT contains fewer sections than the SAT. (2) The PSAT contains items that test your knowledge of usage and mechanics; the SAT does not.

SAT Many colleges use an applicant's SAT score as one factor in deciding whether to admit the student. The test is given nationwide, once a month from October through June except in February. You may repeat the test in the hope of improving your score; however, results of every SAT you take will be reported to the schools to which you apply.

SATs have a math portion and a verbal portion. The verbal portion contains the following sections:

SECTIONS OF THE VERBAL PORTION OF THE SAT

1. **Sentence-completion questions** test your vocabulary. You must choose the appropriate word to fill in a blank within a sentence or passage.
2. **Analogy questions** test your ability to analyze relationships (see the examples on pages 866 and 867).
3. **Critical-reading questions** are multiple-choice questions that test your understanding of two reading passages.

ACT Many colleges use ACT scores to make admissions decisions. Questions on the test—covering English, math, reading, and science reasoning—are all multiple choice. On the English portion, you must identify errors in grammar, usage, mechanics, logic, and organization. The reading portion presents four passages from different fields. You must answer questions about each passage that test your reading and reasoning skills.

ⓛ Learn More

The Standardized Test Preparation Workshop that appears at the end of each chapter throughout this book provides instruction and practice in all of the types of items covered in these tests.

Reflecting on Your Test-Taking Skills

Think about strategies presented in this section and how they apply to you. Use these questions to help you reflect:

- How can I budget my time better while taking tests?
- How can I apply new test-taking strategies when I take tests?

Standardized Test Preparation Workshop

Constructing Meaning From Informational Texts

When you take a standardized test, often you must answer questions about a passage you have read. These questions test your ability to extract meaning from the information provided in the passage. When answering these types of questions, you will be required to do the following:

- Identify the main idea, stated or implied, of a section of the passage.

- Identify the best summary—a concise restating of the key points of the passage.

- Distinguish between facts and nonfacts.

- Recognize the author's point of view and purpose for writing the passage.

The following sample item will give you practice answering these types of questions. To answer the sample question, refer to the passage on the next page.

Test Tip

When answering a question about the main idea of a paragraph or the best summary of a passage, reread the entire paragraph or passage before answering.

Test Item

Read the passage on the next page. Then, read the question below. Decide which is the best answer.

Which of the following represents the author's main purpose in the passage?

A. The author wishes to persuade readers that Elizabethan England was one of the best periods for theater.

B. The author wishes to entertain readers with stories of Elizabethan theater.

C. The author wishes to inform readers about two kinds of theater in Elizabethan England.

D. The author wishes to inform readers about the changing nature of theater in Elizabethan England.

Answers and Explanations

The correct answer is *D*. The author's purpose is informative. The passage gives no opinions on the quality of theater in Elizabethan England (answer *A*). It focuses on facts showing the changing nature of the theater, not on amusing stories (answer *B*). While the passage mentions two kinds of theater, (answer *C*) the two kinds are not the author's main focus.

Practice 1 **Directions:** Read the passage. Then, read each question that follows the passage. Decide which is the best answer to each question.

Before the reign of Elizabeth I, theater companies traveled about the country putting on plays wherever they could find an audience, often performing in the open courtyards of inns. Spectators watched either from the ground or from balconies or galleries above.

When Shakespeare was just twelve years old, an actor named James Burbage built London's first theater, called simply *the theater*, just beyond the city walls in Shoreditch. James Burbage was the son of Richard Burbage—the best actor of Elizabethan times. Actors occupied a strange place in London society during Elizabeth's reign: They were frowned upon by the city fathers but were wildly popular with the common people, who clamored to see them perform in plays. Though actors were considered rogues and vagabonds by some, they were held in sufficient repute to be called on frequently to perform at court.

1 What is the main idea of the second paragraph of this passage?

A London's first theater was built when Shakespeare was just twelve years old.

B Actors were among the celebrities of Elizabethan England.

C When the theater first came to London, the actors met with official disapproval and public popularity.

D Actors in Elizabethan England were glad to leave behind their wandering life to take up quarters in Shoreditch.

2 Which of the following conclusion follows from the passage?

F The royalty of England disapproved of the theater.

G Shakespeare began writing his plays during a period of change in the theater in England.

H Shakespeare was too young to have had a major impact on the changing nature of theater in Elizabethan England.

J Theater was the only form of entertainment available to the public in Elizabethan England.

3 Which of the following is an OPINION expressed in the passage?

A When Shakespeare was twelve years old, an actor named James Burbage built London's first theater.

B Actors were frowned upon by the city fathers but were wildly popular with the common people.

C Before the reign of Elizabeth I, theater companies traveled about the country putting on plays wherever they could find an audience.

D Richard Burbage was probably the best actor of Elizabethan times.

4 Which of the following is the best summary of this passage?

F Actors in Elizabethan England were torn between a wandering life in the countryside and official disapproval in London.

G In Elizabethan England, theater took an important step from a wandering existence in the countryside to a settled one near the city.

H James Burbage made an important contribution to the history of theater in England.

J Theatergoers in Elizabethan England were enthusiastic, celebrating favorite actors and enduring less than ideal viewing conditions.

Workplace Skills and Competencies

Whether your intention is to go to college or to begin your work life right after high school, you will profit from having learned how to read and write carefully and to speak clearly. You will also benefit from knowing other skills, such as how to communicate effectively with others, how to set and achieve goals, and how to solve problems.

The material in this chapter will help you improve your abilities in these areas. It will also offer guidance on budgeting your time and money wisely as you grow more independent. You will learn how to explore career fields through internships and how to apply math and computer skills in daily life.

▲ **Critical Viewing**
What might you learn from this photograph that you can someday apply to a job search of your own? **[Connect]**

Working With People

Just as you learned to work together with teachers and students in high school, you will be expected to interact effectively with people in college and in the workplace. This section offers practical ways to hone your communication skills, working one on one and in groups.

Learn One-on-One Communication

Before you can get a job or gain admission to a college, you must impress an interviewer in a one-on-one situation. The communication skills that serve you well in an interview must then be refined as you engage a variety of other people at work or on campus.

Interviews Typically, internships, jobs, and colleges all require interviews. Learning how to make a good impression during an interview can increase your chances of success.

▶ **KEY CONCEPT** To interview successfully, you must be prepared, professional, and courteous. ■

THE INTERVIEW PROCESS		
Before the Interview	**During the Interview**	**After the Interview**
1. Find out when, where, and with whom the interview is.	**1.** Smile and maintain eye contact.	**1.** In a follow-up letter, restate your interest in the internship, job, or college and extend your thanks.
2. Gather references and prepare your résumé.	**2.** Ask and answer questions concisely.	**2.** When the deadline for a decision arrives, call to check the status.
3. Learn about your potential employer or the college to which you are applying, and prepare questions.	**3.** Thank the interviewer, and ask when a decision will be made.	**3.** If you are applying for a job, and the position has been filled, ask the company to keep your résumé on file.
4. Select a neat, appropriate outfit for the interview.		

⊙ Technology Tip

Computer software often has a built-in feature that helps you prepare a résumé. Type in the word *résumé* at the Help command to investigate this feature.

⟲ Learn More

To learn what information to include in an effective résumé and follow-up letter, see Chapter 16, "Workplace Writing."

Successful Interaction Knowing how to interact well with different people benefits you long after high school. For example, you will find that good communication skills can relieve the tension that may result from dealings with co-workers, clients, supervisors, and classmates.

KEY CONCEPT For successful interaction, listen closely, choose words carefully, and show respect for others. ■

Follow these suggestions for effective interaction:

⊙ Technology Tip

The skills you learn for interacting with people face to face or on the telephone can also be applied to interaction on-line.

KEYS TO SUCCESSFUL INTERACTION

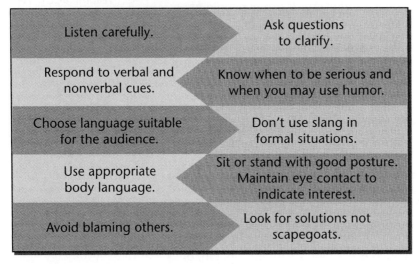

Listen carefully.

Ask questions to clarify.

Respond to verbal and nonverbal cues.

Know when to be serious and when you may use humor.

Choose language suitable for the audience.

Don't use slang in formal situations.

Use appropriate body language.

Sit or stand with good posture. Maintain eye contact to indicate interest.

Avoid blaming others.

Look for solutions not scapegoats.

Exercise 1 Practicing Your Interviewing Skills With a teacher asking the questions, role-play an interview at a company or college. (You might arrange to be videotaped.) Afterward, have the class critique your performance.

Exercise 2 Interacting With Others in Various Situations With other students, role-play the following situations, using the tips for effective interaction noted above as a guide.
1. You must find out why a co-worker has not followed through on his or her portion of a group assignment.
2. You must convince a professor to grant you an extended deadline on a paper.

Learn to Work as a Team

Teamwork requires more than just basic communication skills, because whether you are serving on a committee or preparing a group presentation, conflict invariably arises as you work closely together. Therefore, to interact successfully, group members must know and respect each other's roles.

Roles in Group Discussions Group discussions succeed when members understand their own and each other's roles in the pursuit of a common goal. A group is typically composed of a facilitator, a recorder, and several participants, each with distinct responsibilities.

> **KEY CONCEPT** To realize a common goal, each member of a group must be organized, focused on the issues, and aware of his or her responsibilities. ■

Effective Participation Participants are critical to the success of a group. They must be willing to make suggestions, consider the ideas of others, give and accept criticism with grace, and help smooth tensions that arise.

> **KEY CONCEPT** Effective participation requires a constructive exchange of ideas and a common goal. ■

Follow these suggestions for effective teamwork:

- Share your ideas, and encourage others to do so.

- Listen carefully to all points of view.

- Accept criticism; take nothing personally.

- When you disagree, focus on the idea, not on the person.

- Resolve disputes promptly.

▼ Critical Viewing Based on the details in this photograph, do you think that this group is interacting effectively? Why or why not? **[Evaluate]**

Exercise 3 **Holding a Group Discussion** With five class-mates, hold a group discussion on one of these topics: paths to take after graduation, types of volunteer work, or the impact of computer technology. Choose a facilitator and a recorder for the group, and spend fifteen minutes openly sharing your thoughts and ideas on the topic. End by working together to reach consensus about one idea to share with the class. Select one group member to present the idea.

Exercise 4 **Critiquing a Group Effort** Select an example of poor teamwork from a book or a movie. Read the passage or play the scene for the class. Point out the problems, and explain how the group could have worked better together. Refer to the tips for successful teamwork.

Meetings Discussions can be organized in several different ways. Some discussions are informal, and others are formal. A meeting is a formal group discussion; it is organized to discuss specific ideas and topics. A well-organized meeting has an **agenda** that lists the order of the topics being discussed and assigned roles, such as facilitator, note-taker, and timekeeper. If new issues or questions are raised during the meeting that cannot be solved during the meeting's time limit, all of the people involved should plan to meet again for further discussion.

Exercise 5 **Organizing a Trip to a Local Museum** Working with five or six other students, plan a trip for your entire class to a local museum. Make an agenda to decide where and when you want to go and how you will get there. Assign roles, hold the meeting, and, if necessary, plan to meet again before the trip is finalized.

AGENDA
Project Meeting
October 14

Facilitator: Malcolm
Note-taker: Leslie
Timekeeper: Bill

1. Review and amend agenda
   (All — 5 minutes)

2. Brainstorm for ideas
   (All — 10 minutes)

3. Report of project's progress/difficulties
   (Nicole — 10 minutes)

4. Discussion of project and possible solutions
   (All — 20 minutes)

Moving Toward Your Goals

Put simply, goals are dreams that you plan to achieve in a specific amount of time. They may focus on getting a raise or getting a date, on improving your SAT scores or your backstroke. They may take years to fulfill or a few days. Goals may also conflict with each other, so you must decide which ones are most important.

Personal and Professional Goals

Personal goals, such as overcoming shyness, focus on your development as a person. Professional goals, such as becoming a lieutenant in the military, focus on your career. Though they are different, personal and professional goals may affect each other. To help establish your priorities, you should outline your goals and the strategies needed to achieve them.

Set and Achieve Goals To set a goal, you must define your objective as specifically as possible. To achieve that goal, you must anticipate conflicts and map out a set time for its completion.

> **KEY CONCEPT** Goals require specific definition, realistic planning, and time limits. ■

▲ **Critical Viewing**
What goals might the girls in this photograph set? On what do you base your answer? **[Connect]**

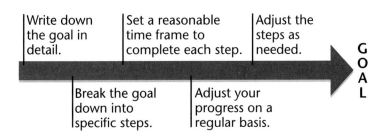

| Write down the goal in detail. | Set a reasonable time frame to complete each step. | Adjust the steps as needed. | G O A L |
| | Break the goal down into specific steps. | Adjust your progress on a regular basis. | |

Internships

An internship may be a goal or a means to achieving one. Internships give people the opportunity to learn about a career by working alongside professionals in the field. Employers benefit because the intern, often unpaid, provides a needed service. Interns may handle basic duties, such as answering phones and opening mail, or career-specific ones, such as compiling statistics or preparing lab experiments.

> **KEY CONCEPT** Internships benefit employers and students alike by providing hands-on learning experiences. ■

 **Research Tip**

To help plan your career goals, investigate fields of interest at the career center of a local college.

> **Exercise 6** Developing an Action Plan to Get an
Internship In your notebook, develop a detailed plan on how
to acquire an internship in a field of your choice. Include in
your plan the steps and resources needed to achieve the goal
and the estimated time each step will take. For example, what
specific skills does the internship require, and how do you get
those skills if you don't already have them? Share your plan
with the class.

Solving Problems With Creative Thinking

While pursuing personal and professional goals, you may
encounter problems. Having the skill to solve problems effectively and efficiently will help you realize your goals and make
you an asset to any profession. By identifying the problem and
evaluating possible options in a methodical manner, you can
select the best solution. Difficult problems may require more
creative thinking to generate a greater number of solutions
from which to choose.

Whether you must find transportation to a new job or housing on an overcrowded campus, you will need to use an organized strategy to isolate the problem and devise a workable
solution.

> **KEY CONCEPT** Solving a problem requires a thorough
grasp of the challenge at hand, a variety of possible solutions,
and a careful analysis of each one. ■

Solve problems by following these steps:

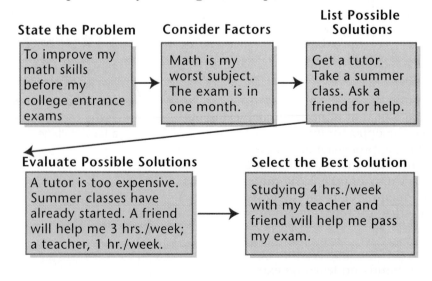

State the Problem
To improve my math skills before my college entrance exams

Consider Factors
Math is my worst subject. The exam is in one month.

List Possible Solutions
Get a tutor. Take a summer class. Ask a friend for help.

Evaluate Possible Solutions
A tutor is too expensive. Summer classes have already started. A friend will help me 3 hrs./week; a teacher, 1 hr./week.

Select the Best Solution
Studying 4 hrs./week with my teacher and friend will help me pass my exam.

Use Creative Thinking Creativity is the ability to put together something new. You can find solutions to problems by thinking creatively—opening your mind to unusual ideas and drawing on the experiences of different people.

KEY CONCEPT Creative thinking requires an openness to new approaches and a wide frame of reference from which to draw ideas. ■

Use the tips below to develop creative problem-solving skills:

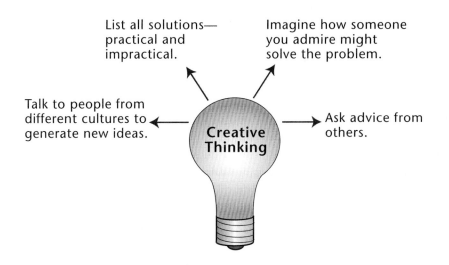

List all solutions—practical and impractical.

Imagine how someone you admire might solve the problem.

Talk to people from different cultures to generate new ideas.

Ask advice from others.

Creative Thinking

Exercise 7 **Solving Problems** As a class, analyze the following problems, generate three possible solutions for each, choose the best one, and explain why.
1. You inadvertently committed to baby-sitting for a neighbor's eight-year-old and to selling refreshments at a college baseball game at the same time.
2. You need a suit for an interview and are short on cash.
3. You started an internship at one company, only to be approached by another with a more interesting offer.

Exercise 8 **Practicing Creative Thinking** Your younger sibling or a neighbor's child is constantly following you and your friends around.With a group, brainstorm for at least five creative solutions that are positive for all parties involved. Evaluate the pros and cons of each potential solution.

Managing Time

Whether you choose the police academy, nursing school, or an apprenticeship with a builder, nearly all professions require the completion of duties in a certain amount of time. Therefore, you should strive to refine your time-management skills.

Proper time management—listing and prioritizing all appointments and activities—helps you accomplish projects, make time for activities, and minimize the impact of interruptions.

KEY CONCEPT Proper time management requires a prioritized list of appointments, activities, and deadlines. ■

Use the following strategies to budget your time well:

- Write appointments, activities, and deadlines on a calendar that you can carry with you.

- Divide large projects into a series of steps.

- Make a to-do list with daily activities ranked from most important to least important. At the day's end, move any unfinished items to the next day.

To-Do List

1. Call Mr. Carroll about math homework.

2. Make an appointment for a haircut.

3. Return movies to video store.

4. Buy flowers for Julie.

Mon 9:30 Project meeting

Tues

Wed 3:00–5:00 Baseball tryouts

Thur 6:00 Drive mom to airport

Fri

Sat 10:30 Help Uncle Mike paint house

Sun

Exercise 9 Analyzing Your Time-Management Skills In your notebook, write down the amount of time you spend on every activity for a week. Tally the amounts at the end of the week (for example, 15 hours on homework, 3 hours driving to activities). Observe how you spend your time, and write down where you need improvement.

Managing Money

New graduates also profit, literally and figuratively, from being wise money managers who make the most of every dollar. Proper money management—planning expenditures, paying your savings account like a bill, and spending less than you make—will

- allot money for what you really want.
- curb impulsive spending.
- provide a cushion for emergencies.

Research Tip

You can find easy-to-understand guides to managing your time and money at your local library.

> **KEY CONCEPT** Wise money managers live within their means, save regularly, and know their goals. ■

Following is a sample budget plan for someone who earns $350 a month, has $210 in expenses, saves at least $140 a month, and wants to buy a $580 car CD player in four months.

My Budget Plan to Buy a Car CD Player	Monthly Income	Monthly Expenses	Monthly Savings
Part-time Job	$350.00		
Car Insurance		$100.00	
Gasoline		25.00	
Club Dues		10.00	
Gifts/Misc.		75.00	
Total	$350.00	210.00	$140.00

> **Exercise 10** **Managing a Budget** Using the figures in the sample budget provided, do four months of budgets, showing how you could manage your money to buy the CD player and still have $100 to buy CDs.

Applying Math Skills

Math and computer knowledge will help you whether your career path takes you into physics or physical education, engineering or catering. From measuring recipe ingredients or board feet to calculating gas mileage or the best buy, math has many practical applications. Computers are ideal when it comes to research and writing.

> **KEY CONCEPT** Math skills enable you to manage money properly, shop economically, calculate measurements, and evaluate certain types of information. ■

Refer to this list for common math applications:

- **Balancing Checkbooks** To keep track of expenditures and to calculate interest earned, you must know basic math.

- **Making Wise Purchases** Faced with multiple choices from stores, mail-order catalogs, and cable and on-line shopping networks, you will need to understand unit prices, credit rates, taxes, and shipping and handling charges to calculate the most economical buys.

- **Calculating Measurements** From baking to building, proper measurements are critical. Besides basic conversions, you should know how to translate metric measures into their U.S. equivalents.

- **Analyzing Statistics** Business reports and daily newspapers often use statistics to support certain points of view. Knowing how to weigh the value of those numbers helps you make informed judgments.

Writing About Math

The ability to produce written explanations of how you go about solving a math problem or keeping a budget is a key skill in both school and business. When writing about math, apply many of the skills you learned in Chapters 10 and 11— "Exposition: Cause and Effect" and "Exposition: Problem and Solution."

> **Exercise 11** Using Math Skills to Prepare a Recipe
Choose a recipe from a cookbook. Imagine that you have only metric measuring cups and spoons. Convert the recipe amounts to fit the tools you have.

> **Exercise 12** Writing About Math Prepare a concise written explanation of a problem you recently solved in math class.

Applying Computer Skills

On the job and in the classroom, you will benefit from quick keyboarding skills, knowledge of software tools to present information accurately and attractively, and the ability to research on the Internet.

> **KEY CONCEPT** Basic computer skills entail the ability to type quickly and accurately, use formatting features, and access Internet information. ■

Use these suggestions to make the most of a computer:

- **Learn formatting techniques**. Use fonts, boldface, bullets, and other features to organize and highlight information.

- **Use spelling, grammar, and language tools.** Find just the right word or catch errors missed during proofreading.

- **Try to type 45 words per minute** or as fast as you can while retaining accuracy.

- **Learn to use the Internet**. With a teacher's guidance, discover the information available on-line.

▲ Critical Viewing How can peers help one another get the most out of using a computer? **[Apply]**

> **Exercise 13** Practicing Your Skills Choose a passage from a book, and practice your keyboarding skills by typing it on the computer as quickly as you can. Time yourself to see how close you are to the 45-word-per-minute goal. Use the spell-check function to check accuracy.

Reflecting on Your Workplace Skills and Competencies

Practice your communication and organizational skills, and write about your progress in your journal. Use the following questions to guide your response:

- What skills would I most like to improve? Why?

- What are my greatest strengths? Why?

- What exercises proved most helpful? Why?

Standardized Test Preparation Workshop

Reading Informational Texts

Some standardized tests assess your ability to read real-world texts, such as flyers, brochures, and advertisements. Often, this involves carefully following a sequence of steps or directions. Look at the example below.

Test Tip

Try to answer multiple-choice questions on your own before you look at the answers that are given.

Sample Test Items

Directions: Read the announcement, and then answer the questions that follow.

Town Meeting
Thursday, April 5 at 8 PM

Issues under discussion:

1. School budget

    • plan for new football stadium

    • increased faculty

2. July 4 celebration

    • parade

    • fireworks

3. Open Forum

Attendance open to <u>all residents.</u> Meeting will begin promptly at 8 P.M. Those wishing to participate in an open forum will have five minutes each. Participation in other discussions is also welcome.

According to the announcement, who will be allowed to participate in the discussion of the school budget?

A   all town residents who attend

B   everyone

C   any town residents

D   school board members

Answer and Explanation

The correct answer is *A, all town residents who attend.* Although any town resident has the opportunity to participate in discussions of the school budget, only those who attend the meeting will be able to take advantage of this opportunity. Answer *B* is too broad, because it does not exclude those who do not live in the town.

Practice 1 **Directions:** Read the passage, and then answer the questions that follow.

Ron had been given the assignment of writing a literary analysis of the poetry of William Wordsworth. To help gather background for his essay, Ron used the AuthorWorks CD-ROM program, which provides extensive background, analyses, critical reviews, and more for Wordsworth and several other authors. After he had installed the software, Ron consulted the page below in the User's Guide. The page provided him with directions on how to navigate through the software.

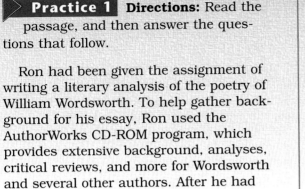

Takes you back a step from your current position.

Takes you to the Author Directory, or Main Menu.

Gives you access to Help.

Gives you access to the Scrapbook, Personal Timeline, Map, and Family History for a selected author.

Gives you access to the Published Work, Reviews, Notes & Letters, and Literary Connections for a selected author.

Gives you access to the Politics & Economics, Science & Technology, Arts, Daily Life, and Literary Trends sections of the program.

Moves you forward and backward through slide shows.

A highlighted speaker icon indicates that there is audio information or music to hear. Select this icon to start or stop the selection.

1 Which of the following types of information would Ron *not* be likely to find in the software?
A critical reviews
B a timeline of key dates in Wordsworth's life
C readings of Wordsworth's poetry by the poet himself
D a family history of the poet

2 What function do the two horizontal arrows serve?
F They allow the user to move back and forth through a slide show.
G They take the user to another author.
H They enable users to scroll through a timeline.
J They take users to the next feature.

3 Why did Ron consult the User's Guide?
A because the software was confusing
B because he wanted to be able to see at a glance how to navigate through the program
C because he was looking for background on Wordsworth
D because he wanted to see what support the software provides.

4 Which of the following is *not* a content feature that the program provides?
F information on daily life and literary trends during the periods in which the authors lived
G literary maps
H video performances of the writers' works
J scrapbooks for selected authors

5 Which of the following best describes how to find information on Wordsworth in the software?
A Click to access the Author Directory or the Main Menu.
B Click the Help button.
C Key in Wordsworth's name.
D Use the Menu Bar.

Citing Sources and Preparing Manuscript

The presentation of your written work is important. Your work should be neat, clean, and easy to read. Follow your teacher's directions for placing your name and class, along with the title and date of your work, on the paper.

For handwritten work:

- Use cursive handwriting or manuscript printing, according to the style your teacher prefers. The penmanship reference below shows the accepted formation of letters in cursive writing.
- Write or print neatly.
- Write on one side of lined $8\frac{1}{2}$" x 11" paper with a clean edge. (Do not use pages torn from a spiral notebook.)
- Indent the first line of each paragraph.

- Leave a margin, as indicated by the guidelines on the lined paper. Write in a size appropriate for the lines provided. Do not write so large that the letters from one line bump into the ones above and below. Do not write so small that the writing is difficult to read.
- Write in blue or black ink.
- Number the pages in the upper right corner.
- You should not cross out words on your final draft. Recopy instead. If your paper is long, your teacher may allow you to make one or two small changes by neatly crossing out the text to be deleted and using a caret [^] to indicate replacement text. Alternatively, you might make one or two corrections neatly with correction fluid. If you find yourself making more than three corrections, consider recopying the work.

PENMANSHIP REFERENCE

For word-processed or typed documents:

- Choose a standard, easy-to-read font.
- Type or print on one side of unlined 8 1/2" x 11" paper.
- Set the margins for the side, top, and bottom of your paper at approximately one inch. Most word-processing programs have a default setting that is appropriate.
- Double-space the document.
- Indent the first line of each paragraph.
- Number the pages in the upper right corner. Many word-processing programs have a header feature that will do this for you automatically.

- If you discover one or two errors after you have typed or printed, use correction fluid if your teacher allows such corrections. If you have more than three errors in an electronic file, consider making the corrections to the file and reprinting the document. If you have typed a long document, your teacher may allow you to make a few corrections by hand. If you have several errors, however, consider retyping the document.

For research papers:

Follow your teacher's directions for formatting formal research papers. Most papers will have the following features:

- Title page
- Table of Contents or Outline
- Works-Cited List

Sybil Luddington:
Female Paul Revere

Megan Mahoney
Language Arts
3rd Period
March 26, 20- -

Table of Contents

.... 6

.... 10

.... 12

.... 15

Cited

Incorporating Ideas From Research

Below are three common methods of incorporating the ideas of other writers into your work. Choose the most appropriate style by analyzing your needs in each case. In all cases, you must credit your source.

- **Direct Quotation:** Use quotation marks to indicate the exact words.
- **Paraphrase:** To share ideas without a direct quotation, state the ideas in your own words. While you haven't copied word-for-word, you still need to credit your source.
- **Summary:** To provide information about a large body of work—such as a speech, an editorial, or a chapter of a book—identify the writer's main idea.

Avoiding Plagiarism

Whether you are presenting a formal research paper or an opinion paper on a current event, you must be careful to give credit for any ideas or opinions that are not your own. Presenting someone else's ideas, research, or opinion as your own—even if you have rephrased it in different words—is *plagiarism*, the equivalent of academic stealing, or fraud.

You can avoid plagiarism by synthesizing what you learn: Read from several sources and let the ideas of experts help you draw your own conclusions and form your own opinions. Ultimately, however, note your own reactions to the ideas presented.

When you choose to use someone else's ideas or work to support your view, credit the source of the material. Give bibliographic information to cite your sources of the following information:

- Statistics
- Direct quotations
- Indirectly quoted statements of opinions
- Conclusions presented by an expert
- Facts available in only one or two sources

Crediting Sources

When you credit a source, you acknowledge where you found your information and you give your readers the details necessary for locating the source themselves. Within the body of the paper, you provide a short citation, a footnote number linked to a footnote, or an endnote number linked to an endnote reference. These brief references show the page numbers on which you found the information. To make your paper more formal, prepare a reference list at the end of the paper to provide full bibliographic information on your sources. These are two common types of reference lists:

- A **bibliography** provides a listing of all the resources you consulted during your research.
- A **works-cited list** indicates the works you have referenced in your paper.

Choosing a Format for Documentation

The type of information you provide and the format in which you provide it depend on what your teacher prefers. These are the most commonly used styles:

- **Modern Language Association (MLA) Style** This is the style used for most papers at the middle-school and high-school level and for most language arts papers.
- **American Psychological Association (APA) Style** This is used for most papers in the social sciences and for most college-level papers.
- ***Chicago Manual of Style*** (CMS) Style This is preferred by some teachers.

On the following pages, you'll find sample citation formats for the most commonly cited materials. Each format calls for standard bibliographic information. The difference is in the order of the material presented in each entry and the punctuation required.

MLA Style for Listing Sources

Book with one author	Pyles, Thomas. *The Origins and Development of the English Language.* 2nd ed. New York: Harcourt Brace Jovanovich, Inc., 1971.
Book with two or three authors	McCrum, Robert, William Cran, and Robert MacNeil. *The Story of English.* New York: Penguin Books, 1987.
Book with an editor	Truth, Sojourner. *Narrative of Sojourner Truth.* Ed. Margaret Washington. New York: Vintage Books, 1993.
Book with more than three authors or editors	Donald, Robert B., et al. *Writing Clear Essays.* Upper Saddle River, NJ: Prentice-Hall, Inc., 1996.
A single work from an anthology	Hawthorne, Nathaniel. "Young Goodman Brown." *Literature: An Introduction to Reading and Writing.* Ed. Edgar V. Roberts and Henry E. Jacobs. Upper Saddle River, NJ: Prentice-Hall, Inc., 1998. 376–385. [Indicate pages for the entire selection.]
Introduction in a published edition	Washington, Margaret. Introduction. *Narrative of Sojourner Truth.* By Sojourner Truth. New York: Vintage Books, 1993, pp. v–xi.
Signed article in a weekly magazine	Wallace, Charles. "A Vodacious Deal." *Time* 14 Feb. 2000: 63.
Signed article in a monthly magazine	Gustaitis, Joseph. "The Sticky History of Chewing Gum." *American History* Oct. 1998: 30–38.
Unsigned editorial or story	"Selective Silence." Editorial. *Wall Street Journal* 11 Feb. 2000: A14. [If the editorial or story is signed, begin with the author's name.]
Signed pamphlet	[Treat the pamphlet as though it were a book.]
Pamphlet with no author, publisher, or date	*Are You at Risk of Heart Attack?* n.p. n.d. [n.p. n.d. indicates that there is no known publisher or date]
Filmstrips, slide programs, and videotape	*The Diary of Anne Frank.* Dir. George Stevens. Perf. Millie Perkins, Shelley Winters, Joseph Schildkraut, Lou Jacobi, and Richard Beymer. Twentieth Century Fox, 1959.
Radio or television program transcript	"The First Immortal Generation." *Ockham's Razor.* Host Robyn Williams. Guest Damien Broderick. National Public Radio. 23 May 1999. Transcript.
Internet	*National Association of Chewing Gum Manufacturers.* 19 Dec. 1999 <http://www.nacgm.org/consumer/funfacts.html> [Indicate the date you accessed the information. Content and addresses at Web sites change frequently.]
Newspaper	Thurow, Roger. "South Africans Who Fought for Sanctions Now Scrap for Investors." *Wall Street Journal* 11 Feb. 2000: A1+ [For a multipage article, write only the first page number on which it appears, followed by a plus sign.]
Personal interview	Smith, Jane. Personal interview. 10 Feb. 2000.
CD (with multiple publishers)	Simms, James, ed. *Romeo and Juliet.* By William Shakespeare. CD-ROM. Oxford: Attica Cybernetics Ltd.; London: BBC Education; London: HarperCollins Publishers, 1995.
Article from an encyclopedia	Askeland, Donald R. (1991). "Welding." *World Book Encyclopedia.* 1991 ed.

APA Style for Listing Sources

The list of citations for APA is referred to as a Reference List and not a bibliography.

Book with one author	Pyles, T. (1971). *The Origins and Development of the English Language* (2nd ed.). New York: Harcourt Brace Jovanovich, Inc.
Book with two or three authors	McCrum, R., Cran, W., & MacNeil, R. (1987). *The Story of English*. New York: Penguin Books.
Book with an editor	Truth, S. (1993). *Narrative of Sojourner Truth* (M. Washington, Ed.). New York: Vintage Books.
Book with more than three authors or editors	Donald, R. B., Morrow, B. R., Wargetz, L. G., & Werner, K. (1996). *Writing Clear Essays*. Upper Saddle River, New Jersey: Prentice-Hall, Inc. [With six or more authors, abbreviate second and following authors as "et al."]
A single work from an anthology	Hawthorne, N. (1998) Young Goodman Brown. In E. V. Roberts, & H. E. Jacobs (Eds.), *Literature: An Introduction to Reading and Writing* (pp. 376–385). Upper Saddle River, New Jersey: Prentice-Hall, Inc.
Introduction to a work included in a published edition	[No style is offered under this heading.]
Signed article in a weekly magazine	Wallace, C. (2000, February 14). A vodacious deal. *Time, 155*, 63. [The volume number appears in italics before the page number.]
Signed article in a monthly magazine	Gustaitis, J. (1998, October). The sticky history of chewing gum. *American History, 33*, 30–38.
Unsigned editorial or story	Selective Silence. (2000, February 11). *Wall Street Journal*, p. A14.
Signed pamphlet	Pearson Education. (2000). *LifeCare* (2nd ed.) [Pamphlet]. Smith, John: Author.
Pamphlet with no author, publisher, or date	[No style is offered under this heading.]
Filmstrips, slide programs, and videotape	Stevens, G. (Producer & Director). (1959). *The Diary of Anne Frank*. [Videotape]. (Available from Twentieth Century Fox) [If the producer and the director are two different people, list the producer first and then the director, with an ampersand (&) between them.]
Radio or television program transcript	Broderick, D. (1999, May 23). The First Immortal Generation. (R. Williams, Radio Host). *Ockham's Razor*. New York: National Public Radio.
Internet	National Association of Chewing Gum Manufacturers. Available: http://www.nacgm.org/consumer/funfacts.html [References to Websites should begin with the author's last name, if available. Indicate the site name and the available path or URL address.]
Newspaper	Thurow, R. (2000, February 11). South Africans who fought for sanctions now scrap for investors. *Wall Street Journal*, pp. A1, A4.
Personal interview	[APA states that, since interviews (and other personal communications) do not provide "recoverable data," they should only be cited in text.]
CD (with multiple publishers)	[No style is offered under this heading.]
Article from an encyclopedia	Askeland, D. R. (1991). Welding. In *World Book Encyclopedia*. (Vol. 21 pp. 190–191). Chicago: World Book, Inc.

CMS Style for Listing Sources

The following chart shows the CMS author-date method of documentation.

Book with one author	Pyles, Thomas. *The Origins and Development of the English Language,* 2nd ed. New York: Harcourt Brace Jovanovich, Inc., 1971.
Book with two or three authors	McCrum, Robert, William Cran, and Robert MacNeil. *The Story of English.* New York: Penguin Books, 1987.
Book with an editor	Truth, Sojourner. *Narrative of Sojourner Truth.* Edited by Margaret Washington. New York: Vintage Books, 1993.
Book with more than three authors or editors	Donald, Robert B., et al. *Writing Clear Essays.* Upper Saddle River, New Jersey: Prentice-Hall, Inc., 1996.
A single work from an anthology	Hawthorne, Nathaniel. "Young Goodman Brown." In *Literature: An Introduction to Reading and Writing.* Ed. Edgar V. Roberts and Henry E. Jacobs. 376–385. Upper Saddle River, New Jersey: Prentice-Hall, Inc., 1998.
Introduction to a work included in a published edition	Washington, Margaret. Introduction to *Narrative of Sojourner Truth,* by Sojourner Truth. New York: Vintage Books, 1993. [According to CMS style, you should avoid this type of entry unless the introduction is of special importance to the work.]
Signed article in a weekly magazine	Wallace, Charles. "A Vodacious Deal." *Time,* 14 February 2000, 63.
Signed article in a monthly magazine	Gustaitis, Joseph. "The Sticky History of Chewing Gum." *American History,* October 1998, 30–38.
Unsigned editorial or story	*Wall Street Journal,* 11 February 2000. [CMS states that items from newspapers are seldom listed in a bibliography. Instead, the name of the paper and the relevant dates are listed.]
Signed pamphlet	[No style is offered under this heading.]
Pamphlet with no author, publisher, or date	[No style is offered under this heading.]
Filmstrips, slide programs, and videotape	Stevens, George. (director). *The Diary of Anne Frank.* 170 min. Beverly Hills, California: Twentieth Century Fox, 1994.
Radio or television program transcript	[No style is offered under this heading.]
Internet	[No style is offered under this heading.]
Newspaper	*Wall Street Journal,* 11 February 2000. [CMS states that items from newspapers are seldom listed in a bibliography. Instead, the name of the paper and the relevant dates are listed.]
Personal interview	[CMS states that, since personal conversations are not available to the public, there is no reason to place them in the bibliography. However, the following format should be followed if they are listed.] Jane Smith. Conversation with author. Wooster, Ohio, 10 February 2000.
CD (with multiple publishers)	Shakespeare, William. *Romeo and Juliet.* Oxford: Attica Cybernetics Ltd.; London: BBC Education; London: HarperCollins Publishers, 1995. CD-ROM.
Article from an encyclopedia	[According to CMS style, encyclopedias are not listed in bibliographies.]

Sample Works-Cited List (MLA)

Carwardine, Mark, Erich Hoyt, R. Ewan Fordyce, and
Peter Gill. *The Nature Company Guides: Whales,
Dolphins, and Porpoises*. New York: Time-Life
Books, 1998.

Ellis, Richard. *Men and Whales*. New York: Knopf,
1991.

Whales in Danger. "Discovering Whales." 18 Oct. 1999.
<http://whales.magna.com.au/DISCOVER>

Sample Internal Citations (MLA)

It makes sense that baleen whales such as the
blue whale, the fin whale, the bowhead whale, the
humpback whale, and the sei whale (to name just
a few) grow to immense sizes (Carwardine 19–21).
The blue whale has grooves running from under its
chin to partway along the length of its underbelly.
As in some other whales, these grooves expand
and allow even more food and water to be taken in
(Ellis 18–21).

Author's last name

page numbers where information can be found

Internet Research Handbook

Introduction to the Internet

The Internet is a series of networks that are interconnected all over the world. The Internet allows users to have almost unlimited access to information stored on the networks. Dr. Berners-Lee, a physicist, created the Internet in the 1980's by writing a small computer program that allowed pages to be linked together using key words. The Internet was mostly text-based until 1992, when a computer program called the NCSA Mosaic (National Center for Supercomputing Applications at the University of Illinois) was created. This program was the first Web browser. The development of Web browsers greatly eased the ability of the user to navigate through all the pages stored on the Web. Very soon, the appearance of the Web was altered as well. More appealing visuals were added, and sound was also implemented. This change made the Web more user-friendly and more appealing to the general public.

Using the Internet for Research

Key Word Search

Before you begin a search, you should identify your specific topic. To make searching easier, narrow your subject to a key word or a group of key words. These are your search terms, and they should be as specific as possible. For example, if you are looking for the latest concert dates for your favorite musical group, you might use the band's name as a key word. However, if you were to enter the name of the group in the query box of the search engine, you might be presented with thousands of links to information about the group that is unrelated to your needs. You might locate such information as band member biographies, the group's history, fan reviews of concerts, and hundreds of sites with related names containing information that is irrelevant to your search. Because you used such a broad key word, you might need to navigate through all that information before you find a link or subheading for concert dates. In contrast, if you were to type in "Duplex Arena and [band name]" you would have a better chance of locating pages that contain this information.

How to Narrow Your Search

If you have a large group of key words and still don't know which ones to use, write out a list of all the words you are considering. Once you have completed the list, scrutinize it. Then, delete the words that are least important to your search, and highlight those that are most important.

These **key search connectors** can help you fine-tune your search:

AND: narrows a search by retrieving documents that include both terms. For example: *baseball AND playoffs*

OR: broadens a search by retrieving documents including any of the terms. For example: *playoffs OR championships*

NOT: narrows a search by excluding documents containing certain words. For example: *baseball NOT history of*

Tips for an Effective Search

1. Keep in mind that search engines can be case-sensitive. If your first attempt at searching fails, check your search terms for misspellings and try again.

2. If you are entering a group of key words, present them in order, from the most important to the least important key word.

3. Avoid opening the link to every single page in your results list. Search engines present pages in descending order of relevancy. The most useful pages will be located at the top of the list. However, read the description of each link before you open the page.

4. When you use some search engines, you can find helpful tips for specializing your search. Take the opportunity to learn more about effective searching.

Other Ways to Search

Using On-line Reference Sites

How you search should be tailored to *what* you are hoping to find. If you are looking for data and facts, use reference sites before you jump onto a simple search engine. For example, you can find reference sites to provide definitions of words, statistics about almost any subject, biographies, maps, and concise information on many topics. Some useful on-line reference sites:

- On-line libraries
- On-line periodicals
- Almanacs
- Encyclopedias

You can find these sources using subject searches.

Conducting Subject Searches

As you prepare to go on-line, consider your subject and the best way to find information to suit your needs. If you are looking for general information on a topic and you want your search results to be extensive, consider the subject search indexes on most search engines. These indexes, in the form of category and subject lists, often appear on the first page of a search engine. When you click on a specific highlighted word, you will be presented with a new screen containing subcategories of the topic you chose. In the screen shots below, the category *Sports & Recreation* provided a second index for users to focus a search even further.

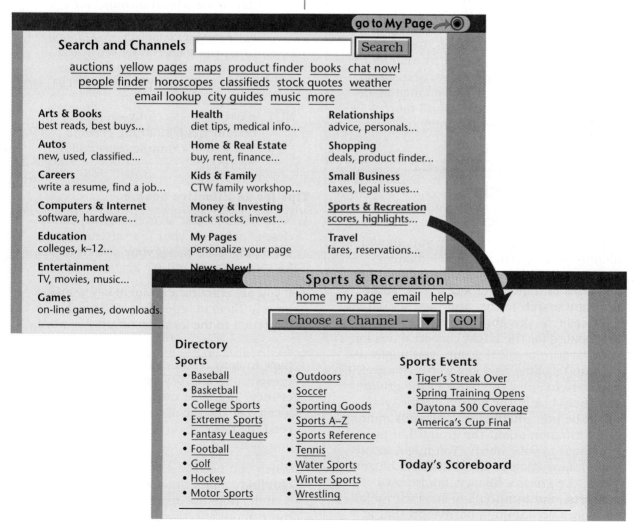

Evaluating the Reliability of Internet Resources

Just as you would evaluate the quality, bias, and validity of any other research material you locate, check the source of information you find on-line. Compare these two sites containing information on the poet and writer Langston Hughes:

Site A is a personal Web site constructed by a college student. It contains no bibliographic information or links to sites that he used. Included on the site are several poems by Langston Hughes and a student essay about the poet's use of symbolism. It has not been updated in more than six months.

Site B is a Web site constructed and maintained by the English Department of a major university. Information on Hughes is presented in a scholarly format, with a bibliography and credits for the writer. The site includes links to other sites and indicates new features that are added weekly.

For your own research, consider the information you find on Site B to be more reliable and accurate than that on Site A. Because it is maintained by experts in their field who are held accountable for their work, the university site will be a better research tool than the student-generated one.

Tips for Evaluating Internet Sources

1. Consider who constructed and who now maintains the Web page. Determine whether this author is a reputable source. Often, the URL endings indicate a source.

   - Sites ending in *.edu* are maintained by educational institutions.
   - Sites ending in *.gov* are maintained by government agencies (federal, state, or local).
   - Sites ending in *.org* are normally maintained by nonprofit organizations and agencies.
   - Sites with a *.com* ending are commercially or personally maintained.

2. Skim the official and trademarked Web pages first. It is safe to assume that the information you draw from Web pages of reputable institutions, on-line encyclopedias, on-line versions of major daily newspapers, or government-owned sites produce information as reliable as the material you would find in print. In contrast, unbranded sites or those generated by individuals tend to borrow information from other sources without providing documentation. As information travels from one source to another, the information has likely been muddled, misinterpreted, edited, or revised.

3. You can still find valuable information in the less "official" sites. Check for the writer's credentials and then consider these factors:

   - Don't let official-looking graphics or presentations fool you.
   - Make sure the information is updated enough to suit your needs. Many Web pages will indicate how recently they have been updated.
   - If the information is borrowed, see whether you can trace it back to its original source.

Respecting Copyrighted Material

Because the Internet is a relatively new and quickly growing medium, issues of copyright and ownership arise almost daily. As laws begin to govern the use and reuse of material posted on-line, they may change the way that people can access or reprint material.

Text, photographs, music, and fine art printed on-line may not be reproduced without acknowledged permission of the copyright owner.

Glossary of Internet Terms

attached file: a file containing information, such as a text document or GIF image, that is attached to an e-mail message; reports, pictures, spreadsheets, and so on transmitted to others by attaching these to messages as files

bandwidth: the amount of information, mainly compressed in bits per second (bps), that can be sent through a connection within a specific amount of time; depending on how fast your modem is, 15,000 bits (roughly one page of text) can be transferred per second

bit: a binary digit of computerized data, represented by a single digit that is either a 1 or a 0; a group of bits constitutes a byte

bookmark: a feature of your Web browser that allows you to place a "bookmark" on a Web page to which you wish to return at a later time

browser: software designed to present material accessed on the Web

bulletin-board system: a computer system that members access in order to join on-line discussion groups or to post announcements

case-sensitivity: the quality of a search engine that causes it to respond to upper- or lowercase letters in different ways

chat room: informal on-line gathering sites where people share conversations, experiences, or information on a specific topic; many chat rooms do not require users to provide their identity, so the reliability or safety of these sites is uncertain

cookie: a digitized piece of information that is sent to a Web browser by a Web server, intended to be saved on a computer; cookies gather information about the user, such as user preferences, or recent on-line purchases; a Web browser can be set to either accept or reject cookies

cyberspace: a term referring to the electronic environment connecting all computer network information with the people who use it

database: a large collection of data that have been formatted to fit a certain user-defined standard

digerati: a slang term to describe Internet experts; an offshoot of the term *literati*

download: to copy files from the Internet onto your computer

e-mail: electronic mail, or the exchange of messages via the Internet; because it is speedier than traditional mail and offers easier global access, e-mail has grown in popularity; e-mail messages can be sent to a single person or in bulk to a group of people

error message: a displayed communication or printout that reports a problem with a program or Web page

FTP site (file transfer protocol): a password-protected server on the Internet that allows the transfer of information from one computer to another

GIF (Graphic Interchange Format): a form of graphics used on the Web

graphics: information displayed as pictures or images instead of text

hits: items retrieved by a key word search; the number tracking the volume of visits to a Web site

home page: the main Web page for an individual or an organization, containing links to subpages within

HTML (HyperText Markup Language): the coding text that is the foundation for creating Web pages

interactivity: a quality of some Web pages that encourages the frequent exchange of information between user and computer

Internet: a worldwide computer network that supports services such as the World Wide Web, e-mail, and file transfer

JPEG (Joint Photo Experts Group, the developers): a file format for graphics especially suited to photographs

K: a measurement of file size or memory; short for "Kilobyte," 1,000 bytes of information (see *bit*)

key word: search term entered into the query box of a search engine to direct the results of the search

link: an icon or word on a Web page that, when clicked, transfers the user to another Web page or to a different document within the same page

login: the procedure by which users gain access to a server or a secure Web site; usually the user must enter a specific user name and password

modem: a device that transfers data to a computer through a phone line. A computer's modem connects to a server, which then sends information in the form of digital signals. The modem converts these signals into waves, for the purpose of information reception. The speed of a modem affects how quickly a computer can receive and download information

newbie: jargon used to describe Internet novices

newsgroup: an on-line discussion group, where users can post and respond to messages; the most prevalent collection of newsgroups is found on USENET

query box: the blank box in a search engine where your search terms are input

relevance ranking: the act of displaying the results of a search in the order of their relevance to the search terms

search engines: tools that help you navigate databases to locate information; search engines respond to a key word search by providing the user with a directory of multiple Web pages about the key word or containing the key word

server: a principal computer that provides services, such as storing files and providing access to the Internet, to another computer

signature: a preprogrammed section of text that is automatically added to an e-mail message

surfing: the process of reading Web pages and of moving from one Web site to another

URL (Uniform Resource Locator): a Web page's address; a URL can look like this:

http://www.phwg.phschool.com or
*http://www.senate.gov/~appropriations/
  labor/testimony*

usenet: a worldwide system of discussion groups, or newsgroups

vanity pages: Web sites placed on-line by people to tell about themselves or their interests; vanity pages do not have any commercial or informational value

virus: a set of instructions, hidden in a computer system or transferred via e-mail or electronic files, that can cause problems with a computer's ability to perform normally

Web page: a set of information, including graphics, text, sound, and video, presented in a browser window; a Web page can be found by its URL once it is posted on the World Wide Web

Web site: a collection of Web pages that are linked together for posting on the World Wide Web

W3: a group of Internet experts, including networking professionals, academics, scientists, and corporate interests, who maintain and develop technologies and standards for the Internet

WWW (World Wide Web): a term referring to the multitude of information systems found on the Internet; this includes FTP, Gopher, telnet, and http sites

zip: the minimizing of files through compression; this function makes for easier transmittal over networks; a receiver can then open the file by "unzipping" it

Commonly Overused Words

When you write, use the most precise word for your meaning, not the word that comes to mind first. Consult this thesaurus to find alternatives for some commonly overused words. Consult a full-length thesaurus to find alternatives to words that do not appear here. Keep in mind that the choices offered in a thesaurus do not all mean exactly the same thing. Review all the options, and choose the one that best expresses your meaning.

about approximately, nearly, almost, approaching, close to

absolutely unconditionally, perfectly, completely, ideally, purely

activity action, movement, operation, labor, exertion, enterprise, project, pursuit, endeavor, job, assignment, pastime, scheme, task

add attach, affix, join, unite, append, increase, amplify

affect adjust, influence, transform, moderate, incline, motivate, prompt

amazing overwhelming, astonishing, startling, unexpected, stunning, dazzling, remarkable

awesome impressive, stupendous, fabulous, astonishing, outstanding

bad defective, inadequate, poor, unsatisfactory, disagreeable, offensive, repulsive, corrupt, wicked, naughty, harmful, injurious, unfavorable

basic essential, necessary, indispensable, vital, fundamental, elementary

beautiful attractive, appealing, alluring, exqui-

site, gorgeous, handsome, stunning

begin commence, found, initiate, introduce, launch, originate

better preferable, superior, worthier

big enormous, extensive, huge, immense, massive

boring commonplace, monotonous, tedious, tiresome

bring accompany, cause, convey, create, conduct, deliver, produce

cause origin, stimulus, inspiration, motive

certain unquestionable, incontrovertible, unmistakable, indubitable, assured, confident

change alter, transform, vary, replace, diversify

choose select, elect, nominate, prefer, identify

decent respectable, adequate, fair, suitable

definitely unquestionably, clearly, precisely, positively, inescapably

easy effortless, natural, comfortable, undemanding, pleasant, relaxed

effective powerful, successful

emphasize underscore, feature, accentuate

end limit, boundary, finish, conclusion, finale, resolution

energy vitality, vigor, force, dynamism

enjoy savor, relish, revel, benefit

entire complete, inclusive, unbroken, integral

excellent superior, remarkable, splendid, unsurpassed, superb, magnificent

exciting thrilling, stirring, rousing, dramatic

far distant, remote

fast swift, quick, fleet, hasty, instant, accelerated

fill occupy, suffuse, pervade, saturate, inflate, stock

finish complete, conclude, cease, achieve, exhaust, deplete, consume

funny comical, ludicrous, amusing, droll, entertaining, bizarre, unusual, uncommon

get obtain, receive, acquire, procure, achieve

give bestow, donate, supply, deliver, distribute, impart

go proceed, progress, advance, move

good satisfactory, serviceable, functional, competent, virtuous, striking

great tremendous, superior, remarkable, eminent, proficient, expert

happy pleased, joyous, elated, jubilant, cheerful, delighted

hard arduous, formidable, complex, complicated, rigorous, harsh

help assist, aid, support, sustain, serve

hurt injure, harm, damage, wound, impair

important significant, substantial, weighty, meaningful, critical, vital, notable

interesting absorbing, appealing, entertaining, fascinating, thought-provoking

job task, work, business, undertaking, occupation, vocation, chore, duty, assignment

keep retain, control, possess

kind type, variety, sort, form

know comprehend, understand, realize, perceive, discern

like (adj) similar, equivalent, parallel

like (verb) enjoy, relish, appreciate

main primary, foremost, dominant

make build, construct, produce, assemble, fashion, manufacture

mean plan, intend, suggest, propose, indicate

more supplementary, additional, replenishment

new recent, modern, current, novel

next subsequently, thereafter, successively

nice pleasant, satisfying, gracious, charming

old aged, mature, experienced, used, worn, former, previous

open unobstructed, accessible

part section, portion, segment, detail, element, component

perfect flawless, faultless, ideal, consummate

plan scheme, design, system, plot

pleasant agreeable, gratifying, refreshing, welcome

prove demonstrate, confirm, validate, verify, corroborate

quick brisk, prompt, responsive, rapid, nimble, hasty

really truly, genuinely, extremely, undeniably

regular standard, routine, customary, habitual

see regard, behold, witness, gaze, realize, notice

small diminutive, miniature, minor, insignificant, slight, trivial

sometimes occasionally, intermittently, sporadically, periodically

take grasp, capture, choose, select, tolerate, endure

terrific extraordinary, magnificent, marvelous

think conceive, imagine, ponder, reflect, contemplate

try attempt, endeavor, venture, test

use employ, operate, utilize

very unusually, extremely, deeply, exceedingly, profoundly

want desire, crave, yearn, long

Commonly Misspelled Words

The list on these pages presents words that cause problems for many people. Some of these words are spelled according to set rules, but others follow no specific rules. As you review this list, check to see how many of the words give you trouble in your own writing. Then, read the instruction in the "Vocabulary and Spelling" chapter in the book for strategies and suggestions for improving your own spelling habits.

abbreviate	athletic	catastrophe	curious
absence	attendance	category	cylinder
absolutely	auxiliary	ceiling	deceive
abundance	awkward	cemetery	decision
accelerate	bandage	census	deductible
accidentally	banquet	certain	defendant
accumulate	bargain	changeable	deficient
accurate	barrel	characteristic	definitely
ache	battery	chauffeur	delinquent
achievement	beautiful	chief	dependent
acquaintance	beggar	clothes	descendant
adequate	beginning	coincidence	description
admittance	behavior	colonel	desert
advertisement	believe	column	desirable
aerial	benefit	commercial	dessert
affect	bicycle	commission	deteriorate
aggravate	biscuit	commitment	dining
aggressive	bookkeeper	committee	disappointed
agreeable	bought	competitor	disastrous
aisle	boulevard	concede	discipline
all right	brief	condemn	dissatisfied
allowance	brilliant	congratulate	distinguish
aluminum	bruise	connoisseur	effect
amateur	bulletin	conscience	eighth
analysis	buoyant	conscientious	eligible
analyze	bureau	conscious	embarrass
ancient	bury	contemporary	enthusiastic
anecdote	buses	continuous	entrepreneur
anniversary	business	controversy	envelope
anonymous	cafeteria	convenience	environment
answer	calendar	coolly	equipped
anticipate	campaign	cooperate	equivalent
anxiety	canceled	cordially	especially
apologize	candidate	correspondence	exaggerate
appall	capacity	counterfeit	exceed
appearance	capital	courageous	excellent
appreciate	capitol	courteous	exercise
appropriate	captain	courtesy	exhibition
architecture	career	criticism	existence
argument	carriage	criticize	experience
associate	cashier	curiosity	explanation

extension	library	particularly	restaurant
extraordinary	license	patience	rhythm
familiar	lieutenant	permanent	ridiculous
fascinating	lightning	permissible	sandwich
February	likable	perseverance	satellite
fiery	liquefy	persistent	schedule
financial	literature	personally	scissors
fluorescent	loneliness	perspiration	secretary
foreign	magnificent	persuade	siege
forfeit	maintenance	phenomenal	solely
fourth	marriage	phenomenon	sponsor
fragile	mathematics	physician	subtle
gauge	maximum	pleasant	subtlety
generally	meanness	pneumonia	superintendent
genius	mediocre	possess	supersede
genuine	mileage	possession	surveillance
government	millionaire	possibility	susceptible
grammar	minimum	prairie	tariff
grievance	minuscule	precede	temperamental
guarantee	miscellaneous	preferable	theater
guard	mischievous	prejudice	threshold
guidance	misspell	preparation	truly
handkerchief	mortgage	prerogative	unmanageable
harass	naturally	previous	unwieldy
height	necessary	primitive	usage
humorous	negotiate	privilege	usually
hygiene	neighbor	probably	valuable
ignorant	neutral	procedure	various
illegible	nickel	proceed	vegetable
immediately	niece	prominent	voluntary
immigrant	ninety	pronunciation	weight
independence	noticeable	psychology	weird
independent	nuclear	publicly	whale
indispensable	nuisance	pursue	wield
individual	obstacle	questionnaire	yield
inflammable	occasion	realize	
intelligence	occasionally	really	
interfere	occur	recede	
irrelevant	occurred	receipt	
irritable	occurrence	receive	
jewelry	omitted	recognize	
judgment	opinion	recommend	
knowledge	opportunity	reference	
laboratory	optimistic	referred	
lawyer	outrageous	rehearse	
legible	pamphlet	relevant	
legislature	parallel	reminiscence	
leisure	paralyze	renowned	
liable	parentheses	repetition	

Abbreviations Guide

Abbreviations, shortened versions of words or phrases, can be valuable tools in writing if you know when and how to use them. They can be very helpful in informal writing situations, such as taking notes or writing lists. However, only a few abbreviations can be used in formal writing. They are: *Mr., Mrs., Miss, Ms., Dr., A.M., P.M., A.D., B.C., M.A, B.A., Ph.D.,* and *M.D.*

The following pages provide the conventional abbreviations for a variety of words.

Abbreviations of Common Titles

Ambassador	Amb.	Lieutenant	Lt.
Attorney	Atty.	Major	Maj.
Brigadier-General	Brig. Gen.	President	Pres.
Brother	Br.	Professor	Prof.
Captain	Capt.	Representative	Rep.
Colonel	Col.	Reverend	Rev.
Commander	Cmdr.	Secretary	Sec.
Commissioner	Com.	Senator	Sen.
Corporal	Cpl.	Sergeant	Sgt.
Doctor	Dr.	Sister	Sr.
Father	Fr.	Superintendent	Supt.
Governor	Gov.	Treasurer	Treas.
Honorable	Hon.	Vice Admiral	Vice Adm.

Abbreviations of Academic Degrees

Bachelor of Arts	B.A. (or A.B.)	Esquire (lawyer)	Esq.
Bachelor of Science	B.S. (or S.B.)	Master of Arts	M.A. (or A.M.)
Doctor of Dental Surgery	D.D.S.	Master of Business Administration	M.B.A.
Doctor of Divinity	D.D.		
Doctor of Education	Ed.D.	Master of Fine Arts	M.F.A.
Doctor of Laws	LL.D.	Master of Science	M.S. (or S.M.)
Doctor of Medicine	M.D.	Registered Nurse	R.N.
Doctor of Philosophy	Ph.D.		

Abbreviations of States

State	Traditional	Postal Service	State	Traditional	Postal Service
Alabama	Ala.	AL	Montana	Mont.	MT
Alaska	Alaska	AK	Nebraska	Nebr.	NE
Arizona	Ariz.	AZ	Nevada	Nev.	NV
Arkansas	Ark.	AR	New Hampshire	N.H.	NH
California	Calif.	CA	New Jersey	N.J.	NJ
Colorado	Colo.	CO	New Mexico	N.M.	NM
Connecticut	Conn.	CT	New York	N.Y.	NY
Delaware	Del.	DE	North Carolina	N.C.	NC
Florida	Fla.	FL	North Dakota	N.Dak.	ND
Georgia	Ga.	GA	Ohio	O.	OH
Hawaii	Hawaii	HI	Oklahoma	Okla.	OK
Idaho	Ida.	ID	Oregon	Ore.	OR
Illinois	Ill.	IL	Pennsylvania	Pa.	PA
Indiana	Ind.	IN	Rhode Island	R.I.	RI
Iowa	Iowa	IA	South Carolina	S.C.	SC
Kansas	Kans.	KS	South Dakota	S.Dak.	SD
Kentucky	Ky.	KY	Tennessee	Tenn.	TN
Louisiana	La.	LA	Texas	Tex.	TX
Maine	Me.	ME	Utah	Utah	UT
Maryland	Md.	MD	Vermont	Vt.	VT
Massachusetts	Mass.	MA	Virginia	Va.	VA
Michigan	Mich.	MI	Washington	Wash.	WA
Minnesota	Minn.	MN	West Virginia	W. Va	WV
Mississippi	Miss.	MS	Wisconsin	Wis.	WI
Missouri	Mo.	MO	Wyoming	Wyo.	WY

Common Geographical Abbreviations

Apartment	Apt.	National	Natl.
Avenue	Ave.	Park, Peak	Pk.
Block	Blk.	Peninsula	Pen.
Boulevard	Blvd.	Point	Pt.
Building	Bldg.	Province	Prov.
County	Co.	Road	Rd.
District	Dist.	Route	Rte.
Drive	Dr.	Square	Sq.
Fort	Ft.	Street	St.
Island	Is.	Territory	Terr.
Mountain	Mt.		

Abbreviations of Traditional Measurements

inch(es)	in.	ounce(s)	oz.
foot, feet	ft.	pound(s)	lb.
yard(s)	yd.	pint(s)	pt.
mile(s)	mi.	quart(s)	qt.
teaspoon(s)	tsp.	gallon(s)	gal.
tablespoon(s)	tbsp.	Fahrenheit	F.

Abbreviations of Metric Measurements

millimeter(s)	mm	liter(s)	L
centimeter(s)	cm	kiloliter(s)	kL
meter(s)	m	milligram(s)	mg
kilometer(s)	km	centigram(s)	cg
milliliter(s)	mL	gram(s)	g
centiliter(s)	cL	Celsius	C

Other Commonly Used Abbreviations

about (used with dates)	c., ca., circ.	manager	mgr.
and others	et al.	manufacturing	mfg.
anonymous	anon.	market	mkt.
approximately	approx.	measure	meas.
associate, association	assoc., assn.	merchandise	mdse.
auxiliary	aux., auxil.	miles per hour	mph
bibliography	bibliog.	miscellaneous	misc.
boxes	bx(s).	money order	M.O.
bucket	bkt.	note well; take notice	N.B.
bulletin	bull.	number	no.
bushel	bu.	package	pkg.
capital letter	cap.	page	p., pg.
cash on delivery	C.O.D.	pages	pp.
department	dept.	pair(s)	pr(s).
discount	disc.	parenthesis	paren.
dozen(s)	doz.	Patent Office	pat. off.
each	ea.	piece(s)	pc(s).
edition, editor	ed.	poetical, poetry	poet.
equivalent	equiv.	private	pvt.
established	est.	proprietor	prop.
fiction	fict.	pseudonym	pseud.
for example	e.g.	published, publisher	pub.
free of charge	grat., gratis	received	recd.
General Post Office	G.P.O.	reference, referee	ref.
government	gov., govt.	revolutions per minute	rpm
graduate, graduated	grad.	rhetorical, rhetoric	rhet.
Greek, Grecian	Gr.	right	R.
headquarters	hdqrs.	scene	sc.
height	ht.	special, specific	spec.
hospital	hosp.	spelling, species	sp.
illustrated	ill., illus.	that is	i.e.
including, inclusive	incl.	treasury, treasurer	treas.
introduction, introductory	intro.	volume	vol.
italics	ital.	weekly	wkly
karat, carat	k., kt.	weight	wt.
left	L.		

Proofreading Symbols Reference

Proofreading symbols make it easier to show where changes are needed in a paper. When proofreading your own or a classmate's work, use these standard proofreading symbols.

insert	I proofr*a*ed.
delete	I p̸ proofread.
close up space	I proof read.
delete and close up space	I proofreade.
begin new paragraph	¶ I proofread.
spell out	I proofread (10) papers. ⓢⓟ
lowercase	I Proofread. ⓛⓒ
capitalize	i proofread. ⓒⓐⓟ
transpose letters	I proofraed. ⓣⓡ
transpose words	I only proofread her paper. ⓣⓡ
period	I will proofread⊙
comma	I will proofread and she will help.
colon	We will proofread for the following errors
semicolon	I will proofread she will help.
single quotation marks	She said, "I enjoyed the story The Invalid."
double quotation marks	She said, I enjoyed the story.
apostrophe	Did you borrow Sylvias book?
question mark	Did you borrow Sylvia's book ?/
exclamation point	You're kidding !/
hyphen	online /=/
parentheses	William Shakespeare 1564–1616

Student Publications

To share your writing with a wider audience, consider submitting it to a local, state, or national publication for student writing. Following are several magazines and Web sites that accept and publish student work.

Periodicals

Creative Kids P.O. Box 8813, Waco, TX 76714

Merlyn's Pen: The National Magazine of Student Writing
P.O. Box 1058, East Greenwich, RI 02818

Skipping Stones P.O. Box 3939, Eugene, OR 97403

The McGuffey Writer McGuffey Foundation School, 5128 Westgate Drive, Oxford, OH 45056

Writing! General Learning Corporation, 900 Skokie Boulevard, Northbrook, IL 60062

On-line Publications

Kid Pub http://kidpub.org/kidpub

MidLink Magazine http://longwood.cs.ucf.edu/~MidLink/

Wild Guess Magazine http://members.tripod.com/~WildGuess/

Contests

Annual Poetry Contest National Federation of State Poetry Societies, 3520 State Route 56, Mechanicsburg, OH 43044

National Written & Illustrated By . . . Awards Contest for Students Landmark Editions, Inc., 1402 Kansas Avenue, Kansas City, MO 64127

Paul A. Witty Outstanding Literature Award International Reading Association, Special Interest Group for Reading for Gifted and Creative Students, c/o Texas Christian University, P.O. Box 32925, Fort Worth, TX 76129

Seventeen Magazine Fiction Contest *Seventeen* Magazine, 850 Third Avenue, New York, NY 10022

The Young Playwrights Festival National Playwriting Competition
321 East 44th Street, Suite 906, New York, NY 10036

Glossary

A

accent: the emphasis on a syllable, usually in poetry

action verb: a word that tells what action someone or something is performing (*See* linking verb.)

active voice: the voice of a verb whose subject performs an action (*See* passive voice.)

adjective: a word that modifies a noun or pronoun by telling *what kind* or *which one*

adjective clause: a subordinate clause that modifies a noun or pronoun

adjective phrase: a prepositional phrase that modifies a noun or pronoun

adverb: a word that modifies a verb, an adjective, or another adverb

adverb clause: a subordinate clause that modifies a verb, an adjective, an adverb, or a verbal by telling *where, when, in what way, to what extent, under what condition,* or *why*

adverb phrase: a prepositional phrase that modifies a verb, an adjective, or an adverb

allegory: a literary work with two or more levels of meaning—a literal level and one or more symbolic levels

alliteration: the repetition of initial consonant sounds in accented syllables

allusion: an indirect reference to a well-known person, place, event, literary work, or work of art

annotated bibliography: a research writing product that provides a list of materials on a given topic, along with publication information, summaries, or evaluations

apostrophe: a punctuation mark used to form possessive nouns and contractions

appositive: a noun or pronoun placed after another noun or pronoun to identify, rename, or explain the preceding word

appositive phrase: a noun or pronoun with its modifiers, placed next to a noun or pronoun to identify, rename, or explain the preceding word

article: one of three commonly used adjectives: *a, an,* and *the*

assonance: the repetition of vowel sounds in stressed syllables containing dissimilar consonant sounds

audience: the reader(s) a writer intends to reach

autobiographical writing: narrative writing that tells a true story about an important period, experience, or relationship in the writer's life

B

ballad: a song that tells a story (often dealing with adventure or romance) or a poem imitating such a song

bias: the attitudes or beliefs that affect a writer's ability to present a subject objectively

bibliography: a list of the sources of a research paper, including full bibliographic references for each source the writer consulted while conducting research (*See* works-cited list.)

biography: narrative writing that tells the story of an important period, experience, or relationship in a person's life, as reported by another

blueprinting: a prewriting technique in which a writer sketches a map of a home, school, neighborhood, or other meaningful place in order to spark memories or associations for further development

body paragraph: a paragraph in an essay that develops, explains, or supports the key ideas of the writing

brainstorming: a prewriting technique in which a group jots down as many ideas as possible about a given topic

C

case: the form of a noun or pronoun that indicates how it functions in a sentence

cause-and-effect writing: expository writing that examines the relationship between events, explaining how one event or situation causes another

character: a person (though not necessarily a human being) who takes part in the action of a literary work

characterization: the act of creating and developing a character through narration, description, and dialogue

citation: in formal research papers, the acknowledgment of ideas found in outside sources

classical invention: a prewriting technique in which writers gather details about a topic by analyzing the category and subcategories to which the topic belongs

clause: a group of words that has a subject and a verb

climax: the high point of interest or suspense in a literary work

coherence: a quality of written work in which all the parts flow logically from one idea to the next

colon: a punctuation mark used before an extended quotation, explanation, example, or series and after the salutation in a formal letter

comma: a punctuation mark used to separate words or groups of words

comparison-and-contrast writing: expository writing that describes the similarities and differences between two or more subjects in order to achieve a specific purpose

complement: a word or group of words that completes the meaning of a verb

compound sentence: a sentence that contains two or more independent clauses with no subordinate clauses

conclusion: the final paragraph(s) of a work of writing in which the writer may restate a main idea, summarize the points of the writing, or provide a closing remark to end the work effectively (*See* introduction, body paragraph, topical paragraph, functional paragraph.)

conflict: a struggle between opposing forces

conjugation: a list of the singular and plural forms of a verb in a particular tense

conjunction: a word used to connect other words or groups of words

connotation: the emotional associations that a word calls to mind (*See* denotation.)

consonance: the repetition of final consonant sounds in stressed syllables containing dissimilar vowel sounds

contraction: a shortened form of a word or phrase that includes an apostrophe to indicate the position of the missing letter(s)

coordinating conjunctions: words such as *and, but, nor,* and *yet* that connect similar words or groups of words

correlative conjunctions: word pairs such as *neither . . . nor, both . . . and,* and *whether . . . or* used to connect similar words or groups of words

couplet: a pair of rhyming lines written in the same meter

cubing: a prewriting technique in which a writer analyzes a subject from six specified angles: description; association; application; analysis; comparison and contrast; and evaluation

D

declarative sentence: a statement punctuated with a period

demonstrative pronouns: words such as *this, that, these,* and *those* used to single out specific people, places, or things

denotation: the objective meaning of a word; its definition independent of other associations the word calls to mind (*See* connotation.)

depth-charging: a drafting technique in which a writer elaborates on a sentence by developing a key word or idea

description: language or writing that uses sensory details to capture a subject

dialect: the form of a language spoken by people in a particular region or group

dialogue: a direct conversation between characters or people

diary: a personal record of daily events, usually written in prose

diction: a writer's word choice

direct object: a noun or a pronoun that receives the action of a transitive verb

direct quotation: a drafting technique in which writers indicate the exact words of another by enclosing them in quotation marks

documentary: nonfiction film that analyzes news events or another focused subject by combining interviews, film footage, narration, and other audio/visual components

documented essay: research writing that includes a limited number of research sources, providing full documentation parenthetically within the text

drafting: a stage of the writing process that follows prewriting and precedes revising in which a writer gets ideas on paper in a rough format

drama: a story written to be performed by actors and actresses

E

elaboration: a drafting technique in which a writer extends his or her ideas through the use of facts, examples, descriptions, details, or quotations

epic: a long narrative poem about the adventures of a god or a hero

essay: a short nonfiction work about a particular subject

etymology: the history of a word, showing where it came from and how it has evolved into its present spelling and meaning

exclamation mark: a punctuation mark used to indicate strong emotion

exclamatory sentence: a statement that conveys strong emotion and ends with an exclamation mark

exposition: writing to inform, addressing analytic purposes such as problem and solution, comparison and contrast, how-to, and cause and effect

extensive writing: writing products generated for others and from others, meant to be shared with an audience and often done for school assignments (*See* reflexive writing.)

F

fact: a statement that can be proved true (*See* opinion.)

fiction: prose writing about imaginary characters and events

figurative language: writing or speech not meant to be interpreted literally

firsthand biography: narrative writing that tells the story of an important period, experience, or relationship in a person's life, reported by a writer who knows the subject personally

five W's: a prewriting technique in which writers gather details about a topic by generating answers to the following questions: *Who? What? Where? When?* and *Why?*

fragment: an incomplete idea punctuated as a complete sentence

freewriting: a prewriting technique in which a writer quickly jots down as many ideas on a topic as possible

functional paragraph: a paragraph that performs a specific role in composition, such as to arouse or sustain interest, to indicate dialogue, to make a transition (*See* topical paragraph.)

G

generalization: a statement that presents a rule or idea based on particular facts

gerund: a noun formed from the present participle of a verb (ending in -*ing*)

gerund phrase: a group of words containing a gerund and its modifiers or complements that function as a noun

grammar: the study of the forms of words and the way they are arranged in phrases, clauses, and sentences

H

helping verb: a verb added to another verb to make a single verb phrase that indicates the time at which an action takes place or whether it actually happens, could happen, or should happen

hexagonal writing: a prewriting technique in

which a writer analyzes a subject from six angles: literal level, personal allusions, theme, literary devices, literary allusions, and evaluation

homophones: pairs of words that sound the same as each other yet have different meanings and different spellings, such as *hear/here*

how-to writing: expository writing that explains a process by providing step-by-step directions

humanities: forms of artistic expression including, but not limited to, fine art, photography, theater, film, music, and dance

hyperbole: a deliberate exaggeration or overstatement

hyphen: a punctuation mark used to combine numbers and word parts, to join certain compound words, and to show that a word has been broken between syllables at the end of a line

I

I-Search report: a research paper in which the writer addresses the research experience in addition to presenting the information gathered

image: a word or phrase that appeals to one or more of the senses—sight, hearing, touch, taste, or smell

imagery: the descriptive language used to re-create sensory experiences, set a tone, suggest emotions, and guide readers' reactions

imperative sentence: a statement that gives an order or a direction and ends with either a period or an exclamation mark

indefinite pronoun: a word such as *anyone, each,* or *many* that refers to a person, place, or thing, without specifying which one

independent clause: a group of words that contains both a subject and a verb and that can stand by itself as a complete sentence

indirect quotation: reporting only the general meaning of what a person said or thought; quotation marks are not needed

infinitive: the form of a verb that comes after the word *to* and acts as a noun, adjective, or adverb

infinitive phrase: a phrase introduced by an infinitive that may be used as a noun, an adjective, or an adverb

interjection: a word or phrase that expresses feeling or emotion and functions independently of a sentence

interrogative pronoun: a word such as *which* and *who* that introduces a question

interrogative sentence: a question that is punctuated with a question mark

interview: an information-gathering technique in which one or more people pose questions to one or more other people who provide opinions or facts on a topic

intransitive verb: an action verb that does not take a direct object (*See* transitive verb.)

introduction: the opening paragraphs of a work of writing in which the writer may capture the readers' attention and present a thesis statement to be developed in the writing (*See* body paragraph, topical paragraph, functional paragraph, conclusion.)

invisible writing: a prewriting technique in which a writer freewrites without looking at the product until the exercise is complete; this can be accomplished at a word processor with the monitor turned off or with carbon paper and an empty ballpoint pen

irony: the general name given to literary techniques that involve surprising, interesting, or amusing contradictions

itemizing: a prewriting technique in which a writer creates a second, more focused, set of ideas based on an original listing activity. (*See* listing.)

J

jargon: the specialized words and phrases unique to a specific field

journal: a notebook or other organized writing system in which daily events and personal impressions are recorded

K

key word: the word or phrase that directs an Internet or database search

L

layering: a drafting technique in which a writer elaborates on a statement by identifying and then expanding upon a central idea or word

lead: the opening sentences of a work of writing meant to grab the reader's interest, accomplished through a variety of methods, including providing an intriguing quotation, a surprising or provocative question or fact, an anecdote, or a description

learning log: a record-keeping system in which a student notes information about new ideas

legend: a widely told story about the past that may or may not be based in fact

legibility: the neatness and readability of words

linking verb: a word that expresses its subject's state of being or condition (*See* action verb.)

listing: a prewriting technique in which a writer prepares a list of ideas related to a specific topic. (*See* itemizing.)

looping: a prewriting activity in which a writer generates follow-up freewriting based on the identification of a key word or central idea in an original freewriting exercise

lyric poem: a poem expressing the observations and feelings of a single speaker

M

main clause: a group of words that has a subject and a verb and can stand alone as a complete sentence

memoir: autobiographical writing that provides an account of a writer's relationship with a person, event, or place

metaphor: a figure of speech in which one thing is spoken of as though it were something else

meter: the rhythmic pattern of a poem

monologue: a speech or performance given entirely by one person or by one character

mood: the feeling created in the reader by a literary work or passage

multimedia presentation: a technique for sharing information with an audience by enhancing narration and explanation with media, including video images, slides, audiotape recordings, music, and fine art

N

narration: writing that tells a story

narrative poem: a poem that tells a story in verse

nominative case: the form of a noun or pronoun used as the subject of a verb, as a predicate nominative, or as the pronoun in a nominative absolute (*See* objective case, possessive case.)

noun: a word that names a person, place, or thing

noun clause: a subordinate clause that acts as a noun

novel: an extended work of fiction that often has a complicated plot, many major and minor characters, a unifying theme, and several settings

O

objective case: the form of a noun or pronoun used as the object of any verb, verbal, or preposition, or as the subject of an infinitive (*See* nominative case, possessive case.)

observation: a prewriting technique involving close visual study of an object; a writing product that reports such a study

ode: a long formal lyric poem with a serious theme

onomatopoeia: words such as *buzz* and *plop* that suggest the sounds they name

open-book test: a form of assessment in which students are permitted to use books and class notes to respond to test questions

opinion: beliefs that can be supported but not proved to be true (*See* fact.)

oral tradition: the body of songs, stories, and poems preserved by being passed from generation to generation by word of mouth

outline: a prewriting or study technique that allows writers or readers to organize the presentation and order of information

oxymoron: a figure of speech that fuses two contradictory or opposing ideas, such as "freezing fire" or "happy grief"

P

parable: a short, simple story from which a moral or religious lesson can be drawn

paradox: a statement that seems to be contradictory but that actually presents a truth

paragraph: a group of sentences that share a common topic or purpose and that focus on a single main idea or thought

parallelism: the placement of equal ideas in words, phrases, or clauses of similar types

paraphrase: restating an author's idea in different words, often to share information by making the meaning clear to readers

parentheses: punctuation marks used to set off asides and explanations when the material is not essential

participial phrase: a group of words made up of a participle and its modifiers and complements that acts as an adjective

participle: a form of a verb that can act as an adjective

passive voice: the voice of a verb whose subject receives an action (*See* active voice.)

peer review: a revising technique in which writers meet with other writers to share focused feedback on a draft

pentad: a prewriting technique in which a writer analyzes a subject from five specified points: actors, acts, scenes, agencies, and purposes

period: a punctuation mark used to end a declarative sentence, an indirect question, and most abbreviations

personal pronoun: a word such as *I, me, you, we, us, he, him, she, her, they,* and *them* that refers to the person speaking; the person spoken to; or the person, place, or thing spoken about

personification a figure of speech in which a nonhuman subject is given human characteristics

persuasion: writing or speaking that attempts to convince others to accept a position on an issue of concern to the writer

phrase: a group of words without a subject and verb that functions as one part of speech

plot: the sequence of events in narrative writing

plural: the form of a word that indicates more than one item is being mentioned

poetry: a category of writing in which the final product may make deliberate use of rhythm, rhyme, and figurative language in order to express deeper feelings than those conveyed in ordinary speech (*See* prose, drama.)

point of view: the perspective, or vantage point, from which a story is told

portfolio: an organized collection of writing projects, including writing ideas, works in progress, final drafts, and the writer's reflections on the work

possessive case: the form of a noun or pronoun used to show ownership (*See* objective case, nominative case.)

prefix: one or more syllables added to the beginning of a word root (*See* root, suffix.)

preposition: a word that relates a noun or pronoun that appears with it to another word in the sentence to indicate relations of time, place, causality, responsibility, and motivation

prepositional phrase: a group of words that includes a preposition and a noun or pronoun

presenting: a stage of the writing process in which a writer shares a final draft with an audience through speaking, listening, or representing activities

prewriting: a stage of the writing process in which writers explore, choose, and narrow a topic and then gather necessary details for drafting

problem-and-solution writing: expository writing that examines a problem and provides a realistic solution

pronoun: a word that stands for a noun or for another word that takes the place of a noun

prose: a category of written language in which the end product is developed through sentences and paragraphs (*See* poetry, drama.)

publishing: a stage of the writing process in which a writer shares the written version of a final draft with an audience

punctuation: the set of symbols used to convey specific directions to the reader

purpose: the specific goal or reason a writer chooses for a writing task

Q

question mark: a punctuation mark used to end an interrogative sentence or an incomplete question

quicklist: a prewriting technique in which a writer creates an impromptu, unresearched list of ideas related to a specific topic

quotation mark: a punctuation mark used to indicate the beginning and end of a person's exact speech or thoughts

R

ratiocination: a systematic approach to the revision process that involves color-coding elements of writing for evaluation

reflective essay: autobiographical writing in which a writer shares a personal experience and then provides insight about the event

reflexive pronoun: a word that ends in -*self* or -*selves* and names the person or thing receiving an action when that person or thing is the same as the one performing the action

reflexive writing: writing generated for oneself and from oneself, not necessarily meant to be shared, in which the writer makes all decisions regarding form and purpose (*See* extensive writing.)

refrain: a regularly repeated line or group of lines in a poem or song

relative pronoun: a pronoun such as *that, which, who, whom,* or *whose* that begins a

subordinate clause and connects it to another idea in the sentence

reporter's formula: a prewriting technique in which writers gather details about a topic by generating answers to the following questions: *Who? What? Where? When?* and *Why?*

research: a prewriting technique in which writers gather information from outside sources such as library reference materials, interviews, and the Internet

research writing: expository writing that presents and interprets information gathered through an extensive study of a subject

response to literature writing: persuasive, expository, or narrative writing that presents a writer's analysis of or reactions to a published work

revising: a stage of the writing process in which a writer reworks a rough draft to improve both form and content

rhyme: the repetition of sounds at the ends of words

rhyme scheme: the regular pattern of rhyming words in a poem or stanza

rhythm: the form or pattern of words or music in which accents or beats come at certain fixed intervals

root: the base of a word (*See* prefix, suffix.)

rubric: an assessment tool, generally organized in a grid, to indicate the range of success or failure according to specific criteria

run-on sentence: two or more complete sentences punctuated incorrectly as one

S

salutation: the greeting in a formal letter

satire: writing that ridicules or holds up to contempt the faults of individuals or of groups

SEE method: an elaboration technique in which a writer presents a statement, an extension, and an elaboration to develop an idea

semicolon: a punctuation mark used to join independent clauses that are not already joined by a conjunction

sentence: a group of words with a subject and a predicate that expresses a complete thought

setting: the time and place of the action of a piece of narrative writing

short story: a brief fictional narrative told in prose

simile: a figure of speech in which *like* or *as* is used to make a comparison between two basically unrelated ideas

sonnet: a fourteen-line lyric poem with a single theme

speaker: the imaginary voice assumed by the writer of a poem

stanza: a group of lines in a poem, seen as a unit

statistics: facts presented in numerical form, such as ratios, percentages, or summaries

subject: the word or group of words in a sentence that tells whom or what the sentence is about

subordinate clause: a group of words containing both a subject and a verb that cannot stand by itself as a complete sentence

subordinating conjunction: a word used to join two complete ideas by making one of the ideas dependent on the other

suffix: one or more syllables added to the end of a word root (*See* prefix, root.)

summary: a brief statement of the main ideas and supporting details presented in a piece of writing

symbol: something that is itself and also stands for something else

T

theme: the central idea, concern, or purpose in a piece of narrative writing, poetry, or drama

thesis statement: a statement of an essay's main idea; all information in the essay supports or elaborates this idea

tone: a writer's attitude toward the readers and toward the subject

topic sentence: a sentence that states the main idea of a paragraph

topic web: a prewriting technique in which a writer generates a graphic organizer to identify categories and subcategories of a topic

topical paragraph: a paragraph that develops, explains, and supports the topic sentence related to an essay's thesis statement

transition: words, phrases, or sentences that smooth writing by indicating the relationship among ideas

transitive verb: an action verb that takes a direct object (*See* intransitive verb.)

U

unity: a quality of written work in which all the parts fit together in a complete, self-contained whole

V

verb: a word or group of words that expresses an action, a condition, or the fact that something exists while indicating the time of the action, condition, or fact

verbal: a word derived from the verb but used as a noun, adjective, or adverb (*See* gerund, infinitive, participle.)

vignette: a brief narrative characterized by precise detail

voice: the distinctive qualities of a writer's style, including diction, attitude, sentence style, and ideas

W

works-cited list: a list of the sources of a research paper, including full bibliographic references for each source named in the body of the paper (*See* bibliography.)

Index

Note: **Bold numbers** show pages on which basic definitions and rules appear.

A

a, an, **646**
Abbreviations
  of academic degrees, 902
  common, 691
  common geographical, 904
  commonly used, 905
  for dates and ordinals, 159
  end marks for, **690, 691**
  for measurements, 904
  state, 903
  of titles, **671,** 902
Abbreviations Guide, **902–905**
Academic Degrees, abbreviations of, 902
Academic Reports, **275**
Accent, **908**
accept, **138, 646**
Acceptance Speech, writing, 44
Acronyms
  in Internet Search, 427
  See also Abbreviations
Action Verbs, **379, 908**
  examples of, 379
  See also Verbs
Active Voice **552, 908**
  using, 554, 555
ACT Scores, 869
adapt, **646**
Ad Campaign, 162–163
Address Book, imagining, 252
Addresses, commas with, **705**
Adjective Clause Fragment, 494
Adjective Clauses, **459, 908**
  commas with, **701**
  essential and nonessential, 459
  introductory words in, 460
Adjective Phrases, **440, 908**
  examples of, 440
  gerund phrases with, 452
Adjectives, 386, **908**
  in adverb clauses, 462
  articles, 387
  compound, 387
  coordinate, 697
  cumulative, 697
  degrees of comparison for, 622
  gerund phrases with, 452
  identifying, 391, 402
  infinitives as, 454
  nouns used as, 387
  numbers as, 389
  predicate, 432
  pronouns used as, 388
  proper, 387, 674–675
  relative pronouns as, 460
  in short story, 80
  verb forms used as, 389

adopt, **646**
Adverb Clause Fragment, 494
Adverb Clauses, **462, 908**
  commas with, **699**
  elliptical, 463
  uses of, 462
Adverb Phrases, **441, 908**
  examples of, 441
  gerund phrases with, 452
Adverbs, **390, 908**
  in adverb clauses, 462
  adverbs modifying, 390
  conjunctive, 398
  degrees of comparison for, 622
  gerund phrases with, 452
  identifying, 391, 396, 402
  infinitives as, 454
  modifying adverbs, 390
  modifying verbs, 390
  nouns functioning as, 391
  as parts of verbs, 390
  relative, 461
Advertisements, 148–167
  defined, **149**
  drafting, 155
  editing and proofreading, 159
  evaluating, 166–167
  model from literature, 150
  prewriting, 151–154
  print, 789
  publishing and presenting, 160
  revising, 156–158
  rubric for self-assessment, 160
  types of, **149**
Advertising, evaluating Internet, 145
affect, 138, **646**
Agenda, for meetings, 876
aggravate, 646
Agreement
  pronoun-antecedent, 262
  proofreading for errors in, 588, 589
  subject and verb, 586–599
Agreement, Rules of, **584–619**
  for ambiguous pronoun references, **611–612**
  for compound antecedents, **601**
  compound subjects, **592–593**
  for confusing subjects, **594–597**
  indefinite pronouns, **604–605**
  in literature, 590
  for number, **601, 602**
  for person, **602**
  reflexive pronouns, **606**
  for relative pronouns, **590**
  subject and verb, **588**
  for vague pronoun references, **608–609,** 614
ain't, **646**
Aircraft
  capitalization of, **673**
  underlining, **731**

all-, **746**
Allegory, **908**
Alliteration, 155, **908**
all ready, already, **647**
all right, alright, **647**
all together, altogether, **647**
Allusion, 839, **908**
Almanacs, **860, 908**
  on Internet, 894
  for research, 255
almost, 501
American Psychological Association (APA) Style, 295, 888, 890
among, **647**
Amounts
  forming possessive for, **750**
  rules of agreement for, **597**
an, **646**
Analogies, 822–823, 834, **866**
  common relationships in, 867
  example, 866
  finding relationships in, 804
Analyses, writing, 331
and, **593, 601**
Anecdotes, 49
Annotated Web Index, 303
Annotating Word Choices, 137
Antecedents, 262, **372**
  compound, 601
Antonyms, **804**
  using, 804
anxious, **648**
any, **596**
anyone, any one, **648**
anyway, **648**
anywhere, 648
APA. *See* American Psychological Association
Apostrophes, **908**
  in literature, 751
  using, **749–753,** 754
Appendix, of textbook, 825
Applications
  examples of, 357
  in workplace, 349
Appositive Phrases, **111, 442, 908**
  identifying, 443–444
Appositives, **111, 442, 908**
  adding details with, 110
  commas with, 113, 701
  essential, **701**
  gerunds as, 451
  identifying, 443
  infinitives as, 454
  nominative pronouns with, 566
  noun clauses as, 464
  objective pronouns with, 569
Appreciative Listening, 784
Argument
  building, 125
  either/or, 135
  evaluating, 124

Acknowledgments

Staff Credits
The people who made up the *Prentice Hall Writing and Grammar: Communication in Action* team—representing design services, editorial, editorial services, electronic publishing technology, manufacturing & inventory planning, marketing, marketing services, market research, on-line services & multimedia development, product planning, production services, project office, and publishing processes—are listed below. Bold type denotes the core team members.

Ellen Backstrom, Betsy Bostwick, Evonne Burgess, **Louise B. Capuano, Sarah Carroll, Megan Chill,** Katherine Clarke, Rhett Conklin, Martha Conway, Harold Crudup, **Harold Delmonte,** Laura Dershewitz, Donna DiCuffa, Amy Fleming, Libby Forsyth, Ellen Goldblatt, Elaine Goldman, Jonathan Goldson, **Rebecca Graziano,** Rick Hickox, Kristan Hoskins, Jim Jeglikowski, Carol Lavis, **George Lychock,** Gregory Lynch, William McAllister, **Frances Medico,** Perrin Moriarty, Loretta Moser, Margaret Plotkin, Maureen Raymond, Shannon Rider, **Steve Sacco,** Gerry Schrenk, **Melissa Shustyk,** Annette Simmons, Robin Sullivan, **Elizabeth Torjussen, Doug Utigard**

Additional Credits
Ernie Albanese, Diane Alimena, Susan Andariese, Michele Angelucci, Penny Baker, Susan Barnes, Louise Casella, Lorena Cerisano, Cynthia Clampitt, Elizabeth Crawford, Ken Dougherty, Vince Esterly, Kathy Gavilanes, Beth Geschwind, Michael Goodman, Diana Hahn, Jennifer Harper, Evan Holstrom, Alex Ivchenko, Leanne Korszoloski, Sue Langan, Rebecca Lauth, Dave Liston, Maria Keogh, Christine Mann, Vicki Menanteaux, Gail Meyer, Artur Mkrtchyan, LaShonda Morris, Karyl Murray, Omni-Photo Communications, Kim Ortell, Patty Rodriguez, Brenda Sanabria, Carolyn Sapontzis, Ken Silver, Slip Jig Image Research Services, Sunnyside, NY, Ron Spezial, Barbara Stufflebeem, Gene Vaughan, Karen Vignola, Linda Westerhoff

Grateful acknowledgment is made to the following for permission to reprint copyrighted material:

Carol Publishing Group, a subsidiary of The Citadel Press
"Meanings" by Eavan Boland. Copyright © 1995 by Alvin Ailey and A. Peter Bailey. Published by The Carol Publishing Group.

Doubleday & Company
"Blindness" Jorge Louis Borges from *The Art of the Personal Essay.* Copyright © 1994 by Phillip Lopate.

James Gorman
"Man, Bytes, Dog." Copyright © 1984 by James Gorman. Originally published in *The New Yorker.*

HarperCollins
Excerpt from *An American Childhood* by Annie Dillard. Copyright © 1987 by Annie Dillard.

Little, Brown, and Company Limited
"Warding Off Wildlife" from *The Practical Gardener: A Guide to Breaking New Ground* by Roger B. Swain. Copyright © 1989 by Roger B. Swain.

William Morrow and Company, Inc.
"Global Language" from *The Mother Tongue* by Bill Bryson. Copyright © 1990 by Bill Bryson.

Pantheon Books, a division of Random House, Inc.
"The Man Who Shouted Teresa" from *Numbers in the Dark* by Italo Calvino. English translation copyright © 1995 by Tim Parks. Published in the United States by Pantheon Books, a division of Random House, Inc., New York. Originally published in Italy as *Primal che tu dica "Pronto"* by Arnoldo Mondadori Editore. Copyright © 1993 by Palomar S.r.l.e., Arnoldo Mondadori S.p.A., Milano. This translation first published by Jonathan Cape, London.

The Poynter Institute
"Snow Dance," Leann Goree (student model). The Poynter Institute, St. Petersburg, FL.

W. W. Norton & Company, Inc
"Miracle on Thirty-Fourth Street" from *Why Buildings Fall Down: How Structures Fail* by Matthys Levy and Mario Salvadori. Copyright © 1992 by Matthys Levy and Mario Salvadori. Published by W. W. Norton & Company, Inc., 500 Fifth Avenue, New York, NY 10110.

Photo Credits

Photo Credits

World Photos/Lionel Cironneau; **299:** Corel Professional Photos CD-ROM™; **300:** Frank Siteman/PhotoEdit; **302:** Culver Pictures, Inc.; **306:** *Fond Memories,* Michael Mortimer Robinson/ SuperStock ; **308:** Darrell Gulin/Tony Stone Images; **309:** Darrell Gulin/Tony Stone Images; **311:** *Sean, Coco and Rumple,* 1991, oil, 50 x 68 inches, March Avery, Courtesy of the artist; **323:** *Paisaje (Cinco Pagodas),* Alejandro Xul Solar. Photo ©Christie's Images; **325:** Karen Mason Blair/COR-BIS; **326:** The Granger Collection, New York; **327:** Photofest; **330:** *Before the Nine O'Clock Bell,* Buckley School Collection/Jane Wooster Scott/ SuperStock; **340:** ©The Stock Market/ Rob Lewine; **341:** image©Copyright 1998 PhotoDisc, Inc.; **342:** ©The Stock Market/Jose L. Pelaez; **344:** The Granger Collection, New York; **348:** ©D. Ermakoff/The Image Works; **358:** image©Copyright 1998 PhotoDisc, Inc.; **360:** *Persistence of Memory,* Salvador Dalí/SuperStock; ©2001 Foundation Gala-Salvador Dalí/ VEGAP/Artists Rights Society (ARS), New York; **364:** *Waterfront Landscape,* 1936, Stuart Davis, National Museum of American Art, Washington, DC/Art Resource, NY; **366–377:** NASA; **379:** Courtesy of the Library of Congress; **381:** Pearson Education/PH College; **382:** Courtesy of the Library of Congress; **386–392:** Corel Professional Photos CD-ROM™; **395–400:** Courtesy of the Library of Congress; **403** & **410** & **413:** Corel Professional Photos CD-ROM™; **415:** Nancy Wolff/Omni-Photo Communications, Inc.; **416:** Corel Professional Photos CD-ROM™; **418:** US Department of Agriculture; **421–423:** Corel Professional Photos CD-ROM™; **426** & **429** & **431:** NASA; **438–544:** Corel Professional Photos CD-ROM™; **549:** NOAA; **550:** Corel Professional Photos CD-ROM™; **552:** Michael Littlejohn/Pearson Education/PH College; **555:** Michael Littlejohn/ Pearson Education/PH College; **562:** Corel Professional Photos CD-ROM™; **565:** Courtesy of the Library of Congress; **567:** NASA; **569:** ©P.

Vauthey/CORBIS-Sygma; **570:** The Granger Collection, New York; **575–587:** Corel Professional Photos CD-ROM™; **588:** Pearson Education/ PH School; **591–629:** Corel Professional Photos CD-ROM™; **638:** NASA; **641:** Corel Professional Photos CD-ROM™; **647–698:** Corel Professional Photos CD-ROM™; **700:** Pearson Education/PH College; **704–726:** Corel Professional Photos CD-ROM™; **729:** W.J. Short/EMG; **737–750:** Corel Professional Photos CD-ROM™; **776:** *Details of a Lost Library,* Stella Waitzkin, Collection of the artist, ©1994 Norman McGrath; **778:** Chris Steele-Perkins/ PictureQuest; **791:** *Effect of the Sun on the Water,* 1905, Andre Derain, ©2001 Artists Rights Society (ARS), New York/ADAGP, Paris/Art Resource, NY; **796:** ©The Stock Market/Charles Gupton; **800:** David Young-Wolff/ PhotoEdit; **803:** ©The Stock Market/ Gabe Palmer/Mug Shots; **805:** Ken Karp/PH photo; **811** & **820:** Corel Professional Photos CD-ROM™; **824:** Ken Karp/PH photo; **832:** David Young-Wolff/PhotoEdit; **835:** CORBIS; **837:** Emmanuelle Dal Secco/Tony Stone Images; **842:** ©Copyright The British Museum; **846:** Bill Aron/ PhotoEdit; **855:** ©Laima Druskis/ Stock, Boston/ PictureQuest; **860:** Harvard University Archives; **863:** United States Department of Labor; **866:** ©The Stock Market/ Jose L. Pelaez; **867:** Silver Burdett Ginn; **868:** ©The Stock Market; **872:** Mary Kate Denny/ PhotoEdit; **875:** © The Stock Market/Tom Stewart; **877:** Walter Hodges/Tony Stone Images

Acknowledgments

Grateful acknowledgment is made to the following for permission to reprint copyrighted material:

Carol Publishing Group, a subsidiary of The Citadel Press
"Meanings" by Eavan Boland . Copyright © 1995 by Alvin Ailey and A. Peter Bailey. Published by The Carol Publishing Group.

Doubleday & Company
"Blindness" Jorge Louis Borges from *The Art of the Personal Essay.* Copyright © 1994 by Phillip Lopate.

James Gorman
"Man, Bytes, Dog." Copyright © 1984 by James Gorman. Originally published in *The New Yorker.*

HarperCollins
Excerpt from *An American Childhood* by Annie Dillard. Copyright © 1987 by Annie Dillard.

Little, Brown, and Company Limited
"Warding Off Wildlife" from *The Practical Gardener: A Guide to Breaking New Ground* by Roger B. Swain. Copyright © 1989 by Roger B. Swain.

William Morrow and Company, Inc.
"Global Language" from *The Mother Tongue* by Bill Bryson. Copyright © 1990 by Bill Bryson.

Pantheon Books, a division of Random House, Inc.
"The Man Who Shouted Teresa" from *Numbers in the Dark* by Italo Calvino. English translation copyright © 1995 by Tim Parks. Published in the United States by Pantheon Books, a division of Random House, Inc., New York. Originally published in Italy as *Primal che tu dica "Pronto"* by Arnoldo Mondadori Editore. Copyright © 1993 by Palomar S.r.l.e., Arnoldo Mondadori S.p.A., Milano. This translation first published by Jonathan Cape, London.

The Poynter Institute
"Snow Dance," Leann Goree (student model). The Poynter Institute, St. Petersburg, FL.

W.W. Norton & Company, Inc
"Miracle on Thirty-Fourth Street" from *Why Buildings Fall Down: How Structures Fail* by Matthys Levy and Mario Salvadori. Copyright © 1992 by Matthys Levy and Mario Salvadori. Published by W.W. Norton & Company, Inc., 500 Fifth Avenue, New York, NY 10110

Note: Every effort has been made to locate the copyright owner of material reprinted in this book. Omissions brought to our attention will be corrected in subsequent editions.

Photo Credits

Building Composite at Dusk, oil on linen, 75 1/2 x 86 inches, Private Collection, DC Moore Gallery; **254:** NASA; **267:** Michelle Bridwell/PhotoEdit; **268:** ©Bob Daemmrich/The Image Works; **269:** Kevin R. Morris/CORBIS; **270:** Photofest; **274:** Corel Professional Photos CD-ROM™; **276–279:** North Wind Picture Archives; **281:** *Benedict Arnold Escapes on a British Frigate,* Brent Silverman, Courtesy of Silverman Studios, Inc.; **289:** ©The Stock Market/Jose L. Pelaez; **291:** Tony Stone Images; **297:** AP/Wide World Photos/Lionel Cironneau; **299:** Corel Professional Photos CD-ROM™; **300:** Frank Siteman/PhotoEdit; **302:** Culver Pictures, Inc.; **306:** *Fond Memories,* Michael Mortimer Robinson/SuperStock ; **308:** Darrell Gulin/Tony Stone Images; **309:** Darrell Gulin/Tony Stone Images; **311:** *Sean, Coco and Rumble,* 1991, oil, 50 x 68 inches, March Avery, Courtesy of the artist; **323:** *Paisaje (Cinco Pagodas),* Alejandro Xul Solar. Photo ©Christie's Images; **325:** Karen Mason Blair/CORBIS; **326:** The Granger Collection, New York; **327:** Photofest; **330:** *Buckley School* Collection/Jane Wooster Scott/SuperStock; **340:** ©The Stock Market/Rob Lewine; **341:** image©Copyright 1998 PhotoDisc, Inc.; **342:** ©The Stock Market/Jose L. Pelaez; **344:** The Granger Collection, New York; **348:** ©D. Ermakoff/The Image Works; **358:** image©Copyright 1998 PhotoDisc, Inc.; **360:** *Persistence of Memory,* Salvador Dali/SuperStock; **364:** *Josephine and Mercie,* Edmund Tarbell, Corcoran Gallery of Art; **366–377:** NASA; **379:** Courtesy of the Library of Congress; **381:** Pearson Education/PH College; **382:** Courtesy of the Library of Congress; **386–392:** Corel Professional Photos CD-ROM™; **395–400:** Courtesy of the Library of Congress; **403 & 410 & 413:**

Corel Professional Photos CD-ROM™; **415:** Nancy Wolff/Omni-Photo Communications, Inc.; **416:** Corel Professional Photos CD-ROM™; **418:** US Department of Agriculture; **421–423:** Corel Professional Photos CD-ROM™; **431:** NASA; **438–544:** Corel Professional Photos CD-ROM™; **549:** NOAA; **550:** Corel Professional Photos CD-ROM™; **552:** Michael Littlejohn/Pearson Education/PH College; **555:** Michael Littlejohn/Pearson Education/PH College; **562:** Corel Professional Photos CD-ROM™; **565:** Courtesy of the Library of Congress; **567:** NASA; **569:** ©P. Vauthey/CORBIS-Sygma; **570:** The Granger Collection, New York; **575–587:** Corel Professional Photos CD-ROM™; **588:** Pearson Education/PH School; **591–627:** Corel Professional Photos CD-ROM™; **636:** NASA; **639:** Corel Professional Photos CD-ROM™; **640:** NASA; **645 698:** Corel Professional Photos CD-ROM™; **700:** Pearson Education/PH College; **704–726:** Corel Professional Photos CD-ROM™; **729:** W.J. Short/EMG; **737–750:** Corel Professional Photos CD-ROM™; **776:** *Details of a Lost Library,* Stella Waitzkin, Collection of the artist, ©1994 Norman McGrath; **778:** Chris Steele-Perkins/PictureQuest; **791:** *Effect of the Sun on the Water,* 1905, Andre Derain, © ARS/Art Resource, NY; **796:** ©The Stock Market/Charles Gupton; **800:** David Young-Wolff/PhotoEdit; **803:** ©The Stock Market/Gabe Palmer/Mug Shots; **805:** Ken Karp/PH photo; **811 & 820:** Corel Professional Photos CD-ROM™; **824:** Ken Karp/PH photo; **832:** David Young-Wolff/PhotoEdit; **835:** CORBIS; **837:** Emmanuelle Dal Secco/Tony Stone Images; **842:** ©British Museum; **846:** Bill Aron/PhotoEdit; **855:** ©Laima Druskis/Stock, Boston/PictureQuest; **860:** Harvard

University Archives; **861:** image © Copyright 1998 PhotoDisc, Inc.; **863:** United States Department of Labor; **866:** ©The Stock Market/Jose L. Pelaez; 866; Monkmeyer; **867:** Silver Burdett Ginn; **868:** ©The Stock Market; **869:** Mary Kate Denny/PhotoEdit; **871:** © The Stock Market/Tom Stewart; **877:** Walter Hodges/Tony Stone Images